Twentieth Century Hangings

by

Peter Wilson

The complete and comprehensive guide to Twentieth Century British executions

London 2002

Twentieth Century Hangings

by

Peter Wilson

*Blackie & Co
Publishers Ltd*

A BLACKIE & CO PUBLISHERS PAPERBACK

© Copyright 2002
Peter Wilson

First published in 2002

A CIP catalogue record for this title is
available from the British Library

ISBN 1 903138 04 3

Blackie & Co Publishers Ltd
107-111 Fleet Street
LONDON EC4A 2AB

Foreword

A conversation overheard on the 4.50 from Paddington:

That's what it says, 'Thou shalt not kill'. Exodus, chapter 20, verse 13. The sixth commandment. Can't get much plainer than that.

And 99.9% of people stick to it too. That's a bigger take up than the seventh and eighth commandments get, that's for sure. There's always exceptions, though.

Exceptions? There's no ifs or buts. It doesn't say, 'Thou shalt not kill except for this and this'.

Yes, but that's self-defence. Kill or be killed.

Well, I know, but we kill people in wartime, don't we?

And what if someone had a knife to your Bobby's throat? You'd kill them wouldn't you?

Well, yes, I suppose I would. But that's self-defence too. In defence of a life.

So there are exceptions! What if you had a burglar in the middle of the night? You wouldn't ask him what he was carrying would you? You'd want to finish him off.

Ah, but I wouldn't want to kill him. Just for a TV or video.

If you didn't he might kill you. You say that but you would if you had to, in self-defence, like you say. If a few more people did it, it might put a stop to them. Damned thieves!

Well, they used to hang thieves, you know. Two hundred years ago they'd have hung a kid for nicking a shilling.

That's ridiculous. But now we've gone to the other extreme. It's open season for burglars and muggers. And you can't let your kids out of your sight these days.

Oh, I think people over-react. You

can't wrap your kids in cotton-wool.

What do you mean? There's kids being abused all the time. Every week you hear of some kid being murdered.

I think you just hear about it more, with TV and that. And it's not every week. Child murder's still quite rare. I've been reading this book. Kids were being murdered in the '20s and '30s too, you know. It's always happened.

Well, I think they should be strung up!

Yes, well, they used to, didn't they? That never stopped the next weirdo though, did it?

Oh, I think it did. They'd think twice if they knew they'd face the rope. We've gone too soft.

All started in the sixties. The pill, free love, abortion, gay love, 'living together'!

Yes. All this rights, rights, rights. Got the right to do anything these days. Can't even smack your kids legs these days.

Well, doing away with the cane, and national service. That started it.

No wonder kids have no discipline these days. Mind you, my Dad hated his army days.

And you wouldn't want anyone slapping your kids about, would you?

Well, my kids never needed smacking. Mind you, our Nancy's boy went off the rails. Got drunk and knocked a cyclist over with his car. Terrible shock. He was banned for three years.

You mean he killed someone?

By accident!

Yes, I suppose. But then I was reading. I mean a lot of people, they kill someone in a fit of rage, you know. They lose control. They don't mean to. My grandad had a terrible temper. Wonder he never killed anyone.

Well, that's what you have courts for. To decide these things.

Oh, I know. But judges and juries are prejudiced sometimes, you know. Did you never see Henry Fonda in 'Twelve Angry Men'? They believe what they want to believe. In this book loads of innocent people got the chop. There was this Somali bloke - never did it. Evans, they didn't believe him because he was simple. Another bloke, Kelly - he was a bit of a gangster, but he didn't do it. They still strung him up.

Well, you're bound to get some mistakes.

What if it's you that's the mistake though? Loads of people have been in jail for years for things they didn't do.

I saw this opinion poll. 75% of people want to bring back hanging.

Well, they can't now. It's against European law. France was the last place, and that's about thirty years ago.

Oh, not another European diktat?

Well, yeah. But we did away with it ourselves before they decided to.

Well, we shouldn't have. The Bible also says, 'An eye for an eye. A life for a life'. That's what I believe. Not that I believe in the Bible. If it's deliberate of course. It's about time the politicians listened.

Yes, but who's to decide who's to live and who's to die?

We should. There should be a referendum.

What! For every case? Some people would have rapists hanged. If you asked a hundred people they'd all have different ideas. If someone beat up your Grandma, you'd want them strung up. I could kill that neighbour of mine sometimes.

Oh, come on. I'm talking about murderers. Especially them who kill kiddies.   Hanging's too good for them.

Well, I don't think execution by opinion poll is a good idea. I think that makes us all murderers. We're just down to their level. Anyway, I don't think hanging is a punishment.

What do you mean? If you kill a little kid, you should pay with your life.

Yes, but when you die, it's over in a flash. That's not punishment. Locked up for life to think about what you did. That's more like it.

Yes, but they don't get life, do they? They're out in a few years.

Well, it should mean life. Anyway, not all of them get out. Look at Hindley.

But why should we pay for them for years? Hang them. Get them out of the way.

And I don't think money should have anything to do with killing someone or not. And they *are* out of the way in prison.

Oh, here's our stop. Anyway, what is this book you've been reading?

So why this book?

I don't know at what age most children realise there is a world beyond their own immediate wants and needs, but my eyes began to settle on further horizons in the early '60s. Kennedy, the Tokyo Olympics, the space race. It so happened that there was also Hanratty, the end of the death penalty, then the Moors murders at that time. These things registered with me.

In reading true crime books, I wanted to know why, for apparently similar crimes, some were hanged and some not. Why were there years when so few were executed and others when there were so many? And the more I read, the more the same names came up time and again - the 'celebrated' cases'. I'd only read about a hundred or so, so who were all the others? Too awful to write about? Too uninteresting?

Though it took a long time, I found out. I discovered that so many tell the same basic story - woman displeases man, so he kills her. I also found out that there is no rhyme or reason why some hanged and others did not. It was always a lottery. The judge, the jury, the lawyers, public opinion, the Home Secretary. Life and death on a whim, the crime itself and the sentence. Touch and go. Your number's up. In the years 1900 to 1964 perhaps 10,000 killers did not hang, too young, too mad, mitigation. These pages reveal those who did hang, including, most disturbingly, twenty potentially innocent citizens.

Revealed are the desolate lives of dysfunctional men, and the wretched lives they inflicted upon powerless women. Lives of poverty and debt, minds scarred, whether by war, mental illness or, above all, by alcohol. Simple men in anger, frustration, tormented by jealousy or greed.

And yet those listed here are merely the exposed mast-head of an enormous sunken wreck of wasted life. Forsaken lives, lonely deaths - all included herein, the villains and victims alike - casualties all. The dark corners of life into which these ultimate outcasts of society withdrew, most of us, manage to avoid.

There, but for the grace of God.

Peter Wilson 2000

Form

The book follows chronologically all British judicial hangings of the twentieth century, and each case is numbered from 001 to 817.

The cases are divided yearly, each section headed by the year and the total number of hangings in that year.

Before the individual cases, the reader will find a table summarising the executions for that year, thus:

1	2	3	4	5	6
248	16 Nov	William REEVE	42		Bedford
249	7 Dec	John THORNLEY	26		Walton
250	7 Dec	Young HILL	28	*American*	Walton
251	22 Dec	Harry THOMPSON	55		Wakefield
252	29 Dec	John McCARTNEY	40		Wakefield

Column 1:	The case number.
Column 2:	The date of execution.
Column 3:	Name of the person executed.
Column 4:	Age at death.
Column 5:	Nationality, if not English.
Column 6:	Place of execution.

Female cases are indicated by (f) following the name.

Each case then follows, thus:

1	**10 August 1915**	Wakefield prison	*T.Pierrepoint/ Willis*
2	**244**		
3	<u>**Walter MARRIOTT**</u>	**24**	

4   ***Stabbed:***   ***Nellie Marriott***, *23, his wife, on 5 June 1915, in Barnsley, W.Yorks.*

5   *Motive:*   *Vengeance.*

6   Marriott, *(b.1891),* claimed that in an argument, his wife went for him with a bottle and a bread knife. Whatever the cause, he stabbed her in the neck with the knife, with a force sufficient to penetrate her body by 15cm, piercing her lung. He was found trying to rouse Nellie, saying, 'Speak to me. What have I done to my lass?'

7   *Read: And May The Lord Have Mercy On Your Soul*

Line 1:	Date and place of execution. Chief/ assistant hangman.
Line 2:	Case number.
Line 3:	Name of person executed, age at death; also any alias. Black or female also noted here.
Line 4:	Means to murder, name and age of victim, date and place of murder.
Line 5:	Motive for murder. 'Drink related' also noted here.
Line 6:	Details of the case.
Line 7:	A recommendation to extended reading.

Following the year section, there may follow an Army, a Firing Squad, an American military, an Irish, or a Jersey supplement, detailing executions carried out under those authorities. These supplements are included for interest only. Please note that Irish execution details are incomplete.

An analysis follows the case studies.

This book is dedicated to

Naomi Farnworth
1926-1932

and the thousands of others so cruelly and
selfishly taken from their loved ones.

"The sentence of the Court upon you is, that you be taken from this place to a place of execution, and you there suffer death by hanging, and that your body be afterwards buried within the precincts of the prison in which you shall have been confined before your execution. And may the Lord have mercy on your soul."

1900

total: *14*

001	9 Jan	Louise MASSET (f)	33	*French*	Newgate
002	6 Mar	Ada CHARD-WILLIAMS (f)	24		Newgate
003	22 May	Henry GROVE	26		Newgate
004	17 Jul	Alfred HIGHFIELD	22		Newgate
005	14 Aug	William IRWIN	61		Newgate
006	16 Aug	Charles BACKHOUSE	24		Armley
007	16 Aug	Thomas MELLOR	29		Armley
008	21 Aug	William LACEY	29	*Jamaican*	Cardiff
009	28 Aug	Charles BLEWITT	33		Armley
010	2 Oct	John PARR	19		Newgate
011	3 Oct	William BURRETT	35		Chelmsford
012	4 Dec	Joseph HOLDEN	57		Strangeways
013	12 Dec	John BOWES	50		Durham
014	27 Dec	James BERGIN	28	*Irish*	Walton

9 January 1900   Newgate prison, London   *James/ W. Billington*

001

Louise Josephine Jemima MASSET   33
female
half-French

Suffocated: ***Manfred Louis Masset**, 4, her son, on 27 October 1899, in London E8.*

Motive: *To clear impediment.*

Masset, *(b.1867)*, a languages and piano teacher, lived in Bethune Road, Stoke Newington, London N.16. An unmarried mother, she boarded out her son to a spinster, Helen Gentle, in Tottenham. In 1899, Masset began an affair with a 19-year old medical student, Eudore Lucas, who lodged next door to her.

Before leaving to spend a weekend in Brighton with Lucas, she collected her son saying that in future he would live with his father in France. At Dalston Junction station the child was suffocated and was inflicted with severe head injuries with a rockery stone supposedly taken from Masset's garden. His naked body was found in a station toilet and his clothes in a waiting room in Brighton. Witnesses identified Masset as having been with the child, and Miss Gentle identified the clothing. Masset claimed that she

1

had left the boy with two women who agreed to look after him for a year for £12. The women were never traced.

The jury reached its verdict in 30 minutes, but some doubt has been cast upon her guilt, with timings that do not fit and suggestions that the baby farmers Sach and Walters, hanged in 1903, were responsible.

Read: Murderous Sussex

6 March 1900   Newgate prison, London   *James Billington*

002

Ada CHARD-WILLIAMS   **24**   *female*

Bludgeoned / strangled: **1 *Selina Ellen Jones*,** 2, on 23 September 1899, in London SW13.
+ *other babies*
Motive: *Financial.*

Williams, *(b.1876),* a married young woman living in Barnes, was a stereotypical 'baby-farmer' whose activities were well-known to her husband, even if he took no direct part in them. Florence Jones, a young unmarried mother, answered Williams' press advertisement about adoption, as probably many had done before her. Williams, who received her mail poste-restante under a pseudonym, met Miss Jones on 31 August at Charing Cross, and took 21-month old Selina in return for a fee, promising to find a good home for her. Miss Jones was shown a house where she was told the child would stay in the interim. When she returned later to pay the £2 balance from the £5 fee, there was no sign of Williams, and Florence went to the police.

Selina's body was fished out of the Thames at Battersea on 27 September. Williams wrote to the police in December, admitting baby-farming, but denying murder. Both she and her husband were charged, though he was later acquitted. Williams' particular style of tying knots was most damning in the evidence against her, linking her with the deaths of many other children found in the river.

Read: And May The Lord Have Mercy On Your Soul.

003

Henry GROVE   26

Bludgeoned: **Henry Smith**, *34, on 24 February 1900, in Enfield, Middlesex.*

Motive: *Vengeance; drink related.*

Grove, *(b.1876)*, was a hawker who kept his horse and cart in his neighbour's yard for the sum of 6d per week. His neighbours, Henry Smith and his wife, ran a sweetshop in Enfield, and gained a little extra income from allowing horses to be kept in the yard at the rear of the premises. By February Grove owed a shilling to Smith, and was told that he should take his horse elsewhere. When Grove, drunk one evening, ignored the order and took his horse to Smith's yard anyway, an argument ensued, which was only broken when Mrs Smith intervened and persuaded her husband to let Grove have his way for now.

Grove though, followed Smith into his house and twice punched him. Still angered, he returned later and attacked the couple with a scythe. Mr Smith sustained two blows to the head, two broken legs, a broken arm and a broken rib. His wife's injuries were less severe. Mr Smith died in hospital on 20 March. After deliberating for an hour, the jury added a strong recommendation to mercy.

Read: And May The Lord Have Mercy On Your Soul.

004

Alfred HIGHFIELD   22

Cut throat of: **Edith Margaret Poole**, *19, on 13 May 1900, in London WC2.*

Motive: *Vengeance.*

Highfield, *(b.1878)*, a labourer at a brewery, had been courting Edith Poole since 1894, and the couple were due to marry in August 1900. On Easter Monday they argued and Edith told Alfred the relationship was over. He in turn blamed her for losing him his job, and though he wrote to her apologising, Edith was adamant that they were finished. Her family, having known Alfred many years, liked him, and Edith's brother invited him for tea in the hope of encouraging a reconciliation.

Still Edith remained adamant, and when the whole family went for a walk after tea, with the couple falling behind the others, Alfred cut Edith's throat when she finally rejected him. He later claimed that he took the razor to cut his own throat, but when Edith struggled with him she was cut accidentally. The jury took two hours considering, but added a recommendation to mercy on account of Alfred's youth and previous good character.

Read: And May The Lord Have Mercy On Your Soul.

14 August 1900   Newgate prison, London   *James Billington*

005

William James IRWIN   61

Stabbed: *Catherine Amelia Irwin, 35, his wife, on 22 June 1900, in London W1.*
Motive: *Sexual rivalry.*

Irwin, *(b.1839)*, a widower, married Catherine in 1888, and fathered four children by her. But by 1899 Catherine had become friendly with a man called Sexton, who would visit her while William was at work. In May the couple parted amicably, and remained friends. Catherine, a draper's assistant, gave money to William after he lost his job, and the couple would see each other regularly. But Irwin was still jealous of Sexton, though his wife claimed there was nothing sexual in the relationship.

On 20 June, Irwin watched Catherine's house, and saw Sexton leave at 11.30pm. The following day he went to borrow money from his wife, but was refused. At 8am the next morning Catherine left for work and Irwin was waiting for her. As she walked along with a friend she refused to speak to William, who pulled a knife and stabbed her in the breast, piercing a lung. Catherine died in hospital later the same day. The jury recommended Irwin to mercy.

Read: And May The Lord Have Mercy On Your Soul.

006

Charles Benjamin BACKHOUSE   24

Shot: *P.C. **John William Kew**, on 10 July 1900, in Swinton, W.Yorkshire.*

Motive: *Vengeance; drink related.*

John Kew, married and a father of four, was the popular village policeman in Swinton. He had served a summons on Fred Backhouse, 19, when he had beaten up his brother Charles' wife Gertie. Fred was charged with assault and was fined £2. The Backhouse brothers resented the policeman's interference into their family's affairs.

On 10 July they bought a revolver and later that evening in the local pub, drummed up support from John Wheeler and William Gibbins. They later continued their deliberations in Wheeler's house, by which time P.C. Kew had been warned of their intentions. He went to their house to confront them, and when Charles answered the door, Kew told him he needed to search him. Charles, *(b.1876),* shot him in the abdomen and passed the gun to Fred who shot him in the hip. Despite his injuries, the policeman managed to arrest the men and to take them to his police house. He died the following day from septic peritonitis.

Both brothers were found guilty of murder, but a strong recommendation to mercy was made in the case of Fred because of his youth and because the fatal wound was the one inflicted by Charles. Fred was reprieved on 14 August, and jailed for life. Charles was hanged with Mellor.

Read: A Date With the Hangman, p51.

007

Thomas MELLOR   29

Drowned: *1 **Ada Beecroft**, 6, and*
                      *2 **Annie Beecroft**, 4, his daughters, on 11 May 1900, in Leeds, W.Yorks.*

Motive: *To clear impediment.*

Mellor, *(b.1871),* had taken up with Priscilla Redshaw while Ada, the mother of his two illegitimate daughters was in an asylum. She died there in

November 1899, and the girls had come to live with Thomas and Priscilla in their Holbeck hovel. Mellor, a gas-worker, drank away most of his 17/- wages, giving Priscilla, a cleaner, only 3/-. They fell into rent arrears and were evicted on 4 May.

After hawking around for a week trying to find a place to stay, Priscilla dumped the girls on Mellor in a pub on the evening of 11 November. He tried the workhouse and relatives, but with nowhere for them to stay, he took them to the Leeds-Liverpool canal at 11pm and pushed them in. They were found floating there the next morning. The jury, strangely, made a strong recommendation to mercy, on account of Mellor's kindness to his children. He was hanged with Charles Backhouse.

Read: Murderous Leeds, p8.

21 August 1900   Cardiff gaol   *James/ W.Billington*

008

William Augustus LACEY   29   *Jamaican*

Cut throat of: ***Pauline Lacey****, 19, his wife, on 6 July 1900, in*
                       Pontypridd, Glamorgan.
Motive: *Vengeance.*

Lacey, *(b.1871),* met Pauline Joseph in Port Tennant through her sister, who was married to a fellow Jamaican. They married at Easter 1900 and moved to Pontypridd when he found work there. The couple argued constantly, and Pauline soon regretted the marriage, writing to her father, who encouraged her to come home. Lacey threatened to kill her if she did so, and refused to go to work for fear that she might leave if he did.

For a week he stayed at home, until he snapped on 6 July when he cut her throat with a razor. Their landlady heard the scream and found Pauline lying beside the murder weapon, Lacey having gone to hand himself in at the police station. He claimed that Pauline had committed suicide when she discovered that Lacey had been having sex with her sister.

Read: And May The Lord Have Mercy On Your Soul.

009

Charles Oliver BLEWITT   33

Cut throat of: ***Mary Ann Blewitt***, *33, his wife, on 8 June 1900, in Leeds, W.Yorks.*
Motive: *To clear impediment.*

Blewitt, *(b.1867)*, a tanner, hailed from Cornwall, but had worked in America from 1884 to 1895, returning to England and marrying Mary Ann Jackson the following year. Blewitt had never been in trouble with the police, and his marriage was said to be happy, no-one ever having heard a cross word between the two. But, after being unemployed for nine weeks, he cut Mary's throat and left her sitting in a chair with a shawl covering her head, which is how their landlord found her when he broke in nine days later.

Blewitt had fled, finding work at a toolmakers in Halifax, where he was arrested on 3 July. He suggested Mary had committed suicide, but this was impossible, as there was no weapon at the scene, and though the first jury, owing to the lack of motive, was deadlocked after 70 minutes, the second convicted him at the retrial after 45 minutes. Blewitt probably just wanted to be free.

Read: Murderous Leeds, p14.

010

John Charles PARR   19

Shot: ***Sarah Willett***, *19, on 27 August 1900, in London E2.*
Motive: *Vengeance.*

Parr, *(b. 1881)*, had served a six-month term for theft, but failed to tell Sarah Willett to whom he became engaged. He also told her he was a French-polisher, though he was unemployed. When she found out he had been economical with the truth in the summer of 1900, she broke off the engagement. On 25 August he told friends he would get her back, or kill her, firing a revolver in the street to show intent.

Two days later, he followed Sarah and her two friends to the music hall. When she refused to buy him a drink, he downed hers. Again following her home, opposite the police station in Bethnal Green Road, when she told him she wanted an honest man, he shot her in the head. He tried a plea of insanity, but the jury, in finding him guilty, recommended mercy on account of his youth.

Read: And May The Lord Have Mercy On Your Soul.

| 3 October 1900 | Chelmsford gaol | *James Billington* |

011

William BURRETT 35

Stabbed: **Ada Gubb Burrett**, 21, his wife, on 25 August 1900, in Plaistow, Essex.
Motive: Vengeance.

Burrett, *(b.1865),* just 8 st, married Ada, a prostitute, in July 1900, but was content to live from her immoral earnings. Ada had hoped marriage would be a way out of her old lifestyle, and pleaded with Burrett to find work. When he failed to do so she threatened to leave him, and many arguments followed. At 7.20am he stabbed her nine times with a bread knife, leaving the door open as he left. A paper-boy saw him leave and spotted Ada in a pool of blood at the foot of the stairs. After making a statement in hospital, Ada died from an abdomen wound at 8.20pm.

Read: And May The Lord Have Mercy On Your Soul.

| 4 December 1900 | Strangeways prison, Manchester |
| | *James Billington/ Warbrick* |

012

Joseph HOLDEN 57

Drowned: **John Dawes**, 9, his grandson, on 5 September 1900, in Bury, Lancs.
Motive: Vengeance.

Joe Holden, *(b.1843),* had turned to drink after his wife had died. He lost his job as an iron turner, and subsequently lost his home. His eleven adult children helped him out, but Holden's resentment of them grew when

8

he was committed to the workhouse. One daughter agreed to put him up, but only while her husband was away in America. His anger swelled. In August 1900, he took his grandson George Eldred, 9, to a quarry and threw a large rock on his head, packing him off back to Bury alone on a tram. Despite evidence that the stone had been forcefully thrown, his daughter believed his account that it had slipped from his hands.

Three weeks later, following a row with George's mother, Holden met another grandson, John Dawes, from school, took him to a quarry and threw him into a 12-metre deep pit. He followed the injured boy down and drowned him in the shallow water at the bottom. He gave himself up to local police, showing no remorse, and blaming his mistreatment at the hands of his children. Apart from John's mother, all his children called for a reprieve, and visited him in prison, as did little George.

Read: Strange Tales from Strangeways, p118.

12 December 1900　　　　Durham gaol　　　*James/ W.Billington*

013

John BOWES　　　50

Bludgeoned:　　*Isabella Bowes, 43, his wife, on 8 September 1900, in Seaham Harbour, Co Durham.*
Motive:　　*Vengeance.*

Bowes, *(b.1850)*, was a drunk who refused to work, content to live off the pickings his wife and 21-year old daughter could earn. Isabella salvaged coal from the beach and sold it to make a living. Bowes often attacked his wife, and falsely accused her of illicit affairs. On 21 August, again drunk, he hit Isabella and ripped his daughter's clothes. The two women had had enough, and left to live with Isabella's uncle. Three weeks later, Bowes found his wife collecting on the beach, and hit her four times on the head with a lump of wood. A policeman found him cradling Isabella, who died in hospital a few hours later. Bowes spent his last hundred days full of remorse.

Read: Murderous Tyneside, p247.

9

014

<u>James Joseph BURGIN</u>   **28**   *Irish*

Shot:	***Margaret Morrison**, 28, on 27 October 1900, in Liverpool, Lancs.*
Motive:	*Vengeance.*

Burgin, *(b.1872),* and Margaret had set Christmas 1898 for their wedding, but postponed the event when he lost his job, deciding to wed sometime the following year. In the meantime her family applied pressure to her because Burgin was a Catholic and she a Protestant, and Margaret called off the engagement. Burgin returned to Ireland.

In July 1900 he came back to Liverpool, and Margaret's mother at first refused him entry to the house. Two days later, though, he was invited to tea, and upstairs the pair became involved in some commotion, her mother discovering Margaret holding a razor, and Burgin having burned his leg with carbolic acid, a bottle of which he was holding.

In October, Burgin bumped into the Morrison family in Bootle, and Margaret and James went on to the theatre together. Walking her home Burgin shot her twice with a revolver. He was arrested the following day at a friend's house. Margaret died a day later. The jury recommended mercy.

Read: And May The Lord Have Mercy On Your Soul.

10 April 1900 Waterford County Gaol *Scott*

PATRICK DUNPHY 74

Poisoned: 1 **Edward Dunphy**, *9, his son, on 29 September 1899,*
2 **John Dunphy**, *11, also his son, on 19 December 1899, both in Waterford.*
Motive: *Financial.*

Dunphy, *(b.1826)*, a former train driver, had been widowed in January 1899, and found it hard to provide for his two youngest sons by menial labouring jobs. He insured both their lives for the sum of £10 to be paid upon their deaths. Edward collapsed in the street in September, his death put down to a form of epilepsy and heart failure. But when John also collapsed in Waterford twelve weeks later, police were alerted.

Edward's body was exhumed and both boys were found to have taken between one and three grains of strychnine. Dunphy had given John a drink of lemonade two hours before his death, and claimed that he had bought poison solely to kill rats. His elder daughter claimed there had never been rats in their house.

Dunphy was tried in March 1900 for the murder of John only, the jury taking only four minutes to reach its verdict. Dunphy's was the first execution in Waterford since 1864, and the poisoner was the oldest man to hang this century in the British Isles.

Read: Master Detective, Nov 97.

1901

total: *15*

015	19 Feb	Sampson SALMON	32		Newgate
016	19 Mar	George PARKER	23		Wandsworth
017	21 Mar	John BENNETT	22		Norwich
018	2 Apr	Joseph SHUTTLEBOTHAM	38		Stafford
019	9 Jul	Valeri GIOVANNI	31	*Italian*	Bodmin
020	30 Jul	Charles WATKINS	54		Maidstone
021	13 Aug	Ernest WICKHAM	30		Wandsworth
022	20 Aug	John JOYCE	36		Winson Green
023	19 Nov	Marcel FOUGERON	25	*French*	Newgate
024	3 Dec	Patrick McKENNA	53		Strangeways
025	7 Dec	John MILLER	67		Newcastle
026	7 Dec	John MILLER	30		Newcastle
027	10 Dec	John THOMPSON	31		Durham
028	13 Dec	Alick CLAYDON	43		Northampton
029	24 Dec	John HARRISON	31		Walton

19 February 1901   Newgate prison, London   *James Billington*

015

Sampson Silas SALMON   32

Cut throat of: **Lucy Smith**, *32, on 15 December 1900, in London E3.*
Motive: *Vengeance.*

Salmon, *(b.1869),* a labourer at a chemical works, took lodgings in Bow with his cousin Lucy, her husband Sam and their daughter in February 1899. He paid them thirteen shillings per week until he lost his job and turned to drink. On 10 December he hit both the Smiths and wielded a knife at them and a neighbour, upon which he was thrown out. When he climbed back through a window they let him stay.

On the morning of 15 December Salmon climbed over the yard wall and waited. When Lucy came out they argued, and Salmon hit her and cut her throat with a knife. Sam returned from work at 8am and found his dead wife with Salmon still there.

Read: And May The Lord Have Mercy On Your Soul

12

016

George Henry PARKER   23   *(aka Hill)*

Shot: **William Pearson**, *43, on 17 January 1901, near Surbiton, Surrey.*

Motive: *Financial.*

Parker, *(b.1878)*, six foot tall and well-built, had been dismissed from the army and was wanted by the police for theft from a theatre. He had recently begun an affair with a married woman and, flat broke, had decided he needed money to smooth along his new relationship. Having bought a revolver a few days previously, he boarded the Southampton to London train at Eastleigh one Thurday afternoon. In the compartment was Mrs Rhoda King, and the two were joined at Winchester by wealthy farmer William Pearson.

As the train approached Surbiton, Parker, having postponed his operation for some 40 miles, went to the lavatory to load his gun, returned and shot Mr Pearson dead, wounding Mrs King in the cheek. Stealing the farmer's money, and throwing the weapon from a window, Parker ran off as the train entered Vauxhall station, but Mrs King raised the alarm, and several men gave chase and caught him. He later said he wished he had killed Mrs King as well. A plea of temporary insanity was rejected.

Read: The Railway Murders, p55.

017

Herbert John BENNETT   22   *i*

Strangled: **Mary Jane Bennett**, *24, his wife, on 22 September 1900, in Yarmouth, Norfolk.*

Motive: *To clear impediment.*

Herbert Bennett *(b.1879)*, and Mary Jane Clarke, were married in 1897, he a grocer's assistant, she his music teacher. They had generally swindled to make a living, selling old violins and running up unpaid credit on a grocery business. He had gone to South Africa but had been deported as a suspected Boer spy. By 1900, living in Bexley Heath, he was working in the Woolwich arsenal, and was involved in the latest of a string of affairs with other women, this time with Alice Meadows, 20. They had holidayed together in Yarmouth and in Ireland.

On 15 September, on Alice's recommendation, Mrs Bennett took off to Yarmouth for a break from it all. Purporting to be Mrs Hood, a widow, she lodged with a Mrs Rudram.

On 20 September Mary Jane was strangled with a bootlace on Yarmouth's south beach. She appeared to have been the victim of a sexual assault. Her real identity was determined by a laundry mark. Her husband was found to be in possession of a watch chain which Mary Jane had been wearing on the day of her death. He was also identified by three other witnesses as having been in Yarmouth on that day. However, another witness placed him in south London, and a Lowestoft newsagent reported that a man with a scratched face and missing a shoelace had been making unusual enquiries about the murder.

Though the evidence weighed heavily against him at his six day trial, and with the jury taking just 35 minutes to determine his guilt, there was considerable doubt in many people's minds. This was underlined when the pole on which the black flag was being raised after his execution snapped and fell to the ground, and, more pertinently, when another woman, Dora Gray, 18, was found murdered on Yarmouth's south beach in identical circumstances in 1912.

Read: The Seaside Murders, p9.

2 April 1901	Stafford gaol	*James/ W.Billington*

018

Joseph Arthur SHUFFLEBOTHAM   38

Cut throat of:	***Elizabeth Shufflebotham**, 32, his wife, on 28 December 1900, in Biddulph Moor, Staffs.*
Motive:	*Vengeance.*

Shufflebotham, *(b.1863)*, already had five children by his first wife when he married Elizabeth, the mother of a further four children of his, on 28 December 1899. Three months later he was fined £2 for an assault on her, and the following October a second summons was issued for a similar offence, which Shufflebotham did not answer. He went off to Yorkshire and found work for a month in a colliery, during which time Elizabeth gave birth to his tenth child.

Returning to Staffordshire in November, he was arrested and this time fined £1. By 3 December, Elizabeth had had enough and went to live with her mother. On their first wedding anniversary, Shufflebotham went to Elizabeth's home, broke down the door, and cut his wife's throat with a razor. He later claimed that she had hit him when he burst in.

Read: And May The Lord Have Mercy On Your Soul.

9 July 1901	Bodmin gaol	*James/ W.Billington*

019

Valeri GIOVANNI   31   *Italian*

Stabbed: ***Victor Baileff,*** *on 15 February 1901, in the south Atlantic.*

Motive: *Vengeance.*

        The Liverpool cargo ship *Lorton* had sailed from Hamburg on 1 April 1900, calling at Portland, Oregon and Durban, where Baileff joined the crew. At the next port of call, Newcastle, Australia, Giovanni, *(b.1870),* signed on. The Italian became the butt of many jokes by Baileff, and when the ship next docked, in Caleta Buena in northern Chile, the two had a fist fight, Giovanni coming off worse.
        Lorton sailed again with a cargo of nitrates on 7 December, bound for Falmouth. By February the teasing by Baileff and others was growing too much for Giovanni. At 6.30am, he stole a knife from the galley and went below decks, where Baileff was repairing a sail. Grabbing from behind round the neck, Giovanni stabbed Baileff eight times, piercing his heart. The ship reached Cornwall in May and the Italian faced a speedy trial.

Read: And May The Lord Have Mercy On Your Soul

30 July 1901	Maidstone prison	*James/ W.Billington*

020

Charles Richard Thomas WATKINS   54

Shot: ***Frederick William Acland Hamilton,*** *46, on 5 April 1901, in Gravesend, Kent.*

Motive: *Vengeance.*

Letitia Hamilton had a daughter from her first marriage when she wed Watkins, *(b.1847)*, in January 1900, the couple living in Rotherhithe. It was only five weeks before she had tired of his drinking, and went to live with her brother in Gravesend. Already hurt, Watkins became angry when Letitia took out a separation order, and anger turned to fury when he was summonsed for falling behind with payments to his estranged wife. Bumping into her brother one day, Watkins started a furious argument, and the following day bought a revolver.

Two days after that, Good Friday, Watkins went to Hamilton's house and hammered on the door. As Frederick opened the window, Watkins let out three shots, hitting his brother-in-law in the lung. Watkins waited calmly outside for police to arrive.

Read: And May The Lord Have Mercy On Your Soul

13 August 1901   Wandsworth prison, London   *James/ W.Billington*

021

Ernest Walter WICKHAM   30

Cut throat of :   ***Amy Euguenie Russell***, 35, on 27 June 1901, in London SW2.
Motive: *Vengeance; drink related.*

Wickham, *(b.1871)*, had been walking out with Amy for some time, and on the evening of 26 June, the two had been seen arguing in a pub. At 1.45am, walking along the street in Brixton, Wickham suddenly pushed Amy against a wall and cut her throat, his crime witnessed from a bedroom window. Police followed a bloody trail to a coffee stall, where the vendor told them a man he knew, Ernest Wickham, had just bought a coffee. He was still caked in dried blood when police roused him from his bed at 4am. Wickham was completely uninterested in the procedings around him, telling the judge, when asked how he would plead, 'Anything you like!'

Read: And May The Lord Have Mercy On Your Soul.

022

John JOYCE   36

Stabbed: ***John Nugent***, *61, on 10 June 1901, in Birmingham, Warwicks.*
Motive: *Vengeance, drink related.*

Joyce, *(b.1865)*, known to everyone as Toby, had been demobbed in 1899, returning to Birmingham after serving in India. Since that time he had been in a running feud with the Nugents, John and his sons Thomas and Michael, who Joyce claimed had attacked him in their home. On 25 May Joyce and Michael had both been hurt in a fight, the case being dismissed by a magistrate.

Two weeks later, the worse for some drink, Joyce, armed with a knife, went to the Nugent home at 9.45pm looking for Michael who was out. John ran to get the police after Joyce had foully insulted him and his wife Elizabeth, but Joyce caught him outside and stabbed him in the abdomen. John Nugent died on his way to hospital.

Joyce was picked up later in a nearby street. Finding him guilty, the jury recommended mercy, believing the Nugents had behaved badly to the murderer.

Read: Murderous Birmingham, p8.

19 November 1901   Newgate prison, London

James Billington/ H.Pierrepoint

023

Marcel FOUGERON   24   *French*

Stabbed: ***Hermann Francis Jung***, *70, on 3 September 1901, in London EC1.*
Motive: *Financial.*

Fougeron, *(b.1877)*, came to London with little English, and little money, in July 1901. Evicted from his lodgings, he was advised to go and see Mr Jung, who ran a jeweller's shop in Clerkenwell, and who was known for helping out foreigners in trouble. Jung, a Swiss watchmaker, had run his shop for forty years, and had already let Fougeron have about £5, when the Frenchman called again on 3 September.

After chatting for about three hours, Fougeron stabbed the old man, probably because he refused him more money, and fled just as Mrs Jung came to investigate the commotion. She gave chase, and a policeman arrested Fougeron. He claimed that Mr Jung was an anarchist who had tried to enlist the Frenchman's help in assassinating Joseph Chamberlain, the Colonial Secretary.

Read: And May The Lord Have Mercy On Your Soul

3 December 1901   Strangeways prison, Manchester
James Billington / H.Pierrepoint

024

Patrick McKENNA   53

Stabbed: ***Anna McKenna***, *50, his wife, on 30 September 1901, in Bolton, Lancs.*
Motive: *Sexual rivalry, drink related.*

McKenna, *(b. 1848)* , a master joiner, had been unemployed for two years and had turned to drink. He and his wife Anna had been forced to take in lodgers to make ends meet. Their latest tenants, Mr and Mrs Palmer, had increased Patrick's anxiety - he had become convinced that Anna and Palmer were having an affair. His daughter-in-law later described the idea as ridiculous.

Though he had found work as a labourer, McKenna continued to drink away most of the family's money, and flew into a rage when Anna refused to hand over any of the money received from a trip to the pawnbroker's.

She fled in fear to her daughter-in-law's house. At 5pm he burst in, and in a noisy exchange, Anna twice dared him to take the knife to her. He did, stabbing her once in the neck. She died soon afterwards.

McKenna fled to his own house, and was found there crouching in the coalhole under the stairs. He was immediately and continuously repentant. 22,000 people signed a petition pleading his reprieve. Standing on the trap, his final words were, 'Oh, Lord, help me!'

Read: A Date With the Hangman, p74.

025, 026

John MILLER   67
John Robert MILLER   30

Stabbed: *Joseph Ferguson, 67, on 20 September 1901, in Cullercoats, Northumberland.*

Motive: *Vengeance, drink related.*

Joseph Ferguson, an itinerant showman, had married John Miller's sister, a well-to-do widow of 85, in 1897.

Miller,*(b.1834),* the owner of fairground roundabouts on Cullercoats beach, infuriated that he may be denied his inheritance, took his simple-minded musician nephew to buy a sheath-knife and to get drunk.

The younger Miller, *(b.1871),* had been kicked in the head by a horse at 7, and spent four months in an asylum. Together they went to Ferguson's home, where the young man stabbed his victim eight times in the neck, chest and hands. The jury found both uncle and nephew guilty after just ten minutes.

The younger man, having spent his final night screaming, went to the scaffold calmly 90 minutes before his uncle - the planned double execution cancelled for fear of an attack by the nephew who felt himself a victim of his uncle's plot.

Read: Murderous Tyneside, p8

027

John George THOMPSON   38

Shot: *Maggie Ann Lieutand, 33, on 16 September 1901, in Newcastle, Northumberland*

Motive: *Vengeance*

Maggie Whistton married a ship's cook in 1898, but separated from him and set up home with John Thompson, *(b.1863),* in March 1901, until that relationship also broke down in July. Thompson, a fitter, could not accept Maggie's decision, and continually pleaded to be taken back.

On 16 September he saw her with a friend and became abusive when she would not talk with him. When she returned to her Gateshead home at about 2.30pm, Thompson was waiting for her. He tried to push his way into her house, and then tried to drag her out, before taking out the revolver he had bought that day and firing a shot. Maggie ran across the street to a neighbour's house, but failed to close the door. Thompson managed to get his arm through and fired two shots, hitting Maggie in the arm and the head.

He was cradling her when police arrived, and Maggie died the following day. Two doctors found Thompson to be suffering syphilitic insanity, but the jury took just five minutes to find him guilty, though they added a strong recommendation to mercy.

Read: True Detective, Sep 98.

---

13 December 1901   Northampton prison   *W.Billington*

028

Alexander CLAYDON   43

Bludgeoned/ stabbed: **Louisa Claydon**, 40, his wife, on 7 July 1901,
                                  in Northampton.
Motive: Vengeance; drink related..

Alick Claydon, *(b.1858)*, a shoe finisher, had once tried suicide, and was said to have fits. His heavy drinking did not help his situation, and in 1899 his wife left him, though the two were again reconciled. After going missing for several days on a drinking binge, Claydon bumped into Louisa in a pub, and the two went home together and retired for the night.

At midnight Claydon rose, went to get a file from the shop, came back home, and battered and stabbed his wife with it. Claydon told his daughter, woken by the commotion, to return to sleep, while he cooked himself some eggs, and then went back to bed beside his dead wife. At 4am he woke again, and went out for a walk, leaving his daughter to find her mother at 10am. He was soon arrested.

Read: And May The Lord Have Mercy On Your Soul

029

John HARRISON   31

Strangled: ***Alice Ann Wright**, 29, on 27 July 1901, in Bickerstaffe,
Lancs.*
Motive: *Vengeance.*

Harrison, *(b.1870)*, became involved with Alice Wright, a married woman, in 1901. She left her husband, and she and Harrison walked from Ormskirk on 26 July, to Skelmerdale and Bickerstaffe the next day, looking for lodgings. They finally rented a cottage, but before leaving just after 1pm, Harrison strangled his mistress, who smashed a window in the struggle.

A woman passer-by saw Alice through the window at 1.20pm, but thought she must be drunk. Harrison returned at 9pm, and immediately reported to his landlord that he had found his wife dead. Though he protested his innocence to the end, blood on Harrison's shirt cuff convinced the jury that only he could have been responsible.

Read: And May The Lord Have Mercy On Your Soul

10 January 1901	Cork County Gaol	*James Billington*

TIMOTHY CADOGAN

Shot:	A gentleman land agent.
Motive:	Vengeance.

Cadogan shot dead a land agent who had evicted him. The night before his execution, he tried to cut his throat with his metal toe-cap. No further details.

11 January 1901	Crumlin Road Gaol, Belfast	*Scott*

WILLIAM WOODS   58

Cut throat of:	**Bridget McGivern**, 40, on 26 September 1900, at Bushmills, Co Antrim.
Motive:	Sadistic pleasure, drink related.

Woods, (b.1843), a pedlar, had by 1890 received over 30 convictions for assault, including one upon a magistrate. He then served nine years of a 12-year sentence for the manslaughter of Mary Irwin, with whom he had been living in Co Derry. Released from a police station at midnight for being drunk, he went home and cut her throat with a scythe, tying her body to a cartwheel and mutilating it with the same weapon. He escaped a murder conviction on provocation grounds.

Bridget was an impoverished widow who lived with her two children in a one-room wooden hut in the hamlet of Eagry near Bushmills. She began a relationship with Woods, but turned down his proposals of marriage on religious grounds- she a catholic, he protestant. Calling on her one evening, he began to drink heavily and Bridget got into bed, as her two sons, aged 2 and 14, slept. Her elder boy awoke to find his mother, her nightdress ripped to shreds, dead on another bed with her throat cut. Woods had walked to a police station and reported the death, explaining, 'We were drunk'. Woods had bought a razor the day before, though he was bearded. The jury took half an hour to find him guilty.

Woods was only the sixth man ever to be hanged in Belfast.

Read: True Detective, Oct 96.

7 March 1901 Mountjoy Gaol, Dublin *Scott/ Binns*

JOHN TOOLE

Murdered: **Lizzie Brennan**
Motive: *unknown*

The pair had been living together. Toole confessed in the condemned cell.

1902

total: **23**

030	18 Mar	Richard WIGLEY	34		Shrewsbury
031	18 Mar	Harold APTED	20		Maidstone
032	25 Mar	Arthur RICHARDSON	30		Hull
033	29 Apr	Charles EARL	56		Wandsworth
034	6 May	George WOOLFE	22		Newgate
035	20 May	Thomas MARSLAND	21		Walton
036	15 Jul	Samuel MIDDLETON	46		Worcester
037	22 Jul	William CHURCHER	35		Winchester
038	30 Jul	John BEDFORD	41		Derby
039	12 Aug	William LANE	48		Stafford
040	13 Aug	George HIBBS	40		Wandsworth
041	30 Sep	James McDONALD	24		Pentonville
042	11 Nov	Henry WILLIAMS	31		Pentonville
043	12 Nov	Patrick LEGGETT		Scottish	Duke Street
044	2 Dec	Harry MACK	29		Strangeways
045	4 Dec	William CHAMBERS	47		Bedford
046	9 Dec	Thomas BARROW	49		Pentonville
047	12 Dec	Jeremiah CALLAGHAN	42	Welsh	Usk
048	16 Dec	Thomas WALTON	31		Durham
049	16 Dec	Thomas NICHOLSON	23		Durham
050	16 Dec	William BROWN	42		Wandsworth
051	22 Dec	William BOLTON	43		Hull
052	30 Dec	George PLACE	28		Warwick

18 March 1902   Shrewsbury prison   *H.Pierrepoint/ Ellis*

030

Richard WIGLEY   **34**

Cut throat of: ***Mary Ellen Bowen***, *28, on 30 November 1901, in Westbury, Shropshire.*
Motive: *Vengeance; drink related.*

Wigley, *(b.1868),* a slaughterman from Berrington, was separated from his wife. He had been seeing Mary Bowen, a barmaid, for some years, but in 1901 she broke off the relationship.

Following a drinking binge, he arrived in Westbury at 10am, wearing his butcher's apron and concealing two knives in its pocket, and went straight to Mary's pub. Not pleased to see him, Mary was reluctant to serve Wigley. He followed Mary into a passage and cut her throat. Wigley tried to claim insanity, citing his mother's confinement in an asylum.

Read: And May The Lord Have Mercy On Your Soul

18 March 1902   Maidstone prison   *W./John Billington*

031

Harold Amos APTED   **20**

i

Stabbed: ***Frances Eliza O'Rourke**, 7, on 31 December 1901, in Southborough, Kent.*
Motive: *Sexual.*

Apted, *(b. 1882)*, a church chorister and the yougest of 12 children, delivered coal and wood for his sick father's business, which Harold had run for two years. He was driving his horse-drawn van near Tonbridge at 4.30pm on New Year's Eve, after delivering calves to Tunbridge Wells.

Frances O'Rourke had been sent on an errand by her tailor father at 2pm, to deliver clothes to Tunbridge Wells, two miles away. She was seen accepting a lift from a van. She was taken to a field, was stripped, raped, and then stabbed behind the left ear. With the knife still entangled in her hair, her naked body was dumped in a pond, where she was found the next morning.

Apted had arrived home at 5pm and gone out with his girlfriend. Blood was found in the vehicle, explained by Apted as animal blood, and small amounts of blood on his clothes did not reflect the girl's wounds. A witness confirmed that Apted was on a different route, but Apted lied about having a knife, and the jury were convinced of his guilt in 50 minutes, though they recommended mercy because of his youth.

Read: True Crime, Mar 98

032

Arthur RICHARDSON   30

Bludgeoned: **Sarah Hebden**, *62, on 28 November 1901, in Hull, E.Yorks.*
Motive: *Financial.*

Richardson, *(b.1872),* was released from a six-month sentence for robbing his aunt, on 20 November 1901. He was Mary Bonar's illegitimate son, and his mother lived next door to her sister, another aunt to Arthur, Sarah Hebden. Sarah was an agent for an insurance company, and paid in the money she had collected every Thursday.

Just eight days after his release, Richardson went to his aunt, battered her to death, stealing the £5 insurance money, a further £5-£10 from the old lady's tea caddy, and a gold watch. Richardson, known to be penniless, drew attention to himself by flaunting a new suit and coat. He was found to be in possession of Sarah's watch. His was Hull's first execution since 1768.

Read: And May The Lord Have Mercy On Your Soul.

033

Charles Robert EARL   56

Shot: **Margaret Pamphilon**, *40, on 6 March 1902, in London SW14.*
Motive: *Vengeance.*

Earl, *(b.1846),* a retired baker, did not get along with his neighbours, the Pamphilons. He blamed them when his wife left him, and his grudge grew to the point where, following an argument in July 1901, he smashed the windows of their house. On 6 March the following spring, Earl bought a revolver, and that evening went to his neighbour's, banging on the door. When Margaret Pamphilon answered, he let out three shots, hitting his neighbour twice in the arm, and once in the forehead. The jury did not bother retiring before reaching its verdict.

Read: And May The Lord Have Mercy On Your Soul.

034

George WOOLFE   22   *C*

Kicked & stabbed: **Charlotte Cheeseman, 22, on**
                              25 January 1902, in Tottenham, Middlesex.
Motive: *To clear impediment, drink related.*

Woolfe, *(b.1880)*, a former soldier, had become Charlotte's boyfriend while her first love was fighting in the Boer War. The girl was hopelessly infatuated and pressed for marriage when she realised she was pregnant. Despite the vindictive letters he wrote to her employers and the punch in the mouth he gave her at new year, she persisted. He insisted to friends that he would soon get rid of her and following a drink in a north London pub, on a freezing night in January, both the worse for drink, he took her to the Tottenham marshes.

There Woolfe, 5'5" and 9st, viciously kicked her in the face and head. As she vainly tried to fend off his blows, he stabbed her seventeen times with a broken chisel. She took several hours to die. Her body was discovered the next morning by a boy recovering his football. Under a false name Woolfe joined the army, but was tracked down to the Surrey Regiment on 6 February.

Woolfe's was the last execution at Newgate, the prison closing two weeks later.

Read: The Hangman's Diary, p156.

035

Thomas MARSLAND   21

Bludgeoned/ cut throat of: **Elizabeth Marsland, 23, his wife, on**
                                      4 April 1902, in Oldham, Lancs.
Motive: *Sadistic pleasure.*

Marsland, *(b.1881)*, a cotton piercer, married Elizabeth in November 1901. From the start he took pleasure in beating his wife. His landlady had seen him three times strike Elizabeth in the mouth, and the couple were thrown out of their lodgings.

Elizabeth left him in February. Marsland gave up his job on 2 April, and met Elizabeth on her way to work two days later. He bought a razor that afternoon and waited for his wife to return from work at 6.15pm. Following an argument, Marsland again punched her to the ground, and slit her throat as she lay helpless.

Read: And May The Lord Have Mercy On Your Soul.

15 July 1902	Worcester prison	*W.Billington*

036

Samuel MIDDLETON   46

Bludgeoned: *Hannah Middleton, 40, his wife, on 10 May 1902, in Foxlydiate, Worcs.*
Motive: *Vengeance; drink related.*

Middleton, *(b.1856)*, was a drunkard who constantly abused his hard-working wife. On the evening of 10 May the neighbours in Foxlydiate, near Redditch, heard another argument between the couple, with the sound of furniture being thrown about. Hannah scratched and bit her husband, and he responded by battering her to death with the poker. He then set the house alight and left. By 3am the blaze had gutted the Middleton house and that of the neighbours. Middleton made a full confession to the police when he was arrested two days later. The jury retired for only four minutes.

Read: Murderous Birmingham, p237

22 July 1902	Winchester prison	*W/ John Billington*

037

William CHURCHER   35

Stabbed: *Sophia Jane Hepworth, 35, on 10 April 1902, in Gosport, Hants.*
Motive: *Vengeance.*

Churcher, *(b.1867),* had lived with Sophia Hepworth since 1889, though she was a married woman. Sophia had a considerable drink problem, and on 10 April a large crowd gathered when she ran down the street completely drunk, and fell in the river. Churcher's patience with her finally ran out when he had to fish her out of the water on his way home from work at 11pm.

A row developed after he had taken her home, and Churcher stabbed Sophia in a frenzied knife attack, wounding her a total of 33 times. Two gashes to the throat proved fatal. The police broke in on 12 April and found Sophia sitting in a chair. The jury made a strong recommendation to mercy on account of Sophia's provocation.

Read: And May The Lord Have Mercy On Your Soul.

| 30 July 1902 | Derby gaol | *W.Billington/ H.Pierrepoint* |

038

John BEDFORD   41

Bludgeoned: *Nancy Price, 48, on 25 June 1902, in Duckmanton, Derbyshire.*
Motive: *Sexual rivalry, drink related.*

Bedford, *(b.1861),* was a miner who lived with his parents at Calow Green. Known as Tommy, he met Nancy Price in 1892. She ran a fish shop in Duckmanton to support her husband Joseph who was much older than her, and was virtually crippled and deaf after two accidents, in the mine and on the railway.

Nancy and Bedford were lovers for ten years without problems between them, he sleeping with her up to four times a week mainly while her husband was staying with their son. But from May 1902 Bedford began to suspect Nancy of seeing another man, and despite her vehement denials, Bedford's jealousy grew. One night he shouted abuse at Nancy and smashed several window panes.

They had both been drinking on the night of 25 June. Joseph was away, and Nancy saw a friend home, returning at 10.45pm. As she sat sewing on the sofa, Bedford, without warning, hit Nancy on the forehead with a poker, and again once behind each ear. They next day in the pub he told disbelieving friends what he had done, and they discovered her body at 11am. The jury took less than five minutes to decide his fate.

Read: Murderous Derbyshire, p25.

039

William LANE   48

Cut throat of: **Elizabeth Dyson**, *46, on 26 June 1902, in West Bromwich, Staffs.*

Motive: *To clear impediment; drink related.*

Lane, *(b.1853),* had been a policeman in Bradford for eleven years before starting his own successful detective agency. Married with two sons, he began an affair in 1896 with Elizabeth Dyson, 40, who came to him concerning her divorce. She had been a dancer and now made her living playing pub pianos.

Often away on business, Lane would take Elizabeth with him as his assistant, but then moved her into the spare room at his family home. It was then that the shine began to fade for Lane, with Elizabeth pressing for marriage, and Lane nervous for his business reputation. He turned her out at Christmas 1899, and the family moved to West Bromwich where Lane built up a new business.

Elizabeth found Lane in March 1902, moving back in, and the affair resuming, but now the business began to suffer, Lane turning to drink and becoming violent towards his wife. She and their sons left him on 23 June, and three days later, after a pub crawl and an argument he cut his lover's throat, almost decapitating her. He told police it was the only way to get rid of her. The jury decided his guilt in just three minutes, but his wife and sons forgave him, visiting him in the condemned cell.

Read: True Crime, Dec 95.

040

George William HIBBS   40

Stabbed: **Miriam Jane Tye**, *57, on 28 June 1902, in London SW11.*

Motive: *Sexual rivalry; drink related.*

Hibbs, *(b.1862)*, a labourer, rented a room in Miriam Tye's Battersea house from January 1900, and the two probably had a sexual relationship. Following a drunken argument on 1 June 1902, Hibbs tried to stab Miriam with a shoemaker's knife, but George apologised when sober, and she forgave him.

But just four weeks later, when Hibbs, again after alcohol, found that Miriam had no clean shirt to give him, he stabbed her in the stomach with the same knife, and was caught red-handed by another lodger who answered the landlady's screams. Miriam died two days later. In taking an hour to reach its verdict, the jury added a strong recommendation to mercy. In the condemned cell Hibbs confessed that he had loved Miriam and was very jealous.

Read: And May The Lord Have Mercy On Your Soul.

30 September 1902   Pentonville prison, London
W/ John Billington/ H.Pierrepoint

041

James MacDONALD   **24**

Stabbed: ***Henry Groves**, 50, on 28 August 1902, in London E1.*
Motive: *Vengeance.*

McDonald, *(b.1878)*, and Groves both had a bed at the Salvation Army shelter, and when McDonald had five shillings stolen while he slept, he blamed the older man, and threatened to kill him.

On 28 August the two got into an argument in a shop near Spitalfields market. McDonald tried to strangle Groves and punched him. Three times a passer-by had to break up the fight, but as they separated McDonald stabbed Groves in the neck, and was held by the witness until police arrived. McDonald's was the first execution at Pentonville prison.

Read: And May The Lord Have Mercy On Your Soul

11 November 1902   Pentonville prison, London

W. Billington/ H.Pierrepoint

042

Henry WILLIAMS   31

Cut throat of: ***Margaret Anne Andrews****, 5, his daughter, on 10
September 1902, in London SW6..*
Motive: *Vengeance.*

Williams, *(b. 1871),* had been with Ellen Andrews, a widow, since
1893, and the pair celebrated the birth of a daughter in 1897, just before
Williams went off to fight in the Boer War. He did not return until July 1902,
and became convinced that Ellen had been unfaithful with a sailor in his
absence, a charge she denied. He did not go back to Ellen, but visited
mother and child in Worthing, promising that he would repay Ellen's
unfaithfulness by breaking her heart.

He took his daughter back to his Fulham home, obsessed with the
fear that she may grow up to be a loose woman like her mother. He put
Margaret to bed and, closing her eyes, cut her throat, before covering her with
a union jack. Though the jury strongly recommended mercy, he made no plea
for clemency, nor sought any reprieve. The man whose executioner
described as 'The bravest man I ever hanged', Williams muttered, 'Lord have
mercy on me' as the trap opened.

Read: And May The Lord Have Mercy On Your Soul.

12 November 1902   Duke Street, Glasgow   *W.Billington*

043

Patrick LEGGETT   *Scottish*

Stabbed: ***Sarah Jane Leggett****, his wife, on 13 September 1902, in
Glasgow, Lanarks.*
Motive: *Vengeance.*

Leggett stabbed his wife in the neck at their home in Wylie's Back
Land, Glasgow, and was rescued from the Clyde after trying to drown himself.

Read: The Encyclopaedia of Scottish Executions

2 December 1902   Strangeways prison, Manchester

W.Billington/ H.Pierrepoint

044

Harry MACK   29   *(real name: Henry McWiggins)*

C

Kicked: ***Esther Elizabeth Bedford**, 26, on 12 August 1902, in Oldham, Lancs.*

Motive: *Sadistic pleasure.*

Mack, *(b.1873)*, and Esther Bedford lived together from June 1902, but it was August before Mack's violence started. Their landlady saw him dragging Esther by the hair and hitting and kicking her on 2 August. Six days later, when he did not like the dinner she served him, he kicked his wife and gave her two black eyes.

The following morning he kicked her awake and hit her in the face with a shovel. Two days after that Mack threw a kettle of boiling water in Esther's face, and when he returned at 9pm, he made a point of hitting her in her scalded face, as well as giving her another kicking. Esther was kicked so hard in the stomach that her bladder ruptured, but before she died she made a statement that Mack had never hurt her. The jury took 20 minutes to decide otherwise. It was in the condemned cell that Mack revealed his true identity.

Read: And May The Lord Have Mercy On Your Soul.

4 December 1902   Bedford gaol   *W.Billington/ Scott*

045

William CHAMBERS   47

Shot: 1 ***Emily Chambers**, 44, his wife and*
                2 ***Mary Oakley**, 67, her mother, on 23 September 1902, in Eversholt, Beds.*

Motive: *Vengeance.*

Chambers, *(b.1855)*, married Emily Oakley in 1892, but she had tired of his ill-treatment by September 1902, and left him, returning to her mother. His anger turned to rage when he received a solicitor's letter on 22 September demanding payments be made to Emily. The following day, at 7pm, he burst into Mary Oakley's house with a shotgun.

Emily, her sister and her sister's daughter were also present. Calmly, and without comment, Chambers raised the gun, and blasted Mary

Oakley through the neck, hitting Emily in the lower face with his second volley. As he reloaded the others fled, and Chambers blasted himself in the face. The shot removed part of his jaw, but Chambers walked into a pub and asked for a drink. The landlord summoned the police.

Read: And May The Lord Have Mercy On Your Soul.

9 December 1902   Pentonville prison, London   *W/ John Billington*

046

Thomas Fairclough BARROW   49

Stabbed: **Emily Coates**, *32, his step-daughter, on 18 October 1902, in London E1.*
Motive: *Vengeance.*

Barrow, *(b.1853),* had lived with his step-daughter since 1887 as man and wife. But arguments started in 1902, and Emily left him when he became violent. Barrow's resentment turned to fury when he was served a warrant for assault.

He went to her lodgings but was refused entry, so he waited for Emily to leave for work. Barrow came up behind her with a knife and stabbed her five times, a blow through the heart proving fatal. The jury considered its verdict without even leaving the courtroom.

Read: And May The Lord have Mercy On Your Soul.

12 December 1902   Usk prison, Monmouthshire   *W/ John Billington*

047

Jeremiah CALLAGHAN   42   *Welsh*

Cut throat of: **Hannah Shea**, *38, on 4 October 1902, in Tredegar, Monmouthshire.*
Motive: *Sexual rivalry; drink related.*

Callaghan, *(b.1860),* and Hannah Shea had four children together, but by 1902, while he was in lodgings, Hannah and the children were in a

34

workhouse. Callaghan, a labourer in Tredegar, was consumed with jealousy over Hannah and other men. Hannah took the children to meet Jeremiah from work, but when he smelled that she had had a drink while waiting for him, he threw her to the ground. Calmer, they later had a drink together, and then set off, Callaghan walking them back home. On the way, with the children present, Callaghan cut Hannah's throat, then went on with the children and joined in a dance at the workhouse.

Read: And May The Lord Have Mercy On Your Soul

16 December 1902	Durham gaol	*W./ John Billington*

048

Samuel Thomas WALTON   31

Shot:
1 **Isabella Walton**, *26, his wife,*
2 **Esther Jane Walton**, *11 mths, their child, and*
3 **Isabella Young**, *53, Isabella's mother, on 11 September 1902, in Middlestone Moor, Co Durham.*
Motive: *Vengeance; drink related.*

Walton, *(b.1871)*, a miner of Middleton Moor, had a rocky marriage. In the summer of 1902, Isabella finally left him, egged on by her mother. On a summons of persistent cruelty, custody of their baby was given to Isabella, and Samuel was ordered to pay 10/- per week. Turning to drink, Walton skipped work and sold all his furniture, leaving his house to stay with parents or friends. Leaving his dog with a friend, he bought a revolver from a pawnbrokers, and at noon went to his mother-in-law's house.

Asking for a receipt for his first payment, he shot Mrs Young through the right eye as she mounted the stairs. He then shot his baby in the head. She died two hours later. Dragging his wife by the hair from the door, he shot her twice in the face through her hand. She managed to run to a neighbour's. When the police arrived, they found Walton with his throat cut, cradling his child. His wife died a week later. The jury did not even retire to consider its verdict. Walton was hanged alongside Thomas Nicholson, telling him, 'Good morning, lad. Keep thy heart up'.

Read: True Detective, Sep 95.

049

Thomas NICHOLSON   23

Strangled: ***Mary Ina Stewart***, *7, on 16 August 1902, in Bill Quay, near Gateshead, Co Durham.*
Motive: *Sexual; drink related.*

Nicholson, *(b.1879),* was a cartman for a farmer in the village of Bill Quay, where he lived with his parents. One Sunday, after drinking in the village pub with a neighbour, he was seen heading for waste ground known as Hilly Fields. He was seen returning two hours later, and leaving the house in the middle of the following night.

On the waste ground at 7.30pm he had met Mary Stewart, returning from an errand to her uncle. She lived in Bill Quay with her widowed father and his mother. Nicholson smothered her with his hand, beating her head and limbs with a stone after her death. He used a knife to open her vagina before raping her. He placed a piece of bread in her mouth and went home, returning later to move her body. She was found in a brickworks yard two days later. Nicholson had blood on his clothes and he lied about staying in the pub until closing time. The jury deliberated for 35 minutes. He was hanged alongside Samuel Walton.

Read: True Detective, Aug 95.

050

William BROWN   42

Kicked: ***Elizabeth Brown***, *41, his wife, in November 1902, in London SW14.*
Motive: *Vengeance; drink related.*

Brown, *(b.1860),* and Elizabeth had married in 1880, but Brown's attachment to drink was a constant headache for his wife. A blazing row at their Mortlake home ended with a sustained attack on Elizabeth, during which Brown hit her in the face and kicked her so heavily on the ground that her breastbone and fourteen ribs were broken. The attack was witnessed through the window by a boy who alerted a neighbour, but Elizabeth called out for her to go away. Mrs Brown was later found dead at the foot of the stairs. Brown wanted the jury to believe that she had been attacked outside the house. It took them one hour to disagree.

Read: And May The Lord Have Mercy On Your Soul

22 December 1902	Hull prison	*W/ John Billington*

051

William James BOLTON   43

Stabbed: **Jane Elizabeth Allen**, on 18 October 1902, in Hull, E.Yorks.

Motive: Vengeance.

       Bolton, *(b.1859),* began an affair with Jane Allen, and so his wife left him. She then went to see Jane, who had no idea Bolton was married. When he called at Jane's lodgings at 11.30pm she told him it was better that they finish the relationship, but, nevertheless, allowed him to stay the night. At 7 the next morning, still in bed, Bolton stabbed Jane three times, and then cut his own throat. Another lodger heard the scream, and found them both on the bed. Recovered, Bolton said that he must have commited the murder in his sleep, and was so appalled upon awakening that he tried to kill himself. The jury did not bother to leave the court before delivering its verdict.

Read: And May The Lord Have Mercy On Your Soul

30 December 1902	Warwick gaol	*H.Pierrepoint/ Ellis*

052

George PLACE   28

Shot: 1 **Eliza Chetwynd**, 60, her daughter
          2 **Eliza Chetwynd**, 20, and her son
          3 **Baby Chetwynd**, 11 days, on 24 August 1902, in Baddesley Ensor, Warwicks.

Motive: Vengeance.

Place, *(b.1874),* a miner, lodged with Eliza Chetwynd and her family for a year, before her daughter found herself pregnant by him. A son was born on 13 August 1902, but Place's girlfriend took a bastardy order out against him, and George left on 21 August.

Determined on revenge, he made threats before witnesses and brandished a revolver in a pub. Eliza, her mother and two brothers were all asleep when Place crept into the house in the early hours of the following day. As the three were all asleep in the same room, Place shot them. The Chetwynd brothers held him until police arrived. Place told them he had intended to commit suicide.

Read: And May The Lord Have Mercy On Your Soul

1902 Executions in Ireland

23 April 1902 Galway County Gaol

Thomas KEELEY

Murdered: *unknown*
Motive: *unknown*

     No details.

30 December 1902 Sligo County Gaol *W.Billington*

James DOHERTY 65

Shot: ***Patrick Doherty**, 25, his son, on 22 March 1902, in Kilclare, Co Leitrim*
Motive: *To eliminate obstacle.*

     Doherty, *(b.1837),* a widower, had a third share with his brother and sister in a prosperous farm in Leitrim, and ran the village post office. Turned down by the parents of a 16-year old whom he wanted to marry, he lived with his son Patrick for whom he had developed a hatred. James had signed a paper selling his share to his son for £100, but accused Patrick of forgery and various other imaginary offences. He eventually offered Patrick £100 to leave the house. Having recently bought a revolver, James went into Patrick's bedroom early one morning, and shot at him, hitting him five times. Patrick jumped from the window and his father shot him again and beat him outside.

     James called for his brother Anthony and the two carried Patrick inside. He had two wounds to the chest, and one each to the head, heart and wrist. His eye had been put out. James had an epileptic fit when Anthony pushed Patrick's arm down and it sprang back. James claimed that his son had committed suicide. One juror prevented agreement, but at the retrial the new jury took only 20 minutes to find him guilty.

Read: Master Detective, Nov 96.

1903

total: **27**

053	3 Feb	Amelia SACH (f)	29		Holloway
054	3 Feb	Annie WALTERS (f)	54		Holloway
055	17 Feb	William HUGHES	42	*Welsh*	Ruthin
056	3 Mar	Edgar OWEN	44		Wandsworth
057	10 Mar	Samuel SMITH	45		Lincoln
058	7 Apr	George CHAPMAN	37	*Polish*	Wandsworth
059	12 May	William HUDSON	26		Strangeways
060	2 Jun	Gustav RAU	28	*German*	Walton
061	2 Jun	Willem SMITH	30	*Dutch*	Walton
062	7 Jun	Charles HOWELL	30		Chelmsford
063	14 Jul	Samuel DOUGAL	57		Chelmsford
064	21 Jul	Thomas PORTER	29		Leicester
065	21 Jul	Thomas PRESTON	24		Leicester
066	28 Jul	Leonard PACHETT	26		Lincoln
067	11 Aug	William TUFFEN	23		Wandsworth
068	10 Nov	Charles SLOWE	28		Pentonville
069	17 Nov	Edward PALMER	24		Devizes
070	1 Dec	Bernard WHITE	21		Chelmsford
071	2 Dec	Charles WHITTAKER	43		Strangeways
072	8 Dec	James DUFFY	46		Durham
073	15 Dec	William HAYWOOD	61		Hereford
074	16 Dec	William BROWN	27		Winchester
075	16 Dec	Thomas COWDREY	36		Winchester
076	22 Dec	Charles ASHTON	19		Hull
077	29 Dec	Emily SWANN	42		Armley
078	29 Dec	John GALLAGHER	30		Armley
079	29 Dec	Henry STARR	31		Walton

3 February 1903   Holloway prison, London   *W.Billington/ H.Pierrepoint*

053, 054

Amelia SACH	**29**		*female*
Annie WALTERS	**54**		*female*

Poisoned/ suffocated:	**1**	*Baby Galley, 3 mths, on 18 November 1902, in London SW1, and*
	+	*c 20 others.*
Motive:		*Financial.*

       The baby-farmers Sach, *(b.1874)*, and Walters, *(b.1849)*, were paid to take away the unwanted babies of mostly unmarried young girls who came to their nursing home in east Finchley for their confinements. The girls believed the children would be found good homes. Sach was the one who negotiated with the unfortunate mothers, and Walters the one who killed the inconvenient infants. They were tried for the murder of specifically, two infants, for whom they had received £25 and £30.

In August 1902 a Miss Galley had come to the nursing home and had handed her baby over for adoption on 15 November. Walters had taken the child home and three days later had poisoned him with chlorodyne. The policeman in whose house Walters lodged had Walters followed. She was found with the corpse at south Kensington station. That they certainly had murdered others was illustrated by the fact that over 300 items of baby clothing were found discarded at the home. The jury took 40 minutes to find then guilty of the murder of baby Galley, but they may also have been responsible for the murder of Manfred Masset, 4, for which Louise Masset was executed in 1900.

Sach was in a state of near collapse at her execution, having to be virtually carried to the scaffold and supported on the trap.

Read: Murder Guide to Eastern & Home Counties, p169.

17 February 1903　　　　　Ruthin prison, Wales　　　*W/ John Billington*

055

William HUGHES　　**42**　　*Welsh*

Shot:　　　**Jane Hannah Hughes**, *32, his wife, on 10 November 1902, in Wrexham, Denbighs.*
Motive:　　*Sexual rivalry.*

Hughes, *(b.1861),* served with the army in India until his return to Britain in 1890. Two years later he married his cousin, Jane Williams, and the couple had four children. Hughes took the death of a child in 1901 badly, and left home, for which he was jailed for three months in 1902.

Jane, meanwhile had become housekeeper to a widower with five children at Old Rhosrobin. Fearful that his wife may be having an affair with her employer, Thomas Maddocks, Hughes became furious when Jane looked to him for support for his own children. He borrowed a shotgun and went to Maddock's house while he was at work. He raised Jane from her bed, and shot her twice as she reached the front door. Hughes handed himself over to a policeman at 3.20am. Before taking his position on the gallows, Hughes removed his boots.

Read: And May The Lord Have Mercy On Your Soul

056

Edgar OWEN   44   *(aka Edgar Edwards)*

Bludgeoned:	**1 John William Darby,** *25*
	2 Beatrice Darby, *25, and their daughter*
Strangled:	**3 Ethel Darby,** *10 weeks, on 1 December 1902, in Camberwell, London SE5.*
Motive:	*Financial.*

Owen, *(b. 1859),* an unemployed clerk living in Leyton, called on Mr and Mrs Darby, who had advertised their grocery business for sale, on 1 December. While John collected the accounts books, Beatrice showed Owen upstairs, where he clubbed her with a 4 kg sash-weight on a rope which he had brought with him. He then strangled the baby. When Mr Darby followed into the upstairs room, he too was bludgeoned by Owen. He dismembered the couple, loading six sacks full of their remains into packing cases.

These, together with furniture from the house, he had transferred to his home in Leyton. Some items were pawned and stock from the shop was sold. Customers were told that the couple had moved to the North. He buried the remains of the Darby family in his garden.

On 23 December, Owen invited a Mr Garland to his house to discuss the sale of the Garland business. He similarly attacked his guest with another sash-weight, but this time his victim managed to escape without serious injury and informed the police. Neighbours reported having seen digging in the garden and the Darbys' remains were revealed. A defence plea of insanity, based on a family history of mental abnormality, was rejected. His final words were, 'I've been looking forward to this'.

Read: Murder by Gaslight, p203.

057

Samuel Henry SMITH   45

Stabbed:	**Lucy Margaret Lingard,** *33, on 18 November 1902, in Grimsby, Lincs.*
Motive:	*Sadistic pleasure, drink related.*

Smith, *(b.1858)*, a fisherman, was stocky and aggressive, especially after drink. He met Lucy Lingard in July 1902 on a tram to Cleethorpes, where she was going for a day out. Lucy had five children, but had been left by her railman husband. She and Smith spent the day together, and then most weekends, before he moved in with her in September.

He soon began to show his true colours, and Lucy suffered many a beating. On 18 November having, literally, dragged Lucy round local pubs, he again began beating her at home. He dragged her by the hair to the kitchen, and then kicked her 12-year old daughter down the stairs. He forced both to kneel, then tormented them by running his fish-gutting knife across their throats and breasts, before finally stabbing Lucy eleven times in the chest.

Her daughter ran out, and by the time police arrived, Smith had stuffed Lucy's body into the coal bunker. Lucy clung to life until 30 November. The jury retired for only seven minutes.

Read: Master Detective Summer Special 97.

7 April 1903   Wandsworth prison, London   *W.Billington/ H.Pierrepoint*

058

George CHAPMAN   **37**   *(ne Severin Antoniovitch Klosovski)*
Polish

Poisoned: **1 Isabella Mary Spink**, on 25 December 1897, in London EC1
2 Elizabeth Taylor, his wife, on 13 February 1901, in London SE1, and
3 Maud Eliza Marsh, 19, his wife, on 22 October 1902, in London SE1.
Motive: *To clear impediment.*

Born in Nargornak in Poland in 1865, as Klosovski, he did not qualify from his training as a surgeon. He came to England in 1888, aged 22, after marrying in Poland and then serving in the Russian army. He bigamously married another Pole in Whitechapel, working as a barber, and went to America from 1890 till 1893. His second 'wife' left him with their two children.

He adopted the name Chapman after living with one Annie Chapman for a year. From 1895 he lived with Mary Spink, whose husband had left her because of her drink problem. She had private means, and the couple moved from Leytonstone to Hastings, where they ran a barbers shop and then moved back to London in 1897 to run the Prince of Wales Tavern off

City Road. Chapman poisoned her, perhaps tiring of her drunkenness, her death being attributed to consumption.

In 1898 Chapman married Bessie Taylor, who had come to work for him as a barmaid. They took a pub in Bishops Stortford, and then the Monument Tavern in Union Street, Borough. He treated her badly and finally poisoned her in 1901, her death attributed to exhaustion from vomiting and diarrhoea. He married new barmaid Maud Marsh later in 1901. He began poisoning her and the couple took another pub, the Crown, also in Union Street. But when Maud's mother and a nurse fell sick after drinking a brandy and soda prepared for Maud by Chapman, suspicions were raised. Chapman finished Maud off quickly, but an autopsy showed antimony poisoning.

After a four-day trial, the jury found Chapman guilty of the murder of all three women, after just eleven minutes' consideration. Chapman, in a state of near collapse, had to be supported on the scaffold.

It has been suggested that Chapman, who beat his women, was suffering from a form of madness brought on by a venereal infection. Another suggestion, that he was Jack the Ripper, is generally rejected.

Read: More Murders of the Black Museum, p242.

12 May 1903   Strangeways prison, Manchester
W.Billington/ H.Pierrepoint

059

William George HUDSON   26

Shot: ***Harry Short**, 23, on 17 February 1903, in Preston, Lancs.*
Motive: *Vengeance; drink related.*

Hudson, *(b.1877)*, was a gunner in the Royal Field Artillery. Born and raised in Birmingham, he had worked as a market porter, but joined the army in 1899 after his wife left him. He had served in India, but was invalided out after being wounded, and was assigned to the Fulward Barracks, Preston. There he had immediately found an antipathy to Bombardier Harry Short. Hudson was insubordinate and had to suffer severe punishments from the Bombardier. He was court-martialled but acquitted on a charge of striking Short.

After a heavy drinking session with two mates, having downed 14 beers and five whiskies, he took a friend's rifle and killed Short with a single shot through the head as he lay sleeping in his bed at 12:30 one night. Two of Hudson's mates told how the gunner had threatened to kill Short, and had confessed that he had done so. They spoke only after the rifle's real owner had come under suspicion. The jury recommended mercy on account of his youth, but Hudson went calmly and coolly to his death.

Read: Strange Tales from Strangeways, p134.

2 June 1903	Walton gaol, Liverpool	*John / W.Billington*

060, 061

Gustav RAU	**28**	*German*
Willem SMITH	**30**	*Dutch*

Drowned:	*1 Alexander McLeod,*
	2 Julius Hersson, and
	3 Patrick Durran, on 8 December 1902,
Shot:	*4 Alexander Shaw and*
	5 Fred Abrahamson on 11 December 1902,
	6 Gustav Johansen on 15 December 1902, and
	7 Alexander Bravo on 17 December 1902, all off the Brazilian coast.
Motive:	*Vengeance.*

The *Veronica*, a British-owned sailing barque, with a complement of 12, had sailed from Biloxi, Louisiana, on 11 October bound for Montevideo with a cargo of timber.

Captain Alexander Shaw, an almost deaf Scot, was a weak captain who handed authority to his brutish first officer, Canadian Alexander McLeod, who regularly beat crewman Smith and threatened to throw him and incompetent seaman Bravo, a native American, overboard. The second officer, American Fred Abrahamson and Irishman Durran had both sexually harassed the teenage crew members. The two Germans, Rau, *(b.1875),* and Otto Monsson, 18, had smuggled revolvers on to the ship, and when rations were cut owing to slow winds, they determined to mutiny against their oppressors. Dutchman Smith, *(b.1873),* and, reluctantly, Ludwig 'Harry' Flohr, 19, joined the cause.

On December 8 they seized their chance, Rau hit McLeod with a steel pin and threw him overboard to drown, Monsson did likewise with the Swede Hersson, and Durran was hit twice by Rau who ordered Flohr and Johansen to throw him over. The captain and second officer were shot and wounded, seeking refuge in their cabin. Three days later they were shot in the head and shoulder respectively, and dispatched overboard. Smith shot Johansen in the head four days later, and two days after that Flohr was ordered to kill Bravo. He was shot three times, falling to the sea from the rigging. The four mutineers spared only the black cook, Moses Thomas, 24.

They set the barque alight and took to the lifeboat, being picked up later by a tramp steamer.

The cook revealed the truth and the four were returned to Liverpool to face seven charges of murder and of piracy. Flohr testified against the others whom the jury took just 12 minutes to convict. They protested their innocence to the end, blaming Thomas for killing the officers after they had killed the crew members. On account of his age and previously good character, Monsson was reprieved and sentenced to penal servitude for life.

Read: The Black Flag, p11.

7 July 1903	Chelmsford gaol	*W.Billington/ Ellis*

062

Charles HOWELL   30

Cut throat of: **Maud Luen**, *19, on 1 June 1903, in Chelmsford, Essex*
Motive: *Vengeance.*

Howell, *(b.1873)*, was stationed at Chelmsford with the Suffolk regiment, and had been dating Maud Luen since he had been there. Howell was said to have changed since returning from the South African war, and was at times found in floods of tears.

He and Maud spent Whitsun Monday together, but she was heard refusing his suggestion to go somewhere, so Howell returned to barracks. At 9.40pm Maud was chatting to a friend when Howell came along, and asked Maud for forgiveness. She agreed, but asked him to leave her alone. As he leaned and asked for a kiss, he cut her throat. The friend's screams alerted a passing army sergeant who took Howell under arrest.

Read: And May The Lord Have Mercy On Your Soul

063

Samuel Herbert DOUGAL   57

Possibly **poisoned**:	*His first two wives, 1885*
Shot:	**Camille Cecile Holland**, *56, on 19 May 1899,*
	near Saffron Walden, Essex.
Motive:	*Financial.*

Dougal, *(b.1846),* was a life-long con-man and seducer of women. He had served in the Royal Engineers from 1866-87, the last ten years being stationed in Halifax, Nova Scotia. His first marriage lasted 16 years and bore him four children, before his wife died suddenly from 'oyster poisoning' in 1885. He quickly remarried, only to lose his second wife in exactly the same way only a few months later.

He returned to England in 1887 with a new woman and their child. She soon tired of his drinking and violence, and there followed a succession of liaisons, including an elderly woman with whom he ran a pub in Ware. Dougal was cleared of arson when the pub burned down and he attempted to claim the insurance. In Dublin in 1892 he married for a third time, to Sarah White, who had two children by him. He later seduced Emily Booty. Having moved in with her, he then proceeded to bring his wife and children along too. His luck ran out in 1896 when he served a year in an asylum for forging a cheque. He tried to hang himself in his cell.

Dougal, 5'7", 11st 7, and bearded, met Camille Holland in 1898. She was wary of him and protective of the £6000 she had inherited. Nevertheless, she succumbed to his winning ways and she bought a farm for them to live in near Saffron Walden. His continual flirting with servant girls exasperated Camille, who threatened to leave. He shot her at point blank range in the back of the head with a revolver, and buried her in the drained moat.

He was now free to spend her money at will, hunt, drink and womanise to his heart's content. He told acquaintances that his wife had left for a yachting holiday. Rumours began to circulate of orgies at the farm, as servant girls became pregnant and numerous women came and went. His wife again returned to him staying till 1902.

Finally, after four years of the good life, a cheque was found to have been forged and the police began to investigate. Dougal fled to London with a woman on 13 March. After five weeks' digging, the body of Camille was found. The bullet in her skull was found to have come from Dougal's revolver. Dougal was arrested trying to change fourteen £10 notes. He confessed to the chaplain on the scaffold.

Read: The Murders of the Black Museum, p134

064, 065

Thomas PORTER   29
Thomas PRESTON   24

Shot: Policeman **William Ariel Wilkinson**, *32, on 25 May 1903, in Sileby, Leics.*
Motive: *To escape arrest; drink related.*

Porter, *(b.1874)*, and Preston, *(b.1879)*, had been out poaching and drinking, when at 10.30pm, they came across local policeman Bill Wilkinson chatting to an acquaintance in the street. Wilkinson had hardly noticed the two men when Porter shot and killed him. The killer had been recognised and police surrounded his house, where the two men threatened to shoot anyone who came near. They held out under siege from 1am to 7am, before giving themselves up. Porter admitted firing the gun, but Preston was held to be equally responsible.

Read: And May The Lord Have Mercy On Your Soul

066

Leonard PACHETT   26

Strangled: **Sarah Ann Pachett**, *25, his wife, on 26 May 1903, in Boultham, Lincs.*
Motive: *Vengeance.*

Pachett, *(b.1877)*, married Sarah in February 1900, but the couple separated in January 1903. In an attempt at a reconciliation, they spent a week together in Derbyshire, but to no avail. Sarah went to work as housekeeper in Boultham, Pachett getting work as a bricklayer in Gainsborough. Pachett visited Sarah twice, but on the second occasion after chatting to her as he left around 7pm, he strangled her manually and left her body in a field, where it was found three days later. In the meantime, Pachett had confessed his crime to a friend.

Read: And May The Lord Have Mercy On Your Soul.

067

William Joseph TUFFEN   23

Bludgeoned: *Caroline Tuffen, 21, his wife, on 23 April 1903, in Thames Ditton, Surrey.*
Motive: *To clear impediment.*

Tuffen, *(b.1880),* and his wife lived first in Wimbledon, then Kingston, finally moving to Thames Ditton in March 1903. Before the month was out Mary Stone had moved in as a lodger, and an affair had begun between her and Tuffen.

Caroline and her husband were heard arguing in the pub on 23 April, and that was the last time she was seen. Tuffen battered her to death and left her upstairs in the house. He and Mary were now free to indulge their desires, a neighbour catching her on his knee on 29 April.

Caroline's brother was suspicious of her disappearance and alerted police who found the body in the house on 7 May, the lovers having fled. They were soon arrested on Norbiton station, and both were charged with murder. Stone was found to be guilty as an accessory after the fact.

Read: And May The Lord Have Mercy On Your Soul

068

Charles Jeremiah SLOWE   28

Stabbed: *Martha Jane Hardwick, 20, on 24 September 1903, in London E1.*
Motive: *Vengeance.*

Slowe, *(b.1875),* had an obsession with Martha Hardwick, a barmaid at the Lord Nelson on Whitechapel road. Martha lived at the pub with her sister, the landlady, and began to avoid serving Slowe when he came in, because of his annoying persistence in asking her out. Determined to avenge Martha's slight to his honour, Slowe left the pub at 10pm, but waited until closing time.

As Martha was seeing customers out, some time after midnight, Slowe sprang upon her in the doorway, and stabbed her repeatedly, crying, 'I've got you now!' He was held by a passer-by until police arrived.

Read: And May The Lord Have Mercy On Your Soul

17 November 1903   Devizes prison   *W/ John Billington*

069

Edward Richard PALMER   24

Shot: ***Esther Swinford**, 19, on 18 September 1903, in Swindon, Wilts.*
Motive: *Vengeance.*

Palmer, *(b.1879)*, was engaged to barmaid Esther, and all preparations were underway for the wedding. Then she discovered that Palmer had not been putting the money she had given him to one side for furniture, but had been drinking it away; so she broke off the engagement. Palmer moved away and found work as a gardener, but began to carry a revolver around with him, to the concern of his brother. Then he took a job at the railway works, back in Swindon, and decided to pay a visit to Esther.

The pub was empty when he arrived, and she was alone in the bar. There he shot her dead. He later claimed that he had taken the gun merely to frighten her, and that it had gone off accidentally.

Read: And May The Lord Have Mercy On Your Soul

1 December 1903   Chelmsford gaol   *W.Billington/ H.Pierrepoint*

070

Bernard WHITE   21

Bludgeoned: ***Maud Garrett**, 20, on 22 May 1903, in Little Warley, Essex.*
Motive: *Sexual rivalry.*

White, *(b.1882)*, a private in the Essex regiment, had dated Maud Garrett for six weeks in 1901 before going off to the Boer War. In his absence, Maud had met and become engaged to another army private. However, upon White's return, they bumped into each other on 21 May, and went for a drink together the following day.

At 10pm, White sneaked out of the camp near Brentwood to see Maud again, and took his cane with him. He beat Maud to death, and returned to the camp at 11pm. Screams had been heard at about 10.30, and when the body was found, marks were found which could have been made by a cane such as White's. Maud's clothing was awry, but there had been no rape. White claimed that Maud had not turned up for the meeting, but blood was found on his clothes and cane.

Read: And May The Lord Have Mercy On Your Soul

2 **December 1903**   Strangeways prison, Manchester   *John Billington/ Ellis*

071

Charles WHITTAKER   43

Stabbed: ***Eliza Range**, 44, on 8 August 1903, in Manchester, Lancs.*
Motive: *Sexual rivalry; drink related.*

Whittaker, *(b.1860)*, a bacon roller, had met Eliza Range in 1901 and had been visiting her house in Collyhurst while her husband was out since February 1903. Eliza, a laundress, had been married three times, lastly for eighteen years and had a son of 15, but she and her husband led largely separate lives. She had a drink problem, but had also started cleaning for a neighbour, and Whittaker grew jealous thinking she may be having an affair. He told her to stop but she told him she would do as she pleased.

He called round at 10.50am after William Range had left for work, and Eliza gave him beer and whisky to drink, before going in the scullery for a wash. Whittaker followed her and stabbed her once above the collarbone, breaking the knife. Her son ran to her aid, and Whittaker fled, but handed himself in to police the following day.

The jury considered for only a few minutes without retiring.

Read: Murderous Manchester, p8.

8 December 1903   Durham gaol   *W/ John Billington*

072

James DUFFY   46

Strangled: ***Ellen Newman**, 40, on 6 September 1903, in*
                  Sunderland, Co Durham.
Motive: *Vengeance; drink related.*

Ellen Newman, a prostitute, left her husband in June 1902 to move in with Duffy, *(b.1857)*, in Grangetown. Both liked their drink and both had matching tempers. In November 1902 Duffy slashed both their throats, with little damage, and got a month in gaol. Ellen took him back upon his release, but Duffy did not work, and relied on Ellen's street earnings. On 6 September, the lodger returned at 11.15pm to find Duffy drunk, arguing with his wife and hitting his 15-year old son. The couple retired for the night, but another argument started in bed, and Duffy strangled her. At 1.45am he walked into a police station to own up.

Read: And May The Lord Have Mercy On Your Soul.

15 December 1903   Hereford prison   *H.Pierrepoint/ Ellis*

073

William HAYWOOD   61

Bludgeoned: ***Jane Haywood**, 60, his wife, on 11 July 1903, in*
                  Leominster, Herefordshire.
Motive: *Sadistic pleasure; drink related.*

Haywood, *(b.1842)*, a quarry labourer, was a man of low intelligence who lived with his wife at Yarpole, their children having grown and left. On the night of 10 July, he decided to sleep at the quarry to be ready for early shift. At 7am next morning he had a drink in the nearby pub, and took beer and whisky back to work with him. An hour later Jane arrived with Haywood's breakfast, and Haywood battered her to death with rocks. In the afternoon no-one at the pub took the drunken old fool seriously when he said he had killed his wife, but at 8.45pm, he turned up again with Jane's body in a wheelbarrow. The landlord called the police. Doctors insisted Haywood was insane, describing him as an imbecile.

Read: And May The Lord Have Mercy On Your Soul

16 December 1903   Winchester prison   *W/ John Billington*

074, 075

William BROWN	**27**
Thomas COWDREY	**36**

Bludgeoned: ***Esther Atkins**, 25, on 6 October 1903, in Aldershot, Hants.*

Motive: *Financial.*

Cowdrey, *(b.1867),* a labourer, met Esther Atkins, a prostitute, in a pub. They were joined there by two soldiers, John Dunbar and William Brown, *(b.1876),* who had slipped from their barracks at 9.30pm. The three men noticed Esther had about £10 on her, and determined to have it, one of them telling a cab driver exactly their intentions. They later beat Esther to death, and probably raped her.

Cowdrey went to the police and told them he had seen two men beating up a woman, taking them to the undiscovered naked body. He later picked Brown out of an identity parade, and when Esther's shoes were found in his possession, he and Dunbar were charged. Only with the cab driver's evidence was Cowdrey's involvement realised by police. After a four-day trial, Dunbar was acquitted.

On the scaffold, Brown confessed, but Cowdrey still blamed the soldier.

Read: And May The Lord Have Mercy On Your Soul

22 December 1903   Hull prison   *W/ John Billington*

076

Charles William ASHTON	**19**

Shot: ***Annie Marshall**, 16, on 20 September 1903, in Scampton, E Yorks.*

Motive: *Financial.*

Ashton, *(b.1884),* was a labourer on a farm at Scampton, near Malton. Annie Marshall was a domestic servant on the same farm, and she left for church at 5.30pm one Sunday. Ashton intercepted her on her way back, beat her and shot her twice in the head with a revolver at 9.30pm, returning to the farm himself at 10pm.

Nine days later he claimed to have found Annie's hat, and suggested to police that her body may have been dumped in the river. The body was indeed where Ashton had foreseen. Police, though, found bloody clothes, a revolver and Annie's purse locked in a box in Ashton's room. The jury recommended mercy on account of his youth.

Read: And May The Lord Have Mercy On Your Soul

29 December 1903   Armley gaol, Leeds   *W.Billington/Ellis*

077, 078

Emily SWANN	**42**	*female*
John GALLAGHER	**30**	

Bludgeoned: **William Swann**, *40, on 6 June 1903, in Wombwell, W.Yorks*
Motive: *Vengeance; drink related.*

Gallagher *(b.1873)*, a miner, nearly 10 stone and 5' 6", lodged with Emily and Bill Swann, a glass-blower, at their home in Wombwell. Swann frequently beat his 4'10", 8 st 10 wife, a mother of eleven children, and evicted Gallagher when he became aware of the relationship between him and his wife.

One day, Emily *(b.1861)*, emerged from their house heavily bruised. On seeing her condition, Gallagher twice went to the house to administer a 10-minute beating to Swann, during which Emily took a poker to her husband. The attack proved fatal. Gallagher fled to Middlesbrough, but was discovered there two months later. The two were tried, sentenced and executed together.

Emily, in a state of near collapse on the morning of their execution, had to be revived with brandy. 'Good morning, love', John greeted her on the scaffold. 'Goodbye. God bless you', she replied.

Read: And May The Lord Have Mercy On Your Soul.

079

Henry Bertram STARR   31

*Possibly **drowned:***	***1 Eleanor Coulthard**, 16, on 23 March 1896, near Clitheroe, Lancs.*
Stabbed:	***2 Mary Hannah Starr**, 26, his wife, on 24 November 1903, in Blackpool, Lancs.*
Motive:	*Sexual rivalry.*

Starr, *(b.1872)*, was tried and acquitted in 1896 of the murder of Nellie Coulthard, a domestic servant with whom he was involved. She had been found in the river Ribble, and Starr, who admitted being with Nellie that night, had been found soaking wet, and very drunk by a policeman at midnight. The couple were said to be very much in love, and the jury clearly thought accident or suicide more likely than murder, as no marks were found on the dead girl.

Starr then moved to Workington, and the travelling salesman took a job as an insurance company rep, but in 1902 he moved to his aunt's boarding house in Blackpool, working in summer as a photographer's canvasser, and in winter as a labourer. He met Mary Hannah Blagg in October, and they married in March 1903, living at her mother's boarding house. Mary became pregnant, and Starr began drinking, getting on very badly with his mother-in-law. He went back to his aunt's in June, and Mary told him that she had a lover. In August a daughter was born, and the two were reconciled for three months, living in their own house, until, tiring again of Starr's drunkenness, Mary moved back to her mother's on 16 November.

Starr waited in the outside toilet all night until Mary came down to let the dog out at 8am. He dived into the house, grabbed a bread knife, and stabbed his wife twenty times. When her mother appeared, he stabbed her in the face and severely beat her. Starr was arrested the following day, the jury taking just four minutes to determine his guilt, without leaving the courtroom.

Read: True Detective Summer Special 92

1903 Executions in Ireland

7 January 1903 Kilkenny County Gaol *W.Billington*

JOSEPH TAYLOR

Murdered: **John Daly**
Motive: Sexual rivalry.

Taylor was having an affair with Daly's wife, Mary, hanged two days later. No further details.

Read: Hangman's Diary, p13.

9 January 1903 Tulamore Gaol *W.Billington*

MARY DALY

Murdered: **John Daly**, *her husband.*
Motive: unknown

Accomplice to Joseph Taylor, with whom she was having an affair and who was hanged two days previously. No further details.

Read: Hangman's Diary, p17.

1904

total: **17**

080	9 Mar	Sidney SMITH	23		Gloucester
081	29 Mar	Henry JONES	50		Stafford
082	29 Mar	James CLARKSON	19		Armley
083	5 Apr	Charles DYER	25		Winson Green
084	31 May	Ping LUN	43	*Chinese*	Walton
085	31 May	William KIRWAN	39		Walton
086	12 Jul	John SULLIVAN	40		Pentonville
087	13 Jul	Samuel ROWLEDGE	37		Northampton
088	26 Jul	Thomas GUNNING		*Scottish*	Duke Street
089	2 Aug	George BREEZE	21		Durham
090	16 Aug	John KAY	52		Armley
091	16 Aug	Samuel HOLDEN	43		Winson Green
092	13 Dec	Joseph POTTER	35		Pentonville
093	13 Dec	Charles WADE	22		Pentonville
094	20 Dec	Edmund HALL	49		Armley
095	21 Dec	Eric LANGE	30	*Russian*	Cardiff
096	29 Dec	Arthur JEFFRIES	44		Armley

9 March 1904 Gloucester prison *W/ John Billington*

080

Sidney George SMITH 23

Cut throat of: ***Alice Woodman***, 21, on 14 December 1903, in Cheltenham, Gloucs.
Motive: *To clear impediment; drink related.*

Smith, *(b.1881),* wrote to girlfriend Alice Woodman, a domestic servant, telling her that if she did not move in with him, against her parents' wishes, it would be all over between them. She went to Smith, and the banns were soon read. Then Smith lost his job, and rapidly got into money troubles, eventually getting notice to quit their home. On 5 December he bought a razor, and though he told a friend that he was going to Worcester to look for work, that plan was abandoned.

Arriving home drunk after 1am, as his wife slept two hours later, he cut her throat, then his own. The pair were discovered on their bed the following afternoon by a neighbour. Smith wept openly as the jury delivered its verdict after a 5-minute retirement.

Read: And May The Lord Have Mercy On Your Soul

081

Henry JONES   50

Cut throat of: **Mary Elizabeth Gilbert**, *48, on 29 January 1904, in Hanley, Staffs.*
Motive: *Sexual rivalry*

    Jones, *(b.1854),* lived in lodgings with Mary Gilbert and their three children.   He became convinced that she was having an affair with their landlord, and arguments got so bad that Jones was given notice to leave. When Jones arrived home at 9pm one night, another row with Mary flared, but the two went peacefully to bed.
    However at 6am, he hit her with a hammer as she slept, and cut her throat.   He had left a note on the mantelpiece, and sent his son for the police. Jones then cut his own throat.   The jury considered its verdict for just four minutes.

    Read: And May The Lord Have Mercy On Your Soul

082

James Henry CLARKSON   19

Cut throat of: **Elizabeth Mary Lynas**, *12, on 27 December 1903, in Guisborough, N Yorks.*
Means: *Sadistic pleasure.*

    Clarkson, *(b.1884),* lived with his father and sister.   They were out on the afternoon of 27 December, when he grabbed young Elizabeth Lynas, on her way home from church.   In his back yard, he grappled with her, bound her and cut her throat with a knife.   He then dumped her body in woods nearby.
    When Elizabeth's bruised body was found the next day, tied hand and foot, searches began, and blood was noticed in Clarkson's yard. Elizabeth's hat was found there, and a bloody knife was still in the kitchen. When arrested, Clarkson was found to have blood on his clothing.   There had

been no sexual assault. The jury took 30 minutes over its considerations, and Clarkson was hanged two days before his twentieth birthday.

Read: And May The Lord Have Mercy On Your Soul

5 April 1904   Winson Green prison, Birmingham   *W./ John Billington*

083

Charles Samuel DYER   **25**   *(aka Charlie Hammond)*

Cut throat of: **Martha Eliza Simpson**, *21, on 4 February 1904, in Birmingham, Warwicks.*
Motive: *Sexual rivalry; drink related.*

Dyer, *(b. 1879),* had served eight years in the army, including three years in Malta, and two in India, before being discharged 'with ignominy' and returning to Birmingham on 9 December 1903. Within days he had met Martha Simpson, a prostitute, and moved in with her on Boxing Day. They moved to a cottage the following month.

On the night of 3 February, Martha went out for a drink with a friend, Margaret Moran, Dyer drinking elsewhere. Martha picked up a client in the pub and the two went back to Margaret's house for a 15-minute encounter. Dyer arrived at Margaret's just as the client was leaving, and he and Martha, both rather drunk, went home together. There they argued, Martha striking him with a poker, and Dyer slitting her throat with a razor as she sat in the armchair. He ran back to Margaret's to confess his crime. The jury took 90 minutes to convict him.

Read: Murderous Birmingham, p16.

31 May 1904   Walton gaol, Liverpool   *W. Billington/ H.Pierrepoint*

084

Ping LUN   **43**   *Chinese*

Shot: **John Go Hing**, *29, on 20 March 1904, in Liverpool, Lancs.*
Motive: *Vengeance.*

Ping Lun, *(b.1861),* had lived in a lodging house for Chinese workers on Frederick Street since September 1903. Much illegal gambling and opium smoking went on at the house, and when Lun arrived home one night, he wanted to place a bet. His good friend, John Go Hing, was running the game and told Lun he would not take a bet from a friend. When Lun realised his bet would have won, he demanded payment, but was again refused.

Angered that Hing still owed him £2 of a previous loan, Lun left and returned with a revolver at 9.30pm. When Hing again refused to pay, Lun fired twice, hitting Hing once in the stomach. As the other gamblers fled, Lun fired two more shots before running out. He was arrested as he returned later that evening. Hing died in hospital three days later. Full of remorse, Lun was hanged alongside William Kirwan.

Read: And May The Lord Have Mercy On Your Soul

31 May 1904   Walton gaol, Liverpool   *W. Billington/ H.Pierrepoint*

085

William KIRWAN   39

Shot: ***Mary Pike,*** *on 26 February 1904, in Liverpool, Lancs.*
Motive: *Vengeance.*

Kirwan, *(b.1865),* a sailor, was convinced his wife was prostituting herself at her sister's house while he was away at sea. Mary Pike, Kirwan's sister-in-law, was at home with Mrs Kirwan when William rushed in with a revolver. He again accused the two women, then fired four shots, two at each, though neither was badly hurt.

While Kirwan reloaded, Mary's lodger ushered both women into the cellar. Kirwan went into the street and fired two more shots, then waited until police arrived. A policeman had taken hold of Kirwan when Mary rushed out of the house to speak to the officer. Kirwan broke free and shot her at close range. Mary Pike died three days later. Kirwan was hanged alongside Ping Lun.

Read: And May The Lord Have Mercy On Your Soul

086

John SULLIVAN   40

Bludgeoned: ***Dennis Lowthian***, *17, on 18 May 1904, in the Indian Ocean.*
Motive: *Sexual rivalry.*

Sullivan, *(b.1864),* was an able seaman aboard the *Waiwera*, and Lowthian a cabin boy, as the ship sailed from London on 6 January 1904, bound for New Zealand. The two developed a sexual relationship, but Sullivan, a Durham native, became obsessed to the point where he was overcome with jealousy if Dennis so much as spoke to anyone else.

By the time the ship arrived at South Africa, Lowthian had had enough and began to distance himself from Sullivan. After he punched the boy in the mouth on 28 March, Sullivan spent a week locked up. Further arguments followed, until one night Sullivan came up behind Dennis at 9pm and smashed his head with an axe.

Read: And May The Lord Have Mercy On Your Soul

087

Samuel ROWLEDGE   37

Shot: ***Alice Foster***, *32, on 15 March 1904, in Northampton.*
Motive: *Vengeance.*

Rowledge, *(b.1867),* was a carpenter who had been engaged to Alice Foster, a domestic servant, since spring 1903. Since then he had lost his job, though his brother finally managed to fix him up with a new one.

Rowledge did not go to work, though he told Alice that he had. Arguments followed, and Rowledge got his revolver out of pawn, and at 7pm went to his mother's where Alice was waiting. Following another row, Rowledge took the revolver and shot Alice three times.

Read: And May The Lord Have Mercy On Your Soul

26 July 1904   Duke Street prison, Glasgow *W.Billington*

088

Thomas GUNNING   *Scottish*

Murdered: ***Agnes Allen**, his girlfriend, in April 1904, in Glasgow, Lanarks.*
Motive: *Vengeance; drink related.*

Gunning brutally murdered his mistress in a drunken frenzy at their home in Bridgeton. No further details.

Read: Encyclopaedia of Scottish Executions

2 August 1904   Durham gaol   *W.Billington/ Ellis*

089

George BREEZE   **21**

Strangled: ***Margaret Jane Chisholm**, 20, on 6 July 1904, in Seaham Harbour, Co Durham.*
Motive: *To clear impediment.*

Breeze, *(b.1883)*, was a miner and amateur footballer, who, following a row with his father, found lodgings with a young married couple, the Chisholms. Breeze slept on the sofa in the couple's bedroom, and the frustration became too much to bear when he and Margaret fell for each other.

Realising the situation was hopeless, Breeze determined to end his and Margaret's suffering. Her husband left for work at 5am, and three hours later Breeze strangled Margaret, going directly to hand himself in at the police station. Determined to hasten his own demise, Breeze pleaded guilty, and was hanged just 27 days after the murder.

Read: And May The Lord Have Mercy On Your Soul.

090

John Thomas KAY   52

Bludgeoned: **Jane Hirst**, *28, on 10 May 1904, in Rotherham, W.Yorks.*
Motive: *Vengeance.*

　　　　Kay, *(b.1852)*, a labourer, met Jane Hirst a couple of months after his wife had died in October 1903. Telling him she was a widow, she moved in with him in January. In fact, her husband, a Sheffield man, had run away to Cardiff the previous September, sick of her continual drunkenness. Her two adult children lived in Sheffield. Jane did not change her ways, continuing to go off with men for days at a time.

　　　　On 7 May, Jane having failed to return home, John tried to hang himself, and having failed, determined to move out, ordering a dray for 10 May. Jane returned on the 9th, and the two retired to bed at 11.30pm.

　　　　Waking in the early morning, Kay smashed Jane's head four times with an axe as she lay sleeping in bed. He claimed to have heard voices telling him to kill her. Such force was used that Jane's brains smeared the bed and walls. Kay then left the house, approached a policeman at 5.45am, and confessed his crime. The jury rejected the plea of insanity in 25 minutes.

　　　　Read: Master Detective, Jun 97.

091

Samuel HOLDEN   43

Stabbed: **Susan Humphries**, *on 2 July 1904, in Birmingham, Warwicks.*
Motive: *Sadistic pleasure; drink related*

　　　　Holden, *(b.1861)*, 5'9" and 12 st, had joined the army in 1890, had served five years in Ceylon, before being decorated four times in the South African War. Working as a market porter, in 1901 he began a stormy relationship with Susan Humphries, characterised by drunken fights.

　　　　One afternoon Susan had gone to a neighbour after Holden had lashed out at her. A few minutes after her return to their house in Coventry Street, Birmingham, Holden stabbed her four times in the neck and shoulder.

The neighbour living opposite saw the whole thing and contacted the police. Susan died on the way to hospital. The jury took 25 minutes to reject Holden's plea of provocation. He died bravely with a cigar still on his lips.

Read: Murderous Birmingham, p23.

13 December 1904   Pentonville prison, London   *W.Billington/ H.Pierrepoint*

092, 093

Joseph POTTER	**34**	*(aka Conrad Donovan)*
Charles WADE	**22**	

Suffocated:	***Matilda Emily Farmer**, 65, on 12 October 1904, in Stepney, London E1.*
Motive:	*Financial*

Potter, *(b.1870)*, a sailor who had served a total of five years of the past decade for striking a superior officer and for housebreaking, and Wade, *(b.1882)*, a labourer, were half-brothers. In May 1904 Potter had hit Miss Farmer in her newsagents shop on Commercial Road, but had fled when a customer arrived.

In October, four days after Wade's release from a robbery sentence, the two tied and gagged Miss Farmer in the back room of her shop at 6am, and proceeded to rob her of her jewellery. A paperboy raised the alarm when he found the shop empty, with a shoe and false teeth on the floor. Miss Farmer was found dead on her bed, hands tied behind her back, and bruised on the face. She had choked on the gag placed in her mouth.

Both men were identified by a witness who saw them leaving the shop at about 6.20am. They were arrested on 26 October, and the jury took 10 minutes to convict. Potter confessed his guilt to the prison chaplain.

Read: True Detective, Summer Special 95.

20 December 1904   Armley gaol, Leeds   *John Billington/ H.Pierrepoint*

094

Edmund HALL   49

Cut throat of: **John Dalby**, *78, on 29 July 1904, in York.*
Motive: *Financial.*

Hall, *(b.1855)*, was discharged from the army in India in 1879 because of melancholia brought on by sunstroke. Living in Leeds he travelled by train to visit his father-in-law, John Dalby, in York, having failed the day before to buy a revolver.

He cut the old man's throat, though Dalby managed to stagger outside into the arms of a neighbour who had heard a rumpus. Hall then emerged and said he would run for a doctor. He was arrested boarding the train back to Leeds. He had Mr Dalby's watch on him.

Read: And May The Lord Have Mercy On Your Soul.

21 December 1904   Cardiff gaol   *W.Billington/ Ellis*

095

Eric LANGE   30   *Russian*   *(ne Eugene Lorenz)*

Stabbed: **John Emlyn Jones**, *37, on 11 September 1904, in Rhonnda, Glamorgan.*
Motive: *Financial.*

Lange, *(b.1874)*, was a Russian seaman born in Riga. For a month in 1901 he had worked in a Rhonnda pub, and three years later paid several visits to the inn, now under new management. At 3.30am he broke in through a toilet window, and removed his boots before climbing the stairs. As he stood at the foot of the bed where the publican, John Jones, and his wife lay, Mrs Jones awoke. As she screamed to her husband, Lange hit her on the head with a file he was carrying.

Mr Jones began to grapple with the intruder, but was stopped by a blow from Lange's knife. The cellarman ran to the bedroom, but too late, for Lange had escaped. A policeman noticed Lange walking by a railway line at 5.30am. As he arrested the dishevelled, shoeless and bloody stranger,

Lange attempted to pull his knife. The officer subdued him with a blow to the head from his truncheon.

Read: And May The Lord Have Mercy On Your Soul

29 December 1904   Armley gaol, Leeds   *John Billington/ H.Pierrepoint*

096

Arthur JEFFRIES   44

Stabbed: ***Sam Barker***, *45, on 12 November 1904, in Rotherham, W.Yorks.*
Motive: *Vengeance.*

Jeffries, *(b.1860)*, and Barker had been friends for more than 25 years. They worked together as miners and both belonged to a gang of six poachers, who supplemented their meagre diet by their nocturnal activities.

Owing to some manner of dispute the other men had gone poaching without Jeffries since October 1904. At 11.15pm on 12 November, the two old friends became involved in a street argument. They tumbled fighting into an alleyway where Jeffries pulled a knife and Barker was stabbed through the heart. He died shortly afterwards. The weapon was never found.

Jeffries was full of remorse for killing his friend, and after 30 minutes' deliberation the jury added a strong recommendation to mercy. His last words were, 'Lord, receive my spirit'.

Read: A Date With the Hangman, p105.

5 January 1904   Londonderry   *W.Billington*

Joseph MORAN

Murdered: *unknown*
Motive: *unknown*

No details.

14 April 1904   Kilkenny County Gaol   *W.Billington*

James CAMPION   45

Kicked: ***Ellen Campion**, 32, his wife, on 29 November 1903, in Coolbawn, Co Kilkenny.*
Motive: *Vengeance.*

Campion, *(b.1859)*, a miner, had a son by his first marriage, and four children by his second wife, Ellen. The two had been for a few drinks on the evening of 28 November when a row developed on the walk home. Ellen, six months pregnant, told her husband she would leave him. He responded by dragging her along by the hair. When she failed to get up, he kicked her six times on the ground, and prevented any of the gathering five witnesses from helping her.

The following morning his eldest son went to look for his step-mother, finding her at 10am in a watery ditch 130 metres from the house. As she was carried in, Campion, bearded and 5'6", again tried to strike her, but she died ten minutes later anyway. Her death was due to a kick to the head, accelerated by exposure.

The jury considered for 35 minutes, but did add a strong recommendation for mercy to their verdict.

Read: Master Detcetive, Mar 98

15 April 1904   Kilkenny County Gaol   *W.Billington*

John KELLY

Murdered: *His wife.*
Motive: *unknown*

No further details.

20 December 1904   Armagh County Gaol   *H.Pierrepoint*

Joseph FEE

Murdered: *unknown*
Motive: *unknown*

Hanged after three trials, the first two juries having failed to agree. No further details.

1905

total: *18*

097	28 Feb	Edward HARRISON	62		Wandsworth
098	29 Mar	John HUTCHINSON	29		Nottingham
099	26 Apr	Alfred BRIDGEMAN	22		Pentonville
100	23 May	Albert STRATTON	22		Wandsworth
101	23 May	Alfred STRATTON	20		Wandsworth
102	20 Jun	Alfred HEAL	22		Wandsworth
103	1 Aug	Ferat Mohamed BENALI	29	*Algerian*	Maidstone
104	9 Aug	William HANCOCKS	35		Knutsford
105	15 Aug	Arthur DEVEREUX	24		Pentonville
106	15 Aug	Thomas TATTERSHALL	31		Armley
107	7 Nov	George BUTLER	50		Pentonville
108	15 Nov	Pasha LIFFEY	24	*Basuto*	Duke Street
109	5 Dec	William YARNOLD	48		Worcester
110	6 Dec	Henry PERKINS	40		Newcastle
111	20 Dec	Samuel CURTIS	60		Maidstone
112	27 Dec	Frederick EDGE	23		Stafford
113	28 Dec	George SMITH	49		Armley
114	29 Dec	John SILK	31		Derby

28 February 1905 Wandsworth prison, London
John Billington/ H.Pierrepoint

097

Edward HARRISON   62

Cut throat of: ***Elizabeth Jane Rickus***, *30, his daughter, on 26 January 1905, in London SE8.*
Motive: *Vengeance.*

Harrison, *(b.1843),* had long mistreated his wife, and when he was sent to gaol for ten days in September 1904 for assaulting her, she left him, encouraged by her daughter.

When released, Harrison took a job as a pub pot-man, but demanded to know where his wife was. His daughter Elizabeth, despite threats, refused to tell him. At her house in Deptford, he cut her throat, nearly severing her head, and left his knife at the scene. He was arrested at his pub workplace.

On the grounds of his wife and daughter's provocation, the jury strongly recommended mercy!

Read: And May The Lord Have Mercy On Your Soul

29 March 1905   Bagthorpe prison, Nottingham
John Billington/ H.Pierrepoint

098

John HUTCHINSON   29

Stabbed: ***Albert Mathews**, 5, on 31 January 1905, in Nottingham.*
Motive: *Vengeance; drink related.*

Hutchinson, *(b.1876)*, left the army in January 1905 and moved to lodgings with George Mathews and his family in the Narrow Marsh slum area of Nottingham. He worked as a labourer, and was of limited intelligence, having been butted in the head by a sheep at the age of 6, and kicked in the head by a horse at 21. He once tried to strangle his own brother.

For a month he seemed to get on well with the Mathews' young son, Albert. After a six hour drinking binge with George, Hutchinson returned home at 5pm and Mrs Mathews went to work.

Hutchinson went berserk when the child threw a poker at him, and stabbed the boy to death with a knife, slashing his whole body, and severing his head. He then went and confessed his crime to a policeman.

Meanwhile, Mrs Mathews had returned home to find her child's head under the sofa. The jury retired for twenty minutes, and as he was taken down, he told them, 'Fuck the lot of you'. A chaplain conducted his confirmation in the condemned cell.

Read: Nottingham...The Sinister Side, p72.

26 April 1905   Pentonville prison, London
John Billington/ H.Pierrepoint

099

Alfred BRIDGEMAN   22

Cut throat of: ***Catherine Balhard**, 48, on 4 March 1905, in London NW1.*
Motive: *Vengeance; drink related.*

Bridgeman, *(b.1883)*, was still friends with his fiancee, even after she broke off their engagement at Christmas, 1904. Her mother, Catherine Balhard disliked him intensely, though. On 3 March, while drunk, he created a disturbance at her home in St Pancras, but the following day he had an evening with his girlfriend at the pub.

They went back to her room at Mrs Balhard's that evening. After coming downstairs, Bridgeman went back up, this time to Catherine's room, where he cut her throat, before running from the house.

He was arrested two days later, still carrying the blood-stained razor. He argued that Mrs Balhard had been saying bad things about him.

Read: And May The Lord Have Mercy On Your Soul.

23 May 1905   Wandsworth prison, London
John Billington/ H.Pierrepoint/ Ellis
100, 101

Albert STRATTON   22
Alfred STRATTON   20

Bludgeoned: *1 **Thomas Farrow** 67, and*
                    *2 **Ann Farrow**, 65, on 27 March 1905, in Deptford, London SE8.*
Motive: *Financial.*

The Stratton brothers, *(b.1883 and 1885)*, had already served jail terms for housebreaking and burglary when they burst past Thomas Farrow in his chandler's store in Deptford High Street at 7 o'clock one morning, wearing stocking masks. Mr Farrow was battered to death in the back parlour, and Mrs Farrow in her bed. She died three days later. The thieves, wearing stocking-masks, got away with only a few pounds. Alfred's mistress, Mary Cromerty, with whom he lived, said he was out on the murder night, and had later destroyed some clothing.

A witness had seen the brothers behaving strangely that morning, and Alfred was arrested on 3 April, Albert a day later. Alfred's thumbprint matched that of one left on the shop's cash-box - the first time fingerprint evidence was used in a murder conviction. The jury considered its verdict for two hours, and the two brothers blamed each other for the murders.

Read: True Detective, Aug 95.

102

Alfred John HEAL   22

Cut throat of: ***Ellen Maria Goodspeed***, *24, on 27 April 1905, in London SE5.*
Motive: *Sexual rivalry.*

Heal, *(b.1883)*, lived with his parents and sister in Camberwell, had courted Ellen Goodspeed since 1903, and was to be married on Easter Monday. But then he lost his job, and the wedding was postponed.

Heal developed a jealousy about a previous boyfriend of Ellen's, who still lived nearby. He became convinced that, not only had she lost her virginity to this man, but that she had borne his child. Arguments began as Ellen vehemently denied his allegations.

Ellen was at Heal's home, and all had gone to bed by 10.30pm, except Alfred and Ellen. At 11.30 he cut her throat and she ran to his parents' room. Ellen began to make a good recovery, and Heal wrote apologising for his actions, but Ellen relapsed, a fever set in, and she died on 7 May. A post-mortem showed that Ellen was, indeed, still a virgin.

Read: And May The Lord Have Mercy On Your Soul

103

Ferat Mohamed BENALI   19   *Algerian*

Cut throat of: ***Hadjou Idder***, *40, on 17 June 1905, in Tenterden, Kent.*
Motive: *Vengeance.*

Benali, *(b.1886)*, was one of five Algerians who shared lodgings in Kent, and who made a living hawking cheap goods door-to-door. Three of them, Benali, Idder, and Idder's brother, Frank Salem, worked in Ashford on 13 June, and two of them, possibly all three, went to Tenterden on 16 June. Sleeping in a field, Benali stated that he awoke to find Idder sexually assaulting him. He hit him with a heavy stick, and cut his throat. The body was found the following morning, and the Algerians were soon rounded up.

Benali and Salem were both charged with murder, as three sets of footprints had been found in the field. Benali admitted the offence, and claimed Salem was not there. The jury believed him, and Salem was acquitted. It seems that Benali confessed in order to save Salem's life.

Read: And May The Lord Have Mercy On Your Soul

9 August 1905   Knutsford gaol   *John Billington/ H.Pierrepoint*

104

William Alfred HANCOCKS   35

Stabbed: ***Mary Elizabeth Hancocks***, *15, his daughter, on 23 March 1905, in Birkenhead, Cheshire.*
Motive: *Sadistic pleasure; drink related.*

Hancocks, *(b.1870)*, was a sheriff's officer with only one arm. He was a bigamist who lived in lodgings with one wife and two young children, aged 4 and 2. His elder daughter Mary, who lived elsewhere, came to visit, and, while his wife was out, he tried to strangle her in his room. The landlady and a lodger answered Mary's screams and interrupted Hancocks. They took Mary to another room when her father pulled a knife. Mrs Hancocks returned, and Bill seemed to calm down.
Mary went again to tend the two children, and her father stabbed her several times in the head, cutting her arms and hands as she sought to defend herself. Hancocks ran out and threw himself in the Mersey, but was fished out and arrested. Mary died four days later. The jury recommended mercy because Hancocks had been drinking. From the condemned cell he wrote letters to both his wives.

Read: And May The Lord Have Mercy On Your Soul

15 August 1905   Pentonville prison, London   *H.Pierrepoint/ Ellis*

105

Arthur DEVEREUX   24

Poisoned: **1** ***Beatrice Devereux***, *25, his wife, and twins sons*
        2 ***Laurence Devereux*** *and*

> **3 Evelyn Devereux**, 1, on 29 January 1905, in Kilburn, London NW6.
>
> Motive: To clear impediment.

Devereux, *(b. 1881)*, his wife of seven years, Beatrice, *(nee Gregory)*, and son Stanley, lived in impoverished conditions in Kilburn. Arthur worked as a chemist's assistant and made applications for better employment, but try as he might, his wages simply did not go far enough.

When his frail wife bore twins in 1904, things became too much for him and he resolved to escape his poverty trap. He poisoned his wife and baby twins and moved with his beloved son, Stanley, 6, sealing the remains of the others in a tin trunk and placing it in storage. With the wages sufficient for his reduced responsibilities, Stanley was found a place in a private school.

After four months, Beatrice's mother tracked him down and found out about the stored trunk. By the time the murder came to light in April, Devereux had fled to Coventry. He claimed that his wife had killed the twins and then taken her own life, but it was shown that he had described himself as a widower in a job application while his wife was still alive, though evidence that his wife was severely depressed was overlooked.

His subsequent ploy of feigning suicide failed to convince and he was condemned by the jury inside ten minutes.

Read: *True Crime Diary.*

15 August 1905	Armley gaol, Leeds	*John Billington/ Warbrick*

106

Thomas George TATTERSHALL   31

Cut throat of:	**Rebecca Tattershall**, 30, his wife, on 3 July 1905, in Wakefield, W Yorks.
Motive:	To clear impediment; drink related.

Tattershall, *(b. 1874)*, was the son of a Wakefield councillor, and ran a plastering business. In Australia in 1893 he suffered head injuries and a rupture in an accident, wearing a truss thereafter. Returning to England the following year, he married Rebecca Stead in 1893, and they had four children, Laura being the eldest. He suffered severe bouts of flu and diphtheria during 1904 and 1905, after which he attempted suicide.

A kind father when sober, drink had a severe effect on him. Several times Rebecca applied for separation, or went to her brother's. In June 1905 the police put Tattershall under surveillance for his wife's protection after he had tried to strangle her.

But one July night as Rebecca got into bed he attacked her, hitting her head with a hatchet and cutting her throat with a razor. Finding her mother bleeding to death, Laura, 10, ran screaming into the street, and police arrested Tattershall several days later. A plea of insanity was rejected by the jury in 12 minutes.

Read: Master Detective, Aug 96.

7 November 1905   Pentonville prison, London   *H.Pierrepoint/ Ellis*

107

George William BUTLER   50

Stabbed: ***Mary Allen***, *45, on 25 September 1905, in London W1.*
Motive: *Vengeance.*

Butler, *(b.1855),* a boot maker, had lived in Marylebone with Mary Allen for three years. He had previously been married, and Mary had got through two husbands. When Mary's son, George Melhuish, came to live with her in July 1905, Butler resented it, and a great dislike grew between the two men.

They came to blows at the end of July, and Melhuish broke Butler's jaw. Butler claimed that Mary had put their son up to it, and as the jaw was slow to heal, Butler having to drink beer through a straw, his anger grew, and threats were made. In their bedroom on the morning of 25 September, Butler stabbed Mary four times, and she died four days later.

Read: And May The Lord Have Mercy On Your Soul

15 November 1905   Duke Street prison, Glasgow   *H.Pierrepoint*

108

Pasha LIFFEY   24   *Basuto*

Murdered: ***Mary Jane Welsh***, *64, on 11 August 1905, in Larkhall, Lanarks.*
Motive: *Sexual.*

Liffey, *(b.1881)*, a native of Mafeking, was touring Scotland with a travelling show. He raped and murdered the elderly miner's wife in Dykehead Road. No further details.

Read: Encyclopaedia of Scottish Executions.

5 December 1905　　　　Worcester prison　　　　*H.Pierrepoint/ Ellis*

109

William YARNOLD　　48

Stabbed:　　　　*Annie Yarnold, 42, his wife, on 4 October 1905, in Worcester.*
Motive:　　　　Sexual rivalry

Yarnold, *(b.1857)*, had spent 28 years in the army, including ten years in India, and service in the Boer war. His wife claimed he beat her and forced her into prostitution, and while he was in South Africa, she left him and took a new lover, George Miles. Yarnold twice bumped into her in a pub, and twice followed her home.

On the second occasion, at 4.30pm, Annie came out to brush her windowsill, and Yarnold stabbed her in the back with a long knife. Her injuries were made worse by a well-meaning neighbour who pulled out the knife, causing severe bleeding.

Yarnold was arrested at 8pm, and Annie died three days later. Deliberating for ten minutes, the jury added a recommendation to mercy, on account of his wife's unfaithfulness. Yarnold's was the first execution at Worcester since 1805.

Read: And May The Lord Have Mercy On Your Soul

6 December 1905　　　　Newcastle prison　　　　*H.Pierrepoint/ Ellis*

110

Henry PERKINS　　40

Possibly murdered:　　　　*A person in Kettering, Northants in 1886.*

Stabbed:	Patrick Durkin, 29, on 13 July 1905, in Newcastle, Northumberland
Motive:	Vengeance; drink related

Perkins, (b.1865), a cobbler, shared a room in a Newcastle lodging house with Patrick Durkin and two other men. Both men were continually drunk and often fought over trivial matters.

On 12 July, they fought twice, the second time Perkins pulling a knife, and the lodging house keeper having to separate them. The following day Durkin, an Irish mason's labourer, came in at 7pm and fell into a drunken sleep on a kitchen bench.

Half an hour later Perkins arrived, also drunk, and, seeing Perkins asleep, went over and stabbed him twice in the throat with a table knife, before running off. He was found in the city centre the next day, and Durkin died in hospital on 19 July.

The jury decided Perkins' fate in ten minutes. It was later revealed that he had been suspected of a murder in Kettering in 1886, but was released for lack of evidence.

Read: Murderous Tyneside, p34.

20 December 1905   Maidstone prison   *H.Pierrepoint/ Fry*

111

Samuel CURTIS   60

Stabbed:	Alice Clover, 34, on 22 July 1905, in Wrotham, Kent.
Motive:	Sexual rivalry.

Curtis, (b.1845), a rag and bone man, had lived with Alice Clover since 1890, but he had treated her badly, and she left him in November 1904. For nine months he trekked around the country searching for her, until in July 1905, he located her, in Wrotham, living with another man.

He bought a knife, and went to the pub were she was drinking. An argument followed, and Annie walked out. Curtis pursued her, and stabbed her twice in the throat. The jury added a strong recommendation to mercy on account of Annie's unfaithfulness.

Read: And May The Lord Have Mercy On Your Soul

112

Frederick William EDGE   23

Cut throat of: **Francis Walter Evans**, *5 mths, on 28 September 1905, in Newcastle-under-Lyme, Staffs.*
Motive: *Vengeance.*

Edge, *(b.1882),* almost certainly had a psychiatric disorder, and would probably now be deemed insane. He eked out a living keeping score in a billiard hall, and from August 1905, lodged with Frank and Rose Evans and their three children, a mining family. When he got into rent arrears he was told he would have to go.

After a last lunch at the house with Rose, he cut young Frank's throat with a razor, and ran out of the house. He gave a parcel of clothes to his sister, and went to the police at 2.30pm to hand himself in. He explained that he had wanted to kill Rose, but did not get the chance.

Read: And May The Lord Have Mercy On Your Soul

28 December 1905   Armley gaol, Leeds   *H.Pierrepoint/ Ellis*

113

George SMITH   49

Stabbed: **Martha Smith**, *50, his wife, on 12 September 1905, in Ilkley, W. Yorkshire.*
Motive: *Sexual rivalry.*

George Smith, *(b. 1857),* had married his wife Martha in 1894, and together they had two children. Martha already had two adult children from an earlier marriage.

A bricklayer by trade, Smith, 5'4", had been unemployed for some time, and his pride was dented at Martha having to go into domestic service to make ends meet. He would beat his wife and made such a scene that she was forced to leave her employment in Leeds, returning to her mother in Wakefield in June 1905. She paid for George's lodgings in Leeds. When Martha took another job as a domestic, Smith became enraged.

On 12 September he stole a knife from his landlady and at 2.30pm went to the Glendennings' house in Ilkley, where Martha had just finished the washing. A terrible row ensued in the kitchen when, to get rid of him for good, Martha told him she had another man.

Smith lunged at his wife, stabbing her 49 times, a severe gash to her neck proving fatal. Smith then carried Martha's body into the cellar. She was discovered by the owner's daughter later that afternoon, and Smith was arrested in Wakefield two days later. After angry uproar from the court's public gallery, the jury returned their verdict within thirteen minutes.

Read Murderous Leeds, p22

29 December 1905   Derby gaol   *H.Pierrepoint/ Ellis*

114

John SILK   **31**

Bludgeoned: ***Mary Fallon**, 51, his mother, on 5 August 1905, in Chesterfield, Derbyshire.*
Motive: *Vengeance; drink related.*

Silk, *(b.1874),* had served with the army in India and South Africa, and upon his discharge in 1903 went to live with his mother in Chesterfield. Mary Fallon had twice been widowed, and then abandoned in 1903 by her third husband. Suffering from sciatica, rheumatism and heart disease, she was a virtual cripple, only able to walk with the use of a crutch.

Silk, the product of her first marriage, was known to be abusive and violent to her when drunk, which was most nights. In the summer of 1904 Mary had taken in a lodger, Thomas Meakin, and he was present at 11pm a year later when a new argument blew up over a lamp.

Silk had come in drunk and when his mother told him to leave the oil lamp alone, Silk slapped her face, smashed a beer bottle and threw the pieces in her face. She retaliated and a scuffle developed in which the lamp was overturned. In the darkness Silk beat his mother about the head and face with her crutch, breaking her nose, and then stamped on her chest.

Meakin ran to several neighbours and then the police, vainly trying to get help. Finding the door locked, he stayed the night with a friend. A paperboy found Mary the next morning at 9.50, and police found Silk awake in bed, with bloody hands and face. The jury considered Silk's fate for fifteen minutes, and the murderer fainted on the scaffold.

Read: Murderous Derbyshire, p38

1905 Executions in Ireland

25 April 1905   Cork County Gaol   *W.Billington/ Ellis*

JOHN FOSTER

Murdered: **William Regan**, *in December 1904.*
Motive: *Financial.*

      Foster, 6'2" and 16 st, was a retired police constable who shared lodgings with US army pensioner William Regan, 5'5". The two were friends, but at 6.30 one evening while walking by the river Lee, Foster killed Regan and dumped his body in the water. He was later found to be in possession of the dead man's gold watch and chain.

      Read: Master Detective, Aug 98.

1906

total: **8**

115	27 Feb	John GRIFFITHS	19	Strangeways
116	10 Apr	Harold WALTERS	39	Wakefield
117	7 Aug	Edward GLYNN	26	Nottingham
118	9 Aug	Thomas MOUNCER	25	Wakefield
119	13 Nov	Frederick REYNOLDS	23	Wandsworth
120	27 Nov	Edward HARTIGAN	58	Knutsford
121	4 Dec	Richard BUCKHAM	20	Chelmsford
122	27 Dec	Walter MARSH	39	Derby

27 February 1906   Strangeways prison   *H.Pierrepoint/Ellis*

115

<u>John GRIFFITHS</u>   **19**

Strangled: ***Catherine Garrity***, *17, on 19 December 1905, at Shaw, Lancs.*
Motive: *Sexual rivalry.*

Jack Griffiths, *(b.1887)*, was a former soldier who had a reputation for a quick temper and violence. He and Kate Garrity both worked in a mill in Shaw, and lived in the same street. They struck up a friendship which was far more serious to him than to her. They quarrelled when he jealously criticised her for talking to any other man and he had been bound over to keep the peace for three months when he punched Kate in the face. But just two weeks later when Kate left home at 8.30 on an evening errand, Griffiths was waiting for her.

He punched her about the face and strangled her with string on waste ground, covering her with sacking. Kate's father discovered her body the next morning. Griffiths had escaped over a wall but was tracked by clogprints traced with blue paint. Blood was found on his clothing, and string in his pocket. In a letter to his mother, he confessed his guilt. The jury took only five minutes to condemn him.

Griffiths, 5' 7", 11 st, cracked jokes in the condemned cell and died smiling.

Read: Strange Tales from Strangeways, p 73.

116

Harold WALTERS   39

C

Internally injured: **Sarah Ann McConnell**, *43,*
                              on 23 December 1905, in Sheffield, W Yorks.
Motive: *Vengeance.*

Sarah McConnell left her husband in September 1905, to go and live with Walters, *(b.1867).* He claimed that Sarah would spend money that he gave her on drink, and that she had been drunk for the past twenty-four hours.

So, after 5pm, he took a terrible revenge of sexual assault. Stripping her almost naked in the sitting room, he first forced a ginger beer bottle violently into her vagina. He then pushed a broom handle between her legs, impaling her to a depth of 50cm, injuring her internal organs, ribs, and even her neck.

Three callers, all seeking to collect money owed, saw Sarah bleeding heavily on the hearth rug, and went for help. The last, a young girl who called before 6pm, saw Walters cradling Sarah and trying to revive her.

Read: And May The Lord Have Mercy On Your Soul

117

Edward GLYNN   26

Stabbed: **Jane Gamble**, *22, on 3 March 1906, in Nottingham.*
Motive: *Sexual rivalry*

Glynn, *(b.1880),* who had known Jane for two years, lived with her in the Narrow Marsh slum district of Nottingham, until she left him for another man, Henry Gibson. He made threats that if he saw them together, he would kill her. As Jane, generally known as Jenny, and Gibson walked home from the pub at 11pm, Glynn was waiting.

He stabbed his former girlfriend repeatedly, and so vicious was his assault, that the knife broke, leaving a 4cm section close to Jenny's spine.

Glynn was arrested in his sister's house at 3.40am, and Jenny died on the morning of the 5 March.

Read: And May The Lord Have Mercy On Your Soul

9 August 1906	Wakefield prison	H/ T.Pierrepoint

118

Thomas Acomb MOUNCER　　　25

Strangled:　　**Elizabeth Baldwin, 31, on 13 May 1906, in Middlesbrough, N Yorks.**
Motive:　　*Sexual rivalry; drink related.*

Mouncer, *(b.1881)*, lived with Elizabeth Baldwin, but was jealous of her friendship with another man. All three had a friendly drink in the pub, and Mouncer and Elizabeth went home together.

In the bedroom, preparing to retire at 12.30am, Mouncer strangled his lover, explaining later that she had insulted him, and gone for him with a knife. At 6.30am, Mouncer walked to a police station and confessed his crime.

Read: And May The Lord Have Mercy On Your Soul

13 November 1906	Wandsworth prison, London	H.Pierrepoint/ Ellis

119

Frederick REYNOLDS　　　23

Cut throat of:　　**Sophia Lovell, 18, on 10 September 1906, in London SE1.**
Motive:　　*Sexual rivalry.*

Reynolds, *(b.1883),* had been courting Sophia Lovell, against her mother's wishes, for eighteen months. When Mrs Lovell died in August 1906, her dying wish was that Sophia would finish with Reynolds, and Sophia did just that.

While out with friends on 8 September, Sophia met Harry Lambourne, and the two went on a date the following evening. A day later, at 9.30pm, Harry and his new girlfriend were out walking, but Reynolds was waiting. He hit Sophia four times, knocking her to the ground, and then cut her throat. Reynolds gave himself up to police at 10.30pm. The jury considered its verdict for just two minutes.

Read: And May The Lord Have Mercy On Your Soul

27 November 1906   Knutsford gaol   *H.Pierrepoint/ Willis*

120

Edward HARTIGAN   58

Bludgeoned: ***Catherine Hartigan**, 45, his wife, on 7 August 1906, in Stockport, Lancs.*
Motive: *Vengeance; drink related.*

Hartigan, *(b.1848),* a hod-carrier, was a powerful and feared man, whose criminal record started at the age of 23. In 1883 he had broken a pub licensee's jaw, and the following year had assaulted his sister. For these and other offences, including theft, he had served two years in prison.

He and Catherine had married in 1889, and she too had a formidable temper, once having assaulted a policeman, and in 1894 caused Edward severe burns by throwing a paraffin lamp at him. Both drank heavily and Hartigan regularly beat his wife, often in front of their four children who by 1906 were aged 9 to 16.

Hartigan had been complaining that his wife had not been feeding him, and when he came home drunk at 6.30pm on 7 August and found his wife asleep in bed, he dragged her out kicking her. He then took a hammer and smashed her skull nineteen times. He was on his way to the police station when a PC caught up with him. Catherine died at midnight.

Read: Murderous Manchester, p14.

121

Richard BUCKHAM   20

Shot: *1 **Albert Watson**, 47, and his wife*
                    *2 **Emma Watson**, 50, on 23 August 1906, in Basildon,*
                    Essex.
Motive: *Vengeance.*

    The Watsons owned a poultry farm and market garden near Basildon, but had come to an arrangement with a neigbouring farmer over water. Mr Buckham gave permission for the Watsons, with no access to water on their own land, to use a pond, 300m from their own home. But Buckham's sons, Robert, 17, and Richard, *(b.1886),* did not like their neighbours, and when they saw Mr and Mrs Watson collecting water at 5.30am, they warned them off.

    When Mr Watson made a curt reply, Richard Buckham blasted him in the back with his shotgun. He then shot Mrs Watson in the chest, and finished her off with a close range shot in the neck. The brothers then took the Watsons' keys and stole a watch and cash from their farmhouse. At 10am they reported to a neighbour that they had found the two bodies. Richard later confessed to the murders, and Robert was acquitted by the court.

    Read: And May The Lord Have Mercy On Your Soul

122

Walter MARSH   39

Cut throat of: **Eliza Marsh**, *22, his wife, on 9 July 1906, in Chesterfield,*
                    Derbyshire.
Motive: *Sexual rivalry.*

    Marsh, *(b.1867),* had spent seventeen years in the army, serving at the battle of Omdurman, before, at the age of 34, marrying 17-year old Eliza Gascoyne in November 1901. He saw further war service in South Africa from December 1901 to June 1902, and finally left the army, a colour sergeant, in August 1903.

The couple took a pub in Sheffield, and then moved to Chesterfield in 1904, where Marsh got a job as a rent collector. By 1906 the couple had two children, but things had gone downhill for them. Eliza was described as lazy, and would often drink, more than once attacking Marsh with a poker. When Marsh responded by beating her, she returned briefly to her father.

On 4 July, Marsh accused her of having sex with the landlord who had called while he was out, and, confronting him with this, he was sacked.

On 5 July a neighbour caught him pinning Eliza down by the arms in the yard, and the following day he threw water at her. She spent two nights with a neighbour but then on 9 July, having had no meals from Eliza for four days, he snapped when she could not be bothered to wash up. He cut her throat as she lay in bed at 5.20pm, almost severing her head, and then went next door to confess. The jury rejected the idea of provocation in twenty minutes.

Read: Murderous Derbyshire, p53.

1907

total: **10**

123	1 Jan	John DAVIS	53		Warwick
124	26 Mar	Joseph JONES	60		Stafford
125	2 Apr	Edwin MOORE	33		Warwick
126	16 Jul	William SLACK	47		Derby
127	7 Aug	Charles PATERSON	37	*St Vincentian*	Walton
128	13 Aug	Richard BRINKLEY	52		Wandsworth
129	14 Aug	Rhoda WILLIS (f)	44	*Welsh*	Cardiff
130	5 Nov	William AUSTIN	31		Reading
131	20 Nov	William DUDDLES	47		Lincoln
132	13 Dec	George STILLS	30	*Welsh*	Cardiff

1 January 1907 Warwick gaol *Ellis/ Willis*

123

John DAVIS   53

Cut throat of: ***Jane Harrison**, 47, on 17 November 1906 in Aston, Warwicks.*
Motive: *Sexual rivalry.*

Davis, *(b.1854),* was a silverer and a religious worker at Garstang docks, Liverpool. He lived with his wife in Aston, Birmingham, but had met pub landlady Mrs Harrison and had begun courting her. Her husband had become mentally ill and she had moved to Aston, but her two adult sons resisted Davis' intentions of moving in.

Davis became increasingly suspicious of a rival and, crazed with jealousy, crept into Jane's home at 10am one morning. A quarrel ensued and Davis cut Mrs Harrison's throat. His victim died an hour later. A crowd held 10st Davis until police arrived. Davis claimed that Jane had cut her own throat because of a bad headache. The jury returned its guilty verdict after only five minutes. Jane had been black-leading the grate, and the razor bore no signs of it.

Read: Murderous Birmingham, p31.

124

Joseph Edwin JONES   60

Bludgeoned/ cut throat of: *Edmund Clarke, 28, on 1 December 1906, in Stafford.*

Motive: *Vengeance.*

Edmund Clarke, a Sunday school teacher, married Ethel Jones in 1902, and the couple lived with Ethel's father, Joseph, *(b.1847)*. He had lost his job in a steel mill, and gambling and drinking had led to money difficulties.

Jones was forced to hand over his property rights to Clarke, and then arguments started, and threats were made by Jones when he claimed Clarke had assaulted him. Ethel had gone out with her two children on the evening of 1 December, and at 8pm, after dinner, Edmund lay on the sofa to sleep. Jones battered him with a poker and then slit his throat with two razors. The jury recommended mercy.

Read: And May The Lord Have Mercy On Your Soul.

125

Edwin James MOORE   33

Burned: *Fanny Adelaide Moore, 52, his mother, on 2 March 1907, in Leamington, Warwicks.*

Motive: *Vengeance; drink related.*

Fanny Moore lived with two of her six children, Bertie, 11, and Edwin, *(b.1874)*, and her husband, a cab driver, who was often out evenings. Edwin would often hit his mother when he had been drinking, as he had been on the evening of 2 March.

He threw his dinner, not to his taste, on the floor, and chased his mother around the room, witnessed by his younger brother. He threw a paraffin lamp at her, and when he caught the unfortunate woman, lit some newspaper from the wick of the lamp, and set fire to her blouse. Mrs Moore had a weak heart and, soon engulfed in flames, died in minutes, despite Moore's efforts to subdue the flames.

Read: And May The Lord Have Mercy On Your Soul.

126

William Edward SLACK   47

Bludgeoned: ***Lucy Wilson***, *40, on 18 March 1907, in Chesterfield,
Derbyshire.*
Motive: *To clear impediment*

Slack, *(b.1860),* had served in the army in India from 1892-7, and received seven years for stabbing a policeman sixteen times in 1899. After his release he worked as a carpenter, then as a painter. Though married, he met Lucy Wilson at the theatre where she was a ticket checker in July 1905, having sex with her on their first encounter. The affair continued up to four times a week for two years, he claimed with her husband's knowledge, and a baby was born in June 1906, which Lucy told Slack was his.

Lucy claimed her husband was unfaithful and gave her no money, and she began to pile on the pressure to run away with Slack. Interrupting him at work, Lucy was told that if she came back he would kill her. When she did the two calmly took a walk, Lucy pushing her pram, when Slack suddenly pulled out a hatchet and began beating her head and shoulders. One of two passers by took him and the baby to the police.

The jury did not retire, and delivered its verdict inside a minute. Long known for his short temper, Slack shouted at the judge, 'You can stick the black cap up your arse', pulled out a handful of his hair and kicked and screamed his way from the dock.

Read: Murderous Derbyshire, p62

127

Charles PATERSON   37   *Black St Vincentian*

Cut throat of: ***Lilian Jane Charlton***, *39, on 29 June 1907, in
Manchester, Lancs.*
Motive: *Vengeance; drink related.*

Lilian Charlton had been separated from her husband for twelve years, but she and her three children were soon to regret her taking up with Charles Paterson in 1906. Of mixed race originating from St Vincent, Paterson was an unemployed sailor, and Lilian's money worries began to escalate. Four times she went to the police when Paterson beat her, and she could not afford the warrant she wanted for his arrest.

She asked him if he had any money and told him to get out when he said he was broke. When he refused, she went upstairs at 5.30pm to pack her own things. Having been drinking, he followed her into the bathroom, cut her throat with a razor, waited for the police, and pleaded guilty to murder.

Read: Murderous Manchester, p19.

13 August 1907	Wandsworth prison, London	*H.Pierrepoint/ Ellis*

128

Richard Clifford BRINKLEY   52

*Probably **poisoned:**1 **Laura Jane Glenn**, 17, in 1893, and*
                                   *2 **Johanna Blume**, 77, on 19 December 1906, in Fulham, London SW6.*
Poisoned: *3 **Richard Beck**, 55, and*
                                 *4 **Elizabeth Beck**, 57, on 20 April 1907, in Croydon, Surrey.*
Motive: *Financial.*

      Brinkley, *(b. 1855),* had married in 1875, but was left a widower with several children eight years later. In 1893 Laura Jane Glenn, 17, with whom he was living, died from arsenic poisoning. It was thought she had committed suicide. Brinkley, a cabinet maker working as a jobbing carpenter, had befriended a 77-year old German widow, Johanna Blume. She lived in Fulham with her grand-daughter.

      On 17 December 1906, a will was made out in her name, witnessed by Reginald Parker and Henry Heard. In it Brinkley was declared sole inheritor of her property and money. Mrs Blume died two days later, apparently of a cerebral haemorrhage. Within a month Brinkley had left his lodgings in Streatham and had moved into the Blume house. The old lady's daughter, Caroline, contested the will, and to prevent her going to court, Brinkley offered to share the estate and also proposed marriage. His offers were declined. It seems that Parker at least had been tricked into signing the will, and that Brinkley risked losing everything in court.

      Parker, 35, was separated from his wife and lodged with Mr and Mrs Beck and their two daughters Daisy, 21, and Hilda, in Croydon. Brinkley called on him on 20 April 1907, to discuss buying his dog. He took with him a bottle of stout. Having drunk some himself, Brinkley asked Parker for water and took the opportunity of being alone to poison the remainder with prussic acid. Parker had suspected Brinkley of previously trying to poison him, and declined the beer. When the Becks returned to the empty house later that evening the stout bottle remained on the table. Richard, Elizabeth and Daisy all took a drink, and very shortly were all violently ill. Hilda alerted a doctor too late to save her parents, though Daisy eventually recovered.

Brinkley at first denied having been in Croydon, but witnesses testified otherwise, including the boy who had sold him the stout. Mrs Blume's body when exhumed failed to show any trace of poison. However, it would seem likely that Mrs Blume and Miss Glenn had both been victims of this poisoner. The jury deliberated for 55 minutes before declaring Brinkley guilty.

Read: Crime Strange But True, p3 .

14 August 1907   Cardiff prison   *H./ T.Pierrepoint*

129

<u>Rhoda WILLIS</u>   **44**   *female*   *Welsh*

Suffocated: ***Baby Treasure,*** *1 day, on 4 June 1907, near Cardiff, Glamorgan.*
Motive: *Financial.*

Rhoda, *(b.1863),* was from a middle-class background. She had raised two families, one by her husband and another by a subsequent lover, but had since fallen upon hard times. Living in Cardiff's slums, she had taken to prostitution as some means of support, and to drink as a lift from her despair. From January 1907 she worked as housekeeper to a man in Pontypool, whom she peruaded to act as her husband in order to make money 'adopting' babies. In April she adopted a 3-week old child, and a month later abandoned it on the steps of a Salvation Army hostel, the baby dying of exposure a week later.

Offered £6 by Maud Treasure, a single girl, to find a home for her one-day old baby, Rhoda, desperate for the money, took the child and then smothered it on the train from Llanishen. The landlady in the lodging house in which Willis was staying, found her drunk and the baby dead. Willis claimed that the baby had died en route to the lodgings. Also known as Rhoda Willis Lascelles and as Mrs Leslie James, she was executed on her 44th birthday.

Read: And May The Lord Have Mercy On Your Soul.

130

William George Thomas Charles AUSTIN   31   *(aka Saunders)*

Strangled: *Unity Annie Butler, 13, on 16 July 1907, in Windsor, Berks.*

Motive: *Sexual*

      Austin, *(b.1876)*, who since coming to Windsor had called himself Saunders, lived with his cousin, Unity Butler, her husband and daughter. He was a drayman, but often preferred to spend his money on drink rather than rent. He became threatening and angry when drunk.

      Of late, Unity and William Butler's marriage had been stormy, with many rows into the early hours; Austin had resented this. The Butler's daughter Unity came home from school one summer afternoon to find her parents out. Going to her room, she was attacked by Austin, 5'7", who gagged her with a handkerchief, tied her hands before her with cord, and raped her. He then strangled her with the same cord.

      Unity's father saw Austin cycle off at about 6pm. He went and got drunk, and gave his watch to a friend, saying he would never see him again. Not until after 11pm, when the mother, Unity came home, was the girl discovered under Austin's bed, skirt raised, underwear missing, and abdomen covered with blood. Austin was found the next day, carrying a letter to the Butlers admitting the crime. He said he was going to drown himself. In court he falsely claimed to have had sex with Unity on many occasions, and to have had an affair with her mother.

      A defence of insanity was rejected inside ten minutes by the jury.

      Read: True Crime, April 95.

---

20 November 1907   Lincoln prison   *H/ T.Pierrepoint*

131

William DUDDLES   47

Bludgeoned: *Catherine Gear, 36, on 8 October 1907, in Sutton Marsh, Lincs.*

Motive: *Vengeance; drink related.*

Duddles, *(b.1860)*, had lodged with William and Catherine Gear for years, but relations between Mrs Gear and the lodger had deteriorated to the extent that Mr Gear punched Duddles when he called Catherine a whore. On the afternoon of 8 October all the neighbours were in for a drinking session, and Duddles went out after 1pm to get some more beer. When he returned Catherine was alone and a row started. She blacked his eye, and Duddles in return battered her with a hammer. He was arrested in the pub at 6.20pm.

Read: And May The Lord Have Mercy On Your Soul

13 December 1907	Cardiff gaol	*H/T.Pierrepoint*

132

George STILLS   **30**   *Welsh*

Bludgeoned: ***Rachel Hannah Stills**, 70, his mother, on 10 September 1907, in Pont-y-cymmer, Glamorgan.*
Motive: *Sadistic pleasure; drink related.*

George Stills, *(b.1877)*, known as 'Notty', lived with his mother and brother John. He often beat his mother after drinking, and the afternoon of 10 September was no exception. After arriving home drunk he battered and kicked his mother to death, then dragged her body into the street, in full view of the neighbours, and, as a final insult, threw the old woman's skirt over her head. He went back in, slammed the door behind him and awaited the arrival of police, summoned by the witnesses.

Read: And May The Lord Have Mercy On Your Soul

1907 Execution in Jersey

19 February 1907   Newgate Street prison, St Helier   *H.Pierrepoint*

Thomas CONNAN

Murdered: *His brother-in-law.*
Motive: *Unknown*

      Connan's was the first execution in Jersey for 41 years. No further details.

1908

total: **14**

133	5 Mar	Joseph HUME	24	Scottish	Inverness
134	24 Mar	Joseph NOBLE	48		Durham
135	24 Mar	Robert LAWMAN	34		Durham
136	12 May	John RAMSBOTTOM	34		Strangeways
137	28 Jul	Fred BALLINGTON	41		Strangeways
138	4 Aug	Thomas SIDDLE	29		Hull
139	5 Aug	Matthew DODDS	43		Durham
140	19 Aug	Edward JOHNSTON	32	Scottish	Perth
141	12 Nov	James PHIPPS	21		Knutsford
142	2 Dec	James NICHOLLS	35		Norwich
143	3 Dec	John ELLWOOD	45		Armley
144	8 Dec	William BOULDRY	41		Maidstone
145	15 Dec	Harry PARKER	32		Warwick
146	30 Dec	Patrick COLLINS	24	Welsh	Cardiff

5 March 1908   Porterfield prison, Inverness   *Ellis/ Willis*

133

Joseph HUME   **24**   *Scottish*

Bludgeoned: ***John Barclay Smith*, *48*, *on 24 September 1907, in Lhanbryde, Moray.***
Motive: *Financial.*

Hume, *(b.1884),* deserting from the army camp at Fort George, was offered work and shelter by John Smith, a road contractor, and the two were seen returning to Smith's home one afternoon. Once there, Hume beat the intoxicated older man about the head with a hammer, and stole a gold watch and some cash. When Hume attempted to pawn the watch in Glasgow, he aroused suspicion and was arrested. His was the first execution in Inverness since 1835, and was to be the last.

Read: Encyclopaedia of Scottish Executions

95

134

Joseph William NOBLE   48

Shot: **John Patterson**, *33, on 1 November 1907, near Gateshead, Co Durham.*
Motive: *Financial.*

Noble, *(b.1860)*, had been a blacksmith for ten years and was popular in his local Gateshead community. Several times he went armed with one of the revolvers he used to repair to steal meat from the Co-op shop in Windy Nook. Exasperated with the thefts, four young employees decided to lie in wait one night.

At 4.30 am, Noble entered the shop with a skeleton key, and the four men pounced. Noble was hit on the head and leg with a hammer, but responded by shooting John Patterson point-blank between the eyes. Christopher Carr was shot in the leg.

Noble was known to the men, but they remained silent until the police received an anonymous tip-off. They then picked him out of an identity parade. The jury took 45 minutes to determine that Noble had not acted in self-defence. His last words were, 'Don't hurt my neck', as he was hanged alongside Robert Lawman.

Read: True Detective Summer Special 96.

24 March 1908   Durham gaol   *H / T Pierrepoint*

135

Robert LAWMAN   34

Stabbed: **Amelia Bell Wood**, *23, on 1 February 1908, in Gateshead, Co Durham*
Motive: *Vengeance; drink related.*

Lawman, *(b.1874)*, a miner living in Elswick, had been left to look after his two sons aged 9 and 6 when his wife deserted him in 1906. He had known Millie Wood for 4 years when he arranged for her to come and stay as his housekeeper in 1907.

Well known for her liking of drink and men, she often stayed out until 2am, coming home drunk, and causing many arguments. She often left Lawman, only to come back a few days later. On 24 January 1908, she finally left, finding a bed in a Gateshead boarding-house. Lawman determined to find her and get her back.

On 31 January he shaved his moustache, took a table knife, and found Millie drunk in a pub. He stayed the night with her, rising at 5am to buy some whisky. Millie's landlady was sent for beer at 11am, delivering it to them in bed. She heard the bedroom door lock, heard moans and then a scream. She fetched the police who barged down the door, finding Millie in a pool of blood. She had found the knife and lunged at Lawman, who hit her in the face with a beer bottle, then stabbed her about the body and in the throat. He then cut his own throat.

The jury took just three minutes to condemn him, and pronouncing himself 'ready to die', he was hanged alongside Joseph Noble, just 52 days after Amelia's murder.

Read: True Detective, Aug 97.

| **12 May 1908** | Strangeways prison, Manchester | *H.Pierrepoint* |

136

John RAMSBOTTOM   34

| **Shot:** | **James MacCraw**, 21, on 21 February 1908, in Manchester, Lancs. |
| Motive: | Vengeance; drink related. |

Ramsbottom, *(b.1874),* a factory worker, married Charlotte MacCraw in October 1907, after getting her pregnant. They lived with their new son in Gorton, until Ramsbottom's drink problem got the better of him and he started threatening his wife, and admitted having sex with another woman. Charlotte returned to the pub in Gorton run by her parents. She refused to go back to him but she did allow him to stay with her at the pub.

When he learned that Charlotte had arranged for furniture to be removed from their home, on 18 February he took time off work to obtain a licence to buy a revolver. He was sacked the following day, and when he returned to the pub on 20th, having been missing two days, Mrs MacCraw told him to get out.

He sat drinking with Charlotte's brother James, a turner, and then he joined Charlotte and the baby in bed. She refused him sex, and he shot her in the breast. Her mother ran to the room to see Ramsbottom standing on the bed holding a gun, wearing only his shirt. Another shot hit a pipe, flooding the room, and then, when James arrived, two more shots hit the young man in the arm and stomach.

Ramsbottom fled across town still in only his shirt, and James died at 8.15 the same morning. Ramsbottom was arrested at his mother's house.

Read: Murderous Manchester, p34.

28 July 1908   Strangeways prison, Manchester   *H.Pierrepoint/ Willis*

137

Fred BALLINGTON   41

Stabbed: ***Ellen Ann Ballington**, 43, his wife, on 25 May 1908, in Manchester, Lancs.*
Motive: *Vengeance.*

Fred Ballington, *(b.1867)*, a butcher from Glossop, had lost his job and had turned to drink. A married man with a son, he normally was a quiet man, but started to act out of character, sometimes disappearing for days. His wife, Ann, turned him out of the house in May 1908.

One Monday, he went as usual with Ann by train to Manchester, but waiting for the return train to depart, he began pleading for 3/- to travel to Blackpool in search of work. The argument continued inside the carriage in front of several witnesses. Ann at first refused to give him any more money to waste and then relented, giving him 1/6.

Infuriated at the pawltry sum, he nevertheless kissed her and made to go, but when she called him lazy and further insulted him, he stepped back and stabbed her in the neck, cutting her face in the process. Ann was three weeks pregnant. He turned the knife on himself and cut his own throat, being arrested at the scene.

The jury took just fifteen minutes to deliver its verdict. The judge wept as he passed sentence, and all were convinced that Ballington welcomed the sentence of death.

Read: A Date With the Hangman, p142.

138

Thomas SIDDLE   29

Cut throat of: ***Gertrude Siddle***, *22, his wife, on 9 June 1908, in Hull, E Yorks.*
Motive: *Sexual rivalry; drink related.*

    Siddle, *(b.1879)*, married Gertrude in 1905, but he was an alcoholic and rarely worked. Gertrude left him in March 1908 and went into lodgings with their two children, taking out a separation order against Siddle. He went to see his wife, to ask her to consider a reconciliation, but noticed a different ring on her finger.
    Carrying his youngest child to the door, about to leave, he suddenly turned and slit Gertrude's throat with a razor. She staggered to a chemist's shop before collapsing, and he waited in the house for police to arrive. Gertrude had pawned her wedding ring, and the replacement had been loaned to her by her landlady.

    Read: And May The Lord Have Mercy On Your Soul

139

Matthew James DODDS   43

Strangled: ***Mary Jane Dodds***, *50, his wife, on 20 February 1908, in Hamsterley, Co Durham*
Motive: *To clear impediment*

    Dodds, *(b.1865)*, married Mary Jane, a widow, in 1905. She had inherited property, some seven houses in Hamsterley near Bishop Auckland, while he worked as a joiner in a colliery, and had a crippled leg.   Their marriage was marked by violent quarrels, which left Mary Jane bruised, or with teeth missing, and turning to drink for comfort. In August 1907 she had revoked her will which had named her husband as beneficiary, but a new one, again to his benefit, was drawn up one month before her death.
    In February 1908, Dodds returned home at 2pm to collect some tools, and cries were heard from the house, to which neighbours were accustomed and paid no heed. At 4pm Dodds rushed to neighbours declaring he had found his wife dead. They discovered her lying by the hearth with the

clothes burned from her charred body. The cinders in the grate, however, were cold. Dodds speculated that his wife had fallen in the fire while drunk.

A coroner decided she had burned to death, and was buried. Suspicions were raised by the will, and by Dodds' story, and when the body was exhumed a month later, doctors declared that Mary Jane had been manually strangled.

Dodds was convicted, and the first ever appeal against a death sentence in England failed.

Read: True Detective, Mar 97.

19 August 1908	Perth prison	*Ellis/ Willis*

140

Edward JOHNSTON   32   *Scottish*

Cut throat of: **Jane Wallace Withers**, *30, on 7 June 1908, in Saline, Fifeshire.*
Motive: *Vengeance.*

Johnstone, *(b.1876),* saw Jane, his partner, kissing another lodger at the boarding house where they lived. Known as a madly jealous man, he took Jane by the neck in mock embrace, and slit her throat. The defence plea of insanity was rejected. Hiis last word was to say 'Goodbye' to his executioner. Ellis replied in kind before springing the trap.

Read: Encyclopaedia of Scottish Executions

12 November 1908	Knutsford prison	*H/ T.Pierrepoint*

141

James PHIPPS   21

Strangled: **Elizabeth Warburton**, *10, on 12 October 1908, in Wharton, Cheshire.*
Motive: *Vengeance.*

Phipps, *(b.1887),* had lost his eye in a stone-throwing incident when he was a child, and had since worn a distinctive white bandage over his glass eye. A painter, he had lost his job in May 1908, and had since attempted suicide twice, by drowning and cutting his throat. Elizabeth Warburton was out playing with some friends, and Phipps may have been an object of fun for them; he later claimed that they had been throwing stones at him.

At 7.30pm, he told Elizabeth to run an errand to buy him some cigarettes, and when she returned, told her to take him to someone's house. Crossing a field, he strangled her and threw her into a ditch. Elizabeth's father and others later began a search for his daughter, and when they saw Phipps, he began to run, but was stopped by a cyclist. He later confessed, 'I wrung her neck for her'.

Read: And May The Lord Have Mercy On Your Soul

2 December 1908   Norwich prison   *H/ T.Pierrepoint*

142

James NICHOLLS   35

Bludgeoned: ***Susan Wilson**, 70, on 11 October 1908, in Feltwell, Norfolk.*
Motive: *Sadistic pleasure.*

Charles Wilson was a travelling umbrella salesman, and left his wife alone for three days on 8 October, while he went about his business. Nicholls, *(b.1873),* was seen entering the Wilsons' house at 2.30pm on 11 October, and was seen dragging the old woman out of the house, and then back in again.

He then battered her to death with an axe, and went to the pub, telling friends that Charles Wilson had just killed his wife. The salesman arrived home at about 4pm to make his awful discovery. Nicholls was arrested in the pub, and the jury took just 15 minutes to deliver its verdict.

Read: And May The Lord Have Mercy On Your Soul

143

John William ELLWOOD   **45**

Bludgeoned: *Thomas Wilkinson, 56, on 31 July 1908, in Leeds, W.Yorks.*
Motive: *Financial.*

     Ellwood, *(b.1863),* had served with the army from 1882 to 1894, including in South Africa. He married Ada in 1886, had four children, and had no financial difficulties. When he lost his job at a dyer's company in April 1908, after a disagreement with a director, he soon found work with an insurance company. But several witnesses recognised Ellwood, 5'10", at the dyer company offices in Fieldhead on 31 July.
     Thomas Wilkinson, a cashier, was beaten about the head ten times with a poker in his office at 2.30pm on the day wages were prepared. Cheques had not yet been cashed, and the killer escaped with only a purse. Blood was found on Ellwood's clothes, though he always maintained his innocence, and the two men were said to have always been on good terms. The jury took 68 minutes to convict him.

     Read: Murderous Leeds, p28.

144

William BOULDRY   **41**

Cut throat of: *Margaret Bouldry, 35, his wife, on 10 October 1908, in Saltwood, Kent.*
Motive: *Vengeance.*

     Bouldry, *(b.1867),* had been left by his wife, who went into lodgings with their young child. Bouldry often visited her there, but, left alone on 10 October, an argument started. Mr Wraight, the landlord, came in and tried to intervene, but was knocked to the floor by Bouldry.
     Margaret fled to the kitchen, pursued by her husband, who proceeded to struggle with her. Wraight again tried to separate the two but failed, and went for assistance. In the time he was away, Bouldry had cut Margaret's throat. She died twenty minutes later, and Bouldry was arrested in nearby Hythe.
     The jury recommended mercy.

     Read: And May The Lord Have Mercy On Your Soul

145

Harry Taylor PARKER   **32**

Bludgeoned: ***Thomas Tompkins***, *61, on 26 August 1908, in Coventry,*
                Warwicks.
Motive: *Vengeance.*

Parker, *(b.1876)*, had, for six long years, held a grudge against two men, baker Mr Mead and his employee Thomas Tompkins. In 1902 Mead had issued a summons for assault against Parker, and the slight had not been forgotten.

At 5am Parker had gone to the bakery, and had got involved in an argument with Tompkins. Picking up a lump of wood, he struck the older man a single blow. The wood, however, was studded with nails, and one of these penetrated Tompkins' skull. Parker admitted the offence, but denied intending to kill.

Read: And May The Lord Have Mercy On Your Soul

146

Patrick COLLINS   **24**   *(aka Noah Percy Collins)*
                                Welsh

Stabbed: ***Annie Dorothy Lawrence***, *19, on 17 August 1908, in*
                Abertridwr, Glamorgan.
Motive: *Sexual rivalry.*

Collins, *(b.1884),* was one of two lodgers with Mr and Mrs Lawrence and their two children, Annie and William. All the men of the house were miners. Collins and Annie began courting, but she ended the relationship in August 1908, and found a new boyfriend.

At 5am, Annie got her brother and the second lodger their breakfast before they left for work, but Collins stayed in bed. At 7am he came to the kitchen and asked Annie for a kiss. When she rebuffed him, he stabbed her seven times with two knives. Mrs Lawrence ran to answer Annie's screams, but Collins burst past her, out of the house. He handed himself in at the police station.

Read: And May The Lord Have Mercy On Your Soul

1908 Execution in Ireland

20 August 1908   Londonderry prison

John BERRYMAN

Crime: *unknown*
Motive: *unknown*

No details.

1909

total: **20**

147	6 Jan	John MURPHY	21		Pentonville
148	23 Feb	Jeremiah O'CONNOR	52	*Irish*	Durham
149	2 Mar	Ernest HUTCHINSON	24		Wakefield
150	12 Mar	Thomas MEAD	33		Armley
151	30 Mar	Edmund ELLIOTT	19		Exeter
152	30 Mar	See LEE	38	*Chinese*	Walton
153	13 Apr	Joseph JONES	39		Stafford
154	8 May	William FOY	25	*Welsh*	Swansea
155	20 May	Marks REUBEN	22		Pentonville
156	20 May	Morris REUBEN	23		Pentonville
157	3 July	John EDMUNDS	24		Usk
158	9 July	Walter DAVIS	37		Wakefield
159	16 July	Alexander EDMONSTONE	23	*Scottish*	Perth
160	20 July	William HAMPTON	23		Bodmin
161	3 Aug	Mark SHAWCROSS	31		Strangeways
162	10 Aug	Julius WAMMER	43	*Norwegian*	Wandsworth
163	31 Aug	Madar Lal DHINGRA	25	*Indian*	Pentonville
164	7 Dec	John FREEMAN	46		Hull
165	8 Dec	Abel ATHERTON	30		Durham
166	14 Dec	Samuel ATHERLEY	30		Nottingham

6 January 1909   Pentonville prison, London

H.Pierrepoint/ Willis

147

John Esmond MURPHY   **21**   *(aka John McDonald)*

Stabbed:	***Frederick George Wilhelm Maria Julius Schlitte***, 47, on 7 November 1908, in London W1
Motive:	Financial.

Murphy, *(b.1888)*, had been taking target practice with his revolver for some time. At noon on 7 November, he walked into the Shaftesbury Avenue branch of the bank Cartnell and Schlitte, and was immediately confronted by Frederick Schlitte, whom he shot without warning.

Schlitte, nevertheless, grappled with the intruder, but was stabbed several times by Murphy with a dagger. His bungled robbery abandoned, Murphy ran out shooting a cabbie in the hand, and a policeman in the shoulder when they got in his way. Two other cab drivers subdued him. Mr Schlitte died two days later.

Read: And May The Lord Have Mercy On Your Soul

23 February 1909   Durham gaol   *H. Pierrepoint/ Willis*

148

Jeremiah O'CONNOR   **52**   *Irish*

Stabbed: ***Mary Donnelly****, 10, on 14 December 1908, in Stanley, Co Durham*
Motive: *Sexual; drink related.*

O'Connor, *(b.1857)*, the son of a Cork tailor, joined the British army to escape his father's profession, and settled with his wife in Sherburn, Co Durham in 1885, finding work in the pits. When Elizabeth died in 1888, he left the five children with in-laws, and became an itinerant, settling in 1905 in Stanley, where he lodged with the Donnelly family. He shared a bed with another lodger in a room also shared by Mary, one of the three Donnelly children.

O'Connor, tall and thin, liked a drink, and was drunk by 4pm on 14 December after being in and out of the house all day. Thomas Donnelly left the house at 7.30pm, his wife sleeping on the divan with the baby.

O'Connor left the house followed by Mary, and was seen with her as late as 9.15. He took her to rough ground three miles away where he violated her by hand, then stabbed her 16 times with a shoemaker's knife, slitting open her torso. He cut his own arms and legs, and was found living rough five days later, claiming a navvy had attacked him and taken the girl. Her body was found the next day. The jury took only eight minutes to decide his fate.

On 16 February the Stanley pit disaster claimed the lives of 160 men, including Thomas Donnelly. O'Connor had worked in the same pit.

Read: True Detective, Aug 97.

107

2 March 1909   Wakefield prison   *H/ T.Pierrepoint*

149

Ernest HUTCHINSON   24

Stabbed: **Hannah Maria Whitely**, *29, on 24 December 1908, in Halifax, W Yorks.*

Motive: *Sexual rivalry.*

Hutchinson, *(b.1885),* met Hannah Whitely in 1907, and lived with her and her daughter Eveline, aged 5, since April 1908. He became suspicious that Hannah was prostituting herself at the house while he was out, and had hit her in November, claiming also that she drank too much. Arriving home on 23 December, he saw a man leaving the house, and found money on the table.

The following morning he stabbed Hannah several times and then cut his own throat. At 9am a neighbour saw Eveline crying at a window, broke in, and found Hannah behind the front door, and Hutchinson on the stairs. In reaching its verdict in 15 minutes, the jury made a strong recommendation to mercy on account of Hutchinson's youth.

Read: And May The Lord Have Mercy On Your Soul

12 March 1909   Armley gaol, Leeds   *H.Pierrepoint/ Ellis*

150

Thomas MEAD   33

Kicked and punched: **Clara Howell**, *30, on 28 November 1908, in Leeds, W.Yorks.*

Motive: *Sadistic pleasure; drink related.*

Mead, *(b.1876),* a gasworker, had lived with Clara Howell, a seamstress, since 1901, and theirs had always been a tempestuous relationship. When drunk, Mead would often beat Clara, who frequently sported black eyes, and neighbours would often hear arguments into the early hours.

Coming home from the pub extremely drunk, Mead stripped Clara, but for her stockings, and then beat and kicked her remorselessly until she was dead, at 1am. Her whole body was a mass of bruising, her nose was broken, and her small intestine ruptured. He may have also used a broom handle to beat her. He then carried her broken body upstairs and hid it in a bedroom corner covered with a pile of rags. He went to work at 9am and stayed the night with friends, to whom he confessed. He was arrested at 10.20pm, the following day.

Read: Murderous Leeds, p37.

30 March 1909   Exeter gaol   *Ellis/ Hyscott*

151

Edmund Walter ELLIOTT   19

Cut throat of: ***Clara Jane Hannaford***, *15, on 17 November 1908, in Plymouth, Devon.*
Motive: *Sexual rivalry.*

Elliott, *(b.1890)*, had been Clara Hannaford's boyfriend for eighteen months, but her parents did not approve of him because he could not hold down a job, and in the summer of 1908, Clara finished with him. Clara took a new boyfriend, a seaman, and while walking to the theatre, they were approached by Elliott, who whispered to Clara about meeting him. After the show, Clara's parents joined the new couple for a drink, but Clara unexpectedly took her leave at 10.30pm.
Elliott met Clara, took her down a lane, hit her in the face and cut her throat, witnessed by two passers-by. While Clara staggered back to her parents, Elliott went to a police station and handed himself in. The jury decided his fate in 15 minutes, but added a recommendation to mercy on account of Elliott's youth.

Read: And May The Lord Have Mercy On Your Soul

30 March 1909   Walton gaol, Liverpool   *H/T.Pierrepoint*

152

See LEE   38   *Chinese*

Shot: ***Yun Yap***, *40, on 4 December 1908, in Liverpool, Lancs.*
Motive: *Sexual rivalry*

In January 1908, in London, See Lee, *(b.1871)*, met Amy Yap Sing, who helped him set up a boarding house in Cardiff. There, in 1904, Amy also met Yun Yap, and Yap and Lee became firm friends. After the Cardiff venture failed, all three made their way to Liverpool, where Amy opened a boarding house, employing Yap as cook. Unknown to Yap or Amy, Lee was beginning to harbour resentments over their friendship. In October 1908, Amy became ill with peritonitis, and was regularly visited by both men.

Yap went to see Amy at 9pm on 4 December, and when Lee returned to her room, he brought with him a revolver. Without a word, he shot Yap who fell at the foot of Amy's bed. Lee was arrested at Lime Street station at 12.30am. Yap died three days later, Lee saying he had no idea why he had shot his good friend.

Read: And May The Lord Have Mercy On Your Soul

13 April 1909   Stafford gaol   *H.Pierrepoint/ Ellis*

153

Joseph Edwin JONES   39

Shot: *Charlotte Jones*, *38, his wife, on 12 November 1908, in Wolverhampton, Staffs.*
Motive: *Vengeance*

Jones, *(b.1870)*, had married Charlotte in 1889, and the two had lived happily together until he hit her on 7 November 1908. She left him, went to live with her mother, and issued a summons against him for assault, for which he was fined £1.

Thinking Joseph was out, Charlotte returned to the house with her mother to collect her things. Jones, a gun owner for some years, was waiting, shot Charlotte, and cut his own throat. He claimed that his wife had slashed him and then shot herself, and the court heard conflicting evidence about whether Charlotte could have commited suicide in this way.

The jury found no reason for suicide, and wondered why she would have used a razor on him when a gun was available.

Read: And May The Lord Have Mercy On Your Soul

154

William Joseph FOY   25   *Welsh*

Dropped: ***Mary Ann Rees***, *33, in Ynysfach, Glamorgan.*
Motive: Vengeance.

        Foy, *(b.1884),* and his lover, Mary Rees, a prostitute, had fallen on hard times and often slept in derelict iron furnaces outside Merthyr Tydfil.
        One particular night, they had gone to the disused foundry with another couple, but 'Sloppy', as he called Mary, walked off after a row with Foy. He followed her, and he said that she had threatened to tell that Foy was living off her immoral earnings, and in a struggle, she had fallen into a pit in the foundry. He returned to the other couple laughing that he had thrown her into the 12m deep pit.
        He confessed to a policeman later that night. Foy went bravely to his death, with a smile and a cigarette on his lips.

        Read: And May The Lord Have Mercy On Your Soul.

155, 156

Marks REUBEN   22
Morris REUBEN   23

Stabbed: ***William Sproull***, *35, on 16 March 1909, in Whitechapel,*
                   London E1.
Motive: Financial; drink related.

        The Reubens brothers, *(b.1886, 1887),* were Jewish pimps and thieves operating from a lodging-house in Rupert St. Two officers from a merchant ship, Sproull and Charles McEachran, picked up what they thought were two prostitutes and were taken back to their room where all four got considerably drunk.
        One of the women was Emily Allen, who had lived since 1906 with Morris Reuben, who had planned the whole thing. The brothers had burst into the room, Morris clubbing Sproull with a walking stick and Marks stabbing him repeatedly. They robbed the dying man of a pocket-watch and about £5.

Both officers had staggered into the street, McEachran in a drunken stupor, Sproull dying of his wounds. Police followed the trail of blood to the lodging house where Morris was arrested after a clasp-knife was discovered hidden. At the trial, the women, Allen and Ellen Stevens, gave evidence for the prosecution, and the jury took ten minutes to decide their fate.

Read: Murder Squad, p33.

3 July 1909   Usk prison   *H.Pierrepoint/ Ellis*

157

John EDMUNDS   24   *C*

Cut throat of: *Cecilia Harris, 59, on 20 February 1909, in*
                        Abersychen, Monmouths.
Motive: *Financial; sexual.*

Jack Edmunds, *(b.1885),* in his desire for cash, had decided on some easy pickings. Cecilia Harris, a widow with heart trouble and brochitis, lived alone on her farm near Pontypool.

At 5.30am, she noticed Edmunds, whom she knew by sight, in her garden with his gun. When she twice told him to go away, he pointed the gun at her, causing her to run inside, locking the door. When he smashed a window to get in, she ran out, but was felled at the garden gate by a shot which injured her in the mouth.

Having raped her outside, Edmunds then led the widow back into her kitchen, where he helped himself to a watch, and 5/6 - all Cecilia's cash. He then cut her throat and banged her head on the floor, before taking his leave.

Despite, her ordeal, Cecilia staggered the 1200m to a neighbour's house, and managed to scrawl a note implicating Edmunds. When arrested at his mother's the next day, he denied being anywhere near the farm, but five witnesses had seen him in the vicinity. Cecilia clung to life for thirteen days, before succumbing to her injuries.

Read: And May The Lord Have Mercy On Your Soul

158

Walter DAVIS   37   *(aka Fred Evans)*

Bludgeoned: ***Hester Harriet Richards**, 51, on 30 March 1909, in Middlesbrough, N Yorks.*
Motive: *Sexual rivalry*

Davis, *(b.1872)*, met Hester Richards, whose husband was working away from home, in 1907. The pair wanted to be together, so, when James Richards returned home, Hester simply told him that Davis was her cousin, Fred Evans, who had come to stay.

The situation too frustrating for them, Davis and Hester ran away together in 1908, first to Leeds, then to Ilkley; but at the end of that year they returned to the sanguine James in Middlesbrough, Davis threatening Hester if she were ever to be a wife to James again.

Left alone in the house from 8.30am, after the husband and lodger had gone to work, Davis battered Hester to death, and went off to Blyth, leaving James to discover his dead wife when he came home later. Davis was arrested on 17 April.

Read: And May The Lord Have Mercy On Your Soul

159

Alexander EDMONSTONE   23   *Scottish*

Strangled: ***Michael Swinton Brown**, 15, on 19 February 1909, in East Wemyss, Fifeshire.*
Motive: *Financial.*

Michael Brown was an apprentice clerk at a linen makers, who weekly took the tram to Buckhaven and back, to collect the wages from the bank. On the tram back, Michael sat next to Edmonstone, *(b.1886)*, who alighted with the boy at School Wynd, East Wemyss. He took Michael to a public lavatory where he strangled him with a knotted handkerchief, and stuffed his cap into his mouth. Edmonstone, an unemployed miner, made off with the boy's satchel containing £80, bought a suit, where the banknotes were later recognised, and made for Glasgow.

Police sought Edmonstone from descriptions given by witnesses, but by the time his bloody clothes were found in a Glasgow hostel, he had moved on to Manchester. He was caught there in March, after being recognised in a wanted poster. He had Michael's watch on him, and made a full confession.

He became deeply depressed in the condemned cell, eating little, and raising concerns about his fitness for the scaffold.

Refs: True Crime, Apr 95.

| 20 July 1909 | Bodmin gaol | *H/T.Pierrepoint* |

160

William HAMPTON   23

Strangled: ***Emily Barnes Trewarthen Tredrea**, 16, on 2 May 1909, in St Erth, Cornwall.*
Motive: *Vengeance.*

Hampton, *(b.1886)*, had worked as a miner in the US for five years, before returning to his home town of St Erth, near Penzance, in November 1907. He lodged with Mrs Tredrea and her four children, becoming engaged to Emily Tredrea at Christmas 1908. Emily's father, also a miner, was living in South Africa.

Soon Emily began to cool towards Hampton, and on 1 May, told him that she hated him. The following evening, while her mother was visiting a neighbour, Emily repeated her declaration, and, in the kitchen, with the 10-year old brother watching, Hampton strangled his fiancee and put her in a chair. The boy ran to get his mother, while Hampton ran off to the neighbouring town of Hayle, and handed himself in to police.

The jury deliberated for fifteen minutes before recommending Hampton to mercy.

Read: Master Detective, Jul 98.

161

Mark SHAWCROSS   **31**

Strangled: ***Emily Ramsbottom**, 26, on 12 May 1909, in Manchester, Lancs.*
Motive: *Sexual rivalry.*

Shawcross, *(b.1878)*, 6'5", had known Emily Ramsbottom since 1902, and had been the man in her life since 1905. The mother of three children, she separated from her husband and then bore two more children to Shawcross. Emily in turn threw him out in January 1908, but he continued to pester her for a reconciliation.

At Christmas 1908 he hit her in the face and tried to strangle her, only to be stopped by her sister, and in March 1909 had hit her on the head with a poker. Shawcross had been sacked from his factory job and had found work as a ship's stoker, and he thought there was mutual attraction between his brother and Emily. He was set on revenge.

He went to the theatre with Emily and they left together at 10.50pm. On a footpath in Gorton he strangled her by hand and tied a handkerchief around her throat. She was found the following morning at 5.30. Shawcross then sent a letter to police admitting his crime, and threatening another, sending a second letter the following day to the foreman who sacked him threatening to shoot him. Before he got the chance he was arrested at his sister's on 20 May.

Read: Murderous Manchester, p42.

162

Julius WAMMER   **43**   *Norwegian*

Shot: ***Cissie Archer**, 24, on 7 July 1909, in London SE1.*
Motive: *Vengeance.*

Wammer, *(b.1866)*, a sailor, had been out with two women on the evening of 2 July, and noticed later that he was missing a gold chain. Five days later, Wammer again went out with the two women, whom he held responsible for the theft, and another of their friends.

At 11.30pm, after stepping into a fishmonger's, he shot Cissie with a revolver. He aimed at the second woman, but missed and hit the shopkeeper in the hand. The gun then jammed, and two passers-by managed to overcome and hold him until police arrived.

Read: And May The Lord Have Mercy On Your Soul.

31 August 1909   Pentonville prison, London   *H./ T.Pierrepoint*

163

Madar Lal DHINGRA   25   *Indian*

Shot: **1 *Sir William Hutt Curzon Wyllie*, 61, and**
               2 *Dr Cowas Lalcaca*, 48, on 1 July 1909, in Kensington,
               London W8.
Motive: *Political.*

Dhingra, *(b. 1884),* a Parsee, only slight at seven stones, was an engineering student who had come to London in November 1906. He bought a revolver in January 1909, and took regular practice at a pistol range, including on the evening of 1 July. He resented the British presence in India, and armed with two guns and a dagger, went to a concert organised by the charitable Imperial Institute in Kensington.

Following the performance, at 11pm, Dhingra approached Sir Curzon Wyllie, a civil servant, and engaged him in conversation. Pulling out his pistol he shot Sir Curzon four times in the head, another bullet going astray. Sir Curzon died instantly.

Dr Lalcaca tried to grab the weapon, but was hit by two more shots. Dhingra then put the gun to his own head, but it misfired. The crowd then subdued the gunman.

The jury reached its verdict without leaving the court. Dhingra was unrepentant to the end, maintaining the right to kill English occupiers.

Read: The Hangman's Diary, p294.

164

John FREEMAN   46

Stabbed: ***Florence Lily Freeman**, 30, on 28 August 1909, in Hull,*
                     E Yorks.
Motive: *Vengeance*

    Freeman, *(b.1863)*, lodged with his younger brother Robert and his wife Florence, and all got on well together, except when they had been drinking. The brothers got drunk one night, and on the way home from the pub, Robert accused John of having an affair with Florence.
    She too was drunk when they arrived home, and Robert also accused her of carrying on with his brother. The two men got into a fight, and Robert was injured over his eye. During the fracas, John got a knife and stabbed Florence in the throat. She managed to stagger outside into the arms of a passer-by. When Robert said he forgave his brother, John said that he could die a happy man.

    Read: And May The Lord Have Mercy On Your Soul

165

Abel ATHERTON   30

Shot: ***Elizabeth Ann Patrick**, 33, on 11 August*
                   1909, in Chopwell, Co Durham.
Motive: *Vengeance.*

    Atherton, *(b. 1879)*, was a miner. Born in Wigan, he worked in several coalfields in the north-east before settling in Chopwell in 1907, lodging with the Patrick family since 1907. Jacob and Elizabeth Patrick had two children, Joseph, 11, and Frances Mary, 12, with whom Atherton became obsessed.
    By the time Frances was 15, Atherton had made several passes at her. He was jealous of the affection she paid her father, and when spurned, began to suggest to villagers that their relationship was incestuous. When Frances told her mother that either he had to leave or she would, Mrs Patrick threw him out.

Atherton, a strongly-built man of only 5 feet 1 inch, found new lodgings, but was still a frequent caller. One day an argument ensued, and Atherton collected his shotgun. When he returned the Patrick family were in the kitchen. He and Mrs Patrick struggled in the doorway. The gun went off, causing no damage, but the second shot hit Elizabeth in the thigh. She died there from the shock of blood loss.

Atherton maintained the killing was an accident, that he had intended only to scare the family. He and his father protested his innocence to the end, though the jury found him guilty after 45 minutes' deliberation. Frances underwent examination to confirm her virginity and to put an end to gossip. Atherton's last words on the trap were, 'You're hanging an innocent man'.

Read: True Detective, Dec 96.

14 December 1909   Bagthorpe prison, Nottingham   *H/ T.Pierrepoint*

166

Samuel ATHERLEY   30

Cut throats of: **1 *Matilda Lambert*,** *27, and his three children*
                 2 *John Lambert*, *8,*
                 3 *Annie Lambert*, *5,*
                 4 *Samuel Lambert*, *2, on 10 July 1909, in Nottingham.*
Motive: Sexual rivalry.

Atherley, *(b.1879),* and Matilda, his common-law wife, with whom he had infamous rows, had three young children during their seven-year partnership. She had left him four times, but always found her way back to Sam. In 1909 he got the idea that Annie, the 5-year old, was the product of an affair between Matilda and her sister's husband, John Watson.

As the family all lay in bed at 3.30am, Atherley slit their throats, and battered the two youngest. Two razors, one broken, and a hammer, were found in the bedroom. Atherley then covered their faces with clothes and cut his own throat, before waking a neighbour by banging on a window.

Read: Nottingham...The Sinister Side, p80.

19 August 1909 Crumlin Road Gaol, Belfast *H.Pierrepoint*

RICHARD JUSTIN **31**

Blugeoned: ***Annie Justin****, 4, his daughter, on 12 March 1909, in Belfast.*

Motive: *To clear impediment.*

Justin, *(b.1878),* a park labourer with Belfast Corporation, had two sons by his first marriage, the eldest aged 11. In 1905, Mary Ellen Thompson had his illegitimate child, and the two were married in 1908.

The shame of a bastard child seemed too much for Justin, who regularly beat the girl. He had been seen punching the child in the yard, and Annie told a neighbour, alarmed by two black eyes, that her father was the culprit.

On 12 March Justin went to a neighbour's, claiming Annie had fallen out of bed. Her body was found to be a mass of bruising. He had beaten her naked body with a cane, had burned her wrists with a poker, and had killed her with blows to the head with a block of wood. Annie died during the two hours it took a doctor to reach the house. Justin tried to blame the neighbour, but the jury found him guilty within 45 minutes. A campaign for his reprieve was raised, pleading that parental authority would be undermined by his hanging.

Read: True Detective, Nov96

1910　　total: *16*

167	15 Feb	William MURPHY	49	*Welsh*	Caernarvon
168	22 Feb	Joseph WREN	23		Strangeways
169	1 Mar	George PERRY	27		Pentonville
170	24 Mar	William BUTLER	62	*Welsh*	Usk
171	25 May	Thomas JESSHOPE	32		Wandsworth
172	14 Jun	James HANCOCK	55		Cambridge
173	12 Jul	Thomas CRAIG	24		Durham
174	14 Jul	Frederick FOREMAN	45		Chelmsford
175	9 Aug	John COULSON	32		Armley
176	9 Aug	John DICKMAN	44		Newcastle
177	15 Nov	Thomas RAWCLIFFE	31		Lancaster
178	22 Nov	Henry THOMPSON	54		Walton
179	23 Nov	Hawley CRIPPEN	48	*American*	Pentonville
180	24 Nov	William BROOME	25		Reading
181	21 Dec	Noah WOOLF	58		Pentonville
182	29 Dec	Henry ISON	45		Armley

15 February 1910　　Carnarvon prison　　*H.Pierrepoint/ Willis*

167

William MURPHY　　**49**　　*Welsh*

Cut throat of:　　**Gwen Ellen Jones**, *36, on 25 December 1909, in Holyhead, Anglesey.*
Motive:　　*Sexual rivalry.*

Gwen Jones and her two children left her husband in 1905, moving in with Murphy, *(b.1861)*. Unable to find work locally, he went to Yorkshire, but by the time Murphy returned to Holyhead in December 1909, Gwen had moved in with another man. He arranged to meet her at 7pm on Christmas Day, but Gwen turned up drunk at 8.30pm, telling Murphy that she was moving away with her new man. She offered him a last bit of passion, and the two went off to a nearby field and had sex.

As Murphy entered Gwen a second time, he began to strangle her, then cut her throat, digging his fingers into the wound, and pulling her head back to maximise the blood flow. He then held her head under the water of a drainage ditch, just to make sure she was dead.. He went to the pub at 9.20pm, and took a friend to see the body. The two then went to the police, where Murphy made a full statement.

Read: And May The Lord Have Mercy On Your Soul

120

22 February 1910   Strangeways prison, Manchester

H.Pierrepoint/ Ellis

168

Joseph WREN   23

Cut throat of: ***John Collins,*** *3, on 28 December 1909, in Burnley,*
                  Lancs.
Motive: *Sadistic pleasure.*

        Wren, *(b.1887),* had fallen on hard times since his discharge from the navy for poor eyesight in 1907. He had no money, and could not afford to make any life for his girlfriend, and the baby she had recently borne. On 28 December 1909, he told his brother that he had not eaten for three days, and wanted to go to prison to be looked after for a while. He intended to kill his own daughter, but as the child was not available, he took the first alternative presented to him.

        John Collins always walked along the street to meet his mother coming home. On that day, he met Wren first. At 5.30pm, he took the boy to a slag heap, and tried to strangle him. When this appeared not to be working, he cut the child's throat with his blunt knife. Wren then sought out the nearest policeman, and confessed.

Read: And May The Lord Have Mercy On Your Soul

1 March 1910   Pentonville prison, London   *H.Pierrepoint/ Willis*

169

George Henry PERRY   27

Cut throat of: ***Annie Covell,*** *27, on 10 January 1910, in Ealing,*
                  Middlesex.
Motive: *Vengeance.*

        Perry, *(b.1883),* a window cleaner, found it hard to get work after leaving the army in 1908. His girlfriend's father felt sorry for him, and offered him lodgings at his house. But when Perry only managed to work for two months in the next two years, Mr Covell thought he was not really trying, and told him to go on 9 January 1910.

        The following day, Perry called round to see his sweetheart, Annie, when only her mother was at home. He stabbed her repeatedly with a bread knife, finishing her off by slashing her throat. As Perry waited, Mrs Covell called the police. The jury decided his fate inside three minutes.

Read: And May The Lord Have Mercy On Yout Soul

| 24 March 1910 | Usk prison | *H.Pierrepoint/ Ellis* |

170

<u>William BUTLER</u>   **62**   *Welsh*   *(real name: Thomas Clements)*

Bludgeoned: **1 *Charles Thomas*, 81, and his wife**
              2 *Mary Thomas*, 74, on 11 November 1909, in Bassaleg, Glamorgan.
Motive: *Financial*

Butler, *(b.1848)*, a former soldier, had spent a total of more than twenty years in prison for theft and violence. Latterly, he worked as an odd job man, drinking away most of his meagre earnings. When he proposed marriage to his landlord's young daughter in September 1909 he was thrown out and then summonsed for uttering threats. Determined to raise the money for a good solicitor, he hatched an elaborate plot.

Wearing his new landlord's boots he sneaked out one evening and entered the home of an elderly couple 800 metres away, breaking a window using the bodice of the young girl to whom he had proposed.

Finding the Thomases asleep in bed, he bashed the old man's head with a candlestick, and hit Mrs Thomas several times in the face with it when she awoke. After bashing Charles four times more he ransacked the place, stealing about £2, but missing a hidden £154. He locked up behind him and left the key on his former landlord's windowsill. The following day he engaged the services of a Cardiff solicitor and returned home secure in the knowledge that he had incriminated others.

When the couple were found dead that evening, Butler's record made him a prime suspect, and when his new landlady testified that she knew he had been out of the house the previous evening, he was charged. Blood was found on his cap and coat, and the jury convicted him in 15 minutes. He fought with the two policemen with him in the dock when he heard the verdict.

Read:: True Crime, Jan 98.

171

Thomas William JESSHOPE   32

Stabbed: ***John Healey***, *43, on 28 March 1910, in London SW9.*
Motive: *Vengeance; drink related.*

       Jesshope, *(b.1878),* for one year the fireman at the Empire Music Hall in Camberwell, was a prolific drunk. He was finally sacked for being drunk on duty on 26 March 1910. Somehow blaming John Healey, the stage carpenter, for his plight, he tried to punch him on the way out. The following morning, Healey was showing the new fireman around the theatre, and descended briefly into the orchestra pit, when Jesshope sprang from behind a chair and stabbed him. A colleague saw Jesshope in the theatre, and he immediately confessed his actions.

       Read: And May The Lord Have Mercy On Your Soul

172

James Henry HANCOCK   55

Stabbed: ***Alfred Doggett***, *59, on 4 March 1910, in Chesterton, Cambs.*
Motive: *Vengeance.*

       Hancock, *(b.1855),* had come to Cambridge from Sheffield in 1894, and had lived with Elizabeth Marshall since 1896. There was bad feeling between Hancock and Elizabeth's brother, Alfred Doggett, for both men were coke merchants, and competitors. The mutual antipathy was worsened when Hancock beat Elizabeth, who went to Doggett for support.
       On 4 March, following another argument with her, Hancock refused to go out on his delivery round. Doggett took Hancock's horse and cart, and took his customers. When brother and sister returned at 5pm, Hancock went to the stable and started a fight with Alfred. He stabbed him, and then told a friend that he had meant to kill Elizabeth.

       Read: And May The Lord Have Mercy On Your Soul

173

Thomas CRAIG   **24**   *(real name Crake)*

Shot:	***Thomas William Henderson***, *22, on 26 March 1910, in Gateshead, Co Durham.*
Motive:	*Sexual rivalry.*

Craig, *(b.1886),* a miner and mechanic, lived in Barnard Castle with his parents. He met Annie Finn, then 16, in 1903, and the two became engaged. When Craig was jailed for seven years for housebreaking and causing grievous bodily harm in 1904, she promised to wait for him. Her letters kept him going, until September 1909, when Annie met another man, and Craig was devastated. Annie, now 23, married Thomas Henderson in February 1910, and Craig wrote to her telling her he would kill her.

Directly he was released on 23 March, Craig set about finding her. Calling at Newcastle, he bought a revolver, and soon tracked Annie down to Gateshead, Henderson's mother taking him to the house unwittingly. After a short conversation in which Annie told Craig, 5' 6", that she preferred her husband to him, he shot Henderson in the back, and Annie in the breast. Henderson died 30 minutes later, but Annie survived.

Craig escaped, but following two burglaries, was tracked down three days later to a cow shed near Corbridge, where he was found sleeping off a hangover. He still had the gun on him. The jury returned after 45 minutes, but added a recommendation to mercy.

Read: True Detective, Jul 95.

174

Frederick FOREMAN   **45**

Bludgeoned:	***Elizabeth Ely***, *35, on 16 May 1910, in Wennington, Essex.*
Motive:	*Sexual rivalry; drink related.*

Foreman, *(b.1865),* and Elizabeth Ely, his common-law wife, were agricultural labourers, living in an old train car in a field. The pair had been arguing in the pub on 16 May, Foreman concerned that Elizabeth had been seeing another man. Back home, they argued, and she told him she was leaving.

In the field he gave her a beating, including with a willow stick, dragging her from one place to another to continue the thrashing. Finally, he left her body by a footpath, with a broken leg, and five severe cuts to the head. Elizabeth died from exposure. He told other workers his wife was dead, before reporting that he had found her body. Blood was found on his clothes and boots.

Read: And may The Lord Have Mercy On Your Soul

| 9 August 1910 | Armley gaol, Leeds | *T.Pierrepoint/ Warbrick* |

175

John Raper COULSON   32

Cut throats of:	**1** ***Jane Ellen Coulson***, 26, his wife, and
	2 ***Thomas Coulson***, 5, his son, on 24 May 1910, in
	Bradford, W.Yorks.
Motive:	Vengeance; drink related.

Coulson, *(b.1878),* an iron-moulder, married Jenny, a weaver, in 1904, but made accusations that she got drunk and went with other men. For this he frequently beat her. Coulson himself had a drink problem, and the house and £580 cash he had inherited when his father died had all been frittered away on alcohol.

Finally, on 23 May, Jenny took out a summons for assault against him, and the following morning at 8am, Coulson took his revenge. He cut the throats of his wife and child with a bread knife, almost severing Jenny's, and left them in their beds. He pawned most of Jenny's things and then, after supposedly looking for his missing wife, went and got drunk again, telling friends in the pub what he had done. Police searched the house at 11pm and Coulson was arrested.

The jury did not retire before giving its verdict.

Read: Murderous Leeds, p45.

John Alexander DICKMAN   44

Possibly **shot:**	**Caroline Luard**, *48, on 24 August 1908, in Sevenoaks, Kent.*
Possibly **bludgeoned:**	**Herman Cohen** *on 8 March 1909, in Sunderland, Co Durham.*
Shot:	**John Innes Nisbet**, *44, on 18 March 1910, near Morpeth, Northumberland.*
Motive:	*Financial.*

Mr Nisbet, a colliery cashier, took the wages from Newcastle to the mine at Widdrington every week. He took his usual train on 18 March, but sharing his carriage was John Dickman, *(b.1867)*, a married man from Jesmond, and father of two daughters. He worked on commission for a bookmaker's, but gambled heavily and had debts of several hundred pounds.

Dickman got off the train at its second stop, Morpeth, and at the next station, Alnmouth, at 12.06pm, Mr Nisbet was found dead under his seat, shot five times in body and head. The leather satchel containing £370 in wages was missing. It was found empty in a shaft near Morpeth the following June.

Dickman was identified as have been in the train carriage, but other witnesses spoke of another man with Mr Nisbet. Bullets of two different calibres had been used, feeding speculation that a second man had been involved. However, police discovered that Dickman had paid off several big debts after the murder, that he had owned a pistol, and that he had lied about going on the train to an interview - all pointing to his guilt. The murder weapons and the money were never recovered. The jury took two and a half hours to decide his fate.

In 1931 it was suggested that Dickman, 5'5" & 11 st 4, may have been responsible for the murder on 24 August 1908 of Caroline Luard, 48, in Sevenoaks, Kent. Mrs Luard had been found dead with two bullet wounds to the head. Her rings were missing. Her husband, Major-General Charles Edward Luard had come under public suspicion and had killed himself under a train when the stress had become too much to bear.

Dickman was also suspected of the murder of a money-lender in Sunderland who was robbed of 30 shillings and axed to death. He may have been in the man's office shortly before the body was discovered.

His last request was to be hanged in his shirt-sleeves. His wish was granted, the arm-straps being removed to allow him to take off his jacket.

Read: True Detective, Jul 96.

177

Thomas RAWCLIFFE   31

Strangled: ***Louisa Ann Rawcliffe****, 27, his wife, on 6 September 1910, in Lancaster.*
Motive: *To clear impediment.*

Rawcliffe, *(b.1879),* had fallen from a window at the age of three, and had been unconscious for seven weeks, his mother claiming that he was never the same since. When he was drunk he would threaten his wife, but otherwise was a good husband. Louisa had been ill, and he later claimed that they had made a suicide pact. After strangling her he was to take rat poison.

At 7pm he strangled his wife on the bed, with all three children asleep in the same room. Her brother called later the same evening, and was told that Louisa had gone out. Then at 6am the next morning, the children still asleep, Rawcliffe called to a passing policeman, 'Come and see what I've done'. The jury took over two hours in its deliberations, but added a recommendation to mercy, on account of Rawcliffe's childhood accident. He fainted on the scaffold.

Read: And May The Lord Have Mercy On Your Soul.

178

Henry THOMPSON   54

Strangled: ***Mary Thompson****, 48, his wife, on 31 July 1910, in Liverpool, Lancs.*
Motive: *Sadistic pleasure; drink related.*

Thompson, *(b.1856),* a docker, married Mary in 1902, and lived with her in lodgings in York street, Liverpool. He was a drinker, fighter and wife-beater, having cut Mary's throat in 1904.

One Saturday night Mrs Thompson had fled terrified into the room of a woman lodger, but was kicked and dragged out by her 12 stone husband, who then beat and strangled her in their own room. After a silent Sunday the lodger and a woman friend tried to get past Thompson, and he hit them both.

They then called the police who later discovered Thompson asleep in bed beside his dead wife on the Monday morning.

Cool to the end, he remarked after sentencing, 'Let them go ahead with it. I don't care. I was never frightened of death'.

Read: And May The Lord Have Mercy On Your Soul.

---

23 November 1910   Pentonville prison, London   *Ellis/ Willis*

179

Hawley Harvey CRIPPEN   48   *American*

Poisoned: ***Kunigunde Mackamotzki**, 36, his wife, on 1 February 1910, in London N7.*
Motive: *To clear impediment.*

Crippen, known as Peter to his friends, was born in Michigan in 1862. He qualified as a doctor of medicine in 1885, and married two years later, fathering a son before his wife died in 1891. In 1893 he was married again to the daughter of a German mother and Polish father, who used the name Cora Turner. They moved to London in 1900, his wife taking the name of Belle Elmore, and moving into Hilldrop Crescent in 1905.

Crippen worked for a medical company and with a weekly wage of £3, was known to be rather mean with money. Trained as an opera singer, Belle was an unsuccessful actress, who gave only one professional performance. She was a short, stout woman, but before she met Peter, himself only 5' 3" and 10 st, she had had several lovers, and continued the practice after their marriage, her husband catching her in bed with their German lodger in 1906. The couple had frequent rows and by that time slept separately.

Crippen himself had in that year begun an affair with Ethel Neave, *(b.1883)*, the typist in his office, whom he had known for three years. She was something of a hypochondriac, and used the preferred name Le Neve. Their love-making was conducted in cheap Paddington hotels, a further drain on Crippen's finances, whereas Belle was given money by her male admirers, and had £600 stashed in the bank. Crippen paid the rent and all bills, Belle spending money on entertaining friends at home.

In December 1909 Belle was threatening to leave and take her money with her. On 19 January 1910, Crippen bought some hyoscine, a sedative. The drug is also used as a sexual suppressant, and it is possible that Crippen had that use in mind - Belle is believed to have had syphilis.

Following an evening at home with friends, it is probable that Crippen administered the poisonous dose in Belle's tea the next morning, 1

February. She will have fallen into a coma and died several hours later. Crippen dismembered the body, and buried the torso, minus bones, genitalia and certain organs beneath the cellar floor. The head, limbs and bones were never found, possibly having been burned in the grate. Crippen told Ethel's friends that she had returned to the U.S.

In February Crippen pawned some of his wife's jewellery, and was frequently seen in Le Neve's company. They spent Easter together in Dieppe. She was noticed to wear Belle's furs and jewels. Ethel moved into Hilldrop Crescent in March, Crippen now announcing that Belle had died of pneumonia in the States. A suspicious friend of Belle's had the police investigate, but they found nothing to concern them when they called at Crippen's house. However, Crippen and Le Neve fled to Belgium.

Concerned about Crippen's flight, the police called again, and on 13 July, discovered Belle's remains, identified by a scar and by clothing in which they were wrapped. Newspapers were alerted.

Crippen and Le Neve took the *SS Montrose* from Antwerp on 20 July, disguised as Mr Robinson and his son. The Captain was alerted by the couple's odd behaviour and he telegraphed to London. When the ship arrived in Quebec on 31 July, the British police were there to arrest them. Returning to England three weeks later, the two were tried separately, she as an accessory. The jury took only 27 minutes to determine Crippen's guilt, but Le Neve was acquitted. Crippen had asserted that Ethel knew nothing of the murder. She visited him on the eve of his execution.

Crippen attempted suicide by cutting an artery in his prison cell, but went smiling to the scaffold, and was buried with a photograph of Ethel. She went to America after the trial, but returned to England six years later, settling in Croydon, marrying and starting a family. She died in 1967, an 84-year old grandmother.

Read: *The Crippen File.*

24 November 1910   Reading gaol   *Ellis/ Willis*

180

William BROOME   **25**   *(aka Brooks)*

Suffocated: ***Mrs Isabella Wilson***, 70, on 15 July 1910, in Slough, Berks.
Motive: Financial.

Broome, *(b. 1885),* a car mechanic and former soldier, lived near Regents Park in London, but his father owned a shop in High Street, Slough, next to a second-hand clothes shop run by a deaf widow who had lived alone for three years.

Broome was aware that Mrs Wilson kept money on the premises, and at 9am on 15 July he went to her shop to relieve her of the cash. Preparing a sandwich in the sitting room at the back, the old lady resisted, and Broome, 5'5" and 11 st badly beat her, then tied her hands across her chest and tied a cushion over her face, suffocating her. He stole £20 in gold coins. She was discovered by her sister-in-law seven hours later.

When questioned, Broome stated that he had been in London applying for a job as a taxi driver, but a search of his rooms turned up an envelope containing the stolen money. Scratches on his face testified to his having been in a struggle. 'I am innocent!' he asserted on the scaffold.

Read: Murder Club Guide to Eastern & Home Counties, p55.

21 December 1910	Pentonville prison	*Ellis/ Willis*

181

Noah WOOLF   58

Stabbed: ***Andrew Simon**, 67, on 28 October 1910, in London N19.*
Motive: Vengeance.

Woolf, *(b.1852),* and Andrew Simon were both residents at a home for the elderly in Upper Holloway. Simon complained about Woolf's rowdy behaviour and irreligious views, and Woolf was asked to leave on 10 June. He was given ten shillings and a weekly wage for three months when he finally went on 4 July.

After the money stopped, Woolf sought revenge. On 27 October, he argued with Simon outside the home, and came back at 10.30 the next morning, going to Simon's room. He asked the old man to withdraw his complaints so that he might come back, but Simon refused, whereupon, Woolf stabbed him eight times.

Read: And May The Lord Have Mercy on Your Soul

Henry ISON   45

Bludgeoned: ***Mary Letitia Jenkin**, 39, on 23 July 1910, in Leeds, W.Yorks.*
Motive: *Vengeance; drink related.*

Ison, *(b.1865)*, had lived with Mary Jenkin, whose real name was Whittaker, since 1897, and the pair were comparatively comfortable financially, though often both were very drunk.

They came home from the pub with friends on 23 July, but Ison got involved in a fight with one of them, and banged his head badly, the guests leaving at 6.30pm. When his wife admitted that she had lost a sovereign Ison had given her, he lost his temper.

Mary crawled out of the house at 8.20 and Ison was seen dragging her back in by her hair, kicking her in the process. Ison said that she fell downstairs and banged her head. He then went to his sister's, and she contacted the police. He was accused of having beaten Mary with a poker, but no blood was found on it, and two doctors disagreed about whether the injuries were consistent with a fall. Perhaps unsure, the jury added a strong recommendation for mercy to their guilty verdict. Ison maintained his innocence to the end.

Read: Murderous Leeds, p55.

1910 Execution in Ireland

4 January 1910   Mountjoy gaol, Dublin

Joseph HEFFERMAN

Crime: *unknown*
Motive: *unknown*

No details.

1911

total: **16**

183	31 Jan	George NEWTON	19		Chelmsford
184	9 May	Thomas SEYMOUR	65		Walton
185	24 May	Michael COLLINS	26		Pentonville
186	20 Jun	Arthur GARROD	49		Ipswich
187	19 Jul	William PALMER	50		Leicester
188	17 Oct	Francisco GODHINO	40	*Italian*	Pentonville
189	17 Oct	Edward HILL	41		Pentonville
190	15 Nov	Frederick THOMAS	37		Wandsworth
191	6 Dec	Michael FAGAN	27		Walton
192	12 Dec	Walter MARTYN	23		Strangeways
193	12 Dec	John TARKENTER	41		Strangeways
194	14 Dec	Henry PHILIPS	44	*Welsh*	Swansea
195	15 Dec	Joseph FLETCHER	40		Walton
196	19 Dec	George PARKER	26		Maidstone
197	21 Dec	Charles COLEMAN	36		St Albans
198	28 Dec	George LOAKE	64		Stafford

31 January 1911   Chelmsford gaol   *Ellis/ Conduit*

183

George NEWTON   19

Cut throat of: ***Ada Roker***, 21, on 24 December 1910, in London E15.
Motive: *Vengeance.*

Newton, *(b.1892)*, lodged with his sister and her husband in Stratford. He had known Ada Roker for three years, and though they had parted several times, they became engaged in June 1910, though they again separated in August. Newton was a very jealous fiance, and twice in December Ada's mother caught the pair apparently having just had a fight. On one occasion, Ada was bleeding from the mouth.

They had a row on the morning of Christmas Eve, and when Newton returned to Ada's home at 7pm, the two were alone in the kitchen. He tied a belt around Ada, fastening her arms to her side, then cut her throat. He barged past her in-coming sister to get from the house, and ran to his brother's, where the police later arrested him.

Read: And May The Lord Have Mercy On Your Soul

9 May 1911   Walton gaol, Liverpool   *Ellis/ T.Pierrepoint*

184

Thomas SEYMOUR   65

Bludgeoned: ***Mary Seymour**, 69, his wife, on 10 March 1911, in Liverpool, Lancs.*
Motive: *Vengeance.*

After many years at sea, Seymour, *(b.1846)*, married his cousin Mary in 1907. She had recently been left £80, and whether or not Seymour had his eye on the cash, his wife tried to keep a tight control on her finances. This led to many arguments, and, in any case, the money was virtually exhausted by 1911. He battered Mary to death with a coal hammer, and shovelled hot ashes from the grate onto her head to soak up the blood. Thus was her state when a female relative called to see her. Indifferent to his fate throughout, Seymour handed himself over to the nearest policeman, and pleaded guilty.

Read: And May The Lord Have Mercy On Your Soul

24 May 1911   Pentonville prison, London   *Ellis/ T.Pierrepoint*

185

Michael COLLINS   26

Cut throat of: ***Elizabeth Ann Kempster**, 29, on 25 March 1911, in London W1.*
Motive: *Vengeance.*

Elizabeth Kempster's husband died in August 1910. She then met Collins, *(b.1885)*, and moved in with her six year old son at Christmas. They lived off Shaftesbury Avenue, and all went well until Elizabeth started to act strangely in March, and would not tell Collins what was wrong.
She ended up not talking to him at all, and when he confronted her with the question, she told him she wanted to live apart. He bought a razor, and, at 5pm, after hitting her in the face with a hammer, cut her throat. He went on to see friends, who went with him to the police station.

Read: And May The Lord Have Mercy On Your Soul

186

Arthur GARROD   49

Cut throat of:	***Sarah Chilvers**, 45, on 5 February 1911, in Ipswich, Suffolk.*
Motive:	*Sexual rivalry; drink related.*

Sarah Chilvers had already been married twice when she and her son moved in with Garrod, *(b.1862)*. He was a jealous man, and confided in Sarah's son, while they were in the pub on 5 February, that he had seen Sarah out drinking with another man. The men got home at 10.30pm, the younger going to bed.

At midnight, when Garrod confronted her about his rival, a row started. Furniture was thrown about before Garrod hit Sarah's head twice with a hatchet, and then cut her throat with his penknife. He slashed his own throat, before Sarah's son could get downstairs. In finding Garrod guilty in 30 minutes, the jury added a recommendation to mercy on account of Sarah's provocation.

Read: And May The Lord Have Mercy On Your Soul

187

William Henry PALMER   50

Murdered:	*A man in South Africa in 1880.*
Possibly murdered:	*A man in Manchester, Lancs.*
Strangled:	***Ann Harris**, 73, on 24 January 1911, in Walcote, Leicestershire.*
Motive:	*Financial.*

Palmer, *(b.1861)*, had murdered a farmer in South Africa in 1880, and returned to England after his release from prison - the death sentence commuted because of his youth. A painter by trade, Palmer, 5'8" and 15 st, was unemployed in 1911 after hawking fish for some time in Manchester, where he had a wife and family.

Preferring life on the road, he went to Lutterworth selling shoelaces door-to-door. Turned out of his lodgings there, Palmer went on to Walcote, where at 3am, he burst open the door of a cottage belonging to Ann Harris, an elderly widow who lived alone. He tied her by the neck with a bandage anchored to a chair, then ransacked her home emptying two purses, but missing 32/- hidden elsewhere.

He went on to Folkestone via London, but was arrested there four days later after the body of Mrs Harris was discovered by her sister at the foot of the stairs.

He was held in custody for five months until Mrs Harris' watch was found in a hotel toilet. Experts disagreed as to how long the watch had been there, and there have been suggestions that it was planted to facilitate a conviction. But police also strongly suspected him of the murder of a man in Manchester. The jury took 72 minutes to decide his guilt.

Palmer was dragged to the scaffold after a struggle in the condemned cell in which he threw himself at his warders.

Read: True Detective, May 96.

---

17 October 1911   Pentonville prison, London   *Ellis/ Conduit/ Lumb*

188

Francisco Carlos GODHINO   40   *Italian*

Bludgeoned: ***Alice Emily Brewster**, 54, on 16 June 1911, in the Arabian Sea.*
Motive: *Vengeance.*

Godhino, *(b.1871),* was a cabin steward and bath attendant en route from Sydney to London on the liner *China*, which left Ceylon for Aden on 7 June 1911. Sleeping on deck for comfort, Godhino was seen walking about at 3am. Alice Brewster was the Italian's line manager, and had been critical of his work at times. Sneaking into the stewardess' cabin, he clubbed her over the head with a porthole key, and attempted to push her body through the porthole.

One of his duties was to wake other crew members, and, at 5.30am, he reported to another stewardess that he had found Alice's body. She was lying on the cabin floor, covered with a mattress. His key was found under running water in a sink, and his trousers bore bloodstains despite an attempt to wash them. He was handed over to UK police upon arrival at London. Godhino, 5'11", 8st 7, was hanged alongside wife-murderer Hill.

Read: Diary of a Hangman, p222.

189

Edward HILL   41

Suffocated: ***Mary Jane Hill***, *43, his wife, on 25 July 1911, in London N1*
Motive: *Sadistic pleasure; drink related.*

Hill, *(b.1870),* had a record of dishonesty and violence and had served ten years for arson. He married on 16 July 1911 but spent the housekeeping money getting drunk and Mary had to borrow from her mother-in-law. Mary worked in a laundry, and the couple occupied lodgings in Kings Cross.

On 24 July Hill, heavily drunk, flew into a rage and cut up the bed. The following day, he again came home drunk, partly strangled his wife with a bandage and then suffocated her with pillows in the bedroom of their house in Caledonia Street. He then set fire to the bed with a paraffin lamp and made off with the 22/- from his mother.

A policeman noticed smoke and flames and Mrs Hill's body was discovered. Hill was arrested in Southwark, and fought with his captors. Hill, only 5', 9st 7, was hanged alongside Italian murderer Godhino.

Read: Diary of a Hangman, p223.

190

Frederick Henry THOMAS   37

Cut throat of: ***Harriet Anna Eckhardt***, *32, on 19 August 1911, in London SE10.*
Motive: *Sexual rivalry.*

Ann Eckhardt had lovers before and during her second marriage, to chief engineer Louis Ernest Eckhardt, 50, who was frequently trading the Thames-Humber route. He knew what she did, but always hoped she might mend her ways. Thomas, *(b.1876),* a bookie from Poplar, was married with three children. He met Ann on a park bench in summer 1910, and she took him back to her place for sex on that first day. As a result, and because he adored Ann, he separated from his wife.

By March 1911, however, Ann had tired of him, and took up with Bruno Koch, a seaman friend of her husband who had been in love with her before her marriage. Thomas continued to pester her, and in August she changed the locks at her Greenwich home so that Thomas could not gain entry.

Even though Eckhardt was on a short leave, Koch called on Ann and the two had sex. There was a banging on the door, and Koch fled to the kitchen fearing the husband was home. Ann answered the door to Thomas, who, aware of the bedroom scene, grabbed a razor from the bathroom, tore off Ann's nightdress, slit her throat, and pushed her down the stairs, before fleeing. Koch also fled when he found the body, fearing he would be blamed. Eckhardt named Thomas as a lover of his wife, and though Koch admitted being in the house at the time of the murder, Thomas eventually confessed. He cut his own throat after his arrest, but survived to hear the jury deliver its verdict after a four hour retirement.

Read: True Crime Summer Special 97.

6 December 1911	Walton gaol, Liverpool	*Ellis/ Brown*

191

Michael FAGAN   27

Bludgeoned: *Lucy Kennedy, 2, on 9 September 1911, in Liverpool, Lancs.*
Motive: *Vengeance; drink related.*

Fagan, *(b.1884),* and his wife, Annie, lodged with Mary Ellen Kennedy and her 2-year old daughter. Both women went out shopping, leaving Fagan, who had been drinking, to look after the child. Annoyed with the child, he hit her with his belt, and may have kicked her, though he denied this. His wife discovered the battered child on the bed when she returned to the empty house. When he came home later, Fagan denied all knowledge of the girl's injuries. Mary called the police, who found Fagan sobbing on his bed. Lucy died two days later.

Read: And May The Lòrd Have Mercy On Your Soul

Walter MARTYN   23

Strangled: **Edith Griffiths**, *25, on 28 September 1911, near Heywood, Manchester, Lancs.*
Motive: *Sexual rivalry.*

    Martyn *(b. 1888)*, a retarded depressive, had been unable to hold down a job, but had eventually found work as a labourer at a Heywood hotel. He began courting Edith Griffiths in December 1910, and became lodger at her widowed step-mother's home. Edith, a cotton-waste operative, had been jilted two years before and had a year-old child. One evening at 8.30 they walked to Plumpton Wood near Heywood, and an argument ensued. Walter said he was considering moving away to find another job, but Edith said if he did that she would find another man. In a rage, Martyn, 5'5" and 11 st, grabbed her by the throat. He strangled her with a scarf and a handkerchief and covered her body with her shawl.
    Martyn confessed to his employer who informed the police. When he was charged, Martyn's father collapsed and died on 2 October. The jury, convinced there was no premeditation, added a strong recommendation to mercy, but this and a public petition failed to move the Home Secretary. Martyn was hanged alongside wife-murderer Tarkenter.

    Read: Master Detective, Nov 96.

John Edward TARKENTER   41

Cut throat of: **Rosetta Tarkenter**, *43, his wife, on 18 July 1911, in Manchester, Lancs.*
Motive: *Sexual rivalry; drink related.*

    Tarkenter, *(b. 1870)*, a spinner who had served in the Boer war, had married Rosetta in 1889, though they had separated four times, once for nine years. They finally were reunited in July 1911, after an eleven-month parting. Tarkenter suspected Rosetta of going with other men while they were estranged.

They moved with their son to Hilton Street, Heyside in June 1911. Tarkenter, 5'4" and 11 st, was a jealous drunkard who regularly argued with and beat his wife. So it was one morning, just four weeks after moving house. After their son had gone to work at 6am, a fight started and Tarkenter cut his wife's throat with a razor in their bedroom, burying her beneath a pile of blankets. Their son alerted the police when he returned at 5.30pm. Tarkenter had gone to see his brother, to whom he had confessed. He told relations that he deserved to die.

Tarkenter was hanged alongside Martyn, the Plumpton Wood murderer.

Read: Diary of a Hangman, p164.

14 December 1911　　　　Swansea prison　　　　　*Ellis/ Willis*

194

Henry PHILLIPS　　　**44**　　*Welsh*

Cut throat of:　　***Margaret Phillips**, 39, his wife, on 26 July 1911, in Knelston, Glamorgan.*
Motive:　　Vengeance.

Phillips, *(b.1867),* had married Margaret in 1898, but when he hit her on 13 July, she left him and went to her mother. It was not the first time they had parted, for she was used to his drunken violence. She issued a summons for persistent cruelty on 22 July, and two days later moved into new lodgings with their four children.

At 6.40am, Margaret had just been chatting in the street with her sister, when Phillips approached her and cut her throat. She collapsed in her sister's arms, and Phillips threatened to kill a man who challenged him. He then went to a pub, and was found by a policeman sleeping in a cornfield later the same day.

Read: And May The Lord Have Mercy On Your Soul

195

Joseph FLETCHER   40

Bludgeoned: ***Caroline Fletcher**, 38, his wife, on 2 September 1911, in Liverpool, Lancs.*

Motive: *Vengeance; drink related.*

Fletcher, *(b.1871)*, was an habitual wife-beater when drunk. Caroline only stayed with him for the sake of their five children, the oldest 17, the youngest just 15 months. Fletcher came in from work at 12.30pm, and then went out drinking. He came home blind drunk later that evening, and when he announced that he was going back out, Caroline locked the door after him. Infuriated, Fletcher hammered on the door until his daughter answered it, and then barged open the locked door to the parlour, to get to his wife.

Though she was holding the baby, Fletcher punched her three times in the face. Caroline passed the child to her daughter and fled to the kitchen, but there he forced her to sit and started hitting her with a chair, ramming its leg into her mouth. He himself got the police, but told them Caroline had fallen down the stairs. His children told the truth to damn him.

Read: And May The Lord Have Mercy On Your Soul

196

George William PARKER   26

Cut throat of: ***Mary Elizabeth Speller**, 26, on 22 July 1911, in Dover, Kent.*

Motive: *Vengeance.*

Parker, *(b.1885)*, lived in lodgings with his girlfriend, Mary Speller, her adoptive mother, and Mary's three children. The women knew Parker's bad temper well; he had kicked one of the children from its bed that summer. Money was the main reason for his poor temper, he had none, and was two weeks in arrears with his rent.

On 22 July, he was told by the landlord to find somewhere else to live. That afternoon, he called Mary to his room, and cut her throat with his razor. Mary ran out into the street with her baby, and there collapsed. A bystander punched Parker as he ran, and held him until police arrived. The jury decided his fate in 15 minutes.

Read: And May The Lord Have Mercy On Your Soul

| **21 December 1911** | St Albans prison | *Ellis/ Willis* |

197

Charles COLEMAN 36

Stabbed: ***Rose Anna Gurney**, 49, on 15 July 1911, in Rickmansworth, Herts.*
Motive: *To clear impediment.*

Coleman, *(b.1875),* had served several prison sentences, one for attempted murder, after cutting his landlady's throat in 1897. His most recent incarceration was for mutilating a dog, after which he was released from St Albans prison on 15 July.

He bumped into an old acquaintance, Rose Gurney, and the two went to a pub. He was seen walking with her at 9.50pm, and then stabbed her, leaving her near a stile. He had blood on his clothes, but his knife was clean. Though the evidence was purely circumstantial, and Coleman claimed that he had left Rose with two men, the jury did not believe him.

Read: And May The Lord Have Mercy On Your Soul

| **28 December 1911** | Stafford gaol | *T.Pierrepoint/ Willis* |

198

George LOAKE 64

Stabbed: ***Elizabeth Loake**, 47, his wife, on 28 August 1911, in Walsall, Warwicks.*
Motive: *Sadistic pleasure.*

George Loake, *(b.1847),* was a good-humoured and well-liked man who had worked for the LNWR railway since the age of 14. In 1903, a widower with nine children, he married Elizabeth Newitt, a divorced mother of two. They lived happily together in Walsall, until George's train was involved in a shunting accident in 1909, in which he suffered head injuries. In severe pain, he the same day threw himself in a canal but was rescued. He became bad-tempered and violent, and started to drink heavily.

In March 1911 he was sacked from his job, also losing his pension rights, and started to fall into debt. In June the family was evicted from their home. Exasperated by George's violence towards her, and his continual suicide attempts, Elizabeth left him and went to stay with her friends, the Dolloways. George went into lodgings. Several times he attempted a reconciliation, and went again to the Dolloway house on Bank holiday Monday. A row with Elizabeth ensued, and George grabbed her, stabbing her in the face and neck six times, witnessed by the Dolloways' eleven year old son. George attempted to cut his own throat, but a policeman hit him with a truncheon, and arrested him.

Elizabeth died shortly afterwards while being attended to by a doctor. Pleas on the grounds of insanity and diminished responsibility were dismissed, the jury taking just over ten minutes to reach its verdict.

Read: Murderous Birmingham, p137.

1911 Execution in Ireland

4 January 1911   Cork gaol

William SCANLAN

Crime: *unknown*
Motive: *unknown*

No details.

1912　total: *10*

199	6 Mar	Myer ABROMOVITCH	28	*Russian*	Pentonville
200	19 Mar	John WILLIAMS	38		Knutsford
201	18 Apr	Frederick SEDDON	40		Pentonville
202	23 Jul	Arthur BIRKETT	22		Strangeways
203	1 Oct	Sargent PHILP	33		Wandsworth
204	5 Nov	Robert GALLOWAY	27		Norwich
205	26 Nov	Gilbert SMITH	35		Gloucester
206	10 Dec	William BEAL	20		Chelmsford
207	18 Dec	Alfred LAWRENCE	32		Maidstone
208	20 Dec	William GALBRAITH	27	*Scottish*	Wakefield

6 March 1912　　　　Pentonville prison　　　　*Ellis/ Lumb*

199

Myer ABROMOVITCH　　　**28**　　*Russian*

Bludgeoned:　　　**1 *Solomon Milstein*,** 35, and his wife
　　　　　　　　　　2 *Annie Milstein*, 37, on 27 December 1911, in London E1
Motive:　　　　　Vengeance.

　　　Abromovitch, *(b.1884),* a Russian Jew and costermonger, frequented the illegal gambling den beneath Milstein's restaurant in Hanbury Street, Spitalfields.　Solomon Milstein ran a lucrative faro game with professional boxer Joe Goldstein, sharing the profits, and boosting the meagre income he gained from the eatery.　They also accepted watches and jewellery to finance loans for the punters.　Abromovitch was one of the losers. Mrs Milstein, however, did not approve of the casino, and her husband agreed that Boxing Day 1911 was to be its last night.　The last customers left at 1am.
　　　Abromovitch stole into the house before 3am, and battered the Milsteins as they lay in bed.　He then poured paraffin over them, and set fire to the bed using hot irons from the fire.　A friend persuaded him to go the police, who found he was wearing Milstein's bloodstained suit beneath his own.

Read: And May The Lord Have Mercy On Your Soul

200

John WILLIAMS   38

Cut throat of: ***Hilda Mary Josephine Williams**, 39, his wife, on 10 December 1911, in Birkenhead, Cheshire.*
Motive: *Vengeance; drink related.*

Williams, *(b.1874),* married Hilda Shawcross in 1908, living in Seacombe. But Hilda found work in domestic service, and the couple parted, as she went to live in Birkenhead. Williams often visited his wife, and they had the day out together on 10 December. They went back to his place, and by the time Williams had to take Hilda to get her bus, he was rather drunk. He dragged his wife into an alleyway and cut her throat, and was arrested at 10.30pm, after drunkenly crying out in the street that he had killed his wife. The jury deliberated for fifteen minutes.

Read: And May The Lord Have Mercy On Your Soul.

201

Frederick Henry SEDDON   40

Poisoned: ***Eliza Mary Barrow**, 49, on 14 September 1911, in London N4.*
Motive: *Financial.*

Seddon, 5'3" and 10 st, was born in Liverpool in 1872, and twice went to sea before the age of 20. He was shipwrecked off Cape Horn and worked as a sheep farmer in the Falkland Islands. A freemason, he had then worked for more than twenty years as an insurance agent.

He was comfortable financially, but was known to be a skinflint. He lived with his wife Mary Ann, 37, a weak-willed woman, his five children, aged 1 to 17, his father, 73, and their servant woman, in Tollington Park, in north London.

In July 1910, Seddon rented the top floor to Miss Eliza Barrow, who moved in with Ernie Grant, 6, an orphan whom she had looked after since his mother died. She was a dirty, untidy woman who drank gin and was generally unpleasant. She did, however, have money, inherited from her mother, and she was very careful with it, rivalling Seddon in her miserliness.

Nevertheless, good salesman that he was, Seddon managed to persuade Eliza that in return for a weekly income, she would be better off turning her assets over to him. In making a new will, she appointed Seddon as executor, to hold her money in trust for Ernie's coming of age.

Miss Barrow came down with vomiting and diarrhoea on 1 September, possibly a result of London's greatest heat wave of the century. Seddon saw his opportunity to get Eliza's money. He sent his wife to buy fly-papers, and poisoned Barrow with the arsenic solution obtained from them. She died on 14 September.

He took the £400 Eliza had in the house, and buried her cheaply in a public grave, not informing any of her relatives. A cousin of hers was angered when he discovered what had happened, and his suspicions were raised. Eliza's body was exhumed and was found to contain 131mg of arsenic. Seddon was charged on 4 December, his wife on 15 January.

Though the evidence was entirely circumstantial, after a ten day trial, the jury took one hour to find him guilty. His wife was acquitted. 250,000 people signed a petition for his reprieve, but Seddon was executed while public attention was more concerned with the *Titanic* which had sunk just four days before. His wife remarried two months later.

Read: The Murders of the Black Museum, p174.

---

23 July 1912   Strangeways prison, Manchester   *Ellis/ Lumb*

202

Arthur BIRKETT   **22**

Cut throat of: **Alice Beetham**, *18, on 20 May 1912, in Blackburn, Lancs.*
Motive: Vengeance.

Birkett, *(b.1890)*, lived with his widowed mother, his grandmother and younger sister in Blackburn, and supported them all by working as a weaver in the local mill. There he met Alice Beetham, his first girlfriend, with whom he fell in love. From April 1912, they went out together a few times, before Alice lost interest and began to give Arthur the cold shoulder. On 17 May, she told him it was all over.

The following Monday at the mill, when Alice refused to speak to him, he grabbed her and cut her throat with a razor, so deeply that the spinal cord was scratched. He then cut his own throat, but his life was saved, albeit for a mere seven weeks. The jury took just 15 minutes to deliver its verdict, and a 60,000 signature petition, signed by Alice's mother, failed to save him.

Read: *True Crime Summer Special 88.*

1 October 1912	Wandsworth prison, London	*Ellis/ T.Pierrepoint*

203

Sargent PHILP   33

Cut throat of:	***Rose Philp***, *35, his wife, on 26 July 1912, in London SE1.*
Motive:	*Vengeance.*

Philp, *(b.1879)*, married Rose Keighley in 1901, and by 1912 the couple had six children. Things turned bad for Philp when he lost an eye in a work accident, and was dismissed. With little money for the youngsters, Rose moved in with her sister in June 1912, and issued a separation order on 8 July. Rose was not in when he called at her sister's on 25 July, but he said he would not pay a penny, swore at her sister, and made threats.

He called again at 11.30 the following morning, and told Rose he was starting a new job. When she told him she would not come back until he had a house for her and the children, he drew a knife, and his wife fled to a neighbour's house. Philp followed her and cut her throat. As he was about to slit his own, he was overpowered by two men answering calls for assistance.

Read: *And May The Lord Have Mercy On Your Soul.*

5 November 1912	Norwich prison	*T.Pierrepoint/ Brown*

204

Robert GALLOWAY   27

Strangled:	***Minnie Morris***, *21, on 16 July 1912, in Walsoken, Norfolk.*
Motive:	*Sexual rivalry; drink related.*

Galloway, *(b.1885),* met Minnie Morris while she was up from London for the fruit picking in Norfolk. He was not, however, her only boyfriend, for she had met fellow Londoner, William Tucker. Galloway regarded Minnie as his, for the summer at least, and when he saw the two in the pub, he threatened them both.

Galloway and Minnie themselves went for a drink together on 16 July, leaving the pub at 2pm. A passer-by noticed them at 2.30 lying, Galloway on top, by the side of the road. He strangled her there, and by the time the onlooker passed again fifteen minutes later, Minnie was lying alone, a cap over her face. He thought she was sleeping. Galloway went to two further pubs, and then walked the mile to Wisbech, and handed himself in to police. The jury considered his fate for just five minutes.

Read: And May The Lord Have Mercy On Your Soul

26 November 1912   Gloucester prison   *T.Pierrepoint/ Lumb*

205

Gilbert Oswald SMITH   35

Cut throat of: ***Rosabella Smith****, 30, his wife, on 21 July 1912, in Dursley, Gloucs.*
Motive: *Vengeance.*

Smith, *(b.1877),* had served in India and South Africa with distinction, and was discharged from the army in November 1906, marrying Rosabella the following year. Though they had no children, the couple got along well enough, until, in May 1912, she left him, and went to live with the neighbours.

On 20 July they chatted at the Dursley Fete, and Smith threatened to kill her. Afraid to go out alone, Rosabella got a neighbour to walk with her the following morning at 7.30. Smith stood in their way and told them not to pass. When his wife went on, Smith ran up to her and cut her throat, then performed the same task, less successfully, on his own.

Read: And May The Lord Have Mercy On Your Soul

206

<u>William Charles Adolphus BEAL</u>   **20**

Cut throat of: ***Clara Elizabeth Carter**, 17, on 12 September 1912, in London E15.*
Motive: *Sexual rivalry.*

      Beal, *(b.1892)*, and Clara Carter were sweethearts, but he was extremely jealous of any attention paid to other men. Walking along a lane in Stratford, he cut her throat, then turned the razor on himself. He crawled to her side and put his arm around her before losing consciousness. Beal had not recovered sufficiently for questioning until 2 October, and then told that Clara had taken the razor from his pocket and cut his throat. Two witnesses, however, had seen the woman fall first, and the razor drop from Beal's hand.
      The jury considered for an hour, before strongly recommending mercy because of Beal's youth.

      Read: And May The Lord Have Mercy On Your Soul

207

<u>Alfred John LAWRENCE</u>   **32**

Bludgeoned/ cut throat of: ***Emily Violet Hubbard**, 47, on 19 August 1912, in Dover, Kent.*
Motive: *Vengeance.*

      Lawrence, *(b.1880)*, was one of the lodgers at the house of William and Emily Hubbard, and it was not long before he and the lady of the house were lovers. Lawrence was a seaman, and on one voyage, in May 1912, the doctor told him he had syphilis. He was home by the end of July, and Emily took his advice to have a medical test.
      Deemed unfit, Lawrence was sacked on 12 August, and Emily was confirmed as having venereal disease three days later. Lawrence later claimed that Emily refused to get treatment, and was having sex with another of her lodgers.
      At lunchtime on 19 August, Emily went to lie down on her bed while her daughter played outside. Lawrence battered her as she lay, five times with a coal hammer, and then cut her throat. He put his fist through the

bedroom window and called to the child to come and see what he had done. He then cut his own throat. The jury decided his fate in 15 minutes.

Read: And May The Lord Have Mercy On Your Soul

20 December 1912   Wakefield prison   *T.Pierrepoint/ Willis*

208

William Wallace GALBRAITH   27

Cut throat of: ***Mary May Galbraith****, 20, his wife, on 14 August 1912, in Middlesbrough, N Yorks.*
Motive: *Vengeance.*

Galbraith, *(b.1885)*, married Mary Kirby in April 1912, and the couple lived with her parents in Middlesbrough, though they moved to his parents' house in Stockton in July. Galbraith lost his job, and following an argument with her mother-in-law, Mary moved back to Middlesbrough.

Galbraith began a depression, though he visited Mary on 12 August and stayed the night. The couple argued the following day, but again he stayed. At 6am the following morning he cut his wife's throat as she lay in bed. Her mother answered her screams, but Galbraith ran past her out of the house, and to the police station.

Read: And May The Lord Have Mercy On Your Soul

1913

total: **20**

209	7 Jan	Albert RUMENS	44		Lewes
210	29 Jan	John WILLIAMS	29	*Scottish*	Lewes
211	29 Jan	Edward HOPWOOD	45		Pentonville
212	4 Feb	Eric SEDGEWICK	29		Reading
213	25 Feb	George CUNLIFFE	28		Exeter
214	19 Mar	Edward PALMER	23		Bristol
215	23 Apr	Walter SYKES	24		Wakefield
216	24 Jun	William BURTON	29		Dorchester
217	8 Jul	Harry LONGDEN	52		Pentonville
218	9 Jul	Thomas FLETCHER	28		Worcester
219	22 Jul	John AMOS	35		Newcastle
220	13 Aug	James RYDER	45		Strangeways
221	13 Aug	Frank GREENING	34		Winson Green
222	14 Aug	Hugh McLAREN	29	*Welsh*	Cardiff
223	1 Oct	Patrick HIGGINS	30	*Scottish*	Calton
224	4 Nov	Frederick SEEKINGS	39		Cambridge
225	26 Nov	Augustus PENNY	30		Winchester
226	27 Nov	Frederick ROBERTSON	26		Pentonville
227	17 Dec	Ernest KELLY	20		Strangeways
228	31 Dec	George LAW	34		Wakefield

7 January 1913 Lewes prison, Sussex

Ellis/ H.Pierrepoint

209

Albert RUMENS 44

Suffocated:	***Mabel Ann Maryan**, 10, on 6 September 1912, near Wadhurst, Sussex*
Motive:	*Sadistic pleasure; drink related.*

Rumens, *(b.1868),* an unmarried casual labourer who lived with his mother at Wood's Green, was said to have the mind of a child, to be an inoffensive man when sober, but not so when he had been drinking. Next door but one to Rumens lived the Maryans, a family of farm labourers, and at 4.50pm Mabel had set off to meet her father from work and to pick blackberries along the way. She met Rumens who took her into Buckland Hill wood and killed her by forcing her face into the ground. He made no sexual assault.

Several people saw them along the way, and a gamekeeper, hearing a scream, saw them at 6.30, telling them to get out of the wood. Rumens fled, but the gamekeeper discovered the girl was dead when she did not respond to his calls. She was clutching Rumen's handkerchief. He recognised Rumens as the man he had seen kissing another gamekeeper two days before, having received a light from him.

Rumens himself called round to the Maryans telling them that he and the girl had been blackberrying, and that she would be home soon. Police arrested Rumens in the pub at 8.30pm. The jury delivered its verdict after 20 minutes.

Read: Murderous Sussex

---

29 January 1913   Lewes prison, Sussex   *Ellis/ Willis*

210

John WILLIAMS   **29**   *(real name, George Mackay;*
                      Scottish   *aka Scottie Shepherd)*

Shot: Policeman **Arthur Walls**, 44, on 9 October 1912, in
                  Eastbourne, Sussex.
Motive: To escape arrest.

Williams, *(b.1884),* was the son of a Church of Scotland minister, who had been gaoled in South Africa as a jewel thief and for burglary. John had been deported in 1907, after serving in the Boer war, and then served three gaol terms in England between 1907 and 1910. He had come to live in London with his girlfriend, Florence Seymour, who became pregnant with his child. He had a poor relationship with his brother, William, and in August 1912 had threatened his sister-in-law with a revolver.

On 2 October, John and Flossie had gone to Eastbourne. Unknown to her, a week later he went to the house of Hungarian aristocrat Countess Sztaray in South Cliff Avenue, intending to burgle the premises looking for jewellery. He was spotted on the portico above the front door by the lady's coachman, and the Countess phoned for the police. When Inspector Walls, a married man with two children, arrived, Williams fired twice at him from the balcony, one shot hitting him in the chest.

Williams, 5'4", made his escape while the officer died at the scene. His trilby hat was left outside the house. Proclaiming his innocence to Flossie, he buried his revolver on the beach, and wrote to his brother asking for money. William Mackay travelled to Bournemouth with Edgar Power, a family friend. They decided that the brothers would return to London together and

Power would follow separately with Flossie, to whom Power had formed an attachment. Instead, Power went to the police.

Williams was arrested at Moorgate station in London on 11 October. Power persuaded Flossie to reveal where the gun was hidden, and when the hat was found to fit Williams, the case against him was convincing. The couple's baby daughter was born at the end of December, but permission for them to marry was refused.

Mother and daughter visited the prisoner on the eve of his execution.

Read: Settings For Slaughter, p43.

---

29 January 1913   Pentonville prison, London   *T.Pierrepoint/ Lumb*

211

Edward HOPWOOD   45

Shot: ***Florence Alice Bernadette Silles**, 34, on 28 September 1912, in London EC3.*
Motive: *Sexual rivalry.*

Hopwood, *(b.1868)*, a married man with three children, was a bankrupt London businessman who lived in Brighton. He had met actress Florence Dudley in Manchester in May 1912, and the two had become lovers. A widow from Ilford, she worked in music halls under her maiden name . Unaware of Hopwood's circumstances, she agreed to marry him, but when he avoided naming the day, she broke off the engagement. Consumed with jealousy, he had her followed in order to check on her movements, and bought a gun on 26 September.

She agreed to meet him in a Holborn restaurant, in order to tell him that their relationship was finished. At 11.45pm they took a taxi to Fenchurch street station, where Hopwood shot her four times in the back as she stepped out, hitting her in the head and lungs. He then shot himself in the head. A will in his pocket indicated he had intended to kill himself. Florence died ten minutes after arriving at hospital.

Read: Master Detective, Jul 94.

212

Eric James SEDGEWICK   29

Stabbed:.   ***Annie Wentworth Davis***, *22, on 24 November 1912, in Eton, Berks.*
Motive: *Vengeance.*

Sedgewick, *(b.1884),* had been discharged from the army in 1902, having served with merit, and met Annie Davis in January 1908. She found work as a domestic servant in Eton, and Sedgewick visited her there several times. Eventually, after much persuading, Annie sacrificed her virginity to him, but when he confessed that he had been with someone else, she broke off the relationship.

He wrote to her, expressing his devotion, but Annie only replied that he should keep away from her. He arrived at 4pm, and, reluctantly, Annie agreed to talk to him in the servants' hall.

When she told Sedgewick her decision was final, he lunged at her, and stabbed her in the breast with a kitchen knife. He showed genuine concern that he had killed the woman he loved.

Read: And May The Lord Have Mercy On Your Soul

213

George CUNLIFFE   28

Cut throat of: ***Kitty Butler***, *26, on 8 November 1912, in Plymouth, Devon.*
Motive: *Vengeance.*

Cunliffe, *(b.1885),* from Wigan, served in the Royal Navy until July 1912, after which he did not hurry himself to find work. He soon met Kitty Butler in Plymouth, and the two lived together. On 2 November, Cunliffe was charged with being drunk and disorderly, and was furious when Kitty refused to pay his fine, and he was forced to serve five days in prison.

Kitty had a friend round when George got back after his release on 8 November, and when he asked Kitty for some money, she told him to get down to the docks and look for work. Having nursed a grudge against her for a week, he immediately grabbed her by the throat. Kitty's friend ran for help, and Cunliffe locked the door behind her, undisturbed to cut her throat and his.

Read: And May The Lord Have Mercy On Your Soul

19 March 1913   Horfield gaol, Bristol   *T.Pierrepoint/ Brown*

214

<u>Edward Henry PALMER</u>   **23**

Cut throat of:	***Ada Louisa James**, 28, on 27 January 1913, in Bristol, Gloucs.*
Motive:	*To clear impediment.*

       Palmer, *(b.1890),* had worked in Canada for a time, and when he could not find a job in Bristol, he began to think that perhaps he ought to go back. His fiancee, Ada James had previously been a prostitute, and was not pleased to hear of Edward's plan. He said that, at 9.30pm, they had an argument in the street, and Ada had thrown her ring at him, telling him that if he emigrated, she would go back to prostitution. Palmer cut her throat with a razor. The passer-by who found Ada, saw her write a note blaming Palmer for attacking her.
       Palmer went to a chemist and bought laudanum, waking an uncle at 4.30am to tell him he had taken poison, and the police were summoned. They found a letter of confession, but also discovered that the day before the attack, Palmer had tried to buy a revolver, and had bought a new razor instead, indicating that the crime was premeditated. Ada died on 28 January.

Read: And May The Lord Have Mercy On Your Soul

23 April 1913   Wakefield prison   *T.Pierrepoint/ Lumb*

215

<u>Walter SYKES</u>   **24**

Cut throats of:	***1 Frances Alice Nicholson**, 7, and* ***2 Amy Nicholson**, 10, her cousin, on 15 November 1912, in Kimberworth, W.Yorks.*

Motive: *To clear impediment*

Sykes, *(b.1889),* had lived with an aunt near Wakefield, but in 1912 had no regular place to live or to work. By August he had made the acquaintance of Amy Nicholson in Kimberworth, near Rotherham. Her parents had moved there from Lincolnshire in 1911 with her aunt's family. In October Sykes took casual work on a fairground, and returned to Kimberworth, having sex with Amy in November.

Three days later, Amy and her cousin Frances disappeared while returning home from a concert rehearsal, being last seen at 8.45pm. Sykes had met the girls and cut their throats with a penknife, leaving them in a hedge 100 yards from Amy's home. Frances' mother found them there the following morning. There had been no sexual assault and the girls were smiling. A post mortem revealed the earlier sexual activity.

Sykes confessed the murders to a stranger in a public toilet and was arrested on 29 December. It seems he killed Amy to stop her telling of her seduction. Imprints of shoes and corduroy trousers in the soil matched those of Sykes, and he told police what he had done with the knife. He retracted his confession several times.

The jury took only six minutes to condemn him. His final words on the scaffold were, 'I'm sorry'.

Read: True Detective, Mar 96.

---

24 June 1913   Dorchester prison, Dorset   *H.Pierrepoint / Brown*

216

William Walter BURTON   29

Shot: **Winifred Mary Mitchell**, *23, on 31 March 1913, in Gussage St Michael, Dorset.*
Motive: To clear impediment.

Burton, *(b.1884),* was a gardener on a Dorset farm, and lived above the village post-office with his schoolteacher wife and their child. Mrs Burton was somewhat older than her husband, and he had begun amusing himself with Winifred Mitchell, a cook at the farm.

When the young woman announced that she was pregnant, he told her they would elope, and thus luring her at 3.30pm to a nearby plantation, where he had dug a hole the previous day, he shot her in the head with a gun he had borrowed, burying her in a shallow grave which lay undiscovered until 2 May.

Letters he had written were found at the farm - sufficient to convince the jury of his guilt. Ironically, Winifred was not pregnant after all.

Read: The Murder Guide to Great Britain, p17.

| 8 July 1913 | Pentonville prison, London | *Ellis/ Willis* |

217

Harry LONGDEN   52

Cut throat of: ***Alice Catlow More***, *27, on 10 April 1913, in London WC1.*
Motive: *Sexual rivalry.*

Longden, *(b.1861),* lived with Alice More, until his persistent complaining about her housekeeping resulted in her leaving him. He believed that she was having an affair with a foreign trader, whom she had met through her work with a society promoting trade with China.

They both denied his allegations when he saw them drinking together on 9 April. In Gordon Square, at 2pm the following day, Longden cut Alice's throat with a butcher's knife, and followed her as she staggered along before cutting his own.

Read: And May The Lord Have Mercy On Your Soul

| 9 July 1913 | Worcester prison | *Ellis/ T.Pierrepoint* |

218

Thomas FLETCHER   28

Shot: ***Lilian Wharton***, *20, on 1 April 1913, in Oldbury, Worcs.*
Motive: *Vengeance; drink related.*

Fletcher, *(b.1885),* had been a railway shunter when in 1906 he and his brother went to America, where they did well gold prospecting in Virginia. He returned in autumn 1911 but spent too much money drinking and boasting and had to take a job as a labourer in the summer of 1912 to earn his fare back to the States. It was then he met and fell for the daughter of a local pub landlord, Lilian Wharton. By Christmas the two were engaged and Fletcher was making plans for the wedding in March, and the trip to Virginia.

But in February 1913 he lost his job, and Lilian's father forbade her to marry. Fletcher was devastated and turned to drink. On 29 March he bought a revolver in a pawnshop and three days later went to the pub where he and Lilian spoke alone in the tap room. He shot her twice, in the ribs and hand, and then shot himself in the temple, losing an eye.

At first it seemed his injuries were worse than Lilian's, but he recovered while Lilian, with a bullet lodged in her intestines, suffered a relapse and died on 8 April. Fletcher claimed her death was accidental, that she was shot while trying to stop him committing suicide.

Read: True Detective Summer Special 90

22 July 1913	Newcastle prison	*T.Pierrepoint/ Willis*

219

John Vickers AMOS   35

Shot:	*1 PC George Bertram Mussell, 31,*
	2 Sarah Ellen Grice, 33, and
	3 Sgt Andrew Barton, 40, on 15 April 1913, in
	Bedlington, Northumberland
Motive:	*Vengeance*

John Amos, *(b.1878)*, had gone to America to seek his fortune, working as a mine foreman, and being badly injured in two mine explosions. Thereafter he had become more withdrawn and morose. He returned to England with his wife Isabella and their three children in 1912, and from January 1913, he took over as manager of the Sun inn in Bedlington, owned by James Irons. Amos paid a £30 bond to Irons, but the owner was determined to cheat him, accusing him of taking stock, and demanding a £46 shortfall.

On 15 April, Irons came to the pub with his new tenants and told Amos to get out, refusing Amos' demand for the return of his bond. After Amos sent his son to buy cartridges, Constable George Mussell arrived. Amos blasted him with his shotgun in the hall, killing him with wounds to the neck and shoulder.

He then shot Mrs Grice, the new tenant's wife, at the cellar door, hitting her in the back of the head. A crowd gathered and more police arrived. Amos, 5'5", 11st 10, warned Sergeant Barton to back off, then felled him with a shot to the chest from 4 yards. After putting the muzzle in his own mouth twice, Amos ran off over nearby fields, where he was later flushed out of a culvert.

Amos claimed that Irons had driven him mad, and there was considerable pity for his plight, 60,000 people signing a petition on his behalf. But the jury took only eight minutes to find him guilty. He was baptised in the condemned cell, and ten days after his execution his widow and her children left for the USA with another man.

Read: True Crime, Feb 95

---

13 August 1913   Strangeways prison, Manchester   *Ellis*

220

James RYDER   45

Cut throat of: ***Elizabeth Ann Ryder***, *43, his wife, on 15 May 1913, in Manchester, Lancs.*
Motive: *Sexual rivalry; drink related*

Ryder, *(b.1868),* a ship's fireman, drank heavily and regularly beat his wife, Elizabeth, a mill worker. Finally deciding enough was enough, in November 1912 Elizabeth moved out with her two sons while Ryder, 5'7", was at sea.

It took him until the following May to find her in Ardwick, but when he did he was sober. After seeing him dry for two days, Elizabeth took him back, and he remained sober for another five days. But then a postcard arrived signed 'With love, P.' It was from Elizabeth's aunt Polly, but Ryder imagined a love rival and the jealousy turned him back to drink.

The three men slept in one room, with Elizabeth in the kitchen, so it was not until the boys had left for work at 5.20am, that he and his wife were left alone. At 8am he took his son's razor and cut Elizabeth's throat with such force that the weapon broke. She was found by her son at 11.45am, and Ryder was arrested in the street at 2.30 that afternoon. He was drunk.

Read: Murderous Manchester, p50.

160

221

<u>Frank GREENING</u>   34

Shot: ***Elizabeth Ellen Hearne***, *27, on 6 April 1913, in Birmingham, Warwicks.*

Motive: *Vengeance*

Greening, *(b.1879)*, a painter, moved in with Elizabeth Hearne in February 1913. Born Elizabeth Pitt she had married but had been separated for nine years, working some time as a prostitute. Though he knew of it when he met her, Greening was angered by Elizabeth's 'business', and their relationship was punctuated by constant rows.

On 26 March 1913, Elizabeth was saved by friends when Greening threw an oil lamp at her, setting her alight. On 6 April he hit her on the head with a lamp, and when she told a friend he threatened to kill her. When Elizabeth refused to accompany him to his mother's, the two had a running argument down the street, culminating with Elizabeth asking him to return his key. He did so, but at 2.30pm he came to see Elizabeth at Edith Mumford's house demanding the key back.

When Elizabeth refused he drew a revolver and shot her three times in the shoulder, stomach and thigh. When Edith ran into the room he shot at her, grazing her head. He was arrested when he arrived home at 9.20. Elizabeth died at 4pm the following afternoon. Greening remained angry to the end, ranting at prison officers and the chaplain in the condemned cell, and swearing all the way to the scaffold.

Read: Murderous Birmingham, p38.

222

<u>Hugh McLAREN</u>   29

Stabbed: ***Julian Biros***, *22, on 23 March 1913, in Cardiff, Glamorgan.*

Motive: *Racism.*

Biros, a Spaniard, was one of a number of transient workers who slept in Cardiff's fuel works, in the hope of each day finding work in the docks. To eke a living, Biros would do odd labouring jobs on ships.

On 22 March, McLaren, *(b.1884)*, was asking around the port for 'that dago', because he wanted to 'slit his throat'. The following morning, McLaren had been through Biros' few possessions, and approached the group of chatting workers that included Biros, at 8.20pm. He suggested making tea, and produced a packet that belonged to the Spaniard. When Biros challenged him, McLaren immediately stabbed him in his side. Biros died that afternoon.

Read: And May The Lord Have Mercy On Your Soul

| 1 October 1913 | Calton gaol, Edinburgh | *Ellis* |

223

Patrick HIGGINS   30   *Scottish*

Drowned: *1 **William Higgins**, 7, and*
                   *2 **John Higgins**, 4, his sons, in November 1911, in*
                   Edinburgh, Midlothian.
Motive: *To clear impediment; drink related.*

Higgins, *(b.1883)*, had served in the army in India, but was discharged due to his epilepsy. He lived in Winchburgh, west Lothian, near Edinburgh, and worked in the local brickworks. He married a local girl, but she died in 1910, leaving him with two young boys, aged 5 and 2, to bring up. Higgins could not cope and turned increasingly to drink. In 1911 he was jailed for two months for neglecting his children, and in November 1911, he took the boys to the Hopetoun quarry, tied them together with sash cord and threw them over into the water below. It is not known if he killed them beforehand.

He told people that he had given the boys away to a woman on a train, and he continued his descent into misery. He slept rough, or at the brickworks, eating there, using his bucket and spade as cooking utensils.

The bodies were discovered in June 1913, remarkably well preserved, and Higgins was arrested. He tried a plea of insanity based on his epilepsy, but to no avail, though the jury entered a recommendation to mercy. A broken man, he admitted that he deserved to die.

Read: True Crime Diary

224

Frederick SEEKINGS   **39**

Cut throat of: **Martha Jane Beeby**, *45, on 28 July 1913, in Brampton, Hunts.*
Motive: *Sadistic pleasure; drink related..*

Seekings, *(b.1874),* a labourer, lived with Martha Beeby, and was in the pub with her on the evening of the Brampton village feast, from 8pm till closing time. Walking home, at 10.30pm, very drunk, he pushed her into a drainage ditch, and then further on the way, cut her throat with his pocket-knife. Villagers who heard noises investigated and found Seekings standing over Martha's body. His claim that she had inflicted the wounds herself were contradicted by experts.

Read: And May The Lord Have Mercy On Your Soul.

225

Augustus John PENNY   **30**

Shot: **Matilda Penny**, *57, his mother, in June 1913, in Copythorne, Hants.*
Motive: *Vengeance; drink related*

Penny, *(b.1883),* lived with his father in Portsmouth after his parents separated. His brother George, a barman, continued to live with their mother in Copythorne. When Matilda came into some money, Gus came over to see if he could extract a share of the £80 from her.

She was not impressed with his sudden show of affection, and he went and got very drunk in George's pub. He told his brother he was taking a drink back for Mum, but used a shotgun to blast her in the head as she lay in bed. George found her there when he returned from work, and a search was made of the area for Gus. A child saw him climbing from a well where he had hidden, and the party found him crouching behind a hedge. Penny pleaded guilty at his trial.

Read: And May The Lord Have Mercy On Your Soul

226

Frederick Albert ROBERTSON   26

Suffocated:	**1 *Nellie Kathleen Robertson*, 2,**
	2 *Frederick Ernest Robertson*, 2, and
	3 *Beatrice Maud Robertson*, 10 mths, his children, on 28 June 1913, in London E5.
Motive:	*To clear impediment.*

Robertson, *(b.1887)*, his wife Lily, and their three children had moved into their ground-floor Clapton flat in June 1913. Just a couple of weeks later, Lily had to go into hospital, and Robertson, who had a wooden leg, was left to look after the youngsters. This was particularly inconvenient, as Fred had recently found himself a new woman.

For a short time the children stayed with a family friend, but then Robertson tried to get the Salvation Army to take them. When they were full up, he decided on more drastic measures, killing the infants, probably by suffocating them, and burying them beneath the floorboards. Telling neighbours that the Army had taken them, Robertson vacated the flat on 12 July. Lily was still in hospital when tenants noticed the smell coming from the Robertson's flat, and the children's bodies were discovered. Arrested on City Road, Robertson claimed that the bodies found were not those of his children.

Read: And May The Lord Have Mercy On Your Soul

227

Ernest KELLY   20

Bludgeoned:	***Daniel Wright Bardsley*, 54**, on 26 July 1913, in Oldham, Lancs.
Motive:	*Financial.*

Kelly, *(b.1893)*, was a friend of Edward Hilton, 17, who had been employed for a time by Mr Bardsley, a newsagent. Hilton knew that Mr Bardsley was in the habit of taking the money from the shop home with him every night, and the two hatched a plot to relieve him of the cash.

Hilton tapped on the shop door at 10.15pm, and when the newsagent let him in, Kelly barged in behind him. They were armed with Kelly's heavy Indian club, and one of them battered Mr Bardsley with it. The shopkeeper was found the next morning, and Hilton was questioned as a suspect. He named Kelly as his accomplice, and both youths blamed each other for striking the blows.

Both were charged with murder, and both found guilty, though Hilton was sentenced to life, on account of his youth, and his being a mental defective. Oldham's people thought Hilton more to blame for the murder, and a huge petition, which included the signature of the mayoress, was organised to gain the same sentence for Kelly. He maintained his innocence throughout.

Read: And May The Lord Have Mercy On Your Soul

31 December 1913	Wakefield prison	*T.Pierrepoint/ Lumb*

228

George Frederick LAW   34

Strangled: ***Annie Cotterill**, 45, on 21 October 1913, in Sheffield, W Yorks.*
Motive: *Vengeance.*

Law, *(b.1879)*, had lodged with the Cotterill family since the spring of 1911, and objected most strongly when they told him they wanted the house for themselves, on 19 October. He told them they would have to carry him out, and made threats, which Mr Cotterill took seriously.

Law was heard walking about during the night, but all except Mrs Cotterill had left for work by 6am. Law came back to the house at 8am, and strangled Annie as she lay in bed. Her husband James found her when he returned from work. Law had gone to the pub, where he said he felt faint, and was arrested at his sister's house. The jury determined his fate in 30 minutes.

Read: And May The Lord Have Mercy On Your Soul

1914

total: *14*

229	26 Feb	George BALL	22		Walton
230	10 Mar	Josiah DAVIES	58		Stafford
231	12 Mar	James HONEYLANDS	21		Exeter
232	24 Mar	Robert UPTON	50		Durham
233	25 Mar	Edgar BINDON	22	*Welsh*	Cardiff
234	14 May	Joseph SPOONER	42		Walton
235	16 Jun	Walter WHITE	22		Winchester
236	28 Jul	Herbert BROOKER	32		Lewes
237	11 Aug	Percy CLIFFORD	32		Lewes
238	4 Nov	Charles FREMBD	71	*German*	Chelmsford
239	10 Nov	John EAYRES	59		Northampton
240	10 Nov	Henry QUARTLY	55		Shepton Mallet
241	12 Nov	Arnold WARREN	32		Leicester
242	23 Dec	George ANDERSON	59		St Albans

26 February 1914   Walton gaol, Liverpool   *Ellis/ Willis*

229

George BALL   22   *(aka George Sumner)*

Bludgeoned: ***Christina Catherine Bradfield***, 40, on 10 December 1913, in Liverpool, Lancs.
Motive: Financial/ sexual.

Ball, *(b.1892)*, worked as a packer for Bradfield's, tarpaulin manufacturers. On 10 December, he attacked his boss' unmarried sister, Christina, at the company shop in Old Hall Street. He sexually assaulted her, beat her savagely about the head with an iron bar, and then with the help of another employee, Samuel Angeles Elltoft, 18, sewed her body into a sack.

By chance, Walter Eaves was waiting for his girlfriend outside the shop, and was hit when the shop's shutter blew down. His bowler hat saved him from any injury. Elltoft called Ball out, and the murderer gave Eaves two shillings for his inconvenience. Eaves was still waiting when the two men emerged from the shop with a tarpaulin-covered handcart. They wheeled the body to the Leeds-Liverpool canal, and dumped it in the water, weighted down with iron.

The bundle was discovered the next day blocking a lock gate. A medallion round Miss Bradfield's neck identified the victim. Elltoft was arrested the same day, and Ball was tracked down to a hostel on 20 December. He had Miss Bradfield's watch in his possession, and bloodstains on his clothes. Eaves identified the two men, Elltoft being found guilty as an accessory, and sentenced to four years. Ball confessed in the condemned cell.

Read: The Christmas Murders, p10.

| 10 March 1914 | Stafford prison | *Ellis/ Brown* |

230

Josiah DAVIES   **58**   *i*

Strangled: **Martha Hodgkins**, *54, on 4 November 1913, in Wolverhampton, Staffs*
Motive: *Financial.*

Davies, *(b. 1856)*, a 5'2", 10st 7 ironworker, unemployed since August 1913, had been confined for some years in a lunatic asylum, though he had been married and had adult children. He lodged in Wolverhampton with Mrs Hodgkins, who was strangled on her bed at 7am, and discovered by a neighbour five hours later. Her purse had been emptied.

The case against Davies was very thin. He had scratches on his hands which he claimed were caused by blackberrying. Davies was hard up but not desperate - his sons helped him out with money. He confessed however, after two months' solitary confinement, to strangling Mrs Hodgkins, and that was enough to convince the jury of his guilt within eight minutes.

Read: Diary of a Hangman, p228.

| 12 March 1914 | Exeter gaol | *Ellis/ Brown* |

231

James HONEYLANDS   **21**

Shot: **Amelia Bradfield**, *18, on 18 October 1913, in Plymouth, Devon.*
Motive: *Sexual rivalry; drink related.*

Honeylands, *(b. 1893)*, was a naval stoker from a family of seafarers. He lodged with Mrs Perry and her daughter, whose husband was in the navy. James and Amelia became romantically involved, but Honeylands had become enraged with jealousy. After arguing with both Amelia and her mother in a pub, he later, in a drunken rage, shot her twice with his revolver. A third shot missed its target. A postman ran after the killer and brought him down.

James confessed his intention to kill, and the jury saw premeditation in his having taken the gun ashore, though it made a strong recommendation to mercy. Honeylands, 5'11" and 11 st, faced the scaffold phlegmatically and died with a smile and a cigarette on his lips.

Read: And May The Lord Have Mercy On Your Soul

24 March 1914	Durham gaol	*Ellis/ Willis*

232

Robert UPTON   **50**

Cut throat of:	***Charles Gribbin**, 64, on 21 December 1913, in Jarrow, Co Durham.*
Motive:	*Sexual rivalry; drink related.*

Elizabeth Burden, 40, had separated from her husband in 1893. Since 1910 she had been housekeeper and mistress to Charles Gribbin in Jarrow, and from March 1912 had a similar arrangement with Robert Upton, *(b.1864)*, a dock labourer, staying with him and his son Joseph, 14, at weekends. Though Gribbin and Upton got on well when sober, the two rivals argued terribly when drunk.

On 9 November 1913, Upton had stormed into Gribbin's house and half-choked him, after which the older man proposed that they should all live together. With other rooms in Gribbin's house sub-let, Burden, Gribbin, Upton and his son all shared a single bedroom until, less than a month later, Elizabeth tired of the situation and left, announcing that she planned to marry Jack Bloy, 54. Both men got considerably drunk on 20 December, and when Upton returned home at 3.30am his son and Gribbin were asleep on the same bed. Blaming Gribbin for driving Elizabeth away, Upton cut his rival's throat, slashing his own as his son ran for a policeman.

The jury rejected a plea of insanity after six minutes, and Upton remained silent during his time in the condemned cell.

Read: Master Detective, Aug 97.

233

Edgar Louis BINDON   **22**   *Welsh*

Shot: ***Maud Mulholland**, 19, on 9 November 1913, in Cardiff,
Glamorgan.*
Motive: *Sexual rivalry.*

Bindon, *(b.1892),* was a footballer with Cardiff City FC, one of their
up-and-coming new talents who had recently been promoted to the first team.
He and his girlfriend Maud, a shop assistant, had been courting for some
time when she told him in the autumn of 1913 that it was all over.

Bindon blamed her ship's captain father, but his jealousy reached
uncontrollable levels when Maud found another suitor.   Bindon received
treatment for depression, and wrote to his mother telling her he would kill
Maud and himself. He went to Maud's house with a revolver on 4 November,
but her father took it from him. He bought another the next day.

One evening he waited for Maud, who was walking home alone at
11pm having been out with the new boyfriend. Bindon shot her five times,
and sat cradling her in the street for five minutes before finding a policeman to
whom he confessed. He later said that he had intended to kill himself, but had
a strong desire to see his mother again.

At his trial in March 1914, the court was told that Bindon's father
had died of a brain disorder, but suggestions of insanity were rejected, though
the jury recommended mercy.   That and a 32,000 signature petition were
dismissed.

Read: Master Detective Summer Special 90.

234

Joseph SPOONER   **42**

Cut throat of: ***Elizabeth Alice Spooner**, 3, his daughter, on 26
February 1914, in Liverpool, Lancs.*
Motive: *Vengeance.*

When Spooner, *(b.1872)*, separated from his wife, Catherine, in 1908, he attempted suicide. They split again in December 1913, and he took it just as bad that time. She moved to her sister with her six children, and took out a summons, under which Spooner was told to pay his wife 12/- a week.

On 26 February, Catherine took out a second summons, for her husband had paid her a total of only six shillings. He spoke to Catherine in the street at 9.30am, then went to collect his young daughter from an aunt, and took her to a sweetshop. He walked her home at 11.45am, and cut her throat in the back yard of his sister-in-law's house. He was arrested nearby at 2.20pm, and told officers he did not know what had made him do it.

Read: And May The Lord Have Mercy On Your Soul

16 June 1914	Winchester prison	*Ellis/ T.Pierrepoint*

235

Walter James WHITE   22

Shot:	***Frances Priscilla Hunter**, 24, on 29 April 1914, in Swindon, Wilts.*
Motive:	*Vengeance.*

White, *(b.1892)*, and Frances, a hotel maid, were very much in love, and were planning marriage, so they went to pay a call on her brother. When they arrived, the landlady would not allow Frances into the house, and when White went back alone, the woman explained that Frances had been living in sin with another man. Walter was devastated, and wrote to his mother and Frances' father telling them that his life was ruined.

At 6pm, he went to the hotel where his fiancee worked, and the pair talked in the back yard, where Frances confirmed that the allegations were true. When White took out his gun, Frances told him, 'For God's sake, do it then', and kissed him, before he blasted her three times. White then asked the hotel manager to call the police.

Read: And May The Lord Have Mercy On Your Soul

28 July 1914 Lewes prison, Sussex *Ellis/ T.Pierrepoint*

236

Herbert BROOKER 32

Cut throat of: *Ada Stone, 29, on 25 April 1914, near Horley, Sussex.*
Motive: *Vengeance; drink related.*

Brooker, *(b.1882),* had served in the navy for twelve years as a gunner, sailing on the *Lusitania* among other vessels. He lived in North Woolwich and worked at the Royal Albert Dock as a lock-keeper. It was there at Christmas 1913 that he had met waitress Ada Stone, married but separated. On Cup Final day, wearing their Burnley colours, they took a ride from London Bridge to Horley, where, both rather drunk, they were seen laughing together. They then boarded the 7.20pm Brighton train, and as the train pulled out, a passenger in the next carriage heard a scream and, leaning out, saw Brooker, 5'7", with a knife.

He had stabbed Ada once in each breast and in the back, and had cut her throat. He leapt out as the train pulled into Three Bridges station, and eight men had to hold him and tie him up until police arrived. Brooker had been carrying the knife with him for a week and problems with marrying seemed the most likely cause of an argument.

The jury added a recommendation to mercy on account of Brooker's previous good character and national service.

Read: Murderous Sussex, p39.

11 August 1914 Lewes prison, Sussex *Ellis*

237

Percy Evelyn CLIFFORD 32

Shot: *Maud Clifford, 24, his wife, on 7 April 1914, in Brighton, Sussex*
Motive: *To clear impediment; drink related.*

Clifford, *(b.1882),* a former theatrical artiste, had served as an engineer in the Boer war, where his right hand was permanently paralysed. He had been living with a woman for six years before meeting Maud Walton in 1909. She promised to give up her work as a prostitute and the couple married in 1911, living in Brixton.

Clifford found little work, and Maud went back to her old occupation, for which Clifford would beat her. She left him in October 1912. His old girlfriend saw him at Christmas 1913 and later said he had a gun and was going to kill himself and his wife because he had no money.

Maud agreed to a trip to Brighton the following April, and Clifford booked a room for three days. On their last night the two got very drunk, and continued to drink whisky the following morning. At about 12.30pm, still in bed, Clifford shot his wife in the temple, and then fired the revolver into his own head. He remained unconscious in hospital for eight days. When he was fit enough to stand trial, the jury took 25 minutes to condemn him to death.

His was the tenth and last execution in Lewes.

Read: Murderous Sussex, p46

4 November 1914	Chelmsford gaol	*Ellis*

238

<u>Charles FREMBD</u>   **71**   *German*

Cut throat of:	**Louisa Frembd**, *52, his wife, on 28 August 1914, in Leytonstone, Essex.*
Motive:	*To clear impediment.*

Born in Germany in 1843, Frembd had lived in the USA before coming to Britain in 1860. He owned a grocery shop in Leytonstone and after the death of his first wife, met Louisa, a widow, in Yarmouth whom he married in May 1913. He claimed his wife had a terrible temper and nagged him constantly.

At 2am in bed, he cut her throat and then his own. Their live-in domestic servant, Dorothy Woolmore, discovered them the next morning. Patched up in hospital, he claimed to have no recollection of the murder, and doctors confirmed evidence of dementia, but the jury's recommendation to mercy was ignored.

Frembd fainted on the scaffold an instant before the drop. He was the oldest person to hang in Great Britain in the twentieth century.

Read: And May The Lord Have Mercy On Your Soul.

239

John Francis EAYRES   59

Cut throat of: *Sarah Ann Eayres, 53, his wife, on 22 August 1914, in Peterborough, Northants.*
Motive: *To clear impediment.*

     Eayres, *(b.1855)*, a 14 st 7 tinsmith, married Sarah in June 1911. Her first husband had died in 1905, leaving her with three children. On 22 August, they had a fight in the street, but had then gone into Peterborough together.
     At 9.30pm Eayres killed his wife because, he said, she had tried him beyond endurance. After she had thrown a sugar basin at him, he cut her throat with a razor in the back yard. The razor was found in his jacket pocket in the house. He then cut his own throat with a penknife, and was found lying next to his wife by the outside toilet. He claimed to have no recollection of the murder.

     Read: And May The Lord Have Mercy On Your Soul

240

Henry QUARTLY   55

Shot: *Henry Pugsley, 59, on 3 June 1914, in Porlock, Somerset.*
Motive: *Vengeance.*

     Quartly, *(b.1859)*, a builder, lived with his sister next door to Henry Pugsley, a fishmonger, and his wife, Fanny. For some time a feud had developed between the two, reaching a head in October 1913, when Pugsley complained to the police that Quartly had barged into his house, swearing at Fanny and shouting to have sex with her. The case against him was dismissed when Quartly explained that Fanny had sexually assaulted her young lodger, Thomas Heard, a friend of Quartly. He had told her she should find a man of her own age.
     When another summons against him arrived on 3 June, Quartly's patience snapped. As Pugsley stood outside his cottage, Quartly fired at him with his shotgun, hitting him in the shoulder, and injuring Alice Middleton, 18, who was nearby.

Pugsley was helped to his house, where he died shortly after the arrival of a doctor. When PC Joseph Greedy arrived he heard a shot from inside Quartly's house. He discovered the culprit in an alcove in his bedroom, where he had tried to shoot himself, but had missed! Quartly pleaded guilty, refusing all attempts to persuade him otherwise. His trial lasted only 12 minutes, and his only regret was not having shot Fanny.

Read: True Crime, July 97

12 November 1914   Leicester prison   *Ellis/ Willis*

241

Arnold WARREN   **32**

Cut throat of: ***James Warren***, *2, his son, on 10 July 1914, in Leicester.*
Motive: *Vengeance.*

Warren, *(b.1882)*, married Ethel in 1906, but he was a heavy gambler, which caused much friction with his wife. She left him when he hit her on 22 May 1914. He was summonsed, bound over, and had to pay his wife 10/- a week towards his son's upkeep. On 10 July, he bumped into Ethel, and told her that he had quit his job, and was putting all his money on a horse. He would kill himself if it lost.

Ethel worked, and their son James was looked after by Warren's mother during the day. At 5.30pm, Warren met his son on his way home to mother, and took him to the recreation fields. They were seen lying on the grass together, for Warren had cut little James' throat, and then taken laudanum. They were found at 8.10pm. The horse had lost.

Read: And May The Lord Have Mercy On Your Soul

242

George ANDERSON   59

Cut throat of: ***Harriet Ann Whybrow**, 31, his step-daughter, on 30 June 1914, in Waltham Cross, Herts.*
Motive: *Vengeance.*

Anderson, *(b.1855)*, married in 1912, but his wife died in June 1914, though he continued to live with her daughter from a previous marriage, Harriet, and her husband, James Whybrow. Anderson and Harriet had, however, developed a sexual relationship, and she was seen sitting on his lap. Arguments with James developed, and on 27 June, Anderson had threatened James and Harriet with an axe. The police were called, and Anderson was put out of the house, sleeping in an outhouse.

He apologised for his behaviour on 29 June, but the following day, after James had left for work at the gunpowder factory, George was back in the house by 10am, drinking beer, with Harriet on his knee. They argued from 1pm to 3pm, and continued in the street, where Anderson cut her throat with a knife. He then went to a pub, where he was arrested. The jury decided his fate in 17 minutes.

Read: And May The Lord Have Mercy On Your Soul

1914 Execution by Firing Squad

6 November 1914   Tower of London

Carl Hans LODY   **39**   *German*

Crime: **Espionage.**

Lody, *(b.1875)*, arrived from the USA at Newcastle on 27 August 1914, and moved to Edinburgh. Ship movements and dockyard security were of primary interest to him. Telegrams he sent to Stockholm were intercepted by MI5, who observed him as he moved on to Rosyth, London, back to Edinburgh and on to Liverpool. He was arrested in Dublin on 2 October 1914.

Read: Shot at the Tower.

1914 Army Executions Overseas

Four English servicemen were executed in France by firing squad:

8 Sep	Thomas J Highgate, 19, of Kent, for desertion
26 Sep	George Ward, 20, of Berkshire, for cowardice
27 Oct	Edward Tanner, 33, of Wiltshire, for desertion
19 Dec	Archibald Browne, 26, of Essex, for desertion

for desertion   3
for cowardice   1

1915

total: **10**

243	15 Jul	Robert ROSENTHAL	22	American	Wandsworth
244	10 Aug	Walter MARRIOTT	24		Wakefield
245	11 Aug	Frank STEELE	28		Durham
246	13 Aug	George SMITH	43		Maidstone
247	17 Aug	George MARSHALL	45		Wandsworth
248	16 Nov	William REEVE	42		Bedford
249	7 Dec	John THORNLEY	26		Walton
250	7 Dec	Young HILL	28	American	Walton
251	22 Dec	Harry THOMPSON	55		Wakefield
252	29 Dec	John McCARTNEY	40		Wakefield

15 July 1915   Wandsworth prison, London   *T.Pierrepoint/ Baxter*

243

Robert ROSENTHAL   **22**   *American*

Crime: **Espionage**

Rosenthal, *(b.1883),* an American of German parentage, had travelled widely in England, and upon arrival in Copenhagen, passed details of British ship movements in Edinburgh, Portsmouth and Hull, to his masters in Holland. His messages were intercepted, and Rosenthal was kept under observation when he returned to the UK. He was arrested in Newcastle, trying to arrange a passage to Bergen. At his trial, held in camera, he named the American, Melton Feder, as a German spy in Berlin. He was the only first world war spy to suffer execution by hanging.

Read: And May The Lord Have Mercy On Your Soul

10 August 1915   Wakefield prison   *T.Pierrepoint/ Willis*

244

Walter MARRIOTT   **24**

Stabbed: ***Nellie Marriott****, 23, his wife, on 5 June 1915, in Barnsley, W.Yorks.*

177

Motive: *Vengeance.*

      Marriott, *(b.1891),* claimed that in an argument, his wife went for him with a bottle and a bread knife. Whatever the cause, he stabbed her in the neck with the knife, with a force sufficient to penetrate her body by 15cm, piercing her lung. He was found trying to rouse Nellie, saying, 'Speak to me. What have I done to my lass?'

Read: And May The Lord Have Mercy On Your Soul

11 August 1915   Durham gaol   *Ellis*

245

<u>Frank STEELE</u>   **28**

Cut throat of: **Nora Barrett**, *21, on 16 May 1915, in Gateshead, Co Durham*
Motive: Sexual rivalry; drink related

      When Nora Barrett, 'Nana' to her acquaintances, and previously known as Nana Spoors, moved in with Frank Steele, *(b.1887),* in January 1915, she gave up her prostitution, for she had a newly born child. She got on well with Frank, despite the early death of the baby and the fact that they both drank heavily, until a letter she had written to the baby's father, Joseph Bell was returned unopened.
      Steele read it and realised Nana still had affection for her previous lover. As she lay in bed sleeping one Sunday morning, Steele cut her throat with a razor, then cut himself superficially on the arm and neck. He told a friend that day, and his mother the next, what he had done, but neither believed him through his drunkenness. His mother finally alerted police on 18 May. The jury took 90 minutes to decide that drink was no excuse for murder.

Read: Murderous Tyneside, p120

246

George Joseph SMITH   43

Drowned:	**1 *Bessie Constance Annie Mundy***, *33, on 13 July 1912, in Herne Bay, Kent.*
	2 *Alice Burnham*, *25, on 12 December 1913, in Blackpool, Lancs.*
	3 *Margaret Elizabeth Lofty*, *38, on 18 December 1914, in London N6.*
Motive:	Financial.

Smith was born in Roman Road, London E3 in 1872, and by the age of seven, he was serving eight years in borstal for petty theft. A lover of poetry and a piano player, he served three years with the Northamptonshire Regiment before receiving a one-year jail sentence for handling stolen goods.

In 1897, aged 25, he became a baker in Leicester, and there, as George Love, married Caroline Thornhill, 18. She pilfered from her employers for him, for which she received a year in jail, he served two, but not until he had bigamously married another woman. Caroline left for Canada in 1899. She remained his only legal wife. Out of prison in 1902, he returned to his second wife, stole her money, and fled. He repeated this performance with several brides over the next six years, until in 1908, he became an antiques dealer in Bristol. In June of that year, in Worthing, he married and deserted widow Florence Wilson, and on 30 July, aged 26, married Edith Mabel Pegler, 28. She had answered his advertisement for a housekeeper, and this became his steadiest relationship.

In 1909, as George Rose, he married Sarah Freeman in Southampton, relieving her of £350 before deserting her. With this money, he and Edith set up a new house together in Southend. In August 1910, at 28, he married Beatrice (Bessie) Mundy, 31, in Weymouth, using the name Henry Williams. He could only manage to get £135 out of her before he left, blaming her in a letter for passing him a venereal disease. He and Edith moved around from Southend to Bristol to London, explaining his absences and new money on business successes.

He was reconciled with Bessie after a chance meeting in March 1912, living with her in Herne Bay. It again proved hard to get at her money, and then he decided on murder. They made out wills in each other's favour, then he drowned her in the bath in July 1912, saying that she had been prone to fits. Though the will was contested, he made £2500 from it. By now he owned seven houses in Bristol. On 31 October 1913, at 31, he married private nurse Alice Burnham, 25, in Southsea. He got £100 from her, and insured her life for £500. Six weeks later, he drowned her in the bath in a Blackpool flat. In September 1914 he married maidservant Alice Reavil in Bournemouth, stealing £100 and jewellery before leaving.

Three months later, as John Lloyd, he married clergyman's daughter Margaret Lofty, 38, in Bath. She had made out her will to him, and he had insured her life for £700. The couple moved to their new home in Highgate, London, where he drowned her on 18 December. This time, the case featured widely in newspaper reports, and a relative of Alice Burnham, and the Blackpool landlady separately reported similarities to the police.

Smith was arrested on 1 February 1915. During the nine-day trial it was revealed that each time he had murdered, Smith, 5'7" and 11 st 7, had slipped the women beneath the bathwater by the legs with one arm, and held their heads under with the other, returning from buying eggs or tomatoes to 'find' them drowned.

Each time the coroner's verdict had been misadventure. Smith constantly made outbursts in court, but the jury took only 22 minutes to find him guilty. Ironically, Miss Pegler reported that Smith himself had taken only one bath in the six years she had known him. Smith cried openly in the condemned cell, protesting his innocence to the end. He had to be supported on the scaffold, so terrified was he. After perhaps a dozen marriages, Smith's only legal wife, Caroline, remarried the day after his execution.

Read: George Joseph Smith

17 August 1915   Wandsworth prison, London   *Ellis/ Brown*

247

George MARSHALL   45

Cut throat of: ***Alice Anderson***, *45, on 3 July 1915, in London SE17.*
Motive: *Sexual rivalry.*

Marshall, *(b.1870)*, a barman, and Alice Anderson were both lodgers at the same Walworth house, and because she would sometimes tidy up for him, or prepare his meals, he believed she was his woman, though there was no romantic involvement on her part. He became jealous at the thought that Alice may be having an affair with an insurance agent, and when he came in from work at 11pm, and found his bed crumpled, he thought Alice and her lover had been using it. He went to her room and cut her throat as she lay there. Alice staggered out of the room and fell downstairs.

Read: And May The Lord Have Mercy On Your Soul

248

William Benjamin REEVE   42

Shot: *Harriet Reeve, 40, his wife, on 5 July 1915, in Leighton*
                   Buzzard, Beds.
Motive: *Vengeance; drink related.*

Reeve, *(b.1873)*, had been unemployed for some time, and spent much of his time drinking, and becoming violent when he had had too much. Shortly after his wife, Harriet, returned from work, at 6.30pm, Reeve got home after a nine-hour binge. After their 16-year old son went out to the cinema, an argument started, and as Harriet sat in the chair, Reeve blasted away her lower face with two barrels of his shotgun. He then cut his own throat and staggered out into the street, where only the quick action of a police officer saved his life, albeit for only another three months. Reeve claimed the gun had gone off accidentally.

Read: And May The Lord Have Mercy On Your Soul

249

John James THORNLEY   48

Cut throat of: *Frances Johnson, 24, on 19 September, in Macclesfield,*
                       Cheshire.
Motive: *Vengeance.*

Thornley, *(b.1865)*, a railway station lamp-man in Macclesfield, was engaged to his foreman porter's daughter, Frances, a ring spinner in a cotton mill. Frances was, perhaps, too vivacious for the moodier Thornley and, though they had been together over two years, the engagement was broken off. Obsessed, the heavily tattooed Thornley began to frequently follow Frances wherever she might go, and had to be warned off by her father.

One night at 3am, when her parents were away, Thornley, 5'6" and 11 st, broke into Frances' home and cut her throat as she lay in her bed. Her friend, Mary Warren, who was staying with her in the next bedroom, heard her screams but was too terrified to intervene. Thornley went downstairs and

wrote several notes confessing his guilt, before throwing himself, ineffectively, in a canal. He was caught on farmland seven miles away two days later.
Hanged with Young Hill, he died silently and bravely.

Read: *Diary of a Hangman, p172.*

7 December 1915   Walton gaol, Liverpool   *Ellis/ Brown*

250

Young HILL   **28**   *American*   *black*

Cut throat of: ***James Crawford**, 25, on 26 July 1915, in Liverpool, Lancs.*
Motive: *Vengeance.*

Hill, *(b.1887),* was a muleteer on the liner *Antillian* which had sailed from New Orleans to Liverpool. After docking in Liverpool on 26 July, Hill had fetched a bucket of water for a sick crewman in the fo'castle. At 7.30pm, he became enraged when James Crawford, a fellow black muleteer, complained the bucket was dirty and went to fetch another. Hill, 5'5" and 12 st, slit Crawford's throat from behind with his razor, and cut him across the back. Crawford died quickly, his jugular severed.
Hanged with John Thornley, on the scaffold he let out a blood-curdling scream and fainted.

Read: *Diary of a Hangman, p172.*

22 December 1915   Wakefield prison   *T.Pierrepoint/ Taylor*

251

Harry THOMPSON   **55**

Cut throat of: ***Alice Kaye**, 27, on 6 November 1915, in Honley, W.Yorks.*
Motive: *Sexual rivalry.*

Thompson, *(b.1860),* had been in a relationship with Alice Kaye for two years, believing she was single. The man whom Thompson had met and

182

believed was Alice's brother was, in fact, her husband, mostly away serving in the army.

By November 1915, Alice was pregnant, and Thompson discovered the truth. The pair argued and Thompson cut Alice's throat, leaving her for dead in the kitchen. Her aunt, Mrs Donkersley, who was staying with Alice during her confinement, forced the door the following morning to discover the body. Thompson approached a policeman on 8 November and confessed all. Letters from Alice to Harry proved he had indeed been misled. The jury deliberated for 30 minutes.

Read: And May The Lord Have Mercy On Your Soul

29 December 1915   Wakefield prison   *T.Pierrepoint/ Baxter*

252

John William McCARTNEY   40   *(aka Harry MacDonald)*

Cut throat of: ***Charlotte Kent**, 29, on 9 September 1915, in Pocklington, W.Yorks.*
Motive: *Vengeance.*

McCartney, *(b.1875),* a private in the East Yorkshire regiment, had married in 1899, but nevertheless took Charlotte Kent for his second bride, the pair living in York lodgings in the names of Harry and Hilda Bertha MacDonald. McCartney became convinced that while he was away on service, Charlotte was seeing other men. He attacked her on 1 August, and their landlady forbade him from staying the night. When he took leave again in September, he came to the house, but Charlotte turned him away. McCartney's response was to cut her throat and then his own. The jury took ten minutes to determine his guilt.

Read: And May The Lord Have Mercy On Your Soul

1915 Executions by Firing Squad

23 June 1915   Tower of London

Carl Frederick MULLER   58   *Latvian*

Crime: ***Espionage***

Muller, *(b.1857),* an ethnic German from Latvia, spoke five languages. He was arrested in London on 2 February, at lodgings he shared with a British woman, after letters in invisible ink were intercepted by censors en route to Rotterdam. A postcard incriminated John Hahn, 28, a Briton, and both men were charged with spying. As one of the accused was a British subject, the pair received trial by jury in open court. It was decided that Hahn had been led astray by Muller, and he received a seven-year sentence.

Read: Shot at the Tower

30 July 1915   Tower of London

Haicke Marinus Petrius JANSSEN   29   *Dutch*
Willem Johannes ROOS   33   *Dutch*

Crime: ***Espionage***

Janssen, *(b.1886),* was arrested on 29 May, after coded telegrams to the Hague were intercepted by censors. Janssen had travelled from Hull to London and Southampton. Further telegrams from Edinburgh by his accomplice, Roos, *(b.1882),* were intercepted. Roos attempted suicide by punching through a window, and entered a plea of insanity. The two men, who had posed as cigar salesmen, were tried in camera.

Read: Shot at the Tower

10 September 1915   Tower of London
17 September 1915

Ernst Waldemar MELIN   49   *Swedish*
Augusto Alfredo ROGGEN   34   *Uruguayan*

Crime: ***Espionage***

Melin, *(b.1865),* a wealthy Swede and former drug-addict, had arrived in England in January 1915. He was arrested in London after censors intercepted a letter in invisible ink from Rotterdam, on 15 April, which contained a £50 payment. Letters from the same company led to the arrest of Roggen, *(b.1881),* in Luss on Loch Lomond. Born in Uruguay to a German father, he had a pistol and invisible ink in his possession. The two were tried together, in camera, and though there was little hard evidence against Roggen, both were sentenced to be shot, the executions taking place one week apart.

Read: Shot at the Tower

19 October 1915   Tower of London

Fernando BUSCHMAN   25   *Brazilian*

Crime: ***Espionage***

Buschman, *(b.1890),* born in France, of a German father and Brazilian mother, had married in 1912 and had a wife in Dresden. He was arrested on 5 June, after a telegram he sent from South Kensington to Rotterdam was intercepted by censors. Buschman had been seeking aircraft information in Southampton and Portsmouth, and had documents concerning troop movements and military bases in his possession. He played the violin while awaiting the firing squad.

Read: Shot at the Tower

26 October 1915   Tower of London

George T. BREECKOW   33   *German   (aka G.T.Parker/*
                                                    Reginald Rowland)

Crime: **Espionage**

      Breeckow, *(b.1882),* born in Poland to German parents, but brought up in the US, was arrested after a letter in invisible ink, in the name of Reginald Rowland, from Bloomsbury to The Hague was intercepted by censors. It contained information about ships and defences in Ramsgate. Breeckow's accomplice in Inverness and Edinburgh, Lizzie Wertheim, was arrested on 9 June. Because she was a British subject, the two were tried by jury in open court. The jury considered its verdict for eleven minutes, and decided that Wertheim was under Breeckow's influence, and she was sentenced to ten years. She died five years later in Broadmoor.

      Read: Shot at the Tower

27 October 1915   Tower of London

Irving Guy REIS   55   *American*

Crime: **Espionage**

      Reis, *(b.1860),* born in Chicago to German parents, arrived in Liverpool, on a false passport, from the USA, on 4 July. Posing as a trader in grain, he travelled to Newcastle, Glasgow, Edinburgh, back to Liverpool, and on to London. Letters to Rotterdam were intercepted by censors, and Reis was arrested on 10 August, having booked a passage from Newcastle to Copenhagen. Reis never revealed his true identity, to avoid shame falling upon his wealthy family.

      Read: Shot at the Tower

27 November 1915   Tower of London

<u>Albert MEYER</u>   **23**   *German*   *Jew*

Crime: ***Espionage***

Meyer, *(b.1892),* born it is believed in Constantinople, lived most of his life in London, where he was known in Whitechapel as a con-man. He was arrested at the Oxford Circus home which he shared with his wife, after letters to The Hague, in invisible ink, were intercepted by censors. Meyer died cursing his captors.

Read: Shot at the Tower

1915 Army Executions Overseas

56 servicemen were executed by firing squad

38 English　　　　　　　　*3 Welsh*
7 Scottish　　　　　　　　*1 west African*
7 Irish

12 Jan	J Ball, 20, of London, in France, for desertion, with F Sheffield, 26, of London, for desertion
22 Jan	George W Latham, 23, married, of Lancashire, in France, for desertion
28 Jan	Thomas Cummings, 27, Irish, in France, for desertion, with Albert Smythe, 22, Irish, for desertion
3 Feb	William Scotton, 19, of London, in Belgium, for desertion
6 Feb	Joseph Byers, 17, Scottish, in France, for desertion, with Andrew Evans, Scottish, for desertion
8 Feb	A Pitts, of Warwickshire, in France, for desertion
11 Feb	George H Povey, 23, of Cheshire, in Belgium, for leaving his post
15 Feb	George E Collins, 20, of Lincolnshire, in France, for desertion
15 Feb	**Richard Morgan**, 32, Welsh, a Private, in France, with **William Price**, 41, Welsh, a Lance-Corporal, for the murder of CSM Hugh Hayes, 32, by shooting while drunk, in Bethune
2 Mar	Alfred Atkinson, 24, of Yorkshire, in France, for desertion
2 Mar	Thomas Hope, 20, Irish, in Belgium, for desertion
6 Mar	James Briggs, Scottish, in France, for desertion
6 Mar	Ernest Kirk, 24, of Yorkshire, in France, for desertion
7 Mar	John Duncan, Scottish, from Glasgow, in France, for desertion
22 Mar	William Walton, 26, in France, for desertion
9 Apr	Isaac Reid, 20, Scottish, in France, for desertion
20 Apr	Joseph S V Fox, 20, of Chippenham, Wilts, in Belgium, for desertion
20 Apr	William J Irvine, 19, of Lancashire, in France, for desertion
20 Apr	William Jones, in France, for desertion
22 Apr	Major Penn, 21, Welsh, in France, for desertion, with A Troughton, 22, for desertion
25 Apr	John Bell, in France, for desertion
26 Apr	James Kershaw, in France, for desertion
17 May	**Alexander Chisholm**, 31, acting Corporal, in France, for the murder by shooting of Lance-Corporal Robert Lewis in Bailleul.
4 Jun	Oliver W Hodgetts, 19, of Worcestershire, in France, for cowardice
10 Jun	George E Roe, 19, of Yorkshire, in Belgium, for desertion
12 Jun	Herbert H Chase, 21, of Lancashire, in Belgium, for cowardice
21 Jun	Thomas Harris, 21, of Kent, in Belgium, for desertion
24 Jun	Ernest A Beaumont, 27, of Leicestershire, in Belgium, for desertion
1 Jul	William J Turpie, 24, of Surrey, in Belgium, for desertion
2 Jul	Thomas Davis, 21, Irish, at Gallipoli, for quitting his post

16 Jul	W Bellamy, 34, in France, for cowardice
16 Jul	Thomas Docherty, 20, Scottish, in Belgium, for desertion
19 Jul	Fatoma, west African, in Cameroon, for cowardice
21 Jul	Herbert F Burden, 17, of Northumberland, in Belgium, for desertion
26 Jul	Ernest Fellows, 29, married with children, of Worcestershire, in Belgium, for desertion, with
	Bert Hartells, 32, of Worcestershire, for desertion
	Frederick Ives, 30, of Worcestershire, for desertion
	John Robinson, 31, of Worcestershire, for desertion
	Alfred D Thompson, 25, of Worcestershire, for desertion
2 Aug	Evan Fraser, 19, Scottish, in France, for desertion
19 Aug	Louis R Philips, 23, Jewish, of Somerset, in Belgium, for desertion
15 Sep	Peter Sands, 27, Irish from Belfast, in France, for desertion
29 Sep	George Mills, 21, of London, in France, for desertion
29 Sep	James Spencer, in France, for desertion
2 Oct	Alexander Lamb, in Belgium, for desertion
3 Oct	George A Irish, *(aka George Lee),* 30, in France, for desertion, with W Smith, 37, for desertion
15 Nov	**Charles W Knight**, 28, of London, a Private, in Belgium, for the murder by shooting when drunk of Private Alfred Edwards
11 Dec	Harry Salter, 24, of Somerset, at Gallipoli, for desertion
21 Dec	J Graham, 21, Irish, in Belgium, for desertion
27 Dec	Patrick J Downey, 20, Irish, in Gallipoli, for disobedience

for desertion	45	*in France*	32
for cowardice	4	*in Belgium*	20
for murder	4	*in Turkey*	3
for quitting post	2	*in Cameroon*	1
for disobedience	1		

1916

total: **9**

253	1 Jan	Lee KUN	27	*Chinese*	Pentonville
254	8 Mar	Frederick HOLMES	44		Strangeways
255	29 Mar	Reginald HASLAM	25		Strangeways
256	3 Aug	Roger CASEMENT	52	*Irish*	Pentonville
257	16 Aug	William BUTLER	39		Winson Green
258	16 Sep	Daniel SULLIVAN	37	*Irish*	Swansea
259	12 Dec	Frederick BROOKS	28		Exeter
260	19 Dec	James HARGREAVES	54		Strangeways
261	20 Dec	Joseph DEANS	44		Durham

1 January 1916   Pentonville prison, London   *Ellis*

253

Lee KUN   27   *Chinese*

Stabbed: ***Clara Thomas**, on 16 October 1915, in London E14.*
Motive: *Vengeance.*

Clara Thomas liked to call herself Elsie Godard since she separated from her husband. She lived with Kun, *(b.1889),* for a time in Poplar, but then moved nearby to a female friend's home. Kun claimed that Elsie refused to pay him back money that she owed, and one evening, armed with a large knife, called on Elsie and her friend. He led Elsie into the yard by her arm, and then immediately stabbed her a number of times. Elsie's friend beat Kun off with a broomstick, and screamed until help arrived.

Read: And May The Lord Have Mercy On Your Soul

8 March 1916   Strangeways prison, Manchester   *Ellis/ Taylor*

254

Frederick HOLMES   44

Cut throat of: ***Sarah Woodall**, 38, on 8 December 1915, in Manchester, Lancs.*
Motive: *Sexual rivalry*

190

Holmes, *(b.1872)*, had known Sarah Woodall some years, but had gone to Ripon for work when he got a letter from her inviting him to come and live with her. Sarah's husband had left her in 1912 because of her addiction to drink and prostitution, and her violent temper - she had once stabbed him with scissors.

In October 1915 her mother had died and left her £250, and though Holmes took up her offer, within a month she was seeing George Wake, whom she had known eight years, behind his back. Holmes caught Wake at home with Sarah and a fight started. Sarah hit Holmes, 5'7" and 11 st, on the head with a shovel, and he stamped on Wake's chest, before clearing off leaving Sarah and Wake together.

Two days later she kicked Wake out, and she and Holmes took new lodgings to make a fresh start. One morning an argument started, Holmes stating that Sarah attacked him with a razor-the back of his jacket had been cut in such a manner-before he punched her on the nose and cut her throat. He slept that night with the body, and the following day the landlady discovered Sarah.

Holmes was arrested the same day at 5.20pm in the street. The jury considered for thitry minutes.

Read: Murderous Manchester

29 March 1916   Strangeways prison, Manchester   *Ellis*

255

<u>Reginald HASLAM</u>   25

Strangled: ***Isabella Holmes Conway***, *35, on 23 December 1915, in Burnley, Lancs.*
Motive: *Sexual rivalry.*

Haslam, *(b. 1891)*, a labourer, and Conway, a cotton-winder, were lovers, both separated from their spouses. Two days before Christmas, Belle had refused Reg entry to her home, and peeping through the letter-box, he had seen another man. Infuriated, he barged down the door, and the couple began a blazing row. In his rage he strangled her in the lounge and sat her in an armchair.

He confessed to a friend and went and told the Burnley police what he had done. Haslam asked for no reprieve when the jury added a strong recommenation to mercy. He later denied any malice and hoped to the end that he might be spared the rope. He fell to his knees to pray on the scaffold, ending with, 'Lord Jesus, Have Mercy on my Soul'.

Read: Master Detective, Mar 96.

256

Roger David CASEMENT   52   *Irish*

Crime: ***High treason.***

     At 6 ft 4 in, Casement, *(b.1864)*, was a pillar of the British establishment. Born in Dublin, Casement was a British citizen, and worked for the consular service from 1895 till 1913. He gained a high reputation for the work he did in Africa and south America, exposing cruelty and slavery in the Belgian Congo and Peru. He was knighted in 1909 and retired in 1913.

     At the outbreak of the first world war, now devoted to Irish nationalism, he went to Germany, and tried to persuade Irish prisoners to fight for the Kaiser. He failed to get backing from the Germans for an Irish revolt, but managed to secure old weapons taken from Russians. He was caught in Tralee Bay on 20 April 1916, trying to land these arms from a German submarine, and was taken to London.

     To head off sympathy from Ireland and America, and any reprieve by the King, private diaries were circulated, in which Casement revealed homosexual tendencies. The smear campaign was orchestrated largely by the assistant commissioner of the Metropolitan Police, Sir Basil Thompson, who was later himself arrested in Hyde Park for a sexual offence. The smear campaign worked, for Casement, stripped of his knighthood, was condemned as a traitor and pervert. His body was finally removed to Dublin in 1965.

Read: Roger Casement-The Flawed Hero

257

William Allen BUTLER   39

Stabbed:	***Florence Beatrice Butler**, 29, on 20 May 1916, in Birmingham, Warwicks.*
Motive:	*Sexual rivalry.*

Butler,*(b.1874),* a foundry worker, went to lodge with Frances Butler, no relation, in July 1915. He began to court her daughter, Florence, the mother of a nine year old girl. She had been separated from her husband for five years. By the following March Florence was pregnant, and then the arguments started, becoming constant. Butler became partcularly incensed by Florence's relationship ship with an older man, Mr Ireland. When on 16 May Butler kicked Florence, Frances gave him a week's notice.

On 20 May, Florence returned from seeing Ireland, who had given her a crab for her supper. As she sat to eat the meal, Butler took out a penknife and stabbed her in the side, puncturing her heart. She managed to stagger to a neighbour before collapsing. Butler handed himself in to the police, later telling his mother in a letter, 'I am sick of life'. The jury took one hour over its deliberations.

Read: Murderous Birmingham.

258

Daniel SULLIVAN   36   *Irish*

Kicked to death:	***Catherine Sullivan**, 35, his wife, on 8 July 1916, in Dowlais, Glamorgan.*
Motive:	*Sadistic pleasure, drink related.*

Sullivan, *(b. 1880),* had left Co Cork and settled in Dowlais as a coker at the steelworks. He met and married a widowed mother of two in 1909, and two further children were born of the union. A heavy drinker, Sullivan returned home one evening and at 9pm, dragged Catherine from her bed, after punching her, demanding supper. 5'11" and 13 st, he kicked his wife from room to room in his heavy boots. She died the following morning.

Sullivan injured several policemen in being arrested. Big Dan's two children were sent to live with his mother in Ireland, the first two children going to the workhouse.

Sullivan went weeping to the scaffold in a state of near collapse.

Read: And May The Lord Have Mercy On Your Soul.

12 December 1916	Exeter prison	*Ellis/ Willis*

259

Frederick BROOKS   28

Strangled: ***Alice Clara Gregory****, 12, on 19 June 1916, in Plymouth, Devon.*
Motive: *Sexual.*

Brooks, *(b. 1888),* a Private in the Worcester regiment first met the Gregory family when he asked them if they had a room for the night in December 1915. He was late from attending a funeral and could not get back. He stayed with them when he was in Plymouth again in March, and on 14 June. The Gregorys were not to know that Brooks had formed an attatchment to the daughter. Five days later, he returned to Plymouth, and took Alice from school in the morning. She accompanied him across some fields, where he sexually assaulted her, before strangling the young girl. At 4.30pm, he approached a policeman to confess his crime. The jury decided his fate in 35 minutes.

Read: And May The Lord Have Mercy On Your Soul

19 December 1916	Strangeways prison, Manchester	*Ellis/ Willis*

260

James Howarth HARGREAVES   54

Bludgeoned: ***Caroline McGee****, 32, on 9 August 1916, in Ashton-under-Lyne, Lancs.*
Motive: *Vengeance; drink related.*

Hargreaves, *(b. 1862)*, and Caroline McGee, who had become his lover at Christmas 1915 while separated from her husband, lived together with his sister in Ashton-under-Lyne. One evening at 11pm, drunk after an evening in the pub, Caroline had brought two soldiers home together with a woman friend and Hargreaves, himself drunk, ate and drank with them happily, though telling Caroline aside that the men could not stay.

After the guests had departed, and James' sister had retired, Caroline undressed for bed, and an argument developed. She threw a bottle at Hargreaves, 5'5" and 13 st 7, who then beat her to death with a poker. The following day he confessed to a policeman and was arrested.

Having boasted to warders of his strength, by the time he reached the scaffold, "his nerve was wholly gone", according to his executioner.

Read: Murderous Manchester

| **20 December 1916** | Durham gaol | *Ellis/ Brown* |

261

Joseph DEANS   44

| **Bludgeoned:** | **Catherine Convery**, 51, on 7 October 1916, in Monkwearmouth, Co Durham. |
| Motive: | Sexual rivalry. |

Deans, *(b. 1872)*, worked from 1897 as a gold miner in South Africa and served there in the Imperial Light Horse. He returned to England in 1913 with £600 and two pensions totalling £2.10s a week, and met widow Catherine Convery in Monkwearmouth in July 1915.

He lavished his money on her, but became sure she was betraying him with other men. He threatened to kill her many times, and told friends that he loved her but was going to see her off. Having failed to buy a gun, he attacked her with an axe, gashing her head, neck and shoulder. She managed to walk to hospital, but died on 13 October. Deans failed in his attempt to kill himself with a razor. He told police he was glad he had killed her, and that he wanted to die. The jury decided his fate in five minutes.

Read: True Detective Summer Special 98.

1916 Execution by Firing Squad

11 April 1916   Tower of London

Ludovico HURWITZ Y ZENDER   37   *Peruvian*

Crime: **Espionage.**

Zender, *(b.1879),* whose grandparents were Swedish, sent telegrams from Glasgow to Christiania, later Oslo, which were intercepted by censors, but had sailed for Bergen on 28 May, by the time the authorities went to arrest him. When he returned to Britain, on 2 July, he was arrested in Newcastle, and was tried in camera, over two days. He purported to be from a canned fish company in Peru.

Read: Shot at the Tower

1916 Army Executions Overseas

108 servicemen were executed, 107 by firing squad, 1 by hanging:

70 English	2 Australian
12 Scottish	1 Gold Coast
9 Irish	1 S African
8 Canadian	1 American
3 Welsh	1 New Zealand

2 Jan	John Robins, of Wiltshire, at Gallipoli, for disobedience
30 Jan	John J Dennis, 19, of Northamptonshire, in France, for desertion
7 Feb	James G Carr, 21, Welsh, in France, for desertion
15 Feb	John Docherty, 20, in France, for desertion
21 Feb	William Hunter, 20, of Co Durham, in France, for desertion
24 Feb	Alfred E Evesleigh, 27, of Surrey, in Belgium, for desertion, with Robert W Gawler, 20, of Kent, for desertion
24 Feb	John T Jones, 21, of Northamptonshire, in Belgium, for desertion
26 Feb	**Thomas Moore**, 23, a Private, of Yorkshire, at Busseboom, Belgium, for the murder by shooting of Staff Sgt James Pick, a Scot, in Busseboom, on 11 February 1916.
27 Feb	James Crozier, 18, Irish, from Belfast, in France, for desertion
3 Mar	**Arthur Dale**, a Private, Scottish, at Mazingarbe, Belgium, for the murder by shooting of Lance Corporal Sneddon, while drunk, in Belgium on 8 February 1916
11 Mar	C Lewis, Scottish, in Belgium, for desertion
19 Mar	J E McCracken, 19, Irish, in France, for desertion, with J Templeton, Irish, for desertion
20 Mar	Abraham Beverstein, 21, Jewish from London, in France, for desertion, with Harry Martin, of Essex, for desertion
23 Mar	F Charles H Bladen, 26, of Yorkshire, in France, for desertion
26 Mar	F Auger, 25, Canadian, in France, for desertion
3 Apr	*N Mathews, S African Private, **hanged** in Egypt, for an unspecified murder*
14 Apr	Edward Bolton, of Cheshire, in France, for desertion
22 Apr	William L Thompson, 27, of Newcastle, in France, for desertion
26 Apr	Henry Carter, 18, of Middlesex, in France, for desertion
30 Apr	A O'Neil, Welsh, in Belgium, for desertion
5 May	William Watts, 29, of Liverpool, in France, for desertion
6 May	James Cuthbert, 20, of Cheshire, in France, for disobedience
10 May	Arthur H Robinson, of Northumberland, in France, for desertion
12 May	J Fox, Scottish, in France, for striking a superior officer
12 May	John W Hasemore, 23, in Belgium, for disobedience
15 May	Albert E Parker, 35, in Belgium, for desertion
20 May	J Thomas, 44, Welsh, in Belgium, for desertion
22 May	William H Burrell, 21, of Sussex, in Belgium, for desertion

29 May	William W Roberts, 34, of London, in Belgium, for desertion
30 May	James Holland, 31, of Cheshire, in Belgium, for cowardice
30 May	H T W Philips, 24, Scottish, in France, for desertion
4 Jun	James Archibald, 20, Scottish from Edinburgh, in France, for desertion
9 Jun	James W Swaine, married, of Middlesex, in France, for desertion
15 Jun	James Molyneaux, of Lancashire, in France, for desertion
26 Jun	John Jennings, of Lancashire, in France, for desertion, with Griffith Lewis, of Lancashire, for desertion
29 Jun	Frederick Harding, 21, of London, in France, for desertion
2 Jul	**Alexander Butler**, of London, a Trooper, in France, for the murder of a comrade by shooting him 5 times
2 Jul	George Hunter, of Co Durham, in Belgium, for desertion
2 Jul	John Smith, 28, of Lancashire, in France, for desertion
9 Jul	James H Wilson, Irish, in Belgium, for desertion
16 Jul	Joseph Brennan, of Liverpool, in France, for desertion, with J Sloan, of Lancashire, for desertion
22 Jul	Arthur G Earp, of Birmingham, in France, for quitting his post
23 Jul	James Cassidy, Irish, in France, for desertion
25 Jul	Frederick S Arnold, 26, American, in France, for desertion
30 Jul	George H Lawton, 36, of Nottinghamshire, married with 5 children, in France, for cowardice
30 Jul	Bertie McCubbin, 22, of Nottinghamshire, in France, for cowardice
30 Jul	John W Roberts, 20, Canadian, in France, for desertion
4 Aug	Come LaLiberte, 25, Canadian, from Montreal, in in France, for desertion
11 Aug	Frederick Hawthorne, 22, of Staffordshire, in France, for cowardice
11 Aug	William B Nelson, 24, of Co Durham, in Belgium, for desertion
17 Aug	Allan Murphy, 27, Scottish, in France, for desertion
17 Aug	Jesse Wilton, 40, of Nottinghamshire, in in France, for quitting his post
23 Aug	E J Reynolds, Canadian, in France, for desertion
24 Aug	Peter Giles, of Northumberland, in France, for desertion
25 Aug	**B De Fehr**, Canadian, a driver, in France, for the murder of his sgt-major, by shooting him in the back
25 Aug	Frank Hughes, 28, of New Zealand, in France, for desertion
26 Aug	J Higgins, Scottish, in France, for desertion
28 Aug	John Bennett, 19, of Hampshire, in Belgium, for cowardice
5 Sep	Herbert Crimmins, 32, of Bradford, in France, for desertion, with Arthur Wild, 24, for desertion
12 Sep	James A Anderson, 30, of Manchester, in France, for cowardice
13 Sep	Charles Depper, 30, of Berkshire, in France, for desertion
15 Sep	Joseph Carey, Irish, in France, for desertion
15 Sep	Albert Rickman, 27, Irish, in Belgium, for desertion
16 Sep	James A Haddock, 32, of Sheffield, in France, for desertion
18 Sep	Peter Black, Scottish, in Belgium, for desertion
22 Sep	Edward A Card, 21, of London, in Belgium, for desertion
28 Sep	Aziberi Frafra, of the Gold Coast, in German E Africa, for casting away his arms

1 Oct	**Francis Murray**, Scottish, a Private, at Noeux-les-Mines, near Lens, France, for 2 unspecified murders
2 Oct	John J Sweeney, 37, Australian, in France, for desertion
3 Oct	Thomas Grant Hamilton, 22, in France, for striking a superior officer, with
	James Mullany, for striking a superior officer
18 Oct	Albert Botfield, 28, of Staffordshire, in Belgium, for cowardice
18 Oct	Harry T Farr, 23, of Yorkshire, in France, for cowardice
25 Oct	Richard Stevenson, 23, of Lancashire, in Belgium, for desertion
27 Oct	Henry Palmer, of Northumberland, in France, for desertion
29 Oct	John Braithwaite, 33, Australian, in France, for mutiny, with
	William E Lewis, 30, for mutiny
29 Oct	Elsworth Young, 19, Canadian, in France, for desertion
1 Nov	Alfred Leonard Jefferies, of Somerset, in France, for desertion
2 Nov	Bernard McGeehan, Irish, in Belgium, for desertion
4 Nov	Robert Loveless Barker, 21, of London, in France, for cowardice
4 Nov	Henry McDonald, 32, of Lancashire, in France, for desertion
6 Nov	John McQuade, Scottish, from Glasgow, in France, for desertion
14 Nov	William G Hunt, 20, of Manchester, in France, for desertion
15 Nov	Alfred T Ansted, 29, in France, for desertion
15 Nov	Hugh Flynn, Scottish, in France, for desertion
21 Nov	Henry H Kerr, Canadian, from Montreal, in France, for desertion
21 Nov	William A Moon, 20, of Cheshire, in France, for desertion
23 Nov	George E Hughes, of Lancashire, in France, for desertion
25 Nov	William H Randle, of Nottinghamshire, in France, for desertion
25 Nov	Reginald T Tite, 27, of Sussex, in Belgium, for cowardice
1 Dec	Albert Ingham, 24, of Manchester, in France, for desertion, with
	Alfred Longshaw, 21, married, of Manchester, for desertion
1 Dec	William H Simmonds, 23, of Middlesex, in Belgium, for desertion
4 Dec	John Cameron, of Northumberland, in France, for desertion
7 Dec	John M Higgins, 24, Canadian, in France, for desertion
7 Dec	Samuel McBride, Irish, in Belgium, for desertion
9 Dec	Ernest Beeby, in France, for desertion
9 Dec	Harry Poole, of Yorkshire, in France, for desertion
10 Dec	Eric Skeffington Poole, 31, of Yorkshire, in Belgium, for desertion
26 Dec	Charles W F Skilton, 20, in France, for desertion
28 Dec	Peter Cairnie, Scottish, in France, for desertion

for desertion	81		*in France*	78
for cowardice	10		*in Belgium*	27
for murder	6		*in German E Africa*	1
for striking officer	3		*in Egypt*	1
for disobedience	3		*in Turkey*	1
for quitting post	2			
for mutiny	2			
for casting arms	1			

1916 Executions in Ireland

3 May 1916 Dublin

Shot by firing squad

Patrick Henry PEARSE **37**
Tom CLARKE
Thomas MacDONAGH

4 May 1916 Dublin

Shot by firing squad

Joseph PLUNKETT
Edward DALY
William PEARSE
Michael O'HANRAHAN

5 May 1916 Dublin

Shot by firing squad

John McBRIDE

8 May 1916 Dublin

Shot by firing squad

Eamonn CEANNT
Michael MALLIN
Con COLBERT
Sean HEUSTON

9 May 1916   Cork

Shot by firing squad

Thomas KENT

12 May 1916   Dublin

Shot by firing squad

James CONNOLLY   48
Sean MacDIARMADA

Crime: **Treason**

       The 15 included seven who were signatories of the Declaration of an Irish republic and who had occupied Dublin's General Post Office on Easter Monday, reading the proclamation from its steps. The re-taking of the GPO by the British cost 450 lives, 132 of them police and soldiers. The main protagonists were rounded up within a week, and were among 90 people sentenced to death. Public outrage at the first fifteen executions spared the remainder, including Eamonn de Valera and Countess Markiewicz.

       Patrick Pearse, *(b.1879)*, was the son of an English father and Irish mother. Interested in Irish history from an early age, he planned the Easter uprising as part of the Irish Republican Brotherhood. He was chosen as president of the provisional government and as commander of its forces. His brother Willie was shot the following day.

       Connolly was born in Edinburgh in 1868 of poor Irish parents. He served in the British army, then worked as a carter, becoming involved in trade unionism. He went to Ireland at the age of 28 and formed the Socialist Republican Party. Returning from seven years in the USA in 1910, he started to organise strikes, and commanded the forces which seized the GPO. Severely wounded in the assault, he was executed sitting in a chair.

       Kent was arrested during mopping-up operations, after his family had been involved in their own actions against police. Plunkett had married his wife Grace in prison the evening before his execution.

      Read: Ireland since the famine.

1917

total: *10*

262	17 Mar	William ROBINSON	26		Pentonville
263	21 Mar	Thomas CLINTON	28	*Welsh*	Strangeways
264	27 Mar	John THOMPSON	43		Armley
265	29 Mar	Leo O'DONNELL	26		Winchester
266	10 Apr	Alec BAKERLIS	24	*Greek*	Cardiff
267	18 Apr	Robert GADSBY	65		Armley
268	16 May	Thomas MCGUINESS	26	*Scottish*	Duke Street
269	16 Aug	William HODGSON	34		Walton
270	18 Dec	William CAVANAGH	29	*Scottish*	Newcastle
271	19 Dec	Thomas COX	59		Shrewsbury

17 March 1917   Pentonville prison, London   *Ellis/ Baxter*

262

William James ROBINSON   26

Stabbed:	*Alfred Williams, 35, on 26 November 1916, in London WC2.*
Motive:	*Financial; drink related.*

Robinson, *(b.1891),* was a former soldier whose war wounds left him with one leg 4 inches shorter than the other. He and John Gray noticed the Canadian soldier, Alfred Williams, with a woman in a pub in Upper St Martins Lane. Following Williams outside, the two men set upon him and he was stabbed behind the ear. Robinson denied that the £27 the Canadian had been passed in the pub was the motive, claiming that he mistook Williams for someone he had had an argument with the previous day, and that he had not intended to kill.

He wrote that he deserved the sentence, but later denied any recollection of having written it. His accomplice had his conviction and 3-year sentence for manslaughter quashed after Robinson's execution.

Read: Diary of a Hangman, p194.

263

Thomas CLINTON   28   *Welsh*

Shot: **Henry Lynch**, *39, on 13 January 1917, in Barrow-in-Furness, Lancs.*
Motive: *Vengeance.*

Clinton, *(b.1889)*, for six months a private in the Welsh Fusiliers, had developed a grudge and a hatred for his sergeant-major, Henry Lynch, who had served with distinction since 1895, and had been wounded in the war. Lynch had Clinton charged with being drunk and disorderly in November, for which the private served seven days and was fined.

For two months, Clinton planned his revenge. One Saturday at 3.25pm, after Lynch had refused permission for Clinton to take his missed lunch, the younger man returned to his superior's office, and with two others present, shot Lynch as he sat writing at his desk. The rifle bullet having hit him in the neck, Lynch died within five minutes. Clinton claimed that the gun had gone off accidentally, but the jury took 20 minutes to decide otherwise.

Read: Master Detective, Oct 98

264

John William THOMPSON   26

Cut throat of: **Lily Tindale**, *13, on 15 February 1917, in Molescroft, E.Yorks.*
Motive: *Sexual.*

Thompson, *(b.1891)*, was a shepherd attached to a farm near Beverley, where Lily Tindale was the daughter of the bailiff. The young girl had gone to the stack yard at 1pm, and Thompson followed her. After a fumbled sexual assault, he cut her throat and covered her body in straw. When her father found her, her clothes were awry, and a plug of tobacco was found nearby. The girl had not been raped. Thompson was arrested, covered in blood, in Beverley at 6pm, and was hanged just forty days later.

Read: And May The Lord Have Mercy On Your Soul

265

Leo George O'DONNELL   26

Bludgeoned: ***William F. Watterton***, *48, on 1 January 1917, in Aldershot, Hants.*
Motive: *Vengeance.*

Sergeant O'Donnell, *(b.1891),* went to Watterton's house to ask permission to marry his daughter, whom he had been courting for some time. She left the men alone to talk, and at 9pm, O'Donnell battered the Lieutenant with a toilet brush, and a jagged stone, leaving his body in a trench. It is thought that Lt. Watterton had turned down the sergeant's request. O'Donnell was condemned when several witnesses testified that he had offered to pay them to secure an alibi.

Read: And May The Lord Have Mercy On Your Soul

266

Alec BAKERLIS   24   *Greek*

Stabbed: ***Winifred Ellen Fortt,*** *19, on 25 December 1916, in Cardiff, Glamorgan.*
Motive: *Vengeance.*

Winifred Fortt's father ran a lodging house for Greek sailors, and his daughter had become very friendly with one of the guests, Alec Bakerlis, *(b.1893).* The young Greek, however, was terribly jealous if Winifred so much as spoke to another man, and her father told him to go, after which Winnie broke off the relationship. She asked a friend to return a ring and some letters, but Bakerlis refused to accept them.

On the evening of Christmas Day, Winifred and a friend were chatting on a bridge, when Bakerlis approached and asked Winifred to return the belongings to him personally. When she removed his ring, he knocked her to the ground, and then stabbed her repeatedly. The Greek ran off, but was stopped by a policeman, and Winifred died of blood poisoning three days later. The jury decided his fate in ten minutes.

Read: And May The Lord Have Mercy On Your Soul

18 April 1917 Armley gaol, Leeds *T.Pierrepoint/ Baxter*

267

Robert GADSBY   65

Cut throat of: ***Julia Ann Johnson***, *54, on 28 February 1917, in Leeds,*
W.Yorks.
Motive: *Sexual rivalry.*

When Gadsby, *(b.1852)*, had been a widower for a year, lodging with his daughter and her husband, he took Julia Johnson for his sweetheart. Married since 1897 and with seven children, she had separated from her husband in 1914. Gadsby accused her of going with other men, and at 9am she ordered him out. In the lounge he cut her throat with a penknife, then went home and left his watch and purse for his two grandsons, before going to the police at 9.20pm. He claimed that Julia had attacked him, and had been cut by accident.

Read: Murderous Leeds, p61.

16 May 1917 Duke Street prison, Glasgow *Ellis/ Willis*

268

Thomas McGUINESS   26   *Scottish*

Punched: ***Alick Imlach***, *5, on 8 March 1917, in Govan, Lanarks.*
Motive: *Sadistic pleasure.*

McGuiness, 4'11" and just 9st, lived with his common-law wife and her five year-old son, Alick. McGuiness was persistently cruel to the child, frequently beating him, and burning him on his hands, arms and legs with cigarettes. He threw Alick down the stairs, and the boy told his mother.
When she went out, McGuiness, a teetotaller, beat the boy until he fell unconscious with blood running from his mouth. Alick died half an hour after his mother returned home. McGuiness left, but when he returned the next morning the police were waiting for him.

Read: Master Detective, Jul 98

269

William Thomas HODGSON   34

Bludgeoned: **1 Margaret Alderson Hodgson**, *37, his wife, and*
                  2 Margaret Hodgson, *3, his daughter, on 16 April 1917, in Wallasey, Cheshire.*
Motive: *To clear impediment.*

Hodgson, *(b.1883)*, a draper's buyer, had married Margaret in September 1910, and had two children, aged 3 and 1. He was also having an affair with a pregnant young waitress. A young man had recently called at the house, asking for gardening work, and Margaret had told him to call back, telling him when her husband would be home, and when not.

At about 9am, Margaret was axed to death in her kitchen, and a moneybox and purse were emptied. Hodgson went for a drink after work, as was his practice, and arrived home to find police at his home, having been alerted by a neighbour who heard the baby crying at 6pm. He claimed that he had left for work at 8.30am, but a neighbour said he had left at 9, putting him within the limits of the time of death. However, no sign of the huge amounts of blood which accompanied the death, were found on him. A spade, mysteriously, was found in the garden.

Read: And May The Lord Have Mercy On Your Soul

270

William James CAVANAGH   29   *Scottish*
                                   (aka William James Thompson)

Stabbed: **Henry Arthur Hollyer**, *27, on 20 June 1917, in Newcastle, Northumberland*
Motive: *Vengeance; drink related.*

Cavanagh, *(b.1888)*, and his pal James Innes, 27, a Scots army deserter, called round to see Cavanagh's girlfriend, Ruby White, a 26 year-old prostitute, on the night of June 20. Ruby had been out drinking with a friend and had met four petty officers on shore leave, Birling, Gough, Grant and

McDonald. They had been joined by two other women and by Henry Hollyer, a leading seaman.

When the pub turned out at 10.30pm, she had invited them all round to her place to continue the party. All went well until one of the women suggested that Cavanagh and Innes, both civilians, should be doing their bit with the services. When one of the sailors chipped in a brawl started.

Cavanagh, 5'3" and 10st 6, who had a record of twenty convictions, struck Hollyer in the face and Innes knocked out McDonald's teeth. Ruby threw glasses and bottles, and then Cavanagh drew his penknife stabbing Gough in the face, and Hollyer five times in the back, chest and neck, before police broke up the fracas.

Hollyer died five days later, Cavanagh claiming that he never intended to kill, thinking the penknife was incapable of inflicting serious injuries. Both he and Innes were tried for murder, Innes being acquitted and Cavanagh receiving a recommendation for mercy after a 30-minute retirement by the jury.

Read: Murderous Tyneside, p126

19 December 1917	Shrewsbury prison	*Ellis/ Willis*

271

Thomas COX   59

Cut throat of:	**Elizabeth Cox**, 49, his wife, on 11 August 1917, in Ludlow, Shropshire.
Motive:	Vengeance.

Cox, *(b.1858)*, and his wife were constantly arguing. They and their two sons, aged 13 and 8, all slept in the same room. At 2.30am, Cox and his wife were still arguing, he accusing her of lying to him. He hit his wife, who then asked the elder son to fetch her a glass of water. Before the boy could do so, Cox slit his wife's throat, told the boy to go back to sleep, and then cut his own neck. At 7.20am, Cox summoned the energy to wake his son, and tell him to go for help.

Read: And May The Lord Have Mercy On Your Soul

1917 Army Executions Overseas

111 servicemen and army workers *(2)* were executed by firing squad:

English	77	*Egyptian*	1
Scottish	11	*Russian*	1
Irish	5	*Australian*	1
Welsh	5	*Nigerian*	1
Canadian	4	*Cypriot*	1
West Indian	3	*Gold Coast*	1

5 Jan	Edwin Leopold Arthur Dyett, 21, Welsh, in France, for desertion
8 Jan	Joseph Tongue, of Liverpool, in France, for desertion
18 Jan	Peter Goggins, 21, of Co Durham, in France, for quitting his post, with
	John McDonald, 28, of Co Durham, for quitting his post, and
	Joseph William Stones, 25, of Co Durham, for casting away his arms
27 Jan	John Taylor, of Lancashire, in France, for desertion
28 Jan	Frederick Wright, in France, for desertion
31 Jan	Alexander Reid, 30, Scottish, in France, for desertion
3 Feb	Ernest W Harris, 20, of Sheffield, in France, for desertion, with
	Robert Murray, for desertion
4 Feb	James Crampton, 42, of Yorkshire, in France, for desertion
6 Feb	Benjamin A Hart, 22, of Suffolk, in France, for desertion
7 Feb	William Murphey, Scottish, in France, for desertion
12 Feb	Frederick Stead, 20, of Yorkshire, in France, for desertion
19 Feb	Robert Burton, 24, of Lancashire, in Iraq, for sleeping at his post, with
	Thomas Downing, 22, of Lancashire, for sleeping at his post
21 Feb	Richard M Jones, 40, married, of Lancashire, in Iraq, for desertion
4 Mar	Ellis Holt, 22, of Salford, in France, for desertion, with
	Frederick Rose, 23, of Yorkshire, for desertion
9 Mar	John Rogers, of Lancashire, in France, for desertion
24 Mar	William Bowerman, 38, married, of London, in France, for desertion
27 Mar	Arthur Hamilton, 31, of Co Durham, in France, for desertion
31 Mar	William E Anderson, 21, of Dorset, in France, for desertion
4 Apr	Frederick Malyon, *c*40, in France, for desertion
6 Apr	George E Gleadow, of Yorkshire, in France, for desertion
10 Apr	William Robinson, of Nottinghamshire, in France, for desertion
11 Apr	Eugene Perry, 21, Canadian, in France, for desertion
19 Apr	John Lewis, 21, of London, in France, for desertion
20 Apr	Harold G Carter, 21, Canadian, in France, for desertion
20 Apr	Joseph Ferguson, 21, Scottish, in France, for desertion
28 Apr	Allassan Mamprusi, of Gold Coast, in German E Africa, for cowardice
14 May	Thomas Hogan, 31, Irish, in France, for desertion

15 May	George Watkins, 31, Welsh, in Belgium, for desertion
19 May	Samuel H Cunnington, 20, of Warwickshire, in France, for desertion
1 Jun	Archibald Brown, Scottish, in Greece, for desertion
3 Jun	Charles M Milligan, 20, Scottish, from Glasgow, in France, for desertion
14 Jun	John W Fryer, 23, of London, in Belgium, for desertion
15 Jun	Arthur E Allsop, 21, in France, for desertion
15 Jun	J Wishard, 24, Irish, in France, for desertion
16 Jun	James Mayers, 25, of London, in in France, for desertion
3 Jul	Gustave Comte, 22, Canadian, in France, for desertion, with Joseph LaLancette, 21, Canadian, in in France, for desertion
3 Jul	Walter Yeoman, 22, of London, in France, for desertion
4 Jul	John E Barnes, 24, of Sussex, in France, for desertion, with Robert Gillis Pattison, 23, of Surrey, for desertion
5 Jul	Robert Hope, 23, Irish, in France, for desertion
6 Jul	'Nicolas', Greek Cypriot, in Greece, for the murder of muleteer Markou Christolis on 14 May 1917
8 Jul	Harry Ashton, 20, of Lancashire, in Greece, for desertion
9 Jul	Denis J Blakemore, 28, of Shropshire, in France, for desertion
10 Jul	Frederick M Barratt, 23, in France, for desertion
12 Jul	William Benham, of London, in France, for desertion
25 Jul	George Cutmore, in Iraq, for desertion
27 Jul	Samuel Sabongidda, Nigerian, in German E Africa, for violence
1 Aug	Frederick Broadrick, of Warwickshire, in Belgium, for desertion
11 Aug	Hubert A Clarke, west Indian, in Egypt, for striking a superior officer
19 Aug	John King, 32, married with 3 children, Australian, in Belgium, for desertion
19 Aug	Frederick Loader, of London, in Belgium, for desertion
20 Aug	Arthur Mitchell, of Lancashire, in France, for desertion
24 Aug	James S Michael, Scottish, in Belgium, for desertion
29 Aug	Stanley Stewart, 21, Scottish, in Belgium, for desertion
30 Aug	Walter Neave, of Yorkshire, in France, for desertion
30 Aug	Albert Parry, of Yorkshire, in in France, for desertion
30 Aug	Thomas W Watts, 21, of Co Durham, in France, for desertion
5 Sep	John J Hyde, of London, in France, for desertion
5 Sep	James Smith, 26, of Lancashire, in Belgium, for desertion
5 Sep	Joseph Stedman, 25, of Liverpool, in Belgium, for desertion
6 Sep	Edward Delargey, 19, Scottish, in Belgium, for desertion
6 Sep	John T Wall, 22, of Worcestershire, in Belgium, for desertion
12 Sep	John H Abigail, 20, of Norfolk, in Belgium, for desertion
12 Sep	Charles Britton, of Warwickshire, in Belgium, for desertion
12 Sep	William Wycherley, 24, married, of Manchester, in Belgium, for desertion
14 Sep	George Everill, 30, married, of Staffordshire, in Belgium, for desertion
19 Sep	Leonard Mitchell, of Yorkshire, in Belgium, for desertion
20 Sep	Herbert Morris, 17, west Indian, in Belgium, for desertion
23 Sep	Charles H Kirman, 32, of Lincolnshire, in France, for desertion
1 Oct	Ernest Mackness, 25, of Leicester, in Belgium, for desertion

4 Oct	Jesse Robert Short, 31, Welsh, in France, for mutiny
4 Oct	John Woodhouse, in France, for desertion
9 Oct	Dimitro Sinizki, 22, Russian, in France, for cowardice
10 Oct	Mahmoud Mohamed Ahmed, Egyptian labourer, in Marseilles, for mutiny
16 Oct	Frederick C Gore, 19, of Kent, in Belgium, for desertion
16 Oct	Norman H Taysum, 25, Scottish, in France, for desertion, with Thomas Ward, 23, Scottish, for desertion
18 Oct	William Alexander, 37, of London, in France, for desertion
20 Oct	Frank W Cheeseman, 29, married, in France, for desertion, with Arthur P Onys, 31, for desertion
22 Oct	Thomas L Moles, 28, of Somerset, in Belgium, for desertion
22 Oct	Ernest Worsley, of Middlesex, in France, for desertion
23 Oct	Frederick Turner, 31, of Northumberland, in Belgium, for desertion
25 Oct	William Jones, Welsh, in Belgium, for desertion
27 Oct	Ernest Bryant, 33, in France, for desertion
27 Oct	Charles B Nicholson, 19, of Yorkshire, in France, for desertion
28 Oct	Stephen Byrne, 30, Irish, in France, for desertion
31 Oct	Thomas Donovan, 20, of London, in Belgium, for desertion
31 Oct	Henry J Webb, of Yorkshire, in Belgium, for desertion
6 Nov	G Hanna, 26, Irish, in France, for desertion
6 Nov	John Taylor, 24, of Staffordshire, in France, for desertion
8 Nov	John B Milburn, of Northumberland, in Belgium, for desertion
14 Nov	William Smith, 20, of Manchester, in Belgium, for desertion
15 Nov	Richard M Davies, of Northamptonshire, in in France, for desertion
21 Nov	Thomas Foulkes, 21, of Manchester, in Belgium, for desertion
22 Nov	Thomas Hawkins, of Surrey, in France, for desertion
22 Nov	Ernest Lawrence, 21, of London, in Belgium, for desertion
22 Nov	T Harry B Rigby, 21, Welsh, in France, for desertion
23 Nov	J S Adamson, 30, Scottish, in France, for desertion
23 Nov	Arthur H Westwood, 20, of London, in Belgium, for desertion
3 Dec	Joseph Bateman, of Staffordshire, in France, for desertion
14 Dec	Frederick W Slade, 24, of London, in Belgium, for disobedience
22 Dec	**James A Mitchell**, 18, west Indian Private, in Palestine, for the murder of an Arab, whose wife Mitchell had assaulted after she had refused his sexual advances.
28 Dec	Charles F McColl, 26, of Yorkshire, in Belgium, for desertion
28 Dec	Harry Williams, of London, in France, for desertion

for desertion	97		
for quitting post	2	*in France*	70
for murder	2	*in Belgium*	31
for striking a superior	1	*in Greece*	3
for mutiny	2	*in Iraq*	3
for violence	1	*in Ger E Africa*	2
for cowardice	2	*in Egypt*	1
for casting arms	1	*in Palestine*	1
for sleeping at post	2		
for disobedience	1		

1918

total: **7**

272	12 Feb	Arthur DE STAMIR	27		Wandsworth
273	21 Feb	Joe JONES	26		Wandsworth
274	2 Mar	Louis VOISIN	50	*French*	Pentonville
275	5 Mar	Verney HASSER	30	*Australian*	Shepton Mallet
276	9 Apr	Louis Van de KERKHOVE	32	*Belgian*	Winson Green
277	17 Dec	John WALSH	35		Armley
278	17 Dec	William ROONEY	51		Strangeways

12 February 1918   Wandsworth prison, London   *Ellis/ Brown*

272

Arthur Harold Victor DE STAMIR   27   *(ne Stamrowski)*

Bludgeoned: ***Edward Kenrick Bunbury Tighe**, 55, on 12 November 1917, in Wimbledon, Surrey.*
Motive: *Financial.*

De Stamir, *(b.1891),* was born in London of French parents in 1891. He had led a life of crime from an early age - convicted of theft at 14, and sent to reform school at 15 for burglary. He lived in Australia for a time, supporting himself there by crime, and returned to England in 1914 to join the City of London Yeomanry. He was imprisoned by them for various offences including threatening an officer. He escaped his detention and took to burglary.

He broke into Winkfield Lodge, Wimbledon, through a window. Captain Tighe had retired separately from his wife at 11.30pm, and de Stamir struck him by his bed with a poker from the dining room. Captain Tighe and his family had moved into the house just five days previously. De Stamir escaped with only two silver watches and a raincoat. The captain died five days later.

Several weeks later, de Stamir was arrested after trying to offer items for sale to a West End jeweller. When his house was searched, Captain Tighe's watches and coat were found. De Stamir claimed that he had been accompanied to the Lodge by another man who had done the killing. He was not believed.

Read: Diary of a Hangman

273

Joseph JONES   26

Bludgeoned: ***Oliver Gilbert Imlay***, *24, on 8 November 1917, in London SE1.*
Motive: *Financial.*

Jones, *(b. 1892),* twice wounded and twice discharged from the army during the Great War, had a history of robbery with violence. Teaming up with Ernest Sharp and Thomas Maguire, two Australian deserters, Jones planned another robbery. The three then lured two Canadian soldiers they had acquainted down a narrow lane off Waterloo Road, beat them up with a truncheon, and robbed them.   John McKinley recovered, but the other Canadian, Oliver Imlay, died three days later of a fractured skull.

When arrested, the Australians both blamed Jones, who had gone out armed with a police truncheon. Sharp received 7 years and Maguire ten years for robbery. Jones' last words of the scaffold were, "God forgive them".

Read: And May The Lord Have Mercy On Your Soul

2 March 1918   Pentonville prison, London   *Ellis/ Taylor*

274

Louis Marie Joseph VOISIN   50   *French*

Bludgeoned/ suffocated: ***Emilienne Gerard***, *32, on 31 October 1917, in London W1.*
Motive: *To clear impediment.*

Emilienne Gerard, a Belgian refugee whose husband was fighting in France, left the NW1 flat paid for by her lover, Louis Voisin, *(b.1875),* during an air-raid on Hallowe'en, and called on him at his home in Charlotte St, W1. There she found him in bed with another woman, Berthe Roche, who had moved in with Voisin while Gerard was in France visiting her husband for two months.

Roche beat Gerard about the head, probably with a poker, and Voisin, 5'3" and 13 st, finished her off by smothering her with a towel. Voisin, a butcher, cut up the body in his cellar and dumped the wrapped torso and limbs in Bloomsbury, WC1, where they were discovered three days later. The head and hands he kept in a barrel in his cellar.

A laundry mark on Gerard's clothing led to her identification, and a photograph of Voisin in her flat, together with an IOU from him for £50, led police to question him. The jury condemned Voisin after 15 minutes. Roche was sentenced to seven years as an accessory after the fact, but died insane one year later.

Read: Diary of a Hangman.

---

5 March 1918   Shepton Mallet Military Prison   *Ellis/ Willis*

275

Verney HASSER   **30**   *Australian*

Shot: ***Joseph Harold Dunkin***, 24, on 27 November 1917, in
              Sutton Veny, Wilts.
Motive: Vengeance.

Hasser, *(b.1888)*, was a private, and Dunkin a Corporal, in the Australian Corps, stationed at Warminster. Hasser had harboured a grudge against his corporal and one night he entered the double room he shared with Dunkin at 10.30pm, and shot him through the head, with a single bullet from a rifle, leaving him sprawled across his bed. When Dunkin was found, it first appeared to be a case of suicide, until forensic experts pointed out that the angle of the shot ruled out that possibility. After a 2-day trial, the jury took 90 minutes to determine Hasser's guilt.

Read: And May The Lord Have Mercy On Your Soul.

---

9 April 1918   Winson Green prison, Birmingham   *Ellis/ Brown*

276

Louis VAN DE KERKHOVE   **32**   *Belgian*

Stabbed: ***Clemence Verelst***, 35, on 13 January 1918, in
              Birmingham, Warwicks
Motive: Vengeance; drink related.

Van de Kerkhove, *(b.1885)*, had sought refuge from the horrors of Great War Belgium in London where he met Clemence Verelst who ran a tea shop with her husband, Pierre Axel. The couple had escaped Belgium in April 1915 working in a Birmingham munitions factory before setting up their business in London. Clemence and Louis ran away together first to Staines and then to Birmingham where he found work in the Austin factory.

Clemence's drink habit soon turned things sour, and she stabbed Louis in the arm when he threatened to leave her. He did so but took her back after constant pleading, only to find Clemence later disappeared with all his furniture. Nevertheless she continued to pester Louis with letters and visits begging for a reconciliation.

He agreed to meet her in a coffee house on 13 January, the two going on to a pub where they drank several whiskies, before booking into the Shaftesbury Hotel. At 10pm Van de Kerkhove became inflamed when Clemence, undressed and ready for passion, admitted to having had another lover. Louis grabbed her by the throat and Clemence sought refuge beneath the bed. He stabbed at her with a knife as she lay there, inflicting injuries to her upper back and abdomen. Louis answered the door wearing only his shirt when a concerned porter went to investigate, and Clemence staggered out in her underwear. Clemence related the events to police before dying on the morning of 15 January.

Read: *Murderous Birmingham, p58*

---

17 December 1918   Armley gaol, Leeds   *T.Pierrepoint/ Willis*

277

John William WALSH   35

Strangled: **Ruth Elizabeth Moore**, 42, on 11 July 1918, in Bottomboat, W.Yorks.
Motive: Vengeance.

Walsh, *(b.1883)*, lived near Wakefield with his brother and lover, Ruth Moore, who was separated from her husband. The couple constantly argued, to the extent that Walsh's brother moved out. Ruth threw Walsh out at least twice, but he always returned, lastly in early July. At 5am, as Ruth lay asleep in bed, Walsh strangled her, before informing the neighbours, and then going to the police. He declared, 'I deserve to swing'.

Read: *And May The Lord Have Mercy On Your Soul*

278

William ROONEY   51

Stabbed: **Mary Ellen Rooney**, *30, on 2 November 1918, in Liverpool, Lancs.*

Motive: *Sexual rivalry.*

Mary Rooney had four children from two marriages, both of which resulted in her being widowed, most recently in July 1918. She moved back to her mother's, where she was courted by her dead husband's brother, William Rooney, *(b.1867).* Mary refused his proposal of marriage, and Rooney threatened her with a knife.

Mary moved away for a time, but when she returned she started courting a soldier lodger of her mother. Rooney became extremely jealous, though the two had a drink together on 2 November. Later, he followed Mary into a shop, and attacked her with a butcher's knife, dragged her into the street, and stabbed her twice more. The manager knocked him to the ground. In his defence, Rooney claimed to have been visited by his brother's spirit.

Read: And May The Lord Have Mercy On Your Soul

1918 Army Executions Overseas

54 servicemen and army workers *(5)* were executed by firing squad

27 English	*2 Welsh*
7 Scottish	*2 American*
7 Canadian	*1 New Zealand*
5 Chinese	*1 Gold Coast*
2 Irish	

24 Jan	John Seymour, Irish, in Belgium, for desertion
9 Feb	Wilfred Clarke, 23, of Co Durham, in France, for desertion
13 Feb	Thomas Hopkins, 26, married, of Lancashire, in France, for quitting his post
17 Feb	Ernest Horler, 26, of Yorkshire, in France, for desertion
24 Feb	Victor M Spencer, 23, of New Zealand, in Belgium, for desertion
2 Mar	E Fairburn, 22, Canadian, in France, for desertion
6 Mar	C Welsh, Canadian, in Belgium, for desertion
7 Mar	**A Wickings**, 28, a Lance-Sgt, at Le Havre, France, for the murder by strangulation of a prostitute in Le Havre
9 Mar	Hector Dalande, married Canadian, in France, for desertion
13 Mar	H E J Lodge, Canadian, in France, for desertion
15 Mar	Arthur C Dagesse, 32, American, in France, for desertion
10 Apr	Henry Hughes, 27, of Sheffield, in France, for desertion
22 Apr	Albert Holmes, 22, married, of Lancs, in France, in desertion
10 May	**James Skone**, 39, married Private, Welsh from Pembroke, in France, for the murder when drunk of Lance-Sergeant Edwin Williams, 42, by shooting, on 13 April 1918 at Gorre
11 May	James Reid, 26, Scottish, in France, for desertion
16 May	Frank O'Neill, 24, of Nottinghamshire, in France, for desertion
19 May	Robert W Simmers, 25, Scottish, in France, for desertion
21 May	Leopold Delisle, 26, Canadian, in France, for desertion
22 May	**R Bell**, 29, a Sapper, at Toutencourt, France, for the murder by shooting of 2nd Lieutenant Wynell Lloyd on 18 April 1918, at Senlis
22 May	John McFarlane, 27, of Liverpool, in Belgium, for desertion
26 May	Malcolm R Richmond, 22, Scottish, in France, for desertion
27 May	William J Earl, 22, of Manchester, in Belgium, for desertion
4 Jun	Thomas Brigham, 22, of Lancashire, in France, for desertion
14 Jun	William T Spry, 29, married with 2 children, of London, in France, for desertion
19 Jun	Stephen M Fowles, 21, Canadian, in France, for desertion
25 Jun	Walter Dossett, 22, of Sheffield, in Belgium, for desertion
26 Jun	**Wang En Jung**, Chinese, near Calais, with **Yang Ch'ing Shan**, Chinese, for the murder of a French woman whilst robbing her cafe
18 Jul	David Stevenson, 23, of Middlesex, in France, for desertion
19 Aug	Arthur Briggs, 27, married with a child, of Nottinghamshire, in France, for desertion

23 Jul	**Cheng Shan Kung**, Chinese, in France, for the murder of another unnamed Chinese coolie
30 July	George Ainley, 20, of Sheffield, in Belgium, for desertion
1 Aug	Frederick Johnson, 40, Scottish, in France, with Harry McClair, 40, Scottish, for desertion
8 Aug	Benjamin O'Connell, 23, Irish, in France, for desertion
9 Aug	**Chao Hsing I**, Chinese, in Calais, for an unspecified murder
10 Aug	William Scholes, 25, Welsh, in Belgium, for desertion
11 Aug	John Swain, of Berkshire, in France, for desertion
12 Aug	Wilson N Ling, 22, Canadian, in France, for desertion
14 Aug	William Baker, in Belgium, for desertion
23 Aug	Henry Hendricks, 46, American, in Belgium, for desertion; the oldest soldier executed in WW1
23 Aug	Joseph Nisbet, 26, of Leicestershire, in France, for desertion
27 Aug	Frederick C Butcher, 26, of Kent, in Belgium, for desertion
10 Sep	Frank Bateman, 28, of Sheffield, in Belgium, for desertion
12 Sep	**Hui I He**, Chinese, in Belgium, for the murder of another unnamed Chinese coolie
12 Sep	Patrick Murphy, 20, of London, in France, for desertion
18 Sep	Robert Young, 21, of Worcestershire, in Salonika, Greece, for desertion
24 Sep	David Gibson, 25, Scottish, in Belgium, for desertion
24 Sep	**John H Paterson**, 28, 2nd Lieutenant, of Middlesex, in Boulogne, for the murder while evading arrest by shooting 3 times, of Sgt Harold Collison, 40, in Calais, on 3 July 1918.
6 Oct	Harry J Knight, in Belgium, for desertion
11 Oct	Lawrence D Elford, 28, married, Scottish, in France, for desertion
7 Nov	Louis Harris, 23, Jewish from London, in Belgium, for desertion
7 Nov	Ernest Jackson, 32, of London, in Belgium, for desertion
10 Nov	**Dezari Barama**, of Gold Coast, a Private, in German E Africa, for an unspecified murder

for desertion	43	*in France*	35
for murder	10	*in Belgium*	17
for quitting his post	1	*in Greece*	1
		in German E Africa	1

1919

total: **13**

279	7 Jan	Benjamin BENSON	41		Armley
280	8 Jan	George CARDWELL	22		Armley
281	8 Jan	Percy BARRETT	20		Armley
282	19 Feb	Joseph ROSE	25		Oxford
283	10 Jul	Henry PERRY	38		Pentonville
284	22 Jul	John CROSSLAND	34		Walton
285	31 Jul	Thomas FOSTER	46		Pentonville
286	8 Aug	Henry GASKIN	27		Winson Green
287	7 Oct	Frank WARREN	41		Pentonville
288	11 Nov	James ADAMS		*Scottish*	Duke Street
289	26 Nov	Ernest SCOTT	28		Newcastle
290	26 Nov	Ambrose QUINN	28		Newcastle
291	3 Dec	Djang Djing SUNG	33	*Chinese*	Worcester

7 January 1919   Armley gaol, Leeds   *T.Pierrepoint /Baxter*

279

Benjamin Hindle BENSON   41

Cut throat of: *Annie Mayne, 29, on 27 August 1918, in Leeds, W.Yorks.*
Motive: *Sexual rivalry.*

Benson lived in a large house in Hunslett, Leeds, with money inherited from his father. In 1914 he employed Charles Mayne as odd-job man, and his wife Anne, as housekeeper. It was not long before Benson and Mrs Mayne had become lovers. Charles caught the two making love and left, leaving Annie to live there as mistress of the house.

In 1916 Benson joined the army and went to war. In his absence Annie took several lovers, always playing the dutiful wife when he came home on leave.

On 26 August 1918, Benson arrived home unexpectedly to find the house empty. Eventually he heard Annie come in with someone, going straight upstairs. She had been out drinking with a young soldier, and Benson caught the two in bed. The soldier fled, and following a row, Benson slept on the sofa. When Annie received two letters the following morning, Benson became enraged with jealousy, slapping her in the face, and then

218

cutting her throat with a razor. She died the same day in hospital. The betrayal and the provocation were not enough to convince the jury.

Read: A Date With the Hangman, p147.

| 8 January 1919 | Armley gaol, Leeds | *T.Pierrepoint / Baxter* |

280, 281

George Walter CARDWELL   22
Percy George BARRETT   20

| **Bludgeoned:** | **Rhoda Walker**, *62, on 16 August 1918, in Pontefract, W.Yorks.* |
| **Motive:** | *Financial.* |

Private Barratt, *(b.1899)*, and Lt-Corporal Cardwell, *(b.1897)*, worked in a colliery, and lived with Cardwell's sister after absconding from their unit in London. Cardwell had served in the army since leaving borstal in 1914, and had been wounded five times in the war. At 4pm, they went to Rhoda Walker's jewellery shop, and with Cardwell outside as lookout, Barrett battered the woman to death before robbing the store. They both went to Cardwell's mother in Halifax, and she pawned some of the items for them. When arrested in Walworth, London, on 20 August, stolen watches belonging to Rhoda were found in their possession. The culprits blamed each other for the murder.

Read: And May The Lord Have Mercy On Your Soul.

| 19 February 1919 | Oxford prison | *Ellis/ Taylor* |

282

Joseph ROSE   25   *i*

Cut throat of:	**1 Sarah Rose**, *19, his cousin, and*
	2 Isabella Rose, *5 mths, his daughter, on*
	28 October 1918, in Shaw-cum-Donnington, Berks.
Motive:	*Sexual rivalry.*

Rose, *(b.1894)*, an albino, had lived since spring 1917 with his cousin and lover, Sarah Rose, in tents at Enbourne, with their baby daughter, and Sarah's mother. The couple and their daughter went to Newbury for the day on 28 October, and were said to be on friendly terms.

Walking back, they stopped by the roadside to eat, and, according to Rose, a man who knew Sarah approached them and cut each of their throats. Rose staggered to passers-by on the road, who found mother and child dead. Rose's tale would have seemed weak, but for the fact that, despite a thorough search of the area, no knife was found.

Read: And May The Lord Have Mercy On Your Soul

10 July 1919	Pentonville prison, London	*Ellis/ Willis*

283

Henry PERRY   **38**   *(aka Henry Beckett)*

Bludgeoned: **1 *Alice Cornish*, 43**
2 *Marie Cornish*, 6,
3 *Alice Cornish*, 15, and
4 *Walter Cornish*, 48, on 28 April 1919, in Forest Gate, Essex.

Motive: Vengeance.

Perry, *(b.1881)*, lodged with the Cornish family, distant relations, in Stukeley road while he was waiting for his demob papers. He had been an army private for eight years, and had been tortured by the Turks after being captured in the Middle East. He had suffered severe head injuries. Perry had seventeen convictions, and had served three prison terms, being last released in November 1916, after serving five years. After an argument, Walter Cornish ordered him out of the house, but he returned on 28 April seeking a bloody revenge.

In the kitchen he battered Mrs Cornish with a poker, and after carrying her to the garden shed, battered her with an axe. He finished her off with a knife in the throat. When the youngest daughter, Marie, arrived home, he smashed her head with a hammer, and threw her down the cellar steps. He hit Alice, the eldest daughter, with the hammer when she arrived, and, before throwing her into the cellar, chopped her in the throat with the axe. Finally, Mr Cornish was cut down with the axe when he got home.

Perry cut off Mrs Cornish's finger to get her ring, and then ransacked the house. Witnesses saw him leaving the house covered with blood, and Mr Cornish managed to stagger outside and tell who had been responsible for the massacre. He died two days later in hospital. Perry was arrested in East Ham a few days later, and confessed all. Despite three doctors certifying him insane, his plea was rejected.

Read: The Hangman's Diary, p230.

22 July 1919   Walton gaol, Liverpool   *Ellis/ Baxter*

284

John CROSSLAND   34

Bludgeoned: **Ellen Crossland**, *35, his wife, on 8 May 1919, in Blackburn, Lancs.*
Motive: Sexual rivalry.

     Crossland, (*1885*), married Ellen in 1903, and they had four children. He was wounded at Mons, and separated from his wife when he returned from the war. He served two months' imprisonment from January 1919, when he fell into arrears with maintenance payments. In March, the two were reconciled, and Crossland moved back in, but after hearing rumours that Ellen had been seeing another man, all unsubstantiated, arguments started, and police put him back out on 2 May.
     Six days later, in the early morning, Crossland let himself into Ellen's home, removed his shoes, and crept into her bedroom. His son, 13, who slept in the same room, said there was no argument, but Ellen was battered to death. Handing himself in for questioning at 11.30am, Crossland claimed that Ellen had banged her head during a row.

Read: And May The Lord Have Mercy On Your Soul

31 July 1919   Pentonville prison, London   *Ellis/ Taylor*

285

Thomas FOSTER   46

Cut throat of: **Minnie Foster**, *33, his wife, on 11 June 1919, in London E2.*
Motive: Vengeance.

Foster, *(b.1873),* married Minnie in 1904, and they had six children. He was a heavy drinker, and regularly beat his wife, though the pair took a friendly walk together on 10 June. The following morning, at 6.45, he attacked Minnie with a razor, and she was badly cut trying to defend herself. Her screams did not stop Foster cutting her throat, but they did alert neighbours, who managed to hold Foster as he ran out. Minnie was found in the bedroom, still clutching her baby. A broken razor lay on the mantelpiece.

Read: And May The Lord Have Mercy On Your Soul

8 August 1919	Winson Green prison, Birmingham	*Ellis/ Taylor*

286

Henry Thomas GASKIN   27

𝒞

Stabbed:	***Elizabeth Gaskin,*** *23, his wife, on 19 February 1919, in Hednesford, Staffs.*
Motive:	*Sexual rivalry*

Gaskin, *(b.1892),* had been sent to reformatory school at 14, and, after marrying Elizabeth Talbot in 1913 and fathering a child, had served two years for theft. Following his release in 1916 he was conscripted into the army and sent to the trenches. Traumatised by his experiences there, he was to exhibit strange behaviour thereafter.

By the time he was awarded leave in September 1917, Elizabeth had had two further children, and by his demob in late January 1919, Elizabeth had another child, all by different fathers. Gaskin went home to his mother and began work as a miner. On 19 February he sent a note to Elizabeth asking her to meet him at 2.30pm. Dragging her into woods he began a two-hour ordeal to take revenge for his wife's infidelities.

He punched her to the ground with several blows to the face. He pushed fists full of snow into her vagina, penetrating her to his elbow, rammed a stick down her throat, and then cut off her clothes. Still conscious, Elizabeth got to her knees only for him to fell her again with a kick to the chin. He then cut her open from genitals to navel, rendering her unconscious by placing his heel on her throat. He then cut her open up to the neck and pulled out her entrails. He severed her head and almost managed to remove a leg, before going to the cinema.

He returned after 8pm, using a wheelbarrow to remove the head, body and clothes to the pond surrounding the gas holder, weighing down the torso by shoving a gas pipe through from the neck to the hip. He reported to the police and made a full confession on 22 February. The jury took 24 minutes to convict him.

Read: Murderous Birmingham, p67.

---

7 October 1919   Pentonville prison, London   *Ellis/ Brown*

287

Frank George WARREN   41   *(aka Burke)*

Strangled: ***Lucy Nightingale**, 27, on 28 July 1919, in London N4.*
Motive: *Financial*

Warren, *(b.1878)*, was a ship's cook who had deserted his merchant ship at Cardiff, taking with him tea, 1500 cigarettes, and 21 bottles of whisky. With the ship's steward, Harold Horatio Morgan, 19, and Olive Parton, 28, whom he had picked up in Cardiff, he went to London. There, at Finsbury Park, the two men met Henry Ball, 66, in a pub, and Morgan, looking for a bed, was invited to his house. He was introduced to Ball's niece, and Morgan paid to spend the night with her, 10/- to Ball, £2 to the woman.

Lucy O'Connor had married James Nightingale in 1918. He left her when she began seeing other men, and returned from Liverpool at the beginning of July. She had gone to lodge with Ball, who was not her uncle, and had entertained men at his house to the financial benefit of them both. Ball's wife had entered an asylum in May.

Morgan and Warren had returned to the house the following night, and Warren went upstairs with Lucy for half an hour. He then hurriedly told Morgan to leave. Ball found Lucy's body trussed up in the bedroom. She had been manually strangled, bound with strips of bed-linen, and wrapped in a sheet with her hands tied behind her back. Warren gave three of her rings to Olive, then shaved his moustache and washed his shirt. A photo of Morgan at the house led to the men's arrest. The jury took just five minutes to acquit Morgan of being an accessory, and to convict Warren.

Read: True Detective, Sep 95.

11 November 1919   Duke Street prison, Glasgow   *Ellis*

288

James ADAMS

Cut throat of: **Mary Kane**, *on 1 August 1919, in Glasgow, Lanarks.*
Motive: *Vengeance.*

Adams and Mary Kane, also known as Doyle, lived together while her husband was away fighting the war in Egypt. Announcing to her lover that she intended to return to her demobbed husband, Adams slit her throat with a razor.

Read: Encyclopaedia of Scottish Executions

26 November 1919   Newcastle prison   *Ellis/ Taylor*

289

Ernest Bernard SCOTT   28

Cut throat of: **Rebecca Jane Quinn**, *25, on 11 August 1919, near New*
                    Delaval, Northumberland
Motive: *Sexual rivalry*

Scott, *(b.1891)*, had been courting Becky Quinn for just three weeks when she told him it was over. Her young child lived with her parents in New Delaval, while she worked as housekeeper to two miners in the village of Bebside two miles away. When Scott suspected that Becky had a new man, he worked out a plot to get even. Taking a day off from the mine, he borrowed a razor from a barman and then, at 9.45am, delivered a message that Rebecca's child had had an accident.
When she returned, Becky and a friend set off across the fields to New Delaval. Scott, 5'5" and 10st 11, was waiting for them. He spoke to Becky and then put his arm round her shoulder, quickly cutting her throat with a razor. After a one hour trial, the jury found Scott guilty without even retiring.

Read: Murderous Tyneside

290

Ambrose QUINN   28

Cut throat of: **Elizabeth Ann Quinn**, 25, his wife, on 9 August 1919, in
                    Newcastle, Northumberland
Motive: Sexual rivalry, drink related.

      Quinn, *(b.1891)*, married Elizabeth Ann in 1914, and by the time he joined the RAF in 1917, they had two children. Quinn did not return to live with Elizabeth's parents, until June 1919, and was immediately angered by Elizabeth's demand for a social life, complaining about her trips to the cinema, and hitting her, and their daughter, when she insisted on going to a street party in July. He then began to hear rumours that his wife had been out with other men while he was away. Though she denied the stories, he left her, first going to his mother's and then to his sister's home on 5 August.
      He threw a knife at her the next day but missed. Three days later he took his brother-in-law's razor and went to the pub, and then waited near Elizabeth's home. When he saw her at 10.30pm he approached her and cut her throat, Elizabeth collapsing on her doorstep. He then ran off and went to the police. Quinn insisted that he had not meant to kill his wife, but the jury retired for ten minutes only before adding a strong recommendation for mercy to their verdict. He was hanged 75 minutes after Ernest Scott.

      Read: Murderous Tyneside

291

Djang Djing SUNG   33   *Chinese*

Stabbed: **Zee Ming Wu**, 41, on 23 June 1919, in Birmingham,
                    Warwicks
Motive: Financial

      Sung, *(b.1886)*, had left his wife in China, and had worked in a Birmingham factory since 1916. He owed fellow Chinaman Wu 30 shillings, but Wu had told him that there was no hurry for its return. Wu had a wife and three children back in Shanghai and had done reasonably well in England, having £240 in his bank account.

Some time on 23 June, the two men went together to Warley woods outside Birmingham, where Sung killed his compatriot. Sung fractured Wu's skull with a piece of timber, and stabbed him in the temple with a screwdriver. Wu also suffered three fractured ribs and had his jaw broken in three places. Sung dragged the body further into the woods where he performed ritualistic mutilations, lacerating both Wu's ears, removing his left testicle through a small incision, and scoring the length of the penis with a knife. Wu's trousers had been carefully removed and replaced.

The following day, Sung had travelled to London and had attempted to withdraw all the money from Wu's bank account. He fled when staff became suspicious. The following day he broke into the home of Kwo Doung Dsou in Shepherds Bush in an attempt at robbery. His acquaintance awoke, and Sung attacked him with a hammer. Wu's body was found on 27 February, and police linked the two crimes. Sung attempted to place the blame on another Chinese at his lodgings, but when he was able to account for his movements, the jury had no problem convicting Sung, reaching its verdict in nine minutes.

Read: Murderous Birmingham, p78

1919 Army Executions Overseas

19 servicemen or army workers *(4)* were executed by firing squad

11 Russian	*2 English*
3 S African	*1 west Indian*
2 Chinese	

20 Jan   **Albert Denny**, west Indian Private, in Italy, for the bayoneting murder of a soldier in Italy in October 1918

15 Feb   **Wan Fa Yu**, Chinese, in France, for an unspecified murder

8 May   **Wang Ch'un Ch'ih**, Chinese, in Belgium, for an unspecified murder

27 May   **Frank O Wills**, 20, a Gunner,in France, for the murder by shooting of an NCO in March 1919 in Paris

Jul   Bitel, Russian, with
Cherbukin, Russian,
Deriagin, Russian,
Elisaieff, Russian,
Kameff, Russian,
Lashkoff, Russian,
Pesochnikoff, Russian,
Posdjeef, Russian,
Sakharoff, Russian,
Taratin, Russian, and
Volkoff, Russian, all Privates, for mutiny in Russia

11 Aug   **Joseph Chandler**, of Lincolnshire, a Private, in France, for the murder of a fellow burglar by shooting, in Calais in 1918

26 Aug   **Abraham Davids**, 24, S African black labourer, in France, with **Willie P Harris**, 23, S African black labourer, for murdering Belgian women

15 Oct   **F Boos**, *(aka Alberts),* 19, S African white, a Private, in France, for the murder of soldier Barend de Vries

for mutiny	11		*in Russia*	11
for murder	8		*in France*	6
			in Belgium	1
			in Italy	1

1920

total: **23**

292	6 Jan	Lewis MASSEY	29		Armley
293	6 Jan	Hyman PERDOVITCH	39	*Russian*	Strangeways
294	6 Jan	David CAPLAN	42		Strangeways
295	10 Mar	William WRIGHT	39		Lincoln
296	28 Mar	William HALL	66		Durham
297	13 Apr	Frederick HOLT	32		Strangeways
298	14 Apr	Thomas CALER	23	*Zanzibar*	Cardiff
299	16 Apr	Miles McHUGH	31		Armley
300	6 May	Thomas WILSON	44		Armley
301	11 May	Herbert SALISBURY	35		Walton
302	11 May	William WADDINGTON	34		Walton
303	26 May	Albert FRASER	24	*Scottish*	Duke Street
304	26 May	James ROLLINS	23	*Scottish*	Duke Street
305	15 Jun	Frederick STOREY	42		Ipswich
306	22 Jun	William ALDRED	54		Strangeways
307	27 Jul	Arthur GOSLETT	44		Pentonville
308	11 Aug	James ELLOR	35		Walton
309	30 Nov	James RILEY	50		Durham
310	30 Nov	Cyril SAUNDERS	21		Exeter
311	30 Dec	Samuel WESTWOOD	24		Winson Green
312	30 Dec	Edwin SOWERBY	28		Armley
313	30 Dec	Marks GOODMACHER	47		Pentonville
314	31 Dec	Charles COLCLOUGH	45		Strangeways

6 January 1920 Armley gaol, Leeds *T.Pierrepoint/ Willis*

292

Lewis MASSEY **29** *(aka Alfred Hird)*

Bludgeoned: **Margaret Hird**, *36, his wife, on 4 November 1919, in Leeds, W.Yorks.*
Motive: *Vengeance.*

Massey, *(b.1891)*, always went by his assumed name of Alfred Hird, and had a mental age of thirteen. He met Margaret Bell, a widow with three children whose husband had been killed in 1915 in France, and married her within a few months at Christmas 1917. A child was born in 1919, and in September that year Hird was demobbed, taking a job as a labourer at a wheelwright's.

Within a short time of being together, he began to beat Margaret, accusing her of leaving the children to go out, and of being drunk. Margaret responded by getting a separation order under which Hird was to pay her 17/- per week. This was increased to 25/- in October, and Hird could not manage on the 58/- he earned.

Convinced she was drinking away the maintenance money, he begged her to take him back but she threatened him with the police. At 9.25pm Margaret was at home with her sister, Elizabeth Hackney, when Hird again called round. Hird pushed his wife down onto the sofa while she was holding the baby, and Elizabeth hit him on the head with a poker. Infuriated, Hird took the weapon and battered both women, Elizabeth escaping upstairs while Hird finished off his wife, who died the following day.

Hird's brother and sister had both been committed to an asylum, but his plea of insanity was rejected.

Read: Murderous Leeds

6 January 1920   Strangeways prison, Manchester   *Ellis/ Baxter/ Taylor*

293

Hyman PERDOVITCH   **39**   *Russian*

Stabbed: ***Solomon Franks**, 49, on 15 August 1919, in Salford, Lancs.*
Motive: *Vengeance.*

Perdovitch, *(b.1881)*, came to England from Lithuania as a teenager in 1898, and served in the British army from 1916, receiving long-term injuries at Ypres the following year. He lived in lodgings in Sedgeley Park, and worked in a garment factory in Salford. His foreman, Solomon Franks, a married man with five children, thought him ambitious, and the disrespect was reciprocated, with Perovitch aware that Franks gave him the worst jobs to do.

At 8.25 one morning, the anger grew too great for Perdovitch. He took the knife he used for cleaning the machinery, and followed Franks as he went through the door to the yard. He stabbed his foreman twice with great force in the back of the neck. The jury deliberated for twenty minutes, and the Russian was hanged alongside David Caplan.

Read: Murderous Manchester.

6 January 1920   Strangeways prison, Manchester   *Ellis/ Baxter/ Taylor*

294

David CAPLAN   42

Bludgeoned:	1 **Freda Caplan**, *33, his wife,*
	2 **Herman Caplan**, *6, and*
	3 **Maurice Caplan**, *3, his children, on 14 October 1919,*
	in Liverpool, Lancs.
Motive:	Vengeance.

Freda Caplan ran a milliner's business from the family home, but did not get along very well with her husband, David, *(b.1878).* She left him on 9 September after he hit her, and following his conviction, a separation order was granted on 8 October. Freda returned to the house on 11 October because her son Maurice was ill, and Caplan blamed her family for the separation, claiming they had interfered.

Furious that his wife would not move back permanently, he battered her and the two children with a flat iron, as they lay in bed. He then cut his throat, all four being found the following day by a neighbour. Caplan was detained in hospital for 17 days. He was hanged alongside Hyman Perdovitch.

Read: Murderous Manchester

10 March 1920   Lincoln prison   *T.Pierrepoint/ Willis*

295

William WRIGHT   39

Strangled:	**Annie Coulbeck**, *34, on 28 October 1919, in Caistor, Lincs.*
Motive:	Sexual rivalry; drink related.

Annie Coulbeck lived alone, but in October 1919, found herself pregnant by her boyfriend, William Wright, *(b.1881)*. He was alarmed by a brooch which Annie had been given by her mother, insisting she had been given it by a new lover. In the pub he had been talking of killing Annie, then went to her house, and strangled her. Annie's body was discovered by a neighbour the following day.

Read: And May The Lord Have Mercy On Your Soul

| 28 March 1920 | Durham gaol | *Ellis/ Baxter* |

296

William HALL   66

| **Cut throat of:** | **Mary Ann Dixon**, 51, on 6 November, in Sunderland, Co Durham. |
| *Motive:* | *Vengeance; drink related.* |

Hall, *(b.1854)*, lived with Mary Dixon, a widow without other family, intermittently from 1918. In September 1919, Mary got a new night job at a lodging house, and left Hall. He went to see Mary at 6pm, and the two went to the pub together, returning to the lodging house. When she refused to let him stay the night, Hall cut Mary's throat. He explained, 'She was a dead wrong woman'.

Read: And May The Lord Have Mercy On Your Soul

| 13 April 1920 | Strangeways prison, Manchester | *Ellis/ Willis* |

297

Frederick Rothwell HOLT   32

| **Shot:** | **Kathleen Harriet Elsie Breaks**, 26, on 23 December 1919, in Lytham St Annes, Lancs. |
| *Motive:* | *Financial.* |

Holt, *(b.1887)*, known as Eric, had an excellent war record on the western front, being invalided out as a Lieutenant, suffering from shell-shock, and its consequent depression and amnesia. After a spell working in Malaya, he returned to Lancashire, living on an inherited income of £500 per year. In 1918 he met Kitty Breaks, a Bradford mill worker, long separated from her husband, and they fell in love. In November 1919, she insured her life for £5000, making Holt the beneficiary.

Just before Christmas 1919, Holt, 6', took Kitty to Blackpool and one night followed her onto the sands at St Annes, where she was taking an evening walk. He shot her three times, and smashed her face beyond recognition. Nearby he buried his revolver and blood-stained gloves. When Kitty's body was discovered by a young boy the next day, Holt's footprints were clearly visible in the sand, and the gun and gloves were recovered.

At the trial the prosecution pointed to the fact that Holt had been living beyond his means, and Kitty's insurance indicated premeditation. The defence, however, made much of its insanity plea. Holt's mother died in a lunatic asylum, and his grandfather and a cousin had also been certified insane. In loyal service to his country, they asserted, he had been driven mad. He had developed a persecution mania, fearing the police were trying to drive him insane. The jury took one hour to dismiss the pleas.

At the appeal extra evidence was cited, that Holt had contracted syphilis in Malaya, underlining the insanity plea. A petition was raised amid considerable public sympathy for Holt. The Home Secretary ordered a medical enquiry into the officer's sanity, but ruled that the sentence should stand.

Read: Vintage Murder of the 20s.

14 April 1920   Cardiff prison   *Ellis/ Willis*

298

Thomas CALER   **23**   *Zanzibar*   black

Cut throats of: **1 Gladys May Ibraim**, 22, and her daughter,
   2 Aysha Ibraim, 8 mths, on 14 December 1919, in Cardiff, Glamorgan.
Motive: Sexual/ financial.

Caler, *(b.1897)*, was a ship's fireman, and it is unclear whether or not he knew Gladys Ibraim when he broke into her house after midnight, eleven days before Christmas. Ahmed Ibraim had gone to London on 12 December, leaving his wife and two children aged 2 years and eight months, for a few days. Caler cut the throats of mother and daughter, raped Gladys'

232

lifeless body, and then ransacked the place. He stole a gramophone, but left behind a suitcase, containing a razor and letters bearing his name. A neighbour discovered the bodies the following day at 12.20pm, with the elder child safe and well in another bedroom. The gramophone was found in Caler's possession, on board his ship. The judge said Caler had committed, "Two of the most cruel and barbarous murders in the annals of crime". Caler sought atonement in praying and reading the Koran in the death cell.

Read: And May The Lord Have Mercy On Your Soul.

16 April 1920   Armley gaol, Leeds   *T.Pierrepoint/ Taylor*

299

Miles McHUGH   **31**

Cut throat of: ***Edith Annie Swainston***, *25, on 24 January 1920, in Middlesbrough, N.Yorks.*
Motive: *Sexual rivalry.*

McHugh, *(b.1889),* lived in Chorley, Lancs, with his wife and two children until January 1918, when the two separated, and McHugh moved to Middlesbrough, gaining work as a labourer. The following June he met Edith Swainston, who had recently broken off her engagement. The two set up home together, and Edith gave birth in March 1919. However, when the former fiance turned up again, McHugh left, returning only to see the child.
During such visits the couple often argued, and on Christmas Day 1919, neighbours intervened when McHugh tried to strangle Edith. A month later the two were seen arguing near a railway arch. McHugh cut Edith's throat, and threw the razor in a river. When arrested he claimed to have found Edith who had carried out a threat to commit suicide. Her wounds could not possibly have been self-inflicted, and the jury sealed his fate within eight minutes.

Read: True Detective, Jun 89.

300

Thomas Hargreaves WILSON   44

Cut throat of: **Annie Maria Wilson**, *46, his wife, on 16 January 1920, in Leeds, W.Yorks.*
Motive: *Vengeance.*

Wilson, *(b.1876),* married Annie Hargreaves in 1917. He was a widower, and she had seven children from a previous marriage, the marital home being completed by Annie's invalid sister-in-law, Harriet Watson. Wilson served in the army from July 1917 until February 1919, and Annie soon found out about his temper when he returned home. She applied for a separation order in November 1919, and Wilson went into lodgings, only to return for an argument periodically, having to be thrown out by police.

At 8pm Wilson had appeared brandishing the court order, with the intension, he claimed, of getting a receipt for the money he had paid Annie. Harriet, a friend and two daughters were present when Annie told him to get out and he accused her of having another man in the house.

When he thought her daughter was going for the police, he pushed Annie onto the settee and her daughter hit him with a picture frame, badly cutting his head. Wilson seized a knife that the women had been cleaning and Annie hid under the sofa. The others ran upstairs and escaped along a window ledge, leaving only Harriet to witness Wilson slashing at his wife. She received ten head wounds, and two gashes to the throat. Wilson attacked a policeman who arrived, cut his own throat, and was knocked unconscious with a truncheon. He was in hospital ten days, and although his brother and sister had died in an asylum, the jury found him guilty within fifteen minutes.

Read: Murderous Leeds

301

Herbert Edward Rawson SALISBURY   35

Shot: **Alice Pearson**, *39, on 21 March 1920, in Formby, Lancs.*
Motive: *To clear impediment; drink related.*

Salisbury, *(b.1885),* had emigrated to the USA in 1900, but had returned to fight for his country in the first world war. In September 1918, he returned from France suffering from trench fever and shrapnel wounds. He met nurse Alice Pearson while he was recuperating in hospital. She was married, her husband also serving in France, but fell in love with Salisbury, and the two took a holiday together when he was discharged. By the time Mark Pearson returned in the spring of 1919, Alice had gone, setting up home with Bert in Southport, and living as man and wife. Salisbury was cited as co-respondent when Pearson sued his wife for divorce later in 1919.

Bert could not get a job, and turned to drink. On 21 March he shot Alice on the banks of the river Alt, outside of Liverpool, and had gone on a drinking binge. When he threatened a man with a revolver, he was taken to the police station, where he told them exactly what he had done, and where Alice's body could be found. No motive ever emerged. The jury took twenty minutes to dismiss his plea of insanity. He was hanged alongside William Waddington.

Read: A Date With the Hangman.

11 May 1920   Walton gaol, Liverpool   *Ellis/ Baxter*

302

William WADDINGTON   **34**

Bludgeoned: ***Ivy Wolfenden**, 7, on 14 February 1920, in Oldham, Lancs.*
Motive: Sexual

Waddington, *(b.1886),* a mill worker, had fought for four years in France in World War One, being injured three times, and reported dead. Unmarried, he had rejoined the army after the war, but had deserted. He lived with his parents and two of his siblings in Oldham. On Valentine's day, he called for a neighbour's child to go to buy cigarettes. Ivy Wolfenden was one of ten children whose mother, Eliza, was widowed. Playing out during a party at her house, Ivy had called at the tobacconist at 3.35pm.

His parents out, and brother George in bed sleeping off a morning's drink, Bill, 5' 6", took the child down to the cellar where he gagged her with paper, and violently raped her. He hit her four times about the head with a coal-hammer, and left the house at 4pm. His sister heard moaning from the cellar when she returned, and Ivy was found there naked from the waist down, with blood and brain matter splashed about. She died as an ambulance arrived. Waddington was arrested in Todmorden the following morning. He denied murder, but blood was found on his trousers.

235

His father claimed that his war experiences had left him mentally unstable. Though many agreed, the jury did not, returning their verdict in ten minutes. Waddington was hanged alongside Bert Salisbury.

Read: *A Date With the Hangman*

| 26 May 1920 | Duke Street prison, Glasgow | *Ellis* |

303, 304

| **Albert James FRASER** | **24** | *Scottish* |
| **James ROLLINS** | **23** | *Scottish* |

Bludgeoned: **Henry Senior**, *35, on 3 February 1920, in Glasgow, Lanarks.*
Motive: Financial.

Fraser, *(b.1896)*, and Rollins, *(b.1897)*, hatched a plan for their girlfriends to entrap men so that they could be robbed. One evening, Gladys White, Fraser's lover, acting as a prostitute in Hope Street, met Henry Senior, and the two travelled by tram to Queen's Park, where Senior produced ten shillings with which to pay for Gladys' services. Fraser and Rollins emerged from the shadows, and savagely beat the unsuspecting punter. Both jaws broken, and his face lacerated and disfigured, Senior was left on the grass to die, while the culprits made off with his coat, watch, shoes and some cash. Ms White testified against the two.

On the scaffold Fraser remarked, 'Cheer up, Jimmy'.

Read: *Encyclopaedia of Scottish Executions.*

| 15 June 1920 | Ipswich prison | *Ellis* |

305

| **Frederick William STOREY** | **42** | *i* |

Bludgeoned: **Sarah Jane Howard**, *27, on 6 February 1920, in Wherstead, Suffolk*
Motive: *To clear impediment*

Storey, *(b.1878),* had been a tram driver in Ipswich since 1899, interrupted only by his war service in the near East. Married with six children, and a seventh expected, his wife stated that he was a kind and caring husband. He first knew Sarah Jane Howard when she worked as a conductress before the war. She was now a housekeeper, but by 1920 had become pregnant, though she was estranged from her husband.

On a cold February evening, she was battered nine times with a hammer near allotments two miles from Ipswich. Witnesses told of Storey's friendship with Sarah, and when bloody clothes and a hammer were found at his home, he was charged. His hammer was not the murder weapon, and his family told that Storey frequently had nose bleeds. He denied having an affair, but could only say he was out walking at the time of the murder. The purely circumstantial evidence was enough to convince the jury within 15 minutes. Storey made no appeal.

Read: True Crime, May 95.

| 22 June 1920 | Strangeways prison, Manchester | *Ellis* |

306

<u>William ALDRED</u>   54

Cut throat of: **Ida Prescott**, *44, on 16 February 1920, in Manchester, Lancs.*
Motive: *Vengeance; drink related.*

Aldred, *(b.1866),* had been unfit for work from 1903 to 1912 because of the condition locomotor ataxy, and had twice been observed for short periods at a mental hospital in 1916. His problems were worsened by his drink problem. He got to know Ida Prescott around Christmas 1918, and had wanted the relationship to become more than platonic. Ida had been widowed with two children, 10 and 12, earlier that year and was not interested, but Aldred persisted in calling to her Clifton home at all times and Ida had to tell him to stay away, a request he ignored.

With a razor he had stolen from a roommate, he called again on Ida at 9.45pm, having been drinking. The two went to the kitchen where he, without warning, cut her throat. Ida's daughter's screams alerted neighbours, and Aldred waited for police to arrive. Pleas of insanity were rejected.

Read: Murderous Manchester

307

Arthur Andrew Clement GOSLETT   44   *SAfrican*

Drowned: ***Evelyn Goslett**, 37, his wife, on 1 May 1920, in Golders Green, Middlesex.*

Motive: *To clear impediment.*

Goslett was born in Cape Town in 1876 to an Englishman and a south African woman. He was dismissed from the navy in South Africa on suspicion of spying for the Germans and was convicted of diamond smuggling in Namibia and released from a German jail in 1912. Married to Evelyn, a widow with three children, in 1914, he first committed bigamy a year later, by which time Evelyn had borne his child.

Masquerading as Captain Arthur Godfrey, RN, he began an affair with Daisy Holt in 1917. When Daisy became pregnant he married her in February 1919, then moved her into his home in Golders Green, telling his wife she was his sister-in-law. Goslett meantime began another affair with Ethel Baker, bigamously marrying her, his sixth bigamous wife, in January 1920, three months after the birth of Daisy's baby.

After his wife discovered the true nature of his relationship with Daisy, and fearing she would report his bigamy, he clubbed her to death with a tyre-lever at 9pm on the tow-path of the river Brent, and dumped her in the water to drown.

He confessed to the murder but claimed he had conspired with Daisy. She denied involvement, and the jury took only eight minutes to confirm his guilt.

Read: True Crime, Sep 97.

308

James ELLOR   35

Bludgeoned: ***Ada Ellor**, 42, his wife, on 27 March 1920, in Hyde, Cheshire.*

Motive: *Vengeance.*

Ellor, *(b.1885),* married Ada, a widow, in July 1907, and was wounded and gassed in the war, thereafter becoming a heavy drinker, and violent towards his wife. Shortly after discovering she was pregnant, in March 1918, Ada received two letters from her soldier husband, the first telling her he had a pregnant mistress, and the second telling her to ignore what he had written in the first.

On 25 March Ada left him and issued him with a summons. Four days later, Ellor went to the lodgings Ada shared with her adult son, and begged her on his knees to come back to him. Left alone to sort things out, Ada refused Ellor's pleas, and he battered her to death with a hammer. At 3.30pm, Ellor handed himself over to a policeman.

Read: And May The Lord Have Mercy On Your Soul

| 30 November 1920 | Durham gaol | *T.Pierrepoint/ Taylor* |

309

<u>James RILEY</u>   50

| **Bludgeoned:** | **Mary Riley***, 43, his wife, on 9 October 1920, in West Auckland, Co Durham.* |
| **Motive:** | *Sadistic pleasure; drink related.* |

Riley, *(b.1870),* a miner, suffered from malaria, contracted during his distinguished war service in India and Greece, and had just one conviction, for drunkenness in 1913. He had been married 20 years, though it was often a tempestuous relationship, particularly when Riley had been drinking. Neighbours called the police on 2 October when he started to beat his wife, but a week later he called round to them at 5.30am to say, 'I've killed her'. He had battered her with a poker and left her dead in the fireplace, and then asked the neighbours to give him an hour before calling the police, which they agreed to.

Two hours later he was arrested just four miles away, the jury deciding his guilt in 35 minutes.

Read: True Crime, Dec 94.

310

Cyril Victor Tennyson SAUNDERS   21

Stabbed: **Dorothy May Saunders**, *16, his cousin, on 23 September 1920, in Plymouth, Devon.*

Motive: *Sexual rivalry.*

Saunders, *(b.1899)*, a Lt-Corporal in the Royal Engineers, stationed in Surrey, planned to marry his cousin, Dorothy, whom he had been courting since 1918. He was angered when he was told, on leave in September, that Dorothy had been out with another boy. When he returned to Surrey, she wrote to him, saying that she could not marry him. There was no other man, but she felt she could not trust Saunders. He returned to Devon on 22 September, and Dorothy agreed to go to the cinema with him. He failed in trying to buy a revolver, so bought a knife instead, and following her into a shop, stabbed her four times.

Read: And May The Lord Have Mercy On Your Soul

311

Samuel WESTWOOD   24

Stabbed: **Lydia Westwood**, *22, his wife, on 11 September 1920, in Birmingham, Warwicks.*

Motive: *Vengeance*

Westwood, *(b.1896)*, had joined the army in November 1915, going to the trenches in February 1917, and being held as a prisoner of war from March to November 1918. He married Lydia Vaughan in July 1920, and the two went to live with his parents in Short Heath, Birmingham. Lydia did not get on with Sam's parents, his mother in particular, and Sam rarely accompanied Lydia to see her parents , who thought him unsuitable for their daughter. The interference of the in-laws created to great a strain for Lydia, and she returned to her mother in Willenhall in September.

She missed Sam and wanted to attempt a reconciliation, taking her mother along to try to find him on the evening of 11 September. Sam had had a couple of pints when they bumped into him on the street at 9pm. He urged Lydia to return to him, promising to find lodgings so they could be alone in peace, but when Alice Vaughan intervened, and Lydia made to go off with her mother, Sam grabbed Lydia and stabbed her in the throat with a penknife. He walked straight down the road and handed himself in at the police station. The jury completed its deliberations in 15 minutes.

Read: Murderous Birmingham

30 December 1920   Armley gaol, Leeds   *T.Pierrepoint/ Taylor*

312

Edwin SOWERBY   28

Cut throat of: ***Jane Darwell**, 19, on 25 October 1920, in Crofton, W.Yorks.*
Motive: *Vengeance.*

    Sowerby, *(b.1892),* was devastated when his girlfriend, Jane Darwell, threw him over. He lost his voice, and barely slept for five weeks. The doctor was called to him, and Edwin told friends that suicide was the only way out. Jane, who was a domestic servant at a guest-house, went to a dance on 25 October, and Sowerby went along as well. He crossed the dancefloor and, in full view of the shocked guests, cut Jane's throat. The jury decided his fate in 20 minutes.

Read: And May The Lord Have Mercy On Your Soul

30 December 1920   Pentonville prison, London   *Willis/ Baxter*

313

Marks GOODMACHER   47

Cut throat of: ***Fanny Zeitoun**, 24, his daughter, on 23 September 1920, in London E1.*
Motive: *Vengeance.*

    Goodmacher, *(b.1873),* a tailor and an orthodox Jew, lived off Commercial Road with his daughter and her husband. Relations in the family had been strained because of Goodmacher's insistence upon orthodox practices, and the young couple eventually moved out. When his son-in-law refused to speak to him on the Day of Atonement, Goodmacher's sorrow turned to anger.

Going to his daughter's house, he destroyed all Fanny's belongings, including jewellery and money, and then cut her throat. Fanny's husband discovered her body, with her father lying beside her, when he returned from work.

Read: And May The Lord Have Mercy On Your Soul

31 December 1920	Strangeways prison, Manchester	*Ellis*

314

Charles COLCLOUGH   45

Cut throat of:	**George Henry Shenton**, *40, on 31 October 1920, in Manchester, Lancs.*
Motive:	Sexual rivalry.

Colclough, *(b.1873)*, a fish seller, and Annie Shelton, were both married, but lived together from July 1920 in Hanley. On 30 October, Annie left Colclough, and returned to her husband. The following afternoon, Colclough went to the couple's house, and called Annie down from the bedroom. When George came down, in shirt and socks only, Colclough attacked him, and cut his throat. He claimed that he had gone to collect £2 in housekeeping money which Annie owed him, and was attacked by her husband.

Read: And May The Lord Have Mercy On Your Soul

1920 Army Executions Overseas

6 servicemen or army workers *(5)* were executed by firing squad:

3 Chinese
2 Irish
1 Russian

14 Feb	**Chang Ju Chih**, Chinese, in France, for the murder of a woman and her three children in Amiens, in November 1918.
21 Feb	**Hei Chi Ming**, Chinese, in France, with **K'ung Ch'ing Hsing**, Chinese, for an unspecified murder
17 Mar	**T Jegoroff**, possibly Russian, a labourer, in Turkey, for an unspecified murder
2 Nov	**James Joseph Daly**, 20, Irish, in Turkey, for mutiny
6 Nov	**Richard Flynn**, Irish, in Turkey, for an unspecified murder

for murder	5	*in France*	3
for mutiny	1	*in Turkey*	3

In addition the following 5 men were shot on unspecified dates probably between 1918 and 1920:

Y Antonio
Y H Louka
S Simeoni
N Thaourdis
Another, unnamed. All were muleteers, probably Greek Cypriots, in Greece, for unspecified murder or murders

1 November 1920   Mountjoy gaol, Dublin

Kevin Gerald BARRY   **18**

Shot: *Three British soldiers, on 20 September 1920, in Dublin.*

Barry, *(b.1902)*, a medical student, was one of four Volunteers who ambushed a party of five British soldiers who were collecting bread from a bakery at 11am in Upper Church Street, Dublin.   As the soldiers were surrendering their arms, as ordered, the IRA men opened fire, killing one soldier, and mortally wounding two others.   Another two soldiers inside the bakery were shot and wounded.   An English officer found Barry, armed with a revolver, hiding beneath a lorry outside the premises.

Following a court martial, there were wide appeals for mercy on account of Barry's youth, but one of his victims had been just 19 years of age, and the IRA had recently killed two soldiers aged just 17.   Though Lloyd George was minded to reprieve the Irishman, out of expediency rather than humanity, the head of the Royal Irish Constabulary threatened to resign if Barry was spared, and consequently he was hanged.

Read: The Black and Tans, p76,89

* 9 other Irishmen were executed by the British in November and December 1920.

1921

total: **8**

315	7 Jan	George LEVER	51		Maidstone
316	4 Feb	Jack FIELD	19		Wandsworth
317	4 Feb	William GRAY	29	S African	Wandsworth
318	2 Mar	George BAILEY	34		Oxford
319	6 May	Frederick QUARMBY	47		Strangeways
320	24 May	Thomas WILSON	43		Strangeways
321	16 Aug	Lester HAMILTON	25	W.Indian	Cardiff
322	22 Dec	Edward O'CONNOR	43		Winson Green

7 January 1921   Maidstone prison   *T.Pierrepoint/ Baxter*

315

George Freeman Quinton LEVER   51

Cut throat of: *Harriet Lever, 35, his wife, on 25 September 1920, in Northfleet, Kent.*
Motive: *To clear impediment.*

Lever, *(b.1870),* had served honourably in the army for twenty years, but was discharged with a nervous disorder, shortly before qualifying for his pension. He and his wife fell into financial problems, and were evicted from their lodgings. Lever remained homeless, and his wife stayed with her first husband's sister. Lever called on his wife, and told her he had found new rooms. His lie was to entice Harriet to the tram depot, where he cut her throat. Harriet managed to stagger to a neighbour's house, while Lever gave himself up to a police officer, handing him the bloody razor.

Read: And May The Lord Have Mercy On Your Soul

4 February 1921   Wandsworth prison, London

T.Pierrepoint/ Baxter/ Willis

316, 317

<u>**Jack Alfred FIELD**</u>	**19**
<u>**William Thomas GRAY**</u>	**29** *South African*

Bludgeoned: ***Irene Violet Munro***, *17, on 19 August 1920, near Eastbourne, Sussex.*

Motive: *Financial.*

        London typist Irene Munro, a Scot, was staying in lodgings near Eastbourne for a week's holiday, her first alone without her mother. She had met Field and Gray soon after her arrival on 16 August, and had walked and had a drink with them. With her holiday money in her handbag, she arranged to meet them again and they went for a walk along the beach. She did not return. Her body was found the following day buried in shingle on the 'Crumbles' beach, her money stolen.

        Witnesses identified the two locals, Field, *(b.1902)*, and Gray, *(b.1892)*, a married man, as walking with a woman towards the sea. She had been arm-in-arm with Gray. Ex-servicemen, both were unemployed labourers, Field with previous robbery convictions, Gray an illiterate convicted rapist, who had come to England with the South African artillery in the Great war. Gray had hit Irene in the mouth and on the head with a walking-stick, breaking her jaw and knocking out her teeth, and then dropped a rock on her head. She was fully clothed and there had been no sexual assault. The murderers attempted to enlist in the army when Irene was discovered.

        Both blamed each other for the murder. Field fell asleep during the court proceedings, and surprisingly, the jury recommended mercy because they felt the crime had not been premeditated.

     Read: The Seaside Murders.

---

2 March 1921   Oxford prison   *Ellis/ Taylor*

318

<u>**George Arthur BAILEY**</u>   **34**

Poisoned: ***Kate Bailey***, *23, his wife, on 29 September 1920, in Little Marlow, Bucks*

Motive: *To clear impediment*

Bailey, *(b.1887)*, had attempted suicide in 1910, and had spent three months in an asylum. He moved with his wife and infant daughter from Ilfracombe to Little Marlow in June 1920. A milkman, he wrote plays and poems, and made inventions, none of which made him any money. He came up with the idea of a new system of singing and advertised for girls to come to a cottage he rented in the village. Alerted by a newspaper, the police observed the cottage for three months up to 22 September, and saw 33 girls come and go. None complained.

On 29 September, Lillian Marks, 16, arrived and was asked to stay the night. She met Mrs Bailey and then went shopping. While she was out Bailey poisoned his wife with prussic acid and hid her body beneath a bed.
That night Bailey entered Lillian's room and attempted to rape her. She left the next day and told her father. When the police searched the cottage on 2 October, they found Kate Bailey's body. She was six months pregnant. Bailey was arrested on Reading station that evening. He claimed his wife had committed suicide, but the jury, which included women for the first time in a murder trial, disagreed after 30 minutes' deliberation.

Read: *True Crime, Nov 97.*

| 6 May 1921 | Strangeways prison, Manchester | *Ellis* |

319

<u>Frederick QUARMBY</u>   **47**

| *Stabbed:* | *Christina Ann Alexandra Smith, 33, on 3 December 1919, in Blackpool, Lancs.* |
| *Motive:* | *Sexual rivalry.* |

Christina had married John Smith in 1913 while eight months pregnant. He left her the following day after she told him that one man was not enough to satisfy her. She moved to Blackpool, her home paid for by John, but she had a succession of lovers, and took money for her favours.

Quarmby, *(b. 1873)*, had money from the family's cotton mill in Stainland near Halifax. He was a keen churchgoer, but was always workshy, though very generous with his money. He met Christina in Blackpool in 1919, and they began a relationship, but her sexual exploits with other men caused him to drink and then to move out. Despite jealous rows they continued to see each other, until Quarmby's jealousy got out of control.

He called at her house, and after fixing her lodger's supper, Christina locked the dining room, undressed and the couple began sexual intercourse. It was then that Quarmby attacked Christina with a knife, almost severing her head. The lodger and Christina's daughter heard a piercing scream and the police were alerted. Quarmby led the officers into the dining room and continued to express his satisfaction at what he had done. A defence plea of insanity was rejected by the jury in 15 minutes.

Read: True Crime SS, 96.

24 May 1921	Strangeways prison, Manchester	*Ellis*

320

Thomas WILSON   43

Shot: *Olive Jackson, 43, on 9 April 1922, in Liverpool, Lancs.*
Motive: *Sexual rivalry.*

Wilson, *(b.1878)*, a sailor, had lodged with George Duff and Olive Jackson since 1916. Olive, a widow with three children, had lived with Duff for twelve years. Wilson imagined a close relationship between him and Olive, but did not seem jealous of George, yet when Henry Roskell gave Olive a friendly kiss under the mistletoe at a Christmas party, Wilson's grudge was born.

After a drink with Duff and Wilson, Olive went to a friend's, and, suspecting that Roskell might be there, Wilson went to collect her at 11pm. On the way home, the two argued, and when Olive told him that she would not be interested in a worm like him, Wilson shot her five times with a revolver. He was arrested on Lime Street station at 11.45 the next morning.

Read: And May The Lord Have Mercy On Your Soul

16 August 1921	Cardiff prison	*Ellis/ Willis*

321

Lester Augustus HAMILTON   25   *West Indian*   *black*

Shot: *Doris Appleton, 17, on 12 February 1921, in Cardiff, Glamorgan.*
Motive: *Sexual rivalry.*

Hamilton, *(b.1896)*, a ship's fireman, met Doris Appleton at the lodging house where he lived and she worked, and the two began a relationship. He had been to the pub with Doris and her mother at 7pm, and stayed on when the women left.

At 8.30pm, he called at Mrs Appleton's house with a friend, whom Doris and her mother did not like the look of. They refused him entry, and when Hamilton suspected that Doris was entertaining a Japanese sailor in the house, and she again refused to let him in, he shot her. He walked a short distance and shot himself in the head, causing himself a serious injury. The jury deliberated for one hour.

Read: And May The Lord Have Mercy On Your Soul

22 December 1921   Winson Green prison, Birmingham   *Ellis/ Wilson*

322

Edward O'CONNOR   43

Cut throat of: ***Thomas O'Connor***, *5, his son, on 31 July 1921, in*
                         Stafford.
Motive: *Vengeance.*

O'Connor, *(b.1878)*, and his wife Elizabeth, had eight children, but Elizabeth had to suffer O'Connor's temper, and eventually left him. She sued him for persistent cruelty, and on 25 July, a summons was served for non-payment of maintenance. He nevertheless called every day, and on 30 July hit Elizabeth. The following night, to overcome the cramped conditions at her lodgings, Elizabeth took two of the children to her mother's, leaving the others at home alone under the 12-year old's supervision.

O'Connor crept into the house at 4am, and, discovering his wife was not there, cut the throats of Thomas, 5, and Mary, 7. He then went to the second bedroom, where Elizabeth, 11, and Edward, 9, suffered the same fate. The other two terrified children escaped his attentions, and O'Connor handed two bloody razors to a policeman at 5am. Thomas died in the house, with the others eventually recovering from the attack.

Read: And May The Lord Have Mercy On Your Soul

1921 Executions in Ireland

14 March 1921   Mounttjoy gaol, Dublin

Frank FLOOD
Patrick MORAN
Bernard RYAN
Thomas WHELAN
and two others

Crime: *Murder, Treason, Levying war*
Motive: *Political*

Five of the six hanged for treason and levying war. The sixth was found guilty of the 'Bloody Sunday' murders of 21 November 1920. Fourteen Irishmen with British connections were simultaneously murdered in their homes at daybreak.

25 April 1921   Mountjoy gaol, Dublin

Thomas TRAYNOR

Crime: *unknown*
Motive: *unknown*

7 June 1921   Mountjoy gaol, Dublin

Edmund FOLEY
Patrick MAHER
William MITCHELL

Crime: *unknown*
Motive: *unknown*

* A further four Irishmen were executed by the British before June 1921.

* 7 prisoners were shot in Ireland from 21 November 1921- opponents of the Irish Free State government.

323	21 Feb	William HARKNESS	30	*Scottish*	Duke Street
324	21 Mar	James WILLIAMSON	37		Durham
325	23 Mar	William SULLIVAN	41		Usk
326	24 Mar	Edward BLACK	36		Exeter
327	7 Apr	Percy ATKIN	29		Nottingham
328	11 Apr	Frederick KEELING	54		Pentonville
329	18 Apr	Edmund TONBRIDGE	38		Pentonville
330	30 May	Hiram THOMPSON	52		Strangeways
331	31 May	Herbert ARMSTRONG	52		Gloucester
332	7 Jun	Henry JACOBY	18		Pentonville
333	10 Aug	Reginald DUNN	24	*Irish*	Wandsworth
334	10 Aug	Joseph O'SULLIVAN	24	*Irish*	Wandsworth
335	11 Aug	Elijah POUNTNEY	48		Winson Green
336	19 Aug	Thomas ALLAWAY	36		Winchester
337	5 Sep	William YELDHAM	23		Pentonville
338	13 Dec	George ROBINSON	27		Lincoln
339	13 Dec	Frank FOWLER	35		Lincoln
340	19 Dec	William RIDER	40		Winson Green

21 February 1922   Duke Street prison, Glasgow   *Ellis/ Willis*

323

William HARKNESS   **30**   *Scottish*

i

Suffocated: **Elizabeth Benjamin**, 14, on 31 October 1921, in Partick, Lanarks.

Motive: Financial.

Harkness, *(b.1892)*, and his wife Helen had a young son and very little money. Nellie planned to rob the rent woman when she came by, but young Elizabeth happened by first. Elizabeth worked in the Jewish family's drapery shop, but on Mondays went door to door selling. When Nellie invited

251

her in at 4pm, she was carrying just about £1.50. Whether William had any part in the attack is not clear, but Nellie said the girl struggled a lot, and admitted stuffing a handkerchief in her mouth.

Elizabeth's hands were tied, and she had been hit on the head with a rivetting tool. Nellie went to get William's brother John, who helped him remove the girl from the wash-house to a neighbour's backyard, where she was found at 7am the following morning.

Finding blood on the Harness' stairs, all three were charged with murder. Charges aginst John were later dropped and he testified against his brother. The jury found husband and wife guilty after a 25-minute retirement, but recommended mercy in Helen's case. William later declared he would hang twice to save his wife, who served 15 years, being released in 1937. John was murdered in a pub brawl in 1926.

Read: True Crime, Apr 99

| 21 March 1922 | Durham gaol | *T.Pierrepoint/ Willis* |

324

James Hutton WILLIAMSON   37

Cut throat of: *Mary Williamson, 38, his wife, on 7 January 1922, in Houghton-le-Spring, Co Durham.*
Motive: *Vengeance.*

Williamson, *(b.1885)*, who lived with his wife and five children in Easington, walked with a limp since being wounded at Salonika. Mary left him in December 1921, and went with the children to her parents, taking out a separation order, by which her husband sent her 30/- every week by post. Williamson stayed with the family over New Year, and stayed again on the night of 6 January, sleeping by the fire.

The following morning, the money did not arrive in the post, and a row developed with Williamson insisting he had sent it, and Mary calling him a liar. In front of two of the children, he cut his wife's throat, and was hacking away at her neck when neighbours arrived. Williamson had indeed posted the money, for two days later it arrived. The jury deliberated for five minutes.

Read: And May The Lord Have Mercy On Your Soul

325

William SULLIVAN   41

Bludgeoned:	*Margaret Thomas, 48, on 26 October 1921, in Pen-groes oped, Monmouths.*
Motive:	*Financial.*

Sullivan, *(b.1881),* was a tramp, and had called on at least two houses in the village near Pontypool on 21 October, asking for water from one, and for bread and cheese from the home of David and Margaret Thomas. Five days later, shortly after Mr Thomas had left for work at 6.30am, Sullivan called again, and battered Margaret to death in her kitchen. The house was locked when David returned at 5pm, and he climbed in through a window to discover his wife's body.

Sullivan was found on 17 November, and continued to plead his innocence, and indeed, his defence suggested that Thomas may have killed his own wife. However, the fact that Sullivan had tried to sell a pair of Thomas' trousers convinced the jury of his guilt in 2 hours 30 minutes. Sullivan's was the last execution at Usk , the prison closing eight days later.

Read: And May The Lord Have Mercy On Your Soul

326

Edward Ernest BLACK   36

Poisoned:	*Annie Black, 50, his wife, on 11 November 1921, near St Austell, Cornwall.*
Motive:	*Financial.*

Black, *(b.1886),* was an insurance salesman from Burnley who had moved to Cornwall and lodged with Annie Nicholls and her illegitimate daughter Marion. Annie and Edward married in August 1914, but by 1919, Black had begun a sexual relationship with Marion, 15, and may have had a mistress elsewhere.

Black had pocketed insurance premiums, and now that claims were being made, he did not have the resources to fund them. His fraud was about to be discovered, and insurance on his wife's life seemed the only answer. A former school-teacher, Annie ran the village sweet shop in Tregonissey, near St Austell, and took ill in November 1921. Edward disappeared on 8

November, and Annie died, apparently of gastro-enteritis, three days later. A post-mortem examination, however, showed the presence of arsenic. On 15 November, a warrant was taken out against Black on fraud charges.

He was tracked down to a hotel in Liverpool, and when the police burst in, on 21 November, Black had cut his throat. He recovered in hospital, and during his two-day trial heard the chemist testify that Black had signed the poisons book for arsenic. The jury considered their verdict for 40 minutes.

Read: True Crime, Jan 95.

7 April 1922	Bagthorpe prison, Nottingham	*Ellis/ Baxter*

327

Percy James ATKIN   29

Buried alive: *Maud Atkin, 27, his wife, on 21 November 1921, in Chaddesden, near Derby.*
Motive: *To clear impediment.*

Atkin, *(b.1893),* a railway guard, had married in 1913, but by 1920 the marriage had turned sour and Maud often stayed with her parents. In the meantime, Percy had met Margaret Milton, telling her his wife had recently died, and he bigamously married her on 14 November 1921. Maud and Percy's lodgers believed the couple were moving to Normanton, and last saw them on 20 November. The next day Percy and Maud decided to go for a walk, to discuss their problems, he claimed. They argued, Atkin stunned her with a blow to the head and then buried her, probably alive, on his allotment.

On 2 December Atkin wrote to a friend saying Maud had died suddenly, and Margaret last saw him on Christmas Day. Maud's body was found on 1 January and Atkin was arrested at his sister's in Surrey the following day. He claimed that he had found Maud dead after he had been searching for the wedding ring which she had thrown at him. In panic, he had buried her in a hole he had made for an apple tree. The jury took less than five minutes to convict him.

Read: Murderous Derbyshire

328

Frederick Alexander KEELING   54

Bludgeoned: ***Emily Agnes Dewberry***, *46, on 24 November 1921, in Tottenham, Middlesex.*
Motive: *Vengeance.*

Keeling, *(b.1868)*, separated from his wife, lived with another woman in lodgings in Tottenham, and supplemented his income by fraudulently claiming a £4 per week pension. Another lodger at the house, Emily Dewberry, discovered this deceit, and reported Keeling to the authorities.

Both were due to appear in court on 24 November, Ms Dewberry as a witness, but Keeling exacted his revenge before she could testify. He hammered her to death in her room, the body being discovered when they both failed to appear in court. Blood was found on Keeling's clothes when he was finally arrested in a pub, on 9 December.

Read: And May The Lord Have Mercy On Your Soul

329

Edmund Hugh TONBRIDGE   38

Poisoned: ***Margaret Evans***, *25, on 14 January 1922, in London E5.*
Motive: *To clear impediment.*

Tonbridge, *(b.1884)*, and Margaret Evans had begun their affair in 1919, and she had borne him a child in November 1920. He paid Margaret 15/- a week until the child was adopted in August the following year. She kept pressing Edmund for marriage, and the demands grew when she found herself pregnant again.

At 7pm, Tonbridge took Margaret for a walk down by the river Lea at Clapton, armed with a bottle of prussic acid. He punched her in the face, then forced the poison down her throat, before dumping her in the river. A policeman, who had seen them walking together, arrested Tonbridge when he heard a splash and saw trhe man alone. Tonbridge tried to convince the jury that Margaret had committed suicide, even having written a letter from a supposed lover beforehand.

Read: And May The Lord Have Mercy On Your Soul

330

Hiram THOMPSON   52

Cut throat of/ Bludgeoned: ***Ellen Thompson****, 49, his wife, on 25 April 1922, at Bamber Bridge, Lancs.*
Motive: *Sadistic pleasure; drink related*

Thompson, *(b. 1870)*, drank heavily, and subjected his wife, Ellen, to frequent physical abuse. The couple shared their home with a married daughter and her husband, and two other of their children, and Thompson's alcohol intake was the cause of many rows. Ellen was alone in the house when Thompson, after a drinking binge, came home one afternoon, cut his wife's throat in the kitchen, and then battered her with an iron heater.

Ellen was discovered at 6pm, at about the time Thompson, in his heavily bloodstained clothes, was telling a neighbour that he had killed her. Arrogant and indifferent to his fate, unmoved by sentencing or scaffold, he had to be shaken awake on the morning of his execution. "One of the most callous brutes I've ever met", Ellis described him.

Read: And May The Lord Have Mercy On Your Soul.

331

Herbert Rowse ARMSTRONG   52

Poisoned: ***Katherine Mary Armstrong****, 48, his wife, on 22 February 1921, in Cusop, Herefordshire.*
Motive: *To clear impediment.*

Armstrong, *(b. 1869)*, a solicitor, freemason and first World War Major, married Katherine Friend in 1907. The couple lived with their three children in the valley of Cusop Dingle in the Welsh borders. He was clerk to the Justices of the Peace in nearby Hay. His wife was sometimes severe with him; Armstrong, with piercing blue eyes, was only eight stone and 5' 6" tall, but they seemed to have a contented life. She suffered from delusions and was commited to an asylum for five months from August 1920. One month after her return home, Katherine died, her death attributed to heart disease.

Later that year, Armstrong was accused of attempting to kill Oswald Martin, 32, a rival solicitor, poisoning chocolates which had been sent to his office, and a scone which Mr Martin ate during a tea to which Armstrong had invited him. Martin's father-in-law, chemist Fred Davies was behind the allegations, and may have tampered with Martin's urine sample. Martin went to the police, Armstrong was charged with attempted murder, and his wife's body exhumed. Armstrong was accused of murdering her with several huge doses of weed-killer containing arsenic, and the defence claim that Mrs Armstrong had committed suicide was, after a ten-day trial, not believed.

Allegations that Armstrong was not faithful to his wife and that he suffered a bout of syphilis were not true. Armstrong maintained his innocence right to the end. His last words on the scaffold were, "I am coming, Kate".

It was later suggested that he was also responsible for the death by poisoning in 1919 of Mabel Greenwood, the wife of a solicitor, who had been acquitted of her murder, in Llanelly.

Read: Dead Not Buried

7 June 1922 Pentonville prison, London *Ellis/ Phillips*

332

Henry Julius JACOBY **18**

Bludgeoned: *Lady Alice White, 65, on 14 March 1922 in London W1.*
Motive: *Financial.*

Jacoby, *(b. 1904),* had been a pantry boy at the Spencer Hotel, Portman St, for three weeks. In the early hours one morning he went to steal from one of the rich guests. Lady White, widow of Sir Edward White, former chairman of the London County Council, had left her room unlocked. As Jacoby shone his torch upon her, Lady White awoke. To stifle her screams, Jacoby hit her several times about the head with the hammer which he had taken from and returned washed to a workman's bag.

Jacoby, who had previously been suspected of stealing from his lodgings, made a full voluntary confession several days later. Despite the jury's strong recommendation to mercy after 40 minutes' deliberation, and public pressure for a reprieve, Jacoby became one of just four 18-year olds hanged this century.

Read: Murder In Low Places

10 August 1922   Wandsworth prison, London

Ellis/ Taylor/ Mills

333, 334

Reginald DUNN	24	*Irish*	*(aka John O'Brien)*
Joseph O'SULLIVAN	24	*Irish*	*(aka James Connelly)*

Shot: ***Sir Henry Hughes Wilson**, 58, on 22 June 1922, in London SW1.*
Motive: *Political.*

Dunne and O'Sullivan, *(both b. 1898)*, had both been wounded fighting in the British army in France during the Great War, O'Sullivan losing his right leg below the knee. They nevertheless became IRA volunteers living in London when Ireland was divided in 1921. Sir Henry had joined the army in 1884, and by 1914 was the Director of Military Operations at the War Office. He was promoted to Field Marshall, and became a Baronet in 1919, and then, in 1922, was elected an MP. He advised the government of Northern Ireland on security matters, and therefore became an ideal target for the IRA, who blamed him for organising the hated Ulster Special Constables, who were held responsible for hundreds of Catholic deaths in recent months.

Dunne and O'Sullivan, a doorkeeper at the Ministry of Labour, shot Sir Henry eight times in the chest, arm, leg and shoulder on his doorstep in Eaton Place, after he had returned home by taxi. The two made their escape, shooting and injuring two pursuing policemen. They were arrested nearby, police rescuing them from an angry mob.

It is not clear whether the killing was ordered by Rory O'Connor's IRA factions opposed to the Free State Treaty, or indeed, by Michael Collins himself, head of the provisional government. Both parties were about to embark on the Irish Civil War. Dunne and O'Sullivan, in a three-hour trial, refused to plead guilty to murder, and were forbidden from reading a written statement to the court. The jury considered for just three minutes.

Read: True Detective, Feb 99.

335

Elijah POUNTNEY   48

Cut throat of: **Alice Gertrude Pountney**, *47, his wife, on 16 April 1922, in Bilston, Warwicks.*
Motive: *Sexual rivalry.*

Pountney, *(b.1874)*, a former blacksmith, and his wife had run the Pheasant Inn in Bilston for six years, the landlord supplementing his meagre income by taking in a lodger and also working as a labourer in the steelworks. There, in December 1921 he was hit on the head by a lump of coal, after which he suffered severe headaches, and became surly and bitter, drinking heavily much of the time. To the horror of his 20-year old son, he first hit Gertrude in January 1922. This was repeated in the public bar in February, when lodger Edmund McCann, a 6' bricklayer, intervened on her behalf.

Pountney, 5'5", became convinced they were having an affair, and appealed to the police to throw McCann out in March, to no avail. On Easter Sunday, with only one customer in the pub, a row developed about whether Gertrude had lent McCann money and was pregnant by him, and in the kitchen, Pountney cut his wife's throat with a knife. He ran out, twice threw himself in a canal, and was twice fished out. Gertrude was not pregnant and a plea of insanity was rejected.

Read: Master Detective Summer Special 94.

336

Thomas Henry ALLAWAY   36

Bludgeoned: **Irene May Wilkins**, *31, on 22 December 1921, at Boscombe, Sussex.*
Motive: *Sexual.*

Thomas Allaway, *(b. 1886)*, chauffeur to Mr Sutton of Boscombe, answered several newspaper advertisements placed by young women seeking employment. One of these, Irene Wilkins, a cook from Streatham in London, took the train to Bournemouth. There, at 7 p.m., she was met by Allaway in his employer's car. He had led her to believe she was to be interviewed for a post as a school cook.

He drove her to a field near Boscombe, where he attempted to rape her, and then killed her with several blows to the head, probably with a car spanner. Arrested at his wife's home in Reading, for stealing Sutton's chequebook, Allaway was identified by tyre-marks at the scene of the crime, his hand-writing on the telegrams he had sent, and by two witnesses who had seen him at the station. Allaway confessed to the murder on the eve of his execution.

Read: True Detective, Feb 96

---

5 September 1922   Pentonville prison, London   *Ellis/ Willis*

337

William James YELDHAM   23

Bludgeoned: **George Stanley Grimshaw**, *54, on 17 May 1921,*
                    near Chingford, Essex.
Motive: Financial.

Yeldham, *(b.1899)*, an unemployed farm labourer from Ilford, had been a submariner in the war. He met Elsie Florence McKenzie in the summer of 1921, and had been living together in poverty ever since. From Edinburgh, she had been a domestic servant, but was working as a prostitute when they met. Yeldham had served six months for stealing a bike in an attempt to raise money for her.

Elsie, 22, met George Grimshaw, a 5' married decorator, at an Easter fair. He became infatuated with Elsie, and the two met often, Elsie accepting money from him. In May they met in Epping Forest but Yeldham had followed them. When he saw Grimshaw kissing Elsie, Yeldham battered Grimshaw with a spanner 26 times. He stole £15 and a watch, and Elsie and he married three days later.

Witnesses had seen the struggle, and Yeldham was identified by a man to whom he sold the watch. The couple were found living rough in Bocking. Elsie was still wearing her only, bloody, dress. Elsie was accused of luring Grimshaw to his death, and both were found guilty, Elsie collapsing in the dock at the verdict. She was, however, granted a reprieve.

Read: True Crime Summer Special 95.

260

338

George ROBINSON   27

Cut throat of: **Frances Florence Pacey**, *18, on 5 September 1922, in Donnington, Lincs.*
Motive: *Vengeance.*

Robinson, *(b.1895),* had been courting Florence Pacey for a year, and he was devastated when she told him, on 9 April, that it was all over, even threatening to kill himself. When the rest of her household had gone to work, and Frances was left alone in the house, at 7.45am, Robinson got in and cut his former girlfriend's throat, leaving his cap in her room to be used as evidence. Frances managed to stagger to a neighbour's, and Robinson went to his mother's, covered in blood. There, he cut his own throat with the razor he had broken slitting Frances. Robinson was hanged alongside Frank Fowler.

Read: And May The Lord Have Mercy On Your Soul

339

Frank FOWLER   35

Shot: **Ivy Dora Prentice**, *18, on 23 September 1922, in Market Deeping, Lincs.*
Motive: *Sexual rivalry.*

Fowler, *(b.1887),* the manager of a smallholding, was said by some to act strangely. Indeed, though he knew Ivy, he had no form of relationship with her, and became extremely jealous when she started seeing Robert Prentice, threatening him in March 1922. On 20 September, Ivy and Robert married, and three days later Ivy's mother, a pub landlady, threw a party, for she herself was to marry a second time two days later.

Fowler came to the pub at 9.30pm, raised his shotgun, and blasted Ivy above the breast. Her mother tackled Fowler, and a second shot smashed a window. Fowler was then overpowered. Ivy's mother still went ahead with her wedding, and Fowler was hanged alongside George Robinson.

Read: And May The Lord Have Mercy On Your Soul

340

<u>William RIDER</u>   **40**

Shot: **Rosilla Patience Barton**, *24, on 7 September 1922, in Harbury, Warwicks.*
Motive: *Vengeance.*

Rosilla Barton, widowed by the Great War in 1916, married Rider, *(b.1882),* in February 1918, little realising he was already married. Though she left him four times after receiving a beating, she kept going back, and stayed with him even after her mother had discovered the truth in February 1922, and sent Rosilla's sister, Winifred, to break the news.

Indeed, Winifred, 15, moved in with the pair, and by August, was herself pregnant by Rider. It was not until Winifred and Rider disappeared together on 26 August, that Rosilla went back to her mother, Rachel, and Winifred eventually returned on 6 September.

The three women were in bed together when Rider sneaked into their house at 7.50am, crept in bare feet to the foot of their bed, and blasted Rosilla through the head with his shotgun. Rachel wrested the weapon from him, and Rider ran out, to be arrested at 9.15am on the roadside.

Read: And May The Lord Have Mercy On Your Soul

1922 Executions in Ireland

17 August 1922   Crumlin Road Gaol, Belfast   *Ellis/ Willis*

SIMON McGEOWN   38

Bludgeoned/ strangled: ***Maggie Fullerton, 8, on 30 May 1922, in Belfast.***
Motive: *Sexual.*

McGeown, *(b.1894),* had enlisted in the army at the age of 14, and was sent to serve in India at 18. His behaviour changed after a bout of malaria, and he was court-martialled and discharged after 18 months. In 1914 he re-enlisted and served three years in France, twice being gassed, being invalided out in 1917, after which he resorted to burglary. Between 1918-22 he served 30 months in prison for six convictions. He became an alcoholic.

At 6pm on 6 May, Maggie Fullerton was sent out to buy sweets. McGeown took her to a nearby plantation where he stripped and raped her. He beat her about the head and strangled her, leaving her naked body on a rubbish tip., where she was found three days later. McGeown, already in custody for burglary, was identified by another girl he had attempted to lure, and by two others who had seen Maggie walking with a man.

The jury took 45 minutes to convict him, and a petition for his reprieve, based on a claim of insanity was rejected. McGeown claimed to the end that he could not remember the murder, so drunk was he.

Read: True Detective, Nov96.

24 November 1922   Dublin   *Shot by firing squad*

Robert Erskine CHILDERS   52

Crime: Possession of firearms

Erskine Childers was born in London to an English father and a protestant Anglo-Irish mother in 1870. Educated at Cambridge, he worked for the civil service in the House of Commons from 1895-1910. A keen yachtsman, he sailed the North Sea and Baltic, gaining inspiration for his famous book, *The Riddle of the Sands (1903).* He married into a Boston Irish family the following year, fathering two sons. He joined the Liberal party in 1910, favouring Irish home rule, but by 1914 was using his boat for running guns from Germany to the Volunteers. Nevertheless, he served with the Naval Air Service in the Great War, in the Low Countries, Turkey and Egypt, leaving as a major.

He joined Sinn Fein while convalescing from flu in 1919, and opposed Collins' acceptance of the Free State in 1921, joining the Republican rebels, and publishing *An Phoblacht.* He went on the run but, weak from sciatica and a chest infection, was captured and beaten. Tried before a Free State special military court, he shook hands with the firing squad at the barracks before his execution, at which he wore no blindfold.

Read: Erskine Childers

8 December 1922	Dublin	*Shot by firing squad*

Liam MELLOWS
Rory O'CONNOR
and two others

Crime: *unknown*
Motive: *Political.*

The four were leading republican prisoners executed in retaliation for the shooting of Sean Hales, a member of the Dail the day before by Republican irregulars. In the following year the Free State government executed **76** other prisoners for outrages committed by their comrades.

Read: Ireland Since the Famine, p467.

1923
total: 17

341	3 Jan	George EDISBURY	44		Strangeways
342	5 Jan	Lee DOON	27	Chinese	Armley
343	9 Jan	Frederick BYWATERS	20		Pentonville
344	9 Jan	Edith THOMPSON (f)	29		Holloway
345	28 Mar	George PERRY	50		Strangeways
346	3 Apr	Daniel CASSIDY	60	Irish	Durham
347	5 Apr	Bernard POMROY	25		Pentonville
348	10 Apr	Frederick WOOD	28		Walton
349	11 Jun	John SAVAGE	50	Scottish	Calton
350	4 Jul	Rowland DUCK	25		Pentonville
351	24 Jul	William GRIFFITHS	57		Shrewsbury
352	8 Aug	Hassan MOHAMMED	33	Yemeni	Durham
353	8 Aug	Albert BURROWS	62		Nottingham
354	10 Oct	Susan NEWELL (f)	30	Scottish	Duke Street
355	30 Oct	Phillip MURRAY		Scottish	Calton
356	1 Nov	Frederick JESSE	26		Wandsworth
357	28 Dec	John EASTWOOD	39		Armley

3 January 1923 Strangeways prison, Manchester *Ellis*

341

George Frederick EDISBURY   44

Cut throat of: ***Winifred Drinkwater***, *50, on 29 July 1922, in Manchester, Lancs.*
Motive: *Vengeance; drink related.*

Edisbury, *(b.1879)*, a painter, had taken up with Annie Grimshaw in 1916. She was separated from her husband, and the two, who called themselves married, shared a drink problem. They took lodgings in Hulme, but developed an acrimonious relationship with another resident couple, the Drinkwaters, the two women being particularly antagonistic to each other.

Peter and Winifred were seen as a respectable couple, but she had a secret problem of alcoholism, and in private momemts would accuse Annie of being a prostitute, and George of living off immoral earnings and claiming a pension under false pretences.

After hearing more insults, and an evening of drinking, Edisbury attacked Mrs Drinkwater on the steps as she returned home, cutting her throat, and then fleeing to his married sister. He slept the night on the floor, and was there when police arrived at 9 the following morning.

Read: *Murderous Manchester, p86.*

---

5 January 1923   Armley gaol, Leeds   *T.Pierrepoint/ Phillips*

342

Lee DOON   **27**   *Chinese*   *(aka Leong Lun)*

Bludgeoned: **Sing Lee,** *34, on 9 September 1922, in Sheffield, W.Yorks.*
Motive: *Financial.*

Doon, *(b.1896),* worked in Sing's laundry.   After employee Lily Siddall had gone home, the two men left alone, Doon battered his employer to death with a series of blows from a blunt instrument, and strangled him. He placed his body in a trunk, and began to dig a pit in the laundry's cellar.
Doon told Lily that Sing had returned suddenly to China, but when she saw him digging the hole, she went to the police. Doon had buried Sing a metre deep inside the trunk, and covered the hole with coal, by the time police arrived.   Doon said the two had quarrelled over Sing's morphine addiction, and that he had killed him in self-defence.

Read: *And May The Lord Have Mercy On Your Soul.*

9 January 1923   Pentonville prison, London   *Willis/ T.Pierrepoint/ Mills*
343, 344   Holloway prison, London   *Ellis/ Baxter/ Phillips*

Frederick Edward Francis BYWATERS   20
Edith Jessie THOMPSON   *female*   **29**
(nee Graydon)

Stabbed: ***Percy Thompson***, *32, on 4 October 1922, in Ilford, Essex*
Motive: *To clear impediment.*

Edith Thompson, *(b.1893)*, a milliner's book-keeper who had been married five years, began an affair with Freddy Bywaters, *(b.1902)*, an old school friend of her brothers and sister, on holiday on the Isle of Wight in 1921. Still only 18, Bywaters, a steward with P&O, was invited by Percy Thompson, a shipping clerk in the City, to lodge with him and his wife at their Ilford home immediately after their holiday together, but was asked to leave when Percy became aware of his wife's adultery. Bywaters had intervened when Percy had hit Edith and denied her a separation.

Between September 1921 and September 1922, Bywaters spent ten months away, working on board ship through five voyages, and staying with his mother in Upper Norwood during his short spells in England. He continued to see Edith whilst on leave, she had more than one abortion, and the couple corresponded frequently while he was away. In her letters Edith alluded to killing herself and to killing Percy - though there was no evidence that she ever attempted to do so.

Percy and Edith were returning from an evening at the theatre, walking from Ilford station along Belgrave Road just before midnight on 4 October 1922. Bywaters had been waiting. With a knife, he attacked Percy, who was cut eleven times in the struggle. Two stab wounds in the back of the neck severed the carotid artery and he bled to death. Mrs Thompson claimed she had no prior knowledge of the attack, but after letters were discovered she too was charged with murder and of conspiring, attempting and inciting to murder.

Her appeals were dismissed and both were found guilty on 11 December. Edith, who was the first woman to hang for sixteen years, was reported to have bled heavily at her execution, possibly due to a miscarriage, though the assistant hangman denied any such event had occured. She had to be carried semi-conscious to the scaffold.

Read: Criminal Justice.

267

345

George PERRY   **50**

Cut throat of: ***Emma Perry***, *48, on 26 December 1922, in Burslem, Staffs.*
Motive: *Vengeance; drink related.*

Perry, *(b.1873)*, had lodged with his brother Edwin, and his wife, Emma, since July 1922. They all had a good deal to drink on Boxing Day, and when their group of friends departed at 1.30pm, Edwin went for a nap. George got into an argument with Emma, who he said had been nagging at him all day, and cut her throat. While Edwin was waking and discovering his wife's body at 4.30pm, his brother was throwing himself into a canal, from where he was soon rescued.

Read: And May The Lord Have Mercy On Your Soul

346

Daniel CASSIDY   **60**   *Irish*

Shot: ***Bernard Quinn***, *30, on 1 January 1923, in Sunderland, Co Durham*
Motive: *Vengeance.*

Cassidy, *(b.1863)*, had been abandoned by his wife, who had returned to Dublin. Though his two daughters still lived close-by, in Sunderland, Cassidy felt his wife had turned them against him. She returned to stay with her daughter on 14 December, in order to attend a new year's party- a party to which her husband was not invited.

Cassidy watched from his own home across the road as the celebration got underway, and by 6pm, his patience was exhausted. He burst in and fired five shots before being overpowered. He had seriously wounded his wife and a daughter, but a bullet had pierced his son-in-law's heart, and he died instantly.

Read: And May The Lord Have Mercy On Your Soul

347

Bernard POMROY   25

Cut throat of: **Alice May Cheshire**, *21, on 6 February 1923, in London NW3.*
Motive: *Vengeance.*

     Pomroy, *(b.1898),* after a three-year romance, had recently become engaged to Alice Cheshire. He had also been conducting an affair with her sister, who by February 1923, was pregnant. Her father demanded that Pomroy tell Alice the truth, so the two went out to the theatre for the evening, while Bernard prepared to make his admission.

     At 11.10pm they took a taxi from Leicester Square, Pomroy directing the driver a circuitous route to Watford, then Hampstead. At 1.30am, passing Swiss Cottage, the driver heard a low cry from the back, but was directed back to Leicester Square, and then asked to drive to a police station. Pomroy had cut his fiancee's throat with a knife. Resisting all attempts to persuade him otherwise, he pleaded guilty.

     Read: And May The Lord Have Mercy On Your Soul

348

Frederick WOOD   28   *(aka George Wood and Ronald Lee)*

Strangled: **Margaret Gilchrist White**, *50, on 18 December 1922, in Cheadle Hulme, Cheshire.*
Motive: *Financial.*

     Fred Wood, *(b.1895),* was a drifter. He had left school at 14, had gone from   job to job, and had a spell in borstal for stealing a bike. He joined the Northumberland Fusiliers in 1914, but received an arm injury in France in 1917 and was discharged with a good record and a pension. In hospital he learned the skills of upholstery.

     He married in Gateshead, fathered a child, and got work in a shipyard, but drink and gambling had got the better of him, and he had begun beating his wife. She left him in 1921, and he took to wandering the country scraping a living doing door-to-door repairs. In 1922 he took lodgings in

Wilmslow, Cheshire, and in the course of his work he called at the home of Margaret White in Bramhall.

Margaret, an unmarried woman, lived with her bank cashier brother John. She asked Wood to reupholster a chair for her when he called at 11.30 am. John White discovered his sister's body in the sitting room when he returned from work at 7 pm. Her hands were tied together with her apron strings, and she had been strangled. No jewellery had been stolen, but cash boxes had been opened and about £2 taken.

Fred Wood's card was found in the house. Wood had travelled from Cheshire to Stockport, Bradford, Middlesbrough and then to Lincoln where he saw his name in a newspaper. He went to a police station there. Wood said that Miss White had had a fit, and that he had tied her hands to prevent her injuring herself. He panicked at the situation, stole some money and then left, Miss White still groaning on the floor. At the trial much was made of whether Wood, 5' 7", could have strangled her with his weak left hand. After an absence of 55 minutes, the jury found him guilty, though with a strong recommendation to mercy.

Read: Master Detective, Oct 96.

11 June 1923	Calton gaol, Edinburgh	Ellis

349

John Henry SAVAGE   50   Scottish

Cut throat of: **Jemima Nicholson**, on 14 March 1923, in Leith, Midlothian.
Motive: unknown; drink related.

Savage, (b.1873), a ship's fireman, was a companion and drinking partner of Jemima Nicholson, otherwise known as Grierson, who had been deserted by her husband. Both had a severe drink problem, and drunk with meths one night, Savage slit her throat with a razor at her home on Bridge Street.

Read: Encyclopaedia of Scottish Executions

350

Rowland DUCK   25

Cut throat of: **Nellie Pearce**, *18, on 3 May 1923, in London SW6.*
Motive: *Vengeance; drink related.*

Nellie Pearce, a prostitute, lodged with Rowland Duck, *(b.1898)*, and his wife and three children, at their Fulham house. Duck had been shelled in the war, and had suffered epilepsy, and a nervous condition ever since, conditions made worse when he had been drinking even a relatively small amount.

He had contacted syphilis from his secret liaisons with Nellie, and demanded of his wife on 2 May, 'Nellie must go'. The following morning, as Nellie lay asleep in bed, Duck cut her throat and, wrapping her in a blanket, dumped her beneath the bed. He then went to a police station to make his confession. The jury deliberated for thirty minutes.

Read: And May The Lord Have Mercy On Your Soul

351

William GRIFFITHS   57

Cut throat of: **Catherine Hughes**, *80, his mother, on 25 May 1923, in Eccleshall, Staffs.*
Motive: *Vengeance; drink related.*

Griffiths, *(b.1866)*, lived with his aged mother, his half-sister and her husband, in a household accustomed to arguments caused mainly by Griffiths heavy drinking. On 25 May, he spent three hours in the pub in the afternoon, and another four hours in the evening, arriving home at 10.30pm, to a torrent of abuse from his mother, who complained of the amount of money her son wasted. She hit him on the head with a candlestick, after which Griffiths slashed at her with a razor, severing her thumb, before cutting her throat. He went to a neighbour, and then to the police, to confess his actions.

Read: And May The Lord Have Mercy On Your Soul

352

Hassan MOHAMMED   33   *Yemeni*

Shot: ***Jane Nagi***, *25, on 12 March 1923, in Jarrow, Co Durham*
Motive: Sexual rivalry

      Jane Brown had married Mohammed Nagi, one of Tyneside's established Arab community, only to be widowed when he was mysteriously murdered in 1922. She had met Hassan, *(b.1890),* a native of Aden, in July of that year in South Shields, and the two formed a relationship. A ship's fireman, he was at sea much of the time, but sent Jane money while he was away, and lived with her while at home. Jane, however, was a notorious drunk, and wasted the money, earning more for herself as a prostitute serving the immigrant community.
      After three months overseas, Hassan was met at Cardiff by Jane on 7 March, and the two returned to Jarrow, intending to marry shortly. Known for her fiery temper - she had tried to strangled Hassan, and had scratched his face on different occasions - on 12 March, Jane got very drunk, looking in cafes for Hassan, and then running away from him when he found her. He followed her to the back of another Arab cafe, where she sat between two men on a sofa. From the doorway he stared at her smoking a cigarette as she told him they were finished. Then he drew a revolver and shot her through the left breast.
      Three Arab men stopped him escaping. Hassan claimed that one of the men, Salem Ali, had shot Jane, and that he had been framed. The jury took three minutes to decide Hassan was to blame. Just 5' and 8 stone, Hassan prayed in Arabic on his way to the scaffold, and bellowed twice 'Allah!' before the drop.

      Read: True Crime, Mar 97.

353

Albert Edward BURROWS   62

Strangled: **1** ***Hannah Calladine***, *28, on 11 January 1920,*
               2 ***Albert Edward Burrows***, *1, his son, on 11 January 1920,*

	3 Elsie Large, 4, on 12 January 1920, near Glossop, Derbyshire.
Motive:	To clear impediment.
Drowned:	**4 Thomas Johnson Wood**, 4, on 4 March 1923, near Glossop, Derbyshire.
Motive:	Sexual.

Burrows, *(b.1861)*, was a farm labourer living in Glossop with his wife Clementine, whom he had married in 1903. In 1918 he began an affair with Hannah Calladine, an unmarried mother of a 2-year old girl, who lived in Nantwich, Cheshire. In October of that year, Hannah gave birth to Burrows' son, and he married her, only to be jailed for six months for bigamy. Hannah took out an order for Burrows to pay for the child, and when he didn't, he received another 21 days in jail.

In December 1919, Hannah turned up in Glossop with her two children, and moved in with him, only for his wife to move out, and slap a maintenance order of her own on him. Burrows fell behind with the rent and could see no way out.

On January 11, Burrows and Hannah took a walk over nearby Symmondley Moor with the baby. He killed them there, probably by strangling, and dumped their bodies down one of the airshafts from the disused mines. The following day, he did the same with Hannah's daughter Elsie. When a neighbour saw him returning without the child, he told her truthfully, 'I took Elsie to her mother'. He told everyone that Hannah had left, and his wife moved back in with him.

For three years no-one was any the wiser, until in March 1923, Burrows took a neighbour's child, Tommy Wood, for a walk over the moors. He perpetrated a savage sexual assault on the boy, and dumped him down the same 30-metre shaft. Burrows may have strangled him first, but the boy died by drowning in the 2 metres of water at the bottom of the shaft. After a huge police search of the area, Burrows told them, nine days later, that he had been on the moor with the boy, and in which area. They searched the shaft and found Tommy's body. The other three victims, now merely a collection of bones, were found on 23 May.

In prison, Burrows approached another prisoner to write a letter from Hannah, saying she was still alive - the prisoner testified against Burrows. He was tried for the murders of Hannah and baby Albert only, and no defence witnesses were called. The jury took only 11 minutes to decide their verdict.

Read: Settings For Slaughter.

<u>Susan NEWELL</u>   **30**   *female*   *Scottish*

Strangled: ***John Johnston**, 13, in June 1923, in Coatbridge, near
                         Glasgow, Lanarks.*
Motive: *Vengeance.*

Susan Newell, *(b. 1893),* lived in a room in Coatbridge, about ten miles from Glasgow, with her husband John, and her daughter by a previous marriage, Janet McLeod, 8. They were an argumentative couple and John had complained to the police in June 1923 that Susan had twice struck him on the head. Their landlord had given them notice to leave. On the day before the murder, John had gone to his brother's funeral and, because of the quarrel with his wife, he had stayed the night at his father's house, and then gone to his sister's.

In the early evening, Mrs Newell had called the passing paperboy, John Johnston, into the house. When he refused to hand over a newspaper without payment, Susan flew into a rage and strangled him, laying his body out on the settee. The following day, she got her daughter to help put the boy in a sack, and then proceeded to wheel the body in a rug-covered cart towards Glasgow, her daughter at times sitting atop the bundle. She accepted a lift from a lorry driver into the city centre. The cart fell from the lorry as they were unloading and from her window a woman noticed a foot and then a head protrude from the sack. The police were called and Mrs Newell was arrested as she dumped the bundle in a courtyard.

Susan told the police that her husband had killed the boy, a story corroborated by her daughter. They were both sent for trial, but Mr Newell was able to show that he was in Glasgow at the time of the murder. He was released and Mrs Newell's plea of insanity dismissed. The jury's strong recommendation to mercy was ignored. On the scaffold, she managed to free her hands and refused the white hood, dying bravely, according to witnesses. She was the first woman to hang in Scotland for more than fifty years.

Read: True Crime Diary vol 2

30 October 1923   Calton gaol, Edinburgh   *Baxter*

355

Phillip MURRAY   *Scottish*

Bludgeoned/dropped: **William Ronald Cree**, on 23 June 1923, in
                           Edinburgh, Midlothian.
Motive: *Vengeance; drink related.*

　　　　Murray lived off the earnings made by Catherine Donoghue working
as a prostitute from her home in Jamaica Street. She returned one evening
with Cree, a Dunfermline man, to find Murray drunk. An argument ensued
between the two men, during which Murray hit Cree on the head with a flat-
iron, and threw him from the upstairs window.

　　　　Read: Encyclopaedia of Scottish Executions.

1 November 1923   Wandsworth prison, London   *Ellis/ Baxter*

356

Frederick William Maximilian JESSE   **26**

Strangled: **Mabel Jennings Edmunds**, 50, on 21 July 1923, in
                           London SE1.
Motive: *Vengeance.*

　　　　Jesse, *(b.1897),* was a boarder at Mabel's lodging house in
Lambeth, but there were many arguments, especially after Jesse borrowed
money from her, and failed to repay the debt. He hatched a plot to kill her and
put the blame elsewhere, strangling her in the bedroom, and beginning to
dismember the body. He told other lodgers Mabel had gone to Sheerness,
then threw an envelope containing her marriage certificate into the Thames,
where it was found on 23 July.
　　　　Jesse wrote a letter purportedly from Mabel's estranged husband,
saying he had killed her and drowned himself. The letter was delivered on 28
July, and two days later police conducted a search of the house, where
Mabel's body was found on the bed, her severed legs on the table. Jesse
then confessed, the jury taking 35 minutes over its deliberations.

　　　　Read: And May The Lord Have Mercy On Your Soul.

357

John William EASTWOOD   39

Bludgeoned: ***John Joseph Clarke**, 49, on 29 July 1923, in Sheffield, W.Yorks.*
Motive: *Sexual rivalry.*

Eastwood, *(b.1884)*, was a pub landlord, who ran off to Blackpool with a woman friend, after his barman, John Clarke, had been over-friendly with Mrs Eastwood. He returned two weeks later, but moved out to lodgings after arguing with his wife. In the early morning, he left his room with an axe, telling his landlord he was going to kill Clarke. He woke the barman and his wife by throwing stones at the bedroom window, and after a struggle, he hacked Clarke to death with an axe-blow to the head. Eastwood went to find a police officer, and Clarke died the following day. The jury decided his fate in 30 minutes.

Read: And May The Lord Have Mercy On Your Soul

1923 Executions in Ireland

8 February 1923   Londonderry gaol

William ROONEY

Crime: *unknown*
Motive: *unknown*

         No details

29 November 1923   Mountjoy gaol, Dublin

Thomas DELANEY

Crime: *unknown*
Motive: *unknown*

         No details

15 December 1923   Mountjoy gaol, Dublin

Thomas McDONAGH

Crime: *unknown*
Motive: *unknown*

         No details

1924 total: *10*

358	2 Jan	Matthew NUNN	24		Durham
359	8 Apr	Francis BOOKER	28		Strangeways
360	18 Jun	William WARDELL	47		Armley
361	30 Jul	Abraham GOLDENBERG	22		Winchester
362	12 Aug	Jean-Pierre VAQUIER	45	*French*	Wandsworth
363	13 Aug	John HORNER	23		Strangeways
364	3 Sep	Patrick MAHON	34		Wandsworth
365	27 Nov	Frederick SOUTHGATE	52		Ipswich
366	9 Dec	William SMITH	26		Hull
367	17 Dec	Arthur SIMMS	25		Nottingham

2 January 1924   Durham gaol   *T.Pierrepoint*

358

Matthew Frederick Atkinson NUNN   24

Cut throat of: ***Minetta Mary Kelly***, *20, on 17 September 1923, in Tanfield, Co Durham.*
Motive: Sexual rivalry.

Nunn, *(b.1900),* a miner, had been courting Minetta Kelly, a clerk, for three months when she found herself pregnant. He wanted to marry her, but she dumped him in June 1923, and he went back to live in Dipton. Minetta, a keen dancer, bumped into her old boyfriend, Joe Hughes, at the music hall on 10 September, and he walked her home, only to find Nunn waiting there for her to return. The two men argued, and both offered to marry Minetta, though she declined both.

She went to see Nunn on 11 September, and he began to see her home at 9.30pm, when he cut Minetta's throat, almost severing her head, then turned the razor on himself, staggering to a friend's house. Nunn tried to claim that Minetta had attacked him, but the injuries could not have been self-inflicted, and the jury took 50 minutes to convict Nunn, though they added a strong recommendation to mercy.

At his execution, the rope broke and Nunn fell, helpless, into the pit. He was hanged again, 25 minutes later.

Read: True Crime, Mar 98.

278

359

Francis Wilson BOOKER   28

Stabbed: ***Percy Sharpe***, *14, on 4 September 1923, in Northenden, Lancs.*
Motive: Sexual.

Booker, *(b.1896),* was an unemployed warehouseman who frequently used to chase naughty boys, and occasionally 'punish' them by caning or spanking. He had also propositioned some sexually. He had met Percy Sharpe at a labour exchange, and had offered him a job. Percy suffered from rheumatic fever, the illness which had led his father to lose his job. He was desperate to find work. The two had gone to Carr's Wood where Booker had assaulted Percy, removing his trousers and lifting his shirt, then stabbed him with a jack-knife below the heart, piercing the liver. He had not had intercourse with the boy. Percy had staggered to nearby Northenden Junction, where the signalman found him at 3 pm. He died in hospital the following morning.

When Booker was seen chastising some boys, the police searched his address where Percy's diary and underpants were found. His braces were discovered on Booker's allotment. The jury decided his guilt in 25 minutes.

Read: Strange Tales from Strangeways

360

William Horsely WARDELL   47

Bludgeoned: ***Elizabeth Reaney***, *60, on 23 February 1924, in Bradford, W.Yorks.*
Motive: Financial.

Wardell, *(b. 1877),* as far as is known, never held down a job. He romanced and overwhelmed women into supporting him. He had lived with Maria Westcott for thirteen years until she tired of his affairs and wastefulness in 1921.

The next female heart to be captivated was that of Hilda Kidd, but she too found it impossible to maintain his expensive tastes. It was while he was living with her that he met and began to woo Mrs Reaney, a well-off widow, who knew him as George Goodson. She fell for his charms, eagerly accepted his suggestion of marriage, and agreed to buy a new home in Buxton. The ideal cottage George had described did not exist. Small items of furniture which Elizabeth believed were being taken to her new house, were in fact being transported by Wardell, 5'7", to his home with Hilda.

When prospective buyers arrived at Mrs Reaney's house on 23 February they were let in by removers who had also arrived only to find a note on the door saying Mrs Reaney had gone to Buxton on urgent business. They found the woman's body in the cellar. She had suffered four blows to the head, probably inflicted by a hammer.

The note on the door was identified as being in Wardell's handwriting. Wardell was arrested four days later. The prosecution identified the motive as robbery, though why Wardell would have found murder necessary to that end remains a mystery. The jury delivered its verdict after an hour's retirement.

Read: Murderous Leeds

30 July 1924   Winchester prison   *T.Pierrepoint/ Willis*

361

Abraham GOLDENBERG   **22**   *(aka Jack Goldenberg)*

Shot: ***William Edward Hall**, 28, on 3 April 1924, in Borden, Hampshire.*
Motive: *Financial.*

Goldenberg, *(b. 1902),* a Lance-Corporal of the East Lancashire Regiment, stationed at Bordon camp in Hampshire, determined to steal enough money so that he could marry his girlfriend. He stole an officer's revolver and one afternoon entered a bank near the camp. He shot the clerk, William Hall, twice in the head at point blank range and escaped with about £1000.

The camp of 6000 soldiers came under suspicion when the bullets used were identified as army issue. Goldenberg attracted suspicion by his unusual curiosity in the case. He admitted going to the bank that day, and described two suspects he said he had seen in a car parked outside. An officer noticed his furtive behaviour in the latrine and £500 of the stolen money was found hidden there. Goldenberg made a full confession and revealed the hidden murder weapon. His plea of insanity was dismissed.

Read: True Crime Diary vol2

12 August 1924   Wandsworth prison, London
T.Pierrepoint/ Willis/ Phillips

362

Jean-Pierre VAQUIER   45   *French*

Poisoned: ***Alfred George Poynter Jones**, 37, on 29 March 1924, in
              Byfleet, Surrey.*
Motive: *Sexual rivalry.*

       Vaquier, *(b. 1879)*, was in January 1924 working in the Victoria
Hotel, Biarritz as a radio operator, when Mrs Mabel Theresa Jones, 35,
arrived to escape the worries of near bankruptcy. A friendship developed
between the two despite their inability to speak each other's language. The
two became lovers, meeting again in Bordeaux and Paris, before one month
later Mabel returned home to her husband at the Blue Anchor Hotel in Byfleet.
       They had married in 1906 and had two children. Alfred Jones was
a heavy drinker and had virtually ruined his business. Vaquier followed her to
England. She visited him in London, and then he came to her hotel on 14
February, his prolonged stay being explained as having to wait for payment for
a sausage machine invention. On 28 March, at a party at the hotel, Vaquier
poisoned a bottle of liver salts with strychnine he had bought in London. The
morning after, a hungover Mr Jones took a dose of salts and died in agony.
       Vaquier was identified by the chemist who had sold him the poison.
He denied murder and denied any affair with Mrs Jones. Upon the verdict,
Vaquier screamed abuse at the judge and had to be dragged from court. His
last words on the scaffold were, 'Vive la France'.

     Read: A Gallery of Poisoners.

13 August 1924   Strangeways prison, Manchester   *Willis*

363

John Charles HORNER   23

Traumatised: ***Norman Widdowson Pinchen**, 5, on 10 June 1924, in
              Salford, Lancs.*
Motive: *Sexual.*

John Horner, *(b. 1901),* a tall, strong man, fair-haired and handsome, was a thief who had just completed six months' hard labour. One summer afternoon he saw Norman Pinchen, 5, playing with his friend Eric Wilson, 8, in Peel Park. He told the boys, 'Come with me and I'll show you something and shove my dicky up yor bottom'. He got rid of Eric by sending him for an ice-cream, and walked hand-in-hand with Norman down to the canal. The pair were seen from a distance on the towpath, and again later, the man carrying the now trousersless boy.

Norman had been raped and viciously assaulted, dying of shock in the process. Horner had then dumped his half-naked body in the canal. The witness summoned the police and Horner was arrested. He continued to protest his innocence, and his girlfriend who had known him seven years said he was incapable of such an act, but the jury decided his fate in 65 minutes.

Read: Strange Tales from Strangeways.

3 September 1924	Wandsworth prison, London	*T.Pierrepoint/ Willis*

364

Patrick Herbert MAHON   34

Bludgeoned?:   *Emily Beilby Kaye, 38, on 15 April 1924, in Westham, Sussex.*
Motive: *Financial.*

Mahon was born in Liverpool in 1889 of Irish parents. He had married his wife Jessie, two years his senior, in 1910, and they had one child. The first of a series of affairs with other women occurred just one year after the marriage. There followed a conviction for forgery, and two prison terms, one for embezzlement, and a five year sentence in 1916 for a hammer attack on a woman in the process of a robbery.

The couple moved to Richmond, Surrey and Mahon got a job as a sales representative for a chartered accountant in the City. In 1923 he began an affair with a secretary at the firm, Emily Kaye. She had £600 in savings, and by 1924 Mahon had promised her a new life together in South Africa. Emily had given Mahon over £400 to make the arrangements. But on 10 April Mahon had met Ethel Duncan, 32, and had arranged to see her again. Mahon had rented a bungalow from 11 April on the Crumbles beach near Eastbourne, the place where Field and Gray had murdered Irene Munro nearly four years before.

Emily travelled to Eastbourne on 12 April and was taken to the bungalow by Mahon, who had earlier that day bought a knife and a saw in London. Emily was now two months pregnant. According to Mahon, 5'11"

282

and 10 stone, Emily flew at him in a rage when he told her the affair was over. He murdered her, probably on the 15th, and stuffed her body into a trunk, before returning to Richmond.

Mahon spent Easter weekend, April 18-21, at the bungalow with Ethel Duncan, she totally unaware of the contents of the trunk in the second bedroom. He returned alone on 22 April and proceeded to dispose of parts of the body, burning the head in the grate. The smell of burning being too much for him, he returned again on the 27th and boiled segments of Emily's body. Various parts he kept in a hat box and a biscuit tin, the quartered torso he stored in the trunk, and various parts wrapped in brown paper were scattered from the window of the train returning him to London.

The knife and Emily's blood-stained scarf and underwear were deposited in Emily's bag in a locker at Waterloo station. Mahon's wife discovered the ticket for the locker and, suspecting her husband of infidelity, asked a friend to investigate. The police were alerted and when Mahon went to claim the bag on 2 May, he was arrested. The remains of Emily Kaye were discovered at the bungalow the following day. A broken axe found at the scene is believed to have been the murder weapon.

Mahon maintained that Emily had accidentally struck her head on a coal scuttle in a struggle. The scuttle was too flimsy to have caused her death. Moreover, the fact that Mahon had purchased the knife before his trip showed premeditation. On the scaffold Mahon had made one last bid to avoid the drop by jumping forward, only to fracture his spine against the trap before the rope broke his neck.

Read: Murders of the Black Museum

27 November 1924   Ipswich prison

365

Frederick SOUTHGATE   52

Stabbed: *Elizabeth Southgate, 58, his wife, on 26 July 1924, in Colchester, Essex.*
Motive: *Vengeance.*

Southgate, *(b.1872),* married Elizabeth in 1921, anticipating the property inheritance she had received, but his wife kept strict control of all her financial assets. She left him, and obtained a separation order on 21 July. Elizabeth was in her back yard when Southgate called five days later, and refused to let him in the house.

When he produced a knife, Elizabeth ran, but her husband caught her, and plunged the weapon into her back. Sixteen-year old John Bruce had witnessed the whole incident, and intervened to stop a further attack by Southgate, who then rode off on his bicycle. The boy carried Elizabeth into her house, as Southgate rode to a mental hospital in Colchester, claiming that he had lost his memory.

Read: And May The Lord Have Mercy On Your Soul

---

9 December 1924   Hull prison   *T.Pierrepoint/ Baxter*

366

William George SMITH 26

Cut throat of: **Elizabeth Bousfield**, *29, on 18 August 1924, in Nottingham.*
Motive: *Sexual rivalry.*

   While seaman Smith, *(b.1898),* was ashore he lodged with his cousin at his uncle's house. His uncle, Thomas Senior, 80, had a housekeeper, Elizabeth Bousfield, the mother of three children, whom Smith had been courting for two years. Smith, Senior and Elizabeth went to the cinema on 13 August, and returned home for supper, after which, Smith claimed, he heard the old man go to Elizabeth's room, and ask her for sex. At 7.40 the next morning, Smith slashed Elizabeth's throat with a razor, and as she ran, collapsing, into the street, Smith went to the police station to hand himself in. He claimed that she had rushed at him with the razor.

Read: And May The Lord Have Mercy On Your Soul

---

17 December 1924 Bagthorpe prison, Nottingham *T.Pierrepoint/ Baxter*

367

Arthur SIMMS 25

Strangled: **Rosa Armstrong**, *9, on 27 June 1924, in Sutton-in-Ashfield, Notts.*
Motive: *Sadistic pleasure.*

Simms, *(b.1899),* had behaved strangely since leaving the army, once tearing his clothes and burning them. At 1pm he waited for his wife's young sister to make her way back to school from having lunch at home, and gave her some money to buy some sweets. He took her down a lane alongside the church, and there strangled her with one of her shoelaces.

She was found in a hedge, still clutching her sweets, in the early hours. There had been no sexual assault. Simms had been seen with Rosa, and he admitted the offence when arrested.

Read: And May The Lord Have Mercy On Your Soul

13 March 1924   Mountjoy gaol, Dublin

Jeremiah GAFFNEY

Crime: *unknown*
Motive: *unknown*

No details

8 May 1924   Crumlin Road Gaol, Belfast   *Willis/ Wilson*

Michael PRATLEY   30

Probably shot: *William J. Twaddell, on 22 May 1922, in Belfast.*
Motive: *Political.*

Shot: *Nelson Leech, 30, on 7 March 1924, in Belfast.*
Motive: *Financial.*

Pratley, *(b.1894)*, a Catholic and a Republican tailor, was charged, along with James Woods, a colonel in the Free State Army, with the murder of Stormont MP, Mr Twaddell. He had been ambushed on a Belfast street by four men, one of whom had shot the MP in the back, another emptying his revolver in the politician as he lay on the ground. The Crown did not proceed with the case.

Two years later, Pratley was one of three men who raided the sculptor's Purdy and Millard as the wages were being made up by four employees. As Nelson Leech grabbed the phone, a warning shot was fired over his head, but when the cashier grabbed the shotgun, he was shot in the abdomen. He died in hospital seven hours later, leaving a wife and four children. The masked men ran off but were pursued by constable Francis Morteshed, who managed to catch Pratley who had an artificial leg.

Pratley refused to name his accomplices, but admitted the robbery, though he denied firing the fatal shot. The jury took 25 minutes to disagree.

Read: True Detective, Nov96.

1 August 1924   Mountjoy gaol, Dublin

Felix McMULLEN

Shot: *A policeman.*
Motive: *Financial.*

     McMullen and another man had robbed a bank. McMullen had shot and wounded the manager, and when pursued by a police officer, McMullen shot and killed him. He admitted that he had fired deliberately, but the jury would not agree a verdict of murder. At his second trial, the jury did.

     Read: Royal Commission on Capital Punishment, p383.

1925

total: **18**

368	24 Feb	William BIGNELL	32		Shepton Mallet
369	31 Mar	William BRESSINGTON	21		Bristol
370	2 Apr	George BARTON	59		Pentonville
371	15 Apr	Thomas SHELTON	25		Durham
372	15 Apr	Henry GRAHAM	42		Durham
373	22 Apr	Norman THORNE	23		Wandsworth
374	26 May	Patrick POWER	41	Irish	Strangeways
375	10 Jun	Hubert DALTON	39		Hull
376	5 Aug	James WINSTANLEY	29		Walton
377	11 Aug	James MAKIN	25		Strangeways
378	14 Aug	William CRONIN	54		Pentonville
379	14 Aug	Arthur BISHOP	18		Pentonville
380	3 Sep	Alfred BOSTOCK	25		Armley
381	3 Sep	Wilfred FOWLER	23		Armley
382	4 Sep	Lawrence FOWLER	25		Armley
383	24 Sep	John KEEN		Scottish	Duke Street
384	12 Nov	Herbert WHITEMAN	27		Norwich
385	15 Dec	Samuel JOHNSON	29		Strangeways

24 February 1925   Shepton Mallet prison   *T.Pierrepoint/ Baxter*

368

William Grover BIGNELL   32

Cut throat of: *Margaret Legg, 37, on 25 October 1924, in Tetbury, Gloucs.*
Motive: *Vengeance.*

Bignell, *(b.1893),* had first met Margaret Legg in 1917, but they had renewed their acquaintance, and she moved in with him in 1924, without telling him she was already married. So it was something of a shock to him when, just two weeks later, she walked out, returning to her husband and child in Swindon. More of a shock was what she left behind, a venereal infection, which caused Bignell a stay in hospital.

When Margaret wrote to him, on 24 October, telling him she wanted him to go and live with her, he decided on his revenge. He persuaded her to run away with him to Tetbury, where they spent an hour in a pub until 10pm, then, in a quiet street, he cut her throat. Bignell approached a policeman to ask where he might get a bed for the night, but, on finding there was none available, confessed all. The jury decided his fate in 20 minutes.

Read: And May The Lord Have Mercy On Your Soul

31 March 1925	Horfield gaol, Bristol	*T.Pierrepoint/ Phillips*

369

William Francis Albert BRESSINGTON   21

Strangled: *Glibert Caleb Amos, 8, on 12 December 1924, in Staple Hill, Gloucs.*
Motive: Sexual.

Bressington, *(b.1904),* an occasional transvestite, had tried to commit suicide in 1915, and had been discharged from the army because he was feeble-minded. A grandfather, an uncle and a cousin had all been long-term residents of mental asylums, and a doctor described Bressington as a 'mental defective' and he was something of a figure of fun in the neighbourhood.
He called on the Amos house while the parents were out, telling William, 12, he was wanted by an aunt, but went instead with Gilbert when the older brother said he was looking after the children. He sexually assaulted the boy, then strangled him with a tie. Bressington told his father, who started fighting with him, before police were called. He admitted murder, but strangely, denied the sexual assault, saying he had lured the boy away for another man. His plea of insanity was rejected.

Read: And May The Lord Have Mercy On Your Soul

370

George William BARTON   59

Cut throat of: **Mary May Palfrey**, *38, on 22 January 1925, in London E6.*
Motive: *Sexual rivalry.*

Barton, *(b.1866),* a widower, started courting his dead wife's sister, Mary Palfrey, after her husband was killed in 1917, and the two had decided on 5 February as their wedding day. They spent the weekend in good spirits with Mary's brother in Norfolk, before returning to the East End on 19 January.

At 10am, according to Barton, Mary told him that, once he had gone to work, a sailor was coming round for sex with her. Barton battered her with a piece of iron pipe, and then slashed her throat as she lay unconscious on the floor. She was found by her son at 12.10pm. The following day, Barton wrote to his own son, asking forgiveness, telling him he did it to avenge his dead wife, and saying he was going abroad. However, he went to the police the next day, and admitted his crime.

Defiant, he told the judge, when passing sentence, 'And may you be hung tomorrow'.

Read: And May The Lord Have Mercy On Your Soul

371

Thomas Henry SHELTON   25

Cut throat of: **Ruth Surtees Rodgers**, *23, on 29 January 1925, in Gateshead, Co Durham.*
Motive: *Sexual rivalry.*

Shelton, *(b.1900),* an engineer, lost his eye in an accident at work in 1915, and had since been unemployed, surviving on his substantial compensation payment. Ruth Rodgers had been his girlfriend since 1918, and his fiancee since 1920. A volatile character, Shelton had been barred by Ruth's mother from their house until 1924.

In March, Ruth began a new job as a clerk at a linoleum factory, where she began to confide in her boss, Walter Schiel, 45. Her father had died in 1917, and she valued Schiel's advice. In November she broke off her engagement, a decision which Shelton refused to accept, following her to and from work.

By Christmas, Shelton, who blamed Schiel for his misery, was telling friends that if he could not have Ruth, then nobody would. He met Ruth from work and was seen leading her by the shoulders. She broke away but was caught on her doorstep by Shelton who cut her throat, and stood shouting in the street, 'I've done her in!'. The jury rejected his plea of insanity in 75 minutes, and Shelton shared the scaffold with Henry Graham.

Read: True Detective, Jun 97.

15 April 1925   Durham gaol   *T.Pierrepoint/ Willis/ Pollard/ Mann*

372

Henry GRAHAM   42

Stabbed: ***Margaret Ann Graham***, 30, his wife, on 21 December 1924, in Sunderland, Co Durham
Motive: Vengeance.

Graham, *(b.1883),* was a window cleaner. He and Margaret had married in 1919, but by August 1924 she had tired of him and had left with their five year old adopted son. He paid the 15/- a week maintenance and sent many letters begging Margaret to come back to him. When his pleas were ignored they turned to threats. Four days before Christmas Margaret had been visiting her sister in hospital with two relatives, when Henry intercepted her in the street.

The two argued and after punching his wife in the face, he stabbed her three times in the back and arm. She broke free and ran, but Henry grabbed her and stabbed her seven more times. He was caught by several men, to whom he handed the knife, saying, 'I hope she's dead'. Margaret died shortly after arriving at hospital. A plea of insanity based on his being blown up in France in 1915 was rejected. He sang in his cell, where he gained 20 pounds in weight before being hanged alongside Thomas Shelton. Neither man spoke on the scaffold.

Read: True Detective, Jul 97.

373

John Norman Holmes THORNE   23

Bludgeoned:	***Elsie Emily Cameron***, *26, on 5 December 1924, in Crowborough, Sussex*
Motive:	*To clear impediment*

Norman Thorne, *(b.1902)*, worked as a mechanic, and was a Sunday-school teacher when he met Elsie Cameron at church in Kensal Rise, London NW6 in 1920. After a spell of unemployment, in 1922 he took on a poultry farm in Sussex, and Elsie came to visit him at weekends, staying in lodgings in the village.

Thorne did not make a very good chicken farmer, living in little more than a shack, and with debt problems. The couple were engaged at Christmas 1922. Elsie worked as a typist, but was rather unstable, receiving treatment for neurosis. Thorne kept putting off setting a wedding date, though their physical relationship became more intense, falling short, he insisted, of full sexual intercourse.

In the spring of 1924, Thorne met Elizabeth Coldicott, with whom he did have sexual relations. In June Elsie lost her job, increasing her neuroses, and when Thorne told her of his new relationship, Elsie lied that she was pregnant, and on 5 December, turned up at the farm ready to move in.

The truth of the events on that day, indeed the causes of Elsie's death, are not clear. Thorne claimed that he returned to find Elsie hanging, but there were bruises to her face and head, which could have been caused by a club, though it seems she died of shock, rather than any injuries. In any event, about six hours after death, Thorne used a hack-saw to dismember her body, burying it under the chicken run, her legs wrapped in newspaper, and her head in a biscuit tin.

When Elsie was reported missing by her father, Thorne at first denied that she had come to the farm, but when villagers reported that they had seen Elsie nearby, he told how she had hanged herself, and how he had cut her up because it looked bad for him. To the jury, the dismemberment did look bad for him, and he was convicted after 30 minutes, though he protested his innocence to the end.

Read: Murders of the Black Museum

374

Patrick POWER   41   *Irish*

Bludgeoned: **Sarah Ann Sykes**, *43, on 11 April 1925, in Pendleton, Lancs.*
Motive: *Vengeance.*

Power, *(b.1884)*, had served 23 years in the army including service in the far east, but had found life tough since his discharge, attempting suicide in December 1924, taking to heavy drinking, and finding no work since. He lodged with James and Sarah Ann Sykes in Pendleton, but had fallen behind with his rent and owed £5, despite having a deposit account containing £40. The Sykes, married for twenty years, ran an ice cream business, and Sarah acted as a medium. Power's feelings for her deteriorated after she twice told him that she could see a figure standing behind him.

At 3pm, after Mr Sykes had left on his delivery round, Mrs Sykes told Power he had three days to pay up or go. Power, who had not had a drink for three weeks, launched a savage attack on his landlady, striking seven blows to the face and chest with a hammer, breaking ribs and both jaws, and then stabbing her twelve times with a knife. Two doctors doubted Power's sanity, but the jury convicted him in ten minutes. Power was hanged just 44 days after his crime.

Read: Murderous Manchester

375

Hubert Ernest DALTON   39

Bludgeoned: **Francis Ward**, *68, on 3 October 1924, in Ingleby Greenhow, N.Yorks.*
Motive: *Financial.*

Dalton, *(b.1886)*, and Francis Ward had been good friends and colleagues on the quarry railroad for many years, but when Ward started talking about his forthcoming holiday, the temptation became too great for Dalton. He battered the older man with his hammer, and dumped the body in a haystack next to Dalton's house, taking two watches and a purse, containing Frank's £12 holiday money and his ticket, from the body.

He went back several hours later to cut his throat. The purse and its contents were later found in his outhouse, and Dalton was found wandering along the railway, having cut his own throat. The first jury could not agree on Dalton's sanity, but the second pondered for just five minutes.

Read: And May The Lord Have Mercy On Your Soul

| 5 August 1925 | Walton gaol, Liverpool | *Willis/ Wilson* |

376

James WINSTANLEY   29

Strangled: **Edith Horrocks-Wilkinson**, *27, on 7 May 1925, in Shevington, Lancs.*
Motive: *Sexual rivalry; drink related.*

Winstanley, *(b.1896),* met Edie Horrocks in 1916 when both were working in a Wigan munitions factory. He was a good cricketer, kind and gentle. She had lived with her parents from the age of 13, having been brought up by her maternal grandmother. The two fell very much in love, but had a quarrelsome relationship, and Jim became morose and depressed, sometimes being violent towards Edith.

In 1918 Edie became a barmaid and met Harry Taylor, by whom she became pregnant. She dumped Winstanley, but returned to him after Taylor emigrated to America in 1922. Two years later, Taylor wrote asking Edie to come with their daughter to the States. Edie alternated between wanting to marry Jim for love, or emigrating for her daughter's security.

Waiting for her emigration papers, she continued to see Winstanley, now working as a miner. The two went on a pub crawl on 8 May, walking to the towpath of the Leeds-Liverpool canal at 9pm. There, whilst making love, Winstanley strangled Edie.

He confessed to his father and sister and was arrested at his brother's home, later taking police to the body hidden in undergrowth on the towpath. Edie's knickers were hanging on a nearby bush. Winstanley first claimed that Edie had asked to be killed, later that he had not intended to, saying that sadism and rough sex were part of their routine. The jury took 25 minutes to determine his guilt.

Read: Master Detective, Jun 94

377

<u>James MAKIN</u>   25

Cut throat of: ***Sarah Elizabeth Clutton***, *24, on 4 May 1925,*
in Manchester, Lancs.
Motive: *Vengeance.*

Makin, *(b.1900)*, had served in the Great war, and had tried suicide three times. He had later lodged with his step-sister and her husband, and had once threatened to kill them. In January 1925 he married, and the young couple went to live with Makin's uncle in Newton Heath. On 4 May his wife and uncle went to work as usual, but Makin had a day's holiday from his job as a bleacher.

He went into Manchester and picked up a prostitute, Sarah Clutton. She was seen arriving home with him at 4pm. After sex Sarah asked for a bowl of water to wash. She was nearing the end of her period, but Makin took this to be a sign of possible disease, and when he asked her, he took her tears to be a sign of confirmation. He smashed a soft drink bottle over her head and then cut her throat with a knife.

Makin's wife discovered the body in the bedroom at 6pm, and Makin, extremely drunk, approached a police officer at 9.45pm to confess. Sarah had no venereal disease.

Read: Murderous Manchester.

378

<u>William John CRONIN</u>   54

Bludgeoned: **1** ***Eliza Cuthbert***, *10 mths, on 23 July 1897.*
Cut throat of: **2** ***Alice Garnett***, *40, on 12 June 1925, in London E14*
Motive: *Sexual rivalry; drink related.*

Cronin, *(b.1871)*, was found guilty of manslaughter in 1897, after battering a strikebreaker's baby to death with a spade. For this offence he served seven years, and did four other stretches in gaol for theft and assault.

A seaman, Cronin was especially violent when drunk, and when Alice Garnett, widowed in 1924, moved in with him, it was not long before she started suffering at his hands. Cronin's sister told him that Alice had been seeing other men while he was away, and at midnight he cut her throat. A neighbour, answering Alice's screams, found her head hanging off. Cronin ran out but was floored by a by-stander, who had his finger cut when Cronin turned the razor on him.

He claimed that someone else had attacked Alice while they both slept, but the jury, contemptuously, did not bother to leave the box in order to reach its decision. Cronin was hanged alongside Arthur Bishop.

Read: And May The Lord Have Mercy On Your Soul

14 August 1925   Pentonville prison, London

Baxter/ Pollard/ Taylor/ Wilson

379

Arthur Henry BISHOP   18

Bludgeoned: *Francis Edward Rix, 26, on 7 June 1925, in London W1.*
Motive: *Financial; drink related.*

Bishop, *(b.1907)*, was a hallboy at the Mayfair home of the High Commissioner for Egypt, Sir George Lloyd, for six months until he was sacked by the butler, Francis Rix, in February 1925.

Bishop had been drinking solidly for three days, when he crept into Sir George's house through a basement window at 1.30am. Rix was sleeping as Bishop entered his room, and to prevent him waking, the teenager axed him to death in his bed. He escaped with a little money, a ring, a watch and a pair of boots. The following day, Bishop handed himself over to police in Sittingbourne, Kent. He had stolen items in his possession.

Hanged with William Cronin, Bishop was one of the four 18-year olds hanged this century.

Read: And May The Lord Have Mercy On Your Soul

380

Alfred BOSTOCK   25

Bludgeoned: ***Elizabeth Maude Sherratt****, 24, on 3 May 1925, near Rotherham, W.Yorks.*

Motive: *To clear impediment*

    Bostock, *(b.1900),* lived in Rotherham with his wife Ethel, and worked as a crane driver at the ironworks. He was a good-looking, strong man, who was immediately attracted, and attractive, to Elizabeth Sherratt, when she took an office job at the same works. They began an affair, and continued with it after Elizabeth quit her job to work at a local cinema. The news, however, that she was pregnant, was not welcome to Bostock. He told friends at work, who would later testify against him, that he had woman problems, and that he would 'do her in'.

    Down by the river at Rawmarsh, he savagely beat her about the head - four crushing blows, which left blood on the bushes and towpath. He threw her dead body into the river. Letters from Bostock were found at the dead woman's home, and witnesses denied his alibi that he had been in the pub at the time of the murder.

    Though the evidence against him was purely circumstantial, the jury took just 15 minutes to find him guilty. He was hanged with Wilfred Fowler.

    Read: A Date With the Hangman

3 September 1925   Armley gaol, Leeds   *T.Pierrepoint/ Wilson/ Pollard*
4 September 1925   *Mann*

381, 382

Wilfred FOWLER   23
Lawrence FOWLER   25

Bludgeoned/ stabbed: ***William F. Plommer****, 33, on 27 April 1925, in Sheffield, W.Yorks.*

Motive: *Vengeance*

    The Fowler brothers, *(b.1900, 1902),* ran a gang in Sheffield, which flourished on beatings and robberies, mainly because witnesses were too frightened to testify against them. When a member of the gang, Trimmer

Welsh, was causing trouble in a pub, William Plommer, a former boxer, had broken his jaw. When Wilfred Fowler came looking for Plommer, with two of his gang members, Plommer's boxing mate, Jack Clay, gave Wilfred a good beating. Now, the Fowlers decided that Plommer needed a good lesson.

The following day the brothers and a gang of nine others turned up at Plommer's door. Plommer, a Scot, with a wife and 11-year old son, faced them. He was punched, kicked, beaten with chains and truncheons, and cut with knives and razors. He died one hour later. The brothers were later picked up, still carrying the blood-stained poker and razor they had used in their savage attack. They were confident that witnesses would again be too scared to testify. But Plommer had become something of a local hero for standing up to the gang. 8000 people attended his funeral, and more lined the streets.

Witnesses did come forward, and seven of the gang were put on trial for Plommer's murder. Two were found not guilty, three guilty of manslaughter, two getting ten years each, another seven years. The brothers were found guilty of murder. Wilfred was hanged alongside Alfred Bostcok on 3 September, his brother faced the same gallows, alone, the following day.

Read: A Date with the Hangman.

| 24 September 1925 | Duke Street prison, Glasgow | *T.Pierrepoint* |

383

John KEEN

Bludgeoned: **Noorh Mohammed**, on 16 May 1925, in Port Dundas, Lanarks.
Motive: Financial.

Keen, together with John McCormack, Robert Fletcher and William Dayer, set upon the Indian pedlar on a stairway of a Clyde Street house. A number of scarves, jumpers and dresses were stolen, and Keen bashed Noorh on the head with a lump of coal. The others also faced assault charges, but Keen alone was found guilty of murder.

Read: Encyclopaedia of Scottish Executions.

384

Herbert George WHITEMAN   27   *(aka Herbert Bloye)*

Bludgeoned: **1** *Alice Mabel Whiteman*, 23, his wife, and her mother,
                     2 *Clara Squires*, 52, on 15 June 1925, in Swaffham,
                     Norfolk.
Motive: Vengeance.

Whiteman, *(b.1898)*, was of low intelligence, and was said to suffer fits.   His wife left him taking their two young children and obtained a separation order in May 1925. He asked her to come back, and wrote a pleading letter, to which he received no reply.

At 1pm, Alice took lunch to her parents, agricultural labourers, as they worked in the fields. Whiteman approached, kissed his children in their pram, and then battered Alice and her mother with a spanner. Alice's father, William Squires, heard the women's screams, and saw Whiteman running away. He went to his brother, admitted what he had done and told him, 'Kiss me goodbye', before going to see his mother to confess to her.

Read: And May The Lord Have Mercy On Your Soul

385

Samuel JOHNSON   29

Stabbed: *Beatrice Philomena Martin*, 23, on 27 July 1925, in
                  Stretford, Lancs.
Motive: Sexual rivalry.

Betty Martin lived in Stretford with her exasperated parents. Since 1919 Betty had been frequenting the Salford Docks area, meeting a succession of men, many of them foreign sailors, generally having a good time and often returning home in the early hours. She could not hold down a job and minded her 5-year old sister while her mother went out to work.

She was jilted by an American sailor in 1924, and then had become more seriously involved with Sam Johnson, *(b.1896)*, whom she had first met in a dockland pub in 1923. He was a labourer on an industrial estate, married with three children, and had become smitten with Betty.

She, however, had not given up her old ways, and in May 1925 met able seaman Jack Hunter, 26, and began an affair with him, taunting Sammy in the process. Johnson was distraught, and followed Betty everywhere. On the evening of 26 July, Johnson had confronted Betty and Jack in a pub, and had then gone to her house and waited in her garden for her to come home. When she eventually returned at 2am, Johnson stabbed her with a dagger seven times in her neck and chest. She died immediately. Johnson went straightaway to hand himself in to police.

He offered no defence at his trial, which lasted only four minutes. Betty's father said that he was glad she was gone.

Read: Strange Tales from Strangeways.

28 July 1925   Mountjoy gaol, Dublin

Cornelius O'LEARY

Bludgeoned: ***Patrick O'Leary***, *45, his brother, on 26 February 1925, in Kilkerrin, Co Cork*
Motive: *Vengeance*

Patrick O'Leary was heir to his dead father's farm, worth £1100. He lived there with his widowed mother of 75 and his sister Hannah. His other siblings, Con and Mary Anne, lived nearby. According to custom, Patrick would get the farm, Mary Anne would inherit £350, and Hannah and Con would have resident rights for life. Patrick was said to be a dominant, burly loud-mouth who remonstrated with Con for working elsewhere.

On a winter night, while he slept, Patrick was bludgeoned to death in his bed with a hammer. His head was found in a sack by a 10-year old boy on 7 March. An arm was in another sack nearby. When questioned, Con said that Patrick had taken a colt to Bandon Fair eight days before. But police suspicions were raised when the colt was found at the farm, when Con and Hannah hesitated over identifying the head, and when Con declared, 'My hands are clean'. All four family members were charged with murder or conspiracy. Mary Anne proved she had been sleeping elsewhere, but died of cancer before the trial. The mother was found to have no case to answer.

Hannah and Con were jointly tried. Patrick had been dismembered crudely with an axe, and blood was found in the bedroom, but Con had arrived for work bloodless. Suspicions grew that Hannah had commited the act. After 30 minutes, the jury found both guilty, but recommended mercy for Hannah. She was reprieved three days before her execution, and was released to a convent in 1942.

Read: True Crime, Dec 97.

5 August 1925   Mountjoy gaol, Dublin   *T.Pierrepoint/ 'Robinson'*

Michael TALBOT   23
Annie WALSH   25   *female*

Bludgeoned: ***Edward Walsh***, *60, her husband, on 24 October 1924, in Carnane, Co Limerick*
Motive: *To clear impediment; drink related.*

Edward, a labourer, and Annie, *(b.1900)*, had been married in 1915. She had been 16, he 50 and, largely due to the huge age difference between the two, the marriage had been a loveless one. Ten years on, the two were still childless. By 1925 Annie had fallen in love with Edward's nephew, Michael Talbot, *(b.1902)*, another labourer, who lived nearby in the village of Carnane, near Fedamore. The two planned to kill Edward and begin a new life in England or America with any compensation payment.

After 10pm on the night of 24 October, Edward was bludgeoned twice with an axe by his fireplace kitchen. The following morning, Annie reported to the police that Talbot had shot her husband after bursting into the house drunk. When Talbot was found hiding in his attic the following evening, he claimed that Annie had axed Edward while he had held his hands. Annie swore her innocence, but Talbot's defence claimed that he had been led on by her.

The two were tried on consecutive days in July 1925, Talbot's jury reaching its verdict in just five minutes, Annie's deliberating for an hour before adding a recommendation of mercy to their guilty verdict. Talbot was hanged first, Annie, her hair having turned grey, had to be carried to the scaffold strapped to a board 45 minutes later. No woman had been hanged in Ireland for 22 years, and Annie Walsh was the last female hanged on the island.

Read: Master Detective, Sep 97.

1926

total: *17*

386	5 Jan	John FISHER	58		Winson Green
387	7 Jan	Lorraine LAX	28		Armley
388	17 Feb	Herbert BURROWS	22		Gloucester
389	2 Mar	John LINCOLN	23		Shepton Mallet
390	9 Mar	Harry THOMPSON	36	*Welsh*	Maidstone
391	9 Mar	George THOMAS	26	*Welsh*	Cardiff
392	16 Mar	William THORPE	45		Strangeways
393	23 Mar	LOCK Ah Tam	54	*Chinese*	Walton
394	24 Mar	Eugene DE VERE	26		Pentonville
395	13 Apr	George SHARPLES	20		Winson Green
396	26 Jun	Louie CALVERT (f)	33		Strangeways
397	27 Jul	Johannes MOMMERS	43	*Dutch*	Pentonville
398	10 Aug	James SMITH	23		Durham
399	12 Aug	Charles FINDEN	22		Winchester
400	2 Nov	Hashankhan SAMANDER	36	*Indian*	Pentonville
401	16 Nov	James LEAH	60		Walton
402	3 Dec	Charles HOUGHTON	45		Gloucester

5 January 1926   Winson Green prison, Birmingham

Willis/ Wilson

386

<u>John FISHER</u>   **58**

Cut throat of:	***Ada Taylor***, *56, on 25 October 1925, in Birmingham, Warwicks*
Motive:	*To clear impediment*

Fisher, *(b.1868),* was discharged from the Royal Marines in 1900 suffering from epilepsy. A machinist, he moved in with Ada Taylor and her daughter in Small Heath in 1912. Jessie Dutton was her daughter from her first marriage, her second husband having walked out in 1910. Fisher lost his job in 1922 and spent most of the next three years on the dole while Ada and Jessie both worked. Problems escalated as Fisher borrowed money from the two women, and as he fell into arrears with the rent. By October 1925, unknown to the women, they faced eviction as nothing had been paid on the house for five months.

With no apparent way out, Fisher determined to kill mother and daughter during their usual Sunday afternoon nap. Jessie, however, decided to go out at 4pm. Fisher first battered Ada with a walking stick as she lay in bed, then cut the throat of his partner as she lay unconscious. Jessie discovered her mother's body when she returned at 10pm. At about the same time, Fisher confessed to an off-duty policeman on a tram. The jury considered for two and a half hours before adding a recommendation to mercy to their verdict.

Read: Murderous Birmingham

| 7 January 1926 | Armley gaol, Leeds | *T.Pierrepoint/ Willis* |

387

Lorraine LAX   28

| *Cut throat of:* | *Elizabeth Lax*, 30, his wife, on 31 August 1925, in Sheffield, W.Yorks. |
| *Motive:* | Vengeance. |

Lax, *(b.1898),* was a heavy drinker and a gambler. His wife, whom he had married in 1920, twice was granted separation orders against him, in 1921 and 1923, but was back with him again by 1925. With their three children in the same room, Lax launched a violent razor attack on Elizabeth, cutting her throat on their bed. He explained later that she had 'come at him'.

Read: And May The Lord Have Mercy On Your Soul

| 17 February 1926 | Gloucester prison | *T.Pierrepoint/ Willis* |

388

Herbert BURROWS   22

Shot:	1 *Ernest George Elton Laight*, 31, and
	2 *Doris Sabrina Laight*, 30, and
Bludgeoned:	3 *Robert Laight*, 1, all on 27 November 1925, in Worcester.
Motive:	Financial.

Living in lodgings in Wylds Lane, Worcester, Burrows, *(b.1904)*, was a probationary police constable, and had little money. He knew Ern and Dolly Laight who ran the Garibaldi pub across the road from his home, and he knew that the takings would be considerable when he popped over for a late night drink on 26 November. What the Laights did not know when Burrows arrived, was that he had a revolver and rubber gloves with him.

Following Ern into the cellar at about 1 a.m., he shot him in the back, and when Dolly came to investigate, he shot her in the chest. He then ransacked the house, fracturing the baby's skull when he began to cry. Having bagged £70, he lit a fire in the cellar, though it did not take hold. Only Joan, aged 6, escaped the massacre.

Casual remarks to a colleague brought Burrows under suspicion, and when his rooms were searched, the money and some Laight belongings were found. Burrows continued to show no remorse, and a plea of insanity was entered, on account of his congenital syphilis. This was rejected, and the murdering policeman later admitted premeditation.

Read: The Hangman's Diary.

2 March 1926	Shepton Mallet Military Prison	*T.Pierrepoint*

389

<u>**John LINCOLN**</u>　　　　**23**　　　　*(ne Ignatius Emanuel Napthali Trebich Lincoln)*

Shot:　　　　***Edward Charles Ingram Richards**, 25, on 24 December 1925, in Trowbridge, Wilts.*
Motive:　　　　*Financial; drink related.*

Lincoln, *(b.1903)*, was a bombardier in the Royal Horse Artillery. On 19 December, his friend, Ian Stewart had met Edward Richards, a salesman for a brewery, in a pub, and had gone back to his house for a game of cards. Stewart told Lincoln of the money Richards had on him, and the two soldiers hatched a plot.

Lincoln took a revolver from the army store on 23 December, and the following night they travelled on Lincoln's motorbike to Richards' house. Richards' employee, with whom he lodged, had left the door open for him when he had retired, and Stewart and Lincoln let themselves in, and helped themselves to drink until Richards got home at midnight.

Richards, confronted by the two men, fired a warning shot from the gun he carried, and Lincoln fired back, hitting the salesman. The two fled on the motorbike, and returned to barracks at 7am. When questioned, Lincoln

305

admitted firing the gun, but claimed he had not aimed it, and Edward had been hit accidentally.

The jury took 15 minutes to dismiss the claim. The case against Stewart was dismissed. Lincoln's father, travelling from overseas, was held up by immigration officers at Dover, and was unable to see his son before he died.

Read: And May The Lord Have Mercy On Your Soul

9 March 1926   Maidstone prison   *T.Pierrepoint/ Willis*

390

Henry THOMPSON   **36**   *Welsh*

Cut throat of: ***Rose Smith**, 41, on 8 February 1926, in Chatham, Kent.*
Motive: *Vengeance; drink related.*

Harry Thompson, *(b.1890)*, a miner, deserted his wife and five children in Pontypridd and moved to the red light district of Chatham where in September 1925 he moved in with Rose Smith, a mother of three whose husband was serving overseas with the Royal Navy. Both were often drunk and quarrelled loudly after a binge.

At 9.30pm on 8 February Rose's three children ran to their neighbour, the 8-year old declaring that Thompson was choking her Mum. Shortly after putting the children to bed, the neighbour heard a scream and Thompson was seen leaving by the back door without hat or shoes. Neighbours found Rose in her kitchen, her head almost severed.

Thompson meanwhile had met a friend in the street and told him, 'I've just cut Rose's fucking head off!' Covered in blood and still clutching the razor, Thompson was led to a policeman, and laughed continuously while being questioned. He supplied no motive, and on the night before his execution, he was heard to sing, 'Show me the way to go home'.

Read: Murder Most Foul 12.

391

George THOMAS   26

Stabbed: ***Marie Beddoe Thomas***, *19, on 6 December 1925, in Pontlottyn, Glamorgan.*
Motive: *To escape situation.*

Thomas, *(b.1900)*, began courting Marie, who was no relation to him, in December 1924, but the two fell out in March, when she wrote him an insulting letter. She apologised, but the relationship was over, and both were soon engaged to new romantic partners.

But George and Marie began meeting again in secret, and by summer the two were talking of marriage again, though they were not in a strong enough financial situation to build a future, and by December, George's frustrations were boiling over. He wrote three letters hinting at suicide, and on 4 December, he bought a knife. Three days later, outside the chapel, he stabbed Marie twice, before plunging the knife into his own chest. The jury deliberated for 50 minutes, but added a recommendation to mercy.

Read: And May The Lord have Mercy On Your Soul

392

William Henry THORPE   45

Cut throat of: ***Frances Clarke***, *39, on 20 November 1925, in Bolton, Lancs.*
Motive: *Sexual rivalry; drink related.*

Thorpe, *(b. 1881)*, had come to Bolton from Blackpool in 1922 and had lodged with Mrs Godfrey and her daughter Frances. He had lost the lower part of his leg during the war, and got a job as watchman on a building site. He and Frances began an on-off relationship, but Billy moved out when Frances became pregnant, and failed to persuade him to marry her. He did not take seriously her friendship with William Clarke, but was devastated to learn that, not having seen her since June, she had married him on 1 August 1925. He received no reply to a love letter, and on 19 November went out on a pub-crawl taking rum home to his lodgings.

Just before 6 am, he broke into Frances' house through a window - her husband having left for work at 5. As she slept in her bed he slit her throat with a glass-cutter. She managed to whisper her attacker's name to her mother before she died. Thorpe made several attempts at suicide before and after his arrest at noon the same day. With a defence of temporary insanity, the jury added a strong recommendation to mercy.

Read: Master Detective, Mar 96.

23 March 1926	Walton gaol, Liverpool	*Willis/ Pollard*

393

LOCK Ah Tam   54   *Chinese*

Shot: **1 *Catherine Lock***, *42, his wife, and his daughters,*
            2 *Doris Lock*, *20, and*
            3 *Cecilia Lock*, *18, all on 2 December 1925, in Birkenhead, Cheshire.*
Motive: *Sadistic pleasure; drink related.*

Lock Ah Tam was born in Canton in 1872, and worked as a ship's steward until he settled in Liverpool, as a clerk, in 1895. He became wealthy and respectable, marrying in 1904, Catherine Morgan, a Welsh woman, and fathering three children. He was the representative in England of three shipping lines, and set up a seamen's club in Liverpool. He was known as a good-natured and generous family man. Often in his social club, he was used to breaking up fights, but in 1918, when doing so, he was hit over the head with a billiard cue by a Russian sailor.

To all who knew him, he then began to undergo a personality change, becoming unpredictable, flaring into bouts of violence amid the usual calm, particularly after he had been drinking. His wife thought he was going mad. Once, at a party, he smashed all the glasses in the fireplace. He lost his usual business acumen, going bankrupt in 1924.

On 1 December 1925, he threw a party to celebrate the 20th birthday and homecoming after nine years in China, of his son, Lock Ling. At 1 a.m. he got into an argument with his wife and loaded his gun. As his son went for the police, Tam went to the scullery and shot his wife and two daughters. He then telephoned the police himself, telling them what he had done. Catherine and Cecilia soon died, but Doris clung to life until 21 January. His defence claimed that Tam had suffered a form of temporary insanity, but the jury decided his guilt within twelve minutes.

Read: Vintage Murder of the 20s

394

<u>Eugene DE VERE</u>   **26**   *Scottish*   *(real name:*
                                                        Ewen Anderson Stitchell)

Bludgeoned/ strangled: **Polly Edith Walker**, *17, on 1 January 1926, in*
                           London NW1.
Motive: *Sexual rivalry*

At 17, de Vere, *(b.1900)*, ran away from home in Renfrew where he had been a tailor's apprentice. He joined the army, and was an air force cadet until his leg was amputated because of a septic foot in 1919. In 1920 he went to London where he earned a pittance playing a barrel organ in the street. He met Polly, a cashier at a Kentish Town outfitters, and took his meals with her, her brother and their widowed mother at their Camden home.

The two went to church together, and Eugene fell in love, though Polly, a sufferer from anaemia and St Vitus' dance, became irritated by his possessiveness. Any attention to other men depressed him, and he once tried to poison himself. Quarrels came to a head over Christmas 1925, and Mrs Walker had decided to tell de Vere he was no longer welcome.

On New Year's Day, de Vere waited for Polly's mother to leave for work at 8.10am, then let himself in the house. He argued with Polly, who called him a beast for not buying her clothes, and bit his finger. He chased her to the bedroom, where he battered Polly six times with a poker and coal tongs which broke with the severity of the attack. He then strangled the unconscious girl with a silk stocking, and left her partly under the bed. He stole watches and jewellery from the house, pawned them, and walked to Hitchin, where he was recognised in a hotel, and arrested. De Vere's claim of provocation was rejected.

Read: True Crime, Aug 93

395

<u>George SHARPLES</u>   **20**

Bludgeoned: **Milly Illingworth Crabtree**, *25, on 13 January 1926, in*
                Ladbroke, Warwicks.
Motive: *Vengeance.*

Sharples, *(b.1906)*, spent four years in a reformatory for breaking into a church, and left Cheshire upon his release, to escape his local reputation, finding work on a Warwickshire farm owned by Arthur and Milly Clark. He was a good worker, and earned 10/- a week, his main love being his wireless set. But Milly told all the workers about George's past, and eventually told him that he would have to find lodgings outside the farm.

Though his wages were increased to 27/9, he had to pay £1 rent, so was worse off. He considered going to Canada, but was told that they would not take anyone with a criminal record. At 9am, he was stripping paint and removing nails from a skirting board, when Milly passed. He suddenly hit her with a hammer, and, wrapping pyjamas around her head, and dragging her to the lounge, continued to rain blows. He then cut his own throat twice, and took poison. The pair were found by the woman's 10-year old daughter.

Read: And May The Lord Have Mercy On Your Soul

26 June 1926   Strangeways prison, Manchester   *T.Pierrepoint/ Willis*

396

Louie CALVERT   **33**   *(nee Gomersall)*   female

Bludgeoned:	**1 John William Frobisher**, *in June 1922, in Leeds, W.Yorks, and*
Bludgeoned/ strangled:	**2 Lily Waterhouse**, *40, on 31 March 1926, in Hunslett, near Leeds.*
Motive:	*Vengeance.*

Louie Gomersal, *(b. 1893)*, was a part time prostitute in Leeds, slight in build and violent in temper. As Louisa Jackson she had in 1922 been housekeeper to John William Frobisher, an elderly widower, who was found dead in a canal in June of that year. Louie, 4'10", later admitted to killing him. By 1925, still unmarried and also known as Louie Jackson, she had two children, one of whom lived with her sister in Dewsbury.

She became housekeeper to Arthur Calvert, a nightwatchman, in March 1925. They became lovers and married the following August. Louie told Arthur she was pregnant, and left him on 8 March 1926, telling him she was going to her sister for the confinement. In fact she became lodger to an old acquaintance in Hunslett, Lily Waterhouse, a widow.

Louie advertised that she could offer a baby a good home, and a 17 year old girl agreed to part with her child. Lily, meanwhile, had noticed that Louie had begun stealing small items from her. Afraid to confront her tempestuous lodger, she took out a summons against her. When Louie realised her friend's actions, she battered her savagely about the head and strangled her. A neighbour saw her leaving the house.

Having collected the child, she returned to her husband, presenting him with his new baby. She returned to Lily's house the following day to pilfer a suitcase-full of household articles. When Mrs Waterhouse failed to appear in court, the police called and found her body. Alerted by the neighbour, they called on Louie and discovered the stolen items. In an attempt to escape a sentence of death, she again falsely claimed to be pregnant. Medical examination proved the lie, and Louie then admitted to her earlier murder.

Read: A Date With the Hangman

---

27 July 1926   Pentonville prison, London   *Baxter/ Willis*

397

<u>Johannes Josephus Cornelius MOMMERS</u>   **43**
Dutch

Cut throat of: ***Augusta Violette Pionbini***, *22, on 7 May 1926, in Thundersley, Essex.*
Motive: *To clear impediment.*

Mommers, *(b.1883)*, was married, but had been seeing Augusta Pionbini for some time. She was putting pressure on the Dutchman to run away with her, but he would not. They went to a pub together, and then for a walk, before arriving at her place at 10pm.

In her kitchen he cut her throat with a razor, and Augusta died 50 minutes later. He claimed that Augusta had committed suicide because he refused to elope, and two experts agreed the wounds were consistent with self-infliction. But, in the jury's eyes, Mommers' bloodstained clothing negated his claim that he had not noticed her cutting her own throat.

Read: And May The Lord Have Mercy On Your Soul.

---

10 August 1926   Durham gaol   *T.Pierrepoint/ Phillips*

398

<u>James SMITH</u>   **23**

Stabbed: ***Catherine Smith***, *26, his wife, on 26 April 1926, in Newcastle, Northumberland.*
Motive: *Sexual rivalry; drink related*

Catherine Scott lived with her parents and her brother and sister in Newcastle. She had married David Weddell in 1918 and had a child by him, but was divorced when she had a second child in 1921 by a tram conductor who paid her 10/- a week maintenance.

In 1924 she started courting James Smith, *(b.1903)*, a ship's fireman, and they married in January the following year. They were to separate four times in all, firstly in February 1925 when Mrs Scott threw him out after he had given Catherine a black eye. From June until February 1926 he was away at sea, but just two weeks after his return they separated again. Smith thought his wife was seeing other men, and disputed whether the child she gave birth to in the spring of 1926 was his.

On 19 August Mrs Scott called the police after Smith had been abusive and drew a dagger. The following day he sailed to Hamburg, returning on 26 August at 9am. After drinking five pints of beer, he went to Catherine's home. Her mother left the couple in the hall as Smith appeared calm, but again a row developed and he stabbed Catherine beneath the collar bone and six times in the lower back before dragging her down the stairs by her hair. He kissed her before running off, and was arrested nearby, handing his knife to the policeman.

Read: Murderous Tyneside.

12 August 1926   Winchester prison   *T.Pierrepoint/ Baxter*

399

Charles Edward FINDEN   22

Strangled: ***John Richard Thompson**, 14, on 5 June 1926, in Alton, Hants.*
Motive: Financial.

Finden, *(b.1904)*, saw John Thompson on the Basingstoke Road after 5pm. The young farm worker had just received his wages of 15 shillings, and had a further shilling with which to buy chicken-feed. Finden struck several blows to John's head, and strangled him with his tie. He then dumped the body in bushes, where it was found by gypsies the following day. Finden gave the 15/- to his wife, telling her it was for labouring work he had done. Though the evidence against him was entirely circumstantial, Finden's lies, and leaky alibis, were sufficient to convince the jury in 45 minutes.

Read: And May The Lord Have Mercy On Your Soul.

400

Hashankhan SAMANDER 36 *Indian*

Stabbed: ***Khannar Jung Baz**, 23, on 9 July 1926, in Tilbury, Essex.*

Motive: *Vengeance.*

  Samander, *(b.1890)*, and Baz, both crew on the *SS China*, tied up in Tilbury docks, had an antagonistic relationship for some time. On 9 May, Baz had attacked Samander with a pair of hair clippers, causing severe cuts on his arm. Baz and his cabin-mate had finished their 4-8am watch, and retired to their berths. At 10am, Samander twice crept into their cabin, and re-entered a third time with a knife, with which he stabbed the younger man. When Baz sprang from sleep, Samander plunged in the knife twice more. The whole episode had been witnessed by the cabin-mate.

  Read: And May The Lord Have Mercy On Your Soul

401

James LEAH 60

Stabbed: ***Louise Leah**, 20, his daughter, on 24 September 1926, in Liverpool, Lancs.*

Motive: *Vengeance.*

  Leah, *(b.1866)*, lived on his farm with his wife and three daughters, all of whom were fed up with their father's drinking and boorishness. Following a row with daughter Elsie and her boyfriend on 23 September, all three women packed and left. The following day, Elsie and her sister Louise returned for some things, and prepared some food for Leah. While Elsie went for a taxi, James stabbed Louise in the throat. She managed to stagger to a neighbouring farm, and Leah was found hiding, having cut his throat with a hay knife. Telling the jury that he could not bear to let Louise go, they recommended him for mercy.

  Read: And May The Lord Have Mercy On Your Soul

402

Charles HOUGHTON   45

Shot: *1 **Martha Gordon Woodhouse**, 57, and*
          *2   **Eleanor Drinkwater Woodhouse**, 65, on 7*
          September 1926, in Burghill, Herefords.
Motive: *Vengeance.*

        Houghton, *(b.1881),* had worked as butler to the two sisters at their
Bughill Court estate near Hereford since 1904.   He had increasingly been
drinking, and the sisters told him that his services would no longer be
required. They offered him two months' wages, but asked him to leave within
24 hours. The following morning, Houghton served the sisters breakfast and
then shot them dead. He then returned to his own room and cut his throat. A
defence plea that epileptic fits made Houghton not responsible for his actions
was rejected.

        Read: The Murder Guide to Great Britain, p165.

1926 Executions in Ireland

15 July 1926   Mountjoy gaol, Dublin

James MYLES

Crime: *unknown*
Motive: *unknown*

    No details

24 November 1926   Mountjoy gaol, Dublin

James McHUGH

Crime: *unknown*
Motive: *unknown*

    No details

9 December 1926   Mountjoy gaol, Dublin

HENRY McCABE

Bludgeoned: **1** *Peter McDonnell,*
                  2 *Joseph McDonnell, his brother and their sisters,*
                  3 *Anne McDonnell and*
                  4 *Alice McDonnell, and servants*
                  5 *James Clarke and*
                  6 *Mary McGowan, on 31 March 1926, at Malahide, Dublin.*
Motive: *Financial.*

        McCabe, a married man with children, was a gardener and servant
at La Mancha, a large house owned by the McDonnells in a village outside
Dublin. As Clarke was milking a cow, McCabe hit him with a spanner. He
then laced the food with arsenic, and as the other five victims lay ill in their

beds, he also battered them to death. He then poured paraffin round the house and set it alight. The mansion was gutted.

Postmortem examinations showed the actual causes of death, and the paraffin can showed the attempt to conceal the crime. When some of Peter McDonnell's clothing was found in McCabe's home, together with bloodstained boots, it was clear the police had the culprit.

Read: Murder Guide to Great Britain, p288.

1927

total: **8**

403	5 Jan	William JONES	22	Armley
404	29 Mar	James STRATTON	26	Pentonville
405	27 Apr	William KNIGHTON	22	Nottingham
406	3 Aug	James MURPHY	29	Wandsworth
407	3 Aug	Frederick FULLER	35	Wandsworth
408	12 Aug	John ROBINSON	36	Pentonville
409	2 Sep	Arthur HARNETT	28	Armley
410	6 Dec	William ROBERTSON	32	Walton

5 January 1927   Armley gaol, Leeds   *T.Pierrepoint/ Baxter*

403

William Cornelius JONES   **22**

Shot: ***Winifred Jones**, 19, his wife, on 10 July 1926, in Halifax, W.Yorks.*
Motive: *Vengeance.*

Jones, *(b.1905),* had married Winifred in October 1925, but she left him after only five months because of his cruelty. After a warning letter from her solicitors, she returned to him, and became pregnant in March 1926. However, she left him again in July. Jones, a territorial army volunteer, took a rifle from the firing range where he told a friend he would shoot his wife. Crouching in a doorway in a Halifax street, he shot Winifred who was out shopping, and was seen doing so. He claimed he had stumbled, and the gun had gone off accidentally. The jury dismissed his version of events in only three minutes.

Read: True Crime Summer Special 94.

29 March 1927   Pentonville prison, London   *Baxter/ Mann*

404

James Frederick STRATTON   26

Stabbed: ***Madge Dorothy Maggs**, 25, on 21 February 1927, in London E8.*
Motive: *Sexual rivalry.*

Stratton, *(b.1901),* lived with his grandmother in Hackney, and had been courting Daisy Maggs since 1920, but at Christmas 1926, she told him it was all over. They still saw each other occasionally, but on 20 February, when Stratton went to Deptford, where Daisy lived with her brother and sister, he found Daisy out with another man.

Stratton sent two messages to Daisy at the White City exhibition where she worked, and she agreed to meet him at Liverpool Street station at 7.30pm. They had a row about her whereabouts the previous evening, and on the train to Hackney, Stratton hit Daisy with an iron tool, and stabbed her with a knife. Stratton jumped out at lights and told the train fireman what he had done. He was executed just 36 days later.

Read: And May The Lord Have Mercy On Your Soul

27 April 1927   Bagthorpe prison, Nottingham   *T.Pierrepoint*

405

William KNIGHTON   22

Cut throat of: ***Ada Knighton**, 55, his mother, on 8 February 1927, in Ilkeston, Derbyshire.*
Motive: *To clear impediment; drink related.*

Knighton, *(b.1905),* a miner, lived in Ilkeston with his parents, Ada and George, an invalid, and his sister, Doris Ivy, 16. He and his mother liked to go and get drunk together, and he was an affectionate son, but, unknown to his parents, he had developed an interest in his sister. Doris slept with her mother, and on 5 February Knighton had entered their room late at night. In his shirt only he had lain on top of Doris, and only when he penetrated her did she realise his intention. She screamed and he ran out, Ada thinking that she had had a nightmare.

Two days later, after a drinking binge, he again came into the room at 1.45am, and, as both women slept, he cut his mother's throat with a razor. Doris awoke, saw William and felt her mother clutching her. She thought Ada was simply not well, but noticed blood when she woke at 6am, and thought it was the result of a coughing fit.

Only at 7.30 when William had been told to fetch his married sister was the wound discovered. It was revealed that Knighton suffered fits, and the Home Secretary referred the case back to the court of appeal before approving the execution.

Read: Murderous Derbyshire

3 August 1927   Wandsworth prison, London

Baxter/ Mann/ Pollard/ Phillips

406, 407

James MURPHY   29
Frederick Stephen FULLER   35

Bludgeoned: *James Stanton, 42, on 14 May 1927, in Purley, Surrey.*
Motive: *Financial.*

Fuller, *(b.1892),* a father of six, whose wife was again pregnant, was a labourer on a building site. He and Murphy, *(b.1898),* hatched a plot to make a little extra money. James Stanton, a single man who lived alone, was nightwatchman at the site in Purley, and was confronted by Murphy and Fuller in the early hours. They battered the guard, stole his wages from his pocket, and an amount of brass and lead from the yard.

Mr Stanton died three days later. When the culprits were arrested in Doncaster on 23 May, they claimed that Stanton had fallen during a fight, and had banged his head accidentally. Fuller's wife gave birth while he awaited his execution.

Read: And May The Lord Have Mercy On Your Soul

408

John ROBINSON   36

Suffocated: ***Minnie Alice Bonati***, *36, on 4 May 1927, in London SW1.*
Motive: *Vengeance.*

Robinson, *(b.1891),* a one-time milkman, barman and bookmaker from Leigh, Lancs, had served in Egypt in the Great War. By 1927 he was a penniless estate agent with an office on Rochester Row. He had married in 1911, but had left his wife and children, and had married bigamously. He met Minnie Bonati, a prostitute, at Victoria station, and took her back to his office. Born Minnie Budd, she was married to an Italian waiter, and had lived for a time with Fred Rolls, sometimes using his name. He reported that she was a violent woman, often drunk.

Minnie asked Robinson for money for sex, and he refused, and he told how she became abusive. He knocked her unconscious and suffocated her with a cushion. Robinson told police that she fell and struck her head. The following day, Robinson dismembered her body, wrapping the parts in brown paper and cloth, and packing them into a trunk, removed them by taxi to the left-luggage section at Charing Cross station. When the smell became too offensive, the police opened the trunk three days later.

A laundry mark gave the police the woman's identity, and they were led to Robinson by the taxi driver, and by a duster which was traced to a snack-bar where Robinson was a regular customer. After a two-day trial, the jury found the estate agent guilty, obviously swayed against Robinson by the dismemberment of Minnie's body.

Read: Murders of the Black Museum

409

Arthur HARNETT   28

Cut throat of: ***Isabella Moore***, *33, on 3 May 1927, in Hemsworth, W.Yorkshire.*
Motive: *Vengeance.*

Harnett, *(b.1899),* was friends with Isabella Moore, and whether or not the relationship was entirely platonic, Isabella's husband, Robert, became jealous, suspecting an affair, and told Harnett to stop calling at the house. On the evening of 3 May, Isabella was alone, her two children in bed, Robert having gone to work at 1pm. Harnett called, and cut her throat.

At 10pm, he told a friend what he had done, handed his watch and medals over, and then went to find a police officer.

Read: And May The Lord Have Mercy On Your Soul

| 6 December 1927 | Walton gaol, Leeds | *T.Pierrepoint/ Phillips* |

410

William Maynell ROBERTSON   32

| *Cut throat of:* | *Evelyn Mary Jennings, 33, on 15 August 1927, in Speke, Lancs.* |
| *Motive:* | *To clear impediment.* |

Evelyn Jennings and Robertson, *(b.1895),* whom she called 'Stiffy', were lovers, and longed to marry, but money problems had gradually made their dream of a life together impossible. On 14 August, Evelyn wrote a letter to her brother telling him of the suicide pact which she and Stiffy had agreed.

At 6pm, they walked together to the woods, and there, Robertson cut both their throats, almost decapitating Evelyn. He managed to stagger out onto the road, and told a passer-by, 'Save her, not me'.

Read: And May The Lord Have Mercy On Your Soul

1927 Execution in Ireland

29 December 1927   Mountjoy gaol, Dublin

William O'NEILL

Crime: *unknown*
Motive: *unknown*

No details

1928

total: **24**

411	3 Jan	Frederick FIELDING	24		Strangeways
412	4 Jan	Bertram KIRBY	47		Lincoln
413	6 Jan	Sidney GOULTER	24		Wandsworth
414	6 Jan	John DUNN	52		Durham
415	7 Jan	Samuel CASE	24		Armley
416	24 Jan	James McKAY		Scottish	Duke Street
417	27 Jan	Edward ROWLANDS	40	Welsh	Cardiff
418	27 Jan	Daniel DRISCOLL	34	Welsh	Cardiff
419	31 Jan	James POWER	33		Winson Green
420	31 Jan	James GILLON	30	Scottish	Wandsworth
421	10 Apr	George HAYWARD	32		Nottingham
422	12 Apr	Frederick LOCK	39		Wandsworth
423	31 May	Frederick BROWNE	47		Pentonville
424	31 May	William KENNEDY	36	Scottish	Wandsworth
425	6 Jun	Frederick STEWART	29		Pentonville
426	28 Jun	Walter BROOKS	48		Strangeways
427	25 Jul	Albert ABSOLOM	28		Walton
428	27 Jul	William MAYNARD	36		Exeter
429	3 Aug	George REYNOLDS	41	Scottish	Duke Street
430	10 Aug	Norman ELLIOTT	23		Durham
431	13 Aug	Allen WALES	25	Scottish	Saughton
432	20 Nov	William BENSON	25		Wandsworth
433	6 Dec	Chung Yi MIAO	28	Chinese	Strangeways
434	11 Dec	Trevor EDWARDS	21	Welsh	Swansea

3 January 1928   Strangeways prison, Manchester   *T.Pierrepoint*

411

Frederick FIELDING   24

Stabbed: ***Eleanor Pilkington***, *23, on 5 November 1927, Rishton, Lancs.*
Motive: *Vengeance; drink related.*

Fielding, *(b. 1904),* and Eleanor Pilkington had been courting for four years when he went to London in March 1927 to join the Metropolitan Police. After an unhappy probationary period he returned to his home village, Clayton-le-Moors, in September and took a job as an iron moulder. However, Eleanor had broken off their relationship just one week after his return. Fielding turned to drink, lost his job and then his home. He pestered Eleanor, smashing a window at her parents' house one night. Distraught, at the end of October he bought a knife, telling the shopkeeper he had a murder to commit.

Eleanor had gone to a fireworks night dance in Great Harwood with two friends and Fielding had gone on a drinking binge, downing ten pints of beer. When Eleanor and her friends returned to their village of Rishton, near Blackburn, Fielding was waiting. He called Eleanor over, and after the two had exchanged angry words, he stabbed her twice in the neck. One hour later, he walked up to a policeman in Blackburn and turned himself in. A defence plea for a manslaughter verdict because of his drunken state was dismissed, and the jury found him guilty
after 15 minutes' deliberation.

Read: *Strange Tales from Strangeways*

4 January 1928	Lincoln gaol	*T.Pierrepoint/ Pollard*

412

Bertram Horace KIRBY   47

Bludgeoned: ***Minnie Eleanor Kirby,*** *46, his wife, on 11 July 1927, in Louth, Lincs.*
Motive: *To clear impediment.*

Kirby, *(b.1881),* was judged insane in 1915, and was discharged from the army. A serious operation further eroded his mental balance in 1925, and he attempted suicide with laudanum in 1927. Once a railway worker, by that time he was selling hardware and clothes, and had very little money. Constant rows with his wife resulted in his 25-year old son leaving home in 1924, though a 10-year old boy still lived with his parents, and Kirby had arranged for him to have lunch with a neighbour on 11 July. After killing Minnie with a single axe blow to the head, Kirby sold some clothes, and went to the pub.

Read: *And May The Lord Have Mercy On Your Soul*

413

Sidney Bernard GOULTER   24

Strangled: **Constance Gertrude Oliver**, *21, on 2 October 1927, in Richmond, Surrey.*
Motive: *Sexual rivalry.*

Goulter, *(b.1904)*, the son of a retired police officer, had behaved strangely since the age of 15. He enjoyed masturbating in front of others, was extremely abusive and sometimes violent. His father was nervous about leaving him alone with his wife and daughter, and neither parent would allow Sidney to be alone or to go out with his sister. Typist Constance Oliver had got to know Sidney and had liked him enough to take him home to meet her parents in Battersea.

While the two were walking in Richmond Park at 7.30pm, Goulter asked Constance for a further date, and when she told him she was seeing another boy that night, he attacked her with her umbrella, stunning her with a blow to the head. He tore her dress to shreds, and despite a huge struggle, managed to strangle her with a strip torn from her clothing. When she was found in undergrowth, there were burn marks at the top of her thighs. A plea of insanity was rejected.

Read: *True Crime, May 97.*

414

John Thomas DUNN   52

Strangled: **Ada Elizabeth Dunn**, *46, his wife, on 25 September 1927, in Sacriston, Co Durham.*
Motive: *Vengeance*

Dunn, *(b.1876)*, was a miner when he married Ada in 1902. They had ten children. In 1907 he spent two months in an asylum, and after serving in the Durham Light Infantry in France, he tried to strangle Ada in 1918, stopped only by his daughter. Over the years he had beaten Ada and burned her clothes, the police had been called, and she had left him many times. By 1927 Dunn was unemployed owing to ill health, and only the three youngest sons remained at home. Ada's plight, however, was no better. She left Dunn again on 18 September, but, begged by him to return, she agreed to do so as housekeeper only, not as his wife.

At 12.30am on 25 September, after a row probably caused by Ada's refusal to sleep with Dunn, he strangled her with a rope, then strung her up on a doorpeg, screaming into the street that his wife had killed herself. Police noticed blood on Dunn's shoulder, and thought suicide was impossible from so low a peg, with so short a rope.

The night after his arrest Dunn was found naked in his cell, having shredded his clothes in a frenzy. His children testified that he was neither a good husband nor father, and the jury decided his guilt in 19 minutes. He spent Christmas writing to relatives, and nursing a bird back to health. During his last night he laughed and joked. Thanking the prison staff, he went calmly to his death.

Read: True Crime, May 97.

7 January 1928   Armley gaol, Leeds   *T.Pierrepoint/ Pollard*

415

Samuel CASE   24

Strangled:	***Mary Alice Mottram**, 22, on 20 October 1927, in Sheffield, W.Yorks.*
Motive:	*Sexual rivalry.*

Case, *(b. 1903),* a miner from Sheffield, had known George Edward Mottram all his life. The two had gone to school together, worked together at the pit, and each acted as best man at the other's wedding. Alice, a buffer at the cutlery factory, had married Teddy in March 1925. He arrived home from work one night at 10.45 to find his wife dead on the kitchen floor.

The following day Case went to the police and confessed to the murder. He claimed that he and Alice had been having an affair, and that she was pregnant by him. As she went to the stove he had inexplicably strangled her with his scarf, then tied a tea towel and a clothes line round her neck. He had stolen her purse to feign robbery.

Case, 5'9" and 12st 8lb, had been unwell for some time, a gum disease causing him to lose all his teeth. A case was made of temporary insanity, but Alice was not pregnant, indeed was menstruating at the time of her death, and it seems more likely that she had rebuffed Case's advances and Case killed her to stop her telling Ted. The jury decided his fate in twenty minutes.

Read: True Detective, May 97

416

James McKAY   *Scottish*

Murdered:	**Agnes McKay**, *his mother, in October 1927, in Glasgow, Lanarks.*
Motive:	*Financial.*

McKay murdered his mother at her home in the hope of receiving an inheritance of £100. He dismembered the body, throwing part in the Clyde, and hiding the remainder in her coal bunker. When part of Mrs McKay's body was discovered in the river, her son calmly confessed to killing her.

Read: Encyclopaedia of Scottish Executions

27 January 1928   Cardiff gaol   *Baxter/ Phillips/ Mann/ Wilson*

417, 418

Edward ROWLANDS   **40**   *Welsh*
Daniel DRISCOLL   **34**   *Welsh*

Stabbed:	**David Lewis**, *on 29 September 1927, in Cardiff, Glamorgan.*
Motive:	*Vengeance.*

Brothers Ted and John Rowlands ran a gang centred in Tiger Bay, Cardiff. Ted had recently been released from a prison sentence for assault. They were angered when Dai Lewis, a former welterweight boxing professional and small-time crook, started running a protection racket on their patch. Acting alone, Lewis, a married man with a family, would make money from bookies and salesmen at Monmouth races. As he left a pub at closing time, four members of the Rowlands gang attacked him, kicking him on the ground, and stabbing him in the throat. He died later in hospital.

The four men were all arrested at a club after the pollice traced phone calls to the hospital, and were all tried for murder. John Rowlands, 30, who did the actual stabbing, was found guilty but insane, and Joseph Price, 42, was acquitted. Edward Rowlands, *(b.1878),* and Daniel Driscoll, *(b.1894),* were both found guilty. Lewis, who died in hospital the next day, had refused to identify his attackers, but others did.

Driscoll remained calm throughout the execution ordeal, telling Rowlands, who had to be assisted to the scaffold, 'Goodbye, Ted. We've both been beaten at the post'.

Read: True Detective Winter Special 88/9.

31 January 1928   Winson Green prison, Birmingham

T.Pierrepoint/ Wilson

419

James Joseph POWER   33

Drowned: ***Olive Gordon Turner***, *18, on 2 July 1927, in Birmingham, Warwicks.*

Motive: *Sadistic pleasure*

Power, *(b.1895)*, was discharged from the police service for unsatisfactory conduct, and latterly was a factory worker. Married with children, he thought himself a victim of a vendetta by certain officers.

Olive Turner and her boyfriend, Charles Broomhead, were taking an evening stroll on the canal towpath at Winson Green when Power accused them of trespassing and asked them to accompany him. For an hour he questioned them, and requested a bribe to let them go. Eventually, Olive made a dash for freedom and, when Charles tried to stop Power pursuing her, he was punched on the jaw.

Power, 15 stone and over 6', caught Olive and told passers by he was a police officer. At 11.30pm a scream was heard. When Charles regained consciousness, he raised the alarm, and Olive was found drowned in the canal at 6am. She had been unconscious when she hit the water, having received a blow to the forehead.

Power simply claimed he had not been there, but he was identified by Broomhead, and by other witnesses. Power already had other charges against him, for rape, assault and demanding money with menaces.

Read: True Detective, Mar 95.

420

James GILLON   **30**   *Scottish*

Cut throat of: *Annie Gillon, 28, his sister, on 20 September 1927, in*
                          Lower Beeding, Sussex
Motive: *Vengeance*

       Gillon, *(b.1898),* a Glaswegian, had been a stoker in the Royal Navy but had been imprisoned after striking a Petty Officer. In 1920 his incestuous relationship with his sister Annie came to light when she gave birth to his daughter, for which Gillon was sentenced to three years.

       He then worked as a miner until in May 1927 when Annie got work as a housemaid near Handcross, her brother joining her a month later as a gardener. Annie lived in the house but James occupied a hut in the grounds. Very possessive of her, James objected to a trip Annie took to Brighton with the chauffeur and cook. Because of the way he had spoken to her, Annie refused to get him his supper that night, and his breakfast the following morning, and refused to speak with him.

       When Annie went into the servants' hall James followed her. He kicked her then slashed her throat with a razor, and stabbed her twice in the back with an army jack-knife, part of which broke off in her spine. He then cut his own throat and pulled Annie onto his knee as he sat on a chair. Gillon left hospital ten days later, but Annie finally died on 28 October. Though one doctor certified Gillon sane, another said he had a persecution complex, and that both his mother and another sister had been confined to asylums. The jury took 15 minutes to decide who to believe.

      Read: Murderous Sussex

10 April 1928   Bagthorpe prison, Nottingham   *T.Pierrepoint/ Pollard*

421

George Frederick Walter HAYWARD   **32**

Cut throat of: *Amy Collinson, 36, on 11 November 1927, in Little*
                          Hayfield, Derbyshire.
Motive: *Financial.*

Known as 'Jerry', Hayward, *(b.1896)*, was a commercial traveller for a soap manufacturers, who lived with his wife in a cottage in Little Hayfield. They had married in 1925 and had a child of three months. Half a mile from his home was the New Inn, run by Arthur and Amy Collinson. Hayward was made redundant in October 1927, and had fallen into debt. He saw the pub as a possible quick source of revenue, though Mr Collinson worked in a builder's yard to make ends meet, leaving Amy to run the pub alone during the daytimes.

On the afternoon of 11 November, Hayward went to the pub and coshed Amy twice with a piece of lead-piping. He then cut her throat, before rifling the place and getting away with £40. Her husband found her body when he returned from work, her hand clasping a carving knife in her throat. Hayward was found to have blood on his hat and tie, and to have paid off some debts the same day. £35 was found hidden in his chimney, and the piping was discovered to have been cut from his kitchen outflow.

Despite protestations of innocence from Hayward, the jury found him guilty after 35 minutes' deliberation.

Read: True Crime, Aug 97.

---

12 April 1928   Wandsworth prison, London   *Baxter/ Mann*

422

Frederick LOCK   39

Cut throat of: ***Florence Alice Kitching***, *28, on 8 February 1928, in London SE1*
Motive: *Vengeance.*

Lock, *(b.1889)*, a widower with four children, had lived with Florence Kitching since 1924, but the relationship was not a happy one, Lock showing early signs of dementia. On 4 February, he punched Florence in the face and brandished a knife at her. Florence's father was ill in Cornwall, and this gave her an added incentive to leave Lock to stew in his own juices.

Her mother came to London, and the night before they were due to depart, Florence, her mother and sister, and Lock, went out for a drink. He asked Florence to come home to prepare dinner for the children, leaving the other women in the pub. Once he had Florence at home, he cut her throat because he could not bear her to leave, then went back to collect the other women. The jury pondered their verdict for just ten minutes.

Read: And May The Lord Have Mercy On Your Soul

| 31 May 1928 | Pentonville prison, London | *Baxter/ Pollard* |
| | Wandsworth prison, London | *T.Pierrepoint / Wilson* |

423, 424

Frederick Guy BROWNE	**47**	*(ne Leo Brown)*
William Henry KENNEDY	**36**	*(aka Patrick*
	Scottish	*Michael Kennedy)*

Shot: ***P.C. George William Gutteridge***, *38, on 27 September 1927, near Romford, Essex.*
Motive: *To escape arrest.*

Browne, *(b. 1881)*, a mechanic from south London, married with a child, had served several jail terms for carrying firearms, car theft and insurance fraud. A powerfully built man, and a tee-totaller, he employed Kennedy as an odd-job man at his repair yard in Lavender Hill. Kennedy, born in Scotland in 1892 of Irish parents, also had served jail terms. His offences included indecent exposure, housebreaking and larceny. The two had met in Dartmoor prison in 1926.

They had stolen a car in Billericay and were driving back to London when they were stopped near the village of Howe Green between Romford and Ongar at about 4.30 a.m. by night-patrol policeman George Gutteridge, a married man. As the policeman was about to write in his book, Browne shot him twice in the face, and, getting out of the car, asking, 'What are you looking at me like that for?', shot him once in each eye as he lay on the ground. The car was later found in Brixton.

The two men were arrested in January and ballistics evidence, used for the first time, proved that a revolver in Browne's possession had been the murder weapon. Kennedy had been married in Liverpool three days before his arrest. He made a full confession, denied by Browne.

Read: Murders of the Black Museum

| **6 June 1928** | Pentonville prison, London | *T.Pierrepoint/ Baxter/ Phillips* |

425

Frederick John STEWART   **29**

Shot: ***Alfred Charles Bertram Webb***, *45, on 9 February, 1928 in London W2.*
Motive: *Financial.*

Stewart, *(b. 1899),* was known as a housebreaker, and on 9 February saw his opportunity to break into a luxury flat in Kensington's Pembridge Square. Mr Webb and his son returned to the flat at 6 p.m. and, noticing the broken glass panel on the front door, his son went to alert the police. Unaware that the burglar was still present, Mr Webb went on in, and as he peered through the frosted glass of the door, Stewart put the revolver to the glass and shot him through the head, making good his escape. Mr Webb died later in hospital.

Police picked up Stewart as he fitted a general description of a man seen leaving the scene. He was identified by a woman whose door he had knocked at while seeking a suitable property to burgle. He later admitted the offence, but claimed the pistol had gone off accidentally. A regular racegoer, he was hanged on Derby-day. His tip to the warders *Felstead* came in at 33-1, though he never lived to hear the result.

Read: Master Detective Summer Special 96.

---

28 June 1928   Strangeways prison, Manchester   *T.Pierrepoint*

426

Walter BROOKS   48

Shot: 1 **Beatrice Brooks**, 39, his wife, and
                   2 **Alfred Moore**, 60, on 4 April 1928, in Preston, Lancs.
Motive: Sexual rivalry.

Brooks, *(b.1880),* had behaved strangely since a serious road accident in 1924, and had spent three days in a mental hospital the following year. Alfred Moore lodged with Brooks and his wife, but it was not long before Brooks suspected the other two of conducting an affair under his own roof. After buying a revolver, he found the two drinking in a pub, and then waited for them to come out. He shot Beatrice and Alfred, and was taken in by a passing policeman.

Read: And May The Lord Have Mercy On Your Soul

427

Albert George ABSALOM   28

Stabbed: ***Mary Alice Reed***, *26, on 11 May 1928, in Liverpool, Lancs.*
Motive: *Sexual rivalry.*

Absalom,*(b.1900),* who had served in the army from 1920 to 1923, met Mary Reed in the mill where they both worked, and the two became engaged. But Absalom was terribly jealous, which made Mary less keen, making him more jealous in turn. By March 1923, Absalom was manager of a relation's fish and chip shop, but Mary's feelings for Albert had cooled considerably.

On 4 May, she took a cycle ride with a neighbour, Bill Cliffe, and Absalom's envy got the better of him. In the street he stabbed her in the throat with a sheath knife, and was stopped from escaping by two passers-by.

Read: And May The Lord Have Mercy On Your Soul

428

William John MAYNARD   36

Bludgeoned: ***Richard Francis Roadley***, *84, on 19 February 1928, near Bude, Cornwall.*
Motive: *Financial.*

Maynard, *(b.1892),* a married farmer and rabbit trapper, broke into the isolated and delapidated cottage of Mr Roadley, a wealthy recluse, in the village of Titson. The old man had left his manor house in Lincolnshire fifty years before, and, hating women, had lived alone ever since.

Maynard killed the old man by a blow to the head with a hammer. Having rifled the house, he buried the proceeds on his father's farm nearby. A neighbour, returning from church found Roadley still alive, but the old man died two hours later. Maynard admitted robbery, but blamed Thomas Harris, who had an unshakeable alibi, for the murder. The jury deliberated for 45 minutes.

Read: Master Detective Summer Special 97.

3 August 1928   Duke Street prison, Glasgow   *T.Pierrepoint*

429

George REYNOLDS   41   *Scottish*

Bludgeoned: **Thomas Lee**, *on 21 March 1928, in Glasgow, Lanarks.*
Motive: *Financial.*

      Reynolds, *(b.1887)*, often visited his friend Thomas Lee, a boilerman, at the bakery where he worked. One night, Reynolds was stoking the fire while his friend took a drunken nap. When Lee awoke a row ensued, with Lee accusing Reynolds of trying to take his job. In the scuffle that followed, Reynolds hit Lee with a branding iron, killing him. He entered a plea of self-defence, but the jury also found him guilty of stealing overalls and some money from his friend.

      Read: Encyclopaedia of Scottish Executions

10 August 1928   Durham gaol   *T.Pierrepoint/ Wilson*

430

Norman ELLIOTT   23

Cut throat of: **William Byland Abbey**, *31, on 16 February 1928,*
                       in Ferryhill, Co Durham.
Motive: *Financial.*

      Elliott, *(b.1905)*, a nurse at Sedgefield mental hospital, had married in January 1928, but until he could raise enough money for their own place, his wife continued to live at her parents pub, and he in quarters at the hospital. He owed money to a workmate,and saw the branch of Lloyds Bank as the answer to his problems.
      At 3pm, William Abbey, a Baptist lay preacher and composer of operettas, was alone in the bank, cashing up before closing. Elliott hit him five times on the head before slitting his throat with a cobbler's knife and escaping with £202. Abbey managed to throw a paperweight through the window, and lived long enough to tell witnesses of his tall attacker.
      Police arrested Elliott four days later after the laundrywoman at the asylum reported his heavily blood-stained shirt. More bloody clothes and £175 was found in his room. He claimed to have won the money gambling. Elliott had paid off his debts and had a new suit and shoes. His story that he

had gone to the bank unwittingly with a gambling acquaintance named Sinclair, and that it was he who had murdered Abbey, was not believed. However, Abbey knew Elliott, but had not named him as the 'tall man', and eight witnesses failed to pick him out. Sinclair, though, was never found. Before his execution, Elliott's wife gave birth to a son, and after it, she remarried.

Read: True Detective, May 97

13 August 1928	Saughton prison, Edinburgh

431

Allen WALES   25   *Scottish*

Murdered:	***Isabella Wales**, 24, his wife, on 5 June 1928, in Leith, Midlothian.*
Motive:	*unknown*

Wales and his wife had lived with her parents in Pirniefield Place for eighteen months since their wedding. It was there that he murdered her. No further details.

Read: Encyclopaedia of Scottish Executions.

20 November 1928	Wandsworth prison, London	*Baxter/ Mann*

432

William Charles BENSON   25

Stabbed:	***Charlotte Alice Harber**, 26, on 6 September 1928, in Coulsdon, Surrey.*
Motive:	*Vengeance.*

Benson, *(b.1903)*, worked in an ice-cream factory, with his best mate Sidney Harber, a married man with two children. Benson went to lodge with the Harbers, but it was not long before an affair had developed between Benson and his pal's wife, Charlotte. Sidney found out in August 1926, and though he threw Benson out, Charlotte managed to persuade him she would be a good wife, and the lodger returned two days later. In 1927, Sidney realised Bill and Charlotte's liaison had resumed, and even though Benson was again expelled, the affair continued, until in April 1928, Charlotte took a room for Benson and went to live with him there.

Benson was contented until, on 5 September, Charlotte announced that this was to be their final night together, that she was returning to Sid. The next day, as Charlotte pushed her pram in a field by the golf course, Benson stabbed her in the breast. Benson found a policeman, and took him to where Charlotte lay. The jury decided Benson's fate inside fifteen minutes.

Read: And May The Lord Have Mercy On Your Soul

6 December 1928   Strangeways prison, Manchester

T.Pierrepoint

433

CHUNG Yi Miao   **28**   *Chinese*

Strangled: ***Wai Sheung Siu**, 29, his wife, on 19 June 1928, in Borrowdale, Cumberland.*
Motive: *To clear impediment.*

Chung, *(b.1900),* was a barrister who met his bride in New York in 1927. She was the daughter of a wealthy Macao merchant, who had inherited all his wealth when he recently died. She had attended Boston University and had opened an art shop in Hong Kong. She had gone to New York for an art exhibition, and after a whirlwind romance, the couple had married in May 1928. They honeymooned in Florida, the Rockies and Niagara, and then took a trans-Atlantic cruise, arriving in the Lake District from Scotland on 18 June.

On the following evening, Chung murdered his wife by a swimming pool near the hotel, strangling her with a cord and leaving her body under an umbrella. He had lifted her skirts and ripped off her knickers to give the impression of rape. Her rings were taken. He told other guests that she had gone to Keswick for shopping.

A farmer discovered the body later the same evening, and, when questioned Chung said that they had been followed by two oriental men earlier in the day. But he immediately raised suspicions because he knew about the robbery, about the rape, and about the place before anyone had mentioned them to him.

The motive remained a mystery, as Chung was entitled anyway to all his wife's money, and the fact that she could not have children would have been more easily solved by divorce than murder. Though the evidence against him was entirely circumstantial, he was convicted after one hours' deliberation by the jury. His appeal was dismissed.

Read: Strange Tales from Strangeways.

11 December 1928	Swansea gaol	*Baxter/ Alfred Allen*

434

Trevor John EDWARDS   21   *Welsh*

Cut throat of:	***Elsie Cook**, 21, on 16 June 1928, in Llanwnog, Montgomeryshire.*
Motive:	*To clear impediment; drink related.*

Edwards, *(b.1907),* and Elsie Cook had been seeing each other for several months, when in June, she discovered she was pregnant, and her mother found out. After a discussion with Elsie's parents, Edwards agreed to marry their daughter, though he had no intension of doing so, for he also had, unknown to any of them, being seeing another, 16-year old girl, during the time he had been courting Elsie.

After drinking with a friend, Edwards met Elsie some time after 6pm, and she waited outside another pub at 8.30 while he had another. He then went up the hillside with the pregnant young woman, and bashed her over the head with a flagon of cider he had taken along for his refreshment. He then strangled her, and finished her off by cutting her throat. The next morning at 10.15, he came down the hillside, and told two men what he had done. On the scaffold, as the trap opened, the assistant hangman, Alfred Allen, failed to move aside in time, and fell into the pit.

Read: And May The Lord Have Mercy On Your Soul

8 August 1928 Crumlin Road Gaol, Belfast

T.Pierrepoint/ Baxter

<u>WILLIAM SMYLIE</u> 28

Shot: 1 *Margaret Macauley, 48, and her sister,*
2 *Sarah Macauley, 43, on 24 May 1928, at Armoy, Co Antrim.*

Motive: *Financial.*

Margaret and Sarah Macauley, unmarried sisters, lived with their two brothers, Andrew and Leslie, on their 300 acre farm at Armoy. Labourers William Smylie and Tommy McCaughan returned from ploughing to eat lunch in the farmhouse while the brothers were repairing a fence.

When McCaughan left for an afternoon off, Smylie was left alone in the house with Margaret. Smylie, *(b.1900)*, shot her in the head at point blank range with a shotgun, and Sarah too was shot in the head when she returned.

He ransacked the bedrooms and stole £30 and a gold watch. A woman servant discovered the sisters in the kitchen an hour later, and called for Smylie, who ran to raise the police. They were alerted when Smylie already knew of a robbery, and the money was found in his boot. The jury found him guilty after 20 minutes, and Smylie made a full confession before his execution.

Read: True Detective, Nov 96.

29 August 1928 Dublin *T.Pierrepoint*

<u>GERARD TOAL</u> 19

Murdered: *Mary Callan, 36, on 16 May 1927, in Faughart, Co Louth.*
Motive: *unknown*

Toal, *(b.1908)*, once a butcher, was a chauffeur and odd-job man for parish priest Father James McKeown in a village near Dundalk. Mary Callan was his housekeeper. While the priest was away in Dublin, Toal murdered Mary, removed her head and legs, and dumped her naked body in a sack in the nearby quarry.

Toal claimed that Mary had said she was going away. McKeown was suspicious as all Mary's clothes were still at the house, but it was a year before a new housekeeper discovered parts of Mary's bicycle in Toal's stables room. The waters of the quarry were searched and Mary's body found. Other than wanting to steal a bicycle, no clear motive was established, unless he had raped Miss Callan and killed to silence her. The jury took less than an hour to decide his fate. Toal protested his innocence throughout.

Read: True Crime, Nov 97.

1929

total: **8**

435	4 Jan	Charles CONLIN	22		Durham
436	20 Feb	Frank HOLLINGTON	25		Pentonville
437	27 Feb	William HOLMYARD	23		Pentonville
438	12 Mar	Joseph CLARK	21		Walton
439	4 Apr	George CARTLEDGE	27		Strangeways
440	7 Aug	James JOHNSON	43		Durham
441	14 Aug	Arthur RAVENY	24		Armley
442	26 Nov	John MAGUIRE	43		Walton

4 January 1929   Durham gaol   *T.Pierrepoint*

435

<u>Charles William CONLIN</u>   **22**

Buried alive: **1** *Emily Frances Kirby*, *64, his grandmother, and her husband,*
2 *Thomas Kirby*, *62, on 22 September 1928, in Norton, Co Durham.*
Motive: *Financial.*

Conlin, *(b.1907),* lodged with his brother-in-law, and earned just 16/6 a week, deciding he would increase his cash flow by taking what he could from his grandmother. On 21 September he stole a car, and took a spade from his home. Driving the four miles to his grandmother's house the following night, he persuaded her to accompany him, leaving her husband to spend the night alone.

He strangled her, then returned the following morning to collect Mr Kirby, who he battered in the same field. He was seen there at 6.20am with a spade. Conlin then used his new money to buy a £21 motor-bike, and showed off £20 in cash to his girlfriend. When the shallow grave was found the next day, it was discovered that the old couple had still been alive when buried.

Read: And May The Lord Have Mercy On Your Soul

436

Frank HOLLINGTON   25   *(aka John Dennis)*

Punched: ***Annie Elizabeth Hatton**, 18, on 17 November 1928, in
               London E9.*
Motive: *Sexual rivalry.*

Hollington, *(b. 1904)*, was violent towards his girlfriend, Annie Hatton, and when she told him the relationship was finished in September, he punched her in the face, refusing to accept the fact. Hollington had arranged to meet Annie, but she failed to turn up, and when he discovered she had been out with another man, he went to confront her.

Annie was a domestic servant to a butcher and his wife, and was babysitting the children and doing some ironing while the couple were at the theatre. Hollington arrived, and asked her about her failed appointmment. When she lied to him, he bound and gagged her, punching her heavily twice. It was enough to kill the young woman, who was found when her employer got home at 11pm. Hollington was arrested on 29 November.

Read: And May The Lord Have Mercy On Your Soul.

437

William John HOLMYARD   23

Bludgeoned: ***William Holmyard**, 72, his grandfather, on 7 December
               1928, in London SW1*
Motive: *Vengeance.*

Holmyard, *(b. 1906)*, an army bandsman who had served in India, before his discharge on 18 November, lived with his father in Pimlico, next-door to his grandfather, who ran a furniture business. On a December afternoon, Holmyard had gone to see his grandfather, seeking his advice in getting a job. The old man insulted the youngster who still owed him £17, and attacked him with a chair. The grandson claimed that he had picked up a pair of coal-tongs and had hit the old man with them in self-defence.

Staggering outside, the old Mr Holmyard was taken to hospital, and his grandson was charged with assault. When his grandfather died three days later, young William had a murder charge to face.

Read: Murderers' London, p138.

12 March 1929	Walton gaol, Liverpool	*T.Pierrepoint*

438

Joseph Reginald Victor CLARK   21   *(aka Reginald Kennedy)*

Strangled: ***Alice Fontaine***, *50, on 28 October 1928, in Liverpool, Lancs.*
Motive: Vengeance.

Clark, *(b.1907),* was brought up by an aunt in Norfolk before going to live with his mother in America in 1923. He returned in 1927, working his passage. He was an amateur hypnotist, but his main source of income was the women whom he managed to trick out of their money.

Many women managed to fall under his spell, at one time four sisters in Liverpool were his mistresses, none of them aware of the others. What many of them certainly must have become aware of was Clark's violent temper when things did not go exactly his way. When he tried in Birkenhead to marry a 17-year old, he was found out, and tried to strangle her - if he could not have her, then no-one would. The woman refused to press charges.

Calling himself Kennedy, he met Agnes Fontaine, 19, a typist, and then moved in to lodge with her and her mother in June 1928. At first fond of Clark, nicknaming him 'Teddy Bear', Mrs Fontaine got wise to his tactics when he fell behind with the rent, and turned him out when she found letters from a previous lover. Not satisfied with the obscene letters which he sent to them, he decided on an even greater revenge when Mrs Fontaine reported him to the police. He entered the house and hid overnight in the cellar. The next morning he strangled Alice with a pyjama cord. He then went upstairs and did the same with young Agnes, cutting her throat for good measure. She survived and ran into the street for help. Clark pleaded guilty, his trial lasting only five minutes.

Read: True Detective Jan '96.

439

George Henry CARTLEDGE   27

Cut throat of: ***Ellen Cartledge***, *25, his wife, on 2 January 1929, in Oldham, Lancs.*
Motive: *Vengeance.*

Cartledge, *(b.1902),* was said to be of low intelligence, and had received treatment for head pains, which deprived him of sleep and concentration. He and his wife, Ellen, had a daughter aged six. At 9am one morning he cut Ellen's throat, and when she was seen collapsing, waving at a window, Cartledge was found in the house, in a dazed condition, with no apparent recollection of events.

He tried to commit suicide in custody, but his insanity was not proven, and the jury, taking 2 hours 45 minutes to reach its verdict, added a recommendation to mercy.

Read: And May The Lord Have Mercy On Your Soul

440

James JOHNSON   43

Cut throat of: ***Mary Ann Johnson***, *39, his wife, on 12 May 1929, in Newcastle, Northumberland*
Motive: *Sexual rivalry*

Johnson, *(b.1886),* a bookmaker, disabled from birth by a malformed leg, had been married to Annie since 1908. Their stormy relationship was due largely to his violent temper when drunk. He had several convictions, dating back to 1917, mostly for being drunk, though he slashed a man with a razor in 1925, and was first sent to gaol in 1927 for stealing purses.

In 1929 the couple lived in two rooms of a house in Elswick, Newcastle with their four youngest children aged between 1 and 13 years. Two elder daughters were married. Unable to pay fines, Johnson spent eight weeks in prison in 1929, and was puzzled why Annie, who had some money, had not paid them for him. He suspected that she was having an affair with his clerk, Billy Ridley, who stayed with Annie for six weeks while Johnson was in jail. In a letter to Annie's sister he vowed revenge, and in an argument on 9 May, Annie hit Johnson with a rolling pin before calling the police to him.

Annie and James went out separately at 6pm on 11 May returning at 11.30, both had been drinking, but neither was drunk. All having retired, Johnson cut his wife's throat as she lay vainly trying to defend herself on her bed. He then blocked the chimney and other airways and turned on the gas, taking to bed in the other room alongside his children. Neighbours alerted police when they heard a thud at 12.30am, and Johnson and the children were led to safety. He had blood stains on his clothes, hands and face. Though two experts maintained that Annie could have inflicted the wounds herself, and Johnson always maintained his innocence, the jury took 20 minutes to determine his guilt.

Read: True Detective, Sep 97.

14 August 1929	Armley gaol, Leeds	*T.Pierrepoint/ Wilson*

441

Arthur Leslie RAVENY   24

Shot:	***Leslie Godfrey White**, 23, on 14 May 1929, in Constable Burton, N.Yorks.*
Motive:	*Vengeance.*

Raveny, *(b.1905),* had served eight years in the Royal Tank Corps without blemish, until a minor offence for which he was confined to barracks. There, he was bullied by Private White, set to guard him. On 10 May, he had threatened to get even with him.

Raveny went absent on 14 May, but was picked up on the road, five miles from Catterick. White was again set to guard him in the back of the van returning him to camp. Raveny shot White, and escaped, eventually being recaptured in a quarry near Newton-le-Willows. He said that White had stolen his gun some time ago to get him into trouble, and had threatened him with it in the van. Raveny had grabbed the weapon and it had gone off accidentally. The threats previously made by Raveny went against him with the jury.

Read: And May The Lord Have Mercy On Your Soul

442

John MAGUIRE   43

Cut throat of: ***Ellen Maguire,*** *42, his wife, on 5 September 1929, in Liverpool, Lancs.*
Motive: *To clear impediment.*

Maguire, *(b.1886),* and his wife Ellen had ten children, varying in age from 24 years to 18 months, and Ellen was again pregnant in September 1929. With eight children still at home, it is likely that yet another mouth to feed proved too much for Maguire to take.

At 1pm he bought a knife, and an hour later Ellen, after a busy morning shopping, doing chores, and getting lunch, was alone with two of the offspring. In a frenzied knife attack, Maguire stabbed his wife in the back, then cut her throat as she lay on the bedroom floor. At 2.30pm he went to tell the neighbours what he had done.

Read: And May The Lord Have Mercy On Your Soul

1929 Execution in Ireland

25 April 1929   Mountjoy gaol, Dublin

<u>John COX</u>   33

Bludgeoned: ***Jacob Kunz***, *in December 1928, in Ardnacrusha, Co Limerick.*

Motive: *Financial.*

Cox, *(b.1896),* murdered the wealthy Jewish shopkeeper during a robbery, beating him to death with a shovel. His defence insisted that the victim's skull was thinner than usual, and that the death could not therefore have been foreseen.

Read: True Detective, Mar 99

1930

total: **3**

443	8 Apr	Sidney FOX	31	Maidstone
444	22 Apr	William PODMORE	29	Winchester
445	13 Jun	Albert MARJERAM	23	Wandsworth

8 April 1930   Maidstone prison

443

Sidney Harry FOX   31

Strangled: ***Rosaline Fox**, 63, his mother, on 23 October 1929,*
in Margate, Kent.
Motive: *Financial.*

Fox, *(b.1899),* originally from Norfolk, travelled the country with his mother, both of them engaged in supplementing their meagre incomes with petty theft and passing stolen cheques, for which he had served several prison terms. They often did a flit without paying the bill for their rooms.

The youngest of four sons, Fox was a homosexual, and an elderly army officer was dismissed from the force after a compromising letter to Fox was found in one of the hotels that he and his mother had vacated. In 1927, he had insured the life of a Mrs Marsh, with whom he had a brief affair, for £6000. Leaving her sleeping with the gas turned on, he stole her jewellery, for which he was jailed. She recovered from the gassing.

In March 1929, Fox insured his mother's life against any accident for £3000, and got her to make out a will. When the policy was expiring, he had it extended, suspiciously, for a mere 36 hours. On 16 October, they booked into the Metropole Hotel in Margate. Fox strangled his mother by hand in her bedroom, and then began a fire with some petrol. Mrs Fox was dragged out of the room unconscious, and died soon after - just twenty minutes before the insurance deadline was up.

She was said to have died from shock and smoke inhalation. However, the insurance company was naturally suspicious, and when the widow's body was exhumed she was found to have been strangled.

The jury considered their verdict for 90 minutes, and Fox made no appeal against his conviction, but neither did he make a confession. He staggered and had to be supported to the scaffold.

Read: The Seaside Murders

444

William Henry PODMORE   29

Blugeoned: **Mr Vivian Messiter**, *57, on 30 October 1928, in Southampton, Hants.*
Motive: *To clear impediment.*

Podmore, *(b.1901)*, was a petty criminal from Leek, Staffs, who was separated from his wife, and who had taken up with another woman, Lily Hambleton. He was wanted for car frauds in Manchester, and had already served several short prison terms. He worked a couple of days repairing a car for Vivian Messiter, the agent of an oil company, working at a depot in Southampton.

Messiter, who had worked for some time in the USA, had been divorced there, and since returning to the UK in September 1928, lived in lodgings, writing to a sweetheart in Canada. He had discovered that Podmore, using the name Thomas, was trying to swindle the company for commission on oil sales. On 30 October, confronted with this knowledge, Podmore, 5'6", hit Messiter three times with a hammer, hitting his head even as he lay unconscious on the floor, and putting out Messiter's left eye.

He then robbed him, and took Lil out for a spin in Messiter's car. He then padlocked the depot, and Messiter's body lay there unfound for almost three months. A private man, only his landlady missed him, and assumed he must have returned to the States.

Meanwhile, Podmore moved on and stole £130 from another job he took in Downton, 15 miles away. When the oil company finally replaced the agent, on 10 January, the body was at last found, decomposed, and gnawed by rats. Police found blood on boxes and the walls. The murder weapon, with Messiter's blood and a single hair on it, was found in the depot. A sales receipt from W.F.Thomas was also found, and a letter from the same man at Messiter's lodgings. Thomas and Podmore were found to be the same man, and he was traced to London.

With little concrete evidence of Podmore's guilt in murder, he was sentenced to six months for the car frauds, followed immediately by another six for the Downton robbery. It was while in prison he confessed the murder to two fellow inmates. The police now felt the circumstantial evidence was sufficient, though Podmore continued to assert his innocence. The jury took one hour to find him guilty.

Read: True Crime Summer Special 94

445

Albert Edward MARJERAM   **23**

Stabbed: ***Edith May Parker****, 23, on 11 April 1930, in Dartford
Heath, Kent.*

Motive: *Sadistic pleasure.*

      Marjeram, *(b.1907),* was said to have suffered a brain absess at the age of five, and to have behaved strangely since. Thrown out of the army for lying, he had attacked his mother several times, and had tried to strangle his 9-year old brother. Stabbing the family cat with a fork, an attempt to gas himself and confessing to a murder he could not have committed in July 1929, were seen as cries for attention. He had worked only five weeks in his entire life. Having bought a knife, with which his mother claimed he had always had a fascination, he went out on Dartford Heath for a walk.

      Also out walking that morning were two sisters, Eva and Edith May Parker, a packer at a Dartmouth factory. Inexplicably Marjeram jumped from some bushes and stabbed Edith in the back, a wound which pierced her lung and spleen. A policeman recalled Marjeram from Eva's description, and he was arrested a few hours later at his parents' home, making a full confession. His plea of insanity was rejected by the jury in fifteen minutes. Marjeram impressed his executioner with his complete indifference to death.

      Read: True Crime, Feb 98.

1930 Execution in Ireland

8 April 1930 Crumlin Road Gaol, Belfast
T.Pierrepoint/ Wilson

SAMUEL CUSHNAN   26

Shot: ***James McCann****, 26, on 16 May 1929, at Millquarter, Co.*
Antrim
Motive: *Financial*

    Cushnan, *(b. 1904),* a catholic farm labourer, 5'2", knew when the rural postman was due to deliver the weekly pension money to the post office at Crosskeys hamlet. On 16 May he did not turn up for work and hid his bicycle and his shotgun in a hedge. When the postman, his friend James McCann, cycled by, he invited him to take a quick drink with him. As he drank from a bottle of poteen, McCann, a single man who lived with his parents, was blasted in the neck from a yard away. £65 was stolen from his bag. Cushnan could not get away by bike as a car had appeared, and was seen crossing the fields. Material from his jacket was found on a nearby bramble bush.

    The jury could not agree a verdict, but at the retrial one hour passed before the guilty verdict.

Refs: True Detective, Dec96.

1931

total: **10**

446	3 Jan	Victor BETTS	22		Winson Green
447	4 Feb	Frederick GILL	26		Armley
448	10 Mar	Alfred ROUSE	37		Bedford
449	16 Apr	Francis LAND	39		Strangeways
450	3 Jun	Alexander ANASTASSIOU	23	*Cypriot*	Pentonville
451	5 Aug	William SHELLEY	57		Pentonville
452	5 Aug	Oliver NEWMAN	61		Pentonville
453	12 Aug	William CORBETT	32		Cardiff
454	10 Dec	Henry SEYMOUR	52		Oxford
455	15 Dec	Solomon STEIN	21		Strangeways

3 January 1931   Winson Green Prison, Birmingham

T.Pierrepoint/ A.Allen

446

Victor Edward BETTS   22

Punched: ***William Thomas Andrews***, *63, on 21 July 1930, in Aston, Warwicks*
Motive: *Financial*

Betts, *(b.1909),* and Herbert Charles Ridley, 23, had known each other five months, and both had a criminal record. They had recently coshed a garage attendant in the course of robbing him. In July 1930 they had been watching the movements of William Andrews. He and his wife worked for a draper's firm, and regularly at 2.30pm William would carry the takings to the bank. While Ridley waited in the getaway car, Betts leapt out, punched Mr Andrews in the temple, grabbed his bag containing £908, and jumped into the car which sped off and was abandoned nearby. Mr Andrews died three days later- the blow being sufficient to crack his thin skull.

The two thieves drove to London and then to Brighton, where they picked up two girls, generally having a high time for a week by the sea. Witnesses recognised the men from police mug-shots, and the pair were arrested in Brighton after they had crashed their car into a ditch. The jury found both guilty of murder after an hour's retirement, but following petitions, Ridley was reprieved.

Read: True Crime Summer Special 97.

4 February 1931   Armley gaol, Leeds   *T.Pierrepoint/ Wilson*

447

Frederick GILL   **26**

Bludgeoned: ***Oliver Preston***, *53, on 25 July 1930, in Keighley,*
                 W.Yorks.
Motive: *Financial*

      Gill, *(b.1905),* worked three days a week as a crane driver at an engineering works, but had fallen into debt. He lodged with his brother in Keighley, but was behind with his part of the rent, and owed the moneylender, Oliver Preston, £3 12s. His girlfriend wanted a summer break in Whitehaven, but Gill could raise no credit. At 6pm he went to see Preston about an extended loan, but was refused.

      Returning to Preston's office about 15 minutes later with a steel bar from the factory, he beat the money-lender about the head, and stole the £80 which was on the premises. Telling his girlfriend Nellie that the horses had come up, they went spending, consumated their relationship, and went off to Whitehaven. Mr Preston was found the following day, and died in hospital two days later. Gill had been seen coming to the office, and blood was found on his overalls and shoes.

      When the jury gave their verdict after one hour, Gill collapsed in the dock. He maintained his innocence.

     Refs: True Crime, Jan 96.

10 March 1931   Bedford gaol   *T.Pierrepoint/ Phillips*

448

Alfred Arthur ROUSE   **37**

Burned to death: *An unidentified man, on 6 November 1930,*
                   near Hardingstone, Northants.
Motive: *To clear impediment.*

      Rouse, *(b.1894),* had received head injuries in France at the age of 21, often cited as the reason for his veracious sexual appetite. He and his wife lived in Barnet. Although he married Lily May Watkins in 1914, they had no children, and his job as a commercial traveller for a garter and braces firm, gave him ample opportunity to begin affairs all over the country, some eighty women falling under his spell, including a 14-year old Scottish girl. He fathered children by the county, and maintenance orders were falling on his doormat. Lily knew of some of these; their domestic servant, Helen Campbell had given birth to Rouse's son in 1925.

By October 1930, Ivy Jenkins in Glamorgan was heavily pregnant by Rouse, his financial problems were growing, and he and Lily were talking of separation. He came up with a half-baked plan to disappear, and build a new identity.

On bonfire night, driving his Morris Minor, he picked up a down-and-out in a pub at Whetstone. At about 1 a.m. in Northamptonshire, he got his passenger drunk, and then rendered him unconscious, either by striking him with a mallet, or by strangulation. He lay the man across the front seats, put a petrol-soaked rag between his legs, and then set the car ablaze by igniting a trail of petrol.

Rouse was seen climbing out of a nearby ditch by two men, and police were able to identify the car as his. He went later the same day to see Ivy in Wales, and was arrested the following day as he returned to London at Hammersmith bus station. He told police that he asked his passenger to refill the tank, as Rouse answered a call of nature, but the evidence pointed at a deliberate fire. The jury took one hour deliberating. The passenger was never identified.

Read: The Vintage Car Murders

16 April 1931   Strangeways prison, Manchester

449

Francis LAND   39

Cut throat of: ***Sarah Ellen Johnson***, *24, on 12 December 1930, in Rochdale, Lancs.*
Motive: *Vengeance.*

Sarah Johnson left her husband of seven years, and went to live with Land, *(b.1892)*, in January 1930, but it was not long before he turned to violence. With a damaged jaw, and bruises to her throat and body, she left him on 2 December, and went to stay with friends. Sarah was approached by Land on 6 December, and was threatened when she refused to go back to him. Three days later, Sarah agreed to go back to Land if he would find a job away from Rochdale. At 9pm that night he cut her throat in his lounge, leaving her on the hearthrug, and going to the pub. When Sarah's friend came looking for her, he told her what he had done.

Read: And May The Lord Have Mercy On Your Soul

450

Alexander ANASTASSIOU   23   *Cypriot*

Cut throat of: ***Evelyn Victoria Holt**, 22, on 26 February 1931, in London W1.*
Motive: *To clear impediment.*

Anastassiou, *(b.1908),* who lodged off Tottenham Court Road, met Evelyn Holt at a Christmas party in 1930, and it was not long before the two were engaged. Evelyn, who lived with an aunt in Shepherds Bush, was a waitress in a west end cafe, and was extremely jealous of any attention Alex paid to other women.

On 26 February, she criticised him for chatting to some girls, and at 11.30pm, in his flat, he told her then that he could not marry her, and that he may go to the US. She flew at him, scratching his face, and the Cypriot then cut her throat with a razor, almost severing her head. His landlady heard Evelyn's screams.

The jury decided Anastassiou's fate in twenty minutes.

Read: And May The Lord Have Mercy On Your Soul

451, 452

William SHELLEY   57
Oliver NEWMAN   61

Bludgeoned: ***Herbert William Ayres**, 45, on 30 May 1931, near Elstree, Herts.*
Motive: *Vengeance.*

Shelley, *(b.1874),* and Newman, *(b.1870),* were itinerant navvies who shared a hut in an area of woodland near Elstree. Known as Moosh and Tiggy, they discovered that Ayres, a neighbouring tramp, known as 'Pigsticker', had stolen some bread and bacon from their hut. Another neighbour, John Armstrong, who was staying the night in the pair's hut, witnessed the pair beating Ayres with an axe and iron bars.

Realising they had killed Ayres, they attempted to dispose of the body by burning it on a smouldering refuse tip. Ayre's body was discovered by another navvy three days later, and the murder weapon was found under the floorboards. It was later revealed that Armstrong had stolen a clock from the hut, and that he, and not Ayres, may have stolen the food for which Ayres was killed.

Read: Murder Club Guide to Eastern & Home Counties

12 August 1931   Cardiff prison

453

William John CORBETT   32

Cut throat of: ***Ethel Louisa Corbett****, 39, his wife, on 25 March 1931, in Caerphilly, Glamorgan.*
Motive: *Vengeance.*

Corbett, *(b.1899)*, a miner, lost his job in November 1930, and began a downward spiral, threatening suicide, and behaving strangely, to the extent that his wife went to the police on 24 March, worried about his conduct. They felt unable to intervene, and the following day, Corbett snapped, hitting Ethel in the mouth. When their daughter defended her mother, he attacked her, to be defended in turn by her mother. He then cut Ethel's throat with his razor, and turned then to his daughter. Ethel, in a last gasp of life, leapt upon Corbett, who then turned the razor upon himself. He told the police that he could remember nothing of the attack.

Read: And May The Lord Have Mercy On Your Soul.

355

454

Henry Daniel SEYMOUR   52

Bludgeoned/ stabbed: ***Anne Louisa Kempson**, 54, on 1 August 1931, in Oxford.*
Motive: *Financial.*

Seymour, *(b.1879)*, had a long history of trouble with the law, first arrested in 1899. He worked as a travelling vacuum cleaner salesman, and in 1930, Seymour attacked and tried to strangle a woman in Paignton, Devon, while giving a demonstration. He was bound over, but did not pay her the £10 he was ordered to. He left his wife and 10-year old son in June 1931, and on 31 July, he returned to the home of Alice Andrews in Oxford, to whom he had sold a cleaner some time before. He told her a story about being robbed and missing his last bus, and she and her husband agreed to let him stay the night. Mrs Andrews noticed Seymour had a new hammer and chisel with him as he left the next morning.

He then walked to the house of Mrs Kempson, just ten minutes away - she too had been a customer of his. A widow of ten years, she let him in, and in the hallway he hit her from behind with the hammer. He hit her again on the forehead, and dragging her body into the dining-room, stabbed her right through the neck with the chisel, severing an artery. He ransacked her home, but escaped with only a few pounds, missing the larger stash she had hidden in the bedroom.

Seymour went from there to a hotel in Aylesbury, from where he sent his thanks and a postal order to Mrs Andrews. Unable to pay his bill, the hotel owner had kept Seymour's suitcase. Mrs Kempson was found by a relative two days later, and Alice Andrews was able to tell the police about Seymour. In his case at Aylesbury, police found the hammer, and Seymour himself was found in lodgings in Brighton on 15 August. Planning his next robbery, he had bored two holes in the floor of his rooms, to watch the owner hiding her money below.

Though the case against him was entirely circumstantial, there was no forensic evidence, and no-one saw him at the widow's house, and though six witnesses said they saw Mrs Kempson up till 1.30pm, compromising the time of death, and therefore Seymour's guilt, the jury took 38 minutes to find him guilty.

Read: Murder Squad, p99.

455

<u>Solomon STEIN</u>   **21**

Strangled:	***Annie Riley**, 28, on 3 October 1931, in Manchester, Lancs.*
Motive:	*Sadistic pleasure.*

Stein, *(b.1910)*, a machinist in a raincoat factory, lived with his mother in Hightown. Leaving the cinema in Manchester one night at 10.30, he was approached by Annie Riley, who asked for his help in looking for an hotel. Finding one, Annie asked him if he wanted to stay the night with her. The somewhat inexperienced Stein agreed and the couple booked in. The following morning Stein, 5'4", rose and dressed, and seeing Annie sleeping, for no apparent reason, strangled her with his tie. He was seen leaving at 8am. Riddled with guilt, he went to the police to confess at 5pm on 5 October. Stein, a Jew, insisted on pleading guilty to the murder charge.

Read: Murderous Manchester

31 July 1931   Crumlin Road Gaol, Belfast

THOMAS DORNAN   47

Shot: *1 **Margaret Aiken**, 28, and her sister*
                 *2 **Isabella Aiken**, 20, on 22 May 1931, in Skerry East,*
                 Co Antrim
Motive: *To clear impediment*

     Dornan, *(b. 1884),* a married man, was the owner of 20 acres and was the sexton of a local presbyterian church. In January 1930, local girl Isabella Aiken had his child. She lived with her pareents and three siblings on a nearby smallholding. Dornan had to quit his post as sexton after the birth, and he agreed to pay 6/- per week maintenance. After a year Dornan ceased paying.
     On a May day the Aiken sisters were among others cutting peat from the bog, Dornan twice came to the field, on the second occasion firing at the sisters with his shotgun. As the women ran, Dornan continued to shoot at them, and emptied his gun into them as they lay in each other's arms on the ground. Margaret was hit four times, Isabella, six. Dornan walked into a river and had to be dragged out. A defence based on insanity was rejected by the jury inside 32 minutes.

     Read: True Detective, Dec96.

456	3 Feb	George RICE	32		Strangeways
457	23 Feb	William GODDARD	25		Pentonville
458	9 Mar	George POPLE	22	*Welsh*	Oxford Castle
459	27 Apr	George MICHAEL	49	*Danish*	Hull
460	28 Apr	John ROBERTS	23		Armley
461	28 Apr	Thomas RILEY	36	*Irish*	Armley
462	4 May	Maurice FREEDMAN	36		Pentonville
463	18 May	Charles COWLE	19		Strangeways
464	23 Nov	Edward HUTCHINSON	43		Oxford Castle

3 February 1932   Strangeways prison, Manchester   *T.Pierrepoint*

456

George Alfred RICE   **32**

Suffocated: ***Constance Inman***, *9, on 22 September 1931, in Manchester, Lancs.*
Motive: *Sexual.*

Rice, *(b. 1900),* was a simple-minded loner from Bolton who had moved to Manchester in the spring of 1930. He had one eye and was unemployed and illiterate, having worked only briefly in a hotel. Those with whom he lodged in Manchester's Victoria Park district knew him as George Price. Together with other parents in the area, Christopher and Lillian Inman had been worried about a prowler on a bicycle who had recently been trying to entice children. They therefore were extremely concerned when their daughter Connie failed to return home one evening. She had last been seen by a friend at 6.30 pm.

Her body was found at the bottom of a garden the following morning at 8.20. She had died elsewhere some time after midnight and had been carried there. Her knickers had been removed, though there seemed to be no sign of sexual assault, and doctors first thought strangulation had been the cause of death.

Police were alerted to Rice after a routine house-to-house call at his address. Appearing suspicious, Rice was questioned more closely and confessed to having been with the child. He said he had found her and cuddled her. It was later discovered that death had been caused by squeezing her chest. Rice was charged, and when at the trial it was said that Connie could have been raped, the jury took 45 minutes to decide Rice's guilt.

He was in a state of near collapse at his execution and had to be half carried to the scaffold. Rice, however, did not own a bicycle.

Read: Strange Tales from Strangeways.

23 February 1932	Pentonville prison, London	*Baxter/ Phillips*

457

William Harold GODDARD   25

Bludgeoned: ***Charles William Lambert****, 57, on 27 November 1931, in London E16.*
Motive: *Vengeance.*

Goddard, *(b.1907)*, worked on the barge *Speranza*, tied up at Dartford. He did not get on very well with the skipper, Charles Lambert, and when Goddard asked for his mail, one of the two letters he received was from his fiancee. Lambert handed the letter over and used insulting terms to describe the young woman, at which Goddard punched him. He then battered the skipper with a coal hammer, and partly strangled him with rope. He took Lambert's watch and made off to Ipswich, where he went to a police station on 30 November. He said the skipper had died accidentally.

Read: And May The Lord Have Mercy On Your Soul

9 March 1932	Oxford Castle	*T.Pierrepoint*

458

George Thomas POPLE   22   *Welsh*

Kicked: ***Mabel Elizabeth Mathews****, 56, on 19 December 1931, near Burford, Oxfords.*
Motive: *Financial.*

Pople, *(b.1910)*, was an army private on a month's leave who cycled from Bath to London, and then, on his way back to his home town of Brecon, noticed Mrs Mathews, a farmer's wife, cycling on the Oxford-

Cheltenham road at 8pm, with an acetylene lamp on her bike. He decided he wanted the new light and made a grab for it. He knocked Mrs Mathews to the ground with two blows to the back of the head, and then repeatedly punched and kicked her 23 times, fracturing her jaw and eleven ribs, and causing huge internal injuries. He also partly strangled her, but left his duffle-bag at the scene, and it was traced to him. Pople had robbed Mrs Mathews of a half-crown.

Arrested in Abergavenny on 20 December, Pople, married with a young child, told the court that he had become tangled in his pedal and that Mrs Mathews had been killed as they rolled down a slope. The fact that he had stolen the lamp and the woman's groceries went against him, the jury deciding his fate in 43 minutes. Pople wept openly as sentence was passed.

Read: True Crime, Nov 98.

27 April 1932	Hull prison	*T.Pierrepoint/ Pollard*

459

George Emanuel MICHAEL   **49**   *Danish*   *black*

Stabbed: ***Theresa Mary Hemstock***, *47, on 31 December 1931, in Hull, E.Yorks.*
Motive: *Vengeance.*

Michael, *(b.1883),* a seaman of Caribbean origin, married Theresa Hemstock in 1929. He served eleven months for stabbing her and her daughter, but then she took him back. Following further brutal treatment, Theresa went to the police on 12 December 1931 to admit her bigamy, Michael only then realising that she already had a husband.

He immediately left her and went into lodgings, but went to her home on new year's eve, and smashed all her windows, threatening her into the bargain. A policeman was called, and as he was talking to the pair, Michael pushed past him, and stabbed Theresa six times with a knife, then turning the weapon on himself. The jury deliberated for 50 minutes.

Read: And May The Lord Have Mercy On Your Soul

460

John Henry ROBERTS   23

Bludgeoned: ***Victor Albert Gill***, 55, on 11 December 1931, in Pudsey,
                    W. Yorks
Motive: *Financial*

Roberts, *(b.1909)*, had been unemployed, but continued to draw dole after Albert Gill had taken him on. Gill was a Bradford greengrocer and pig breeder who had done well for himself, and lived in a large house in Laisterdyke with his wife and their grown up children. Roberts had fallen into debt and owed 35/-. He received an order to pay 8/-.

On 11 December, after making deliveries, the two men went to the piggery. There Roberts, 5'3", beat Gill about the face and head with a brick and hammer. He relieved his boss of a roll of notes containing up to £50, dragged his victim to a shed and took the horse to its stables. Gill's son found the body at 12.40am after his father had failed to return home.

Roberts was taken from his bed and arrested. He claimed that he had left Albert with another man at the piggery, but when it was shown that the horse he had taken had trampled in blood he changed his story. He claimed that when he had dropped a barrel of potatoes, Gill had sworn at him, cursed his mother, and had attacked him. No spilled potatoes were found, and when it was shown that Roberts had been spending freely that night, the jury took only 35 minutes to convict him. He was hanged alongside Thomas Riley.

Read: True Crime, Dec 97.

461

Thomas RILEY   36   *Irish*

Bludgeoned: ***Elizabeth Castle***, 53, on 16 December 1931, in Lepton,
                    Huddersfield, W.Yorks.
Motive: *Vengeance.*

Riley, *(b.1896)*, was victim to a mustard gas attack whilst serving in the army in France in 1915, and suffered the effects of lupus, a skin disfigurement of tuberculosis. He survived on a disibility pension since losing his job as a miner. From Wigan, he moved in search of work to Huddersfield in July 1931, meeting Elizabeth Castle in a pub there. A widow for a year, she worked as a cleaner and took Riley in as a lodger in August, soon becoming his lover.

The two got on very well together, until Elizabeth demanded one day that he fetch more firewood. An argument developed during which Elizabeth called him 'an Irish bastard', and Riley battered her three times across the head with a hammer. He dragged her body from the lounge to a pantry, covering her with a rug. He fled to Bradford then Leeds, where he went to the police to confess on 19 December. He was hanged alongside John Roberts.

Read: True Crime, Feb 98.

4 May 1932	Pentonville prison, London	*Baxter/ Wilson*

462

Maurice FREEDMAN   36

Cut throat of: **Annette Friedson**, 23, on 26 January 1932, in London EC2.
Motive: Vengeance.

Freedman, *(b.1896),* had been a policeman, but latterly had taken to betting, and his marriage was in trouble. In August 1930, he had become friendly with Annette Friedson, a typist, but her parents had become aware of the situation in October 1931, and made plain to their daughter their opposition to the liaison. Freedman had become extremely agitated when Annette told him it was all over. Indeed, she became so worried for her safety, that her brother escorted her daily to work in the City.

At 9.15 one morning, though, Freedman waited for her inside her workplace, and slit her throat with a razor. He left the weapon on a bus. He told police that he had threatened to kill himself with the razor if Annette did not take him back, and that she had taken it and cut her own throat. He had thrown the razor, he said, into a canal, and was caught out in a lie. A bus conductor who had found the knife identified him. The jury took 15 minutes deliberating.

Read: The Hangman's Diary, p154.

463

Charles James COWLE   19   *C*

Strangled: **Naomi Annie Farnworth**, *6, on 22 March 1932, in Darwen, Lancs.*
Motive: Sexual.

Cowle, *(b. 1913),* a lonely and retarded youth, had a criminal record dating back to the age of 9, when he hit a 2-year old with a brick and left him for dead. He spent five years in borstal. He lived in Darwen with his parents, but they went out to work while he was unable to hold down a job. They were next door-but-one to Albert and Henrietta Farnworth, whose daughter Annie sometimes came home for lunch. Cowle had met her from the chip shop one lunchtime and enticed her back to his house with chips.

There, at about 3 pm, he perpetrated a most brutal assault upon her, hiding her body in a tin trunk in the bedroom he shared with his parents. When the alarm for Annie was raised after 6 pm, he had helped search local woodland. Police were told later by a schoolfriend that Annie had been seen in the chip shop with Cowle's jug.

Annie had lain beneath Cowle's bed for three days when police searched the house. They found her naked from the waist down with bruising to her arms, lips and genitals. She had been raped and a cord was tightly tied around her neck. Her fists were still clenched tightly. Annie's knickers, coat and hat were found in a suitcase.

The defence showed there was a history of insanity in Cowle's family, and to hide the body in a place where his parents were bound to discover it sooner rather than later, demonstrated Cowle's madness. The jury was not convinced.

Read: Strange Tales from Strangeways

464

Ernest HUTCHINSON   43

Suffocated: **Gwendoline Annie Warren**, *37, on 11 September 1932, in Maidenhead, Berks.*
Motive: To clear impediment.

Gwen Warren left her husband, and moved in with Hutchinson, *(b.1889)*, in June 1932. She took her two children with her, a son of 12, and Hutchinson's own new baby. The son was sent to stay with an aunt for a few days on 10 September, so that Hutchinson could take his chance. After clubbing Gwendoline on the head with a hammer, he piled a mattress, cushions and bedding on top of her, and suffocated her, spending the night himself in the spare room. Hutchinson would not let the boy back in on his return, and his aunt later forced the door with the help of a neighbour on 14 September.

Hutchinson, 5' 7", was in the company of a prostitute when arrested the next day in Southend. He said he had found the woman under the bedding, and tried to pin the blame on her estranged husband. The jury deliberated for 70 minutes, and Hutchinson received the sentence with a broad smile.

Read: And May The Lord Have Mercy On Your Soul

1932 Executions in Ireland

13 January 1932   Crumlin Road Gaol, Belfast

EDDIE CULLENS   28   *American*

Shot:	***Ahmet Musa**, 26, on 2 September 1931, at Seskin, Co Antrim*
Motive:	*To eliminate impediment*

Musa, a Turk, was part of a fairground attraction which featured the oldest man in the world, 156-year old Zaro Agha. He and Assim Redvan had taken the act to New York where they had teamed up with Cullens, *(b. 1904),* originally a Cypriot Jew who had underworld connections. He arranged for the team to go to England, and it seems intended to kill Musa at the end of August in Liverpool, where a pick-axe and shovel were found in a rented garage. His motive is unclear, but it appears Cullens may have been involved in gun-running, or there may have been a dispute about sharing the circus fees.

The four men travelled by car to Belfast on August 28. Musa and Cullens met two women and drove to Bangor for the day. Two days later the two drove into the country near Carrickfergus where Cullens shot the Turk twice in the head.

To impede identification, he cut off Musa's clothes, which were found later in a Belfast street. His naked body, wearing only a bathing cap was discovered in a field. One of the young women told that such a bathing cap had been in Cullen's car. He returned to Liverpool telling that Musa had returned to Turkey.

The jury decided Cullens' guilt in 32 minutes, and he became the only Jew to be hanged in Ireland.

Read: True Detective, Dec96

29 December 1932 Mountjoy prison, Dublin   *T./A.Pierrepoint*

Patrick McDERMOTT   28

Shot:	***John McDermott**, 30, his brother, on 4 September 1932, near Creggs, Co Roscommon*
Motive:	*To clear impediment.*

McDermott, *(b.1904),* lived with his brother Patrick and sister Kate outside the village of Creggs. John had inherited Rossmoylan farm from his father on the condition that he pay £100 each to his siblings. The farm, however, showed little profit, and he was unable to pay. Moreover, Patrick had to do most of the heavy work as John kept poor health. Over the past five years, they had been broken into four times by a previous employee who had never been paid for work undertaken at the farm. Attending the trial of the intruder on 3 September, Patrick was heard to remark that the same would never happen to him.

That night, getting in at midnight, he told his sister he was going to the cow-sheds. Instead, he waited for his brother to return. When he did so, at 12.30am, he blasted two rounds from the shotgun he had borrowed from his neighbour two days before. One hit John in the chest killing him.

Patrick called no doctor or priest, but went to the police at 7 the next morning, claiming he had found his brother's body. At the trial it was also claimed that the brothers were both vying for the attentions of the same girl. The jury took four hours to decide McDermott's fate. This was Albert Pierrepoint's first execution.

Read: Master Detective, Feb 98

1933

total: **9**

465	2 Feb	Jeremiah HANBURY	49		Winson Green
466	8 Jun	Jack PUTTNAM	31		Pentonville
467	20 Jun	Richard HETHERINGTON	36		Walton
468	25 Jul	Frederick MORSE	32		Bristol
469	10 Aug	Varnavas ANTORKA	31	*Cypriot*	Pentonville
470	11 Oct	Robert KIRBY	26		Pentonville
471	6 Dec	Ernest PARKER	25		Durham
472	19 Dec	William BURTOFT	47		Strangeways
473	28 Dec	Stanley HOBDAY	21		Winson Green

2 February 1933   Winson Green prison, Birmingham

T./ A. Pierrepoint/ Wilson

465

Jeremiah HANBURY   **49**

Bludgeoned/ cut throat of: ***Jessie Payne****, 39, on 17 October 1932, in Brockmoor, Staffs.*
Motive: *Sexual rivalry*

Hanbury, *(b.1884),* had been invalided out of the army after serving in the middle east. He worked in Brockmoor at the ironworks, but his wife died in 1928, and the works closed in 1929 making him unemployed. He took in lodgers to make ends meet, and it was at about that time that he began an affair with the wife of his life-long friend, James Payne, a lorry driver. Jessie, a nurse, was the daughter of a wealthy industrialist, and the mother of four children.

When she began seeing another man in the summer of 1932, she told Jerry the affair was over. He became depressed and suicidal and threw out his lodgers. One afternoon, he went to the Paynes' house while James was away, hit Jessie three times in the face with a hammer, and severed her head with a razor. He then cut his own throat. A neighbour saw him leaving the house covered in blood. He was quickly arrested and required 17 stitches in his neck wound.

His defence was based on a family history of mental problems, but the jury took only 15 minutes to seal his fate. He sang for his last two hours in the condemned cell, and laughed as he was being restrained.

368

His last words were, 'Be good everybody, and thank you for all your trouble'.

Read: True Detective, Sep 96

---

8 June 1933   Pentonville prison, London   *Baxter/ Cross*

466

Jack Samuel PUTTNAM   31

Strangled: ***Elizabeth Mary Standley**, 44, his aunt, on 4 March 1933, in London N4.*
Motive: *Vengeance.*

Puttnam, *(b.1902)*, had borrowed a total of £35 from his aunt, Elizabeth Standley. He went to see her in her home on Blackstock road, Finsbury Park, at 9.30am, after her husband and two lodgers had left for work. They got into an argument about the unpaid debt, and she accused him of having an affair with his brother's wife. He first punched her, then stabbed her with a metal skewer, before strangling her with the flex from her radio.

He left her under the bed where she was found at 12.30pm. He withdrew the confession he had made, but was identified by a bus driver, who saw him running from the house.

Read: And May The Lord Have Mercy On Your Soul

---

20 June 1933   Walton gaol, Liverpool

467

Richard HETHERINGTON   36

Shot: ***1 Joseph Nixon**, 76, and his wife*
          ***2 Mary Ann Nixon**, 75, on 19 February 1933, in Newby, Westmorland.*
Motive: *Vengeance.*

Hetherington, *(b.1897)*, had a farm neighbouring that of the Nixons. Nixon claimed Hetherington owed him money, and Hetherington in turn claimed Nixon owed him for work he had done on their farm. In October 1932 the police had been called after Hetherington had been issuing threats, but it was another five months before he made good his menace.

On 17 February he bought a shotgun, and two days later, at 6pm, he shot the old couple in their bungalow, before setting light to the building, which was gutted. The gun was found in Hetherington's barn. The jury took 3 hours and ten minutes over their deliberations, and Hetherington tried to hang himself in his cell on 3 May.

Read: And May The Lord Have Mercy On Your Soul

25 July 1933   Horfield gaol, Bristol

468

Frederick MORSE   32

Drowned: ***Doris Winifred Brewer**, 12, his niece, on 23 February 1933, in Taunton, Devon.*
Motive: *To clear impediment; drink related.*

Morse, *(b.1901)*, a worker in a lime quarry, lived with his parents and, from 1928, with his niece, Doris, usually known as Dorothy, who looked more like 16 than her 12 years. There had been rumours that Morse was, in fact, Doris' natural father.

In February 1933, it became known that Dorothy was pregnant, and the blame was firmly put at Morse's door, though he denied it. He took Dorothy to a pub one afternoon, and thereafter to inspect some rabbit traps. He claimed that he left the girl sheltering from the rain for 45 minutes, during which time she must have fallen into the river.

The police suspected that Morse took Doris to the river, where he plied her with a good deal of rum, before hurling her into the water. Dorothy's body was found snagged in an overhanging branch. In a later confession, claimed by some to have been manufactured by police, Morse claimed the two had a suicide pact, and that they had both jumped in together. The jury deliberated for one hour.

Read: Master Detective, Jan 99.

469

Varnavas ANTORKA   31   *Cypriot*

Shot: ***Boleslar Pankorski***, *35, on 12 May 1933, in London W1.*
Motive: *Vengeance.*

Antorka, *(b.1902),* had arrived in London from Cyprus in 1928, and had found work washing up in a restaurant in Soho square. He was reluctant, however, to take orders, and when he was slow to put some plates to warm, the head chef, Boleslar Pankorski, told him to hurry up or he would be sacked. When Antorka answered him back, he was dismissed on the spot, and went home to collect his gun.

He returned at 1pm, and grabbed the chef as he reached the foot of the stairs. There followed a struggle during which Pankorski was shot. Two other employees ran to help, and one was wounded in the leg when Antorka let off two more shots.

Read: And May The Lord Have Mercy On Your Soul

470

Robert James KIRBY   26

Strangled: ***Grace Ivy Newing***, *17, on 6 July 1933, in Chadwell Heath, Essex.*
Motive: *To clear impediment.*

Kirby, *(b.1907),* had seen his father gaoled for four years for the attempted murder of his mother, and was no stranger to family violence. He had been courting Grace Newing for only three months when she found herself pregnant. On 6 July, Kirby called round to her parents, who allowed him to wait for her return from late shift at work. The household all retired at 10.30pm, and Kirby was alone when Grace got back at 11pm. He strangled her with cord, and then ran to his mother's, where he confessed, before repeating the same at his brother's house. The police were called, and Kirby was arrested at another brother's at 6am. The jury deliberated for 15 minutes before adding a recommendation to mercy.

Read: And May The Lord Have Mercy On Your Soul

471

Ernest Wadge PARKER   25   *(aka Scott)*

Bludgeoned: ***Lily Parker,*** *36, his sister, on 25 June 1933, in Stanley,*
                    Co Durham.
Motive: Vengeance.

      Parker, *(b.1908)*, in 1917 spent six months in a mental hospital, where his mother had died after a two-year stay, in 1914. He and his twin brother ran the family fruit business, but his father and sister were always finding fault, and on 20 November 1932, he hit his father, and was bound over. After hitting Lily in April 1933, he was told to keep away from the house, but he returned just four days later and hit her again, for which he got two months hard labour.

      He was released on 17 June, and went straight to the house, making threats. The police were called when, on 25 June, he broke into the house at 9am, and hit Lily. The police were called again when he returned at 1pm. Then, while his father was out, he returned at 3.30pm, and axed his sister to death on her bed. Lily's daughter ran for the police, whom Parker told, 'She asked for it, and she got it'.

Read: And May The Lord Have Mercy On Your Soul

472

William BURTOFT   47

Bludgeoned: ***Frances Levin***, *61, on 19 July 1933, in*
                    Cheetham, Manchester, Lancs.
Motive: Financial.

      Mrs Fanny Levin, separated from her husband for 37 years, lived with her two brothers and her two daughters in a wealthy area of Manchester. The family were Jewish antique dealers. One hot July afternoon, Mrs Levin was lying on her settee sewing, when a man entered the house, and beat her with a bar from the kitchen grate so forcefully that the walls, carpet and sofa were spattered with blood. Her maid, Freda Phillips, 17, saw a man leaving the drive from her upstairs window, but did not see his face. No antiques were stolen, only 9 shillings from a purse. Mrs Levin died four hours later in the Jewish hospital.

William Burtoft, *(b.1886),* an unemployed seaman with one eye, was arrested for drunkenness a week later. Still drunk on meths, he confessed to the murder. No-one picked him out from identity parades, his fingerprints did not match those at the scene, and no blood was found on his clothing. He claimed that the confession had been forced, and that he had been offered whisky to co-operate. After deliberating for over two hours, the jury believed the police's version of events and found him guilty.

Read: Strange Tales from Strangeways

28 December 1933   Winson Green prison, Birmingham   *T./A. Pierrepoint*

473

Stanley Eric HOBDAY   **21**

Stabbed:	***Charles William Fox***, *24, on 27 August 1933, in West Bromwich, Staffs.*
Motive:	*Financial.*

Hobday, *(b.1912),* 5'5", had a history of housebreaking. At 1.40am on 27 August, he broke into a house in West Bromwich, by cutting the glass in a rear window. The owner, Charles Fox, 6', a married metal stripper with a son of 8 months, was woken by his wife, who had heard movement downstairs, and by candlelight, he saw the open window and closed it. He did not realise that Hobday was still in the room, and as he turned he was felled by seven blows with a knife. Hobday escaped as Fox staggered upstairs and collapsed at his wife's feet, the knife still in his back. She raised the alarm by shouting out of the bedroom window.

Hobday, meanwhile, entered the premises of Mr Newton, the butcher, half a mile away. He had a shave there, had a drink of milk, stole £7, and continued on his way. He next stole a car and drove off to High Legh, 70 miles away in Cheshire, where the vehicle overturned. Hobday was careless; his fingerprints were on the milk bottle at Newton's, and on the car's starting handle. He had cut his elbow on the glass, and mended a tear in his sleeve with the butcher's cotton. Most damning was his size 4 footprint outside the Fox window. After a three-day trial, the jury considered their verdict for 45 minutes.

Read: Murderous Birmingham

7 April 1933   Crumlin Road Gaol, Belfast   *T./ A. Pierrepoint*

HAROLD COURTNEY   23

Cut throat of: *Minnie Reid, 23, on 27 July 1932, at Derryane, Co Armagh*
Motive: *To clear impediment*

Courtney, *(b. 1910)*, a lorry driver, had known Minnie Reid for five years.   She worked as a domestic servant, and became pregnant in December 1931.   She wrote to Courtney asking to meet him, and he drove her to a country lane.   There he cut her throat with his father's stolen razor, which was found several yards away.   Witnesses saw his car.

Minnie's heavily pregnant body was found a week later in dense undergrowth.   Her glove had been stuffed into her neck wound.   Courtney, engaged to be married to a higher class young lady, denied any sexual involvement with Minnie, and the defence case stressed the possibility of suicide.   The prosecution asked why Minnie would go to so remote a spot to take her life, and then throw away the razor after the deed.

The jury failed to agree a verdict, but a second jury found him guilty, adding a recommendation for mercy.   When Courtney fought his way to the gallows, his execution had to be delayed by an hour.

Refs: True Detective, Dec96.

1933

JOHN FLEMING   34

Bludgeoned: ***Ellen Fleming***, *his wife, on 26 July 1933, in Drumcondra, Dublin*
Motive: *To clear impediment.*

Fleming, *(b. 1900)*, was a shoe salesman, and began an affair with waitress Rita Murtagh.   He told her that he was single and lived with an aunt.   When Rita became pregnant she began to press for marriage, and the pair selected rings in February 1933.

The following month Fleming began to poison his wife with chocolates laced with strychnine.   When Rita began to hear rumours that John was married, his patience snapped and, in the kitchen of their terraced house, he beat Ellen to death with punches and hammer blows.

Read: Murder Guide to Great Britain, p284.

1934

total: **9**

474	3 Jan	Roy GREGORY	29	Hull
475	6 Feb	Ernest BROWN	35	Armley
476	6 Apr	Louis HAMILTON	25	Armley
477	3 May	Reginald HINKS	32	Bristol
478	4 May	Frederick PARKER	21	Wandsworth
479	4 May	Albert PROBERT	26	Wandsworth
480	9 Oct	Harry TUFFNEY	36	Pentonville
481	14 Nov	John STOCKWELL	19	Pentonville
482	19 Dec	Ethel MAJOR (f)	42	Hull

3 January 1934   Hull prison   *T.Pierrepoint/ Phillips*

474

Roy GREGORY   **29**

Bludgeoned: ***Dorothy Margaret Addinell**, 2, on 9 March 1933, in Scarborough, N.Yorks.*
Motive: *To clear impediment.*

Gregory, *(b.1905),* lived with his girlfriend, an unmarried mother of a 2-year old, who gave birth to his child in February 1933. Gregory had been a grocer's assistant, but lost his job around that time, and scraped a living repairing boots. He told his sister that he wanted the older child adopted, and by 9 March the child had gone. Gregory had smashed Dorothy's head seven times with a hammer. The same day he asked a neighbour if he could use her cellar as a workshop, and buried the child's body there.

Both his sister and the neighbour told police of their suspicions about the child's disappearance, and, dissatisfied with his adoption story, they began digging in the cellar. Gregory then said that he had thrown the child onto the bed after she had messed herself, and that she had banged her head on the wall. He had buried her on Scalby beach. The police, however, found the body in the cellar on 3 August. The jury reached its verdict after 40 minutes.

Read: Master Detective Summer Special 97.

475

Ernest BROWN   35

Possibly shot:	**1 Evelyn Foster**, *28, on 6 January 1931, in Otterburn, N.Yorks.*
Shot:	**2 Frederick Ellison Morton**, *28, on 5 September 1933, near Towton, N.Yorks.*
Motive:	*Sexual rivalry.*

    Brown, *(b.1899)*, was something of a law unto himself, having been birched for theft, and undergone army discipline for assaults and desertion. A widower with one child, he boasted of many female conquests, one of whom was Dorothy Morton, 26, whom he had first bowled over in 1930. He worked as a groom for her husband on their cattle farm near Towton, between York and Leeds. By the summer of 1933, Dorothy, mother of a 2-year old child, had grown tired of her lover, his fits of jealousy and bad temper, and when Frederick had asked Brown to mow the lawn, he had walked out, saying it was beneath him. When he wanted his job back, Dorothy would not stand up for him, and her husband would only offer him work as an odd-job man. His anger with Frederick, and his insane jealousy got the better of him when Dorothy began seeing another man.

    On 5 September, Brown came to the farm, and waited for Mr Morton to arrive home. As his car coasted into the garage at 11.30pm, Brown followed it in, and shot the owner with a shotgun blast to the stomach. He went outside and shot again. Dorothy ran upstairs with her daughter and housekeeper, Ann Houseman - Brown calling out that he had been shooting rats. They stayed there for hours, too frightened to come out, until about 3.30 a.m., when there was an explosion. Brown had set fire to the garage with petrol, and the building was ablaze. The women ran out into the fields, the phone lines having been cut. Brown was arrested when the police arrived, and the jury sealed his fate after one hour's deliberation.

    It has been suggested that Brown was responsible for the unsolved death of Evelyn Foster, 28, on 6 January 1931 in Otterburn, N. Yorks. The taxi driver was found badly burned next to her blazing car. Before dying she had told of the man who had set her and the car alight. Police suggested she may have died in the process of firing the car herself for insurance purposes. Brown's last words were ambiguous, 'Ought to burn', or 'Otterburn'.

Read: Settings For Slaughter

6 April 1934   Armley gaol, Leeds   *T.Pierrepoint/ Alfred Allen*

476

Louis HAMILTON   25

Cut throat of: **Maud Hamilton**, *22, his wife, on 26 December 1933, in Bradford, W.Yorks.*
Motive: *Vengeance.*

Hamilton, *(b.1909),* married Maud Hay in July 1933, and the heavily pregnant bride gave birth just a few weeks later. She left him alleging cruelty and returned to her mother on 22 December, leaving the baby, for whom she did not seem to care, with a sister. On 23 December, he went and dragged Maud home, pulling her by the hair and kicking her, and grabbing her brother by the throat. She returned to her mother's at 4am with a bruised neck and took out a summons for assault. The summons was served on Boxing day, and again Hamilton went round, but failed to see Maud who sought refuge at a neighbour's house.

The police were informed, but Hamilton, armed with a knife taken from his sister, grabbed Maud, who was pregnant again, as she left her neighbour's and dragged her into her mother's house alone. Before friends could kick the door down, he had cut Maud's throat. When they got in seconds later, the men dragged Hamilton outside and beat him up. The jury found him guilty in twelve minutes, but added a strong recommendation to mercy.

Read: Murderous Leeds

3 May 1934   Horfield gaol, Bristol

477

Reginald Ivor HINKS   32

Gassed: **James Pullen**, *84, his father-in-law, on 1 December 1933, in Bath, Somerset.*
Motive: *Financial.*

Hinks, *(b.1902),* was a small-time crook, a stealer of handbags and the like, who worked as a vacuum cleaner salesman. Early in 1933, he had got to know Constance Jeffries, the mother of a small child, who had been divorced for adultery.

When Hinks heard of her wealthy old father, he insisted on an early marriage, and once wed, immediately set about trying to get his hands on the old man's money. Solicitors made it very difficult for him, though Constance managed to get hold of £900, with which Hinks bought a house in Bath. He decided that the old man's death would be the best way to easy money. He dismissed the male nurse who cared for Mr Pullen, and under Hinks' care, the senile pensioner was on a regime of stiff walks and a reduced diet. Hinks would even abandon him on busy roads.

When none of this worked, he tried drowning the old man in the bath, but covering himself too carefully, he called the police and fire-brigade too early, the old man survived. Now desperate, while Dorothy was out, he hit the old man on the head, and dragged him to the gas oven, turning on the taps. It was found that the bruise on his head was inflicted while he was still alive, and that he was incapable of switching on the taps himself. Dorothy gave birth to another child a year after her husband's arrest.

Read: The Murder Guide to Great Britain

4 May 1934	Wandsworth prison, London

T./ A.Pierrepoint/ Cross/ Phillips

478, 479

Frederick William PARKER   21
Albert PROBERT   26

Bludgeoned:	*Joseph Bedford, 80, on 13 November 1933, in Portslade, Sussex.*
Motive:	*Financial.*

Parker, *(b.1913)*, a labourer from Hove, and Probert, *(b.1908)*, a fitter from Dover, met in a hostel in Brighton. Together they robbed Mr Bedford, a reclusive bachelor and talented musician, in his general store on a Monday evening in November 1933. Probert beat the man repeatedly with a tyre lever to get him to reveal the whereabouts of his takings, banging his head against the floor. They escaped with about £6. At 10pm a policeman saw Mr Bedford stagger in the shop and fall onto a display case.

The pair were arrested for loitering in Worthing on 16 November and identified by a witness as having been 'hanging about' Mr Bedford's shop. Parker admitted the attack, not realising that Mr Bedford had died a few hours later from the injuries inflicted, and fainted in court eight times. Though Probert denied his involvement, the jury damned them in 35 minutes.

Read: Murders of the Black Museum

480

Harry TUFFNEY

Bludgeoned: *Edith Kate Longshaw, 38, on 30 June 1934, in London W2.*
Motive: *Sexual rivalry.*

Tuffney, *(b.1898),* was of a rather unstable family, with his mother, two brothers and an aunt all having been confined to asylums. When he moved to lodgings in Paddington in May 1934, he met Edith Longshaw, who also rented a room, and the two began courting. Tuffney discovered a letter from a rival called Sidney, and, it appeared, Edith was about to move in with him. On 29 June, Tuffney bought an axe, and the following night stayed with Edith in her room until late, and once she had fallen asleep, he axed her with a single deep blow to the head. He spent the next four hours trying to gas himself, before handing himself in to the police.

Read: And May The Lord Have Mercy On Your Soul

481

John Frederick STOCKWELL   19

Bludgeoned: *Dudley Henry Hoard, 40, on 7 August 1934, in London E3.*
Motive: *Financial.*

Stockwell, *(b.1916),* had lived with relatives, in children's homes and with foster parents from the age of ten, his father having been killed in the war, and his mother dying in 1926. He worked in a cinema in Bow road and at 7.40 one morning, having seen his fiancee off to work, woke the manager, claiming that he had lost 10/- at work.

Stockwell, 5'10", attacked Mr Hoard with an axe, and clubbed Mrs Hoard when she intervened. He stole the safe keys and made off with £100. Mr Hoard, a failed actor who had run the cinema since February 1934, was found soon afterwards in the circle by a cleaner, and he died without regaining consciousness later the same day. Mrs Hoard, who fully recovered, was not able to identify the attacker.

Stockwell, meanwhile, put into effect his plan to feign suicide. He deposited the money in a railway station locker, then left his clothes on a Lowestoft beach. A suicide note to the police confessing to the murder was found to have been postmarked after the clothes were found, and Stockwell was arrested in a Great Yarmouth hotel. The jury recommended mercy on account of Stockwell's youth.

Read: True Crime, Oct 98.

19 December 1934	Hull prison	*T/ A.Pierrepoint*

482

<u>Ethel Lillie MAJOR</u>   **42**   *(nee Ethel Brown)*   *female*

Poisoned: **Arthur Major**, *44, her husband, on 24 May 1934, at Kirkby-on-Bain, Lincs.*
Motive: *To clear impediment.*

Ethel Brown, *(b.1892)*, and Arthur Major, a labourer and lorry driver, had married in 1918, but by May 1934 their relationship had deteriorated to such an extent that sometimes Ethel and the couple's fourteen-year old son, Lawrence, did not sleep in the family home, but at the house of Ethel's father, Tom Brown, 75, a mile away at Roughton.

In 1915 Ethel had had an illegitimate daughter who lived with Tom. She was a profligate spender and was known in the village as an argumentative woman, but Arthur was a bully and a long-time heavy drinker. He had also been having an affair with a neighbour. She stole strychnine from her father, a gamekeeper who used it to kill vermin, and twice administered it to her husband in his tea on 22 and 24 May. An anonymous letter prompted an autopsy which showed 1.27 grains of strychnine in Arthur's body. Mrs Major had been seen feeding a neighbour's dog which was later found dead. The dog was also found to have been poisoned. Ethel was arrested on July 9.

The jury's strong recommendation to mercy after an hour's retirement was ignored, and Ethel Major was the first woman to hang for eight years. She had to be supported on the gallows, having been in a state of collapse for two days.

Read: A Date With the Hangman

483	1 Jan	Frederick RUSHWORTH	29		Armley
484	7 Feb	David BLAKE	29		Armley
485	13 Mar	Charles LAKE	37		Pentonville
486	2 Apr	Leonard BRIGSTOCK	33		Wandsworth
487	16 Apr	Percy ANDERSON	21		Wandsworth
488	9 May	John BAINBRIDGE	24		Durham
489	30 May	John BRIDGE	25		Strangeways
490	25 Jun	Arthur FRANKLIN	44		Gloucester
491	10 Jul	Walter WORTHINGTON	57		Bedford
492	16 Jul	George HAGUE	23		Durham
493	29 Oct	Raymond BOUSQUET	30	*Canadian*	Wandsworth
494	30 Oct	Alan GRIERSON	27		Pentonville

1 January 1935   Armley gaol, Leeds   *T.Pierrepoint/ Cross*

483

Frederick RUSHWORTH   29

Buried alive: His 24-day old child, on 25 March 1934, near Middleham, N.Yorks.

Motive: To clear impediment.

Lydia Crome, from Hartlepool, had married in 1927, but after three children, was thrown out by her husband in 1930. Leaving the children with her mother, she worked as a servant at a holiday camp at Carperby, north Yorkshire, where she lived in a caravan. It was there, in January 1933, age 23, now Lydia Binks, that she met Fred Rushworth, *(b.1905)*, a local farm labourer. The two had sex only a few times, but by Christmas she realised she was pregnant by him.

Fearful for her job, she gave birth alone in the caravan on 1 March, and then claimed that she was looking after the baby of a friend. Under pressure from her boss to return the child, Lydia wrote to Rushworth, who arranged to meet mother with child at Wensley Bridge. Handing the child in a basket over to its father, Lydia, who had a mental age of 13, watched as he dug a hole and buried the child.

Rumours about the baby's disappearance led police to question Lydia, who took them to the shallow grave. The two were tried together, Rushworth claiming that he thought the child was already dead when he buried it. After 2 hours and 35 minutes, the jury found both guilty, but added the strongest recommendation to mercy in the case of Lydia. Her sentence was commuted to life imprisonment on 28 December, six days before her execution date.

Read: True Detective, Jul 93.

7 February 1935   Armley gaol, Leeds   *T.Pierrepoint/ Alfred Allen*

484

David Maskill BLAKE   **29**

Strangled: ***Emily Yeomans***, *23, on 16 October 1934, in Leeds, W.Yorks.*
Motive: *Sexual.*

Blake, *(b.1906)*, had raped an old woman while on army service in India, and in 1929 had received three years for beating and robbing a young girl. An unemployed steel erector, Blake had gone out drinking with Albert Schofield on 16 October 1934, and had gone on to meet Emily Yeomans, a waitress, at about 7.40. He had first met her three weeks before and they had been out on three or four dates since. Blake, 5'7", had then taken her to Middleton woods, raped her, and then strangled her with her scarf at 9pm.
Emily was found at 8.30 the next morning, and hours later Blake was married, with Schofield as his best man. His wife, Jean, had given birth to his son the previous March, but the couple continued to live apart, even after the wedding. Blake was so preoccupied with the death, that on his second night as a married man, he had met a complete stranger, Arthur Jubb, and had asked to stay the night at his house. Jubb and others became suspicious of Blake's obsession, and the police were informed.
Blake was arrested on 24 October. It was his best man who produced the most damning testimony, Blake having told him that he was meeting Emily, and actually seeing the two together before the murder. Blake had given Emily's powder compact to Jubb as a gift for his wife. He always maintained his innocence, and forensic evidence of pubic hair fitted both Blake and the first man arrested as a suspect, Joseph Talbot. The jury gave its verdict after 75 minutes.

Read: A Date With the Hangman

485

Charles Malcolm LAKE   37   *(aka George Frank Harvey)*

Bludgeoned: ***George Hamblin**, 40, on 26 October 1934, in London SW3.*
Motive: *Financial.*

Lake, *(b.1898),* and Hamblin were both residents of the Poor Law Institution in Chelsea. Hamblin made a little extra money for himself by taking small bets, and Lake lost rather more than he could afford to him. Cornering Hamblin in the storeroom at 4.30pm, Lake battered him with a hammer, and stole his money pouch. Lake then accompanied a woman friend to the cinema, and did not return to the institution for three days, whereupon he was arrested. Known to be hard up, Lake had £3 on him, and a postal order belonging to the dead man. Tried under the name of Harvey, Lake did not want his sick mother to know the truth.

Read: And May The Lord Have Mercy On Your Soul

486

Leonard Albert BRIGSTOCK   33

Cut throat of: ***Hubert Sidney Deggan**, 36, on 19 January 1935, in Chatham, Kent.*
Motive: *Vengeance; drink related.*

Brigstock, *(b.1902),* was stoker petty officer on *HMS Arethusa* tied up in Chatham, and had been reported for three minor offences by Chief Petty Officer Hubert Deggan. After spending several hours drinking in pubs, Brigstock, a married man, returned to the ship, and saw Deggan sleeping alone in the mess. He slit his throat with a razor, and handed the weapon to another sailor, admitting what he had done.

Read: And May The Lord Have Mercy On Your Soul

487

Percy Charles ANDERSON   21

Strangled: ***Edith Constance Drew-Bear**, 21, on 25 November 1934, near Ovingdean, Sussex.*
Motive: *To clear impediment.*

Anderson, *(b.1914)*, a motor mechanic, and Miss Drew-Bear, a cinema usherette, had had a relationship, which it seemed, he was more eager to terminate than she. It also seemed that she was jealous of any attention he paid to other women. At 5pm on a golf-course, Anderson shot Edith with a revolver five times in the head and back, and then strangled her to death with his silk scarf. He dumped her body in a water tank, and then boarded a bus soaking wet, minus his shoes, and was recognised by the conductor.

Anderson claimed the two had quarrelled, that he had gone for a swim in the sea, and then could remember nothing. At his home, police found an assortment of weapons, including a knife and a home-made pistol, ammunition from which matched that which had been found in Emily's body. The jury heard that Anderson suffered headaches and blackouts but reached its verdict within forty minutes.

Read: Murderous Sussex

9 May 1935   Durham gaol

488

John Stephenson BAINBRIDGE   24

Bludgeoned/ cut throat of: ***Edward Frederick Herdman**, 75, on 31 December 1934, in Bishop Auckland, Co Durham.*
Motive: *Financial.*

Bainbridge, *(b.1911)*, had worked as a junior clerk in a solicitor's office, before joining the Durham Light Infantry. Returning from his station in Hampshire on 22 December, for Christmas leave, he paid a visit to Mr Herdman, his former managing clerk, and a neighbour. The old man advised Bainbridge to make a will, and the soldier called at 12.30pm on new year's eve, to get it drafted. He called again at 6.15pm, and left with Herdman's daughter at 7.50, and was in his parents at 8pm.

He went back to his neighbour, battered him with a poker, and cut his throat with a pen-knife, before going to a jewellers at 8.20, and then on to a party in Gateshead. It seemed unlikely that Bainbridge would have time to commit the offence, but he had been hard up, and had suddenly enough money to buy a ring for his fiancee, and cash left over. He sent £36 in bloodstained notes to Hampshire, and his story that he had borrowed it from a married woman, whom he was not prepared to name, was not believed.

Read: And May The Lord Have Mercy On Your Soul

30 May 1935   Strangeways prison, Manchester

489

John Harris BRIDGE   25

Cut throat of: ***Amelia Nuttall***, *23, on 14 April 1935, in Salford, Lancs.*
Motive: *To clear impediment.*

Bridge, *(b.1910),* lived in Broughton and worked as a driver and warehouseman for a jewellery company. He had been courting Amelia Nuttall since 1928, and the two had become engaged in 1932, with the wedding planned for June 1935. Bridge's problem was that in 1934 he had fallen for another woman, Eileen Earl. Eileen had tried to solve the problem by finding herself another boyfriend, but by February 1935 she knew it was Bridge she wanted, and the two became lovers. Bridge broke the news of another woman to Amelia on 6 April, but stopped short of ending things with his fiancee.

At 7pm, an hour after her father had gone out, he went to see Amelia. Telling her it was all over, she became hysterical. He slapped her and then dazed her with a blow from the poker. He then cut her throat with a bread knife, and turned out drawers to suggest robbery. Amelia was discovered by her father at 10.15pm. At first, he admitted going to the house, but denied murder, but he confessed the following morning, stating that Amelia had attacked him with the poker after he slapped her. The jury retired for 50 minutes. Bridge was hanged just 46
days after killing Amelia.

Read: Murderous Manchester

490

Arthur Henry FRANKLIN   44

Shot: **Bessie Gladys Nott**, *28, on 8 May 1935, in Gloucester.*
Motive: *Sexual rivalry.*

      Franklin, *(1891),* lived with his brother by Hanham woods, where Henry and Bessie Nott were neighbouring smallholders. Arthur and Bessie began an affair, and in November 1933, Bessie moved in with the brothers, leaving her 10-year old son with her husband.
      By May 1935, though, she had had enough, and decided to return to Henry, leaving at 10am. No sooner had she left his house, than Arthur shot her in the back, and again as she lay on the ground. Henry had come out of his house when he heard the shot, but was chased back by Franklin, who caught up with his rival, and seriously wounded him with another blast. Franklin pleaded guilty at his trial.

      Read: And May The Lord Have Mercy On Your Soul

491

Walter Osmond WORTHINGTON   57

Shot: **Sybil Worthington**, *27, his wife, on 9 March 1935, in Broughton, Hunts.*
Motive: *Sexual rivalry.*

      Walter Worthington's first wife had died in 1919, leaving 13 children. Walter, *(b. 1878),* was a shy and religious man, a tee-totaller who was a well-liked chicken farmer and handyman in the village of Broughton.
      He met his second wife while doing some electrical repairs in the village pub, the Crown, where Sybil's sister, Bertha Wright, was the landlady. Within six weeks they were married. The quiet life, however, was not for Sybil, who often went to the Crown, and stayed out late.   Worthington confided his jealousies to his vicar. When Sybil began seeing Bertha's son, Lionel, 18, more often, going out on his motor-bike, Walter's jealousy grew.
      One evening, while two of his sons were at home, and Sybil was getting ready to go out yet again, Walter wrote a suicide note. He went into

the living room, took down his shotgun, and when Sybil entered, he shot her in the chest. His defence claimed that he had intended the gun for himself, and that it had gone off accidentally. The jury decided Walter's guilt in twelve minutes, figuring that the pressure required to fire the gun was too great for the shot to have been anything but deliberate.

Read: True Crime Summer Special, 96

| 16 July 1935 | Durham gaol | *T.Pierrepoint* |

492

George HAGUE   23

Cut throat of:	***Amanda Sharp***, *20, on 6 May 1935, in Langley Park, Co Durham.*
Motive:	*Vengeance.*

Hague, *(b.1912),* the youngest of 13 children, had lost his job as a bus conductor in October 1934. He had courted Amanda Sharp since Christmas 1934, but five months later she was tiring of him. He wanted to accompany her to a bonfire party, in celebration of the jubilee, but she made an excuse that the matron of the hospital where she worked as a kitchen maid, had forbidden the young women from being accompanied by their boyfriends.

The two attended the party separately, but Hague waited on the hospital driveway at 11.30pm, for Amanda to return. He appeared from behind bushes when she approached with a friend, and asked to speak to her. Moments later, he cut her throat with a razor, and was seen lying on top of her. He was arrested at home an hour later, and relied on a plea of insanity.

Read: True Crime, Aug 98

493

Raymond Henry BOUSQUET   30   *Canadian*
(aka Del Fontaine)

Shot: ***Hilda Meek***, *19, on 10 July 1935, in London SE11.*
Motive: *Sexual rivalry; drink related.*

Bousquet, *(b.1905),* a married man from Winnipeg, was a professional boxer under the name Del Fontaine, and had begun an affair with Hilda Meek in 1933. By 1935 he was tiring of Hilda, and was considering returning to Canada, but she managed to persuade him to stay, though it was not much longer before he realised that she was being unfaithful.

They had spent the early evening in several Kennington pubs, and Bousquet had passed Hilda a letter, threatening to kill her if she continued her alternative relationship. She said he was too much of a coward to do that, and left for home. He followed her there, and discovered her on the phone, arranging a meeting for 10pm. A blazing row developed, and when her mother came to investigate, he shot them both. The two women managed to run into the street, and Bousquet was arrested.

Read: And May The Lord Have Mercy On Your Soul

30 October 1935   Pentonville prison, London   *Baxter/ Pollard*

494

Alan James GRIERSON   27

Bludgeoned: ***Louise Berthe Gann***, *62, on 22 June 1935, in London NW1*
Motive: *Financial*

Grierson, *(b.1908),* had attended private school, the son of a solicitor, but was lazy, and became a small-time con-man to support himself, serving several prison terms for fraud, including one whilst living in Australia. Returning to London in the summer of 1935, Grierson, 5'9", took a job as a car salesman, and met the shy and naive Mary Gann, a shop assistant.

Mary lived with her mother, and Grierson wormed his way into the trust of both, Mrs Gann allowing him to stay in the flat near Regents Park of some friends who were away. He arranged a seaside trip with both women, and got Mary out of the way by arranging to pick her up by car at Earls Court.

Instead he went to the flat where he he smashed Mrs Gann six times about the head with a flat iron, and made off with valuables. Mary later found her mother who died within hours.

Grierson was found in lodgings in Weybridge. Having been identified by a jeweller as the man who had sold him a cruet set stolen from the flat at the time of the murder, Grierson was condemned by the jury after 25 minutes' deliberation.

Read: True Crime Summer Special 92

495	16 Apr	Dorothea WADDINGHAM (f)	36		Winson Green
496	12 May	Buck RUXTON	37	*Indian*	Strangeways
497	30 Jun	Frederick FIELD	32		Wandsworth
498	14 Jul	George BRYANT	38		Wandsworth
499	15 Jul	Charlotte BRYANT (f)	33	*Irish*	Exeter
500	5 Aug	Wallace JENDEN	57		Wandsworth
501	16 Dec	Christopher JACKSON	24		Durham

16 April 1936   Winson Green prison, Birmingham   *T./ A. Pierrepoint*

495

Dorothea Nancy WADDINGHAM   **36**   *(Mrs Thomas*
                                female   *Leech)*

*Probably **poisoned**:*   **1 Loisa Baguley**, *89, on 12 May 1935, and her daughter*
Poisoned: **2 Ada Louise Baguley**, *50, on 11 September 1935, in Nottingham.*
Motive: *Financial.*

    Waddingham, *(b.1900),* a widow since 1930, with three children, had a criminal record for theft and fraud dating from 1925, and had served three months' jail. She had previously worked as a factory hand and as a workhouse orderly, then in 1934 set up a nursing home in Devonshire Drive, Nottingham, with her lover, Ronald Joseph Sullivan, 39, who was separated from his wife. They had two children together, the last born in January 1936. Neither Nancy nor Joe, as they called each other, had any nursing qualifications.

    In January 1935, Loisa Baguley, 6 years a widow, and her unmarried 16-stone bed-ridden daughter, Ada, were placed in Waddingham's care. In exchange for cheap life-long care, Ada changed her will to make Waddingham and Sullivan sole beneficiaries of the £1600 estate. Eight days later on 12 May, Loisa Baguley died. When Ada died on 11 September, Waddingham's rush to arrange a cremation aroused suspicion and a post-mortem revealed 3 grains of morphine which Waddingham admitted administering. Loisa's exhumed body also contained morphine.

Sullivan was found to have no direct involvement and was discharged. After a two-hour retirement, the jury's strong recommendation to mercy was ignored.

Read: Murders of the Black Museum

12 May 1936   Strangeways prison, Manchester

496

Buck RUXTON   **37**   *(ne Bikhtyar Rustomji*
                        Indian   *Rakanji Hakim)*

Strangled: **1 Isabella Ruxton**, *(nee Kerr), 35, and*
                        2 Mary Rogerson, *19, on 15 September 1935, in*
                        Lancaster.
Motive: *Sexual rivalry.*

Ruxton, *(b.1899),* was a Bachelor of Medicine, a parsee originally from Bombay, who had come to England in 1925, meeting Isabella Van Ees three years later. He anglicised his name by deed poll in 1929. In 1930 he and Isabella had moved to 2 Dalton Square, Lancaster, where he had acquired a new practice.

Isabella, a Scot, had previously been married to a Dutchman, but took the name Ruxton, though they never married. They had three children, but their relationship was tempestuous, violent rows followed by violent sex. Ruxton was constantly making accusations of infidelity against Isabella.

When Isabella returned home late from a Blackpool trip, Ruxton, insane with jealousy, strangled her and then murdered the children's nursemaid, Mary Rogerson, presumably because she had been a witness. He dismembered both bodies and particularly destroyed identifying traits. He told Mary's parents that the two women had left for a holiday in Edinburgh. He dumped the remains in a ravine near Moffat in Scotland on 17 September where they were found twelve days later. Ruxton had asked a friend to take care of the three children, aged 4, 5 and 7, while his wife was away.

Ruxton was suspected when Mary's mother told the police she was missing. Some clothing found with the bodies was identified as having come from the Ruxton house and three charwomen testified to bloodstains in the house. The jury delivered its verdict after one hour. Ruxton's appeal was rejected, and he wrote a confession in the condemned cell.

Read: Medical Murders

497

Frederick Herbert Charles FIELD   32

Probably **strangled:**	**1 Nora Upchurch**, 20, on 1 October 1931, in Clapham, London W1, and
Strangled:	**2 Beatrice Vilna Sutton**, 46, in April 1936, in London SW4.
Motive:	Sadistic pleasure.

Nora Upchurch, a 20-year old prostitute, was found gagged, strangled with her belt in an empty locked premises on Shaftesbury Avenue, on 2 October 1931. Field, *(b.1904),* a signwriter and electrician, told how he had given the key to a potential gentleman buyer. An inquest returned an open verdict, but the police had their suspicions about Field, a married man with a daughter. In July 1933 he confessed to the crime, saying he had known Nora eight months and that she had been demanding money not to tell his wife and boss of their clandestine affair. He was charged with murder. But Field withdrew his confession, claiming he only wanted to clear his name. His description of the murder had differed from the actuality, and he was acquitted.

In April 1936, Field, now a deserter from the RAF, strangled to death Beatrice Sutton, a middle-aged prostitute and widow, in her Clapham flat. He again confessed to the murder, and then withdrew his admission, but this time his description of the victim's injuries were too close to the truth and the jury convicted him inside fifteen minutes.

Read: True Crime Summer Special 89

498

George Arthur BRYANT   38

Strangled:	**Ellen Margaret Mary Whiting**, 36, on 21 May 1936, in Dover, Kent.
Motive:	Sexual rivalry.

Ellen Whiting lived with her husband William and three children in Folkestone, until she met Bryant, *(b.1897),* and began an affair in October

1935. While William was away, Ellen took the children and moved in with Bryant in Dover, but, once the dust had settled, William and Ellen continued to meet once a week. She saw him last on 16 May, and made arrangements for the following week. Bryant got home at 2.30pm on 21 May, and gave the children money to go to the cinema. At 4.30pm, he hit Ellen over the head with a bottle, and then strangled her. At 5.40pm, he went to a police station and confessed.

Read: *And May The Lord Have Mercy On Your Soul*

15 July 1936   Exeter prison   *T./ A. Pierrepoint/ Phillips*

499

Charlotte BRYANT   **33**   *(nee Charlotte McHugh)*
                          female   *Irish*

Poisoned: ***Frederick Bryant**, 39, her husband, on 22 December 1935, in Sherborne, Dorset.*
Motive: *To clear impediment.*

Frederick Bryant had met Charlotte McHugh, *(b.1903)*, in Londonderry in 1921 whilst serving as a military policeman. They married the following year. He had since worked as a farm labourer. Charlotte was an unkempt, toothless and illiterate woman who was well-known for selling her sexual favours, to which Fred had no objection, welcoming the extra cash.

Charlotte had five children between 1923 and 1934, and in December 1933 began an affair with Leonard Parsons, a gipsy pedlar and horse dealer who was an occasional lodger with the Bryants. In between times he lived with another woman by whom he had four children.

Keen to have Parsons to herself, Charlotte began poisoning her husband in May 1935. Parsons finally left the Bryants' tied cottage in October 1935, not as keen as Charlotte was on a permanent relationship. The fourth attempt on Frederick's life had the desired effect.

A post-mortem revealed 4.09 grains of arsenic and a search of the house revealed the presence of weed-killer. Lucy Ostler, an old widow who had recently come to lodge at the house testified to seeing Charlotte disposing of weed-killer, and of coaxing Frederick into a drink of Oxo the night before he died. Parsons gave evidence that Charlotte had declared that her husband would soon be dead, and she would be free to marry him.

Read: *Murders of the Black Museum*

500

Wallace JENDEN   57

Cut throat of: *Alice Whye, 38, on 23 May 1936, in Croydon, Surrey.*
Motive: *Vengeance; drink related.*

Jenden, *(b.1878),* lived in a hut on an allotment, and met Alice Whye in 1935. She was separated from her husband, and had taken the two children to live with her mother. She soon found that Jenden was an extremely jealous man, and sometimes threatened her.

After a good few drinks, Alice went back to the hut with Jenden, where he stabbed her, and cut her throat. When Alice failed to return home the following day, her mother contacted the police, who arrived at the hut just in time to prevent Jenden, blind drunk, from cutting his own throat. Alice's body was found on the floor of the shack. Jenden confessed, but then changed his story, saying that he had found her body, and had taken it to the hut.

Read: And May The Lord Have Mercy On Your Soul

501

Christopher JACKSON   24

Bludgeoned: *Harriet May Ferris Linney, 62, his aunt, on 30 June 1936, in Sunderland, Co Durham.*
Motive: *Financial.*

Jackson, *(b.1911),* lived in Chester-le-Street, but was in arrears with his rent, and owed money on several loans. While his uncle was at Carlisle races, at 6pm Jackson called on his aunt in Sunderland. When he asked her for money, she began calling him names, and he responded by punching her twice in the face, and hitting her over the head four times with a beer bottle. Her neighbour found Mrs Linney at 8pm. Jackson had been seen getting on a bus near the Linney house, and was found to have suddenly cleared his debts. £9 and some bloody clothes were found locked in his suitcase.

Read: And May The Lord Have Mercy On Your Soul

1937

total: **9**

502	4 Feb	Max HASLAM	23	Strangeways
503	10 Feb	Andrew BAGLEY	62	Armley
504	27 Jul	Philip DAVIS	30	Exeter
505	12 Aug	Horace BRUNT	32	Strangeways
506	13 Aug	Leslie STONE	24	Pentonville
507	17 Aug	Frederick MURPHY	53	Pentonville
508	18 Nov	John RODGERS	22	Pentonville
509	7 Dec	Ernest MOSS	28	Exeter
510	30 Dec	Frederick NODDER	44	Lincoln

4 February 1937   Strangeways prison, Manchester

502

Max Mayer HASLAM   **23**

Bludgeoned: ***Ruth Clarkson***, *74, on 19 June 1936, in Nelson, Lancs.*
Motive: *Financial.*

Haslam, *(b.1914),* a 4 ft 7 in dwarf, had heard rumours that Ruth Clarkson, an old woman who lived alone, was worth a few bob. He battered her to death in her living room, and hanged her dog from a bedpost after it had attacked him. He got away with several hundred pounds, and some jewellery. Ruth was discovered on 22 June, when police, alerted by concerned neighbours, forced an entry. Two lodgers with whom Haslam stayed, having read press reports, went to the police after he had shown them some jewels, and spoke of killing a dog. One of them said that Haslam had offered him £200 to help dump a body in the swamp.

Read: And May The Lord Have Mercy On Your Soul

396

503

<u>Andrew Anderson BAGLEY</u>   **62**   *(aka John Smith)*

Strangled: ***Irene Hart****, 16, on 12 September 1936, in Rotherham, W.Yorks.*
Motive: *Sexual rivalry.*

Bagley, *(b.1875)*, and his retarded son lodged with his daughter and her husband in rather cramped conditions, such that Bagley shared a bedroom with his son-in-law's daughter from a previous marriage, Irene Hart. Bagley, who slept on a mattress on the floor, developed a fixation for the girl, thinking of her as his girlfriend. When she went to the cinema with two boys on 29 August, he shouted at her when she returned, though he later apologised.

Two weeks later, the two were left alone in the house from 9.30am. Bagley strangled Irene with a clothes line, stuffed some newspaper in her mouth, and removed some of her clothes. Her mother later discovered Irene stuffed in a tin trunk,, Bagley having disappeared. He was arrested thirty miles away in Hucknall, on 23 October.

Read: And May The Lord Have Mercy On Your Soul

504

<u>Philip Edward Percy DAVIS</u>   **30**

Bludgeoned: ***1 Wilhelmina Vermadell Davis****, 33, his wife, and*
    2 Monica Rowe*, 15, his niece, on 21 April 1937, in Tuckingmill, Cornwall.*
Motive: *Vengeance*

Davis, *(b.1907)*, had been certified insane and committed to an asylum in 1925. By 1937 he had been married several years and lived with his wife and niece near Camborne. Without apparent reason or motive, he battered both to death with a hammer, and then rented a garage from a neighbour, where he buried the naked bodies. He told people that his wife had left him, and taken his niece with her, but six days later he was seen moving barrows-full of soil around the garage. Satisfying local gossip, the neighbour inspected the garage, and called police when he noticed a foul smell. At his trial, Davis offered no explanation, and though one doctor said he was insane, three others declared him responsible for his actions.

Read: And May The Lord Have Mercy On Your Soul

12 August 1937   Strangeways prison, Manchester

505

Horace William BRUNT   32

Shot: *Kate Elizabeth Collier, 54, on 24 April 1937, near Ashbourne, Derbyshire.*
Motive: *Vengeance*

Brunt, *(b.1905)*, had known Elsie Kate Collier since 1932, and the two had been courting since June 1935. Brunt worked as a lorry driver but lost his job and was unemployed for five months before finding work as a hotel yard hand in April 1937. Elsie's parents did not like Brunt, thinking him unsuitable for their daughter. They ran a chicken farm at Bradley near Ashbourne, and Hugo Collier and his daughter went to the Derby market as usual at 8.30am on April 24.

Brunt cycled to the farm at 12.30pm when Kate Collier was feeding the chickens. Taking the shotgun from above the kitchen door, he blasted Mrs Collier in the back of the head from a distance of two metres. He took some money and cycled off. Witnesses saw Kate feeding the chickens, and saw Brunt cycling to and from the farm. Husband and daughter made the bloody discovery on their return at 2.45pm. Brunt at first gave a false alibi, then confessed, claiming that Mrs Collier had attacked him with a poker, and that he took the gun off her, firing by accident. The jury took 40 minutes in deliberating.

Read: Murderous Derbyshire

Leslie George STONE   24

Strangled:	***Ruby Anne Keen***, *23, on 11 April 1937, in Leighton Buzzard, Beds.*
Motive:	*Sexual rivalry; drink related.*

     Stone, *(b.1913)*, a building labourer, had first met Ruby Keen in 1931, and they had been sweethearts, but when Stone had joined the Royal Artillery and was posted to Hong Kong in 1932, Ruby had put him out of her mind. Indeed she had had several boyfriends since, and by 1937 was engaged to a policeman. Ruby, a factory worker, lived with her widowed mother and brother and sister, and after Stone had left the army in December 1936, the two of them met by chance.

     On the night of 11 April, they had drinks in several pubs, and were overheard in heated discussion, Stone pleading with Ruby to break off her engagement, and to marry him. They were seen entering a lover's lane near Ruby's home, and there the arguments continued when Stone tried to kiss her. When Ruby called him a 'dirty devil', Stone punched her on the chin and tore off most of her clothes. Kneeling on the ground beside her, he strangled Ruby with her scarf, and fled, too scared to go through with the rape. Soil was found in the knee of Stone's new suit, and a thread from Ruby's slip in his jacket.

     The jury, taking 25 minutes in deciding, asked whether he would still be guilty if rape, and not murder, had been intended, and they were directed that this was the case. This direction formed the basis of his appeal, which failed.

     Read: Murders of the Black Museum

Frederick George MURPHY   53

*Probably **cut throat of:***	**1 *Katherine Peck***, *in London EC3.*
Cut throat of:	**2 *Rosina Field***, *49, on 13 May 1937, in London N1.*
Motive:	*Sexual.*

Katherine Peck was found in the street near Aldgate with her throat cut. Murphy had been seen with her that night, and was charged when two men told police that Murphy had admitted to them that he had committed the murder. However, he was acquitted when one of the men failed to testify. Indignant that he had been wrongly charged, Murphy smashed a window at the Home Office, and spent two weeks in prison as a result.

Some time later, in 1937, he took a prostitute, Rosina Field, to the furniture warehouse where he worked on Islington Green. There he cut her throat. The next day, he reported to his employers that there was a body in the building. The police unravelled Murphy's elaborate alibi, and witnesses had seen him entering the warehouse with the woman.

Read: Murder Guide to London, p138.

18 November 1937   Pentonville prison, London   *T.Pierrepoint/ Pollard*

508

John Thomas RODGERS   22

Strangled: ***Lilian Maud Chamberlain**, 25, on 26 August 1937, in Northwood, Middlesex.*
Motive: *Financial.*

Rodgers, *(b. 1915)*, was a barman at the same pub as barmaid Lilian Chamberlain. She lived opposite the pub with her husband, a restaurant car worker on the railways, who was frequently away from home. On his day off, Rodgers turned up at Lily's door after she had got in from work at 10.45pm. He battered and strangled her, before changing into her husband's clothes and making off.

When neither turned up for work the following day, the body was found, and the suspect identified. Rodgers was arrested later at Golders Green station. He claimed he had got back late and needed a bed for the night, discovering Lily's body when he entered the house. Asked why he then made off in her husband's clothing, he said, 'With me it's self first and self last'. No clear motive was established.

Read: And May The Lord Have Mercy On Your Soul

509

Ernest John MOSS   28

Shot: **Constance Bennett**, *19, on 7 August 1937, in Woolacombe, Devon.*
Motive: *To clear impediment.*

Ernie Moss, *(b. 1909)*, once a policeman, had found work as a taxi driver. He was known as an honest man, though separated from his wife and two children. He met Kitty Bennett, a laundry girl, and rented a bungalow for her on Woolacombe Sands, once the two had become lovers. She told her parents that she was going there to get married, but Moss had decided he wanted to end the relationship.

One week later on a hot afternoon, he shot her from behind, then ran into the street and told a policeman what he had done. He ran off but was later arrested after her body had been found on her bed, her face blown away. She had apparently been taken by surprise, and there had been no sexual assault. Moss pleaded guilty and remained silent.

Read: True Crime Summer Special, 96.

30 December 1937   Lincoln prison

510

Frederick NODDER   44   *(aka Frederick Hudson)*

Strangled: **Mona Lilian Tinsley**, *10, on 6 January 1937, near Worksop, Notts.*
Motive: *Sadistic pleasure.*

Nodder, *(b.1893)*, some time motor engineer, some time lorry driver, had been sacked from several jobs for being drunk and for lying. He had left his wife, and was wanted for non-payment of support for an illegitimate child. He had been thrown out of several lodgings for being dirty and untidy and for not paying rent. In 1934 he had lived with the Grimes family in Sheffield, and had moved on in 1935 to live with the family of Mrs Grimes' sister, the Tinsleys, in Newark. Known to them as Fred Hudson, and to the children as Uncle Fred, he had left in October 1935, again for not paying rent.

By 1937, he was renting a cottage in the village of Hayton, near Worksop. On 5 January, he met Mona from school, and took her back to his home. Some time on the following day he strangled her with a ligature and dumped her body in a nearby river. Witnesses had seen him with the child on a bus, and in his garden. Nodder claimed the girl had wanted to go to see her aunt, and he had put her on a bus for Sheffield the day after her disappearance. With no evidence of murder, despite his home and grounds being virtually taken to pieces, Nodder was charged with abduction, and sentenced to seven years on 10 March. On 6 June, Mona's body was found in the river Idle about 30 miles from Hayton, and Nodder was again tried, this time for her murder.

Read: True Detective, Summer Special 95.

1938

total: **8**

511	8 Mar	Walter SMITH	33		Norwich
512	20 Apr	Charles CALDWELL	49		Strangeways
513	26 May	Robert HOOLHOUSE	21		Durham
514	8 Jun	Jan MOHAMED	30	*Bengali*	Walton
515	12 Jul	Alfred RICHARDS	38		Wandsworth
516	19 Jul	William GRAVES	38		Wandsworth
517	26 Jul	William PARKER	25		Durham
518	1 Nov	George BRAIN	27		Wandsworth

8 March 1938   Norwich prison   *T.Pierrepoint*

511

<u>Walter SMITH</u>   **33**

Shot: ***Albert Edward Baker**, 28, on 22 October 1937, in Felixstowe, Suffolk.*
Motive: *Vengeance.*

Smith, *(b.1905),* was mate on the barge *East Anglia* which dockled at Felixstowe in October 1937, to unload its cargo of barley. Albert Baker, the captain of the barge, was Smith's best friend, but the two had an unexplained disagreement, and Smith shot his pal once in the head and twice in the heart.

Smith went ashore, getting very drunk in several pubs, and left open the boat's hatches, which led to the discovery of Baker's body. Smith claimed he had no memory of the murder, but mentioned his friend being shot dead before the means of murder had been disclosed.

Read: And May The Lord Have Mercy On Your Soul

512

Charles James CALDWELL　　　49

Stabbed:　　*Eliza Augustina Caldwell, 40, his wife, on 11 February 1938, in Rochdale, Lancs.*
Motive:　　*Vengeance.*

Caldwell, *(b.1889),* was an internee in Switzerland in the first world war, when he met his Swiss wife, Eliza. The couple and their two children moved to Rochdale, but Caldwell became unemployed, and financial problems grew. After regular rows over money and Caldwell's drink habit, Eliza left him, and served him with a summons for cruelty, desertion and wilful neglect, on 7 February.

Eliza rebutted his frequent attempts to persuade her to return, and while she was talking to a friend in the street, Caldwell approached and asked his wife a final time to return to him. When she refused, he drew a knife, and stabbed her near the heart. He told police, 'I want the rope now'.

Read: And May The Lord Have Mercy On Your Soul

513

Robert William HOOLHOUSE　　　21　　　*i*

Stabbed:　　*Margaret Jane Dobson, 67, on 17 January 1938, near Wolviston, Co Durham.*
Motive:　　*Vengeance.*

Hoolhouse, *(b.1917),* with a mental age of 14, and his parents had lived in a labourer's cottage on the Dobson's farm outside Wolviston until, in 1933, a dispute arose, and the Hoolhouses had been evicted. They moved to a village four miles away. Mrs Dobson, who had run the farm with her husband for over thirty years, left home before 5pm on 17 January and was found stabbed and raped on a farm track 17 hours later. Two drunken strangers had been seen in the area.

Seeking someone with a motive, police arrested Hoolhouse, who was found to have scratches on his face and blood and hairs on his clothes. Footprints found at the scene, however, did not fit Hoolhouse, and there were people prepared to support his alibi that he was at home at the time of the murder, and became scratched falling off his bicycle the following morning. Expecting an acquittal, his defence called no witnesses, and, unexpectedly, the jury found him guilty after a four-hour retirement. Despite a petition of 14,000 signatures, no reprieve was forthcoming.

Read: And May The Lord Have Mercy On Your Soul

8 June 1938   Walton gaol, Liverpool

514

Jan MOHAMMED   30   *Bengali*

Bludgeoned: ***Aminul Haq***, *20, on 11 April 1938, in Liverpool, Lancs.*
Motive: *Vengeance.*

Mohammed, *(b.1908),* and Haq were engine room crew on the same ship, and fell into a violent argument on 15 March 1938, when Haq hit Mohammed in the face with an iron bar, causing him the loss of several teeth. Haq was transferred to the *SS Kabinga*, also tied up in Liverpool docks.

Seeking his revenge, Mohammed tried to board the ship on 9 April, but was prevented. Two days later, he succeeded, and hid for three hours, until Haq returned to the ship. He then beat him to death with a heavy file.

Read: And May The Lord Have Mercy On Your Soul

12 July 1938   Wandsworth prison, London   *T/ A.Pierrepoint*

515

Alfred Ernest RICHARDS   38

Bludgeoned: ***Kathleen Richards***, *37, his wife, on 30 May 1938, in*
                 Welling, Kent.
Motive: *Vengeance.*

Richards, *(b.1900),* was, according to all who knew him, an honest and hard-working man, the father of three children. When his wife went out with a female friend to the cinema in February 1938, and returned late, he hit the roof, sparking a huge row, and telling Kathleen she would go or he would kill her. The pair had lived with Kathleen's sister and her husband, and she regularly returned to visit.

On the last such occasion, 11 May, Kathleen left a message for Alfred that she intended to take the children on an outing on 1 June. On 30 May at 11am, assuming Alfred had left for work, Kathleen again called to see her sister, but Richards battered her to death upstairs, and then tried to strangle her. He handed himself in to a police station less than an hour later.

Read: And May The Lord Have Mercy On Your Soul

19 July 1938	Wandsworth prison, London	*T.Pierrepoint/ Phillips*

516

William James GRAVES   38

Strangled:	*Tony Ruffle, 1, his son, on 26 March 1938, in Dover, Kent.*
Motive:	*To clear impediment.*

When Queenie Ruffle gave birth in January 1937, neither she nor the father, William Graves, *(b.1900),* could look after the child, and he was fostered out. Both parents shared equally the 15/- a week cost, but after October, Graves failed to pay any further money.

Concerned to lessen the financial burden to himself, Graves told Queenie that he had found alternative, and cheaper, foster parents in Canterbury, and told her to meet the prospective parents at Ashford station. Graves himself turned up and took the child. He later said he intended to abandon little Tony, but when the child started to cry, Graves strangled him with his coat, and left the body under a bush. Queenie, concerned by press reports, identified her child. The jury decided Graves' fate in ten minutes.

Read: And May The Lord Have Mercy On Your Soul

517

William PARKER   25

Strangled: **1** *Jane Ann Parker*, 23, his wife, and his children
                         2 *Theresa Shirley Parker*, 13 months, and
                         3 *Cecil Edward Parker*, 2 months, on 22 April 1938, in
                         Newcastle, Northumberland
Motive: To clear impediment

        Parker, *(b.1913)*, a miner, married Jane Ann Daley on Boxing Day 1936, and she gave birth to a daughter the following March and a son in February 1938. Parker had fallen into poor attendance at work, and the consequent money problems had led to arguments.
        According to Parker, one Friday night while he popped out for 15 minutes to buy cigarettes, his wife had strangled the two children, and then had flown at him with a poker upon his return. He had battered her with a hammer six times in retaliation. He then tied a string tightly around her neck-the ultimate cause of death-and carried her upstairs to bed. He acted as a golf caddy over the weekend as usual, and it was Monday evening before he went to the police to tell them of what had occurred before fainting.
        They found Mrs Parker on her bed covered in three coats, and the children in another room, still with string tightly knotted round their necks. Parker was charged with all three murders, and the jury agreed that it was he who had the motive and inclination to kill, not his wife.

        Read: Master Detective Summer Special 98.

518

George BRAIN   27

Stabbed: *Rose Muriel Atkins*, 30, on 12 July 1938, in Wimbledon,
                         Surrey.
Motive: To clear impediment.

        Brain, *(b.1911),* was a van driver, who at 11pm on 12 July 1938, picked up 'Irish Rose', a prostitute known to him for some time. He was her favourite of about six regular clients, and a row developed when he announced his intention to marry and to stop seeing Rose.

Brain hit her with the starting handle, and stabbed her to death. Emptying her bag of four shillings, Brain, 5'7", dumped Rose on a road in Wimbledon, running over the body, in some attempt to feign a road accident. Rose was identified only on 15 July. Tyre marks helped identify the van, which was found abandoned. The interior was marked with blood, and Rose's handbag, left inside, bore the fingerprint of the man identified as the driver. His employers, a bootmakers, said they wanted him for stealing £32.

Brain was arrested on cliffs at Sheerness, Kent, two weeks later. The jury delivered their verdict on him after only fifteen minutes. The rather plump Brain lost considerable weight awaiting his execution.

Read: True Detective Winter Special 90/1

1939

total: **7**

519	8 Feb	John DAYMOND	19	Durham
520	21 Mar	Harry ARMSTRONG	38	Wandsworth
521	29 Mar	William BUTLER	29	Wandsworth
522	7 Jun	Ralph SMITH	41	Gloucester
523	10 Oct	Leonard HUCKER	30	Wandsworth
524	25 Oct	Stanley BOON	27	Wandsworth
525	26 Oct	Arthur SMITH	26	Wandsworth

8 Fenruary 1939   Durham gaol   *T.Pierrepoint*

519

John DAYMOND   19

Bludgeoned: ***James Irwin Percival***, *68, on 9 November 1938, near Wigton, Cumberland.*
Motive: *Financial.*

Daymond, *(b.1920),* had worked for James Percival in the summer of 1938, haymaking on his farm at Aikhead, near Wigton. On 8 November, he called to ask Mr Percival's son if he could help him, as he was penniless, and had not eaten all day. He was turned down, and spent the night sleeping on a farm.

The following morning he battered both father and son with a pickaxe in the engine room of their farm, though only managed to secure the 2/8 that old Mr Percival had in his pocket. Daymond was found hiding in a hayloft at 1.30pm. The jury added a strong recommendation to mercy, on account of his youth.

Read: And May The Lord Have Mercy On Your Soul

520

Harry ARMSTRONG   38

Strangled: ***Peggy Irene Violet Pentecost***, *17, on 1 January 1939, in London SE1.*
Motive: *To clear impediment.*

        Armstrong, *(b.1901),* worked as a steward at a boys' school, though he had a long history of crime. In 1925 he was jailed for 15 months for knifing his pregnant girlfriend in the throat.   In 1928 he got three years for housebreaking, and in 1932 was convicted of attempting suicide and of a firearms offence. He was released in 1936. He became engaged to Peggy Pentecost from Brighton, who worked as a school clerk in Tonbridge, telling her he was a schoolmaster. She fell in love with him, but he feared he might lose his job if she exposed his deception.
        The two booked into a hotel at Waterloo as man and wife on New Year's Eve 1938, and the following day he strangled her manually during rough sex, stuffing a handkerchief and the corner of the quilt into her mouth. A chambermaid discovered her naked body the next day. He picked up a woman in a nearby pub and went with her to Paddington. She remembered a tattoo on his arm, and he was identified through police records. The jury deliberated for 37 minutes.

        Read: True Crime Summer Special 97

521

William Thomas BUTLER   29

Stabbed: ***Ernest Percival Key***, *64, on 24 December 1938, in Surbiton, Surrey.*
Motive: *Financial.*

        Butler, *(b.1910),* an unemployed driver, lived with his wife and two children in Teddington, Surrey, and had a record of housebreaking. On the morning of Christmas Eve, he entered Ernest Key's jewellery shop in Surbiton, intent on robbery. The owner was stabbed 31 times in the face, neck and head, and had cuts on his arms where he had tried to fend off the blows. Butler escaped with some jewellery, and Mr Key was left to be found by his son and daughter about midday. He died on the way to hospital.

The murderer, however, had left behind his bowler hat with hairs inside it. It was traced to Butler, who claimed to have killed in self-defence. The jury rejected his version of events after a two-day trial.

Read: Murders of the Black Museum, p359

7 June 1939   Gloucester prison   *T./ A. Pierrepoint*

522

Ralph SMITH   **41**

Cut throat of: ***Beatrice Delia Baxter**, 53, on 4 March 1939, in Swindon, Wilts.*
Motive: *Sexual rivalry.*

Smith, *(b.1898)*, had a son by his wife who had died in 1925. A one-time seaman and steelworker in Hartlepool, he had gone to Swindon from Cirencester in September 1938, taking work as a labourer at the gasworks, and lodging at the house of Beatrice Baxter, a widow since 1935 and the mother of three adult children. She had two great loves, dancing and cycling. The two got on well together and became dance partners. He imagined they would marry, but Beatrice wanted no romance from the friendship. Things deteriorated when Smith became jealous of rival dance partners, and started arguments with his landlady.

On 10 January she called the police because of Smith's behaviour, and the following day he took new lodgings. The following month he lost his job for persistent drunkenness, and he moved to Bristol to start anew.

But Smith could not get Beatrice out of his mind, and he returned to Swindon, knocking on her door at 7pm. She was getting ready to go out to a dance with her lodger and his girlfriend, but went outside to speak to Smith. After a brief conversation, he slashed her across the back of the neck with a razor and went to the police station to hand himself in. Smith's was the last execution in Gloucester.

Read: Master Detective, Feb 98.

523

Leonard George HUCKER   30

Stabbed: ***Mary Alice Maud Moncrieff,*** *60, on 16 August 1939, in London NW2.*

Motive: *Vengeance.*

      Hucker, *(b.1909),* had a brief affair with Beatrice Fullick, while he lodged with her and her mother, Mary Moncrieff, in Willesden in 1939. Frequent rows with Mary caused Hucker to leave, and though Beatrice continued to see him, she also had another boyfriend on the side.

      Finally, Beatrice told Hucker it was all over on 11 August. Four days later he bought a scout's knife, and the following day, after Beatrice had left for work at 9am, he called to see Mary. He stabbed her, and pushed her down the stairs into the cellar. She was found there with the knife still embedded in her chest. He handed himself into police at 3.45pm. He claimed that Mary had blamed him for making Beatrice pregnant, a claim which his former girlfriend vehemently denied.

      Read: And May The Lord Have Mercy On Your Soul.

524, 525

Stanley Ernest BOON   27
Arthur John SMITH   26

Bludgeoned: ***Mabel Maud Bundy,*** *42, on 4 July 1939, in Hindhead, Surrey.*

Motive: *Sexual, drink related.*

      Boon, *(b.1912),* and Smith, *(b.1913),* were soldiers stationed at Thursley camp. Smith had been drinking in a hotel bar with Boon and an old mate from service in India, Joseph Goodwin, when he got talking to Mabel Bundy, a maid at another hotel nearby. When he walked her back to the staff entrance, Boon and Goodwin followed. Mabel resisted having sex with Smith when she realised the others were present. She was found there, battered to death and sexually assaulted, the next morning.

Goodwin testified that Smith had torn Mabel's clothes and the two were on the floor having sex, when Boon, extremely drunk, had battered the woman twice in the face, before also raping her. Smith claimed that she had consented to sex. Boon said that he was prepared to rape Mabel, but that Goodwin had pushed him aside to have her for himself. Blood and semen stains indicated that all three had been involved in the rape of the maid. The three soldiers were tried together, Goodwin being acquitted, after one hour's consideration by the jury.

Read: Master Detective, Sep 98

1940 total: *15*

526	7 Feb	Peter BARNES	32	*Irish*	Winson Green
527	7 Feb	James RICHARDS	29	*Irish*	Winson Green
528	27 Mar	Ernest HAMMERTON	25		Wandsworth
529	24 Apr	William COWELL	38		Wandsworth
530	11 Jul	Vincent OSTLER	24		Durham
531	11 Jul	William APPLEBY	27		Durham
532	31 Jul	Udham SINGH	37	*Indian*	Pentonville
533	8 Aug	George ROBERTS	29		Cardiff
534	10 Sep	John WRIGHT	41		Durham
535	31 Oct	Stanley COLE	23		Wandsworth
536	26 Nov	William COOPER	24		Bedford
537	10 Dec	Carl MEIER	24	*Dutch*	Pentonville
538	10 Dec	Jose WALDEBERG	25	*German*	Pentonville
539	17 Dec	Charles VAN DEN KIEBOOM	26	*Dutch*	Pentonville
540	24 Dec	Edward SCOLLER	42		Durham

7 February 1940   Winson Green prison, Birmingham
T/ A.Pierrepoint/ Phillips/ Cross

526, 527

Peter BARNES   **32**   *Irish*
James RICHARDS   **29**   *Irish*

Blew up: 1 **Elsie Laura Ansell**, *21*,
        2 **Gwilym Rowland**, *50*,
        3 **James Corbett** *Arnott, 15*,
        4 **James Clay**, *81, and*
        5   **Rex Gentle**, *30, on 25 August 1939 in Coventry, Warwicks.*
Motive: Political.

        Irishmen Barnes, *(b.1908)*, and Richards, *(b.1911)*, were IRA agents. Richards, the 'operating officer' was sent to Coventry in May 1939 as part of 'S-plan', a campaign to further British withdrawal from Northern Ireland by means of terrorism. Barnes joined Richards from London in August 1939, and together with another, unidentified, agent manufactured a bomb of

414

potassium chlorate, with a timing device. The bomb, in a suitcase, was left in Broadgate on a bicycle near a parked car, exploding at 2.30 p.m. and causing five deaths and considerable damage.

Barnes and Richards were traced through the bicycle number and were further implicated by explosives found beneath the stairs at Richards' address. They were charged with the single murder of Elsie Ansell, as were Joseph Hewitt, his wife Mary, and her mother Brigid O'Hara, the Irish family with whom Richards lodged. The members of the family were found not guilty. Richards admitted IRA membership, but Barnes denied any involvement. The jury deliberated for 30 minutes.

Read: The Murder Guide to Great Britain, p180.

| 27 March 1940 | Wandsworth prison, London | *Phillips/ Riley* |

528

Ernest Ernest HAMMERTON   25

| **Stabbed:** | ***Elsie May Ellington**, 28, on 16 January 1940, in London SE17.* |
| Motive: | *Vengeance.* |

Hammerton, *(b.1915),* had been courting Elsie Ellington for some time, but had only stayed at her lodgings once before, sleeping on the sofa. Elsie promised to marry Ernest and he went to stay with her on 8 January, remaining this time for a week, with similarly modest sleeping arrangements.

On the evening of 15 January, Elsie would not go to the cinema with Hammerton, and the two had gone out separately, with it becoming apparent to Ernest that Elsie had changed her mind about the wedding. At 8.40 the following morning in the scullery, he stabbed Elsie 24 times, leaving the knife embedded in her heart. When the landlady came down in response to Elsie's screams, Hammerton rushed out, declaring he was going for a doctor. He was arrested as he alighted from a train in Manchester.

Read: And May The Lord Have Mercy On Your Soul.

24 April 1940   Wandsworth prison, London   *T.Pierrepoint/ Cross*

529

William Charles COWELL   38

Bludgeoned: ***Anne Farrow Cook***, *33, on 21 August 1939, near Burgess Hill, Sussex.*
Motive: *Sadistic pleasure*

　　　　Cowell, *(b.1902)*, was a night orderly in the same Brighton hospital where Annie Cook worked, having given up work as a professional dancer. They met at 7.30pm to go to a visiting circus, but went instead to woods near Burgess Hill, where Cowell clubbed Annie to death with two blows from a piece of wood. He went back later and dragged her body forty metres to hide it in undergrowth.

　　　　He was seen coming out of the wood that night, but returned to the body on each of the next five nights. When Annie was reported missing, Cowell went to the police on 22 August to tell them that though they had met, Annie had not wanted to attend the circus and they had parted. He eventually confessed under questioning. The jury deliberated for forty minutes.

　　　　Read: Murderous Sussex.

11 July 1940   Durham gaol   *T./ A. Pierrepoint*

530, 531

Vincent OSTLER   24
William APPLEBY   27

Shot: P.C. ***William Ralph Schiell***, *on 29 February 1940, in Coxhoe, Co Durham.*
Motive: *To escape arrest.*

　　　　Ostler, *(b.1916)*, and Appleby, *(b.1913)*, a coffin-maker, had carried out a string of 12 burglaries from grocer's stores, and were in Coxhoe's Co-op when they were disturbed by police officers. Bursting out through the front window, they made a run for it across fields to their getaway car.

　　　　Ostler shot PC Shiell in the stomach, and in a dying deposition, the officer claimed that someone had cried, 'Let him have it. He is all alone'. The two men were arrested on March at their homes in Bradford, Ostler pulling a gun from under his pillow. Appleby confessed, but denied knowledge of a gun. Both men were convicted on the grounds that the two were united in a common resolution, but the jury recommended mercy for Appleby.

Read: True Detective, Oct 95.

| 31 July 1940 | Pentonville prison, London | *Cross/ A.Pierrepoint* |

532

Udham SINGH   37   *(aka Mohamed Singh Azad)*
                        Indian

Shot: ***Sir Michael O'Dwyer**, 75, on 13 March 1940, in London SW1.*
Motive: *Political.*

Udham Singh, *(b.1903)*, a Sikh from the Punjab, worked as a mechanic and lived at Mornington Crescent. His brother had been one of hundreds killed in the Amritsar massacre of 1919. He consequently deplored British policy in India, and was angered at the difficulties of getting a British passport. He had deserted from the army, and had been involved in gun-trafficking. He came to England in 1935.

Armed with a knife, and a revolver which he said he had bought from a soldier in a pub, he went to the Caxton Hall where a meeting of the East India Association and the Royal Central Asian Society was taking place. A lecture had just finished when Singh walked down to the front of the Hall and fired six shots into the group on the platform.

Sir Louis Dane, 84, a former Lieutenant Governor in the Punjab, had his arm broken by a bullet, President of the Association and former Governor of Bombay, Lord Lemington, 79, had his wrist injured, Lord Zetland, Secretary of State for India, was hit twice in the chest, but escaped serious injury. Sir Michael O'Dwyer, Dane's predecessor in the Punjab, was hit twice in the back, injuries to his heart, lung and kidney proving fatal. Singh expressed regret at having killed only one.

Attlee and Gandhi both condemned the outrage. Singh's appeal was dismissed. In 1974 Singh's body was returned to India, cremated as an Indian martyr.

Read: Murders of the Black Museum

533

George Edward ROBERTS   29

Bludgeoned: ***Arthur John Allen**, 38, on 4 February 1940, in Cardiff, Glamorgan.*
Motive: *Financial; drink related.*

Roberts, *(1911)*, a married man, and Allen, who had not previously met, were both guests at a party on 3 February, and left at the same time in the early hours. They walked off together, and Roberts offered the older man a cup of tea at his house before going on home.

As Allen sat in a chair, Roberts hit him with an iron bar, took about £5 from his wallet, and items of clothing. At 4.30am, using a false name, Roberts took the badly injured man to a police station. Allen died in surgery later that day. Unfortunately for Roberts, he was identified by someone in the police station who knew his real name.

Read: And May The Lord Have Mercy On Your Soul

534

John William WRIGHT   41

Bludgeoned: ***Alice Wright**, 43, his wife, on 22 May 1940, in Bishop Auckland, Co Durham.*
Motive: *Financial*

Wright, *(b.1899)*, married for fifteen years, with three children, claimed that his wife, Alice, had been having affairs with other men. They argued on the evening of 21 May over an insurance policy, and the following morning, Wright went to check if the policy on his wife's life was still valid.

Before lunch, he axed Alice to death in the kitchen, where she was found by her children coming home to eat. Wright returned to the house, and put a coat over his wife's body, in feigned concern. Blood on his shirt helped convince the jury of his guilt.

Read: And May The Lord Have Mercy On Your Soul

31 October 1940   Wandsworth prison, London

     T.Pierrepoint/ Morris/ Kirk/ Critchell

535

Stanley Edward COLE   23

Stabbed: ***Doris Eugenia Girl***, *29, on 23 August 1940, in Wimbledon, Surrey.*

Motive: *Sadistic pleasure; drink related.*

Cole, *(b.1917)*, had only one conviction, for shopbreaking and stealing cigarettes, in 1938. He became friendly in April 1940, with Doris Girl, a married woman with a daughter of 8. Whether Doris and Cole were having an affair is not clear, but he sometimes would sleep on the sofa at her home.

They had been to the pub for four hours, before going home to consume a little more. There was no argument, and no provocation, but Cole saw a knife on the table, and without motive or reason, he plunged it into Doris' back. At 12.40am, he arrived in tears at the police station, to inform them of his actions. The jury convicted him in 35 minutes.

Read: And May The Lord Have Mercy On Your Soul

26 November 1940   Bedford gaol   *T/ A.Pierrepoint*

536

William Henry COOPER   24

Bludgeoned: ***John Joseph Harrison***, *68, on 5 July 1940, in Thorney, Cambs.*

Motive: *Financial.*

Cooper, *(b.1916)*, had worked on John Harrison's farm until he was sacked in April 1940, and a few months later he determined to get his revenge. He knew that Mr Harrison paid his workers every Friday, so at 7.30am, Cooper hid in the chicken hut, where the old man fed the birds every morning. Cooper was seen entering the coop. He smashed Harrison over the head with a glass bottle, but got away on his bicycle with only 30 shillings, for the workers had unusually been paid the day before. Harrison died a few days later, and the jury decided Cooper's guilt in just fifteen minutes.

Read; And May The Lord Have Mercy On Your Soul

10 December 1940	Pentonville prison, London	*Cross/ A.Pierrepoint/ Kirk*
10 December 1940	Pentonville prison, London	*Cross/ A.Pierrepoint/ Kirk*
17 December 1940	Pentonville prison, London	*Cross/ Morris*

537, 538, 539

Carl MEIER	**24**	*Dutch*
Jose WALDEBERG	**25**	*German*
Charles Albert VAN DEN KIEBOOM	**26**	*Dutch*

Crime: **Espionage.**

Meier, *(b.1916),* Waldeberg, *(b.1915),* and van den Kieboom, *(b.1914),* were German spies who, sent to pose as refugees, were captured at bayonet point soon after landing in Britain by submarine in September 1940. Meier had aroused suspicion after trying to get a drink out of pub hours. They were equipped with radio transmitters, and large amounts of Sterling. Their mission was to send back as much information as they could about the war effort.

As civilians, they were tried together in a court, but van den Kieboom, a Dutch citizen born in Japan, and known as a petty criminal in Holland, entered an appeal, which though later withdrawn, led to his execution being delayed a week beyond the double hanging of Meier and Waldeerg.

Read: True Detective, May 99

24 December 1940	Durham gaol	*T.Pierrepoint*

540

Edward SCOLLER	**42**

Stabbed:	**Beatrice Barbara Scoller**, *35, his wife, on 12 August 1940, in Middlesbrough, N.Yorks.*
Motive:	*Vengeance; drink related.*

Scoller, *(b.1898),* and his wife appeared to have a happy enough relationship, until they argued in July 1939 over some furniture which Beatrice sold to her brother. The following spring, they argued again over money which had not yet been paid by her brother, and on both occasions Beatrice had briefly walked out on Edward for a few days.

On 31 July, there was a further disagreement over money and their son's attempts to find a job, and this time Beatrice left her husband again.

Scoller got very drunk on 12 August, and, seeing his wife in the street, asked her to come back home. When Beatrice said that getting a new house was a condition, Scoller stabbed her. He went home, slashed his wrists and hanged himself. He remained in hospital for five weeks, and the jury took 65 minutes debating his fate.

Read: And May The Lord Have Mercy On Your Soul

Executions in the Channel Isles

During the German occupation, *July 1940-May 1945*, the number of foreign workers executed by the Germans is unknown. Many hundreds died, mainly from exhaustion, but also from beatings. The line between murder and execution is, in these circumstances, so blurred that, were accurate figures available, they would, in any circumstances, be meaningless.

It is known that several German soldiers were executed for offences including desertion and stealing food, largely towards the end of the occupation. No Channel Islands subjects were executed by the German authorities.

1941

total: **15**

541	11 Feb	Clifford HOLMES	25		Strangeways
542	6 Mar	Henry WHITE	39		Durham
543	9 Apr	Samuel MORGAN	28	*Irish*	Walton
544	9 Jul	George ARMSTRONG	39		Wandsworth
545	24 Jul	David JENNINGS	21		Dorchester
546	31 Jul	Edward ANDERSON	19		Durham
547	6 Aug	Karl DRUCKE	25	*German*	Wandsworth
548	6 Aug	Robert PETTER	34	*German*	Wandsworth
549	4 Sep	John SMITH	32		Strangeways
550	19 Sep	Eli RICHARDS	45		Winson Green
551	31 Oct	Antonio MANCINI	39		Pentonville
552	12 Nov	Lionel WATSON	30		Pentonville
553	3 Dec	John SMITH	21		Wandsworth
554	10 Dec	Karel RICHTER	29	*German*	Wandsworth
555	23 Dec	Thomas THORPE	61		Leicester

11 February 1941   Strangeways prison, Manchester

541

Clifford HOLMES   25

Shot/ stabbed: ***Irene Holmes**, 23, his wife, on 10 October 1940, in Manchester, Lancs.*
Motive: *Vengeance; drink related.*

      Holmes, *(b.1916),* was a soldier with the Royal Engineers, who had seen service in Palestine and had been involved in the Dunkirk evacuation. While he was stationed in Aldershot, his wife and two children lived in Longsight, Manchester, the separation giving Holmes' time to dwell on his wife's possible unfaithfulness. Four times he wrote to Irene so accusing her, using foul language. Eventually, falsely accused, Irene applied for a separation order and moved from the family home.
      On 5 October, Holmes took compassionate leave to sort out the marital problems, and Irene's order was granted three days later. On 9 October, finding her lodgings, he punched Irene, leaving her with a black eye, and she sought legal advice.

But the following night at 8.45, having drunk four pints, and armed with his rifle, Holmes went back shooting the lock off Irene's door. He fired five more shots, hitting his wife three times in the arm and twice in the trunk, stabbing her five times with his bayonet. He claimed the rifle jammed when he tried to shoot himself. With his children screaming, he then lifted her on to a sofa, where he tried to reach into her chest wound to remove the bullet, and fondled her beneath her skirt. Two doctors suggested early signs of schizophrenia, or sexual obsession and neurosis.

Read: Murderous Manchester

6 March 1941   Durham gaol   *T.Pierrepoint*

542

Henry Lyndo WHITE   **39**

Cut throat of: ***Emily Wardle**, 34, on 19 January 1941, in South Shields, Co Durham*
Motive: *Sexual rivalry.*

White, *(b.1902)*, an unemployed labourer, had a wife, Annie, who was blissfully unaware that for the past seven years her husband had had a mistress. His mistress, Emily Wardle, whom he visited at her parents' home three days a week, was blissfully unaware that he was married. But when White thought that Emily was perhaps seeing another man, his pride could not stand that he should be two-timed. He stopped Emily coming from her mother's, grabbed her by the coat and started hitting her in the face.
A passing 17 year-old, William Elliot, intervened, and though Emily begged him to take her to her grandmother's house, White became calmer and told him there was nothing to worry about. As William walked on, White cut Emily's throat with a razor. Running back, William escorted Emily to a seat in a shop, where White turned up and cut his own throat and wrist. He was later treated for superficial wounds. Emily died in the shop.

Read: Murderous Tyneside

9 April 1941 Walton gaol, Liverpool *T.Pierrepoint/ Morris*

543

Samuel MORGAN 28 *Irish*

Strangled: **Mary Hagan**, *15, on 2 November 1940, in Liverpool, Lancs.*
Motive: *Sexual.*

Morgan, *(b.1913)*, was a soldier posted with the Irish Guards to the Seaforth barracks in Liverpool. Just before seven on the evening of 2 November, he met Mary Hagan, who had nipped out to buy a newspaper. He took her to a concrete blockhouse, an invasion fortification, and there raped and strangled her with his bare hands. In an agitated state, he then went and had a drink in a pub.

Near the body was found a piece of bandage containing ointment only issued to military personnel. When questioned at the barracks, Morgan was found to have a cut thumb, his sister later testifying that she had dressed it in just such a bandage. Soil found on Morgan's uniform matched that on the blockhouse floor. He was detained by police on 15 November, and charged with Mary's murder.

Read: Master Detective Summer Special 90.

9 July 1941 Wandsworth prison, London *T.Pierrepoint/ Wade*

544

George Johnson ARMSTRONG 39

Crime: **Espionage.**

Armstrong, *(b.1902)*, a communist from Newcastle, had served as a ship's engineer for Britain between 1939 and 1940, before going to the USA in 1941. There, he offered his services to the German consul, and it was arranged for him to travel back to the UK, to spy on British shipping movements. He was arrested soon after arriving by tanker in Cardiff. His trial in camera lasted one day.

Read: True Detective, May 99

24 July 1941   Dorchester prison

545

David Miller JENNINGS   21

Shot: **Albert Farley**, 65, on 26 January 1941, in Dorchester,
                Dorset.
Motive: *Financial; drink related.*

      Jennings, *(b.1920)*, had joined the army in 1938, and had been evacuated from Dunkirk in May 1940. Stationed at Dorchester, Jennings received a letter from his fiancee, telling him the relationship was over, and went out on a pub crawl.
      Late at night he sneaked out of camp with his rifle, telling a mate that he was going to commit a robbery. First he broke into an office, but in trying to shoot open a safe, all he got was a cut face from flying metal. He then went to the NAAFI, where he was confronted by the nightwatchman, Albert Farley. Jennings shot him, and stepped over the body to take the petty cash box. He owned up to the crime back at the barracks. His was the last execution at Dorchester.

Read: And May The Lord Have Mercy On Your Soul

31 July 1941   Durham gaol   *T.Pierrepoint*

546

Edward Walter ANDERSON   19

Bludgeoned: **William Anderson**, 63, on 11 June 1941, near Durham.
Motive: *Financial.*

      Anderson, *(b.1922)*, was a porter at a Tynemouth hotel until March 1941, after which he went to Hull to seek work. His blind great-uncle, William Anderson, lived with a nephew in Belmont, and was known by all the family to keep his money upstairs at home.
      After 7am, William was left alone at home, and Edward called, axing the old man by the front door. As well as cash, Edward Anderson escaped with some personal belongings. William was discovered by his housekeeper who arrived at 10am, and died eight days later. His shoes, macintosh and pen were found in Edward's lodgings.

Read: And May The Lord Have Mercy On Your Soul

6 August 1941   Wandsworth prison, London

                                                     T/ A.Pierrepoint/ Kirk/ Cross

547, 548

Karl Theodore DRUCKE	**25**	*German*	*(aka Francois de Deeker)*
Robert PETTER	**34**	*German*	*(aka Werner Henrich Walti)*

Crime: **Espionage.**

         Drucke, *(b.1916)*, a successful businessman in Germany, and Petter, *(b.1907)*, were parachuted by seaplane onto the coast near Banff at the beginning of June 1941, and separated to make their ways south to begin their spying missions. One made it only twenty miles before being arrested on Portgordon station. He was found to be carrying a radio, a pistol, money and a German sausage. His compatriot got as far as Edinburgh. They were tried together at the Old Bailey in June 1941.

        Read: True Detective, May 99

4 September 1941   Strangeways prison, Manchester   *T.Pierrepoint*

549

John SMITH   **32**

Shot: **Margaret Ellen Knight**, *28, on 18 May 1941, in Whitworth, Lancs.*

Motive: *Vengeance.*

         Smith, *(b.1909)*, was a member of the home guard, and Margaret Knight, his girlfriend since November 1940, was in the Salvation Army. By March, Margaret was pregnant, and though Smith was keen to marry her, Margaret cooled the relationship. They still occasionally saw each other, but Smith was unable to rekindle Margaret's feelings. He followed her as she walked home at 3pm, from an army meeting, and from behind he was seen raising his rifle and aiming at his ex-girlfriend. The single bullet he fired passed right through Margaret's body and killed her almost instantly. Smith told police he had aimed over her head.

        Read: And May The Lord Have Mercy On Your Soul

T.Pierrepoint/ Cross

550

Eli RICHARDS   45

Bludgeoned: *Jane Turner, 64, on 29 March 1941, in Birmingham, Warwicks.*
Motive: *Sexual; drink related.*

Richards, *(b.1896)*, divorced and illiterate, had served in the army from 1915-18, being injured at Ypres, and had enlisted again in 1940, receiving a leg wound in France which had resulted in a limp ever since. He had a long-standing drink problem, but held down a job at ICI.

Jane Turner, separated from her husband for two years, had been thrown out of her lodgings on 27 March for persistent drunkenness, and the following evening was seen by witnesses drinking in a pub with Richards and then boarding a tram with him. Two Home Guard patrolmen spoke to the couple at Bournville after they had heard Jane scream at 11.30pm.

Some time later, following an argument over beer, Richards battered Jane about the head with either his walking stick or a beer bottle, also fracturing her ribs. An attempt at rape was unsuccessful. Jane was found on the pavement at 4.45 the next morning, naked from the waist down, her knickers and false teeth lying nearby. At her foot was a broken bottle-neck, and a walking stick. Richards at first denied being with the woman, but later stated that he had left her without harming her. He had scratches to his face, and pieces of glass in his underpants. The jury took 35 minutes to convict.

Read: Murderous Birmingham

31 October 1941   Pentonville prison, London   *A.Pierrepoint / Wade*

551

Antonio MANCINI   39

Stabbed: *Harry Distleman, 36, on 1 May 1941, in London W1.*
Motive: *Vengeance.*

Babe Mancini, *(b.1902)*, was a London gangster who ran a club in Wardour Street. On 20 April he barred two men who had been involved in a fight. The pair, Scarface Distleman, who had six convictions for assault, and Edward Fletcher, returned eleven days later, and chased Mancini upstairs.

The fight between them in the snooker hall of a neighbouring club involved billiard cues and balls, chairs and knives. With forty people present, Fletcher was stabbed in the wrist, and Distleman beneath the left armpit, severing an artery. He died after staggering outside into the street. Mancini claimed it was self-defence, but the witnesses refuted that. His appeal went to the House of Lords, but was rejected. Smiling before being led out, his last word on the scaffold was, 'Cheerio'.

Read: *Murders of the Black Museum*

12 November 1941   Pentonville prison, London   *T.Pierrepoint/ Critchell*

552

Lionel Rupert Nathan WATSON   30

Poisoned:	***1 Phyllis Elizabeth Crocker****, 28, and her daughter,*
	2 Eileen Alice Crocker*, 18 mths, on 20 May 1941,*
	in Greenford, Middlesex.
Motive:	*To clear impediment.*

Watson, *(b.1911)*, a bakelite moulder, was married, but separated, with four children. In the spring of 1940 he met Phyllis Crocker, who had moved to Greenford with her daughter and elderly mother at the outbreak of war. Watson moved in with them, and after the death of Phyllis' mother in November, married her, telling her that his divorce had come through. It had not.

In April 1941 Phyllis found she was pregnant, and within a month she and her daughter were dead, poisoned by cyanide. Watson buried them in a shallow grave in the garden by the coal-shed. A neighbour, alerted by Watson's attention to the flagstones, and the disappearance of mother and child, alerted the police. They were found on June 30. Watson claimed he had found the two dead in the kitchen, and buried them, afraid that his bigamy would be discovered.

Watson had access to cyanide at work, he had tried to cash Phyllis' savings certificate, and had withdrawn money from her account. Furthermore, he was found to have been dating a 17-year old from his factory since Phyllis' death. The jury returned their verdict after twenty minutes.

Read: *Master Detective, Oct 95*

3 December 1941   Wandsworth prison, London   *A.Pierrepoint/ Harry Allen*

553

John Ernest SMITH   21

Stabbed: ***Christina Rose Dicksee**, 24, on 29 October 1941, in London SE1.*
Motive: *Vengeance.*

Smith, *(b.1920),* and Christina were very much in love. While she was away on holiday, he wrote nine letters a day to her, and her correspondence reciprocated his feelings. The two became engaged in April 1941, with the blessing of both sets of parents, though hers advised waiting a while, mainly because of the war's uncertainties. Smith became convinced they were trying to split up the couple, and suspected Christina might cool towards him. When she came to his home, he stabbed her 34 times.

Read: And May The Lord Have Mercy On Your Soul

10 December 1941   Wandsworth prison, London   *A.Pierrepoint/ Wade*

554

Karel Richard RICHTER   29   *Czech*   *(aka Fred Snyder)*

Crime: **Espionage.**

Richter, *(b.1912),* a strongly-built ethnic German, at 6ft 4in and 15 stones, had parachuted into Britain near London Colney, Herts on 13 May 1941. For 24 hours he had hidden in a copse, burying his parachute and flying gear, and emerging at dusk in a suit and overcoat, bearing a food package and £600 and $6000 in cash. He had hidden his radio set in the copse for later retrieval.

He had hardly covered 400 metres when a passing lorry driver stopped to ask directions. When the German refused to help, the driver reported the man to a police constable, and he was arrested less than a mile from his landing point. He was convicted after a four-day closed trial.

As the hangman arrived to take him to his death, the spy dived head first into the cell wall, and then had to be subdued by four warders. Breaking his wrist-straps he again broke free, having to be subdued again. On the scaffold, he jumped as the trap opened, and the noose caught him under the nose as he fell, breaking his neck nevertheless. His executioner described the events as his toughest session on the scaffold.

Read: True Detective, May 99

23 December 1941　　　　Leicester prison　　　　*T/ A.Pierrepoint*

555

Thomas William THORPE　　61

Cut throat of:　　**Nellie Thorpe**, *47, his wife, on 14 July 1941, in Leicester.*
Motive:　　　　　*Sexual rivalry.*

　　　Thorpe, *(b.1880),* had married Nellie in 1915, but she had left him in March 1941, after he had become violent, kicking her once. He accused her of going with other men, and at 5.30pm he came up behind her as she walked home from work with some friends. He cut Nellie's throat with a razor, and then his own.

Read: And May The Lord Have Mercy On Your Soul

1941 Execution by Firing Squad

14 August 1941   Tower of London

<u>Josef JAKOBS</u>   **43**   *German*

Crime: ***Espionage***

   Jakobs, *(b.1898),* a naturalised German, born in Luxemburg, was a non-commissioned officer sent to monitor weather conditions to assist bombing raids. He was equipped with a transmitter, a pistol and £500 cash. Parachuted into Ramsey Hollow, Hunts on 31 January 1941, he broke his ankle and was quickly apprehended by two farm workers, and arrested by the Home Guard after only twelve hours in Britain. As a serving officer, he was tried by court-martial and sentenced to be shot, strapped in a chair. His was Britain's last execution by firing squad.

   Read: Shot in the Tower.

1941 Executions in Ireland

7 January 1941	Mountjoy gaol, Dublin

Daniel DOHERTY   29

Bludgeoned: **Hannah Mary Doherty**, *30, on 19 April 1940, in Ardmalin, Co Donegal*
Motive: *To eliminate impediment*

Doherty, *(b. 1912)*, an illiterate farmer, lived with his 44 year old American wife and his aged mother, near Malin Head, two minutes walk from the home of his second cousin. Hannah, unmarried at 30, was not the virgin her parents assumed. She had already given birth to one child, and in 1940 found herself pregnant again. She had secret liaisons with Daniel at a nearby widow's house, and both had sought advice on procuring an abortion.

On 19 April Hannah took an evening walk to meet her lover on the hillside at Ireland's most northerly point. They smoked several cigarettes together before Daniel strangled her, and hit her sixteen times on the face and head with a rock. He carried her body 120 metres to hide her in furze bushes. Her father discovered her body the next day. Police found blood on Daniel's trousers and discovered he had been lying about the clothes he had been wearing. Some garments were found burned. The defence depended on showing insanity, but the jury found him guilty after 90 minutes' deliberation.

Read: Master Detective, Oct 96.

23 April 1941	Mountjoy gaol, Dublin	*T./ A. Pierrepoint*

Henry GLEESON   38

Shot: **Mary McCarthy**, *39, on 21 November 1940, in Marlhill, Co Tipperary*
Motive: *To clear impediment*

Moll McCarthy farmed her land near New Inn, and had a reputation as a loose woman, seducing many of the local men, and provoking the hatred of most of the village wives. Never married, and the mother of seven children, she had at one time suffered a burned roof in retaliation for her offences.

She was found shot twice in the face on the morning of 21 November, and police arrested her unmarried neighbour, Henry Gleeson, *(b.1903)*, accusing him of fathering one of Moll's children. Gleeson managed his uncle's farm, and was charged with murder after his cousin, Tommy Reid, had been held by police for thirteen hours and severely beaten.

Not knowing whether Moll had been murdered that morning or the previous evening, the police seemed to adjust the evidence to fit Gleeson's conviction, which they secured after a jury retirement of over two hours. The jury, however, seemed unsure, for they added a strong recommendation to mercy.

Read: Murder at Marlhill

1942

total: **19**

556	30 Jan	Arthur PEACH	23			Winson Green
557	11 Mar	Harold TREVOR	62			Wandsworth
558	25 Mar	David WILLIAMS	33			Walton
559	15 Apr	Cyril JOHNSON	20			Wandsworth
560	30 Apr	Frederick AUSTIN	28			Bristol
561	1 May	Harold HILL	26			Oxford Castle
562	24 Jun	Douglas EDMONDSON	29			Walton
563	25 Jun	Gordon CUMMINS	28			Wandsworth
564	7 Jul	Jose KEY	34	*Gibraltarian*		Wandsworth
565	7 Jul	Alphonse TIMMERMAN	28	*Belgian*		Wandsworth
566	21 Jul	Arthur ANDERSON	52	*Greek*		Wandsworth
567	10 Sep	George SILVEROSA	23			Pentonville
568	10 Sep	Sam DASHWOOD	22			Pentonville
569	10 Sep	Harold MERRY	40			Winson Green
570	6 Oct	Patrick KINGSTON	38			Wandsworth
571	28 Oct	William COLLINS	21			Durham
572	3 Nov	Duncan SCOTT-FORD	21			Wandsworth
573	6 Nov	Herbert BOUNDS	42			Wandsworth
574	31 Dec	Johannes DRONKERS	46	*Dutch*		Wandsworth

30 January 1942   Winson Green prison, Birmingham

T.Pierrepoint/ Critchell

556

Arthur PEACH   23

Shot:	***Kitty Lyon**, 18, on 21 September 1941, near Walsall, Staffs.*
Motive:	*Financial*

Kitty Lyon, whose father had recently died, and her best friend Violet Richards went for a Sunday stroll blackberrying at Rushall outside Walsall. Private Peach, *(b.1919)*, 5'7", a signaller, had gone absent from his unit in Devon with a stolen revolver, and was staying with his parents in Walsall.

At 11am the two young women passed Peach on the path by a railway tunnel. As they walked away Peach, determined to steal the handbag Kitty carried, shot and hit Violet in the back. Kitty ran off but was caught by Peach who shot her behind the right ear. He returned to Violet, hitting her with the gun butt as she lay on the ground. She received twelve wounds to the head, fracturing her skull, both forearms were broken and two teeth knocked out. He made off with the bag and the 15/- it held.

The incident was witnessed by a teenage boy who, with Violet, gave a description of the soldier involved. The weapon was found in a ditch and was traced to Peach's unit. Peach was arrested at his parents' home at 2.30am the following night and was identified by the survivor, but still insisted that he had been with another soldier who was responsible. He made no confession before his death.

Read: True Crime, Jan 98

---

11 March 1942   Wandsworth prison, London   *A.Pierrepoint/ Morris*

557

Harold Dorian TREVOR   62

Bludgeoned/ strangled: ***Theodora Jessie Greenhill**, 65, on 14 October 1941, in London W14.*
Motive: *Financial.*

Trevor, *(b.1880),* was an extreme recidivist, spending 41 of the last 42 years in prison, on charges of theft and fraud - he had never committed a violent crime. He had again just been released when he answered an advertisement about a flat to let. Mrs Greenhill, the widow of an army Major, her second husband, lived alone in Elsham road, west Kensington, and was letting her home in order to escape war-torn London.

Trevor called on her on 14 October, and gave her a deposit on the rent. As she sat at her desk and began to write the receipt, Trevor hit her over the back of the head with a beer bottle, which shattered on impact. He strangled the old woman with a ligature, and placed a handkerchief over her face. He stole £5 and some jewellery and left. Mrs Greenhill was found later by her daughter. Trevor pawned two of her rings, but had left fingerprints, and his own name on the receipt. He was later arrested in Rhyl. It is thought Trevor had wanted to be caught, so unused was he to life outside prison.

Read: Murders of the Black Museum

436

558

David Roger WILLIAMS   33

Traumatised: ***Elizabeth Smith***, *28, on 30 November 1941, in Morecambe, Lancs.*
Motive: *Sexual rivalry.*

Williams, *(b.1909)*, an aircraftsman, and his girlfriend Elizabeth Smith, were very fond of each other, but his obsession with her went way beyond her feelings for him. He went from his lodgings to meet her at 5.45pm, and the two argued, apparently over a soldier whom she had been seeing.

Passing over a bridge, Williams hit her, catapulting her into the river below, and, standing in the water himself, held Elizabeth's head under until she struggled no more. She managed to stragger to get help, but died on 2 December from complications due to shock and pneumonia.

Read: And May The Lord Have Mercy On Your Soul

15 April 1942   Wandsworth prison, London   *T.Pierrepoint/ Critchell*

559

Cyril JOHNSON   20

Bludgeoned/ strangled: ***Maggie Smail***, *29, on 6 February 1942, in Ashford, Kent.*
Motive: *Vengeance.*

Johnson, *(b.1922)*, was a soldier in the West Yorkshire regiment, who had been dumped by his fiancee in October 1941, after which he developed a mistrust, indeed, hatred of women. He met Maggie Smail the following month, and the two went to dances together, becoming good friends, rather than lovers.

On 5 February, the two returned rather late, and Johnson was invited to spend the night on the sofa at Maggie's home, which she shared with her sister. The following morning, Johnson battered her with a poker as she lay in bed, and strangled her with her scarf. She was found wearing only her pyjama top. He wrote to his former fiancee confessing, saying that both women had teased him. Johnson was recommended to mercy on account of his youth.

Read: And May The Lord Have Mercy On Your Soul

30 April 1942   Horfield gaol, Bristol

560

Frederick James AUSTIN   28

Shot: *Lilian Dorothy Austin, 22, his wife, on 31 January 1942, in Bristol, Gloucs.*
Motive: *To clear impediment.*

Austin, *(b.1914),* and his wife Lilian lived in Colchester, until he was stationed in Bristol, where Lilian took lodgings to be near him. There was, however, another woman in the soldier's life, and Lilian found a letter from her rival in Austin's kitbag on 28 January.

Several arguments followed, until, three days later, as Lilian was sitting by the fire darning, Austin shot her with his rifle. He rushed to tell Lilian's landlady that there had been an accident, that he had not known the gun was loaded, but the jury did not give him the benefit of that doubt, though he was recommended to mercy.

Read: And May The Lord Have Mercy On Your Soul.

1 May 1942   Oxford Castle

561

Harold HILL   26

Stabbed: *1 Doreen Joyce Hearne, 8, and*
              2 Kathleen Trendle, 6, on 19 November 1941, near Penn, Bucks.
Motive: *Sadistic pleasure.*

438

Hill, *(b.1916),* from Yoxford, Suffolk, was a private in the Royal Artillery, who had two previous convictions for assaults on young girls. On 19 November 1941, Doreen Hearne and Kathleen Trendle were leaving school in the village of Penn, when Hill offered them a ride in an army lorry. Other children saw him and one remembered the number of the lorry.

He drove the girls four miles to Rough Wood and strangled them to unconsciousness. He then stabbed Doreen six times in the chest, and three times in the neck, Kathleen receiving eleven stab wounds in her neck. There was no sexual assault, and Hill's motive is unknown.

At the scene where the bodies were found 40 metres apart three days later, Hill had left a handkerchief bearing a laundry mark, and fingerprints on Doreen's gas mask container. Tyre marks near the bodies matched with those on the identified lorry, and Hill was arrested. Blood was found on his uniform. A defence plea of schizophrenia was rejected.

Read: Murder Squad, p147

---

24 June 1942   Walton gaol, Liverpool

562

Douglas EDMONDSON   29

Strangled: *Imeldred Maria Osliff, 28, on 7 February 1942, in Southport, Lancs.*
Motive: *Vengeance.*

Edmondson, *(b. 1913),* had travelled to New Zealand as an apprentice boatman at 16, and had joined the navy in 1933. From the age of 17 he and Imeldred had been lovers. During the war he had seen active service in Shanghai and Dunkirk, and had been bombed on the *Ark Royal* and injured in the blitz.

As a stoker Petty Officer, he had a good record. Edmondson had asked Imeldred to marry him several times, but was always refused. He claimed that they had last been intimate in December 1940, before which she had had a miscarriage, and he had tried to cut his wrists. He increasingly fantasised and told pointless lies.

Edmondson met another nurse in August 1941, marrying her after a swift elopement. Imeldred became jealous and wrote many letters to both Douglas and his wife. The two arranged to meet on 7 February and went for a drink. In a park he had asked her for some money. He said she became angry and abusive, and that in a rage he had strangled her. Her naked body was found the following morning.

439

Edmondson was arrested in Birmingham two days later. Admitting the killing, he relied on a plea of insanity, which the jury rejected inside 20 minutes.

Read: Master Detective, Apr 96

25 June 1942   Wandsworth prison, London   *A.Pierrepoint/ Kirk*

563

Gordon Frederick CUMMINS   28   *C*

Probably strangled:	**1 Maple Church**, 19, in October 1941, in London NW1
	2 Mrs Humphries, in October 1941
Strangled:	**3 Evelyn Margaret Hamilton**, 40, on 8 February 1942, in London W1
	4 Evelyn Oatley, 35, on 8 February 1942, in London W1
	5 Margaret Florence Lowe, 43, on 11 February 1942, in London W1
	6 Doris Jouannet, 33, on 13 February 1942, in London W2.
Motive:	*Financial.*

Cummins, *(b.1914),* a Yorkshireman, married in 1936, but had no children, and was in aircrew training with the RAF, billeted in St Johns Wood. He had a history of losing jobs through dishonesty. During the blackout, he would frequent west end pubs and clubs, picking up prostitutes or women willing to have a good time with servicemen while their husbands were away. His motive for murder was money.

Cummins met Evelyn Hamilton, a chemist's assistant, in the early evening of 8 February. She worked in Essex, but was in London en route to her home in Newcastle. Taking her to an air-raid shelter in Montagu Place, Cummins strangled her and stole her bag containing £80. There was no sexual assault.

Later the same evening, he picked up Evelyn Oatley, a former chorus-line girl, and prostitute, also known as Nita Ward. In her flat in Wardour Street, he strangled her with a silk stocking and cut her throat. Before leaving, he used a tin-opener to severely mutilate her genitals. He left the weapon, bearing his fingerprints, at the scene.

Three days later he went home with another prostitute, Margaret Lowe. At her home in Gosfield Street, he again used a silk stocking to

440

strangle her, and then mutilated her genitals with a razor blade and a knife. She was later found by her daughter.

The following day, 12 February, he attempted to strangle two women. Greta Haywood had run when he tried to kiss her. When interrupted in his strangulation, he fled leaving behind his gas mask. A little later, Mrs Mulcahy screamed when he attacked, and again he fled, this time leaving his belt.

The following day, he met Doris Jouannet, the wife of a hotel manager in Sussex Gardens. Also known as Doris Robson, she often entertained servicemen while her husband was out. Cummins again strangled and mutilated in his familiar way, leaving Doris' husband to find her.

The gas mask and belt led police to Cummins, who was found to have stolen items in his possession, and to match fingerprints left near his victims - Cummins was left-handed. He was arrested on 16 February. His wife believed his insistent claims of innocence, but the jury convicted him in thirty minutes. The two earlier murders were later attributed to him.

Read: *Murders of the Black Museum*

7 July 1942   Wandsworth prison, London
                                          A.Pierrepoint/ Kirk/ Wade/ Critchell

564

<u>**Jose Estella KEY**</u>   **34**   *Gibraltarian*

Crime: **Espionage.**

Key, *(b.1908),* as a Gibraltarian, was a British subject, who spied for Germany and Franco on the Rock, reporting movements of all forces. When he was arrested, he had lists of various ship movements, and was suffering from syphilis.

He was sent to London for a four-day trial in May 1942. He was hanged with the Belgian spy, Alphonse Timmerman.

Read: *True Detective, May 99*

441

7 July 1942   Wandsworth prison, London

A.Pierrepoint/ Kirk/ Wade/ Critchell

565

Alphonse Louis Eugene TIMMERMAN   **28**   *Belgian*

Crime: **Espionage.**

    Timmerman, *(b.1914),* as a ship's steward before the war, had visited many British ports. His experience was particularly useful when he offered his services as a spy to Germany. He was sent to Glasgow in the autumn of 1941, posing as a refugee. When arrested, Timmerman was carrying a great deal of British and American currency, and had invisible ink. He was hanged with the Gibraltarian spy, Jose Key.

    Read: True Detective, May 99

21 July 1942   Wandsworth prison, London

566

Arthur ANDERSON   **52**   *Greek*   *(real name: Apergis)*

Shot: ***Pauline Barker**, 45, on 31 May 1942, in London NW6.*
Motive: *Vengeance; drink related.*

    Pauline Barker had twice been married when she moved in with Anderson, *(b.1890),* but arguments soon followed, mainly because he would not help around the place, and because he claimed Pauline's mother hated him. He hit Pauline, and threatened to shoot her, but by 27 May, after she had gone to a party without him, he had had enough, and he moved out of their lodgings, and went to his parents.
    At 1pm on 31 May, Anderson went to see Pauline briefly, and then went to the pub. After much drinking, at 7pm he returned to Pauline's flat, and shot her in the kitchen. He returned to the pub, handed his revolver to the landlord, and was arrested there at 7.45pm.

    Read: And May The Lord Have Mercy On Your Soul

10 September 1942   Pentonville prison, London
A.Pierrepoint/ Wade/ Morris/ Kirk
567, 568

George William SILVEROSA   23
Samuel Sydney DASHWOOD   22

Bludgeoned: *Leonard Moules, 71, on 30 April 1942, in London EC2.*
Motive: *Financial.*

  Dashwood, *(b.1920),* and Silverosa, *(b.1919),* a machinist from Pitsea in Essex, were two ex-Borstal boys. Dashwood had stolen a revolver, and one afternoon in April 1942 they met in a cafe and decided on a robbery.
  At 1 p.m. they burst into Leonard Moules jewellery shop on Hackney Road, Bethnal Green, as the old man was closing up. Dashwood felled the owner with a blow from the revolver, and battered him across the head four more times as he lay on the floor. He silenced Mr Moules' barking dog with a blow between the eyes. Silverosa, meanwhile, robbed the safe of a number of rings. Mr Moules died nine days later in hospital without regaining consciousness.
  The police found that a soldier had seen the two with the gun in the cafe, and had overheard their names mentioned in their conversation. Silverosa, whose palmprint was found on the safe, immediately confessed his part, blaming Dashwood for the killing. Three days before his execution, Silverosa injured two warders by attacking them with a poker.

  Read: Murder Squad, p155.

10 September 1942   Winson Green prison, Birmingham
T.Pierrepoint/ Critchell
569

Harold Oswald MERRY   40

Drowned: *Joyce Dixon, 27, on 29 March 1942, in Birmingham, Warwicks.*
Motive: *To clear impediment*

  Merry, *(b.1902),* was an aircraft inspector who lived in Redditch with his wife Florence and their five children. The couple had been married 17 years when Merry began an affair with a typist at his works, Joyce Dixon. Joyce seemed to have overcome the mental health problems which had affected her from 1931 to 1938. Mrs Merry found out about the two-month liaison in September and threw her husband out.

In March 1942 he took Joyce to a London hotel in the hope of speeding up a divorce, but after Joyce's mother found out Harold was married, the pair had to continue meeting in secret.

On 29 March they took a walk and discussed the situation they both regarded as hopeless. They decided on a suicide pact, and wrote a note to that effect which they both signed. In a field at the back of Joyce's home, Merry strangled Joyce with his tie, and dragged her unconscious to a pond into which he dumped her. He tried to strangle himself, but kept coming round when he hit the water. He went to his wife's house, telling her that he had fallen in a river, and she allowed him to have a bath. When Joyce failed to return home, her brother went to the Merry house, and found Harold there trying to strangle himself with an electric flex.

Read: Murderous Birmingham

6 October 1942   Wandsworth prison, London   *A.Pierrepoint/ Morris*

570

Patrick William KINGSTON   **38**

Strangled: ***Sheila Margaret Wilson**, 11, on 15 July 1942, in London SE13.*
Motive: *Sadistic pleasure.*

Kingston, *(b.1904)*, had a mutilated left hand, and walked with a limp since being caught in a bomb blast in November 1940. He lodged a few doors away from the Wilson family, to where Sheila had returned from her evacuation in Dorset in May 1942.

Kingston had asked Sheila to come out later and run an errand for him, and at 8.20pm, after having her dinner, she left, her mother assuming a neighbour had asked her to run to the shop. Kingston took her to his room where he strangled her with cord, leaving her body beneath trhe floorboards. She was found there on 20 July. Kingston pleaded guilty.

Read: And May The Lord Have Mercy On Your Soul

571

William Ambrose COLLINS   21

Bludgeoned: ***Margaret Mary Rice***, *23, on 13 June 1942, in Newcastle,*
                    Northumberland
Motive: *Sexual; drink related.*

Collins, *(b.1921)*, a slim, good-looking merchant navy apprentice, described by a doctor as vain, conceited and effeminate, had been out drinking on 12 June when he came across Mrs Rice walking on Newcastle's Town Moor at about midnight. Margaret Liell, a WAAF corporal, and her husband, Patrick Rice, an army officer, had been married in April 1942, and had stayed in lodgings during his two-day embarkation leave. She had seen him off on his train and was walking home.

Collins smashed her in the face four times with his revolver butt, from which pieces were broken off, stripped her from the waist down, raped her and dumped her body on a grass verge behind some road repairs. He returned to the body at 2am to steal various objects, including a watch, gloves and a compact, but had then cast them away in drains on his way home.

When Margaret was found at 8.40am, the trail led virtually to his door, and the broken and bloody rifle was found in his lodgings. Collins could offer no explanation other than madness and drunkenness. The jury found him guilty within twenty minutes.

Read: Master Detective, Dec 97.

572

Duncan Alexander Croall SCOTT-FORD   21

Crime: ***Espionage***

Scott-Ford, *(b.1921)*, a native of Plymouth, was a merchant seaman on the route between Britain and Lisbon. He had been dismissed from the Royal Navy in 1939 after altering a pay-book. He was approached there by German agents who paid him £18 to pass them information.

After he had done so, they refused to pay more, blackmailing him into working for them, with the threat that they would let the British authorities know of his activities if he refused. When arrested he was found with lists of ship details and movements, and of air cover. He was tried in October 1942.

Read: True Detective, May 99

6 November 1942   Wandsworth prison, London   *T.Pierrepoint/ Critchell*

573

Herbert Hiram BOUNDS   42

Cut throat of: ***Elizabeth Bounds***, *39, his wife, on 21 August 1942, in Croydon, Surrey.*
Motive: *Vengeance.*

Bounds, *(b.1900)*, had married in 1923, but four of the couple's children had died, leaving only a nine-year old daughter. Bounds had not worked since the autumn of 1941, and the family were confined to a single room. Bounds complained of stomach pains, visiting the doctor numerous times, convinced he had cancer.

Elizabeth was at the end of her tether with him, hitting him, and threatening to poison him if he did not stop malingering and get a job. On 21 August, after she had been waving a knife at him, he cut her throat with a razor at 6pm, their daughter running from the room screaming, and Elizabeth collapsing on her way to a doctor. Bounds handed himself to a police officer. He said he could not take any more after all the years of nagging.

Read: And May The Lord Have Mercy On Your Soul

31 December 1942   Wandsworth prison, London   *A.Pierrepoint/ Wade*

574

Johannes Marinus DRONKERS   46   *Dutch*

Crime: **Espionage.**

Dronkers, *(b1896)*, a member of the Dutch nazi party, had worked as a seaman, and then for the post office. Offering his services to the

Germans, he underwent training with the aim of going to England to report on troop movements, especially those of US and Canadian forces.

On 16 May he embarked for Britain in a small yacht, but was picked up by a trawler. He claimed at first to be a Dutch refugee, but later admitted his intentions.

Read: True Detective, May 99

1942 Execution in Ireland

2 September 1942   Crumlin Road Gaol, Belfast   *T./A. Pierrepoint*

THOMAS WILLIAMS   19

Shot: Constable **Patrick Murphy**, *38, on 5 April 1942, in Belfast*
Motive: *To escape arrest*

On Easter Sunday 1942 all nationalist commemorations of the 1916 rising were banned, but a parade was planned, and it was the task of Williams and five other IRA supporters to distract the police in order that it might go ahead.

The six were to fire over the police's heads, pass their weapons to two women, and escape to a safe house. However, the police immediately pursued the gunmen who, with the two women, ran into a house on Cawnpore Street. Police reinforcements surrounded the building. Williams, *(b. 1923)*, drew his gun and opened the back door, only to be confronted by Constable Murphy, a father of nine.

They exchanged shots. Williams was wounded, and Murphy's gun jammed. The other gunmen, Joe Cahill, 19, Henry Gordner, 19, Patrick Simpson, 18, William Perry and John Oliver, all arrived and the policeman was shot five times, once in the head. Twenty policemen forced the men's surrender.

Williams, thinking his wounds would prove fatal, confessed to firing the shots, but all six were charged with murder, the two women with abetting. The jury took just five minutes to determine their guilt. To prevent sectarian trouble, the Northern Ireland government reprieved all but Williams on 31 August. They were released in 1949. Williams went peacefully to his execution, praying continuously.

Read: True Detective, Jan 97.

1943

total: *16*

575	26 Jan	Franciscus WINTER	40	*Belgian*	Wandsworth
576	27 Jan	Harry DOBKIN	49	*Russian*	Wandsworth
577	10 Feb	Ronald ROBERTS	28		Walton
578	24 Mar	William TURNER	19		Pentonville
579	31 Mar	Dudley RAYNER	26	*Burmese*	Wandsworth
580	6 Apr	Gordon TRENOWETH	33		Exeter
581	29 Apr	August SANGRET	29	*Canadian*	Wandsworth
582	10 Jul	Charles RAYMOND	23	*Canadian*	Wandsworth
583	3 Aug	William QUAYLE	52		Winson Green
584	3 Aug	Gerald ROE	41		Pentonville
585	10 Sep	Trevor ELVIN	21		Armley
586	24 Sep	Charles GAUTHIER	25	*Canadian*	Wandsworth
587	19 Nov	Terence CASEY	22		Wandsworth
588	15 Dec	Charles KOOPMAN	23		Pentonville
589	22 Dec	John DORGAN	47		Wandsworth
590	29 Dec	Thomas JAMES	26		Walton

26 January 1943   Wandsworth prison, London   *A.Pierrepoint/ Critchell*

575

Franciscus Johannes WINTER   **40**   *Belgian*

Crime: ***Espionage.***

　　　　Winter, *(b.1902),* from Antwerp, was a ship's steward who posed as a refugee when he landed at Gourock on the Clyde on 31 July 1942, but was detained upon arrival. Carrying £100 in various currencies, his mission was to spy and report on convoy movements.

　　　　Read: True Detective, May 99

Harry DOBKIN   49   *Russian*

Strangled: **Rachel Dubinski**, *47, his wife, on 11 April 1941, in London SW8.*
Motive: *To clear impediment.*

Dobkin, *(b.1894),* and his wife Rachel, both Russian-born Jews, married in 1920, but separated just three days later. Nevertheless, a son was born nine months later, and there began twenty years of hassle for Dobkin. Maintenance orders were placed on him right up until the time his child was twenty years old, and Dobkin was jailed several times for non-payment. His wife also blackmailed him with embarrassing revelations if he did not pay. By 1941, he had had enough.

He was fire-watcher at a chapel in Kennington, and there he strangled his 5' wife, cut off her head and severed her limbs below the knee and elbow joints. Those remains were then partially burned. Her hair, eyes, facial features, hands and feet were all removed to prevent identification, and were never recovered. He buried her in lime beneath a stone slab in the chapel crypt.

The chapel was bombed during the war, and clearance of the site did not begin until July 1942, when a handbag, and then the first bones, were uncovered. Mrs Dobkin was identified by her dental records. The cause of death was established by locating a small broken bone in her neck. Dobkin, by this time a builder, collapsed when the jury gave its verdict of guilty after twenty minutes' consideration, though it did recommend mercy.

Read: Forty Years of Murder, p58.

Ronald ROBERTS   28

Bludgeoned: **Nellie Pearson**, *39, on 5 October 1942, in Barrow-in-Furness, Lancs.*
Motive: *Financial*

Roberts, *(b.1915),* was a shipyard worker who shared a flat in Barrow with Mrs Catherine Worrell and her son Jack, 17. Jack and Catherine had separate bedrooms, and Roberts slept on the sitting room sofa. He missed much time from work owing to his ulcerated legs, and fell into debt, pilfering from club money, for which he acted as treasurer. When the accounts needed to be seen, he took his first opportunity to get some money.

Mrs Pearson, who lived with her husband, daughter and aged mother, called every Monday afternoon to collect money for a mail-order catalogue. Roberts attacked her with a hammer, and stabbed her in the throat as she lay dying. He then put her body into an alcove of Catherine's room behind a camp bed. He claimed to have been out at the cinema when Mrs Pearson called. Three days later, police, making house-to-house calls, searched the flat and found the body. The jury convicted Roberts within 15 minutes.

Read: True Detective, Nov 95.

24 March 1943   Pentonville prison, London   *T.Pierrepoint/ Critchell*

578

William Henry TURNER   **19**

Strangled: ***Ann Elizabeth Wade***, *82, on 2 January 1943, in Colchester, Essex.*
Motive: *Financial.*

Turner, *(b.1924)*, had stolen clothes from lodgings in which he had stayed on 29 December. He moved on to a new room the following day, and on 2 January, called at Ann Wade's house, and offered to do a little gardening for money. He then strangled her as she bent over a chair in her kitchen. Pushing the body under the bed, he stole some cash, returned to his lodgings, stole some belongings from there, and left.

When arrested, he made a full confession, but said the old woman had gone limp as soon as he held her. Turner was found guilty after a retrial, the first jury having failed to agree.

Read: And May The Lord Have Mercy On Your Soul

579

Dudley George RAYNER   26   *Burmese*

Bludgeoned: ***Josephine Rayner****, 19, his wife, on 8 February 1943, in London SE20.*
Motive: *To clear impediment.*

    Rayner, *(b.1917),* a native of Rangoon, was a sergeant in the Pioneer Corps, and had married his compatriot, Josephine Colalucion, a member of the ATS, in August 1942. She went to join her unit in November, and Rayner missed her terribly. In three months they had only one brief meeting, and Rayner began to imagine the temptations his wife may succumb to while separated from him.
    On 6 February, they began a long-awaited leave together near Penge. After breakfast the following morning, as he was cleaning shoes, Rayner, apparently suffering a brainstorm, picked up a hammer and battered his wife to death. He pleaded guilty, and the whole trial lasted a mere nine minutes.

    Read: And May The Lord Have Mercy On Your Soul

580

Gordon Horace TRENOWETH   33

Kicked to death: ***Albert James Bateman****, 61, on 24 December 1942, in Falmouth, Cornwall.*
Motive: *Financial*

    Trenoweth, *(b.1910),* a Falmouth docker, lived at his parents' house with his five children. His wife had been sent to an asylum in January 1941, and Trenoweth had been jailed for not paying his contribution to her welfare. He was freed on 21 November.
    Albert Bateman had been an accountant in Southport before taking his tobacconist shop with his wife. As he was closing up on Christmas Eve, Trenoweth came in, knocked the older man to the ground, and stamped on his head. Mr Bateman drowned in his own blood. About £5 was stolen. A revolver was left on the counter, which bore fibres from Trenoweth's coat. He

was arrested at home at 3.30am on Christmas Day. After the murder, he had gone to Truro to meet a woman friend, and had been free with his money.

Blood was found on his jacket, but not on his shoes, and no fingerprints were on the revolver, but oil from the gun was found in his jacket pocket. His family testified that he could not have been in the shop at the time of the murder. The jury struggled with these variables for two hours, adding a strong recommendation to mercy to their guilty verdict, believing Trenoweth had not intended to kill.

Read: Master Detective Summer Special 88.

29 April 1943   Wandsworth prison, London   *A.Pierrepoint/ Critchell*

581
                                                    •
                                                    i
August SANGRET   29   *Canadian*

Bludgeoned: ***Joan Pearl Wolfe***, *19, on 14*
                    September 1942,
                    near Godalming, Surrey.
Motive: *To clear impediment.*

Sangret, *(b.1913)*, 5'5" and 10 stone, was an illiterate mixed-race Cree from a poor family in Saskatchewan. He served six months for violent assault in 1932, and three months for threatening a married lover in 1938. He also had vagrancy and theft convictions. Sangret had worked as a farm labourer before joining the Regina Rifles in 1940. Physically A1 and of average intelligence, by the time he was shipped to England in March 1942, Sangret had been detained twice for four times going AWOL.

He had first contracted VD in 1930, and by 1942 had been hospitalised five times, urethritis resulting in an obstructed bladder. He had already had three sexual partners in Britain by the time he met Pearl Wolfe in a Godalming pub on 17 July. They first had sex two hours later in a field.

Pearl had first dated soldiers in 1939, and the latest had returned to Canada just two days before. Pearl told Sangret she was pregnant on 30 July. He offered to marry her and had 'Pearl' tattooed on his arm, without questioning whether he was the likely father. He built a wigwam in woods near his base, and overnight they stayed there or in a cricket pavilion, Sangret slipping back into camp at 6am.

Around the 14 September in woods on Hankley Common, Pearl was stabbed three times in the head with a hooked knife, and cut seven times on the forearm as she attempted to defend herself. She ran and tripped, smashing her teeth, and as she lay face down on the earth, was clubbed with a thick birch branch, shattering her skull. She was later dragged 400 metres, and buried face down beneath heather in a shallow grave. Her body was found there by soldiers on exercise on 7 October. The birch branch, still with Pearl's hair attached, was found a short distance away.

Sangret said he last saw Pearl on the morning of 14 September, and had searched for her for days. When the murder weapon was found in a wash-house at his camp, police were convinced. Sangret was charged on 6 December, though no blood was found on his clothes. He declared 'I did not do it. Someone did, but I will have to take the rap'. The jury took two hours considering the evidence, and added a strong recommendation for mercy to their guilty verdict. It has been suggested that Sangret was framed by a guilty fellow serviceman.

Read: The Wigwam Murder

10 July 1943   Wandsworth prison, London   *T.Pierrepoint/ Wade*

582

Charles Arthur RAYMOND   **23**   *Canadian*

Stabbed: ***Marguerite Beatrice Burge,** 22, on 30 January 1943, near Goodwood, Sussex*
Motive: *Sadistic pleasure*

Raymond, *(b.1920),* a French Canadian soldier, had taken a screwdriver from his toolbox and was driving an army lorry when he stopped to offer Marguerite Burge a lift. A WAAF for two years, Marguerite, from Bedhampton, was on her way to a date, and was seen getting into the lorry at 3.40pm. Raymond drove the lorry to a lay-by, where it was seen at 4.15. He stunned Marguerite with a punch to the jaw, then dragged her into a field where he stabbed her with the screwdriver, four times to the head and three times to the trunk, but there was no sexual assault. He signed for some petrol while he was out.

He passed by the same spot the next day with fellow soldier Arthur Patry and they saw the body, though neither reported it for fear of trouble with the army. When the body was found by two home guard men at 12.40pm on 31 January, the screwdriver, a balaclava and a glove were also found. Linked firmly with the crime, Raymond tried to implicate Patry, but his alibi was solid. The jury deliberated for twenty minutes.

Read: Murderous Sussex

583

William QUAYLE   52

Strangled: ***Vera Clark**, 8, on 5 May 1943, in Birmingham, Warwicks.*
Motive: Sexual.

Quayle, *(b.1891),* a works security guard, lived in Ladywood, Birmingham, where he asked Vera Clark to run a message for him on her way home from school. She was last seen delivering him potatoes at 5pm. He stripped, bound and raped the young girl, strangling her with twine. He later took her body in a cart to a bombed out house in Edgbaston, where he buried her beneath a pile of bricks. Quayle was abrupt, denying he had seen Vera, when her parents called round the next day.

When they fetched the police, they found Vera's coat in Quayle's cellar, and her skipping rope down his armchair. He eventually confessed under questioning, and took them to Vera's body, naked but for socks and a single shoe, the twine still holding her wrists and ankles. Quayle claimed to have had a brainstorm, brought on by drink after his wife had left him the previous week. Awaiting trial, Quayle tried to kill himself by swallowing objects. Amongst other items, an open safety pin was removed from his stomach.

Read: Master Detctive, Jul 94

584

Gerald Elphinstone ROE   41

Gassed: ***Elsie Elphinstone Roe**, 43, his wife, on 17 May 1943, in*
      Barnet, Herts.
Motive: Vengeance.

Roe, *(b.1902),* was seen at 6.50am, struggling with his wife, clad only in her pyjamas, outside their house. An hour or so later, he coshed her six times and dragged her to the kitchen where he switched on the gas. He was seen leaving with two suitcases. Neighbours smelled the gas later that morning and the police broke in, finding Elsie already dead. Roe was arrested in Highcliffe, Hants, his clothes still bloody from the attack.

Read: And May The Lord Have Mercy On Your Soul

| 10 September 1943 | Armley gaol, Leeds | *T.Pierrepoint/ Kirk* |

585

Trevor ELVIN   21

Bludgeoned: **Violet Wakefield**, *20, on 4 May 1943, in Barnsley, W.Yorks.*
Motive: *Sexual rivalry.*

Elvin, *(b.1922),* an engineer at a glassworks, had been courting Violet Wakefield for some time, and marriage was considered, when she abruptly told him, on Easter Saturday, that everything was off. He suspected that she had found another suitor, and when they met on 3 May, Elvin and Violet argued, though they agreed to meet again the following morning. They were seen walking together near a fairground at 8am, and shortly after, Elvin battered her to death. He travelled to Otley, and then on to Blackpool where he was arrested.

Read: And May The Lord Have Mercy On Your Soul

| 24 September 1943 | Wandsworth prison, London | *A.Pierrepoint/ Riley* |

586

Charles Eugene GAUTHIER   25   *Canadian*

Shot: **Annette Elizabeth Frederika Christina Pepper**, *30, on 15 March 1943, in Portslade, Sussex.*
Motive: *Sexual rivalry*

Annette Pepper was married with an eight-year old daughter, but since her husband was taken as a prisoner-of-war she had taken several lovers from the contingent of French Canadians stationed near Portslade.

She had had an on-off relationship with sergeant William Rendall since November 1941, but then met Charles Gauthier, *(b.1918),* a married man, in January 1943. Both soldiers were aware of the other's involvement, and when Annette announced in March that she was pregnant, the two met and argued over her. On 15 March she took both men to her home, but there told Gauthier that she loved Rendall. He slapped her and left.

Gauthier stole a bren gun from his camp and returned, firing three bullets through the front door, hitting Rendall in the ankle. He left for help through the back, where Gauthier next took the gun. Promising Annette that he would not fire if she came downstairs, he shot as soon as she appeared, hitting her in the neck. He moved the gun to pump three more shots into her stomach as she lay there.

He was arrested nearby by the home guard. The jury remained deadlocked after an hour, and it took a retrial to declare him guilty, the second jury adding a strong recommendation to mercy after 20 minutes consideration. Annette had been seven weeks pregnant.

Read: Master Detective Summer Special 98

19 November 1943   Wandsworth prison, London   *A.Pierrepoint/ Critchell*

587

Terence CASEY   22

Strangled: **Bridget Nora Mitton**, 45, on 13 July 1943, in London SW15.
Motive: Sexual; drink related.

Casey, *(b.1921),* a private in the Royal Army Medical Corps, was on leave, staying with relatives in Fulham. He spent the evening of 13 July getting drunk in a Putney pub, pestering a barmaid, and then hanging around outside. He followed an Irish woman, Bridget Mitton, when she left the pub at 11pm. Bridget called on a friend on her way home, and resumed her journey, followed again by Casey, at 11.35.

He sexually assaulted her in a garden, removing some of her clothes, and then strangled her. An air-raid warden discovered him with Bridget shortly after the murder had been committed. The jury took 45 minutes to convict Casey, though they added a recommendation to mercy.

Read: And May The Lord Have Mercy On Your Soul

588

Charles William KOOPMAN   23

Bludgeoned: *1 Gladys Lavinia Brewer, 22, and her daughter,*
               2 Shirley Brewer, 2, on 8 September 1943, in London
               W5.
Motive: *Vengeance; drink related.*

Koopman, *(b.1920),* had first met Gladys Brewer in 1938, but the two had separately married, he to Patricia, in 1941. He introduced the two women in 1942. Gladys' husband was away in the navy, and Koopman, an aircraftsman, and Patricia went to stay with Gladys on 5 September. Three days later, after going out for a drink, an argument started when Koopman began to tease Gladys by turning down the light while she was reading.

He battered her to death with a hammer, and then turned the weapon on the child when she began to cry. The murders were discovered by neighbours the following afternoon, along with air force clothes, and a note to Gladys' husband, apologising for the killing, but adding that Gladys was an immoral woman. The couple were arrested in Slough, and though both were initially charged with murder, the charges against Patricia were subsequently dropped.

Read: And May The Lord Have Mercy On Your Soul

589

John Joseph DORGAN   47

Strangled: *Florence Elizabeth Agnes Dorgan, 61, his wife, on 30*
               July 1943, in Brighton, Sussex.
Motive: *Sadistic pleasure; drink related.*

Dorgan, *(b.1896),* had served on the Somme, where he suffered shell-shock, and had then transferred with the army to India, where he suffered malaria. There, in 1927, he had met and married Florence Pentecost, a widow fourteen years his senior, and mother of three children. Her family hated him, not least for the fact he was an alcoholic. He left the army in 1936 and the couple moved to Brighton. In 1939 he was called up as a reservist and was sent to France, developing a stomach ulcer.

Dorgan worked as a waiter and then a postman until he lost his job in July 1943. The quarrels with his wife, a cleaner at a bank, grew in intensity, and after a drinking binge in Brighton pubs, he strangled her, knotting a tie round her throat and shoving her under the lodger's bed. Waiter Charles Fyfe found her there, and Dorgan was arrested later the same day, having sold most of his wife's belongings. He confessed, and the jury delivered its verdict in thirteen minutes.

Read: Master Detective Summer Special 97.

29 December 1943   Walton gaol, Liverpool

590

Thomas JAMES   **26**   *black*

Strangled: ***Gwendoline Sweeney**, 28, on 17 August 1943, in Liverpool, Lancs.*
Motive: *Sexual; drink related.*

James, *(b.1917)*, known as 'Knocker', and his friend George Dias, had been out drinking on the night of 17 August, and were seen with Gwen Sweeney in three pubs. Witnesses reported seeing her, extremely drunk, with two black men at various times after leaving the last pub. Knocker told Dias to leave him alone with Gwen, after which he took her to a bombed out house, where, after sex, he strangled her manually, and stabbed her repeatedly between the legs.

Shortly after, at 10.15pm, he got into an argument with a man who had asked what he was doing outside the murder site. James had knocked the torch from his young daughter's hand. James confessed what he had done to Dias the next morning, and, after seeing the corpse for himself, Dias went to the police.

Read: And May The Lord Have Mercy On Your Soul

1943 U.S. Military Hangings in Britain

12 March 1943   Shepton Mallet prison, Somerset   *A.Pierrepoint*

David COBB   **21**   *American*

Shot: *Robert J. Cobner, on 27 December 1942, in Desborough, Northants.*
Motive: *Vengeance.*

Cobb, *(b.1922),* a private in the 827th Engineers Battalion, was on guard duty at his base, when approached by Cobner, the duty officer. Cobb told him he was tired of guard duty, and refused to stand to attention when ordered. The sergeant of the guard was called to arrest the private, but Cobb pointed his rifle at the man, at which point Cobner stepped forward to perform the arrest himself. Cobb shot him through the heart.

Parliament had in 1942 passed the United Staes of America (Visiting Forces) Act, under which accused members of the American forces in Britain would be handed over for trial by US courts. Cobb was the first of eighteen US servicemen to be executed in Britain under US law.

Read: And May The Lord Have Mercy On Your Soul

25 June 1943   Shepton Mallet prison, Somerset

Harold A. SMITH   **25**   *American*

Shot: *Harry Jenkins, on 9 January 1943, in Swindon, Wilts.*
Motive: *To clear impediment.*

Smith, *(b.1918),* a private at Chisledon camp, went absent after being paid on new year's day, and took the train to London, where he joined up with a fellow absconder. He returned to camp a week later, having spent all his money. His unit, however, had moved on, so Smith ate, slept, and stole a pistol from the store. The following day he was stopped by another private, Harry Jenkins, and both men drew their weapons. Quicker on the draw, Smith shot Jenkins, and fired at another soldier who approached. Fleeing to London, Jenkins was arrested when asked for ID by a policeman.

Read: And May The Lord Have Mercy On Your Soul

14 December 1943   Shepton Mallet prison, Somerset

<u>Lee DAVIS</u>   **25**   *Black American*

Shot: ***June Lay****, 19, on 28 September 1943, in Marlborough, Wilts.*

Motive: Sexual.

      Davis, *(b.1918),* was hanging around looking for a likely target for his sexual frustration. June Lay had met her friend, Muriel Fawden, a nurse, at 7.45pm, and were walking towards the hospital, when they were approached by Davis. When they walked on, he called after them to stop, or he would fire. Training his rifle on them, he ordered the women to get into some nearby bushes, but they tried to run for safety. June was shot dead, and Muriel was forced to the shrubbery, where she was raped. The weapons of all local Americans were examined, and Davis arrested. His last words on trhe scaffold were, 'Oh, God. I'm going to die'.

    Read: And May The Lord Have Mercy On Your Soul

2 June 1943   Mountjoy gaol, Dublin

BERNARD KIRWAN   35

Bludgeoned: *Laurence Kirwan, 31, his brother, on 22 November*
               1941, near Tullamore, Co Offaly.
Motive: *Vengeance*

    Laurence and Bernard Kirwan, *(b.1908),* inherited Ballycloughan, a 70 acre farm near Tullamore, when their mother died in 1937. Laurence ran the farm alone until his brother was released in 1941 from serving a sentence in prison for armed robbery. However, Laurence refused to let Bernard eat in the farmhouse. A neighbour had once seen Bernard attack his brother with a knife.
    Five months after his release Bernard murdered Laurence, cut up his body, using skills acquired in the prison butchers and from cutting up pigs, burned the limbs and head in a boiler, and dumped the torso in a sack in a drain on the bog a mile and a half away. Bernard then took over the running of the farm, spending money freely . Despite police suspicions, it was not until the sack was found the following May that anyone was aware of Laurence's true fate. The jury took 3 hours and 20 minutes to decide Kirwan's fate.

Read: True Crime, Oct 97.

1943

WILLIAM O'SHEA   25

Accessory to shooting: *Maureen O'Shea, his wife, on 15 March 1943,*
                          near Ballyhane, Co Waterford
Motive: *To clear impediment*

    O'Shea, *(b.1918),* and his wife did not have a happy marriage, despite their new baby. Maureen was jealous of William's friendship with Thomas White, 16, with whom her husband would sit up till all hours playing cards. Together William and Thomas plotted to get rid of Maureen. White set fire to the house on 19 February 1943, but Maureen escaped with the child.
    They then hatched a scheme whereby while the young couple were taking their evening walk, White would come up behind and shoot her. He would warn William by first tapping him on the shoulder. The plan worked and

462

White shot Maureen dead, but as Thomas was ruled mentally sub-normal, and therefore unfit to stand trial, William was tried alone. As he had provided the cartridge and had lured her to her murder, he was found guilty.

Read: Murder Guide to Great Britain, p294.

1944

total: **12**

591	2 Feb	Christos GEORGHIOU	37	*Greek*	Pentonville
592	3 Feb	Mervin McEWAN	35	*Canadian*	Armley
593	16 Mar	Ernest DIGBY	35		Bristol
594	16 Mar	Oswald John JOB	58	*German*	Pentonville
595	13 Apr	Sidney DELASALLE	39		Durham
596	6 Jun	Ernest KEMP	21		Wandsworth
597	23 Jun	Pierre NEUKERMANS	28	*Belgian*	Pentonville
598	12 Jul	Joseph VAN HOVE	27	*Belgian*	Pentonville
599	12 Jul	John DAVIDSON	18	*Scottish*	Walton
600	26 Jul	James GALBRAITH	26		Strangeways
601	8 Aug	William COWLE	31		Leicester
602	8 Aug	William MEFFEN	52		Leicester

2 February 1944   Pentonville prison, London   *A.Pierrepoint/ Morris*

591

Christos GEORGHIOU   **37**   *Greek*   *(aka Chris Trihas)*

Stabbed: ***Savvas Demetriades**, 43, on 25 October 1943, in London W1.*

Motive: *Vengeance; drink related.*

Georghiou, *(b.1907)*, and Demetriades were friends and partners in a Cardiff cafe, until Georghiou accused his colleague of pocketing thirty shillings from the takings. The older Greek dissolved the partnership, but there was further antagonism when Demetriades invited Chris' girlfriend to a party. Georghiou moved to London in April 1943, and the two old friends did not see each other until Demetriades, in the capital on business, bumped into Georghiou in a cafe on 24 October. They did not speak.

Georghiou got considerably drunk the following lunchtime, and at 3pm saw Demetriades walking on Old Compton Street. They exchanged blows, and as Savvas stumbled to the ground, Chris stabbed him three times. He was arrested at a former girlfriend's home at 10am the following morning.

Read: And May The Lord Have Mercy On Your Soul

592

Mervin Clare McEWAN   35   *Canadian*

Bludgeoned: **Mark Turner**, *82, on 3 April 1943, in Halifax, W.Yorks.*
Motive: *Sadistic pleasure; drink related.*

McEwan, *(b.1909)*, a soldier, had gone absent in February 1943, and lived in an old hut in a Halifax park. He had been befriended by old Mark Turner, who invited McEwan and another pal to his house on 2 April for a few drinks. The two guests left, but McEwan returned at 1am and helped himself to food and drink. When Turner woke, McEwan battered him to death.

Empty bottles and some of the Canadian's clothes were found the following morning when the body was discovered. McEwan fled to Manchester, and by the time he was arrested on 23 June, he was living with a woman under the name of James Aston.

Read: And May The Lord Have Mercy On Your Soul.

593

Ernest Charles DIGBY   35

Bludgeoned: **1 Baby Digby**, *his child, around 1941, and*
        2 Dawn Digby, *25 days, his daughter, on 15 November*
        1943, in Milborne Park, Somerset.
Motive: *To clear impediment.*

Digby, *(b.1909)*, had married in 1931, and had fathered three children by his wife, but was separated when his mistress had his child. Digby took the child away, and because of financial restraints, said he had her adopted. He then met Olga Hill, and in March 1943, now a sergeant in the Royal Artillery, he bigamously married her. Olga gave birth to a child, Dawn, on 21 October, and when Ernest came home on leave in November, he determined that this child should go the same way as the first.

At 10.30am the couple and the child were walking to the railway station, when Digby fell behind and battered the baby to death with the suitcase he was carrying. He was later seen burying some rubbish, before returning to his unit on 19 November. Olga claimed to know nothing of the child's death, but both were tried for murder. Olga, 29, was acquitted, Digby being convicted inside 15 minutes.

Read: Master Detective, Dec 98.

16 March 1944   Pentonville prison, London   *A.Pierrepoint/ Kirk*

594

Oswald John JOB   **58**   *German*

Crime: **Espionage.**

Job, *(b.1886)*, a businessman born in London of German parents, lived in Paris from the age of 25. After the fall of France to the Nazis, he offered his services as a spy. He travelled to England via Lisbon, arriving in Bristol on 1 November 1943. Letters he sent to his spymasters were intercepted.

Read: True Detective, May 99

13 April 1944   Durham gaol   *A.Pierrepoint*

595

Sidney James DELASALLE   **39**

Shot: ***Ronald John Murphy***, *23, on 4 February 1944, in Co Durham.*
Motive: *Vengeance.*

Delasalle, *(b.1905)*, and the other airmen were lined up in their quarters for bed inspection by the flight sergeant, Ronald Murphy, but Delasalle was in no mood for paying respect to undeserving younger men. He complained about the rations, and challenged Murphy to a fight when he did not receive a satisfactory response to his complaint. Delasalle, who had a Burmese wife in Brighton, was confined to camp for two weeks. On 4

February, in the tea queue, he went berserk with his rifle, killing Murphy and wounding four others.

Read: And May The Lord Have Mercy On Your Soul

6 June 1944   Wandsworth prison, London   *A.Pierrepoint/ Morris*

596

Ernest James Harman KEMP   21

Strangled: ***Iris Miriam Dealey***, *21, on 14 February 1944, in Eltham, London SE9.*
Motive: *Sexual.*

Kemp, *(b.1923)*, was a private in the Royal Artillery, who deserted and escaped detention in February 1944, taking jobs as a porter and driver. Miriam Dealey, an aircraftswoman since 1942, had been visiting her fiance on weekend leave and caught the 11.25pm train from Charing Cross to return to base at Kidbrooke. From Lewisham station, she walked part way with a couple, and they were joined by Kemp, who walked on alone with Miriam towards the camp.

When he touched Miriam's breasts she resisted and he pulled her down by some allotments. He strangled her with her scarf to prevent her struggles. Kemp removed her lower clothing after death, but did not rape her. He left behind footprints and a glove, and was identified by the couple in Lewisham. Reaching its decision in 15 minutes, the jury added a recommendation to mercy, believing that Kemp did not intend to kill.

Read: True Crime, Jan 95.

23 June 1944   Pentonville prison, London   *A.Pierrepoint/ Riley*

597

Pierre Richard Charles NEUKERMANS   28   *Belgian*

Crime: ***Espionage.***

Neukermans, *(b.1916),* was invalided out of the Belgian army in 1938, and then helped to run his father's business, before agreeing to spy for the Germans. He flew to Poole via Lisbon on 16 July 1943. He said he had escaped German occupation, and was given work as a clerk for the Belgian government in exile. The information he sent back to Germany on Belgian troops was intercepted.

Read: True Detective, May 99

12 July 1944   Pentonville prison, London   *A.Pierrepoint/ Wade*

598

Joseph Jan VAN HOVE   27   *Belgian*

Crime: **Espionage.**

Van Hove, *(b.1917),* worked as a waiter in Antwerp, and got involved in the black market, which is where he met contacts who asked him to spy for Germany. He spent time watching his compatriots in a labour camp in France, before attempting to get to Britain, first via Switzerland, and then via Sweden, arriving there on a German ship. He reached Leuchars on 11 February 1944, but was immediately arrested, and admitted his intentions under interrogation. His trial lasted two hours.

Read: True Detective, May 99

12 July 1944   Walton gaol, Liverpool

599

John Gordon DAVIDSON   18   *Scottish*

Strangled: ***Gladys May Appleton***, *27, on 19 March 1944, in St Helens, Lancs.*
Motive: *Sexual; drink related.*

Private Davidson, *(b.1926),* was stationed at Burscough, ten miles from St Helens, where he had gone for a drink with friends on a Sunday night.

He had tried to pick up a mate's girlfriend, and later alone, had followed a young woman to her door asking for a kiss. Unsuccessful, at about 11pm he came across Gladys Appleton, a cleaner at the Co-op, walking home from seeing her boyfriend. When she rejected his advances, he threw her to the ground and punched her in the face. Tearing away her clothes under her coat, he strangled her with her scarf, stuffing the ends in her mouth, and violently raped her. Her breasts were savagely bitten.

Police searched the kitbags of hundreds of soldiers until they found boots that matched prints at the murder scene and at the previous woman's house. Under questioning, Davidson admitted the crime and fibres from Gladys' dress were found on his coat. The jury retired for 34 minutes before adding a recommendation to mercy to the verdict. Davidson had turned 18 on 5 March, and was one of the four 18-year olds hanged this century.

Read: Master Detective, Summer Special 95.

26 July 1944   Strangeways prison, Manchester

600

James GALBRAITH   26

Bludgeoned: *James William Percey, 48, on 6 April 1944, in Salford, Lancs.*
Motive: *Financial; drink related.*

Galbraith, *(b.1918),* was a chief steward with a police record waiting to be hired in Salford, where he lived with his mother. Percey, a Canadian chief radio officer on the *Pacific Shipper,* had returned from crossing the Atlantic on 1 April. A widower, he kept himself to himself and stayed aboard ship in Salford dock except to visit Mary Gibbons, an Irish prostitute.

Having spent two days with her, he returned to the ship very drunk at 3pm on 6 April. He was accompanied by Galbraith who was seen drinking earlier with the Canadian, and the two had a drink in Percey's cabin. There Galbraith attacked him with an axe, almost obliterating his face, before making off with the £88 Percey had just been paid. He went on to spend much of it on women, and the fresh notes were later found to be Percey's.

Read: True Detective, Feb 96.

469

601

William Alfred COWLE   31

Stabbed: **Nora Emily Payne**, *32, on 18 May 1944, in Leicester.*
Motive: *Vengeance.*

Cowle, *(b.1913)*, married but separated, had been dating Nora Payne, a clerk, since 1941. She wrote to him telling him the relationship was off, so Cowle determined on one last attempt to get her to change her mind. After lunch at home, Nora left to return to work at 1.40pm, and Cowle was waiting for her. When she again insisted she was finished with him, he stabbed her in the neck with a dagger, before approaching a policeman to confess. He was hanged alongside William Meffen.

Read: And May The Lord Have Mercy On Your Soul

602

William Frederick George MEFFEN   52

Cut throat of: **Winifred Ellen Stanley**, *38, his step-daughter, on 29 February 1944, in Derby.*
Motive: *Sexual rivalry.*

Meffen, *(b.1892)*, had suffered bouts of malaria since his army days in India in 1909. He lived with his wife, two daughters and step-daughter in Derby. He and Winifred, for whom he had developed an undisclosed attachment, worked for the same cable company. When she started dating George Birks in November 1943 his jealousy burst forth, telling her not to see him. When she stayed out all night on 22 February, Meffen sat in his chair crying all night, and accused her of sleeping with Birks. She denied his accusations, and was later proved to still be a virgin.

On the 28 February he wrote a letter spelling out his intentions, and the following morning at 7am followed Winifred into the bathroom, locking the door. He cut her throat, then left the house and handed himself over to the first policeman he saw. He claimed Winifred and he had loved each other until Birks came along. He was hanged alongside William Cowle.

Read: Murderous Derbyshire

1944 U.S. Military Executions in Britain

10 February 1944   Shepton Mallet prison, Somerset

T.Pierrepoint/ Riley

Hanged

John H. WATERS   39   *American*

Shot: ***Doris M. Staples**, 35, on 14 July 1943, in Henley-on-Thames, Oxon.*
Motive: *Sexual rivalry.*

Waters, *(b.1905)*, from New Jersey, had separated from his wife in 1928, and while stationed near Henley, had met Doris Staples in February 1943. A month later she found that she was pregnant and Waters gave her £5 for an abortion. By July Doris had decided to cool the relationship, flaunting the fact that she had been dating other US servicemen. Waters went to the draper's shop where Doris worked and shot her five times, twice in the chest, twice in the legs, and once in the arm. She died within two minutes.

When the shots were heard, police surrounded the building, and eventually forced an entry after firing in tear gas. Waters was found in the toilet having shot himself through the chin. His injuries were life threatening, and by the time of his court-martial, Waters was severely scarred and partially blinded.

Read: Master Detective, Aug 98

16 March 1944   Shepton Mallet prison, Somerset

Hanged

John C. LEATHERBERRY   24   *Black American*

Strangled: ***Henry Claude Hailstone**, 28, on 7 December 1943, near Colchester, Essex*
Motive: *Financial*

Harry Hailstone was a big heavy man, a bachelor who lived in lodgings in Colchester. A taxi-driver, he got a call at 11pm one night to take two US GIs to Birch, 5 miles outside the town, where there were five US army camps. His Vauxhall was found abandoned the next day, fifteen miles away near Clacton. A jacket and raincoat were inside, the latter traced to a

Canadian captain who reported that it had been stolen by a black American soldier. Hailstone's body, his face covered in blood, was found on 9 December, near Birch camp.

Private George Fowler was traced. He said that he and another private, John Leatherberry, *(b.1920)*, had gone to London on 5 December, spending two days in drinking and sexual exploits with women. When they returned to Colchester, Leatherberry suggested 'rolling' a cab driver. While Fowler got out of the cab to urinate, Leatherberry had begun hitting Hailstone, and dragged his body onto the back seat. They both robbed him and rolled his body under a fence down an incline.

Police estimated they had got away with £12. At the January court-martial in Ipswich, Leatherberry denied all knowledge of the crime, claiming to have been in a London club at the time. Witnesses, however, refuted this. Both men were found guilty of murder and robbery, Fowler receiving life, Leatherberry, death.

Read: The Essex Triangle

26 May 1944	Shepton Mallet prison, Somerset

Hanged

Wiley HARRIS   24   *American*

Stabbed: *Harry Coogan, on 6 March 1944, in Belfast.*
Motive: *Vengeance.*

Private Harris, *(b.1920)*, and private Robert Fils were drinking in a Belfast pub when they were approached by Coogan, who asked them if they would like some female entertainment. Coogan introduced Eileen Magaw, who accepted Harris' money, and took him to an air-raid shelter, while Coogan kept watch outside.

The Irishman called out that the police were coming before Harris could even begin his sexual encounter, but Eileen refused to hand back the money. As she ran off, she dropped some change, and as Harris bent to pick up the money, Coogan hit him in the face. In retaliation, Harris stabbed him 17 times.

Read: And May The Lord Have Mercy On Your Soul

30 May 1944   Shepton Mallet prison, Somerset

Shot

Alex F. MIRANDA   20   *American*

Shot: ***Thomas Evison****, on 5 March 1944, in Broomhill, Devon.*
Motive: *Vengeance; drink related.*

Miranda, *(b.1924),* went into Broomhill from his camp, and got considerably drunk. He was picked up by a policeman for urinating in the street, and was escorted back to his billet. Once back he started shooting off his drunken mouth, and went to where his sergeant, Tom Evison, was sleeping, and shot him dead. Miranda faced a ten-man firing squad.

Read: And May The Lord Have Mercy On Your Soul

11 August 1944   Shepton Mallet prison, Somerset

Hanged

Eliga BRINSON   24   *American*
Willie SMITH   24   *American*

Raped: *Dorothy Holmes, on 4 March 1944, in Bishops Cleeve, Gloucs.*

Dorothy Holmes had been to a dance with her American soldier boyfriend, Edward Hefferman, and the two were walking home when they realised they were being followed by two men. Brinson and Smith, *(b.1920),* hit Hefferman in the face with a bottle, and while he ran to get help, Dorothy was dragged into a nearby field and raped in turn by the two GIs. Plastercasts of footprints found at the scene led directly to the arrest of the two.

Read: And May The Lord Have Mercy On Your Soul

12 October 1944   Shepton Mallet prison, Somerset

Hanged

Madison THOMAS 25 *American*

Raped: *Beatrice Maud Reynolds, on 26 July 1944, in Gunnislake, Cornwall.*

    Thomas, *(b.1919),* followed Beatrice Reynolds after she left work at the British Legion at 10.40pm. In an attempt to get rid of him, she chatted to a friend at her gate, but Thomas approached and asked the friend for a kiss.
    Beatrice walked on towards home, but Thomas dragged her over a hedge into a field, where he hit her, then raped her, and stole her watch. Beatrice picked him out at a parade of all the soldiers at the camp. Her blood was still on his trousers.

    Read: And May The Lord Have Mercy On Your Soul

28 November 1944   Shepton Mallet prison, Somerset

Shot

Benjamin PYEGATE 24 *American*

Stabbed: ***James E. Alexander,*** *on 17 June 1944, in Westbury, Wilts.*
Motive: *Vengeance.*

    Pyegate, *(b.1920),* had been out drinking in Westbury, but had arrived too late to be served at the recreation hall, so went back to camp in a filthy mood. He got into an argument with four men, including James Alexander, whom Pyegate rendered helpless with a kick to the crotch, before stabbing him in the neck.

    Read: And May The Lord Have Mercy On Your Soul

1945

total: **19**

603	9 Jan	Horace GORDON	28	*Jamaican*	Wandsworth
604	30 Jan	Andrew BROWN	26	*Irish*	Wandsworth
605	31 Jan	Arthur THOMPSON	34		Armley
606	8 Mar	Karl HULTEN	23	*American*	Pentonville
607	13 Mar	Arthur HEYS	37		Norwich
608	5 Sep	Howard GROSSLEY	37	*Canadian*	Cardiff
609	7 Sep	Thomas RICHARDSON	28		Armley
610	6 Oct	Erich KOENIG	20	*German*	Pentonville
611	6 Oct	Joachim PALME-GOLTZ	20	*German*	Pentonville
612	6 Oct	Kurt ZUCHLSDORFF	20	*German*	Pentonville
613	6 Oct	Heinz BRUELING	22	*German*	Pentonville
614	6 Oct	Josep MERTINS	21	*German*	Pentonville
615	31 Oct	Robert MAURI	32		Wandsworth
616	16 Nov	Armin KUEHNE	21	*German*	Pentonville
617	16 Nov	Emil SCHMITTENDORF	31	*German*	Pentonville
618	19 Dec	John AMERY	33		Wandsworth
619	21 Dec	John YOUNG	40		Pentonville
620	21 Dec	James MCNICOL	28	*Scottish*	Pentonville
621	29 Dec	Robert BLAINE	24		Wandsworth

9 January 1945   Wandsworth prison, London   *A.Pierrepoint/ Wade*

603

Horace Beresford GORDON   **28**   *Jamaican*
black

Stabbed: ***Dorothy May Hillman***, *18, on 7 September 1944, near Grafham, Surrey.*
Motive: *Sexual.*

Gordon, *(b.1917)*, serving with the Royal Canadian Ornance Corps in England since October 1941, was stationed at Francombe, Surrey, and was returning the women's bicycle he had borrowed when he saw Dorothy Hillman walking by the road. Dorothy, eight months pregnant, had left home at 6.20pm, to walk the dog, and buy some cigarettes.

Gordon dragged her to the hedge, tried to sexually assault her, and when she resisted and slapped his face, he stabbed her eleven times. Dorothy survived long enough to identify Gordon, who had blood on his uniform, and chewed the same chewing gum as wrappers found at the scene. After giving birth to a stillborn child, Dorothy succumbed to her injuries fifteen days later. The jury deliberated for 95 minutes.

Read: And May The Lord Have Mercy On Your Soul

30 January 1945   Wandsworth prison, London   *A.Pierrepoint/ Wade*

604

<u>Andrew BROWN</u>   **26**   *Irish*

Punched: ***Amelia Elizabeth Ann Knowles,*** *69, on 18 September 1944, in Arundel, Sussex.*
Motive: *Sexual/ financial; drink related.*

       Amelia Knowles ran the Old Curiosity shop from the front room of her squalid home in Arundel. Unmarried, she had lived alone since the death of her father in 1934. Somewhat eccentric, she often screamed out at night, and neighbours ceased to pay any heed since several unnecessary calls to police. On 14 September a woman passer-by had seen two airmen loitering near the shop at 11pm, one calling the other 'Paddy'.
       Just after midnight four days later, aircraftsman Brown, *(b.1918),* from Belfast, had been out drinking and passed the shop on his way back to base. He knocked on the door when he heard Miss Knowles shouting to herself. When she opened the door, he barged his way in, chased her into the passage and punched her several times, stealing a roll of ten ten-shilling notes, but missing £128 more. He raped her before he left.
       Police found Amelia, naked from the waist down, at midday having been alerted by a milkman. With the passer-by's evidence, police interviewed all Irishmen and airmen named Patrick on the nearby bases. When Brown's alibi of having been with mates broke down, he confessed. He led police to stolen items from the shop hidden beneath a bridge. Pleading guilty to manslaughter, Brown was condemned by the jury in just eleven minutes.

Read: True Detective, Dec 97.

605

Arthur THOMPSON   34

Strangled: **Jane Coulton**, *69, on 21 September 1944, in Bradford, W.Yorks.*
Motive: *Financial; drink related.*

Thompson, *(b.1911),* a Lance Corporal from Bootle, was due to face disciplinary proceedings for his part in a brawl on 22 September. He had joined the army in 1926 at age 15 and served five years. In 1932 he contracted syphilis, and received head injuries in 1936, but had rejoined the forces in September 1944.

He went AWOL on 21 September and after drinking fifteen pints broke into the Nags Head in Bradford at 1am, punching and strangling the landlady with a stocking when she disturbed him. He escaped with a cash bag and some jewellery, but missed £119 kept in a drawer. Mrs Coulton was discovered at 7am. Thompson, meanwhile, paid off his debts to friends and fled to Halifax then Burnley, swapping his uniform for new clothes. He was arrested in a pub near Morecambe on 24 September, and hid two rings and two brooches in the police car which took him.

Read: Murderous Leeds

8 March 1945   Pentonville prison, London   *A.Pierrepoint/ Critchell*

606

Karl Gustav HULTEN   23   *American*

Shot: **George Edward Heath**, *34, on 7 October 1944, in London W4.*
Motive: *Financial.*

Hulten, *(b.1922),* a Swedish American, was a private with the US paratroopers stationed in Britain. He had been absent without leave for seven weeks when he met Elizabeth Maud Jones, 18, a Welsh girl, in October 1944. He went by the name 'Ricky' and she by her stage-name, Georgina Grayson. She worked as a stripper, and had a flat in Hammersmith. She had married in Wales when only sixteen, but had left her husband the same day when he hit her, and she had come to London in January 1943.

Both Ricky and Georgina were fantasists, playing out the role of gangster and moll which they had admired in the movies. Daily, they would drive around west London in a stolen army truck, mugging cyclists and pedestrians for money and personal belongings. They slept together in the van, or in Georgina's flat, but Hulten stopped short of full intercourse, finding a rash on her stomach distasteful. He also continued to see another girlfriend. One night Hulten and Jones nearly killed a woman to whom they had given a lift. They hit the woman with an iron bar and threw her in the Thames.

On 7 October, they hailed a taxi driven by George Heath. He was told to stop after a mile, and Hulten shot him in the back with a pistol, the girl going through the driver's pockets as the American drove on. A cigarette case, a silver pencil and 19 shillings was their haul. Mr Heath's body was dumped in a ditch in Staines. Foolishly, Hulten continued to use the taxi, and was arrested getting into it in Hammersmith on 10 October. He still had his gun with him.

Both Hulten and Jones were charged with murder, Hulten claiming the girl had encouraged him, seeking excitement, and Jones claiming she had acted under duress. The trial lasted six days, and both were sentenced to hang. The jury made a recommendation to mercy in Jones' case, and she was reprieved two days before her execution date. She was released in 1954.

Read: Murders of the Black Museum

13 March 1945   Norwich prison

607

Arthur HEYS   37

Suffocated:	***Winifred Mary Evans**, 27, on 8 November 1944, near Beccles, Suffolk.*
Motive:	*Sexual; drink related.*

Heys, *(b.1908)*, was an aircraftman in the RAF, married with a young family. He was stationed in Suffolk, one mile from the women's RAF camp. At about midnight, Winifred Evans, a radio operator, and her friend, Margaret Johns, had returned from a dance to their billet, and Winifred had continued on to the aerodrome, where she was due on duty. Margaret had then found a drunken man in the women's wash-house, and had told him to get out. The man was Arthur Heys, and he set out on the same path which Winifred had taken, towards the men's camp.

When he caught up with Miss Evans, he attacked her. He pushed her to the ground, face down, and raped her from behind with considerable force. She was bruised internally, and the large amount of blood found around her genitals was not entirely due to her menstruation. Winifred, who had previously been a virgin, died as Heys knelt on her chest, pushing her face into the mud. She was asphyxiated. Margaret Johns picked Heys out at the unit's pay parade, and police found blood on his tunic, together with mud and hairs which matched samples taken from the body.

The jury took forty minutes to find him guilty. Heys smuggled a letter out of Norwich prison, supposedly from the real murderer saying that Heys was innocent. The letter contained details only the murderer could have known and when the handwriting was found to match his own, even the slightest doubt as to his guilt was dismissed.

Read: Forty Years of Murder, p113

5 September 1945   Cardiff prison

608

Howard Joseph GROSSLEY   **37**   *Canadian*

Shot: **Lily Griffiths**, *29, on 12 March 1945, in Porthcawl, Glamorgan.*
Motive: *To clear impediment.*

Grossley, *(b.1908),* came to England with the Canadian army in 1941, leaving his wife back home. It was not long before he met Lily Griffiths, and the two lived together, a son being born in 1943. By the end of the war, Grossley did not want to return to Canada, and decided suicide was preferable.

On a country walk with Lily he told her his plans, and produced his gun. She tried to wrestle the gun from him, but Lily was hit when the gun went off. Lily's deathbed testimony backed up Grossley's claims, but the jury decided the weapon had been aimed, and the Canadian was found guilty of murder.

Read: And May The Lord Have Mercy On Your Soul

609

<u>Thomas Eric RICHARDSON</u>   **28**

Bludgeoned: ***Dr David Walker Dewar***, *42, on 29 April 1945, in Leeds, W.Yorks.*
Motive: *Sexual rivalry.*

          Richardson, *(b.1917)*, an engineer and single, had been having an affair for a year with Laura Walker, a married woman, whose husband was serving in Italy. He was infatuated with her, and was enraged with jealousy when he became aware that she was also seeing other men. One of these others was a Scottish doctor, David Dewar, who himself was married and had had several affairs. Though he liked a drink, he was a good, popular doctor, and his association with Laura dated back a full decade.
          At 1am on 29 April 1945, as he was getting out of his car outside his home, Dewar was attacked by Richardson, 5'6". His head was smashed by ten blows with an axe, which Richardson said he later threw into the river Aire, though it was never found. Dewar was found at 8.10 the next morning. Mrs Walker told the police that Richardson had admitted to the crime, and he was arrested on 21 May. After a 90-minute retirement, the jury's strong recommendation to mercy was rejected.

          Read: True Crime, Nov 99.

6 October 1945   Pentonville prison, London
                              A.Pierrepoint/ Wade/ Harry Allen

610, 611, 612, 613, 614

<u>**Erich KOENIG**</u>	**20**	*German*
<u>**Joachim PALME-GOLTZ**</u>	**20**	*German*
<u>**Kurt ZUCHLSDORFF**</u>	**20**	*German*
<u>**Heinz BRUELING**</u>	**22**	*German*
<u>**Josep MERTENS**</u>	**21**	*German*

Strangled: ***Wolfgang Rosterg***, *35, on 23 December 1944, in Comrie, Perthshire.*
Motive: *Vengeance.*

Sergeant-Major Rosterg was one of 3500 German prisoners-of-war held at Comrie camp. Captured in Normandy in July 1944, he was an anti-Nazi, though he was held together with other POWs. They blamed him when their plan to escape from the POW camp in Devizes, where Rosterg acted as an interpreter, was discovered. 32 were arrested, and all were transferred to Scotland on 21 December 1944.

Several men took Rosterg from his bed in the middle of the night, and subjected him to a mock trial, where they sentenced him to die. Ignored by Polish guards, they severely punched and kicked him, put a rope around his neck, and dragged him to a latrine where Goltz, the Commanding Officer, hanged him by the neck from a water pipe.

No investigation took place until the following April, and, with witnesses guaranteed anonymity, eight men were tried in July by a British court martial, two being acquitted, a third, Rolf Herzig, being sentenced to life, and the other five to death. They were hanged, singly and in pairs, wearing their uniforms.

31 October 1945   Wandsworth prison, London   *A.Pierrepoint/ Kirk*

615

Ronald Bertram MAURI   32

Strangled: ***Vera Guest***, *18, on 11 July 1945, in Hillingdon, Middlesex.*
Motive: *Vengeance.*

Mauri, *(b.1913)*, a lorry driver, felt that the Nottingham police had framed him for a robbery of cigarettes, and declared that he wanted to commit suicide. He claimed also that his girlfriend, Vera Guest, wanted to die with him. He strangled her to death with her scarf in her house at 5.30pm, then wrote a series of letters, to his employer, to his mother, and to Vera's parents, admitting his crime, and claiming that he would commit suicide when he had killed six times more.

One of his victims was to be his brother's wife, whom he claimed was unfaithful. He added that he would shoot any policeman who stood in his way. He was eventually tracked down to Monmouthshire, and police cornered him in a wood, shooting him in the head. His injuries did not prove serious enough to deprive the hangman.

Read: And May The Lord Have Mercy On Your Soul

16 November 1945   Pentonville prison, London   *A.Pierrepoint/ Riley*

616, 617

<u>Armin **KEUHNE**</u>	**21**	*German*
<u>Emil **SCHMITTENDORF**</u>	**31**	*German*

Kicked/ punched: **Gerhardt Rettig**, *25, on 24 March 1945, near Sheffield, W.Yorks.*
Motive: *Vengeance.*

In the prisoner-of-war camp near Sheffield, an escape tunnel was discovered by the British guards on 24 March 1945. After Rettig, an anti-Nazi, was seen passing a note to a sentry, the rumour swiftly got round that he was the informer responsible for the disclosure.

At 5.30pm, he was chased by a gang of about twenty prisoners back to his hut, where he was punched and knocked about. Outside a crowd of about a hundred gathered, all shouting for revenge. Rettig was dragged outside and beaten to death by the mob. Schmittendorf, *(b.1914),* was seen kicking him in the head. Four men were tried, with witnesses guaranteed anonymity, but only Keuhne, *(b.1924),* and Schmittendorf were convicted.

Read: And May The Lord Have Mercy On Your Soul

19 December 1945   Wandsworth prison, London   *A.Pierrepoint/ Critchell*

618

<u>John **AMERY**</u>   **33**

Crime: ***High treason.***

Amery, *(b.1913),* was the son of the Secretary of State for India in the wartime coalition government, Leo Amery. His brother, Julian, himself to be a politician, had been a war-hero, parachuting behind enemy lines. John, however, had proved an embarrassment to the family.

Reckoned to be mentally abnormal, he had been bankrupt at the age of 25, and had 74 convictions for motoring offences. He imagined that his father's status would give him protection. After gun-running for Franco in the Spanish civil war, his fascist commitments took him to Germany in 1942. He tried to persuade the British prisoners of war to fight for the Nazis, and lectured in Germany and occupied Europe, extolling the virtues of Nazism, condemning the Jews and British policy.

Captured in Italy on 7 July 1945, Amery was flown to London where he pleaded guilty to treason. His brother made a futile attempt to show that John had taken Spanish nationality. His trial lasted a mere eight minutes.

Read: Hangman, p209.

21 December 1945   Pentonville prison, London

A.Pierrepoint/ Morris/ Wade

619

John Riley YOUNG   40

Bludgeoned: **1** **Frederick Benjamin Lucas**, *52, and his wife,*
                  2 **Cissie Clara Lucas**, *51, on 6 June 1945, in Leigh-on-Sea, Essex.*
Motive: Financial.

Mr Lucas and his wife owned a jeweller's shop in Leigh-on-Sea. Young, *(b.1905)*, a builder from Ilford, had managed to swindle £3000 out of Lucas with which to buy sovereigns. At 9 o'clock one morning, Young called at their house and told Lucas there were no coins, that he had spent the money on a car.

Young said that when Lucas flew into a rage he retaliated. He hit the husband six times about the head with a chair leg, which broke with the violence of the assault. He then attacked Mrs Lucas three times with the edge of a wooden board, and then gave each of them one final blow with the flat of the board. Mr Lucas died almost immediately, but Mrs Lucas lingered in life for another eight hours or so.

Their bodies were discovered by their 17-year old daughter when she returned from work. Young fled to his sister's where he twice tried to gas himself and attempted to slash his wrists. When police arrived at his hospital bedside, Young confessed all. He was hanged at 8am, 90 minutes before McNicol.

Read: True Detective Summer Special 93.

21 December 1945   Pentonville prison, London

A.Pierrepoint/ Morris/ Wade

620

<u>James McNICHOL</u>   **28**   *Scottish*

Shot: ***Donald Alfred Richard Kirkaldie***, *27, on 17 August 1945, in Thorpe Bay, Essex*
Motive: *Vengeance*

McNicol, *(b.1927)*, from Motherwell, was a sergeant with the 494th Heavy Anti-Aircraft Battery stationed at Thorpe Bay. He had been out with a female private four times, but she threw him over on 15 August. The following night there was a big party for VJ Day, and McNicol had become enraged when his girl was talking to an RAF man. He emptied a drink over the flier's head, and tried to pick a fight with Leonard Cox, another sergeant, when he intervened.

    Their bickering continued all evening, and in the early hours, picking up a rifle from the armoury, McNicol went to the nissen hut where Cox and several others slept. He fired through a window, seriously injuring Cox, but also hitting Donald Kirkaldie in the jaw and killing him. Kirkaldie, from Ramsgate, was a married man with a young child. McNicol was seen on the esplanade and arrested. The jury retired for one hour. McNicol was hanged after Young, at 9.30am.

Read: True Crime, Nov 95.

29 December 1945   Wandsworth prison, London   *A.Pierrepoint/ Kirk*

621

<u>Robert BLAINE</u>   **24**   *(aka Reginald Douglas Johnson)*

Bludgeoned: ***John Alexander Ritchie***, *on 14 September 1945, in London W1.*
Motive: *Financial.*

Blaine, *(b.1921)*, a soldier who had several convictions for theft dating back to 1938, was out in the west end with a friend he named as Jack Connolly, who had picked up a brick as a weapon to use on any likely victim.

    Captain Ritchie, a Canadian soldier, staying in London at the officers' club of the YMCA, had been dining with a friend, and was walking through Soho after leaving the restaurant at 10pm. He was battered with the brick, and two soldiers were seen running away. When Blaine was picked up, he had £5 on him, along with the Captain's bank and cheque books. Of Connolly there was never any trace.

Read: And May The Lord Have Mercy On Your Soul

1945 U.S. Military Hangings in Britain

8 January 1945   Shepton Mallet prison, Somerset   *A.Pierrepoint*

Ernest Lee CLARK	**22**	*American*
Augustine M. GUERRA	**20**	*American*

Strangled: ***Betty Green***, *15, on 22 August 1944, in Ashford, Kent*
Motive: *Sexual; drink related.*

Betty Green had been to the fair at Newton in Ashford with a friend where the two had met and flirted with two of the many American airmen stationed in the area. Her father, meanwhile, was drinking in his local pub where two more American airmen, Corporal Clark, *(b.1922)*, and Private Guerra, *(b.1924)*, were getting very drunk. Betty stayed on at the fair after her friend had left, and then set off to walk home at about 10.20pm. She was seen walking alone by a cyclist. At about the same time, Mr Green noticed Clark and Guerra leave the pub.

The two Americans bumped into Betty as they walked along a path near the railway. They dragged her into a field and both raped her. She was strangled manually and discovered the following morning by railwaymen. The murderers had left behind semen and hair in the girl's grasp. Betty's friend identified the airmen at the fair, and her father picked out the airmen in the pub.

Forensic tests proved Clark and Guerra were the culprits. Clark, court-martialled on 24 September, admitted the rape but denied murder; Guerra, court-martialled three weeks later, said the girl had consented to sex.

Read: True Detective Summer Special 91

17 March 1945   Shepton Mallet prison, Somerset

Robert L. PEARSON	**25**	*American*	*black*
Parson JONES	**25**	*American*	*black*

Crime: **Rape.**
Victim: *Joyce Brown, on 3 December 1944, in Chard, Somerset.*

Joyce Brown, eight months pregnant, left her home at 8pm. She was followed by the two soldiers, who dragged her through a gate and into an orchard, where they both raped her at knifepoint. All soldiers on the American base near Chard were inspected, and Pearson and Jones, *(b.1920)*, were found to have wet and muddy uniforms. The men tried to claim that Joyce had consented to sex with them, but the bruises on the woman, and her advanced pregnancy nailed the lie.

Read: And May The Lord Have Mercy On Your Soul

7 April 1945   Shepton Mallet prison, Somerset

William HARRISON   23   *American*

Strangled: ***Patricia Wylie**, 7, on 25 September 1944, in Killycolpy, Co Tyrone.*
Motive: *Sexual.*

Harrison, *(b.1922)*, a private in the US air force and native of Kentucky, had several times gone AWOL, and had been stationed in Ulster from 1942. He had become friendly with the Wylie family in the summer of 1943. Patrick Wylie, father of four, owned a small farm on the shores of Lough Neagh, and earned extra income as a fisherman. Harrison often took meals with the Wylies, and sometimes went to the pub with Patrick.

Telling Mrs Wylie he wanted to repay their kindness by buying a present, she agreed that Patricia should accompany Harrison to the shops at 3.30pm. Instead he took the child to a field, where he punched her in the face, raped and then strangled her. When Patricia had not returned by 7pm, Patrick contacted the police, and the girl's near naked body was found in a haystack.

Read: Master Detective, May 98.

8 May 1945   Shepton Mallet prison, Somerset

George E. SMITH   25   *American*

Shot: ***Sir Eric Teichman**, 61, on 3 December 1944, in Attlebridge, Norfolk.*
Motive: *Sadistic pleasure.*

Smith, *(b.1920)*, and fellow American serviceman Leonard Wojtacha were seen leaving their camp on Sunday morning. They went to woods near Attlebridge, and began shooting at birds and animals, including a cow they saw.

Sir Eric and his wife had just finished Sunday lunch and heard the shots from the nearby wood. He went to investigate, and upon approaching the strangers, was shot through the head by Smith. After Sir Eric's body was discovered at midnight, Smith and Wojtacha were questioned. Smith alone bore responsibility and was executed on VE Day.

Read: And May The Lord Have Mercy On Your Soul

15 June 1945   Shepton Mallet prison, Somerset

Aniceto MARTINEZ   22   *American*

Crime: **Rape.**
Victim: *Agnes Cape, 75, on 6 August 1944, in Rugeley, Staffs.*

Martinez, *(b.1923),* was a guard at a prisoner of war camp near Rugeley. He left the camp late at night and broke into the house of Agnes Cape at 3.15am. No money was stolen, but the old woman was raped. Only one soldier was found to have been out of camp that night, and fibres from Agnes' bedroom were on his clothing.

Read: And May The Lord Have Mercy On Your Soul

1945 Execution in Ireland

19 March 1945

JAMES LEHMAN   *Canadian*

Poisoned:	***Margaret Lehman***, *his wife, on 19 March 1944, at Rathmines, Dublin.*
Motive:	*To clear impediment.*

Lehman had met Margaret Hayden in Aldershot while he was a soldier and she a NAAFI worker. They married in February 1940. By 1944 Lehman ran a retail coffee business in Dublin and he and his wife had two children with another on the way. But James had become friendly with a nurse, to whom he had declared that he was single.

One evening in March, he laced his wife's rum with a large dose of cyanide, and she died on the way to hospital. Lehman escaped, and avoided capture for some months by the use of various aliases. He maintained that Margaret had committed suicide.

Read: Murder Guide to Great Britain, p285.

1946　　total: **24**

622	3 Jan	William JOYCE	40			Wandsworth
623	4 Jan	Theodore SCHURCH	27			Pentonville
624	8 Jan	William BATTY	27			Armley
625	31 Jan	Michael NIESCIOR	29	*Polish*		Wandsworth
626	9 Feb	John LYON	21	*Scottish*		Barlinnie
627	5 Mar	Charles PRESCOTT	23			Durham
628	19 Mar	Arthur CLEGG	42			Wandsworth
629	26 Mar	Arthur CHARLES	34			Durham
630	2 Apr	Marian GRONDKOWSKI	33	*Polish*		Wandsworth
631	2 Apr	Henryk MALINOWSKI	25	*Polish*		Wandsworth
632	6 Apr	Patrick CARRAHER	40	*Scottish*		Barlinnie
633	9 Apr	Harold BERRY	30			Strangeways
634	24 Apr	Martin COFFEY	24			Strangeways
635	28 May	Leonard HOLMES	32			Lincoln
636	17 Jul	Thomas HENDREN	31			Walton
637	7 Aug	Walter CLAYTON	22			Walton
638	10 Aug	John CALDWELL	19	*Scottish*		Barlinnie
639	6 Sep	David MASON	39			Wandsworth
640	6 Sep	Sydney SMITH	22			Wandsworth
641	16 Oct	Neville HEATH	29			Pentonville
642	1 Nov	Arthur BOYCE	45			Pentonville
643	13 Nov	Frank FREIYER	26			Wandsworth
644	19 Nov	Arthur RUSHTON	31			Walton
645	10 Dec	John MATHIESON	23			Pentonville

3 January 1946　　Wandsworth prison, London　　*A.Pierrepoint/ Riley*

622

William JOYCE　　**40**　　*(aka Lord Haw-Haw)*

Crime:　　**High treason.**

　　　　Joyce was born in 1906 in the USA, the son of Anglo-Irish parents who had taken American citizenship. When they returned to the UK, they retook British nationality. Joyce was a 1930s fascist, involved in street fights and rabble-rousing. At the outbreak of war he went to Germany, and from 18 September 1939 until 1945, he worked as a Nazi propagandist, broadcasting to Britain. He took German citizenship in September 1940.

490

'Germany calling...Germany calling', became his notorious trademark, and the British public became used to his morale-sapping calls expressing the hopelessness of Britain's war effort, and encouraging surrender. He was dubbed 'Lord Haw-Haw' by Jonah Barrington, a newspaper journalist. Joyce was shot in the thigh and captured on the Danish-German border on 28 May 1945, and charged with treason, but his case went to the House of Lords, which had to decide whether a German citizen could be a traitor to the UK. They ruled that Joyce had travelled on a British passport, and therefore enjoyed the rights and bore the responsibilities of any British subject. The guilty verdict was upheld.

Read: Lord Haw-Haw & William Joyce, The Full Story

4 January 1946   Pentonville prison, London   *A.Pierrepoint/ Riley*

623

Theodore William John SCHURCH   27

Crime: **High treason.**

Schurch was born in London in 1919 of Swiss parents, and joined the British Union of Fascists in 1934. He entered the army in 1936, but was captured by the Italians while serving in north Africa, and was engaged by them as a spy. He was used, under the name of Captain Richards, to spy on the other detainees in the PoW camp in Italy, and then sent to France and Switzerland on spying missions. When returned to England he was identified as the treacherous Richards and charged.

Read: And May The Lord Have Mercy On Your Soul

8 January 1946   Armley gaol, Leeds   *T.Pierrepoint/ Harry Allen*

624

William BATTY   27

Shot: **Samuel Hammond Gray**, *33, on 14 August 1946, in Bradford, W.Yorks.*
Motive: *Vengeance*

491

Batty, *(b.1919)*, had a long criminal record, having been in court sixteen times, and in gaol or borstal four times for stealing, larceny or housebreaking. He met Nellie Gray in 1942, a year after her husband went to Burma with the army. After four years happily together, Nellie tried to break things off as her husband's return came closer, but Batty threatened to kill himself if she did.

Samuel Gray came home on 11 August, and Batty went round the same day. When Nellie shut the door in his face he fired a revolver outside. Nellie told Sam of her affair, but decided to stay with her husband. Three days later, at 10.30pm, Batty returned and when Sam opened the door Batty shot him in the stomach. Batty was arrested as he arrived at his mother's at 12.30am. The jury deliberated for 25 minutes.

Read: Murderous Leeds

31 January 1946   Wandsworth prison, London   *A.Pierrepoint/ Wade*

625

Michael NIESCIOR   **29**   *Polish*

Stabbed: ***Charles Elphick***, *42, on 22 October 1945, in Portslade, Sussex*
Motive: *Sexual rivalry*

Niescior, *(b.1927)*, came to England after being invalided out of the Polish navy, taking employment as a chef at a Brighton nursing home. He met Jessie Eileen Elphick at a dance hall in May 1944, her husband having been away at war since 1942. The two fell in love and she wrote to her husband telling him she had found someone else but omitted to mention that Michael had moved into their Portslade home in April 1945.

So when Charles Elphick returned home in August 1945 he was somewhat shocked to find Niescior in his bed while Jessie was in the bath. After all three spent the night under the same roof, Jessie left with Michael the next day, but continued to return daily to cook her husband's dinner. This led to rows with Michael, and two weeks later she returned to her husband. In his anger Niescior smashed the windows of the Elphick house and Jessie took Michael back, sharing both men for a month.

At 11.20pm, armed with a knife, Niescior woke the couple up and Charles, having armed himself with a hammer, took on the Pole, both stumbling outside, where Charles was stabbed in the head, trunk and arms. Niescior gave himself up to police and Elphick died at 9.40 the next morning.

492

The jury deliberated for 65 minutes, before adding a strong recommendation to mercy on account of provocation.

Read: *Murderous Sussex*

---

9 February 1946　　　　　　Barlinnie prison, Glasgow　　　*A.Pierrepoint*

626

<u>**John LYON**</u>　　　　　**21**　　　　　*Scottish*

Stabbed:　　　　***John Brady**, 19, on 20 October 1945, in Glasgow, Lanarks.*
Motive:　　　　*Sadistic pleasure.*

　　　　John Brady had returned to his Glasgow home on 16 October having been demobilised from the Royal Navy. His younger brother Thomas was a member of the Iona Boys street gang. Arrivng home from a dance at 10.30 one Saturday night , John was told of a commotion down the street, and went in search of his brother.

　　　　Eight of the Dougie Boys, a rival gang, were pursuing a lone teenager, but John Brady became their target. Thomas found his brother dying in the street from bayonet wounds to his head. Lyon, *(b.1925),* was identified as one of the culprits, who had gone out armed with bayonets and a revolver.

　　　　He and two others, Alexander Crosbie, 18, and John Lennie, were convicted of murder. A fourth youth got three years for assault. Crosbie and Lennie were reprieved on 6 February. Lyon's execution was the first at Barlinnie, and Scotland's first for 18 years.

Read: *True Crime, Mar 96*

---

5 March 1946　　　　　　Durham gaol　　　　　*T.Pierrepoint*

627

<u>**Charles Edward PRESCOTT**</u>　　　　**23**

Shot:　　　　***Sarah Jean Young**, 19, on 19 November 1945, in Wigton, Cumberland.*
Motive:　　　　*Vengeance.*

Prescott, *(b.1923)*, a Royal Marine, had been dating Belle Young, 18, for some time when she broke off with him on 26 October. Belle had been seeing another man and Prescott's anger grew to the point where he threatened her with a dagger four days after the split.

On 7 November he went to the farm where Belle lived with her parents, her sister, Sarah, and her brother, and fruitlessly lay in wait for her for forty-eight hours. Some days later, Belle was at home looking at some photos with her brother, sister and two workers. From 100 metres away, Prescott fired his rifle at the window, the shot hitting Belle's sister. The police were called when he announced in a library what he had done. He claimed the gun had gun off accidentally.

Read: And May The Lord Have Mercy On Your Soul

19 March 1946   Wandsworth prison, London   *A.Pierrepoint/ Morris*

628

Arthur CLEGG   **42**

Drowned: ***Jill Clegg**, 11 days, his granddaughter, on 30 October 1945, in London.*
Motive: *To clear impediment.*

When Joan Clegg gave birth to a daughter on 19 October, the whole thing was kept quiet for, not only was Joan not married, but her father, Arthur Clegg, *(b.1904)*, was most probably the father. Plans were made for adoption, and when Joan came home from hospital, the baby stayed there.

But the plans fell through, and Clegg collected his granddaughter eleven days later, at 5pm. On the way home he dumped the child in the Thames, and told Joan that he had found friends willing to put up little Jill. The baby's body, complete with name tag, was washed up on 6 November, though Clegg maintained that he had handed her to a woman on the steps of the adoption agency.

Read: And May The Lord Have Mercy On Your Soul

629

Arthur CHARLES   34   *black*

Shot: ***John Duplessis***, *35, on 29 November 1945, in South Shields, Co Durham*

Motive: *Sexual rivalry; drink related.*

Charles, *(b.1914),* a seaman, had moved in with Hannah Burns, married but separated, in October 1943. Their somewhat stormy relationship survived the best part of a year, despite Charles hitting her when he suspected that she had been seeing other men during his absences at sea. In November 1944 he had been in a fight with the man who replaced him in Hannah's affections, John Duplessis, a black South African ship's fireman who had come to England from Cape Town in 1942.

The two men returned to England on the same ship on 28 November, and the following day were together with Hannah and another three friends laughing and joking in a cafe. Duplessis went on to the pub, getting home at 11pm. When Hannah opened the door to dispose of some water, Charles was standing there armed with a revolver. He told John to stand up and when he refused shot him five times where he sat, hitting him in the arm, abdomen and twice in the thigh. Hannah went to the police at midnight. Duplessis survived 32 days, before succumbing to septicaemia on new year's eve.

Read: *Murderous Tyneside*

630, 631

Marian GRONDKOWSKI   33   *Polish*
Henryk MALINOWSKI   25   *Polish*

Possibly *shot*:   ***1 Frank Everitt***, *56, in October 1945, in Southwark, London SE1.*

Shot: ***2 Reuben Martirosoff***, *39, on 1 November 1945, near Notting Hill, London W11.*

Motive: *Financial; drink related*

Grondkowski, *(b. 1913)*, and Malinowski, *(b. 1921)*, had met while serving in the Foreign Legion in north Africa in 1941, and shared a flat in Ilford. Grondkowski had fought in the Spanish Civil War and in the French army, Malinowski in the defence of Warsaw in 1939. Both came to England in 1943 and joined the free Polish army.

The pair knew Reuben Martirosoff, an Armenian black-marketeer, and went drinking with him on 1 November. He was found slumped at the wheel of his car, shot through the head and robbed of £160. The murder weapon, a revolver, was found at Grondkowski's lodgings. Each accused the other, and Grondkowski was accused by Malinowski of the murder in similar circumstances of taxi driver Frank Everitt, 56, two weeks earlier in Southwark, though no proof ever surfaced. Grondkowski was hanged at 9am, Malinowski one hour later.

Read: Forty Years of Murder, p157.

6 April 1946	Barlinnie prison, Glasgow	*A.Pierrepoint*

632

Patrick CARRAHER   40   *Scottish*

Stabbed:	**1 James Sydney Emden Shaw**, 23, in August 1938, in Glasgow, Lanarks.
	2 John Gordon, 39, on 23 November 1945, in Glasgow.
Motive:	*Sadistic pleasure.*

Though from a decent working-class family and only 5'6", Carraher, *(b.1906)*, became a hard man of the Gorbals district. An alcoholic street-fighter known as 'Carry', he lived by housebreaking, and had served his first of 14 prison sentences at the age of 17. Since then, he had spent more than ten years behind bars, including two for possessing explosives. While there, he had been the ringleader in a prison riot.

In August 1938, he had killed soldier James Sydney Emden Shaw, 23, in a fight, by stabbing him in the neck. He was drunk, was found guilty of culpable homicide, and was sentenced to three years. Now known as 'Killer', in 1943, he received three years for a razor attack in which no-one was injured.

In November 1945, Carraher's brother-in-law, Daniel Bonner, got involved in a fight with the three Gordon brothers. Carraher joined in. He was on licence from an assault charge at the time. John Gordon, a soldier, had just been released after spending five years as a German prisoner-of-war. He was not directly involved with the fight, but, from behind, Carraher stabbed

496

him in the neck with a chisel. The soldier died in hospital later. This time, the court was not so lenient with the killer, the jury deciding his fate in 20 minutes.

Read: True Crime Diary vol 2, p106

9 April 1946   Strangeways prison, Manchester

633

<u>Harold BERRY</u>   **30**

Stabbed: **Bernard Philipps**, *37, on 3 January 1946, in Winsford, Cheshire.*
Motive: *Financial.*

Berry, *(b.1916)*, a married man with four children, worked in a bacon factory, and was having an affair with Irene Winn, whose soldier husband was away on service. Berry told Bernard Philipps, a moneylender's manager, that he wanted to secure a loan on some property, and the two left Philipps' office at 11am, the manager with £50 in his wallet.

Out in open country, Berry stabbed Philipps with a commando knife and robbed him. Berry and Irene travelled first class for two days around London on the proceeds. Mr Philipps' body was found on 5 January, and his wallet and cigarette lighter were found in Berry's possession. His own wife testified that Berry owned such a commando knife.

Read: And May The Lord Have Mercy On Your Soul

24 April 1946   Strangeways prison, Manchester

634

<u>Martin Patrick COFFEY</u>   **24**

Shot: **Henry Dutton**, *72, on 26 November 1945, in Manchester, Lancs.*
Motive: *Financial.*

Coffey, *(b.1922)*, entered Mr Dutton's shop at 2.30pm, and asked the shopkeeper to see an overcoat, before pulling out a pistol and demanding money. When the old man tried to struggle with his assailant, Coffey fired two shots, hitting Mr Dutton in the thigh and the stomach. He managed to stagger outside, before collapsing on the pavement and being taken to hospital.

Coffey bragged to friends about the robbery, claiming he had netted over £2000. He and the friends were picked up on an unconnected matter, but when Mr Dutton died on 30 November, one of Coffey's associates told police what he knew. The jury took 45 minutes to convict.

Read: Murderous Manchester, p194.

28 May 1946   Lincoln prison

635

Leonard HOLMES   32

Strangled: **Peggy Agnes Holmes**, *29, his wife, on 19 November 1945, in Walesby, Lincs.*
Motive: *To clear impediment; drink related.*

Holmes, *(b.1914)*, lived in a bungalow with his wife and six children, but hankered after May Shaw whom he had met in 1943 while he was a soldier. May had promised to marry Holmes if ever anything happened to his wife. Holmes drank quite happily with his parents and Peggy in the pub on the night of 18 November, but at 2am he battered his wife with a coal hammer, and finished her off by strangling her.

He took the kids to school, arranged for them to stay with their grandparents, and then went off to Huddersfield to see May. He told her Peggy had left him, and they were now free to be together. Holmes brother found Peggy's body, and Leonard was arrested on the way back to Walesby. He tried to claim that Peggy had been flirting with soldiers, and was about to leave him.

Read: And May The Lord Have Mercy On Your Soul

636

Thomas HENDREN   31

Stabbed:	***Ella Valentine Staunton***, *41, on 20 May 1946, in Liverpool, Lancs.*
Motive:	*Vengeance*

Hendren, *(b.1915)*, had seen wartime action in Singapore with the merchant navy, and had worked as a ship's baker until January 1945. Thereafter things started to go wrong for him. Unable to hold another job down, he stole money from a factory, and then from his sister. His fiancee broke off their engagement after he had infected her with VD, and twice he tried to kill himself, with gas and pills, for which he served a short prison term.

For five years he had been a client of Ella Staunton, who ran a brothel in the basement of her manicure lounge in Tempest Hey. A former ballroom dancer, Ella French had been married for four years until 1938, and was suspected of running the brothel since 1940.

On the afternoon of 20 May, Hendren visited Ella, and asked her for a loan of £10. He felt she owed him for all the money he had paid her over the years. When she refused, he bludgeoned her with a case-opener, strangled her with flex and stabbed her in the heart. By chance, the police had the place under surveillance, and heard the fracas. They questioned Hendren as he left, but let him go, not discovering Ella's body until they entered the premises ten minutes later.

He was found in a Salford toilet two days later, with items stolen from Ella on him. He made a full confession, and unsuccessfully relied on an insanity plea.

Read: True Detective, Oct 97.

637

Walter CLAYTON   22

Strangled:	***Joyce Jacques***, *23, on 12 April 1946, in Morecambe, Lancs.*
Motive:	*To clear impediment; drink related.*

Clayton, *(b.1924)*, had a wife in Morecambe, and was in the army, having served mainly in Burma. Not much of his leave in April 1946 was spent with his wife, for he met Joyce Jacques, a former WAAF, and went to stay with her from their first encounter.

They spent much of 12 April drinking, finally leaving the pub at 8pm and going back to her place. Having failed to borrow a dagger earlier, he killed Joyce, his lover for just seven days, by strangling her, and returned to the pub at 9pm. He later met his wife on the pier, and told her what he had done. He was arrested at home at 2am.

Read: And May The Lord Have Mercy On Your Soul

10 August 1946   Barlinnie prison, Glasgow   *A.Pierrepoint*

638

John CALDWELL   **19**   *Scottish*

Shot: ***James Straiton**, 65, on 26 March 1946, in Glasgow, Lanarks.*
Motive: *Financial.*

Caldwell, *(b. 1927)*, had been released from borstal in mid-July, and had since conducted several armed burglaries in the Dennistoun area of Glasgow. His 57-year old father, James, acted as his fence. On 26 March John and his 15-year old accomplice entered the home of retired Detective Sergeant James Deekan.

Returning from the cinema with his wife at 8pm, Deekan saw a light on, and went to get his ex-policeman neighbour, Jim Straiton, to help. When they went in they saw the two youths at the top of the stairs. Caldwell, 5'5", missed with the first shot of his Colt-45, and Straiton managed to hit him on the head with his truncheon. But two more shots were fired, one hitting Straiton in the stomach.

A fingerprint left in another burgled house led police to Caldwell. Charges against the accomplice, a mental defective, were dismissed.

Read: True Crime, Apr 96.

6 September 1946

Wandsworth prison, London
A.Pierrepoint/ Critchell/ Harry Allen

639

David Baillie MASON   39

Strangled: ***Dorothy Louisa Mildred Mason**, his wife, 37, on 28 May 1946, in Wallington, Surrey*

Motive: *Vengeance*

Mason, *(b. 1907),* a milling operator, lived in Wallington with his wife Dorothy, a cleaner and hairdresser, and their 3-year old son, David. Dorothy was not happy and regretted having the child. On 28 May she did not collect her son from nursery and his father was called to get him.

Dorothy returned home at 10.30pm and, according to Mason, smothered the child in his cot, an act of which her own brother said she was quite capable. In fact, it was later determined that the child died from morphine poisoning. His habit of not sleeping had annoyed Dorothy. In his distress, for Mason doted on his child, he strangled his wife by hand, put her into her nightdress and into bed. At 4am he fetched a doctor saying his wife had had a bilious attack.

The jury did not accept his son's death as provocation, and condemned him in 40 minutes. He was hanged with Sydney Smith.

Read: Master Detective, Nov95.

6 September 1946

Wandsworth prison, London
A.Pierrepoint/ Critchell/ Harry Allen

640

Sydney John SMITH   22

Shot: *John Whatman, 72, on 2 March 1946, near Hastings, Sussex.*

Motive: *Financial.*

Smith, *(b. 1924),* some-time glazier, lived in Markyate, Herts, having moved from his parents home in Lunsford Cross, Sussex in 1944. They had been tinkers until Sidney's teenage years, and he was illiterate, having received no schooling. He bought a revolver from his father in January 1946.

On the evening of 2 March, Smith called at the isolated wooden cottage owned by John Whatman in Hollington, near Hastings. Whatman, a widower, was a horse and cattle dealer, and lived alone. Outside the house

Smith twice shot the old man at point blank range, once in the back of the neck and once in the shoulder, and dragged his body towards an outhouse where he covered it with an overcoat. He then ransacked the cottage and opened the safe, stealing perhaps £25 and several watches. He threw the revolver into a hedge down the lane. Mr Whatman's body was found in the snow by an employee the following morning.

Sydney Smith had been seen in the area and was traced to Markyate by a signed £5 note. Police found him in possession of Mr Whatman's watch, some ammunition and £29. Smith confessed, but said that he had acted in self-defence after the old man had refused to buy the gun and had attacked him. The jury took under 30 minutes to decide his guilt. He was hanged with David Mason.

Read: True Crime, Apr 96.

16 October 1946   Pentonville prison, London   *A.Pierrepoint/ Kirk*

641

Neville George Clevely HEATH   29

Suffocated:	**1 Margery Aimee Brownell Gardner**, *32,* *on 20 June 1946, in Notting Hill, London W11,*
Cut throat of:	**2 Doreen Marshall**, *21, on 3 July 1946,* *near Bournemouth, Hants.*
Motive:	*Sadistic pleasure.*

Heath, *(b.1917),* had a record for housebreaking, theft and fraud, and had served a Borstal term from 1938. He was twice court-martialled and dismissed from the RAF, in between serving in the South African air force. There he had been married for three years and had fathered a son before being divorced in 1945.

Blond, blue-eyed Heath's particular pleasure was sado-masochistic sex. As a boy, he had committed assault, and again in South Africa, before being caught in March 1946 whipping a naked woman in a hotel room in Notting Hill. No charges were brought.

In May he was similarly interrupted by a hotel detective when the screams of willing participant Margery Gardner were heard. On 15 June, Yvonne Symonds, 19, had been his overnight guest at the hotel, and five days later, after an evening clubbing in Kensington, Margery again accompanied Heath to his hotel room. She was an occasional film extra, and was separated from her husband.

According to their usual pleasure, Margery was bound hand and foot on the bed, and Heath began to whip her with a metal-tipped riding switch. As Heath's frenzy grew, he stifled Margery's screams with a gag. Seventeen times he hit her face and upper body with the whip and punched her in the face. Hit bit off her nipples and twisted the whip, or possibly a poker, inside her vagina, causing severe bleeding.

Only then did he relieve Margery of her suffering by suffocating her, probably with a pillow. There was no evidence that intercourse had taken place. Her body was discovered on the bed, covered with a sheet, by a chambermaid the following afternoon.

While the police were searching for Heath, he met Doreen Marshall in Bournemouth, on holiday from London to recuperate from a bout of flu. Using an alias, Heath offered to walk her to her hotel after midnight on 3 July. In Branksome Dene Chine, threatening her with a knife, they both stripped. He bound and gagged her and then slit her throat. There was bruising on her head and shoulders and cuts on her hands resulting from her attempts to fend him off. Unlike Margery, Doreen's mutilation took place after death. He cut open her torso in a 'Y' from breasts to genitals. He used a branch to split open her anus and vagina, slashed at her breasts and bit off one nipple. Her body was discovered the next day. He re-entered his hotel through a window and was seen sleeping in his room at 4 a.m.

Two days later, sure of his alibi, he went to the police under his alias to assist them with inquiries. He was, however, recognised from photos of Heath which had been circulated. The riding switch was discovered in his hotel room, and he was identified as having sold Doreen's ring and watch. Heath was charged with the murder of Margery Gardner only. The defence's plea of insanity was rejected, and the jury of eleven men and one woman took one hour to find him guilty.

Read: Murders of the Black Museum

1 November 1946   Pentonville prison, London   *A.Pierrepoint/ Critchell*

642

Arthur Robert BOYCE   45

Shot: ***Elizabeth McLindon**, 41, on 8 June 1946, in Belgravia, London SW1.*
Motive: *Vengeance.*

Boyce, *(b.1901)*, a married man with a grown-up family, had served eighteen months for bigamy. He was a painter-decorator on Brighton pier, who supplemented his income with illegal bookmaking. He was wanted for passing dud cheques. One of these was used to pay for an engagement ring for Elizabeth McLindon whom he had met in April 1946.

With fake references from Boyce, she had managed to secure herself a job as housekeeper in the home of King George II of Greece, in Belgravia. The King was yet to move in, and in the few weeks since she had been there, Miss McLindon had worked as a high-class prostitute, entertaining wealthy men at the house.

The ring Boyce had given her was reclaimed on the morning of 8 June, and when Boyce called later the same day, an argument ensued. As Elizabeth sat in the library and picked up the telephone to call the police, Boyce shot her in the neck. He copied her keys and locked her within the library. He then sent letters saying he had tried to phone her, to deflect suspicion.

When the body was found six days later, the letters gave police their lead. A man testified that his pistol had been stolen from a Fulham hostel some months before, and he had suspected Boyce. Empty shell cases from the pistol were the same as from the murder weapon. Boyce tried to implicate Elizabeth's former lover William Matlow, but the jury were convinced of his guilt in 75 minutes.

Read: Forty Years of Murder, p159.

13 November 1946   Wandsworth prison, Manchester   *A.Pierrepoint/ Kirk*

643

Frank Josiah FREIYER   **26**

Strangled: ***Joyce Brierley,*** *19, on 20 September 1946, in London SE7.*
Motive: *To clear impediment.*

Freiyer, *(b.1920),* had joined the RAF in 1938, and had then served with the 8th army at El Alamein in 1942. He and Joyce Brierley had been together for some weeks, but Freiyer had begun to tire of her. In September, with his mother, they went to Canvey Island, and Frank seemed rather downcast on his return.

Despite her feelings for him, Joyce told Freiyer that he could finish with her if he so wished, and the two went to the park at 9.30pm. The couple kissed, but there was a struggle as he began to strangle her. Joyce managed to bite his nose, but finally succumbed to his pressure.

Read: And May The Lord Have Mercy On Your Soul

504

644

Arthur RUSHTON   31

Stabbed: ***Catherine Cooper***, *18, on 2 September 1946, in Birkenhead, Cheshire*
Motive: *Vengeance*

Rushton, *(b.1915)*, from Birkenhead, joined the army in 1938, and married his wife Josephine, whom he met on leave in Bootle, in 1940. He was then posted overseas until 1945, during which time he heard that he wife was being unfaithful. Upon his discharge he returned to live with his parents. He met Rene Cooper early in 1946, and the two fell in love. He told her about his wife, but a divorce was too expensive at the time. He considered re-enlisting to facilitate an easier separation, and he and Rene were engaged on 30 June, her 18th birthday. However, Rene's parents soon discovered Rushton was already married, and the engagement was broken off.

Rushton called to see his love several times, and she promised to wait for him, but on 2 September outside her house, Rushton punched her in the face, and stabbed her with the dagger which he had given her as a present, and which she was returning. He went to the hospital, and on discovering Rene was dead, Rushton drank a bottle of disinfectant. He claimed he did not know what had happened at the house, and stated that he did not want to live.

Read: True Crime, Nov 97.

10 December 1946   Pentonville prison, London
                                                    A.Pierrepoint/ Harry Allen

645

John Fleming McCready MATHIESON   23

Strangled: ***Mona Victoria van der Stay***, *46, on 20 July 1946, in Holloway, London N7.*
Motive: *Sexual; drink related.*

Mathieson, *(b. 1923)*, was an able seaman in the Royal Navy. He had been torpedoed in 1943, his ear-drum being perforated. He spent three days stranded on a raft, and was taken as a prisoner-of-war by the Germans.

There he had stolen and crashed a vehicle, receiving head injuries. Based in Portsmouth, he had in the summer of 1946 taken lodgings in Finsbury Park. On 20 July he had got very drunk in two Holloway pubs, downing beer and several double gins.

Mrs van der Stay was married to an assistant cinema manager and the mother of five children. She and her parents had been music hall weight-lifters, and she was preparing a theatre company trip to Australia. She had left home at 8pm to go to see a *Tarzan* film. It seems that she had met Mathieson at a bus stop on her way home.

He was arrested at midnight when a cafe owner complained of his drunkenness. He remained in police cells, when Mona's body was found the next morning near the vestry of St Luke's church by two seven-year old choirboys. She was naked above the waist and a coat had been thrown over her. There had been no sexual assault, and her handbag containing £12 had not been touched. Her ID card was found in Holloway road, but three of her clothing coupons were found on Mathieson in the cells. He admitted meeting a woman, but said that she had fought him and he had punched her. He was too drunk to remember anything else.

It appeared that drink had got the better of Mathieson's attempt at rape, but It was strange that the strong woman had not put up more of a struggle. The jury took 50 minutes to deliver its verdict, at which Mathieson merely smirked.

Read: True Detective, Nov 96

1947

total: *12*

646	3 Jan	Stanley SHEMINANT	35		Walton
647	30 Jan	Albert SABIN	21		Armley
648	27 Feb	Walter ROWLAND	39		Strangeways
649	18 Mar	Harold HAGGER	45		Wandsworth
650	26 Mar	Frederick REYNOLDS	39		Pentonville
651	15 Apr	David WILLIAMS	26		Wandsworth
652	20 Jun	Eric BRIGGS	40		Armley
653	14 Aug	William SMEDLEY	38		Armley
654	21 Aug	John GARTSIDE	24		Armley
655	19 Sep	Christopher GERAGHTY	20		Pentonville
656	19 Sep	Charles JENKINS	23		Pentonville
657	30 Dec	Eugeniusz JURKIEWICZ	34	*Polish*	Bristol

3 January 1947   Walton gaol, Liverpool   *Wade*

646

Stanley SHEMINANT   **35**

Bludgeoned: *Harry Berrisford, 20, on 17 May 1946, in Hanley, Staffs.*
Motive: *To clear impediment*

When Harry Berrisford was called up to the catering corps in 1945, his mother, Margaret, took in lodgers, Sheminant, *(b.1912)* and his girlfriend occupied the front parlour. Sheminant, from Southampton, had separated from his wife in 1939, and came to Staffordshire in 1943, working as a bus driver. He injured a leg in a car accident in February 1946, and had been off work since. A gambler, he had accrued debts, and supplemented his income by selling the piano from his room, and Harry's bike and best suit, unknown to Mrs Berrisford.

When the private returned on brief leave in May, he found out about the suit and bike and an argument followed. Sheminant struck Harry with a hammer. He sawed through a joist in the floor to accomodate the body, then lay new linoleum on top. He told Harry's mother, returning later from work, that her son had been called away suddenly. Sheminant and his girlfriend, threatend to keep quiet, continued to sleep on a mattress above the corpse.

On 19 July, Margaret forced the door after a strange smell had raised her suspicions. Finding the piano gone, and the floorboards disturbed, she called the police, who found her son's body. They waited for Sheminant to return home. He was wearing the soldier's shoes, and had his pen. The jury convicted Sheminant in 30 minutes.

Read: True Crime, Dec 95.   .

---

30 January 1947   Armley gaol, Leeds   *Wade/ Kirk*

647

Albert SABIN   **21**

Shot: ***Dr Neil Macleod**, 52, on 21 September 1946, in Leeds, W.Yorks.*
Motive: *Financial.*

Sabin, *(b.1926),* from Birmingham, was an army private who acted as a guard at a prisoner-of-war camp near Leeds. At 2pm he waited outside Dr Macleod's surgery and was seen leaping into his car as he departed. Macleod, from Skye, was married with two sons and had come to Leeds in 1938, having fought at Jutland in 1916. Sabin made him drive to a disused colliery at Topcliffe where he shot him with a revolver four times in the head and chest, dragging his body from the car to a ditch where he was found an hour later.
Sabin drove the car back to his camp and hid the doctor's coat and bag there, stealing £20. He claimed the gun had gone off by accident after Macleod had tried to 'interfere' with him.

Read: Murderous Leeds

---

27 February 1947   Strangeways prison, Manchester   *A.Pierrepoint*

648

Walter Graham ROWLAND   **39**

Strangled: **1 *Mavis Agnes Rowland**, 2, his daughter, on 2 Mar 1934, in Mellor, Derbyshire.*

Probably bludgeoned:	**2 Olive Balchin**, *40, on 19 October 1946, in Manchester, Lancs.*
Motive:	*Vengeance.*

Rowland, *(b. 1908)*, married Annie Schofield in 1932 after attempting to strangle her in 1927. He had served a term in borstal for that offence. His first wife had died nine months after their marriage in 1930. In 1934 he was sentenced to death for strangling his 2-year old daughter Mavis. He was reprieved and released in 1940 to serve in the Royal Artillery. Since his demobilisation in 1946, he had worked as a labourer and lived in a hostel for ex-servicemen.

On 19 October Rowland murdered Olive Balchin, a prostitute, with a shoemaker's hammer, found nearby, on a bomb site near Deansgate. Her body was found by two children the following day. Rowland had syphilis which he thought he had contracted from Olive, whom he knew as 'Lil'. Dust, hair and blood found on Rowland's clothing matched the bomb site and the victim, though witness evidence was inconclusive.

Another man, David Ware, 39, admitted to the killing, but later retracted the confession. There was no forensic evidence against him, though his claim to have paid Olive ten shillings for sex that night on the bomb site, matched with money found on the dead body. Ware committed suicide in Broadmoor in 1954, after the attempted murder with a hammer of another woman in 1951. He again admitted his guilt for the 1946 murder. Rowland maintained his innocence to the end, reprieved for a murder he probably did commit, and hanged for one he probably did not.

Read: Murder In Low Places

8 March 1947	Wandsworth prison, London	*A.Pierrepoint/ Critchell*

649

Harold HAGGER   45   *(aka Sydney Sinclair)*

Strangled:	**Dagmar Peters**, *47, on 31 October 1946, on Wrotham Hill, Kent.*
Motive:	*Financial.*

Hagger, *(b. 1902)*, worked as a lorry driver for a firm in Cambridge. Known as 'Basher' or otherwise as Sydney Sinclair, he had a string of sixteen convictions, including assault on a woman. In the early morning of 31 October 1946, en route to delivering bricks to a mill in East Malling in Kent, he gave a lift to Dagmar Peters, waiting by the roadside of the A20. She was a single woman of Polish origin, real name Petrzywalski, of very limited means who lived alone near her aged mother in Kingsdown. She journeyed weekly to London to visit her sister-in-law, often taking lifts from passing motorists.

Hagger strangled her from behind in his cab, using the woman's scarf as a ligature. He drove on a short distance before dragging her body into roadside shrubbery, where it was later discovered by a passing driver who had noticed a single shoe by the kerb. The woman's purse, key, string-bag and attache case were missing. No sexual assault had been made, and robbery seems to have been the motive, however unlikely the victim.

Having discovered the brick delivery, the police questioned Hagger in Cambridge. He admitted the killing, claiming that he had been angered when Miss Peters had tried to steal from his jacket hanging in the cab. On a cold morning, the prosecution suggested, he would have been wearing it. Hagger was not believed.

Read: Settings For Slaughter, p288.

| 26 March 1947 | Pentonville prison, London | *A.Pierrepoint/ Kirk* |

650

Frederick REYNOLDS   39

Shot: **Beatrice Greenberg**, 40, on 17 December 1946, in London N5.
Motive: *Vengeance; drink related.*

Reynolds, *(b.1908),* and Beatrice Greenberg had been having a relationship for eighteen years, even though both were married. He would pass her house and whistle, and if her husband was out, she would signal him to come in.

On 17 December, there was no answer to his musical salute, so Reynolds went back later when Beatrice let him in. When she told him he could not stay because her husband was about to return, he shot her.

Read: And May The Lord Have Mercy On Your Soul

651

David John WILLIAMS 26

Bludgeoned: **Margaret Williams**, *26, his wife, on 6 February 1947, in Merton, Surrey.*
Motive: *Vengeance.*

Williams, *(b.1921)*, was left by his wife in January 1947, and Margaret went into lodgings in Merton. She was granted maintenance. Williams failed in repeated attempts to get her back, and attempted to gas himself on 2 February.

Williams then rose early to be outside Margaret's lodgings when she left for work. He again urged her to come back to him, but when she refused, he hit her over the head with a hammer, and banged her head against the road several times. Williams claimed that Margaret had double-crossed him.

Read: And May The Lord Have Mercy On Your Soul

652

Eric Charles BRIGGS   40

Stabbed: **Gertrude Briggs**, *47, his wife, on 10 February 1947, in Leeds, W.Yorks.*
Motive: *To clear impediment.*

In 1932 Briggs, *(b.1907)*, met Gertrude Dugdale, who had a daughter Irene, 10, from her first marriage. The two married in 1934, Gertrude giving birth again, and Irene becoming the mother of four children. Briggs was the father of them all. Gertrude was aware of this and many arguments followed, with Briggs' wife threatening to sell herself on the streets if he did not stop.

While his wife was working washing up at a hotel, Briggs and Irene, now 25, had sex before he slipped out of the house at midnight, his step-daughter sleeping. He waited for Gertrude to approach and then stabbed her in the neck with a hacksaw blade. She had 47 small cuts and three deeper wounds and was found at 12.30am.

The police called for Briggs at 4.45am when he still had blood on his hands and clothes. He confessed but later withdrew his statement. Private Dennis Wood, 19, also confessed, and knew various unpublished details. He had attacked two women over the previous five weeks, and was later found guilty but insane of attempted murder on those charges.

Read: Murderous Leeds

14 August 1947   Armley gaol, Leeds   *Wade/ Kirk*

653

William SMEDLEY   38

Strangled: *Edith Simmonite*, 27, on 7 March 1947, in Sheffield, W.Yorks.
Motive: *Vengeance.*

Smedley, *(b.1909)*, lived in a hostel, and was a regular client of prostitute Edith Simmonite. He claimed that she pestered him, usually for money, and he thought that it was she who had stolen some money from him. Smedley and a friend from the hostel had a drink with Edith, and the three walked back to the lodgings, where the friend left the other two. They went to a derelict house and had sex, after which, Smedley said, Edith told him she had venereal disease. He then strangled her with her scarf. Smedley had not slept in his bed that night, and he confessed to his sister.

Read: And May The Lord Have Mercy On Your Soul

21 August 1947   Armley gaol, Leeds   *Wade/ Critchell*

654

John Edward GARTSIDE   24

Shot: 1 *Percy Baker*, 45, and his wife,
          2 *Alice Baker*, 43, on 20 May 1947, in Standedge, W.Yorks.
Motive: *Financial.*

Gartside, *(b. 1923)*, ran a shop in Uppermill, West Yorkshire. He lived with his parents nearby, on the Pennines between Oldham and Huddersfield. Only 300 metres away was the farm where Percy Baker and his wife Alice lived.

Gartside went to the farm on 20 May armed with a revolver and a rifle, presumably to commit burglary. When the Bakers returned home and disturbed him, he killed Alice with a single revolver shot to the head at close range. Percy was shot in the chest with the rifle, and finished off with two revolver shots to the head. That night he buried the naked bodies on Brun Moor, 200 metres from the roadside. He stole the couple's car, and arranged for their furniture to be collected and taken to his premises in Uppermill.

Friends of the Bakers raised the alarm when they found the removers at work. Percy's signature was found to have been falsified and Gartside was found driving his car. His explanation was that the couple had quarrelled while he was there arranging the sale of some of their furniture. They had both been shot while struggling with the guns. The ballistics evidence did not match Gartside's story and he was found guilty.

Read: *Settings For Slaughter*

19 September 1947   Pentonville prison, London
                                        A.Pierrepoint/ Critchell/ Harry Allen

655, 656

Christopher James GERAGHTY   20
Charles Henry JENKINS   23

Shot: ***Alec de Antiquis**, 34, on 28 April 1947, in Tottenham St, London W1.*
Motive: *To escape arrest.*

Jenkins, *(b.1924)*, who had a record of assault, had been in borstal with Geraghty, *(b.1927)*, also of Bermondsey, south London. Together with Terence Peter Rolt, 17, who also had a record for robbery, they broke into a jeweller's shop in Charlotte St on a Monday afternoon in April, armed with weapons stolen from a shop two days before. The firm's director was clubbed with a gun and a shot was fired.

The robbery and their planned escape in a stolen car were bungled. They escaped empty-handed on foot, and Alec de Antiquis, married with six children, drove his motor-cycle across their path. He was shot in the head by Geraghty, who claimed he had only fired tthe revolver to frighten the man.

513

Traced through trade numbers found in a raincoat in a nearby office block, all three were found guilty, Rolt being detained as a minor. He was released in June 1956. Jenkins' brother, Thomas, had been found guilty of manslaughter for a similar offence in 1944.

Read: Murders of the Black Museum

30 December 1947   Horfield gaol, Bristol

657

Eugeniusz JURKIEWICZ   **34**   *Polish*

Strangled: ***Emily Bowers***, *75, on 13 September 1947, in Middlezoy, Somerset*
Motive: *Sexual; drink related.*

Jurkiewicz, *(b.1913),* had been a soldier since 1928, fighting in the Polish campaign in 1939, and then being taken to a Siberian labour camp for two years. After serving in Italy for two years, the staff sergeant came to England in 1946, and came to Middlezoy resettlement camp near Bridgwater in August 1947. Like many of his compatriots he enjoyed the dances in Emily Bowers village pub.

Emily had been a widow for 20 years, and had come to Middlezoy from Brixham in 1940. An elderly lodger had died in 1946, and, living alone, she was advertising for another. Many locals abandoned her pub when the Polish troops started to frequent it. On 12 September she had been dancing with Jurkiewicz and had kissed him on the neck. Thinking this was an invitation for sex, the worse for drink, he returned later through a downstairs window. He stifled her screams as he raped Emily, then strangled the old woman.

The jury decided his fate in 22 minutes.

Read: Master Detective, Jun 95.

658	7 Jan	George WHELPTON	31		Armley
659	3 Feb	Evan EVANS	22	*Welsh*	Cardiff
660	6 Feb	Stanislaw MYSZKA	23	*Polish*	Perth
661	19 Feb	Walter CROSS	21		Pentonville
662	18 Nov	Stanley CLARK	34		Norwich
663	19 Nov	Peter GRIFFITHS	22		Walton
664	2 Dec	George RUSSELL	45		Oxford
665	9 Dec	Clifford WILLS	31	*Welsh*	Cardiff
666	30 Dec	Arthur OSBORNE	28		Armley

7 January 1948　　　　Armley gaol, Leeds　　　　*Wade/ Kirk*

658

George Henry WHELPTON　　　31

Strangled:　　1 **Alison Gertrude Parkin**, *48, and her children,*
　　　　　　　　2 **Joyce Parkin,** *23,*
　　　　　　　　3 **Maurice Parkin**, *15, on 9 October 1947, in Doncaster,*
　　　　　　　　W.Yorks.
Motive:　　　*Vengeance.*

　　　Whelpton, *(b. 1917),* was a bus driver who had served in North Africa during the war. He and Mrs Parkin, a widow, had been lovers for some time even though he was married. Following an argument over money, he strangled Alison and her two children in the living room of their home, using two knives to mutilate the sexual organs of all three. He had then gone upstairs to bed.
　　　Leaving the bed covered in blood, urine and excrement, he left at 7am and went to his mother's. A neighbour, finding the door wide open, discovered the bodies at midday. Maurice's trousers were pulled down and his genitals cut off. They had been stuffed into Alison's mouth, a cigarette butt in her vagina. Another stub had been shoved down Joyce's throat. Both women were naked.
　　　Arrested at work, Whelpton claimed that Alison had discovered him in bed with Joyce. Almost certainly insane, he was, nevertheless, condemned by the jury.

Read: Master Detective Summer Special 93

3 February 1948   Cardiff prison

659

<u>Evan Haydn EVANS</u>   **22**   *Welsh*

Punched/ kicked to death: ***Rachel Allan***, *76, on 12 October 1947, in Wattstown, Glamorgan.*
Motive: *Vengeance; drink related.*

Evans, *(b.1926),* a 4' 11" colliery worker, lived in the Rhondda with his parents and sister. Getting drunk in the local pub, he got into an argument with the local old washerwoman, Rachel Allan, to whom he had been making lewd suggestions.

When the pub closed, Evans followed Rachel down the street. As she reached her house, where she lived a poverty-stricken life alone but for her cats, she was again accosted by Evans. When she called him a pig, he punched her to the ground and jumped on her face, continuing to kick her as she lay dying. He sexually assaulted her and stuffed a match up her nose as he lit a cigarette and went on his way.

Rachel's neighbour found her by the yard door, with her skirt over her head, and naked below. Evans, who had been seen arguing with Rachel in the street, denied all knowledge of the assault, but the suit he had been wearing on the evening of the attack was found in the Evans' sofa. It was covered in blood, as were his shoes. The turn-ups of his trousers contained blood and skin tissue. The jury decided his fate in 40 minutes.

Evans' was the first hanging in Wales for 20 years.

Read: Master Detective Summer Special 91.

6 February 1948   Perth prison

660

<u>Stanislaw MYSZKA</u> **23** *Polish*

Bludgeoned: ***Catherine McIntyre***, *47, on 26 September 1947, in Kenmore, Perthshire.*
Motive: *Financial.*

Myszka, *(b. 1925),* from the Polish army in exile had for two years lived at a resettlement centre near Loch Tay. He was of low intellect and his wife and children were in France. For three months he had been casually employed on a farm in Old Meldrum, Aberdeenshire, from where he stole a shotgun.

On the morning of 26 September, 1947, he bound Mrs McIntyre with bootlaces and gagged her with a scarf on her son's bed at her house in Kenmore, near Aberfeldy. He battered her over the head with the butt of a shotgun and stole £86, some clothes and her wedding ring. Mrs McIntyre's husband was a head shepherd and the money had been the wages of the shepherds on the farm.

Myszka, 5'6", was identified by a taxi driver who had later taken him to Perth, from a railway ticket specially issued to the armed forces, by hairs on a razor blade, and by the sawn-off shotgun found in a bracken hideout near the McIntyre house. Arrested on 2 October, he was found to be carrying Mrs McIntyre's wedding ring.

Read: True Detective Summer Special 96

19 February 1948   Pentonville prison, London   *A.Pierrepoint/ Harry Allen*

661

Walter John CROSS   21

Strangled: ***Percy Bushby**, 55, on 14 November 1947, in Barking, Essex.*
Motive: *Financial.*

Cross, *(b.1927)*, a married man, had got to know Walter Bull in October 1947, and the two had taken some items to sell at Mr Bushby's shop on 20 October and 12 November. Percy was a watchmaker, virtually lame, and lived alone behind his shop. The two young men had noticed a wallet stuffed with money, and planned a robbery.

Bull failed to turn up, so Cross went ahead alone, strangling the old man when he interrupted him after breaking in. A neighbour found Mr Bushby at 9.30pm. Cross' wife was due to give birth in February 1948.

Read: And May The Lord Have Mercy On Your Soul.

18 November 1948   Norwich prison

662

Stanley Joseph CLARKE   34

Stabbed:	*Florence May Bentley, 32, on 16 June 1948, in Great Yarmouth, Norfolk.*
Motive:	*Financial.*

Clarke, *(b.1914),* met Florence Bentley while she was working as a chambermaid at his brother's guest house. The two dated, but when Clarke proposed, she turned him down, and Clarke then told her he would kill her. In June, Clarke went to the hotel and followed Florence when she went about her duties upstairs. He produced a butcher's knife, and chasing her down the stairs, he stabbed her three times. Clarke then telephoned the police.

Determined to die, Clarke dived down the steps in the dock, and pleaded guilty, the court proceedings lasting just four minutes.

Read: And May The Lord Have Mercy On Your Soul.

---

19 November 1948   Walton gaol, Liverpool   *A.Pierrepoint*

663

Peter GRIFFITHS   22   *C*

Probably murdered:	**1 Sheila Fox**, 6, in 1944, in Farnworth, Lancs.
*Prob. **bludgeoned/ stabbed:***	**2 Jack Quentin Smith**, 11, in March 1948, in Farnworth, Lancs.
Bludgeoned:	**3 June Anne Devaney**, 4, on 15 May 1948, in Blackburn, Lancs.
Motive:	*Sexual; drink related.*

Griffiths, *(b. 1926),* was a flour-mill packer. Six feet tall, he had been a Guardsman, leaving the service at the beginning of 1948. On the evening of 14 March, he went on a drinking spree, downing 13 pints of beer and two shorts. He found himself outside the Queens Park Hospital in Blackburn.

Walking into a children's ward, he looked round before selecting June Anne Devaney. She had been admitted ten days earlier suffering from pneumonia, and was due to be discharged the following day. He took her to a secluded part of the grounds and sexually assaulted her, possibly raping her. When she cried, he swung her by the leg, smashing her head on a boundary wall. He had left behind fingerprints on the bed and on a bedside bottle.

46,000 adult males were fingerprinted in Blackburn, and Griffiths was arrested on 12 August, fibres from his clothing matching those found on the child and in the hospital. The jury decided his fate within 23 minutes. Police suspected Griffiths of the murder of Sheila Fox, who had disappeared four years earlier, and of Quentin Smith, 11, found dead by a railway embankment. He had been stabbed and beaten, as had his friend, David Lee, 9, who had escaped. Many other Lancashire child assaults were also attributed to him.

Read: A Date With the Hangman, p16

2 December 1948   Oxford prison

664

George RUSSELL   45

Suffocated: ***Minnie Freeman Lee***, *94, on 30 May 1948, in Maidenhead, Berks.*
Motive: *Financial.*

Russell, *(b.1903)*, was a convicted thief and housebreaker. He called on Mrs Lee, an old recluse, on 30 May. Married to a barrister and widowed in 1926, she lived alone, her only son having been killed in the Great War. Her large house was in a state of disrepair, and she lived in a single ground-floor room.

Russell claimed he had called about a gardening job. He hit her about the head with her shoe and bound and gagged her, shutting her in a trunk in the hallway. He ransacked the house, but found nothing of value - Mrs Lee was by now broke. She suffocated from the gag placed in her mouth.

Police, alerted by a milkman, found a single partial fingerprint on a cardboard box and were able to identify it as belonging to Russell. He was arrested in St Albans on 6 June, wearing a scarf belonging to Mrs Lee.

Read: Murder Club Guide to Eastern & Home Counties, p30.

665

Clifford Godfrey WILLS   31   *Welsh*

Stabbed: **Sylvina May Parry**, *32, on 8 June 1948,*
in Pontnewydd, Monmouths.
Motive: *To clear impediment.*

Wills, *(b.1917)*, was unemployed and lived with his mother. For some time he had been conducting a clandestine affair with a married woman who lived nearby. Sylvina May Parry, a petite blonde, was a machine operator at a lacquer works. She and her husband, a steel worker, had a 14-year old son. Sylvina would meet Wills sometimes at his home, but more often at hers while her husband worked shifts.

At 2pm one June day she left work early, supposedly to do some shopping, and went home to entertain Wills. After sex, as she was dressing, he strangled her, hit her on the back of the head with a spanner, and then stabbed her. He stuffed her sleeve down her throat.

Mr Parry reported Sylvina missing the next day, but returned home to find his wife's body under a bed in the box room. She wore black stockings and cami-knickers beneath a raincoat. An unused condom clung to her thigh. Neighbours told police that Wills was a regular visitor, and his fingerprints matched those on Sylvina's handbag, and his shoes matched a footprint in the bathroom. He was found at home having taken an overdose of sleeping pills. He admitted the affair, but denied murder.

Read: True Crime Summer Special 93

666

Arthur George OSBORNE   28

Stabbed: **Ernest Hargreaves Westwood**, *70, on 25 September*
1948, near Halifax, W. Yorks.
Motive: *Financial.*

Osborne, *(b. 1921)*, was known as a housebreaker. He married in 1944 and had three children, but his wife was confined to a mental hospital, and the children put in care. Unemployed, he burgled the home of Mr

Westwood, who lived alone in Southowram, on 25 September. The old man still worked in the local mill, and also acted as a debt collector.

When Mr Westwood disturbed Osborne and threw something at him, he was stabbed with a screwdriver, and died in hospital the same day without regaining consciousness. The £14 he had collected was stolen. Osborne, however, had left a fingerprint, and he was arrested on a train in Sutton, Surrey. He had been due to get bigamously married the same day. Osborne was hanged on his 28th birthday.

Read: True Crime Diary vol 2, p278.

24 November 1948   Mountjoy gaol, Dublin   *A.Pierrepoint*

<u>William GAMBON</u>   28

Bludgeoned: ***John Long***, *39, on 22 August 1948, in Dublin.*
Motive: *Vengeance.*

      Gambon, *(b. 1920),* and Long had become firm friends when they met in hospital in Dublin in 1940. Their friendship, based largely on loneliness, survived Long's moving to England in 1942. Each week Long would send money to his unemployed pal, and when Gambon married in April 1948, Long arranged to take a summer break to visit Gambon that summer. Mrs Gambon had gone to stay with a cousin so that Long could be accomodated in the single room that she and her husband shared.

      When he arrived Long gave Gambon £5 for his wife, and the two friends went out for a drink. They returned to the bed-sit at 2.30am, Long getting into bed, and then agreeing to a game of cards. Gambon won £60 from Long and an argument began. He refused to return all the money to his already over-generous friend, offering only £30. Long swore at Gambon and started to insult his wife, and a fight started.

      Gambon, 5'6", fearing for his safety, reached for an iron bar and hit Long, 6'6", before he could get out of bed. The next day Gambon gave £1 to a friend and bought a padlock for the room. The police were tipped off two days later, and Gambon was arrested. The jury reached its verdict in 65 minutes.

      Read: Master Detective, Oct 97

1949

total: *16*

667	12 Jan	Margaret ALLEN (f)	42		Strangeways
668	27 Jan	George SEMINI	24	*Maltese*	Walton
669	22 Mar	Kenneth STRICKSON	21		Lincoln
670	29 Mar	James FARRELL	19		Winson Green
671	21 Apr	Harry LEWIS	21		Pentonville
672	2 Jun	Dennis NEVILLE	22		Armley
673	21 Jun	Bernard COOPER	40		Pentonville
674	28 Jul	Sidney CHAMBERLAIN	31		Winchester
675	4 Aug	Robert MACKINTOSH	21	*Welsh*	Swansea
676	4 Aug	Rex JONES	21	*Welsh*	Swansea
677	10 Aug	John HAIGH	40		Wandsworth
678	16 Aug	William DAVIES	31		Wandsworth
679	28 Sep	William JONES	31		Pentonville
680	13 Dec	John WILSON	22		Durham
681	13 Dec	Benjamin ROBERTS	22		Durham
682	30 Dec	Ernest COUZINS	49		Wandsworth

12 January 1949   Strangeways prison, Manchester   *A.Pierrepoint*

667

Margaret ALLEN   **42**   *female*

Bludgeoned: ***Nancy Ellen Chadwick**, 68, on 29 August 1948,
at Rawtenstall, Lancs.*
Motive: *Sadistic pleasure.*

Allen, *(b.1906),* a bus conductress from 1942-6, one of 22 children, had lived alone since her mother's death in 1943.   She suffered from depression, brought on by the menopause, and had once tried to gas herself. She badly neglected herself and her home. She was a lesbian and liked to be known as 'Bill'.

On 29 August, Nancy Chadwick, an eccentric, miserly housekeeper called at Allen's house, where she lived alone. Eventually having invited her in, Allen 'on the spur of the moment' battered her over the head several times with a hammer. She hid the body in the cellar, removing it to the roadside opposite her house after dark, where it was found next morning. She had robbed the old woman and dumped her bag in a river at the back of the

523

house. Her interest in the case aroused suspicion and she made a speedy and full confession.

Less than 1% of the villagers were prepared to sign a petition for a reprieve such was her unpopularity, and a plea of insanity was rejected. The court case lasted only five hours, and the jury sat for only fifteen minutes. She was the first woman to be hanged for more than 12 years.

Read: Lady Killers

27 January 1949   Walton gaol, Liverpool   *A.Pierrepoint/ H.Allen*

668

George SEMINI   24   *Maltese*

Stabbed: ***Joseph Gibbons**, 23, on 8 October 1948,*
       in Newcastle-under-Lyme, Staffs.
Motive: *Vengeance*

Semini, *(b.1925)*, had come to England in 1940 and joined the RAF. He was invalided out in 1944 and had become a miner in Staffordshire in 1947, living in a miners' hostel in Knutton. He liked to spend weekends drinking with girlfriends. On an October Friday he had been to the cinema with his latest sweetheart and they had taken the bus to Newcastle where they intended to have a drink.

Walking along the street the two were insulted by a drunk, Joseph Gibbons from Liverpool, a labourer at Stafford gasworks, who made sexist and racist remarks. Two of his mates appeared, and Semini slapped Gibbons in the face, stabbed him in the heart with a five-inch sheath knife, and fled. Semini's girlfriend answered a police appeal and Semini was identified by Gibbon's friends.

Semini denied stabbing Gibbons, but a photograph of him posing with just such a knife three weeks before proved damning. He claimed that he had been subject to blackouts since 1944 and knew nothing of the stabbing. The jury deliberated for an hour, and finding him guilty, asked for his state of mind to be examined. Doctors found him to be sane.

Read: True Crime, Dec 97

22 March 1949   Lincoln prison

669

Kenneth STRICKSON   **21**

Bludgeoned: ***Irene May Phillips****, 46, on 19 November 1948, in Nottingham.*
Motive: *Sexual*

Strickson, *(b.1927)*, was an inmate at Bagthorpe borstal, having spent most of his life in institutions since his father's suicide in an asylum, by swallowing a fork. Strickson helped in the cleaning of the chapel, where he made, not for the first time, a sexual suggestion to the matron, Mrs Phillips, who had been there two years. When she rejected his advances, he beat her about the head sixteen times with two chairs, breaking the legs clean off. He stole her keys, but having failed to escape, went to the governor and admitted his crime.

Read: Nottingham...The Sinister Side, p43.

29 March 1949   Winson Green prison, Birmingham   *A.Pierrepoint/Kirk*

670

James FARRELL   **19**

Strangled: ***Joan Mary Marney****, 14, on 21 November 1948, in Birmingham, Warwicks.*
Motive: *Sexual.*

Farrell, *(b.1930)*, had gone absent from his Preston unit on 19 November and had returned to his father's home in Kingstanding. He had been an unruly child, and his mother had been in an asylum since 1945. The following day, Farrell had tried to gas himself, his father finding him unconscious. The day after that he went to the cinema where he got talking to Joan Marney, who told him she was 17. She had gone there with two friends, whom she told to go on without her.

Taking her to a nearby beauty spot at Sutton Park, Farrell attacked Joan, hitting her in the face, and strangling her manually. He stuffed a corner of her raincoat in her mouth to stifle her cries. There was no sexual assault. He then dumped her body in hollybushes, where she was found at 11.45am the next day. Farrell reported himself absent without leave to police at 10pm that day, and made a full confession when questioned about the murder.

Read: *The Hangman's Tale, p11.*

21 April 1949   Pentonville prison, London   *A.Pierrepoint/ Harry Allen*

671

Harry LEWIS   21

Bludgeoned: **Harry Saul Michaelson**, *50, on 26 December 1948, in Paddington, London W1.*
Motive: *Financial.*

Harry Michaelson was a cartoonist and commercial artist who lived in a Paddington basement flat with his wife. She was away for the Christmas holidays, and Harry was sleeping there alone. Lewis, *(b.1938),* a Welshman who had a record for petty theft, was out of money. Wandering the streets he noticed the window to Michaelson's flat was open, and saw the opportunity of easy money. He stole £5 from Harry's trouser pocket but the artist awoke and confronted him. Lewis hit him across the head and body with a steel chair - the first thing that came to hand. As Lewis made his escape through the bedroom window, Harry staggered out of his front door and collapsed. Despite emergency surgery in hospital, he died shortly after.

Fingerprints on the chair led police to Lewis, who was arrested on 18 January. The defence claimed that Mr Michaelson had died not from his injuries but from the surgery he had undergone. The jury did not accept that, but did recommend mercy.

Read: *Murders of the Black Museum*

2 June 1949   Armley gaol, Leeds   *Wade/ Harry Allen*

672

Dennis NEVILLE   22

Strangled: **Marian Poskitt**, *21, on 19 February 1949, in Dewsbury, W.Yorks.*

526

| *Motive:* | *Vengeance* |

Neville, *(b.1927)*, was a schizophrenic who worked as a glazier's mate. After taking part in the D-Day landings, he had been taken prisoner by the Germans who beat, starved and isolated him. Freed by the allies, he returned to England to find that his brother had been killed in Burma and that his parents had separated. Soon after, his father was killed in a street brawl, the killer being acquitted. Neville, living with his mother and two sisters, became very disturbed and was an out-patient at Leeds Infirmary.

His girlfriend was Marian Poskitt, a mill weaver, whom he had known for 11 years. But by 1949, Neville was cooling the relationship. He said that she admitted having sex with another man in November 1948, and that she was pregnant. Neville and Marian then had intercourse once only. They both attended a dance separately on 19 February, but Marian asked Neville to walk her home.

On a cricket pitch they had sex, and then Marian told him that everyone would assume the child was his, and that he would have to take responsibility for it. Neville, powerfully built, then punched the girl, breaking her jaw. He continued to hit the unconcious Marian, spreading blood over a nearby stone wall, and then strangled her to death. Blood and semen were on Marian's clothes, as they were on Neville's. He made a full confession, and the jury delivered its verdict after one hour.

Read: True Crime, July 95

21 June 1949   Pentonville prison, London   *A.Pierrepoint/ Kirk*

673

Bernard Alfred Peter COOPER   40

| **Strangled:** | ***Mary Elizabeth Cooper**, 38, his wife, on 1 April 1949, in London W12.* |
| **Motive:** | *To clear impediment* |

Cooper, *(b.1909)*, was a painter and decorator who in 1949 lived in Shepherds Bush with his pregnant wife and their three children. She was unaware that from the autumn of 1948 until February 1949 her husband had been forcing their 14-year old daughter Sheila into having sex with him. Mary thought his tea-time visits to her bedroom were to help with homework. Then Sheila became pregnant, but still did not tell her mother who the father was. Cooper told doctors his daughter had been raped and was too distressed to tell the police - they performed an abortion.

527

On 1 April Mary discovered the truth, and railed hysterically at her husband, who responded by strangling her with a stocking and putting her under the bed. Cooper told Sheila her mother was dead, and fled. He was arrested five days later sleeping in a school bike shed. He immediately confessed all. The jury sealed his fate within eleven minutes.

Read: True Detective, Sep 96.

28 July 1949   Winchester prison   *A.Pierrepoint/ Harry Allen*

674

Sidney Archibald Frederick CHAMBERLAIN   31

Strangled: ***Doreen Primrose Messenger**, 15, on 18 February 1949, near Exeter, Devon*
Motive: *Vengeance*

Chamberlain, *(b.1918),* a lorry driver and rag and bone man, had a mental age of 11, though he had served in the RAF and was married. In 1940 he had received two years for intent to commit robbery armed with a hammer. By 1949 he had begun an affair with teenager Doreen Messenger, who worked for a book-binders, having left school at 14.

On alternate nights Chamberlain would drive her to Haldon Moor for love-making. He was besotted with her, as letters revealed, and it seems could not bear the relationship to reach its inevitable ending. When she told him, 'I would rather die than go home', he took her literally and strangled her. Her jaw was bruised, and her body, naked except for stockings, was found dumped in a copse the following morning.

He might have got away with it had he not driven straight through a road block, set up after an escape from Dartmoor. He crashed the car into a wall, and when police searched it, they discovered a torn piece of Doreen's dress. The jury retired for 30 minutes.

Read: True Detective, Jun 95.

675

Robert Thomas MACKINTOSH   **21**   *Welsh*

Strangled: **Beryl Beechey**, *16, on 3 June 1949, in Aberavon, Glamorgan.*

Motive: *Sexual.*

Mackintosh, *(b.1928)*, was a quiet, law-abiding furnace-man at Port Talbot steelworks, who had seen action in the Middle East. He lived with his parents, friends of the Beechey family with whom they had previously lodged. Robert was at home alone preparing for a lads' night out when Beryl Beechey called at 7pm to repay 10/- owed to Mrs Mackintosh.

Mackintosh, overcome with lust, violently raped Beryl in his bedroom and strangled her with cord. He dumped her over a wall onto a railway embankment near the back of his home. Her body was discovered there at six the next morning, her clothing ripped apart and covered with blood - due to the violence of the rape upon the young virgin.

When Mrs Beechey reported that Beryl had been on an errand to the Mackintosh house, Robert fell under suspicion, and blood was found in his bedroom. Mackintosh admitted the crime but a plea of temporary insanity was entered. The jury took 15 minutes to reject it. He was hanged alongside Rex Jones.

Read: True Crime, Aug 96.

676

Rex Harvey JONES   **21**   *Welsh*

Strangled: **Beatrice May Watts**, *20, on 5 June 1949, in Nantybar, Glamorgan.*

Motive: *Sexual; drink related.*

Jones, *(b. 1928)*, a shy and pleasant miner from Duffryn Rhondda, had known Beatrice Watts for about six months. He had been to the miners' club and she to a dance when they bumped into each other at the bus stop at 10.30 one Sunday night. He was a bit drunk and Beatrice responded to his kisses. The two went to the nearby forest and made love, there was no sign of any struggle, but immediately afterwards, Jones strangled Beatrice.

The following morning he telephoned the police and confessed to the crime. He could offer no explanation of it, and a plea of temporary insanity was made. The jury took only five minutes to decide his guilt, but did add the 'strongest possible' recommendation to mercy. He was hanged alongside Robert Mackintosh.

Read: True Crime, Aug 96.

10 August 1949   Wandsworth prison, London   *A.Pierrepoint/ Kirk*

677

<u>John George HAIGH</u>   **40**

Bludgeoned:	1 ***William Donald McSwann***, *34, on 9 September 1944, and his parents*
	2 ***William Donald McSwann***, *67, and*
	3 ***Amy McSwann***, *57, in July 1945, in London SW7*
Shot:	4 ***Dr Archibald Henderson***, *41, and his wife*
	5 ***Rosalie Henderson***, *36, on 16 February 1948*
	6 ***Olive Henrietta Helen Olivia Robarts Durand-Deacon***, *68, on 18 February 1949, in Crawley, Sussex.*
Motive:	*Financial.*

Haigh was born in Lincolnshire in 1909 to strictly religious parents, and was brought up in Yorkshire. A small man, accomplished at the piano and organ, he married briefly in 1934. He always had little interest in sex, and was deserted by his wife after he was sent to prison, the first of three terms he served for theft and fraud. He came to London in 1936, and took a job as an amusement arcade manager for Mr and Mrs McSwann. He gambled his money away, and devised a plan to get more. A bad car accident in 1944 was blamed by some for his later taste for blood.

Resuming his acquaintance with the McSwanns, he tricked William, the son, to his house in south Kensington, where he coshed him and disposed of his body by pieces through a mincer. When the parents followed ten months later, Haigh made £4000 plus property on their stolen assets. In 1945 Haigh went to live at the Onslow Court Hotel in Kensington. In 1948, he tricked the Hendersons, a GP and his wife, into a business venture, and separately shot them in the head, disposing of them in the acid tub in Crawley. He made £8000 out of their assets.

Mrs Durand-Deacon, a stout little widow, had being staying at the Onslow Court since 1943. She and Haigh struck up an acquaintance, and she became interested in how he may have been able to help in the manufacture of false finger-nails. Haigh invited her to his 'factory' in Crawley, in fact a mere storeroom. He shot her there in the back of the head, and, stripping her of all valuables, tipped her into the tub of acid. He and another hotel guest reported the widow missing, but police became suspicious of him. His storeroom rendered a cleaner's ticket for Mrs Durand-Deacon, a revolver and bloodstains on the wall. They became aware that he had pawned her jewellery.

Haigh made a full confession, believing that where no body was found, no conviction could follow. Outside the storeroom, where Haigh had emptied the acid, the remaining sludge was taken away for examination. In the 14kg of fat were bone fragments, gallstones, a red handbag, and a set of dentures, positive proof of the victim's identity. Haigh admitted to drinking his victims' blood, and to three extra murders - thought to be fantasy to aid his insanity plea. He did, however, drink his own urine. The trial lasted only two days, and the jury returned their verdict in just seventeen minutes.

Read: Haigh: The Mind of a Murderer.

16 August 1949   Wandsworth prison, London   *A.Pierrepoint/ Kirk*

678

William John DAVIES   31

Stabbed: ***Lucy Wilson**, 37, on 8 March 1949, in Eastbourne, Sussex.*
Motive: Sexual rivalry

Davies, *(b.1918)*, had been a kitchen porter at Eastbourne's Grand Hotel from October 1948 until he was sacked after missing work, following an accident in which he broke his right hand. He had lived with Lucy Wilson, nee Kirby, since 1945. She had been separated from her husband since he joined the army in 1942. Lucy imagined Bill was carrying on with another woman at their lodgings, and left him on 5 March. For two days Davies, who was shy and suffered a stutter, pestered her at the cafe where she worked, begging her to come back, but she told him she was dating another man.

On 8 March he went to the cafe with a knife. When Lucy went upstairs to set tables he followed her up. A row developed and Davies stabbed her three times in the face, dislodging Lucy's left eye. She staggered down before collapsing in the street. Davies was sitting at a table crying when police arrived. Lucy eventually died of pneumonia, caused by complications of her injuries, on 23 March. The jury was retired for 18 minutes. His last words on the scaffold were, 'I'm sorry'.

Read: True Crime, May 97.

28 September 1949   Pentonville prison, London

A.Pierrepoint/ Harry Allen

679

William Claude Hodson JONES   31

Shot: ***Waltraut Lehman**, 24, in July 1945, in Rotenburg, Lower Saxony, Germany.*
Motive: *Vengeance.*

Jones, *(b.1917)*, had a short temper ever since being kicked in the head by a horse at the age of seven, and had no schooling until he was 13. He was, in 1945, in the Pioneer Corps, as part of the occupation force in Germany after the war.

Walking in the woods near Rotenburg, he met Waltraut Lehman a few times, merely passing the time of day. She was collecting flowers there, when Jones again approached. He thought she said something insulting to him, and he shot her. British soldiers were quizzed when her body was found, but Jones was on his way back to England by that time.

In 1948 Jones was a farmer. On 18 November he gave a letter to a friend admitting his crime three years earlier. The letter was passed on to army authorities who had Jones arrested.

Read: And May The Lord Have Mercy On Your Soul

13 December 1949   Durham gaol   *Wade/ Dernley*

680

John WILSON   22

Strangled: ***Lucy Nightingale**, 25, on 13 August 1949, in Cold Hesleden, Co Durham.*
Motive: *Vengeance; drink related.*

Wilson, *(b.1927)*, a miner, met Lucy Nightingale in a pub on 12 August, and arranged to meet her again the next day. Lucy, the wife of a seaman, spent most of the day on a pub crawl with Wilson, later going to a fairground and to the fields.

When she told Wilson he could have sex for ten shillings, he beat her, raped her, and then strangled her with her scarf. In the early hours he went and confessed to his sister. Wilson handed over the watch and ring he had stolen from Lucy to the police. He was hanged alongside another miner, Ben Roberts.

Read: And May The Lord Have Mercy On Your Soul.

13 December 1949   Durham gaol   *Wade/ Harry Allen/ Kirk*

681

Benjamin ROBERTS   22

Shot: ***Lilian Vickers***, *21, on 15 August 1949, in Chilton, Co Durham.*
Motive: *Sexual rivalry.*

Roberts, *(b.1927)*, a miner, became smitten with the girlfriend of his workmate Alan Neal. Neal and Lilian came to tea with Roberts on 14 August, and Roberts showed his friend his revolver. Lilian left, and the two men went to the pub at 6.30pm. At 11pm they met Lilian, and all went back to Roberts' house again, having supper with his parents and sister.

As they left, Alan and Lilian were seen kissing by Roberts, who came out and went to the allotments. The couple followed him, but once there, Roberts shot Lilian, and then turned the gun on himself. He collapsed on the girl's body, but succeeded only in causing himself severe neck injuries. He was hanged alongside another miner, John Wilson.

Read: And May The Lord Have Mercy On Your Soul.

30 December 1949   Wandsworth prison, London
                                   A.Pierrepoint/ Harry Allen
682

Ernest Soper COUZINS   49

Shot: ***Victor Desmond Elias***, *30, on 3 August 1949, in Canterbury, Kent.*
Motive: *Vengeance.*

Couzins, *(b.1900)*, met Mabel Rose while he was in the army in 1941, and though they were both married, they began an affair. He borrowed £50 from Mabel's daughter, and some seven years later, when Mabel's husband had put a stop to the affair, had still managed to repay only half of the debt.

Now Mabel's son-in-law, Victor Elias, demanded that Couzins pay the balance. At 7am he went to Victor's workplace and shot him with his revolver, then stabbed him and cut his throat, shoving his body in a cupboard. He then went up to the manager's office, where Mabel was cleaning, and told her what he had done.

Read: And May The Lord Have Mercy On Your Soul.

1950

total: **20**

683	6 Jan	Daniel RAVEN	23		Pentonville
684	8 Mar	James RIVETT	21		Norwich
685	9 Mar	Timothy EVANS	25	*Welsh*	Pentonville
686	28 Mar	George KELLY	27		Walton
687	29 Mar	Piotr MAKSIMOWSKI	33	*Polish*	Winson Green
688	30 Mar	Walter SHARPE	20		Armley
689	19 Apr	Albert JENKINS	37	*Welsh*	Swansea
690	7 Jul	Roman REDEL	23	*Polish*	Winchester
691	7 Jul	Zbigniew GOWER	23	*Polish*	Winchester
692	11 Jul	George BROWN	23		Durham
693	13 Jul	Ronald ATWELL	24		Bristol
694	13 Jul	John WALKER	48		Durham
695	16 Aug	Albert PRICE	32		Wandsworth
696	30 Oct	Paul HARRIS	28	*Scottish*	Barlinnie
697	14 Nov	Patrick TURNAGE	31	*S.African*	Durham
698	24 Nov	Norman GOLDTHORPE	40		Norwich
699	28 Nov	James CORBITT	37		Strangeways
700	14 Dec	Edward WOODFIELD	49		Bristol
701	16 Dec	James ROBERTSON	33	*Scottish*	Barlinnie
702	19 Dec	Nicholas CROSBY	22		Strangeways

6 January 1950   Pentonville prison, London   *A.Pierrepoint/ Kirk*

683

Daniel RAVEN   23

Bludgeoned:	**1 Leopold Goodman**, 49, and **2 Esther Goodman**, 47, on 10 October 1949, in Edgware, Middlesex.
Motive:	Vengeance.

Daniel Raven, *(b.1927)*, was a Jewish advertising agent living in Edgware with his wife, in the house bought for them by her wealthy businessman father, Leopold Goodman. Mr and Mrs Goodman, both Russian Jews, lived only 500 metres from their daughter. They had recently suffered a burglary.

Raven's wife of 18 months, Marie, had given birth to a son in a maternity home, and four days later, on 10 October, Raven and his in-laws had visited her there. On his way home from seeing his wife, Raven called at the Goodman's, where he battered Esther seven times and her husband 14 times about the head with the aluminium base of a T.V. aerial. They were found later in the evening by another relative. He had found no evidence of a break-in or of theft.

Suspicious of Raven's smart and fresh clothes so late, the police checked Raven's house. They found a suit covered in blood burning in the boiler, and traces of blood on his shoes. Raven at first blamed the killings on Mr Goodman's enemies from illegal deals he had made, then, to explain away the blood, told of how he and found the bodies and panicked. All else having failed, at his appeal he tried a plea of insanity. The court did not believe that, either, the jury delivering its verdict after 50 minutes.

Read: Murders of the Black Museum

8 March 1950   Norwich prison

684

<u>James Frank RIVETT</u>   **21**

Strangled: *Christine Ruth Cuddon, 17, on 5 November 1949, in Beccles, Suffolk.*
Motive: *Vengeance.*

Rivett, *(b.1929)*, had been dating Christine Cuddon some time, but he felt sure her father was about to insist that she put a stop to it. At 9pm they went to a local school, where, after having sex, Rivett strangled Christine. He went back home and took his father's shotgun, intending to commit suicide, but his nerve failed him. He went to a friend at 11.30pm, to confess what he had done. A total of five doctors testified that Rivett was insane and, probably schizophrenic, unfit to plead. However, two juries found him fit to do so, and after a statutory medical inquiry, he was executed.

Read: And May The Lord Have Mercy On Your Soul.

685

Timothy John EVANS   25   *Welsh*

Strangled: *1 Beryl Susanna Evans, 19, his
                    wife, and
                    2 Geraldine Evans, 1, his daughter, on 8 November
                    1949, in London W11.*
Motive: *To clear impediment.*

Evans, *(b.1925)*, was born in south Wales and had come to live in London in 1936. He was a small, slight man, illiterate and with a low level of intelligence. He had married a London girl, Beryl, and they had a daughter, Geraldine, in September 1949. Evans worked as a van driver, and they had come to live on the top floor of 10 Rillington Place, Notting Hill, with their landlord, John Christie, and his wife Ethel. Evans and Beryl had been going through a bad patch in their marriage and he was known to sometimes lash out at her. He was also known to lie and to tell exaggerated stories. When Beryl became pregnant again, the couple were faced with the prospect of real financial problems.

Beryl and her baby were strangled to death on 8 November 1949. Two weeks later, Evans went to the police in Merthyr Tydfil and told them he had killed his wife and put her body down the drain outside the house. When the police found the drain empty, he told them that Christie had killed his wife in the course of performing an abortion on her. He made no mention of the baby being dead. The bodies were found wrapped in a tablecloth in an outside washhouse. Crucially, in a further change of story, he admitted the killings, though he later retracted this, again blaming Christie. Evans was tried for the murder of the baby only. The jury considered for 35 minutes before finding him guilty.

It was not until 1953 that the verdict was questioned, for then six more women were found dead at Rillington Place, and Christie was hanged for their murders. An inquiry then upheld the verdict against Evans. Christie had gassed his victims, and gas had not been used on Beryl. But a further inquiry in 1966, found that while Evans probably had killed his wife, he had not killed his daughter, the crime for which he had been tried. He was given a full pardon, the only time British justice had acknowledged an error in its use of the death penalty. The truth of the matter, beyond a reasonable doubt, will probably never be known.

Read: Ten Rillington Place

686

George KELLY   27

Shot: **1 Leonard Thomas**, 44, and
                   2 John Bernard Catterall, 25, on 19 March 1949, in
                   Liverpool, Lancs.
Motive: Financial.

The cameo cinema in Webster Road, Wavertree, was raided on 19 March at 9.30pm by a man armed with a revolver. His accomplice remained outside as look-out. The manager, Mr Thomas, and his assistant, Mr Catterall, were counting the takings when the gunman burst into the box-office. Six shots were fired and the two men died at the scene, Mr Thomas killed with a single shot to the chest, Mr Catterall by three shots to the hand, chest and back. The culprits escaped, and it was not until six months later that George Kelly and Charles Connolly, 26, were apprehended after a tip-off by Jackie Dickson, a prostitue, and Jimmy Northam, her pimp.

Kelly, *(b.1923),* a self-important small-time gangster, had been known to the police since the age of ten, and had been court-martialled by the navy. There was no forensic evidence against them, and the gun was never found. When the two men were tried together, the jury failed to agree on a verdict. Tried again, separately, Kelly was sentenced to hang. Connolly was jailed for ten years, having pleaded guilty to robbery to escape the rope. On his way to the scaffold. Kelly soiled himself, a story spread with some pleasure to diminish the heroic reputation of a small-time thug.

In 1996 Connolly claimed that he and Kelly had been the victims of a set-up, that the tip-offs resulted from police bribery, and that George 'Judd' Johnson was the real killer, and Kelly's brother Joey the look-out. Kelly's case was at last referred to the Court of Appeal in 2001.

Read: The Cameo Conspiracy

687

Piotr MAKSIMOWSKI   33   *Polish*

Cut wrists of: **Dilys Doreen Campbell**, 31, on 31 December
                            1949, in Beaconsfield, Bucks.

| Motive: | Sexual rivalry; drink related. |

Maksimowski, *(b.1917)*, worked as a dustman in Slough. A Polish refugee who was living at a camp at Great Bower Wood near Beaconsfield, he had been having an affair with Dilys Campbell for five months before she admitted that she was not a widow, but that she was still living with her husband.

After spending the evening together in a Windsor pub, the couple went together to Great Bower Wood, where Maksimowski slashed her wrists, and then her throat. She bled to death.

He turned himself in at a Beaconsfield police station at 3.45am, claiming that they had a suicide pact because neither of them could end the affair. Maksimowski's wrist showed only superficial cuts, and the jury did not believe his version of events. His request to be shot rather than hanged was ignored.

Read: Master Detective Summer Special 98

| **30 March 1950** | Armley gaol, Leeds | *Wade/ Harry Allen* |

688

Walter SHARPE   20

| *Shot:* | ***Abraham Harry Levine***, *50, on 16 November 1949, in Leeds, W.Yorks.* |
| *Motive:* | *Financial.* |

Sharpe, *(b.1930)*, had been a troublesome youth since his father died in Italy in 1943. He and his pal, Gordon Lannen, 17, had both been sacked from their jobs in a surgical appliance factory in August 1949, and the two broke into a gunsmiths on 14 November, stealing five weapons.

Five days later, at 10.15am, they burst into Abraham Levine's jewellery shop. When Mr Levine resisted their demands, he was coshed on the nose and temple with the gun butt, and then shot in the stomach. Several people tried to give chase, but more shots were fired at the pursuers. The pair were picked up looking suspicious in Southport on 18 November. Lannen confessed to the killing, and told police where the revolver had been thrown into a river. The jury deliberated for twenty minutes before finding both men guilty, Lannen being detained at His Majesty's pleasure.

Read: Murderous Leeds

19 April 1950   Swansea prison

689

<u>Albert Edward JENKINS</u>   **37**   *Welsh*

Bludgeoned: *William Henry Llewellyn, 52, on 10 October 1949, in*
                 Rosemarket, Pembrokeshire.
Motive: *Vengeance.*

Jenkins, *(b. 1913),* was a tenant farmer on William Llewellyn's land, and was negotiating to buy his 28 acre holding. At 11am Llewellyn went on his bicycle to discuss the deal with Jenkins, whose wife and child were out at a country fair. Jenkins, presumably snubbed by his landlord, battered the older man to death on his doorstep, wrapped him in a tarpaulin and carried his body on a tractor to the claypit, where he buried him in a shallow grave.

Blood was found at Jenkins' door, and on his clothes, the tarpaulin was seen on his tractor, he was seen at the pit, and cycling Llewellyn's bike. Jenkins claimed he had handed over £1000, but was found to have been £136 overdrawn. The jury sealed his fate after 105 minutes.

Read: And May The Lord Have Mercy On Your Soul.

7 July 1950   Winchester prison   *A.Pierrepoint/ Kirk/ Harry Allen/ Dernley*

690, 691

<u>Roman REDEL</u>   **23**   *Polish*
<u>Zbigniew GOWER</u>   **23**   *Polish*

Shot: *Robert Taylor, 30, on 13 March 1950, in Bristol, Gloucs.*
Motive: *Financial; drink related.*

The two unemployed Poles, *(both b.1927),* had each deserted from the Polish Corps, and settled in England in 1947, working as dock labourers until February 1950. Redel had recently married. Still drunk from a binge the previous evening, they robbed a sub-branch of Lloyd's Bank at North View, of £28 and were attempting to get away by bus when a crowd stopped the vehicle and pursued them on foot.

Redel was brought down by judo enthusiast Bob Taylor, a bachelor who had served in the Mediterranean during the war. In the struggle Mr Taylor was shot in the head by Redel, who later claimed the gun had gone off

540

accidentally. Gower, some way ahead of Redel at the time of the killing, claimed he did not know the gun was loaded and had no part in the murder, though he had badly beaten another pursuer. The pair were caught by six unarmed officers, one of whom brought Redel down with a rugby tackle.

The jury considered for one hour, and despite a strong recommendation to mercy in his case, Gower's appeals against the death sentence were rejected. Bob Taylor was posthumously awarded the George Medal.

Read: The Hangman's Tale, p93

11 July 1950　　　　　　Durham gaol　　　　　　*A.Pierrepoint*

692

George Finlay BROWN　　　23

Strangled:　　**Mary Victoria Longhurst**, 23, on 10 March 1950, in North Shields, Northumberland
Motive:　　Sexual

Brown, *(b.1927)*, was the third man in quick succession that Mary Longhurst had living with her and her four year old daughter in her North Shields bedsit. When Mary turned her attentions to Frank Boucher, Brown left in March 1950, returning to his mother. Though he had stayed only a month, he had lasted longer than the others. He continued to harass Mary, however, wanting a reconciliation, and she complained to the police on 9 March.

Brown, frustrated, approached a woman in the street at 10.30 the next night asking unsuccessfully for sex. He then went to Mary's, where he found the key in the lock as she had just popped out, returning at 10.55pm. They argued and the sound of furniture being thrown and of screams could be heard by other residents. With the toddler cowering beneath the bed, Brown tied Mary to the bedhead with string and removed her knickers. He then strangled her with a length of the twine and made his escape. The jury did not believe his denials, and convicted him in 35 minutes.

Read: Murderous Tyneside

693

Ronald Douglas ATWELL   24

Strangled/ bludgeoned: *Lily Irene Palmer, 26, on 15 April 1950, in*
          Bridgwater, Somerset.
Motive: *Sexual rivalry.*

Atwell, *(b.1926),* was a gasworks labourer. He met Lily in a cinema, and bumping into her again, had asked her out for a drink. Lily was a simple-minded woman, who was waiting for a place in a psychiatric hospital. They walked to a nearby farm, and, Atwell explained, he rejected Lily's sexual advances after she had told him that she had been with other men, the latest just a few hours earlier. She then became insulting and abusive, and he began hitting, kicking and strangling her.

He dumped her body, naked but for shoes and stockings, in a nearby hedge. The landlord of the pub identified Atwell, and the jury took just six minutes to decide his fate.

Read: The Hangman's Tale, p106.

694

John WALKER   48

Bludgeoned: *Francis Henry Wilson, 45, on 29 April 1950, in*
          Brompton, N.Yorks.
Motive: *Vengeance.*

Walker, *(b.1902),* first met Gladys Wilson in 1944, while he was a soldier. Upon his demob in 1947, he went to lodge with her and her husband, Frank, who would sometimes give his wife a hiding. Her old feelings for Walker soon surfaced, and before long they were sharing the double bed, and Frank was relegated to the spare room.

Frank tolerated the situation, until on 29 April, Gladys gave him five shillings, rather than his usual allowance of ten. When the men were left alone, Gladys having gone to the cinema, Frank threatened to smack his wife for her meanness, whereupon, Walker, only 5' tall, attacked him, axing him six times in the scullery. When she returned, Gladys thought her husband had gone to bed, and Walker left the following morning. He was arrested in Bishop Auckland.

Read: And May The Lord Have Mercy On Your Soul

16 August 1950	Wandsworth prison, London	*A.Pierrepoint/ Allen*

695

Albert PRICE   **32**

Bludgeoned:	**1 Doris Maude Price**, *26, his wife, on 3 June 1950, in New Malden, Surrey, and his children*
Suffocated:	**2 Jennifer Valerie Price**, *3, and*
	3 Maureen Ann Price, *17mths, on 5 June 1950, in Bognor, Sussex*
Motive:	*To clear impediment.*

Price, *(b.1918)*, was a painter and decorator, who lived a happy family life in New Malden with his wife and two young daughters. But Price ran into money problems, and tried to gamble his way out. The debts built up, and when he received notice to quit his prefab for non-payment of rent, it was the final blow. Rather than subject his family to indignity, he decided to kill them all.

He smashed his wife's head nine times with an axe as she slept, and then took the children to Bognor. There he drugged them with sleeping pills before suffocating them both in their pushchair and leaving them in dense shrubbery. He was later found sleeping in a deck chair in London's Green park. In finding the happy family man guilty in forty minutes, the jury added a strong recommendation to mercy.

Read: Master Detective Summer Special 97.

696

Paul Christopher HARRIS   28   *Scottish*

Stabbed: ***Martin Dunleavy**, 38, on 7 July 1950, in Glasgow, Lanarks.*
Motive: *Vengeance; drink related.*

Paul Harris, *(b.1922)*, was married with a young baby. He and his brother Claude, 30, liked a drunken street brawl. On 7 July, they and two friends were in a pub drinking. They got involved in a fight over a woman, and they badly injured a man by pushing a glass into his face.

Moving on to a nearby tenement, the four became involved in another brawl. One man was repeatedly kicked in the head, and another was hit with a bottle. Martin Dunleavy, himself drunk, was stabbed in the face with a broken bottle. He died hours later in hospital.

The brothers were both found guilty of murder, with a recommendation to mercy, a third man being acquitted. To save his brother, Paul confessed to the act, and Claude's execution was delayed. His sentence was commuted to life on 4 November. Paul's last request to his wife was not to let their son drink.

Read: True Crime, Apr 96

697

Patrick TURNAGE   31   *South African*

Strangled: ***Julia Beesley**, 78, on 29 July 1950, in Stockton-on-Tees, Co Durham.*
Motive: *Vengeance; drink related.*

Turnage, *(b.1919)*, had his home near Durban, South Africa, though born in India. He was third engineer on the SS *Absalon*, which sailed up the Tees in July 1950, for a three-day stay. Turnage disembarked determined to satisfy his sexual desires. Julia Beesley lived in Stockton with her son. She had worked as a prostitute for years, and still, despite her age, did occasional trade.

The two, both somewhat drunk, met in a pub, departing in a taxi. Turnage took her to the ship, but she refused to go aboard, taking her leave. Turnage followed her. It seems he took offence when she wanted £1 from him for sex. He strangled her and dumped her in a ditch near the docks, covering her in a mound of grass.

She was found by chance the following day, less than twenty-four hours before Turnage's ship was due to sail. He pleaded guilty, prefering death to incarceration. The court proceedings took just seven minutes.

Read: The Hangman's Tale, p116.

| 24 November 1950 | Norwich prison | *Kirk/ Dernley* |

698

Norman GOLDTHORPE   40

Strangled: **Emma Howe**, *66, in August 1950, in Yarmouth, Norfolk.*
Motive: *Sexual; drink related.*

Goldthorpe, *(b.1910),* only 5 feet tall, had turned to drink after his wife had eloped with a soldier. He began an affair with Marguerite Myers in Yorkshire, where he knew her and her husband. They had gone together to Yarmouth, but she had grown tired of his unstable temper and had left him. He turned to drink to console himself, and to the comforts of cheap sex.

He could not find Emma Howe, the local old prostitute, in her usual pub, so set off to her home. Unfortunately for him, he was seen entering and leaving. He had sex with her and then strangled her in her bed. Eight minutes was all it took for the jury to make their decision.

Goldthorpe was heard to snort for several seconds after the drop. Kirk was never to conduct another hanging.

Read: The Hangman's Tale, p129.

699

James Henry CORBITT   37

Strangled: ***Eliza Wood***, *36, on 20 August 1950, in Ashton-under-Lyne, Lancs.*
Motive: *Sexual rivalry; drink related.*

Corbitt, *(b.1913)*, a toolmaker, had been having an affair with Eliza Wood for eighteen months, sharing lodgings at her mother's in Manchester. James had recently become jealous of another boarder, Tommy, and Eliza had suffered a cut head when Corbitt attacked her in mid-July. James and Eliza, both drunk, booked into an Ashton inn for the night, but at 11.30pm, after having sex, Corbitt punched Eliza in the mouth then strangled her first with a necklace, then manually when the string broke.

He left the inn at 7.45am having written 'Whore' on her forehead in ballpoint pen. He was arrested at his lodgings two days later and his diaries revealed that he had planned to kill her when he had 'won her affection completely'. His plea of insanity was rejected.

Read: Murderous Manchester.

14 December 1950   Horfield gaol, Bristol

700

Edward Isaac WOODFIELD   49

Strangled: ***Ethel Merinda Worth***, *65, on 20 September 1950, in Bristol, Gloucs.*
Motive: *Financial.*

Woodfield, *(b.1901)*, whose sister and brother lived next door to Ethel Worth, had known the old woman some time. He had already borrowed a total of £3 from her, when he went again to see her on the afternoon of 20 September. When she refused him, he battered her with a lemonade bottle, and as she slumped into her chair, begging him to stop, he strangled her to death, making off with a watch, binoculars, and some money.

Ethel was found by her son at 5.30pm. Woodfield had been seen hanging around the house, and when questioned, made a full confession. The jury decided his fate after three hours.

Read: And May The Lord Have Mercy On Your Soul

701

James Ronald ROBERTSON   33   *Scottish*

Ran over: ***Catherine McCluskey****, 40, on 28 July 1950, in Glasgow, Lanarks.*
Motive: *To clear impediment.*

      Robertson, *(b.1917)*, previously an aero-engine inspector, had been a police constable for five years. He was married with two children. He was, however, also having an affair with Catherine McCluskey, an unmarried mother of two children, one of them Robertson's. On a road in the south of Glasgow, Robertson, 6', knocked Catherine unconscious with a rubber truncheon, and then ran over her twice, killing her. As he had contrived, her body was later found there, apparently the victim of a road accident.
      The car was found abandoned nearby, and though skin, hair and blood was found under the vehicle, there was no impact damage. It was found to belong to P.C. Robertson, but also to have been stolen. Stolen goods were found in his house. He told that he had accidentally run Catherine over, trapping her under the car, and manoevred to try to set her free. It seems Catherine had been pressuring her lover to be rehoused, and Robertson wanted rid of the problem. The jury did not believe him, taking one hour to convict by a majority decision.

Read: The Vintage Car Murders

19 December 1950   Strangeways prison, Manchester

A.Pierrepoint / Dernley

702

Nicholas Persoulious CROSBY   22

Cut throat of: ***Ruth Massey**, 19, on 8 July 1950, in Leeds, W.Yorks.*
Motive: *Sexual; drink related.*

Crosby, *(b.1928)*, a gypsy who hawked linoleum, met Ruth Massey, a seamstress, in a Leeds hotel, where he was with two friends and she was having a drink with her sister-in-law and a friend. Crosby offered to walk her home at 9.50pm, and cut her throat at 11pm on waste ground where she was found at 8.20 the next morning.

Arrested the day after the murder, having already confessed to his cousin, Crosby told that they had met someone else on the way home, and Ruth had gone off with him. He later said that he was so drunk that he did not know if he had killed her. The jury dismissed his version of events in 55 minutes.

Read: Murderous Leeds

1951

total: **15**

703	4 Jan	Frank GRIFFIN	40		Shrewsbury
704	26 Jan	Nenad KOVACEVIK	29	*Yugoslav*	Strangeways
705	3 Apr	William WATKINS	49		Winson Green
706	25 Apr	Joseph BROWN	33		Wandsworth
707	25 Apr	Edward SMITH	33		Wandsworth
708	26 Apr	James VIRRELS	56		Wandsworth
709	8 May	James INGLIS	29	*Scottish*	Strangeways
710	9 May	William SHAUGHNESSY	48		Winchester
711	12 Jun	John DAND	32		Strangeways
712	3 Jul	Jack WRIGHT	30		Strangeways
713	19 Jul	Dennis MOORE	22		Norwich
714	19 Jul	Alfred REYNOLDS	24		Norwich
715	15 Sep	Robert SMITH	30	*Scottish*	Saughton
716	24 Oct	John O'CONNOR	29		Pentonville
717	11 Dec	Herbert MILLS	19		Lincoln

4 January 1951   Shrewsbury prison   *A.Pierrepoint/ Morris*

703

Frank GRIFFIN   **40**

Bludgeoned: ***Jane Edge**, 74, on 6 September 1950, in Ketley, Shropshire*
Motive: *Financial; drink related.*

Griffin, *(b.1911),* a married man from Bolton, had come to Shropshire in search of work, but he quit his job at the steelworks on 2 September and, suffering depression, had begun to drink heavily. On 6 September, already drunk, he called at the Queen's Head in Ketley, where the landlady, Mrs Edge, served him two pints, and then offered him a cup of tea.

When she went to the kitchen, Griffin emptied the till, only to be caught red-handed as the landlady returned to the bar. As she shouted, he gripped her by the throat and then hit her 19 times with a pint mug. He then took her to the lounge and sat her on a sofa.

Mrs Edge, a widow, had run the pub for 22 years, and lived there with her younger son. She was discovered at 5.30pm when her elder son called round. Witnesses placed Griffin in the vicinity, and he was found to have a large amount of silver coin, and bloody clothes.The defence centred on whether the drink excused the action. Deliberating for 145 minutes, the jury decided it did not.

Read: Master Detective, Dec 95.

26 January 1951   Strangeways prison, Manchester
A.Pierrepoint/ Harry Allen

704

Nenad KOVACEVIK   29   *Yugoslav*

Bludgeoned: ***Radomir Djorovic***, *26, on 8 November 1950, near Ramsbottom, Lancs.*
Motive: *Vengeance.*

Kovacevik, *(b.1922),* a partisan, and Djorovic, a nazi supporter, fought on opposite sides in Yugoslavia during the war, with Kosacevik losing his father and five siblings to the enemy. Refugees in England, both men met in finding work at a Blackburn paper mill.

One Sunday they were both invited to a mutual friend's for dinner, and walked together. When the rain started, they took shelter in an old hut, and conversation turned to the war. Djorovic made fun of Nenad's family, and a fight started, with Kovacevik picking up an axe to batter his compatriot to death. The body was found the following morning, and the bus taking Nenad to London was intercepted at Cannock. He was found to have the dead man's coat, watch and wallet on him. The jury deliberated for 85 minutes, and Kovacevik fought with his gaolers all the way to the gallows.

Read: And May The Lord Have Mercy On Your Soul

3 April 1951   Winson Green prison, Birmingham
A.Pierrepoint/ Harry Allen

705

William Arthur WATKINS   49

Drowned: ***Baby Watkins***, *10 mins old, his son, on 21 January 1951, in Birmingham, Warwicks*
Motive: *To clear impediment*

Watkins, *(b.1905),* who was hard of hearing, was married but separated. He had lived in Balsall Heath, Birmingham for five years with Florence May White and their 3-year old son. Florence gave birth to a second son on 21 January, but Watkins immediately took the child to the bathroom. He later declared that as he was bathing the infant it slipped and drowned in the water.

Neighbours alerted the police when they saw neither mother nor child, knowing that no-one had been in attendance at the birth. Police found the infant inside a pillow-case face down in the water. The jury believed only that Watkins had intended to relieve himself of a further financial burden, reaching their verdict in two and a half hours.

Read: Murderous Birmingham

25 April 1951   Wandsworth prison, London
A.Pierrepoint/ Harry Allen/ Herbert Allen/ Dernley
706, 707

Joseph BROWN   33
Edward Charles SMITH   33

Suffocated: *Frederick Gosling, 77, on 11 January 1951, at Chertsey, Surrey.*
Motive: *Financial.*

Mr Gosling, known as 'Old Gossy', ran a corner grocery shop. Brown and lorry driver Smith, *(both b.1918),* made a bungled attempt to rob the shop early on 11 January. They had been accompanied by Brown's younger brother Frederick, 27, acting as look-out, but customers disturbed them.

Later the same evening, Mr Gosling was burgled. He was hit over the eye and tied up on the bed, the thieves escaping with about £50. Mr Gosling had been gagged with a duster and suffocated. Frederick Brown claimed his brother and Smith had returned alone to the shop. He was believed over others who claimed Frederick with an unknown accomplice were themselves guilty. 'Leave me alone', Smith told the hangman, 'I'll walk on my own'.

Read: Master Detective Summer Special 90.

26 April 1951   Wandsworth prison, London   *A.Pierrepoint/ Dernley*

708

James VIRRELS   56

Stabbed: **Alice Kate Roberts**, *40, on 29 January 1951, in Worthing, Sussex.*
Motive: *Vengeance.*

Alice Roberts was a widowed mother of five. Her husband, a merchant seaman, had been killed at sea during the war. Virrels, *(b.1895),* a labourer, had taken up lodgings at her home in Worthing in September 1950, and the two had got on so well that they had become engaged. A row developed between the two when Virrels complained that the jam sandwiches, which Alice gave him daily as a packed lunch, were becoming monotonous.

Virrels stabbed her 39 times, including ten blows to the chest, and then continued to batter her five times with an axe. He later claimed that she had come at him with a dagger. Her eldest son of 14 later found his mother's bloodied body in the kitchen when he returned from school. Virrels fled to his brother's, where he admitted to the crime. He was said to suffer blackouts as a result of brain disease, but was certified sane. The jury took 85 minutes to decide its verdict. Virrels soiled himself on the way to the scaffold.

Read: The Hangman's Tale, p155.

8 May 1951   Strangeways prison, Manchester   *A.Pierrepoint/ Dernley*

709

James INGLIS   29   *Scottish*

Strangled/ bludgeoned: **Alice Morgan**, *50, on 1 February 1951, in Hull, E.Yorks.*
Motive: *Vengeance; drink related.*

Inglis, *(b.1922),* was a Scot who had ended up in Hull after his army days. He had spent a spell in a psychiatric hospital, and after his discharge in 1945, had never been able to hold down any of his labouring jobs for long, moving from lodgings to lodgings. He spent most of his money on drink and prostitutes in Hull's docks area.

In January 1951, he was lodging with Herbert Bell and Amy Gray in the east of the city. It was at this time that he met Alice Morgan, a local prostitute. She had been married, had two children, but was now divorced and working the streets, servicing the local seamen. For Alice, Inglis was just another customer at £5 a time, but Inglis seemed to think of Alice as his woman.

On 1 February, Inglis packed in his latest job at the shipyard, taking the money owed to him. He spent it in the pub with Alice. He took her home, but when she told him that with no money he could not afford her, and that there were plenty who could pay to stay the night with her, he flew into a rage and beat Alice remorselessly with his fists, and strangled her with a stocking, leaving her dead on her sitting-room floor.

Two days later, Amy Gray started asking Inglis about rent money. He beat her across the back of the head and strangled her, taking money from the gas meter and her purse as he went. Amy survived the attack. Alice's body was found on 4 February, and Inglis was tracked down to a nearby Salvation Army hostel.

At his trial he asked to be hanged as soon as possible. He ran to the gallows and was dispatched within seven seconds.

Read: The Hangman's Tale, p163

9 May 1951　　　　　　　Winchester prison

710

William Edward SHAUGHNESSY　　48

Bludgeoned/ strangled:	**1 Marie Alexine Shaughnessy**, *46, his wife, on 18 December 1950, and*
Strangled:	**2 Joyce Shaughnessy**, *20, his daughter, on 19 December 1950, in Portsmouth, Hants.*
Motive:	*To clear impediment.*

Shaughnessy, *(b.1903)*, lived with his wife Marie, and five of their six children. While the children were out, he bashed and then strangled Marie, hiding her body in the cupboard under the stairs. The following day, he strangled his daughter Joyce, leaving her body on her bed, while taking the remaining children to London. He allowed his 16-year old son to return the following day, and he discovered his sister's body, calling the police who found Shaughnessy's other victim. He was arrested on 23 December, and tried for the murder of his wife only. The jury deliberated for 100 minutes.

Read: And May The Lord Have Mercy On Your Soul

553

711

<u>John DAND</u>   32

Stabbed: ***Walter Wyld**, 72, on 27 January 1951, in York.*
Motive: *Vengeance; drink related.*

Dand, *(b.1919)*, had been invalided out of the army in 1949, suffering from a stomach ulcer, and was in receipt of an army pension. Walter Wyld, a fit septuagenarian, was a former rugby league player, and now a widower. He was on friendly terms with Dand, the two playing dominoes together most weekends in the pub. Wyld had loaned Dand's wife £3 for work clothes, and though it had been repaid, Dand reborrowed the same amount. The couple moved to Kirkcaldy in November 1950, but separated, Dand returning to York alone two months later.

Wyld wrote to Dand asking for the return of the money as his rates were due to be paid. After drinking with a friend, Dand called on Wyld, who had himself returned home from a whist drive at 10pm. Dand, now a press operator, had other debts, and could not repay the old man. An argument ensued, and Dand attacked Wyld, who put up a terrific fight from the lounge through to the kitchen, despite being battered about the head, and stabbed three times in the chest and back with a bayonet. Neighbours found the body, a cushion over the face, the following lunchtime. Letters from Dand and his wife were found, and the former soldier was arrested. The jury considered its verdict for 65 minutes.

Read: True Detective, Ap98

712

<u>Jack WRIGHT</u>   30

Strangled: ***Mona Mather**, 28, on 8 April 1951, in Tyldesley, Lancs.*
Means: *Sexual rivalry*

Wright, *(b.1921)*, a miner from Tyldesley, had in three years got away with three assaults on women who would not press charges. He met Mona Mather in the summer of 1950, but their acquaintance lasted only two months, for Wright very quickly became jealous of Mona's attention to other men. Walking together, Mona had started talking to a rival, and had told Wright to walk on if he did not like it. He did, and he did not see her again until she tapped him on the shoulder in a pub in April 1951.

They went together to a fair and Wright agreed to walk Mona home over the common after midnight. The two kissed, then Wright strangled her, the pair being seen by a passing couple. He carried Mona to a field behind the colliery, had sex with her, then finished her off with her scarf. She was found at 6am, and Wright was arrested that evening in Manchester. He claimed at first to have left Mona at the fair with two men, but the jury rejected his plea of insanity after a three-hour retirement.

Read: Master Detective Summer Special 93.

19 July 1951   Norwich prison   *A.Pierrepoint/ Dernley*

713

Dennis Albert Reginald MOORE   22

Strangled: ***Eileen Emily Rose Cullen**, 21, on 3 February 1951, in Norwich, Norfolk.*
Motive: *Vengeance.*

        Labourer Moore, *(b.1929),* had tried to strangle both a colleague in the army during a play-fight, and a previous girlfriend. He had met Eileen Cullen in 1950, and the pair were just two weeks away from their wedding. She was pregnant, and the couple had been together to the doctor to see if all was progressing well. They had then gone shopping, and later for a walk on the outskirts of the city, but Moore had taken a knife with him. A row developed when Eileen refused, not for the first time, to have sex with Moore.

        He strangled her in a cow-shed, and then cut her throat. So full of remorse was he, that he led police to the scene, and threw himself upon his dead fiancee, expressing his love for her.

        He was hanged with Alfred Reynolds.

Read: True Crime, Feb 96.

714

Alfred George REYNOLDS   24

Shot: ***Ellen May Ludkin***, *19, on 8 February 1951, in East Dereham, Norfolk.*
Motive: *Vengeance.*

    Reynolds, *(b.1927)*, who had a mental age of eleven, had been courting Ellen Ludkin since the summer of 1948. She found herself pregnant in October 1950, and her parents gave their consent to marriage, so long as Reynolds got himself a job. Reynolds found labouring work, and all was well until he was sacked. Ellen's father forbade them from seeing each other again.

    Mr Ludkin turned Reynolds away from the house on 7 February, but the following day the couple went for a walk together, and in a bike shed near her home, Reynolds shot her. He claimed that she had suggested a suicide pact when he had threatened to kill himself, and that Ellen had pulled the trigger herself. However, this was shown not to have been the case - the jury taking forty minutes to convict.

    He was hanged with Dennis Moore, who had murdered his girlfriend just five days earlier than Reynolds.

    Read: True Crime, Feb 96.

715

Robert Dobie SMITH   30   *Scottish*

Shot: *Police sergeant* ***William Gibson***, *35, on 22 May 1951, in Dumfries.*
Motive: *Sadistic pleasure.*

    Rab Smith, *(b.1921)*, had served on minesweepers in the navy during the war, and worked as electrician at ICI. On 17 May he had a row with his 17-year old girlfriend, and she finished with him. He blamed her parents who felt he was too old for her. He went out and got drunk. His depression was compounded the following day when the young son of a neighbour of whom Smith was very fond fell to his death.

On his 30th birthday, having broken into his father's shed to get his shotgun, he forced his brother to saw off the barrel, to write a letter saying, 'When I go out this door, I will shoot the first policeman I see', and then to phone the police reporting a man going berserk with a gun. Sergeant Gibson and two constables drove to investigate.

Finding Smith, Sgt Gibson opened the car door as Smith took the shotgun from under his coat. He blasted Gibson in the face, and shot PC Hope in the arms. PC Campbell grabbed the gunman. A plea of insanity was rejected by the jury in 32 minutes.

Read: True Crime, Feb 96.

24 October 1951   Pentonville prison, London   *A.Pierrepoint/ Harry Allen*

716

John O'CONNOR   29

Stabbed: ***Eugenie le Maire**, 82, on 11 August 1951, in London W14.*
Motive: *Sexual; drink related.*

O'Connor, *(b.1922),* lodged with Eugenie le Maire in West Kensington, and after he returned from an extensive pub crawl on 10 August, the old lady made tea for him. He repaid his landlady's kindness by strangling her to unconsciousness before raping her and then retiring to bed. He got up again, no doubt worried about the consequences of his actions, and stabbed Eugenie through the heart. The jury's verdict took only ten minutes in arriving.

Read: And May the Lord Have Mercy On Your Soul

11 December 1951   Lincoln prison   *A.Pierrepoint*

717

Herbert Leonard MILLS   19

Strangled: ***Mabel Tattershaw**, 48, on 3 August 1951, in Nottingham.*

557

Motive: *Sadistic pleasure.*

   Mills, *(b.1932)*, an unemployed clerk who was on probation for theft, was a lonely and slightly crippled youth who fancied himself as an artist and poet and who fantasized about committing the perfect murder. On 2 August he went to a cinema in Nottingham, where he lived, and got talking to Mabel Tattershaw, a housewife with two teenage daughters, who, with nothing better to do than be flattered by a young man- her husband was in prison- agreed to meet him the next day. They walked to an orchard in Sherwood Vale, where Mabel lay down, and Mills covered her with her coat. He beat her across the head, possibly with a blunt object, and then, kneeling on her shoulders, strangled her. Hiding the body in bushes, he neither robbed, nor sexually assaulted her.

   He thought with no motive and no evidence, he was in the clear. However, he became impatient for the crime to come to light, and on 9 August he telephoned the *News of the World* telling them he had found a body, asking for money for the story. Mills had £1000 of gambling debts to pay off. The call was traced and Mills took the police to the orchard. Eventually he admitted the crime to newspapermen. In fact, he had not committed the perfect murder, forensic evidence linked him with hairs and fibres on the dead woman. The jury decided his fate in 25 minutes.

   Mills' heart continued to beat for 20 minutes after the drop.

Read: True Crime, Aug 93

1952   total: **25**

718	1 Jan	Horace CARTER	31		Winson Green
719	15 Jan	Alfred BRADLEY	24		Strangeways
720	6 Feb	Alfred MOORE	36		Armley
721	26 Feb	Roy HARRIS	24		Strangeways
722	21 Mar	Takir ALI	40	*Bengali*	Durham
723	12 Apr	James SMITH	21	*Scottish*	Barlinnie
724	25 Apr	Alfred BURNS	21		Walton
725	25 Apr	Edward DEVLIN	22		Walton
726	7 May	Ajit SINGH	27	*Indian*	Cardiff
727	27 May	Backary MANNEH	25		Pentonville
728	29 May	Patrick DEVENEY	42	*Scottish*	Barlinnie
729	8 Jul	Harry HUXLEY	42		Shrewsbury
730	15 Jul	Thomas EAMES	31		Bristol
731	22 Jul	Frank BURGESS	21		Wandsworth
732	12 Aug	Oliver BUTLER	24		Oxford
733	3 Sep	Mahmood MATTAN	29	*Somali*	Cardiff
734	5 Sep	John GODAR	31		Pentonville
735	30 Sep	Raymond CULL	25		Pentonville
736	30 Sep	Dennis MULDOWNEY	41		Pentonville
737	9 Oct	Peter JOHNSON	24		Pentonville
738	23 Oct	Donald SIMON	32		Shrewsbury
739	12 Dec	Eric NORCLIFFE	30		Lincoln
740	17 Dec	John LIVESEY	24		Wandsworth
741	23 Dec	Leslie GREEN	29		Winson Green
742	24 Dec	Herbert APPLEBY	20		Durham

1 January 1952   Winson Green prison, Birmingham

A.Pierrepoint/ Dernley

718

Horace CARTER   31

Suffocated: ***Sheila Ethel Attwood**, 11, on 1 August 1951, in Birmingham, Warwicks.*

Motive: Sexual.

C

Carter, *(b.1921),* lured Sheila Attwood into his house with sweets. He was a labourer and lived with his brother-in-law in the same street as Sheila. In his bedroom, he raped her, then, fearing identification, attempted to suffocate her. Sheila resisted his bungled attempts, and Carter turned to strangling her with string and putting his fingers down her throat. He finally succeeding in his task by binding her airways with cloth and pushing her face into the pillow, then binding her limbs with string. He waited until his brother-in-law had gone out before taking the body out and dumping it behind a nearby hedge, where a neighbour discovered it the following morning. He admitted his guilt when questioned by police.

Carter's only defence was insanity. His sister was considered a mental defective for nine years until her death, and his brother was in an asylum from 1934 to 1941. Carter had shot himself in the chest while in the army because the weather was bad. He was said to be indifferent to his own or anyone else's fate. The jury arrived at its verdict in 15 minutes.

Read: Murderous Birmingham

15 January 1952   Strangeways prison, Manchester

A.Pierrepoint/ Stewart

719

Alfred BRADLEY   24

Bludgeoned: ***George Camp***, *58, on 12 August 1951, in Manchester, Lancs.*
Motive: *Vengeance; drink related.*

Bradley, *(b.1927)*, a petty thief from Macclesfield, was 17 when he first met one-eyed George Camp in 1945. The two had begun a sexual relationship, Camp paying 'Joyce', as he called Bradley, £3 or £4 every time the two had sex.

Camp was a nightwatchman on a building site in Wythenshawe, and the two went there together after drinking ten pints in a local pub. After Camp had penetrated Bradley, he refused to hand over any money. When the young man said he did not want sex with Camp any more, a quarrel ensued, Camp threatening to tell Bradley's family of their illegal liaisons. Bradley, 5'6" and stocky, battered Camp with a 20kg plank of wood and an axe, breaking his ribs and jaw, and leaving with £16 of his money. Camp was found dead in his hut the following morning.

The police were given a description of a young man seen playing cards with Camp a few days before, but made no progress with the investigation. In October, when Bradley was in gaol for theft, he admitted the murder. He later retracted the confession, naming two men he claimed were guilty. His trial was halted when he threw a Bible at the judge. He had described details only the murderer would have known, and his testimony was not believed, the jury delivering its verdict after 55 minutes.

Read: True Crime, Apr 97.

720

Alfred MOORE   36

Shot: *1 Det. Insp.* **Duncan A. Fraser**, *45, and*
          2 P.C. **Arthur Jagger**, *42,   on 15 July 1951, near*
          Huddersfield, W. Yorkshire.
Motive: *To escape arrest.*

          Alfred Moore, *(b.1916),* was a poultry farmer who lived with his wife
and four children at Whinney Close Farm in Kirkheaton, near Huddersfield.
He had sent his two eldest girls to a private school, and his resources were
run low. He had served eight months for desertion in 1943. Local police
suspected him of hundreds of burglaries in local offices and houses, stealing
cash and stamps, to supplement his income. They decided to set a trap for
him, lying in wait outside the farm, in the hope of catching him red-handed
with stolen goods.
          At about 2 a.m. Moore appeared. P.C. Jagger approached him, but
as he questioned him, Moore pulled a gun and shot Jagger in the abdomen.
He then shot Detective Inspector Fraser three times, the last at point-blank
range through the heart. Fraser died on his way to hospital.
          When reinforcements arrived at the house, Moore claimed he had
been in bed since midnight, but police found recently burned stamps and
dollar bills in the grate, a stash of rings, gold and silver items and 157 keys.
As P.C. Jagger was dangerously ill, an identity parade was hastily convened,
at which he picked out Moore, and at a special court session at his bedside,
his evidence of the shootings was heard. Arthur Jagger died the following
morning. The murder weapon was never found.
          Despite arguments about the accuracy of identification by torchlight
at night, the jury took fifty minutes to give its verdict.

          Read: Settings For Slaughter, p97

721

Herbert Roy HARRIS   24

Bludgeoned: **Eileen Harris**, *22, his wife, on 8 December 1951, in Flint.*
Motive: *Vengeance*

Roy Harris, *(b.1928)*, a silk worker, had served with the Welsh Guards in Palestine. Born in Coventry, he married Flint girl Eileen in 1948, and they had three children, the last born in October 1951. Living with Eileen's parents had put a strain on the marriage, and the couple had separated and reconciled several times since their wedding.

By the end of 1951 both were living with their respective parents, but still saw each other several times a week. They had arranged to go to the cinema together, but Eileen had gone without Roy, and he waited for her to come out. They were seen walking away quite happily. But being stood up had annoyed Roy and an argument developed.

On a bridge, he clubbed Eileen with several stones, one of 25kg, and with an iron bar. She was found by a passer-by at 9.30pm. Harris then fled to London, where he was arrested in an hotel the following day. He claimed the killing had been unintentional, and the jury, after 48 minutes' deliberation, added a strong recommendation to mercy.

Read: Master Detective, Mar 97

---

21 March 1952   Durham gaol

722

<u>Takir ALI</u>   **40**   *Bengali*

Stabbed: ***Evelyn McDonald***, 25, on 20 November 1951, in South Shields, Co Durham.
Motive: *Sexual rivalry.*

In 1943 Evelyn McDonald had left her widowed mother in Sunderland at 17 because she was pregnant. She settled in South Shields and worked as a cleaner in various Indian cafes, serving the seamen who had settled in the town. There in 1944 she met Montez Ullah from what was then east Pakistan. A ship's fireman, he took Evelyn to live with him, but he went home in the summer of 1947, intending a six-month stay.

In 1948 Evelyn began a relationship with Ullah's cousin, Takir Ali, *(b.1912)*, a short and slight seaman. Evelyn would stay nights with Ali, but would not move in with him. Ullah returned in 1950 and in 1951 Ali went to sea for several months, sending Evelyn £5 every fortnight.

When he returned in October Evelyn told him their relationship was over. The two had a fight in the street in 14 November, and then a few days later, Ali went for a drink with Evelyn and a friend, and then,walking home outside a cinema, he stabbed her with a flickknife twice in the back, then through the heart.

Arrested nearby, he claimed that Evelyn's friend was lying, that someone else was responsible. The jury took 35 minutes to disagree.

Read: True Crime, Nov 97

12 April 1952   Barlinnie prison, Glasgow   *A.Pierrepoint/ Wade*

723

<u>**James SMITH**</u>   **21**   *Scottish*

Stabbed:	***Martin Malone***, *34, on 16 November 1951, in Glasgow, Lanarks.*
Motive:	*Sadistic pleasure.*

Martin Malone was a steam pipe boiler coverer, and had been married to his wife Mary, 31, for 13 years. They had 2 children. His wife had gone with a friend to the dance-hall on Royston Road, Glasgow, and Martin had joined them there at 9.30, accompanied by his friend of 12 years, William Loudon, 38. It was a fund-raising night for pensioners and about 250 people were present.

Shortly after arriving Martin noticed his friend in a tussle with a man in the foyer and went over to offer assistance. Loudon was stabbed in the right hip and Malone in the chest. Witnesses identified labourer James Smith, *(b.1931)*, as having been seen brandishing a knife. He had given a policeman the slip, but was picked up the following day at a relative's house.

He said that he had helped another man who earlier was being punched by Malone and Loudon, and that they had come back later to take revenge on him. He had stabbed Loudon in self-defence and Malone by accident. The jury deliberated for 100 minutes before finding him guilty. His appeal centred upon a second knife found in the dance-hall, but was dismissed.

Read: True Crime, Aug 96

25 April 1952   Walton prison, Liverpool

A.Pierrepoint/ Dernley/ Stewart/ Smith

724, 725

Alfred BURNS   21
Edward Francis DEVLIN   22

Bludgeoned: ***Beatrice Alice Rimmer***, *54, on 20 August 1951, in Waverley, Liverpool, Lancs.*

Motive: *Financial.*

Labourers Burns, *(b.1931),* and Devlin, *(b.1930),* from Manchester, lay in wait for reclusive widow Mrs Rimmer at her home in Cranborne Road, having broken in through a kitchen window. The woman was rumoured to keep large sums of money in the house. When she returned home that evening she was severely beaten about the head twelve times with a torch and left to die in her hallway.

Her son, 24, found her the following evening. Underworld informers pointed to Burns and Devlin who claimed they were involved in a Manchester robbery at that time, an alibi backed up by witnesses. Despite a large campaign protesting their innocence, their appeals were turned down. Later, in the condemned cell, one of the men confessed.

Read: True Detective, Mar 97

7 May 1952   Cardiff prison

726

Ajit SINGH   27   *Indian*

Shot: ***Joan Marion Thomas***, *27, on 30 December 1951, in Bridgend, Glamorgan.*

Motive: *Vengeance.*

Singh, *(b.1925),* came to Britain in 1949, starting his own drapery business, then working in the steelworks after the business folded. Rather lonely since his wife died in 1950, in March 1951 he met Joan Thomas while she was working on a market stall belonging to the clothing store for which she worked. The two began a slow courtship - Singh, a Sikh with full beard and turban, was only allowed to walk her home two weeks later.

He dined with her parents, but they turned hostile when marriage was mentioned. So the two began to meet in secret. By November, however, the novelty had worn off for Joan, and she told Singh it was all over. He could not accept this, and began to call at the house, follow Joan, and wait for her. He told her he would shoot her if she did not take him back. Joan took him his dinner on Christmas Day, and tried to persuade him to accept her decision.

On 30 December he followed Joan and a friend onto a bus to the hospital. When they disembarked, he fired four shots, hitting a woman passer-by in the ear, but striking Joan twice in the back. He turned her over, and shot her once in the heart. Putting the gun to his own forehead, he fired twice, but the gun was out of ammunition. He then cradled Joan's body in his arms until police arrived.

The jury retired for thirty minutes, before adding the strongest possible recommendation to mercy to their verdict. The Home Office allowed a cremation at Pontypridd before Singh's ashes were interred in the prison.

Read: True Detective, Aug 91.

27 May 1952	Pentonville prison, London	*A.Pierrepoint/ Smith*

727

Backary MANNEH   25   *black*

Stabbed: *Joseph Aaku, 28, on 4 January 1952, in London NW1.*
Motive: *Vengeance.*

Manneh, *(b. 1927)*, and Aaku both worked at Euston station, and lodged at the same address, where Aaku supplemented his income by drug dealing. It was during an argument over narcotics that Manneh attacked Aaku, slashing his face and stabbing him in the neck several times, then stealing a gold watch.

Police found a large quantity of hemp in Aaku's room, but also two types of blood, and Manneh fell under suspicion when it was learned he had badly cut his hand. He claimed it had been injured when he was mugged, but Manneh had warned a woman friend not to mention it to the police. When it was discovered that he had sold Aaku's watch for £2, the police arrested Manneh in hospital on 14 January, his cut having turned septic.

Many arrests for drug dealing were made following the discovery of Aaku's diary.

Read: And May The Lord have Mercy on Your Soul

29 May 1952   Barlinnie prison, Glasgow   *A.Pierrepoint/ Wade*

728

Patrick Gallagher DEVENEY   **42**   *Scottish*

Strangled: ***Jeanie Deveney**, 37, his wife, on 26 February 1952, in Glasgow, Lanarks.*
Motive: *Sadistic pleasure.*

Deveney, *(b.1910)*, had met Jeanie Todd whilst on army leave in 1939. They had known each other only one week when they married. He was discharged from the army in 1942, being described as 'psychopathic'. By 1952 the couple had five children, but frequently argued. Neighbours described Deveney as hot-tempered.

On the afternoon of 26 February, Deveney attacked his wife, hitting her on the forehead with a coal-hammer, and strangling her with a tie. He then took his daughter and walked into a Greenock police station to tell them he had killed his wife. She was found fully-dressed under a pile of bed-clothes next to her bed. Doctors having described Deveney as having no mental disease, the jury took 40 minutes to convict him.

Read: True Crime, Aug 96

8 July 1952   Shrewsbury prison   *A.Pierrepoint/ Allen*

729

Harry HUXLEY   **42**   *Welsh*

Shot: ***Ada Royce**, 32, on 29 December 1951, in Holt, Denbighs, Wales.*
Motive: *Sexual rivalry.*

Huxley, *(b.1910)*, had been in the army from 1940 to 1945, by which time his sweetheart, Ada, was married with two children. From 1945, Huxley worked as a labourer at the same industrial estate where Charles Royce was a machinist, but he had soon met Ada again and the two had begun an affair. In 1947 Ada had a second son, and told Huxley he was the father. He gave money for the boy, but gradually Ada began to cool the relationship, refusing to leave her husband.

In December 1951, Huxley borrowed a shotgun from a friend with which to shoot pheasants. On Christmas Day, he saw Ada and her sister in a pub, and bought them a drink, Ada leaving in disgust when Huxley got rolling drunk, and began waving the shotgun around in the bar.

Four days later he again saw Ada in the pub, and told her the gun had been intended for her. Followed by him along the street, Ada threatened to report him to the police if there were any more threats, and again refused to leave Charles. Huxley shot her, and then shot himself in the chest. He claimed in court that the gun had gone off by accident, but after two hours of deliberation, the jury rejected his evidence.

Read: True Crime, Apr 97.

15 July 1952	Horsfield gaol, Bristol	*A.Pierrepoint*

730

Thomas EAMES 31

Stabbed: ***Muriel Elsie Bent****, 26, on 27 February 1952, in Plymouth, Devon.*
Motive: *Sexual rivalry.*

Eames, *(b.1921),* was known as a shy, but a kind and gentle man whose wife and daughter had left him during the war. He had then returned to his parents in Plymouth, where he worked as a labourer. He met Muriel Bent in 1947 and married her, escaping imprisonment when his bigamy was discovered. Muriel stayed with him, and the two had a daughter, though by 1951 Muriel had had enough and left him. When Eames saw her walking with another man, he became withdrawn and moody.

He told her there was a letter for her, to entice her to his house. A workmate saw him sharpening a knife into a dagger, and was concerned that Eames had not slept for days. When Muriel called round at 6pm, Eames had not eaten for four days, and immediately flew into a rage, hitting her. He said that Muriel kissed him, and as she did so he stabbed her in the back. As she fell he stabbed her again in the chest, to 'prevent her lingering'. He then went to his brother-in-law, who took him to the police. In finding him guilty, the jury added a strong recommendation to mercy, but on the scaffold Eames told his warders, 'I am quite happy to go'.

Read: True Crime, Jun 97.

731

Frank BURGESS   21

Strangled: **Johanna Hallahan**, *22, on 21 April 1952, in East Croydon, Surrey.*
Motive: *Sadistic pleasure.*

Burgess, *(b.1931)*, was a porter at a Croydon hotel, but was on probation after attacking a taxi driver. His room was close to that of Johanna Hallahan, who also worked at the hotel, and who was engaged to be married. On their day off, Burgess went to ask Johanna for the loan of £1, but then strangled her. He broke into her electricity meter, and then his own, and then made off. When neither turned up for work on 23 April, the alarm was raised.

Read: And May The Lord Have Mercy On Your Soul

732

Oliver George BUTLER   24

Strangled: **Rose Margaret Meadows**, *21, on 19 May 1952, in Horley, Oxon.*
Motive: *Sexual rivalry.*

Butler, *(b.1928)*, and Rose both worked in an aluminium factory, and were very much in love. On 16 May, Butler, from Grimsbury, moved in with Rose and her parents in Wroxton. He was, however, married with three children, and his wife refused to divorce him. The couple could see only an unhappy future together.

Taking a spring walk, the two made love in a field near Horley, and then, according to Butler, Rose remarked that this was a good place to die, and dared her lover to kill her to end their miserable dilemma. He strangled her, then ran crying to a level crossing keeper asking him to phone the police. He told them he wanted to hang to be with Rose. Butler told how Rose had frequently talked of suicide, but a witness had seen her laughing with Butler shortly before the murder. The jury considered for 45 minutes, adding a strong recommendation to mercy.

Read: True Crime, May 95.

733

i

Mahmood Hussein MATTAN   **29**
Somali

Cut throat of: ***Lily Volpert**, 41, on 6 March 1952, in Cardiff, Glamorgan.*
Motive: *Financial.*

The Volperts, a Jewish family, had run a shop in Tiger Bay for many years. In 1952 Lily Volpert, 4' 10", was the locally popular proprietress, and she lived behind the shop with her mother, sister and niece. Mattan, *(b.1923)*, a 5' 8" unemployed labourer from British Somaliland, had arrived from Aden in Tiger Bay's multi-racial community as a seaman during the war. In 1947 he married 17-year old Laura Williams against the wishes of her family, and to the abuse of her community. The couple had three sons.

The shop's bell rang at 8.05 one windy evening and Lily, used to late customers, had interrupted her supper to answer it. From behind, she was silently grabbed by the hair and her throat was slit with a razor, almost severing her head. When local seaman William Archbold entered the shop, the murderer hid behind a tailor's dummy. Discovering Lily's body, Archbold immediately ran for the police. The killer helped himself to cash from the shop, perhaps £100, and left. The police arrived before Lily's family was aware of what had happened.

A Jamaican witness, Harold Cover, said he saw Mattan leaving the shop and another said that he had been flashing money around after the murder - Mattan liked to gamble but was usually broke. Though the killer would have been covered in blood, police found only traces on Mattan's shoes and no forensic tests were made. No trace of the missing money was found on him.

Mattan denied any knowledge of the murder and remained indignant throughout. But the circumstantial evidence was enough to convince the jury of his guilt after 85 minutes. Mattan's family continued to plead his innocence, but police remained convinced, later stating that local shopkeepers were in fear of the Somali's violence. However, Mattan was not picked out at any identity parade, the woman who saw him flashing money only came forward a week after the murder after a reward had been offered, and Cover had been a gambling acquaintance of Mattan's, and may have had a grudge. He himself was jailed for life in 1969 for the attempted murder of his daughter with a razor.

Mattan was reburied in 1996, and his conviction was finally quashed by the Court of Appeal in February 1998.

Read: Mail on Sunday, 1.12.96

734

John Howard GODAR   31

Stabbed: ***Maureen Jones Cox**, 20, on 6 June 1952, in Uxbridge, Middlesex.*
Motive: *Sexual rivalry.*

    Godar, *(b.1921),* had been courting Maureen Cox for ten months, but she was cooling the relationship after discovering that Godar was divorced, and the father of a child. They took a taxi in Uxbridge, and the driver was told to make for Maple Cross, Herts, but the pair had hardly begun their journey, when Maureen told Godar that she had made a date with another man, whereupon he stabbed her twenty times in the face, twenty times in the chest, and eight times in the throat. The taxi driver was then asked to proceed to the nearest police station.

    Read: And May The Lord Have Mercy On Your Soul

30 September 1952   Pentonville prison, London
                                     A.Pierrepoint/ Smith/ Stewart

735

Raymond Jack CULL   25

Stabbed: ***Jean Frances Cull**, 17, his wife, on 29 June 1952, in Northolt, Middlesex.*
Motive: *Sexual rivalry; drink related.*

    Cull, *(b.1927),* a labourer known as Johnny, met and began a sexual relationship with 15-year old Jean Caton in 1950. Six months later, when she turned 16, Jean went to live with her lover. The arguments soon started, Cull easily offended by any attention paid by Jean to other men. On one occasion the police were called. However, when Johnny was in hospital for kidney stones, Jean did indeed see another man. Nevertheless, the two married in March 1952, with Jean's date of birth forged. She still spent much time with her parents, who were separated, and by June Jean had decided Johnny was not going to be a permanent fixture.

Madly jealous, Cull waited outside her father's house till 2.30am for Jean to return from a date with a new boyfriend, then spent the rest of the night with her, leaving for work at 6.45am.

Later that day he received a letter from his wife telling him it was all over. Drunk, he broke into Mr Caton's house armed with a bayonet at 11.30pm, and stabbed Jean to death in her bed. The wound went through her arm, and penetrated her lung by 35cm. He then chased her father, clad only in underpants, down the street. Cull broke into a shop to phone 999 before going to his sister's. The jury retired for 55 minutes before adding a recomendation to mercy to its guilty verdict.

Read: Master Detective, Oct 97.

30 September 1952   Pentonville prison, London

A.Pierrepoint/ Smith/ Stewart

736

Dennis George MULDOWNEY   41

Stabbed:	***Countess Krystyna Skarbek**, 36, on 15 June 1952, in London SW5.*
Motive:	*Sexual rivalry.*

Muldowney, *(b.1911),* a night porter at the Reform Club, had met the Countess whilst they were working on a liner in 1951, and a friendship had developed. Krystyna was a Polish aristocrat who had received the George Medal and the Croix de Guerre for her wartime intelligence work in Hungary, Turkey, France and Italy. She had settled in London and changed her name to Christine Granville. She had become engaged to a wartime colleague, spurning Muldowney by burning his letters.

Intense with jealousy, Muldowney waited for her at her Earls Court hotel residence after her evening dining out. He approached her and stabbed her in the heart. He made no attempt to escape, and pleaded guilty. The jury's decision took only three minutes to arrive.

Read: The Hangman's Diary, p319.

571

9 October 1952   Pentonville prison, London   *A.Pierrepoint/ Harry Allen*

737

Peter Cyril JOHNSON   **24**

Bludgeoned: ***Charles Mead**, 24, on 28 June 1952, in London E2.*
Motive: *Vengeance.*

Johnson, *(b.1928),* had a long record of violence, but was good friends with Charles Mead, a fellow street trader in Bethnal Green. The two got into an argument on 28 June, and in the ensuing fight, Johnson hit Mead on the head with an 8kg concrete block. The prisoner struggled with his warders in court, and had to be taken down. The jury took 30 minutes to decide his fate.

Read: And May The Lord Have Mercy On Your Soul.

23 October 1952   Shrewsbury prison

738

Donald Neil SIMON   **32**

Shot: **1 *Eunice Marjorie Joyce Simon**, 28, his wife, and*
      2   *Victor Brades, 27, on 21 June 1952, in Slough,*
      Bucks.
Motive: *Sexual rivalry.*

Simon, *(b.1920),* and Eunice had married in 1943, and had emigrated to Canada, but returned four years later, as she had become home-sick. Eunice left Donald in November 1951, mainly because of his heavy drinking, and had begun seeing Victor Brades. The couple were making their way home at 11.40pm, after an evening in the pub, when Simon approached, and shot his wife twice, Brades four times. Brades died at the scene, but Eunice survived until the following day. Simon was discovered cradling his wife, crying, 'What have I done?'

Read: And May The Lord Have Mercy On Your Soul

12 December 1952   Lincoln prison

739

Eric NORCLIFFE   30

Stabbed: ***Kathleen Vera Norcliffe**, 23, his wife, on 25 June 1952, in Warsop, Notts.*
Motive: *Vengeance.*

      Norcliffe, *(b.1922),* had married Kathleen in 1943, and served in the war as an RAF gunner, but it was not until April 1952, that the couple got a home of their own. Thereafter the relationship deteriorated, and a change soon came upon Eric. He used to do certain domestic chores, but he chided his wife for not completing them, and he developed a melancholia. When he failed to prepare dinner as usual, Kathleen set about the task, giving Eric the job of cutting the cabbage, and then criticised him, calling him a 'bastard'. He took the knife and stabbed her twelve times.

    Read: And May The Lord Have Mercy On Your Soul

17 December 1952   Wandsworth prison, London   *A.Pierrepoint/ Dernley*

740

John Kenneth LIVESEY   24

Stabbed: ***Stephanie Marie Small**, 49, on 26 July 1952, in London SE10.*
Motive: *Vengeance.*

      Livesey, *(b.1928),* a miller operative, had married Pamela Small, 23, in 1950. They had a son of 15 months and lived unhappily with Pamela's parents and two sisters, Collen, 18, and Pat, 13, crammed into a council flat on Blackheath Hill. Tensions built up and Livesey had applied to rejoin the army, but Pamela had hidden the letter telling him to report on 24 July. On the 16th Livesey hit his father- in-law, who needed stitches to an eye injury.

      Harry Small, 63, a factory foreman, had married his Anglo-Indian wife while serving in India in 1918. They had moved to the flat in Greenwich with their five children in 1948, and relations with Pamela had been strained since her marriage. On the evening of 26 July, while Colleen was in Southend, and Pamela visiting friends, Harry and Pat went to watch TV at a neighbour's, leaving Livesey and Stephanie alone at home with baby Paul.

573

Between 9 and 11 pm, as Stephanie was about to get into bed, Livesey stabbed her 24 times in the neck and back. Livesey ran off but was arrested in Ramsgate four days later, wearing a raincoat under which he was naked but for a new shirt. He claimed his clothes had been stolen while he bathed in the sea. Traces of blood were found on his coat and shoes and in his hair and fingernails.

He denied any knowledge of the murder, saying he had thought about his problems and had left home at 9.30. The all-male jury took 35 minutes to decide they did not believe him. While stripping the corpse after his execution, assistant hangman Syd Dernley commented upon the 'magnificent' size of Livesey's genitals. He received no more invitations to assist at hangings.

Read: True Detective, July96

---

23 December 1952   Winson Green prison, Birmingham
A.Pierrepoint/ Dernley

741

Leslie GREEN   29

Bludgeoned: ***Alice Wiltshaw**, 62, on 16 July 1952, in Barlaston, Staffordshire.*
Motive: *Vengeance; financial.*

Green, *(b. 1923),* had four convictions for theft and had served a term in Borstal. From 1937 to 1949 he had served in the army and air force, marrying in that time and fathering a daughter in 1946. In 1950 he had gone to work as chauffeur and gardener to Frederick Cuthbert Wiltshaw, a wealthy pottery maker, at their village mansion in Staffordshire. In May 1952, Mr Wiltshaw sacked Green after he had used the car without permission.

Green knew when the two maids had their day off, and on 16 July went to the house to take revenge. Finding Mrs Wiltshaw in the kitchen, he felled her with a one metre log. Having rifled the house, stealing £3000 worth of jewellery, he returned to Mrs Wiltshaw, who had managed to crawl into the hall. He beat her with a vase and brass bowl, breaking her nose and jaw, then took a poker to twice stab the woman in the face and abdomen. Mrs Wiltshaw's body was later discovered by her husband.

Green left behind a footprint and a pair of gloves, discovered in the garden. When police called at Green's house in nearby Longton, his wife told them he had been missing for two weeks. He had become 'engaged' to an Irish nurse in Leeds, and had given her two of Mrs Wiltshaw's rings. Green went to the police of his own accord, but denied any involvement. However, the footprint matched his shoe, and a cut on his thumb corresponded to a tear in the gloves.

Read: True Detective Winter Special 88/9

24 December 1952   Durham gaol   *Wade/ Allen*

742

Herbert APPLEBY   20

Stabbed: ***John David Thomas***, *29, on 21 September 1952, in Middlesbrough, N.Yorks.*
Motive: *Sexual rivalry; drink related.*

Appleby, *(b.1932)*, from Grangetown, Middlesbrough, was a sling-loader at the docks, and was known as a quiet and well-mannered young man. Following damage at birth, he sleepwalked, had epilepsy and also a squint, but he had spent two years in the army in the middle-east.

With his girlfriend, Lillian Robbins, 20, known as 'Dolly', he attended the wedding of a friend, and the reception at a local pub. However, when he saw the groom's step-brother, John Thomas, sitting with his arm round Dolly, Appleby was overwhelmed with jealousy. He walked the 200m to his home and returned with a kitchen knife. As Thomas sat, still with his arm round Dolly, Appleby stabbed him in the chest once. He then took a taxi to the police station to turn himself in.

Appleby's defence centred on temporary insanity, brought about by lack of sleep and food, and too much drink. Following his conviction, his father and Dolly raised a petition for his reprieve, to no avail. His last words were to thank the prison staff for their kindness.

Read: True Detective, Jan 96

743	2 Jan	John ALCOTT	22		Wandsworth
744	26 Jan	George SHAW	25	*Irish*	Barlinnie
745	28 Jan	Derek BENTLEY	19		Wandsworth
746	24 Feb	Miles GIFFARD	27		Bristol
747	19 May	John TODD	20		Walton
748	15 Jul	John CHRISTIE	55		Pentonville
749	30 Jul	Philip HENRY	25		Armley
750	18 Sep	Louisa MERRIFIELD (f)	46		Strangeways
751	20 Oct	John GREENWAY	27	*Welsh*	Bristol
752	17 Nov	John REYNOLDS	31	*Irish*	Leicester
753	17 Dec	Stanislaw JURAS	43	*Polish*	Strangeways
754	18 Dec	John WILKINSON	24		Wandsworth
755	22 Dec	Alfred WHITEWAY	22		Wandsworth
756	23 Dec	George NEWLAND	21		Pentonville

2 January 1953   Wandsworth prison, London   *A.Pierrepoint/ Smith*

743

John James ALCOTT   **22**

Murdered: **1 Peter Helm**, in 1948, in Germany.
Stabbed: **2 Geoffrey Charles Dean**, 27, on 22 August 1952,
                near Aldershot, Hampshire.
Motive: Financial.

In 1948 Alcott, *(b.1931)*, had, with a Czech accomlice, murdered Peter Helm, a German civilian, while stationed with the Grenadier Guards in Germany. He was sentenced to death, but as his mother had not been informed of the nature of his trial, he was reprieved on a technicality. He had convictions for theft from an early age.

Three years later, a railway fireman living in Eltham, Alcott, 6', had been hanging around Ash Vale railway station for two days. While the booking clerk Geoffrey Dean, a married man with a daughter of 5, was working late one night Alcott had at 8.45pm, walked into the booking office and stabbed Dean more than twenty times, first fatally to the neck, and including two wounds to the heart. He stole £168 from the safe.

Together with a bloody jacket, the knife was later found in the chimney at the Aldershot boarding-house where Alcott lived. When arrested arriving home, he was found to be carrying £109. Confessing to the crime, his claim to have had a mental blackout was dismissed. The jury took 30 minutes to convict.

Read: True Detective Winter Special 90/1

26 January 1953	Barlinnie prison, Glasgow	*A.Pierrepoint*

744

George SHAW   25   *Irish*

Bludgeoned: **Michael Connelly**, *79, on 15 August 1952, near Lanark.*
Motive: *Financial.*

Michael Connelly had come to Scotland from Ireland at the age of 26. He had done some labouring work at Huntlygate Farm in 1932 and had been allowed to stay in a 6'x4' shack there rent-free ever since. Known as 'Old Mick', he drew his pension weekly and had saved enough for his funeral, though he possessed little.

George Shaw, *(b.1928),* had left Ireland when he was 15 and lived with his girlfriend and their three children in Lanark, but he had recently lost his job as a farm labourer. He and his Irish friend George Dunn, 22, were seen near the farm on 15 August.

On the 24th two walkers found Old Mick dead in his hut, slumped over a fruit box. He had been battered from behind with a lemonade bottle. Shaw's girlfriend became suspicious over money which George suddenly had, and reported him to the police. Witnesses said the two Irishmen were seen in a hotel on the 17 August, flush with cash. Shaw admitted being near the farm with Dunn but denied murder. Both men were wearing Connelly's socks, and Dunn's bootprints were found near the shack. The jury deliberated for 105 minutes and found both men guilty of murder by an 11-3 majority. Dunn, with a mental age of 8, was sent to a mental institution, Shaw to the scaffold.

Read: True Crime, Aug 96

Derek William BENTLEY   19   *i*

Accomplice to shooting of: **P.C. Sidney George**
Miles, *42, on 2 November*
1952, in Croydon, Surrey.
Motive: *To escape arrest.*

Bentley, *(b.1933),* lived with his parents in Norbury, SW16. He worked occasionally as a dustman or removal man, but had a mental age of 11, was illiterate, and had a record for shop-breaking. His parents tried to discourage his friendship with Christopher Craig, 16, a Camberwell garage-hand, whom Derek looked up to. On 30 October 1952, Craig's brother Niven, 26, had been jailed for 12 years for armed robbery.

Three days later, Craig, armed with a revolver and a knife, went out with Bentley determined on burglary. Bentley had a knife and knuckle-dusters on him. They were seen entering a warehouse in Croydon at 9.15pm, and the police soon arrived. On the warehouse roof Bentley was seized by Det. Con. Frederick Fairfax. Bentley was reported to have shouted, 'Let him have it, Chris!' and Craig shot Fairfax in the shoulder. As P.C. Miles arrived on the roof, Craig shot at him and he was hit over the left eye, dying instantly. More police arrived, shots were exchanged, and when Craig's revolver was emptied, he jumped the 8m from the roof, fracturing his spine.

The court took the view that though Bentley was in police custody at the time of the murder, his call was incitement to kill. The jury took 75 minutes to find both guilty, Bentley receiving a recommendation to mercy, and Craig being detained as a minor. He was released in 1963. An outcry was raised to prevent Bentley from hanging, with 200 M.P.s signing a petition, and 5000 protested outside the jail on the day of his execution.

In July 1998, the court of appeal ruled that, though the case against Bentley was "a substantial one, albeit not overwhelming", Lord Goddard's summing up amounted to a mistrial, and Bentley's conviction was finally quashed. There has since been speculation that PC Miles was in fact shot accidentally by one of his colleagues.

Read: Let Him Have It, Chris

746

Miles William GIFFARD   27

Bludgeoned: *Charles Henry Giffard, 53, and*
                     Elizabeth Giffard, 56, his parents, on 7 November 1952,
                     near St Austell, Cornwall.
Motive: *Financial.*

Charles Giffard was Clerk to the Magistrates. He and his wife, who lived in Porthpean on the Cornish south coast, were disappointed with their son, Miles, *(b.1926)*.   Miles was schizophrenic, perhaps induced by a childhood nanny who would lock Miles in a cupboard. He was expelled from Rugby public school, and failed in his law studies, and at everything else he attempted. He did serve three years in the navy, but thereafter frittered away a £750 inheritance, and came home to his parents when attempts at self-sufficiency in Bournemouth and London failed. He did, however, fall in love with Gabrielle Vallance, 19, from Chelsea. Then his father forbade him from using his car and from taking trips to the capital.

On 7 November, Miles battered his father over the head, killing him with lead piping as he worked in the garage. He went to the kitchen and battered his mother about the head and body. She was still alive as he tipped both parents over the nearby cliffs, a 40m drop. Having cleaned up the blood, he took his father's car to London, pawning some of his mother's jewellery before meeting Gabrielle. He told her what he had done, confessing all to the police on his arrest. His plea of insanity was rejected by the jury in 35 minutes.

Read: Landmarks in C20 Murder, p175

747

John TODD   20

Bludgeoned: *George Walker, 82, on 14 January 1953, in Aintree,*
                     Lancs.
Motive: *Financial.*

Todd, *(b.1933)*, was seen by two schoolboys getting his clocks repaired at the bric-a-brac shop owned by George Walker. Todd locked the door and then axed the old man to death, leaving him at the foot of his stairs. Neighbours, disturbed by Mr Walker's two dogs' constant barking, discovered his body the next day. Five days later, Todd's girlfriend told her father that Todd had admitted commiting the crime, and the police were contacted. Todd's shoes matched bloody footprints found in the shop, and his raincoat was bloodstained.

Read: And May The Lord Have Mercy On Your Soul

15 July 1953   Pentonville prison, London   *A.Pierrepoint/ Smith*

748

John Reginald Halliday CHRISTIE   **55**

Strangled:	**1 *Ruth Fuerst***, *21, on 24 August 1943.*
	2 *Muriel Eady*, *32, on 7 October 1944.*
probably	**3 *Beryl Evans***, *20, on 8 November 1949, and*
possibly	**4 *Geraldine Evans***, *1, her daughter, on 8 November 1949.*
	5 *Ethel Christie*, *his wife, 54, on 14 December 1952.*
	6 *Rita Nelson*, *25, on 2 January 1953.*
	7 *Kathleen Maloney*, *26, on 12 January 1953.*
	8 *Hectorina McLennan*, *26, on 3 March 1953, all in London W11.*
Motive:	*Sexual/ to clear impediment.*

Christie, *(b.1898)*, was a thin, weak man, a liar and a hypochondriac. He married Ethel in 1920, but they separated for ten years in 1923 when he left his native Yorkshire to live in London. He was sacked from a succession of jobs for petty theft, and served several short prison terms for stealing, the last in 1933. In 1938, he and Ethel moved into 10 Rillington Place, W11, and he worked as a special constable during the war, and in a succession of clerical jobs thereafter.

It was while Ethel was visiting her family in 1943, that he killed his first victim, Ruth Fuerst, an Austrian woman. His pattern was to render the women unconscious with gas, then to rape them, killing them by strangulation while achieving orgasm. He would then masturbate over their bodies.

Beryl and Timothy Evans were lodgers at the house. It seems that Christie killed Beryl in a similar way, after he offered to conduct an abortion on her. It is not clear whether Christie or Evans killed the baby. In any event, Evans hanged for both murders in March 1950.

It is probable that Christie killed his own wife to free himself for more murder, or because she had made a discovery. She was strangled, but there was no sexual assault, the couple had not had sex together for over two years. Free at last, Christie conducted three murders of prostitutes in quick succession at the beginning of 1953.

With no money, Christie left Rillington Place on 20 March, to roam London's streets. The new tenant discovered the bodies of the three prostitutes papered into a cupboard on 24 March. Mrs Christie was under the floorboards and his first two victims were found buried in the garden. Pubic hair from four of his victims was found in a tobacco tin. Christie was arrested near Putney bridge on 31 March. He was tried only for the murder of his wife, but confessed to all the killings, except that of baby Geraldine. The jury decided his fate after 85 minutes' deliberation.

Rillington Place, later renamed Rushton Close, was demolished in 1972.

Read: Ten Rillington Place

30 July 1953   Armley gaol, Leeds   *A.Pierrepoint/ Rickard*

749

<u>Philip HENRY</u>   **25**   *black*

Bludgeoned: ***Flora Jane Gilligan**, 76, on 10 March 1953, in York, N.Yorks.*
Motive: *Sexual; drink related.*

Henry, *(b.1928)*, was a private in the Kings Own Yorkshire Light Infantry, camped in York. From Stockton, Henry had served in Malaya and Korea, returning to England in December 1952. On 10 March, he went into the city and consumed 9 pints of beer. He failed to break into one house, but saw an open window next door, and entered the home of Miss Gilligan, who had lived alone since the death of her sister in 1948.

He raped her then beat her to death with a washing-dolly, throwing her naked body head-first from an upstairs window into her yard below, in an attempt to suggest suicide. He did not take the money which was in the house. He did, however, leave behind finger and boot prints. 467 men in the nearby camp were fingerprinted and Henry, due for an overseas posting a week later, was arrested, protesting his innocence. The jury's retirement, including a visit to the house, lasted a total of 3 hours 18 minutes.

Read: Master Detective, Aug 95.

18 September 1953   Strangeways prison, Manchester

A.Pierrepoint / Stewart

750

Louisa MERRIFIELD   46   *female*

Poisoned: ***Sarah Ann Ricketts***, *79, on 14 April 1953 in Blackpool, Lancs.*
Motive: *Financial.*

At the end of March 1953, Louisa Merrifield, *(b.1907)*, and her third husband Alfred, 71, were appointed as housekeepers to Mrs Ricketts at her bungalow in Devonshire Road, Blackpool, after answering a newspaper advertisement. Mrs Merrifield had had twenty such jobs in the past three years, and she had previously served a prison term for ration book fraud. Mrs Ricketts' son changed her will in the couple's favour despite his mother complaining of not being given enough food.

Mrs Merrifield poisoned Mrs Ricketts with rat poison, containing phosphorus, mixed with rum. She had found her on the bedroom floor at 3.15 a.m., but did not call a doctor until the following afternoon. Despite attempts by Merrifield to get her cremated 'at once', a post-mortem was ordered - she had been fit and well during a medical examination the day before her death.

A witness testified that Mrs Merrifield had bragged that the old woman would soon die and that the couple would be well-off, and a spoon covered with a rum residue was found in Merrifield's bag. Alfred was identified as having bought rat poison but after six hours the jury failed to reach agreement on his part in the murder. He was not re-tried, and died in 1962.

Read: Lady Killers

20 October 1953   Horfield gaol, Bristol   *A.Pierrepoint/ Harry Allen*

751

John Owen GREENWAY   27   *Welsh*

Bludgeoned: ***Beatrice Ann Court***, *68, on 2 June 1953, in Swindon, Wilts.*
Motive: *Vengeance*

Greenway, *(b.1926)*, a quiet and reserved man, lived with his parents in Pontypridd until September 1952 when he moved to Swindon and took a job as a machine operator. He had known Christopher Percy for five

582

years in south Wales and the two men formed a sexual relationship. Percy went with Greenway to Swindon, but did not tell him that he was married and seeking a divorce.

Both men shared a room in lodgings with the Courts, but they and the third lodger soon began to complain about the appalling food. On 29 May, Percy left a note for Greenway saying he had gone, unable to bear the food any longer. Unable to contact his lover through his sister, Greenway contemplated suicide, and then four days after Percy's departure, at 11.45 pm, Greenway shouted for Mrs Court. He showed her the letter from Percy and blamed her for his heartbreak. He hit her about the head several times with a household axe, and injured Mr Court, an invalid with heart trouble, on the hand when he tried to intervene. Police arrived to find Greenway sitting in the scullery crying.

He pleaded guilty, and refused to see any visitors while awaiting his execution.

Read: Master Detective, July 96.

17 November 1953   Leicester prison   *A.Pierrepoint/ Stewart*

752

John Christopher REYNOLDS   **31**   *Irish*

Strangled: **Janet Mary Warner**, *12, on 22 May 1953, in Blaby, Leics.*
Motive: *Sadistic pleasure.*

Reynolds, *(b.1922)*, a labourer, had stabbed and badly injured a woman on Barry beach in 1945. He was sentenced to three years, citing 'depression' as his excuse. In 1953, he had been hanging around the canal towpath in Blaby for ten days, waiting for a suitable victim, when Janet Warner, the daughter of a company director, came along with her dog. Diverting from the towpath, Janet entered the adjacent spinney to collect bluebells, when Reynolds pounced, strangling her with a stocking he had been carrying for the purpose. There was no sexual assault. Two young boys witnessed the attack.

Reynolds was arrested two days later in Leicester. Confessing to the murder, his trial lasted a mere four minutes. He told the court, 'I am happy to die'.

Read: True Crime Summer Special 94.

17 December 1953   Strangeways prison, Manchester

753

Stanislaw JURAS   43   *Polish*

Strangled: *Irene Wagner, 29, on 16 September 1953, in Halifax.*
                   W.Yorks.
Motive: *Sexual.*

Juras, *(b.1910)*, a mill worker, lodged with other Poles at the boarding house run by Karol and Irene Wagner, German speaking Poles who had come to the UK after the war. Juras, married in Poland, and said to be uneducated, highly strung and of limited intelligence, had developed something of an obsession about his landlady, a biscuit factory worker, though she was said to fear him.

Karol, 54, went away to Blackpool on 14 September, and two days later, perhaps spurned by her, Juras raped and manually strangled Irene in his room, and switched on the gas. Other tenants heard a scream, and turned off the gas, but Juras refused to leave his room, escaping later through a window. Irene was found naked in his bed, a scarf tied round her throat. Juras was soon found hiding in a nearby yard, and immediately confessed to the murder. The jury took ten minutes to condemn him.

Read: True Detective, Jun 99

18 December 1953   Wandsworth prison, London   *Wade/ Rickard*

754

John Francis WILKINSON   24

Bludgeoned: *Miriam Susan Gray, 5, on 15 August 1953, in London*
                    SW12.
Motive: *Sexual*

Charlotte Schreiber lived with her second husband, and her only child, from her first marriage, in Balham. Hermann and Charlotte took in lodgers to make ends meet, and little Miriam slept on a divan in the kitchen.

In June 1953, John Wilkinson, *(b.1929)*, a furnaceman, came to lodge with them. In the early hours he came down from his room to take two bottles from the cellar. He took the leg of a chair from his bedroom and battered Miriam as she slept, holding her by the neck as he attempted to rape her. He then set fire to the divan, took some food in a suitcase, smashed the french windows in the lounge and ran off. Rising half an hour later, Hermann quickly put out the smouldering fire and discovered Miriam's body. Wilkinson was arrested in Esher the following day.

The trial heard that Wilkinson, one of ten children, had been disturbed since childhood, was psychopathic but sane. The jury decided his fate after 45 minutes' retirement.

Read: True Crime, Jan 97.

22 December 1953   Wandsworth prison, London

A.Pierrepoint/ Broadbent

755

Alfred Charles WHITEWAY   **22**

Bludgeoned/ stabbed: **1 Barbara Songhurst**, 16, and
    2 Christine Reed, 18, on 31 May 1953, in Teddington, Middlesex.
Motive: Sexual.

Whiteway, *(b.1931),* a labourer, was a married man, though, owing to housing problems, his wife, 19, lived with her parents in Kingston, Surrey, and Whiteway with his, in Teddington. He had convictions for theft. He was responsible for more than twelve rapes in the Teddington area, and may have been the man who by night roamed nearby woodland, dressed only in a loin-cloth.

On 24 May, Whiteway attempted to rape a 56-year old woman, and did rape a girl of 14 in woods at Oxshott, about ten miles from his home. They had been attacked with a meat cleaver. A week later, Christine Reed and her friend Barbara Songhurst were cycling home along the Thames towpath at about 11.30 p.m.

Probably in only his loin-cloth, Whiteway raped Barbara then stabbed her three times in the back and battered her with a cleaver. He fractured Christine's skull with the axe, and stabbed her in the chest and back ten times. He then raped her. Christine was still alive when both girls were thrown in the river.

Barbara had recognised Whiteway, probably his reason for turning to murder. Her body was found in the river at Richmond, a few miles downstream, the following day, Christine's near the same point five days later. Whiteway was detained at the end of June in connection with the Oxshott assaults.

Questioned about the murders, he eventually confessed. The cleaver he had used was found in the police car in which he had been transported. Whiteway was tried for the murder of Barbara Songhurst only. The jury deliberated for 47 minutes before reaching its verdict.

Read: True Detective Summer Special 88

23 December 1953   Pentonville prison, London
A.Pierrepoint/ Harry Allen

756

George James NEWLAND   21

Bludgeoned: ***Henry John Tandy***, 65, on 30 May 1953, in Orsett, Essex.

Motive: *Financial.*

'Ginger' Newland, *(b.1932),* had become friendly with Henry and Honor Tandy while stationed in Essex during the war, and had been kind to them both. Now a metal caster, living in Walthamstow, Newland called on the couple in May 1953, and they were delighted to see him once again. But Newland was hard up for money, and wanted a new suit. He had come armed with a claw-hammer, and first battered Honor with it, before killing Henry by the same means.

Honor eventually recovered after a lengthy hospital stay. Newland, who escaped with just over £8, admitted the offence, and said he was sorry for doing it.

Read: And May The Lord Have Mercy On Your Soul

1954

total: **17**

757	5 Jan	Robert MOORE	26	*Canadian*	Armley
758	8 Jan	Czeslaw KOWALEWSKI	33	*Polish*	Strangeways
759	26 Jan	Desmond HOOPER	27		Shrewsbury
760	27 Jan	Wilhelm LUBINA	42	*Polish*	Armley
761	14 Apr	James DOOHAN	24		Wandsworth
762	22 Apr	Albert HALL	48		Armley
763	23 Apr	John LYNCH	45	*Irish*	Saughton
764	28 Apr	Thomas HARRIES	24	*Welsh*	Swansea
765	17 Jun	Kenneth GILBERT	21		Pentonville
766	17 Jun	Ian GRANT	24		Pentonville
767	22 Jun	Milton TAYLOR	23		Walton
768	23 Jun	George ROBERTSON	40	*Scottish*	Saughton
769	11 Aug	William HEPPER	62	*Spanish*	Wandsworth
770	12 Aug	Harry FOWLER	21		Lincoln
771	1 Sep	Edward REID	24		Armley
772	1 Sep	Rupert WELLS	53		Wandsworth
773	15 Dec	Stylou CHRISTOPHI (f)	53	*Cypriot*	Holloway

5 January 1954   Armley gaol, Leeds   *Wade/ Smith*

757

Robert William MOORE   **26**   *Canadian*

Shot: ***Edward Watson**, 27, on 31 May 1953, in Fewston, N. Yorks.*
Motive: *Vengeance.*

Moore, *(b.1928)*, came to England at the age of five, and served in the army from 1944, marrying in 1950, and fathering a son a year later. He and Watson were both second-hand car dealers. Watson, from Leeds, had sold a defective car to Moore at a Harrogate auction, and Moore had determined on revenge. After buying a rifle he lured Watson back to the Harrogate area with the offer of a good bargain, and suggested a spot of pheasant or rabbit shooting.

Moore shot Watson five times to the upper torso on the Primrose Cottage Plantation, stole the £126 Watson had brought with him, and buried him in woods. A witness testified that Moore had recently bought a rifle and had been seen loading a spade into the boot of his car. He later confessed after trying to gas himself. The jury took 100 minutes to decide his fate.

Read: Murderous Leeds

8 January 1954   Strangeways prison, Manchester

758

Czeslaw KOWALEWSKI   33   *Polish*

Stabbed:	***Doris Douglas***, *29, on 6 October 1953, in Leeds, W.Yorks.*
Motive:	*Sexual rivalry.*

Kowalewski, *(b.1921)*, was from a well-off Polish family who lost everything in the Nazi occupation. After his release from a PoW camp, he settled in Scotland as a miner in 1947, coming to Leeds two years later. He met Doris Douglas, usually known as Doris Allen, in a Leeds pub in April 1953, and, keen to settle down and start a family, soon proposed to her.

He did not know that she was well-known to police through drink and prostitution. She agreed only to live with him, and told him that at weekends she had to stay with her mother. In fact, from Friday night to Monday morning, she earned 10/- looking after the needs of a 60-year old man elsewhere in the city. Kowalewski was tipped off by a friend, but Doris said the old man was a friend of her mother whom she merely helped.

One Monday, however, tired of his jealousy, Doris did not return to Czeslaw, but the two soon ran into each other in a pub. They drank together and walked till 11.45pm, during which time Kowalewski, 5'8", fought with a Ukrainian acquaintance who insulted Doris. The man was hospitalised for several days. The Pole followed Doris to the old man's flat, but was thrown out by him.

He returned at 12.50am and kicked the door down, stabbing Doris through the head, and in the abdomen as she lay on the ground. He was arrested five days later. The jury reached its guilty verdict in 15 minutes. Awaiting execution, in an attempt to bleed to death, Kowalewski ripped the skin from his penis.

Read: True Detective Winter Special 88/9

759

Desmond Donald HOOPER   27

i

Drowned:	***Betty Selina Smith***, *12, on 21 July 1953, in Shrewsbury, Shropshire*
Motive:	*Sexual*

      Hooper, *(b.1927),* a gardener, lived with his wife and two young children in temporary housing at Atcham camp, Shrewsbury. Betty Smith sometimes used to mind Hooper's children, living nearby with her widowed mother Dorothy and four siblings. At 8.30pm, Betty went to the Hoopers' but failed to return home. Dorothy went there before midnight, but Mary Hooper had not seen Betty, and Desmond was not back. He returned at 1.40am, claiming he had been to feed a neighbour's pigeons, and that Betty had left for home at 10.30.

      Her body was found submerged in water in a disused air-shaft of an underground canal. She had been partially strangled with a tie in an oat field, then dropped unconscious, head first into the shaft where she drowned. She had fractured ribs and skull. A jacket in the shaft belonged to Hooper.

      It emerged that Betty had been giving sexual favours to some men, and Hooper suggested that a local storeman, who admitted having borrowed the jacket, had wanted to get even with Dorothy Smith for hitting one of his children, and that he had sexually propositioned her.

      A petition, and messages of sympathy from Mrs Smith for Hooper, failed to gain a reprieve.

      Read: True Detective, Apr 95

760

Wilhelm LUBINA   42   *Polish*

Stabbed:	***Charlotte Ball***, *39, on 25 June 1953, in Barnsley, W.Yorks.*
Motive:	*Sexual rivalry.*

      Lubina, *(b.1912),* a miner, had known Charlotte Ball since 1948, but had lodged with her and her disabled husband for less than a year.

He fell for his landlady, but this led to arguments, and at the beginning of June, Charlotte had slapped Lubina's face. The two were alone when another row developed, and the Pole stabbed Charlotte six times in the chest. He then ran to his bedroom, smashing his head into a mirror, cutting his face, and stabbed himself three times in his chest.

Read: And May The Lord Have Mercy On Your Soul

14 April 1954　　　Wandsworth prison, London　　*A.Pierrepoint/ Harry Allen*

761

James Reginald DOOHAN　　　　**24**

Shot:　**Herbert Victor Ketley**, *40, on 9 February 1954, on the Isle of Sheppey, Kent*
Motive:　*Vengeance.*

Doohan, *(b.1930),* a labourer from Queensborough on Sheppey, had been courting Yvonne Deighton, 18, for three years. He was infatuated with her and expected to be able to arrange a wedding date soon. But on 8 February she told him that she could not marry him as his feelings were not reciprocated. Doohan blamed Yvonne's step-father, motor mechanic Herbert Ketley, for the split.

Borrowing a shotgun from a friend, Doohan told Ketley that someone had been hurt on nearby Rushenden marshes, and the two went there together, Doohan concealing the gun under his coat. Once on the marshes, with Ketley walking before him, Doohan shot him at close range in the back of the neck.

He then went directly to a police station to hand himself in. His plea of insanity was rejected by the jury in 65 minutes.

Read: True Crime Summer Special 91

762

Albert George HALL   48

Bludgeoned: ***Mary Hackett**, 6, on 12 August 1953, in Halifax, W.Yorkshire.*
Motive: *Sadistic pleasure.*

Mary Hackett had gone out to play on 12 August and failed to return home. She had been taken across the road to the Congregational Church, where George Hall, *(b.1906),* was the caretaker. He had some time previously been a patient in a psychiatric hospital, and he killed Mary either by hitting her across the back of the head with a blunt instrument or by banging her head against a wall. She had not been sexually assaulted.

He buried her body beneath the labyrinthine crypt. Police had searched the hall, but had another look when the pile of chairs and pews in one corner, and the opened tins of paint, placed there by Hall to mask any smells of decomposition, aroused their suspicions. Mary's body was uncovered on 12 September. Hall had mentioned the cause of death before it was publicly known, and was subsequently charged.

Read: Murder Squad, p212

23 April 1954   Saughton prison, Edinburgh

763

John LYNCH   45   *Irish*

Strangled: **1 *Margaret Johnson**, 3, and*
               2   *Lesley Sinclair, 4, on 11 December 1953, in Edinburgh, Midlothian.*
Motive: *unknown.*

Lynch, *(b.1909),* a labourer, murdered the two young girls in a lavatory in Marshall's Court, Greenside. No further details.

Read: Encyclopaedia of Scottish Executions.

764

Thomas Ronald Lewis HARRIES   **24**   *Welsh*

Bludgeoned:	**1** *John Harries*, *63, and his wife*
	2 *Phoebe Mary Harries*, *54, on 16 October 1953,*
	near St Clears, Carmarthenshire.
Motive:	*Financial.*

       John and Phoebe Harries were farmers at Llanginning. Their adoptive nephew Ronald, *(b.1930)*, was married with a baby daughter, and worked for his father, a butcher, in nearby Pendine. He murdered them with a hammer when they returned from the Harvest Festival service on 16 October, burying their bodies in a field adjoining the farm.

       He told neighbours that the couple had gone away to London, but police became suspicious as the cows had not been milked and a joint was left in the oven. The couple had not returned after three weeks and when Ronald tried to cash a cheque for £909 from his uncle, he became chief suspect. The cheque, originally for £9, had been altered.

       Expecting the murderer to check the burial site, officers placed thread across all entry points to the farm. Sure enough, they found one piece broken, and uncovered the bodies nearby, on 16 November.

       The circumstantial evidence was enough for the jury to convict after 88 minutes.

       Read: True Crime, Aug 95

                                     A.Pierrepoint/ Rickard/ Grant/ Smith

765, 766

Kenneth GILBERT   **21**
Ian Arthur GRANT   **24**

Suffocated:	*George Frederick Smart*, *55, on 9 March 1954, in*
	London SW7
Motive:	*Financial.*

       Gilbert, *(b.1933)*, and Grant, *(b.1930)*, both from Fulham, were porters at Olympia, but Gilbert had previously worked at the Aban Court Hotel in South Kensington. The two broke into the Aban Court through a cellar at

2.30am, and soon confronted the night porter, George Smart, who had worked there for 16 years. Grant punched him in the stomach, and Gilbert broke his jaw. They tied his hands behind his back, stuffed a bandage and a serviette in his mouth, and tied his ankles.

They then ransacked the reception and bar, making off with £2 cash, and cigarettes worth £7. Mr Smart tried ringing the alarm with his head, and had managed to free his hands, but had suffocated on his gag, his nostrils filled with blood. He was discovered at 7.45am.

Gilbert told a workmate about the job, and gave him a ticket to collect the cigarettes at Victoria station. Instead he went to the police. The two men denied intending to kill the porter, but the jury found them guilty in 20 minutes. Theirs was the last double execution in Britain.

Read: True Detective, Mar 95.

| 22 June 1954 | Walton gaol, Liverpool |

767

Milton TAYLOR   23

Strangled: ***Marie Bradshaw***, 25, in 1954, in Nantwich, Cheshire.
Motive: Vengeance.

Taylor, *(b.1931)*, described by a doctor as a 'moron', had been to borstal, but had managed to keep out of trouble since. He began an affair with a married woman, Marie Bradshaw, who lived in his street, and the two eventually ran away to Crewe together.

In Nantwich, low on funds, they spent the night in a disused hut, but when Marie continued to talk, Taylor was unable to get to sleep, so he strangled her with his tie. He later declared that 'Everyone should strangle somebody'.

Read: And May The Lord Have Mercy On Your Soul

768

George Alexander ROBERTSON   40

Stabbed: *1 Elizabeth McGarry, 39, his ex-wife, and*
          2 George Robertson, 18, his son, on 28 February 1954,
          in Glasgow, Lanarks.
Motive: *Vengeance.*

Robertson, *(b.1914)*, had divorced in 1950, and Elizabeth had continued to live with her two children, George, 18, and Jean, 16, in Tron Square, Glasgow. She had a short-lived second marriage, before her first husband returned in January 1954. Arguments soon followed, caused, it seems, by George objecting to his former wife staying out late. He disappeared for a few days around 24 February, but returned one night at 2.30 am.
          Dragging Elizabeth from her bed, he forced her to strip and kneel in the kitchen. Disturbed by the commotion, George Jr emerged to find his mother, in her bra only, at his father's feet. George then stabbed his son in the head, and as the teenager fled, his father stabbed his daughter as he pushed her back on her bed. He then took his wife outside, stabbed her in the stomach, and carried her back inside, dumping her by the cooker. George then pursued his son to a neighbour's house, where he stabbed him again, carrying the body back home to an armchair.
          When the police arrived, George had his head in the gas oven. Two knives were found, one a 12-inch stiletto. The jury took one hour to find him guilty of murder, and of assaulting his daughter, with danger to life. His was the last execution in the Scottish capital.

          Read: True Crime, Mar 99

769

William Sanchez de Pina HEPPER   62   *Spanish*

Strangled: *Margaret Rose Louise Spevick, 11, on 4 February*
          1954, in Hove, Sussex.
Motive: *Sexual.*

Hepper, *(b.1891),* had once been a spy for Britain in Portugal. Born in Spain of a Gibraltarian father and Spanish mother, he married in 1919 and returned to England in 1939 after 11 years away. He worked as a wool merchant in London and then as a translator for the BBC, but had resigned after suffering head injuries in a car crash in 1946. An asthmatic, he had then taken to working as an artist. He rarely saw his five children or his wife, with whose infidelity he was obsessed.

Margaret, known as Margot, a friend of Hepper's daughter, had come to stay with him in Hove for a few days after breaking her arm. Whilst painting the child's portrait in his studio, Hepper raped and strangled her with her sling. Margaret's mother found her daughter's naked body when she came to collect her on 7 February.

Hepper had fled to Spain, where he was arrested a few days later after a tip-off from his uncle. His defence centred on his impotence and claims of amnesia and hallucinations, in which he thought he was attacking his wife. His one previous conviction had been for larceny in 1916. The jury deliberated for 85 minutes.

Read: The Art of Murder,p27

| 12 August 1954 | Lincoln prison | *A.Pierrepoint/ Allen* |

770

Harold FOWLER   21

Stabbed: ***Kenneth Joseph George Mulligan,*** *27, on 19 May 1954,*
                  in Nottingham.
Motive: *Sexual rivalry.*

Kenneth Mulligan, a miner, had married his wife Doreen, a shop assistant, in December 1947, and a daughter was born to them in 1949. But in December 1952 Doreen had by chance met Harry Fowler, *(b.1933),* an engineer's labourer, during a trip to the cinema, and the two became lovers. After a row with Ken, Doreen and her daughter moved out to lodgings in November 1953, continuing to see Fowler, who lived nearby. In March 1954 she gave birth to a son, believed to be her husband's, and Ken began writing asking Doreen to come home.

At 9.30pm on 19 May, Ken called round to Doreen's lodgings to ask her once more to return. But he found Doreen and Fowler on the bed together, and he punched his rival and pulled Doreen from the bed. Fowler lunged at Mulligan with a sheath knife, hitting him with such force that it penetrated his stomach by 17cm. He died the following morning in hospital.

Fowler tried to obtain a manslaughter conviction based on provocation, a course rejected by the jury in 70 minutes.

Read: Master Detective, Jun 97.

| 1 September 1954 | Armley gaol, Leeds | *Wade/ Smith* |

771

Edward Lindsay REID   24

Dropped: ***Arthur White***, *40, on 3 April 1954, in Bradford, W.Yorks.*
Motive: *Vengeance; drink related.*

Reid, *(b.1930)*, shared an attic room in a Bradford boarding house with Arthur White from March 1953. The two were generally on good terms, but on 3 April, they argued over dinner. That evening they both got drunk at separate pubs, returning to the house after 10.30pm.

It seems that Reid attacked White in the bedroom and then tipped him from the window, White landing 10m below in the yard. He was found there at 10.45pm, and blood had been wiped up in the attic room. Reid denied any argument had taken place and suggested White had fallen from the window before he got back, but Reid had a bruised hand. White sustained a fractured skull, jaw and cheekbone, two broken legs and a broken back, doctors claiming that some of the injuries must have been inflicted before the fall. The jury found Reid guilty after 75 minutes.

Read: Murderous Leeds

| 1 September 1954 | Wandsworth prison, London | *A.Pierrepoint/ Stewart* |

772

Rupert Geoffrey WELLS   53

Strangled: ***Nellie Officer***, *46, on 9 May 1954, in Kingston-upon-Thames, Surrey.*
Motive: *Vengeance; drink related.*

Wells, *(b.1901),* met Nellie Officer in 1952, and moved in with her at Christmas 1953, but Wells had a drink problem which caused Nellie, a barmaid, to become somewhat frightened of him. She asked a customer to walk her home one night, and to check the house when they arrived. Nellie was so nervous that the man stayed the night, sleeping on the sofa. No sooner had Nellie's protector left, than Wells arrived at 9.15am.

He strangled Nellie, and left her sitting in the armchair, while he went and got drunk in the pub, eventually confessing his crime to the landlord. Wells was on sedatives, and his defence relied upon showing that the mix of drugs and drink left him incapable of intent. After 51 minutes, the jury dismissed the claims.

Read: *And May The Lord Have Mercy On Your Soul*

15 December 1954	Holloway prison, London	*A.Pierrepoint*

773

Stylou Pantopiou CHRISTOPHI   53   *female*   *Cypriot*

Strangled/ bludgeoned: **Hella Christophi**, *36, on 29 July 1954, in London NW3.*
Motive: *To clear impediment.*

Stavros Christophi, a waiter in a West End restaurant, and his German wife Hella, who worked in a boutique, married in 1939 and had three children. In 1953 his illiterate mother, Stylou, *(b.1901),* came from Cyprus to live with them at their house in South Hill Park, Hampstead. The two women did not get on, and Stavros had decided to send his mother back to Cyprus.

At about 11 p.m. on 29 July, Stylou battered Hella over the head with an ashplate, fracturing her skull, and strangled her with a rope. Using paraffin and paper, she attempted to burn the body in the back garden. She had then run outside telling a couple in a car that there had been a fire.

Hella's body, dressed in briefs only, was found outside the french windows. Her wedding ring was found in Stylou's room. A witness testified that he had seen Stylou stirring a fire in the garden.

Stylou had been tried in Cyprus in 1925 for the murder of her own mother-in-law with a burning torch down her throat. On that occasion she was acquitted. On this occasion, having been found sane by three doctors, she was hanged.

Read: *Lady Killers*

1954 Execution in Ireland

Michael MANNING 24

Suffocated: ***Catherine Elizabeth Cooper****, 65, on 18 November 1953, in Limerick.*
Motive: *Sexual; drink related.*

  Manning, *(b.1930)*, was a carter from Limerick, a married man. At 9.25pm, after visiting a friend, Catherine Cooper, an unmarried hospital sister, left for home. She was noticed by Manning, also walking home after an evening getting very drunk in several pubs. He dragged her to the roadside, punching her in the face, breaking her nose and several ribs. Her dentures were smashed and Manning stuffed grass down her throat to stifle her screams. She choked on it. He was disturbed by a passing vehicle, having failed to rape her.

  His hat and her beret led the police to Manning, who confessed his crime, blaming the drink. The jury took 3 hours to convict him. His was the last execution in the Irish republic.

Read: True Detective, Apr 95.

1955

total: *12*

774	29 Mar	William SALT	43		Walton
775	14 Apr	Sydney CLARKE	33		Wandsworth
776	4 May	Winston SHAW	39		Armley
777	24 May	James ROBINSON	27		Lincoln
778	21 Jun	Richard GOWLER	43		Walton
779	12 Jul	Kenneth ROBERTS	24		Lincoln
780	13 Jul	Ruth ELLIS (f)	28	*Welsh*	Holloway
781	26 Jul	Frederick CROSS	34		Winson Green
782	27 Jul	Norman GREEN	23	*Scottish*	Walton
783	2 Aug	Corbett ROBERTS	46	*Jamaican*	Winson Green
784	9 Aug	Ernest HARDING	42		Winson Green
785	12 Aug	Alec WILKINSON	22		Armley

29 March 1955   Walton gaol, Liverpool

774

William Arthur SALT   43

Drowned: ***Dennis John Shenton**, 6, on 16 December 1954, in Trentham, Staffs.*
Motive: *Vengeance.*

Salt, *(b.1912)*, had been involved in two road accidents, and a mining mishap, which left him a somewhat neurotic individual. He lodged with Annie Shenton and her six-year old son, and the two had set 18 December 1955 as their wedding day. Salt omitted to mention to Annie that he was already married. He collected young Dennis from school at 10am, telling teachers that the boy was going to see his grandmother.

Instead the two took a walk, hand in hand by the canal. Salt later explained that the boy was getting on his nerves, so he swung him round by the hand, and dumped him in the water. Getting home at 6pm, Salt told Annie that Dennis had gone to his sister's, but Annie insisted that they go to collect him. Salt ran away from her on the way to the station, and stayed the night with friends.

Annie called the police, and Salt was arrested the next day in the pub, where he admitted what he had done, and led police to find Dennis' body floating in the canal.

Read: And May The Lord Have Mercy On Your Soul

775

Sydney CLARKE   33

Strangled:	***Rose Elizabeth Fairhurst***, *45, on 9 February 1955, in London SE1.*
Motive:	*Sadistic pleasure; drink related.*

Clarke, *(b.1922)*, approached Rose Fairhurst as she sat drinking in the pub with a woman friend, and offered her ten shillings to satisfy his immediate sexual desire. They left the bar together at 9.30pm, and went to an old bomb site, where Clarke found a dumped mattress. It seems that Rose was not keen to perform on so dirty a berth, and Clarke turned nasty, beating her and tearing off her clothes in a frenzy.

He strangled her, and satisfied himself, for semen was found on Rose's thigh. By 10.30pm, he was in another pub, propositioning another woman. He arrived back at the hostel where he lodged at midnight, and was arrested there the next day, claiming in the face of numerous witness statements, that he was in Bristol at the time.

Read: And May The Lord Have Mercy On Your Soul

776

Winston SHAW   39

Stabbed:	***Jean Cave Tate***, *24, on 3 December 1954, in Knaresborough, W.Yorks.*
Motive:	*Vengeance.*

Shaw, *(b.1916)*, and his wife Florence had separated within two months of their marriage in 1937. By the time she resurfaced, in 1953, Shaw had been living with Jean Tate for two years, and they had two children. Nevertheless, Florence moved in with them, and it took until October 1954 for Jean to get fed up with the arrangement. Shaw took new lodgings for Jean and himself, but left the children with Florence.

When someone from the NSPCC called to see Jean in November she told them she was locked in her flat and could not see her children. Shaw had kicked her and the leg wound had needed seventeen stitches. As a result, she and the children were moved to a secret address.

It took Shaw until 3 December to find her, and he bought a knife and an axe in preparation for his visit. At 9.15pm he called round, stabbing Jean twenty times, and then axing her head a further five times. He was arrested at 11.30 that night in his lodgings, where the knife was found. He claimed that another man was in the flat when he got there.

Read: Murderous Leeds.

24 May 1955   Lincoln prison   *A.Pierrepoint/ Harry Allen*

777

James ROBINSON   27

Strangled: ***Mary Ann Dodsley**, 83, on 15 December 1954, in Skegby, Notts.*
Motive: *Sexual; drink related.*

Robinson, *(b.1928),* a turkey farm labourer, broke into the house of Mary Dodsley, 5'2", late at night by breaking a window. He had attempted to rape her, and then strangled the old woman, leaving her under a pile of bedclothes. Police found a palm-print on the smashed pane, and after 68 local residents were tested to find a match, Robinson was arrested. A heavy drinker who lived with his mother, Robinson could prove that he was in the pub until 10pm, and though one expert put the time of death between 10pm and 1am, another stated that between 9pm and 10pm was more likely.

Although Robinson maintained his innocence to the end, the jury found the palm-print damning, despite the doubt over the times, after a deliberation of 6 hours 35 minutes.

Read: Master Detective, Mar 99

21 June 1955   Walton gaol, Liverpool   *A.Pierrepoint/ Stewart*

778

Richard GOWLER   43

Stabbed: ***Mary Catherine Boothroyd**, 53, on 15 March 1955, in Seacombe, Lancs.*

Motive: *Vengeance*

Gowler, *(b.1912),* was a ship's rigger, from West Hartlepool. Separated from his wife, he went to lodge with Mrs Boothroyd, a widow, and her daughter Margaret, 20, in 1951. Then in 1954, Mrs Boothroyd's other daughter, Mavis Thompson, left her husband, and came to stay with her baby of 18 months. Before long, Gowler and Mavis had begun an affair. Mrs Boothroyd found out and Gowler was forced to leave. He called round many times, but Mavis was no longer interested, and police had to be called more than once. Mavis failed to keep three dates to see Gowler, and finally, he broke into the house in the early hours and went to Mavis' room.

When she screamed he stabbed her 13 times with a 50cm marlinspike, and when her mother came out, he stabbed her three times in the face, and five times in the chest. Margaret raised the alarm, and Gowler was arrested on New Brighton pier. Somehow, Mavis survived to testify against him. The jury retired for 45 minutes. Walton's governor described Gowler as the bravest condemned man he had seen.

Read: True Crime, Nov 95

12 July 1955   Lincoln prison   *Wade/ Stewart*

779

Kenneth ROBERTS   24

Strangled: ***Mary Georgina Roberts**, 18, on 10 May 1955,*
                   in Scunthorpe, Lincs.
Motive: *Sexual*

Roberts, *(b.1931),* a warehouseman, lived at his mother-in-law's with his pregnant wife and two children in Winterton, Lincs. The couple had finally been alloted a council house on 9 May 1955. The following evening Roberts was picked up outside a Scunthorpe club by a prostitute.

Mary Roberts, no relation to her client, had been a clerk, but was now an unemployed, unmarried mother of an 18-month old son. She was again pregnant. The two went to a woodyard and had sex, after which Roberts strangled Mary with her scarf. When he got home, Roberts confessed to his mother-in-law, and the police were called.

Read: True Crime Summer Special 95.

13 July 1955   Holloway prison, London   *A.Pierrepoint / Harry Allen*

780

<u>Ruth ELLIS</u>   28   *female*   *(nee Ruth Neilson)*   *Welsh*

Shot: ***David Moffet Drummond Blakely**, 25, on 10 April
                1955, in London NW3.*
Motive: *Sexual rivalry.*

Ruth Ellis was born in 1926 in Rhyl, to a Belgian mother and a cellist father, real name Hornby. They had moved to London in 1941, and Ruth had a son to a married Canadian GI in 1944. She had worked as a nude photographic model and then embarked on a career as a nightclub hostess, and prostitute, in Mayfair. She married an alcoholic dentist in 1950, and had a daughter by him, but the couple remained together only one year, Ruth then returning to her club work.

She was made manageress in 1953, and in the club shortly afterwards met David Blakely, *(b.1929)*, embarking on a tempestuous relationship, characterised by their mutual unfaithfulness and jealousy. Blakely, obsessed by his motor racing, had lived on an allowance from his mother and began to live off Ellis' money, beating her in moments of anger. They set up house together in Egerton Gardens in Kensington at the end of March 1955, but Blakely soon left Ellis, and she had the latest of five or six abortions in early April.

On Good Friday, Ellis called to see Blakely at a friend's house in Hampstead, but he refused to see her. The police were called when she became noisy. By Easter Sunday she was crazed with feelings of jealousy and injustice, and, given a revolver by Desmond Cussen, 33, another sometime lover, she was driven by him to the Magdala pub where Blakely was drinking with friends. She waited for him to come out and fired six shots at him. One hit a passer-by in the hand, and four hit Blakely, one in the leg, one in the arm and two in the back.

Ellis resisted all attempts to reprieve her, and thanked the judge for his death sentence, after the jury had retired for just 23 minutes. Taking catholic communion on the morning of her execution, she was the last woman to be hanged in Britain. Her son committed suicide in 1982. An argument was later put forward that manslaughter on the grounds of diminished responsibility would have been a safer verdict. The Court of Appeal agreed in 2002 to hear the case.

Read: Ruth Ellis

26 July 1955   Winson Green prison, Birmingham

A.Pierrepoint/ Harry Allen

781

Frederick Arthur CROSS   34

Stabbed: ***Donald Haywood Lainton**, 28, on 25 February 1955,
in Great Heywood, Staffs.*
Motive: *Sadistic pleasure.*

Cross, *(b. 1921)*, a Londoner, lived in a nissan hut in Great Heywood with his wife and children until she left him to go and live with her lover in north Wales. When she ignored his pleading letters, he became suicidal and turned to drink. He lost his job at a cement works and lacked the courage to make good his desire for death.

Drinking one lunchtime in a local pub, he got talking to a Stockport insurance agent, who had been stranded there by the worsening blizzard. Telling Donald Lainton he could direct him to a pub with food, he instead got the businessman to drive to a nearby lane where he stabbed him ten times in the head and chest with a pair of scissors. He was found there several hours later, and survived in hospital until the following morning. One wound had penetrated his brain through his eye socket.

Cross went and told his mother what he had done, and she telephoned the police. Cross said that he had murdered so that he would be hanged, but expressed sorrow that Mr Lainton had been a married man. He refused legal aid and pleaded guilty, the trial lasting only seven minutes. As his execution approached, Cross changed his mind and pleaded for a reprieve, having almost to be dragged to the scaffold.

Read: True Crime, Feb 96

27 July 1955   Walton gaol, Liverpool   *A.Pierrepoint*

782

Norman William GREEN   23   *Scottish*

Stabbed: ***1 William Richard Harmer**, 11, on 27 August 1954, and
2 Norman Yates, 10, on 11 April 1955, both in Wigan,
Lancs.*
Motive: *Sadistic pleasure*

Green, *(b.1932)*, was born in Aberdeen, and had lived in Wigan with his widowed mother and brother since 1940. He had worked at a corn miller's since 1951. On 27 August he attacked two young boys, stabbing one of them, Billy Mitchell, 7, with a penknife. Three hours later, he followed Billy Harmer, stabbing him ten times in the chest, and once, fatally, in the neck, leaving him for dead in an old depot.

Eight months later, on Easter Monday at 9.30pm, he took Norman Yates, who was out on an errand for his mother, to waste ground near to his home at Ince, in Wigan. He stabbed the boy three times in the chest and once, fatally, in the neck. Matching the description of the wanted man, Green was questioned at work, and suddenly confessed to Norman's murder, saying he was sorry for the boy's mother. He later admitted Billy's killing. Tried only for the latter crime, Green was described as an epileptic who murdered in an attempt to kill his own alter ego. There was no sexual motive. The jury considered his plea of insanity for 3 hours 30 minutes before delivering its verdict. Green's execution was the last by Albert Pierrepoint.

Read: True Detective, Jun 97

2 August 1955   Winson Green prison, Birmingham   *Wade/ Harry Allen*

783

Corbett Montague ROBERTS   **46**   *Jamaican*

Bludgeoned: ***Doris Acquilla Roberts**, 41, his wife, on 31 May 1955, in Birmingham, Warwicks.*
Motive: *Vengeance*

Roberts, *(b.1909)*, a father of two adult daughters, had married Doris in Portland, Jamaica, and had come to England, working as a building site labourer, in July 1953. His wife and daughter had joined him in Aston a few months later, and they had then been joined by his daughter's husband, and his wife's brother, with whom Doris and Corbett had to share a room. The Roberts' marriage had often been quarrelsome, mostly because of money, each accusing the other of stealing.

Doris and her daughter moved out in 1955, leaving Corbett sharing with ten or so other west Indians, and in May Corbett lost his job through poor timekeeping. His wife moved back in shortly after, but the arguments continued.

When, at 7.40am, Doris took the money Corbett had put out on the table ready to start his new job, he saw red. When she refused to give back the money, and put it down her blouse, he attacked her with a hammer. When its shaft broke he took another and continued to smash her head. He went round to see his daughter, but when she was out he confessed to her landlady, then going straight to the police at 8.30am to do the same. He made no appeal, and was hanged just 63 days after his crime. The jury took eight minutes to find him guilty, and Roberts was the last man hanged for murdering his wife.

Read: Master Detective, May 99

9 August 1955   Winson Green prison, Birmingham   *Wade/ Stewart*

784

Ernest Charles HARDING   42

Strangled: ***Evelyn Patricia Higgins***, 10, on 8 June 1955, near
              Fillongley, Warwicks.
Motive: Sexual.

Harding, *(b.1913)*, was a bricklayer who lived in Coventry with his wife of 22 years and their two children. A friendly man and caring husband, he was punched in 1952 and hit his head on a pavement, fracturing his skull. Since then he had been moody and bad-tempered. Possibly epileptic, he had dizzy spells and 'indecent impulses'. He received several convictions, none involving violence or children.

One wet day he claimed to a workmate that his car was playing up, and in view of the weather would not go to work. After visiting a pub and a cinema he drove round inviting young girls to ride in his car. Two girls refused, but at 5pm they noticed Patsy Higgins get in the car. She had been to the hairdressers on her way home from school. Harding, a well-built man, drove Patsy, a slim girl of 4' 10", seven miles outside Coventry, raped her, strangled her and cut her neck with a knife. The passenger door had no handle.

A young boy collecting car numbers alerted the police to Harding. Invited to the police station the next day, Harding instead was found trying to kill himself in his car with a hose from the exhaust. Under questioning, Harding admitted the crime, though he claimed not to remember cutting Patsy. Dismissing suggestions of insanity, the jury found him guilty.

Read: True Detective, Feb 97.

785

Alec WILKINSON   22

Bludgeoned/ stabbed: ***Clara Farrell**, 50, on 1 May 1955, in Wombwell, W.Yorks.*
Motive: *Vengeance; drink related.*

Alec Wilkinson, *(b.1933)*, a miner, described as intelligent, honest, friendly and hard-working, married Maureen Farrell in August 1954, and the young couple went to live with his parents. Maureen, however, became unhappy with the domestic arrangements, and returned to the home of her own mother and father.

Her mother, Clara, had worked locally as a prostitute, and was known as the 'Green Linnet'. Alec made repeated attempts to get his wife to return to him, but was rebuked by her mother, who suggested that Alec could not properly support her, and that Maureen may have to turn to prostitution to make ends meet. Alec's resentment of his mother-in-law grew, and after spending much of 30 April drinking, determined to kill her. After midnight he entered through Clara's unlocked door. When she swore at him, he punched her and repeatedly banged her head on the floor, then stabbed her.

When Maureen arrived home and intervened she was knocked out by a punch. Wilkinson piled up furniture in the hallway and set fire to it, dragging Clara's legs into the flames. Escaping through the back, Alec ran down the street elated, while neighbours attended the scene. Wilkinson confessed to a nightwatchman who called the police.

Wilkinson told the court that he was not sorry for what he had done. Glowing references and a 35,000-strong petition could not save him. His was to be the last execution for 23 months.

Read: Master Detective, Aug 91.

1956

total: *0*

1957

total: **2**

| 786 | 23 Jul | John VICKERS | 22 | Durham |
| 787 | 4 Dec | Dennis HOWARD | 24 | Winson Green |

23 July 1957　　　　　Durham gaol　　　　　*Allen/ Smith*

786

John Willson VICKERS　　　　**22**

Punched/ kicked to death:　*Jane Duckett, 72, on 14 April 1957, in Carlisle, Cumberland.*
Motive:　　　　　　　　　*Financial.*

Vickers, *(b.1935)*, a labourer from Penrith, received the first of his many convictions for theft at the age of 11. He had discussed with his roommate the possibility of robbing the local sweetshop, and had made two unsuccessful attempts to break in during April 1957.

Jane Duckett had come with her sister from Appleby to run the shop in 1917, and was alone since her sister's death in 1953, and the recent disappearance of her dog. She had £882 hidden in her wardrobe. At 1am on 14 April, Vickers was dropped off near the shop, having received a lift from a dance in Penrith. He broke into the shop through a cellar window and tried to hide when he heard Miss Duckett coming downstairs. However, she found him and he proceeded to punch her and kick her as she fell to the ground.

He ransacked the upstairs rooms, but failed to find the money. Held on suspicion of another theft, police were alerted by scratches on his face. Vickers later confessed to the crime and to the previous break-in attempts. His shoe prints were found in the cellar and fibres from his socks were found in the old woman's hand. He denied any intention to seriously harm Miss Duckett.

Under the new Homicide Act 1957, which limited capital murder, Vickers had to be shown to have intended grievous harm in the furtherance of theft. Though he had no previous convictions for violence, he was convicted and his appeal dismissed. His was the first execution for 23 months. A 1981 review concluded that his conviction was sound.

Read: True Detective, Jan 97.

4 December 1957   Winson Green prison, Birmingham
Harry Allen/ Rickard

787

Dennis HOWARD   24

Shot: ***David Alan Keasey****, 21, on 17 May 1957, in Dudley,*
                 Worcs.
Motive: *Financial.*

Howard, *(b. 1933),* owned two revolvers and a pistol, all unlicenced. Armed with the pistol he decided on a gentlemen's outfitters as a likely target for a hold-up. David Keasey was engaged to be married and already owned his own business.

As he was about to close up for the day at 5.30pm, Howard, 5'10", entered the shop and demanded the money from the till. Mr Keasey struggled with the attacker who shot him once in the back. Howard fled empty handed, seen by a teenager outside the store. Four days later, Howard stopped a man in the street at gunpoint and demanded that he empty his pockets. Howard had boasted of the murder to a friend who informed the police. The murder weapon, along with the revolvers, were found at his home in Smethwick.

Read: Murderous Birmingham

1958

total: **5**

788	5 May	Vivian TEED	24	*Welsh*	Swansea
789	11 Jul	Peter MANUEL	31	*Scottish*	Barlinnie
790	12 Aug	Matthew KAVANAGH	32		Winson Green
791	3 Sep	Frank STOKES	44		Durham
792	17 Dec	Brian CHANDLER	20		Durham

5 May 1958   Swansea prison   *Stewart/ Robson*

788

Vivian Frederick TEED   **24**   *Welsh*

Bludgeoned: **William Williams**, *73, on 15 November 1957, at Fforestfach, Glamorgan*
Motive: *Financial.*

Teed, *(b.1934),* a labourer, had a criminal record dating back to the age of 13, for offences of vandalism and theft, and he had served separate terms of three and two years in gaol for assault. During service with the RAF, he had gone AWOL several times, and was described as a compulsive liar. He had been one of several buiders employed to renovate Mr Williams' post office five miles from Swansea, where Teed lived with his pregnant girlfriend. He had since been unemployed.

At 8pm he knocked at Mr Williams' door and barged his way in when the old man answered. He felled the postmaster with a hammer and rained down 27 blows as he lay on the floor. Having failed to find the keys to the safe, he fled. Mr Williams was found the following morning. Teed boasted of his crime to a friend who alerted the police.

The jury took 4 hours and 45 minutes before agreeing a verdict and Teed's was the last execution in Wales.

Read: Master Detective Summer Special 95.

789

Peter Thomas Anthony MANUEL   31   *Scottish*

Strangled:	**1 Helen Carlin**, *in September 1954, in Pimlico, London SW1.*
Motive:	*Sexual.*
Bludgeoned:	**2 Anne Kneilands**, *17, on 4 January 1956, in East Kilbride, near Glasgow, Lanarks.*
Motive:	*Sexual.*
Bludgeoned:	**3 Anne Steele**, *55, on 11 January 1956, in Glasgow.*
Motive:	*Financial.*
Stabbed:	**4 Ellen Petrie**, *in June 1956, in Glasgow.*
Motive:	*Financial.*
Shot:	**5 Marion Watt**, *45, and also her sister,* **6 Margaret Brown** *and her daughter,* **7 Vivienne Watt**, *16, on 17 September 1956, in East Kilbride.*
Motive:	*Financial.*
Shot:	**8 Sydney Dunn**, *36, on 8 December 1957, in Edmondbyers, Co Durham.*
Motive:	*Financial.*
Strangled:	**9 Isabelle Cooke**, *17, on 27 December 1957, in Mt Vernon, Glasgow.*
Motive:	*Sexual.*
Shot:	**10 Peter Smart**, *45, along with his wife,* **11 Doris Smart**, *and their son,* **12 Michael Smart**, *11, on 1 January 1958, in Uddingston, near Glasgow.*
Motive:	*Financial.*

      Manuel was born in New York in 1927, his family returning to Britain in 1932. From the age of twelve he was in trouble with the law. He had numerous convictions for burglary, robbery, rape and indecency. He was in prison from 1946 to 1953 for housebreaking and rape. In September of 1954 he committed his first murder, that of the Pimlico prostitute Helen Carlin.

      He killed six times in 1956, Anne Steele, a spinster, was battered to death, and Ellen Petrie was stabbed, in the course of robberies at their homes. Anne Kneilands, 17, was found on a golf course with her head split open. Though she had not been raped, Manuel had indulged his underwear fetish and items of her clothing were missing. Then in September he burgled the Watt house in East Kilbride. Mrs Marion Watt, her sister and daughter were all found shot dead. Her husband was held for two months on suspicion of the murders.

Manuel served another prison term for a year from October 1956. He had not been free for long before he struck again, on 8 December 1957, shooting Sydney Dunn, a taxi driver, through the head in County Durham. He then cut his victim's throat. Back in Glasgow, three weeks later, he sexually assaulted and murdered Isabelle Cooke, 17, burying her near naked in a shallow grave.

Just three days later, on New Year's Day, he shot dead all three members of the Smart household in Uddingston whilst committing burglary.

Following this latest crime, Manuel and his father were arrested on 13 January. Housebreaking tools were found at their home. In custody Manuel admitted to the Smart killings, and confessed to those of Kneilands, Cooke and the Watts. He was charged with those eight murders, but was acquitted in the case of Anne Kneilands through lack of corroborative evidence.

Having dismissed his defence lawyers, he was convicted of seven murders, and admitted to those of the other three women in the condemned cell. An inquest later found him guilty of Mr Dunn's murder.

Manuel was one of Britain's most notorious serial killers.

Read: The Hunting Down of Peter Manuel

12 August 1958   Winson Green prison, Birmingham   *Harry Allen/ Cunliffe*

790

Matthew KAVANAGH   32

Strangled: *Isaiah Dixon, 60, in April 1958, in Rugby, Warwicks.*
Motive: *Financial; drink related.*

Kavanagh, *(b.1926),* had stood trial in 1957 for the murder of Mrs Evelyn Ulla, 35, in Birmingham. She had died from pressure on the vagal nerve in the neck. Kavanagh claimed that she had dropped dead while adjusting her scarf. The case against him was dismissed.

A year later, in Rugby, unemployed and broke, he was turned out of the hostel where he had been staying. Drunk, he returned to the hostel, where he helped the drunken old lodger Dixon to his room, then strangled him with his own tie and robbed him.

He took the £5 he had obtained and told a cafe owner what he had done.

Read: The Hangman's Diary, p275.

3 September 1958   Durham gaol   *Harry Allen*

791

Frank STOKES   44

Bludgeoned: ***Mrs Linda Violet Ash***, *75, on 14 April 1958, in Gosforth, Northumberland.*
Motive: *Financial.*

Stokes, *(b.1914),* a bald and stocky man of 5'10", had a record dating back to 1923, for larceny, house-breaking and demanding money with menaces. A former hotel porter in Leeds, he answered an advertisement in a newsagent's window for a gardener at the boarding house run by the elderly widow, Mrs Ash. She offered him 3/6 an hour, and an argument developed when Stokes demanded 3/10.
Ordered out, he took a hammer and beat the woman four times about the head in her kitchen. He searched her bedroom, and made off with her purse, containing probably £2. She died the next day. The newsagent where he answered the ad gave a description, and 11 days later, Stokes gave himself up in a London police station at 1am. The jury took 15 minutes to convict him of capital murder.

Read: True Crime, Mar 97.

17 December 1958   Durham gaol   *Stewart/ Cunliffe*

792

Brian CHANDLER   20

Bludgeoned: ***Martha Annie Dodd***, *83, on 11 June 1958, in Darlington, Co Durham.*
Motive: *Financial.*

Chandler, *(b.1938)*, from Middlesbrough, had received probation for theft in 1957, and had then joined the Royal Army Medical Corps. The private had gone AWOL from Catterick on 8 June and headed for Darlington. There he met two 18-year old girls with whom he planned to go to London. Needing money for the venture, one of the girls told of an old woman who kept money in her flat. They decided they would have to kill her to prevent identification.

Martha Dodd had lived alone since her husband's death in 1949, though her son visited regularly. Once a professional singer, she and her husband had run a domestic service agency. Chandler's girlfriend 'cased the joint' on 10 June, asking Mrs Dodd for work, and after staying the night together in a hotel, Chandler went to the widow's home the next day at 3pm with the same ruse.

He battered the old woman 19 times with a hammer, 12 blows falling to the head. She was discovered in her kitchen by a neighbour at 10pm. Chandler had managed to steal only £4. He told his girlfriend what he had done, and the two stayed the night together at a friend's. Told that they were wanted for questioning, the pair went to a police station.

Chandler said that the girl and he had gone together, and that it was she who had killed Mrs Dodd. The jury's verdict went against him after 75 minutes.

Read: Master Detective, May 97.

1959

total: **6**

793	10 Feb	Ernest JONES	39		Armley
794	28 Apr	Joseph CHRIMES	30		Pentonville
795	8 May	Ronald MARWOOD	25		Pentonville
796	14 May	Michael TATUM	24		Winchester
797	14 Aug	Bernard WALDEN	33		Armley
798	5 Nov	Guenther PODOLA	30	*German*	Wandsworth

10 February 1959   Armley gaol, Leeds   *Harry Allen/ Smith*

793

Ernest Raymond JONES   39

Bludgeoned: ***Raymond Turner****, on 30 September 1958, in Lepton, W.Yorks.*
Motive: *Financial.*

Jones, *(b.1920),* had broken into the Co-op store near Huddersfield in 1957, and decided to make a return visit a year later. On 29 September, he told a friend that he would soon have 30,000 cigarettes to sell, and the following night at 9pm, he entered the shop, and had secured the cigarettes and some clothing, when he was surprised by Richard Turner, the manager, who was just locking the safe. He hit the manager, fracturing his skull, and told a friend what he had done. He had managed to get away with a total of £75 from the safe.

Read: And May The Lord Have Mercy On Your Soul.

28 April 1959   Pentonville prison, London   *Harry Allen/ Rickard*

794

Joseph CHRIMES   30

Bludgeoned: ***Nora Summerfield****, 60, on 31 December 1958, in Hillingdon, Middlesex.*

Motive:	Financial.

Chrimes, *(b. 1929),* and Ronald Pritchard, 18, broke into Mrs Summerfield's bungalow on new year's eve, battering the widow with a tyre lever, before stealing a clock, a cigarette case, and some smaller items including spoons.

Chrimes told a friend what he had done, even before Nora's body was found on 2 January. Both men were arrested on 6 January, and both blamed each other for the killing. At the trial the prosecution offered no evidence against Pritchard, and he testified against Chrimes. After more than an hour in retirement, the jury found Chrimes guilty of capital murder, and Pritchard was sent to borstal for his part in the robbery.

Read: And May The Lord Have Mercy On Your Soul.

8 May 1959   Pentonville prison, London   *Harry Allen/ Robinson*

795

Ronald Henry MARWOOD   25

Stabbed:	**P.C. Raymond Henry Summers,** *23, on 14 December 1958, in London N7.*
Motive:	*To escape arrest; drink related.*

About twenty youths were involved in a gang fight outside a dance hall on Seven Sisters Road on the night of 14 December. Axes, knives and bottles were being used when Marwood, *(b.1934),* and his friends arrived.

Marwood, a scaffolder, had already drunk ten pints of brown ale. He had recently celebrated his first wedding anniversary and had no criminal record. P.C. Summers, on duty, was attempting an arrest, when Marwood stabbed him in the back with a ten-inch knife. The youths scattered and Marwood went into hiding until 27 January, when he confessed to the crime, though denying the intention to kill.

Later retracting the confession, he denied having a knife. The jury considered its verdict for three hours. On the day of his execution, about 1000 youths outside Pentonville had to be restrained by mounted police.

Read: True Crime Summer Special 91

796

Michael George TATUM   24

Bludgeoned: **Charles Frederick Barrett**, *85, on 16 January 1959, in Southampton, Hants.*
Motive: *Financial.*

Tatum, *(b.1935),* an unemployed projectionist, and his wife Mary had married in 1957. They moved from London in 1958, and in December Mary got the job as housekeeper to Mr Barrett, a cavalry captain of the Boer War. The couple lived with him and another lodger who had been there four years.

Following a row with Mary, Tatum left on 9 January, but returned a week later when he knew the old man would be alone. Letting himself in with copied keys at 7.30am, Tatum began to search the house for money. In the bedroom Tatum disturbed Mr Barrett, hitting him three times over the head with a souvenir knobkerrie, an African club. He escaped with £7 from Barrett's wallet. Found when his lodger returned from night-work, Mr Barrett died in hospital the same day.

Tatum, a schizophrenic, admitted the robbery, but claimed he was working with an accomplice he named in court. The accused man had an alibi, and the jury decided Tatum's guilt in 40 minutes.

Read: Master Detective, Mar 95.

797

Bernard Hugh WALDEN   33

Shot: 1 **Neil Saxton**, *20, and*
           2 **Joyce Moran**, *21, on 7 April 1959, in Rotherham, W.Yorks.*
Motive: *Sexual rivalry.*

Walden, *(b.1926),* a disabled physics lecturer in a Rotherham college had proposed marriage to Miss Moran, a clerk at the college, with whom he had become obsessed, and had been rejected. At 7.30pm, Joyce and her boyfriend, ex-student Neil Saxton were talking in a corridor near the general office, when Walden went to his locker, took out a revolver, shot

Saxton, and then turned the gun on Joyce. He shot her six times, the last three into her back as she lay on the floor.

Walden drove off, and was arrested in Reading on 1 May. Walden was said to suffer chronic paranoia.

Read: And May The Lord Have Mercy On Your Soul.

5 November 1959   Wandsworth prison, London   *Harry Allen/ Rickard*

798

<u>Guenther Fritz Erwin PODOLA</u>   **30**
   German

Shot: Det. Sgt. ***Raymond William Purdy***, *40, on 13 July 1959,*
               in London SW7.
Motive: *To escape arrest.*

Podola was born in Berlin in 1929. His father was killed at Stalingrad and his mother was raped by the conquering Russians. After the war he lived with a woman and fathered a child. He emigrated to Canada in 1952, but was deported in 1958 after a year in jail for burglary. He came to London in May 1959 and supported himself by again housebreaking.

In July he stole £2000 worth of furs and jewels from Mrs Verne Schiffman, 30, and then later attempted to blackmail her. His calls were traced and police arrested him at South Kensington tube station. He escaped but the two police officers caught up with him nearby. He pulled a pistol and shot Detective Sergeant Purdy, married with two children, through the heart. A palm print led to his identification, and a suspicious hotel-keeper led to his arrest in a Kensington hotel room.

Podola was injured when the bedroom door was knocked down, and the pistol used in the murder was found hidden in the hotel attic. He feigned amnesia at his trial, but the jury decided his fate after 90 minutes.

Read: Murders of the Black Museum

1959 Execution in Jersey

| 9 October 1959 | Newgate Street Prison, St Helier | *Harry Allen* |

<u>Francis Joseph HUCHET</u>   32

| **Shot:** | ***John Perree***, *45, on 30 March 1959, near Mont a la Brune, Jersey.* |
| *Motive:* | *Financial* |

      Huchet, *(b.1928)*, a sewerage worker, had got talking to Perree, a bachelor who worked for the roads department, in a pub on Easter Monday, and had become interested in the wad of £5 notes the older man had on him. The two men went walking on the beach at 11.15pm, and while Perree, a veteran of the Sicily landings, urinated on the sand, Huchet blasted him in the face twelve times with a shotgun, and relieved him of £50-60.

      After burying him in the sand, Huchet's car got stuck, and he stole a lorry to tow it out. The body was discovered five days later by a family playing on the dunes. Perree's glass eye was found six feet from the body.

      The murder weapon was found to be a gun stolen from a lodger of Huchet's mother. Any doubt as to Huchet's guilt was dispelled by an anonymous letter he wrote trying to shift the blame. The jury of 24 persons returned their unanimous verdict after 90 minutes. Huchet's execution, only the second in the Channel Islands this century, was also the last.

Read: True Crime Summer Special 97.

1960

total: **4**

799	1 Sep	John CONSTANTINE	22		Lincoln
800	10 Nov	Francis FORSYTH	18		Wandsworth
801	10 Nov	Norman HARRIS	23		Pentonville
802	22 Dec	Anthony MILLER	19	Scottish	Barlinnie

1 September 1960   Lincoln prison   *Allen/ Rickard*

799

John Louis CONSTANTINE   22

Bludgeoned: ***Lily Parry**, 75, on 23 April 1960, in Nottingham.*
Motive: *Financial.*

  Lily Parry had lived above her general store in Summers Street for 30 years. A widow with arthritis, she shared her home with her dog and her 15-year old papergirl lodger. Early one Saturday, Constantine, *(b.1938),* a married box-maker, broke in through a back door. Surprised by Mrs Parry, he hit her with his jemmy, and escaped with £20-30. Lily's young lodger discovered her groaning in her bedroom at 7 am.
  Police rounded up known criminals, including Constantine, who admitted the assault, and directed police to the jemmy in a nearby canal. When Mrs Parry died five days later, he changed his story. He had been downstairs petting the dog while his accomplice had carried out the attack. However, the man he named produced witnesses who solidly backed his alibi. The jury took 105 minutes to reach their verdict.

Read: Master Detective, Mar 96.

Wandsworth prison, London
Pentonville prison, London

Harry Allen/ Rickard
Stewart/ Robinson

800, 801

Francis Robert George FORSYTH   18
Norman James HARRIS   23

Kicked to death: ***Allan Edward John Jee***, *23, on 25 June 1960, at Isleworth, Middlesex.*
Motive: *Financial; drink related.*

     Harris, *(b.1937),* an unemployed driver, and 'Flossie' Forsyth, *(b.1942),* a labourer, together with coalman Christopher Louis Darby, 23 and labourer Terence Lutt, 17, having been drinking, and intent on robbery, ambushed engineer Alan Jee on his way home from an evening with his fiancee at 11.30 p.m. in an alley by a footpath.

     Lutt punched him and Forsyth kicked him in the head. Jee, who had been carrying no money, died on 27 June. Harris was questioned after boasting to friends of his exploits. After the jury had spent 40 minutes deliberating, all four were found guilty. Lutt was detained as a minor, and Darby given a life term. Forsyth was one of four 18-year olds executed this century.

     Read: Master Detective, May 95.

Barlinnie prison, Glasgow   *Allen/ Stewart*

802

Anthony Joseph MILLER   19   *Scottish*

Bludgeoned: ***John Cremin***, *55, on 6 April 1960, in Glasgow, Lanarks.*
Motive: *Financial.*

     Queens Park recreation ground was a haunt of Glasgow's homosexuals. Tony Miller, *(b.1941),* and his friend, James Denovon, 16, went there many times over at least six months, Denovon meeting men in the public toilet, offering them sex acts, then leading them outside where Miller would jump them.

     One April night, John Cremin, himself a known thief from Dundee, was their victim. Denovon allowed Cremin to fondle him, then Miller came from behind and hit him across the head with a metre-long piece of wood.

They stole a chequebook, a knife, a watch and £67, but bragged about it to friends in their local cafe.

In October, while Denovon was being questioned about another matter, and after being charged in August with committing an indecent act, he confessed the crime to police, but blamed Miller for the killing. Miller did not speak in his own defence in court, and despite his youth, the jury took 30 minutes to find him guilty, and Denovon not guilty of capital murder. The younger boy was detained at Her Majesty's pleasure, eventually being released in 1969, and Miller became the youngest person to be hanged in Scotland this century.

Read: True Crime, Aug 96

1961

total: **7**

803	27 Jan	Wasyl GNYPIUK	34	*Polish*	Leicester
804	9 Feb	George RILEY	21		Shrewsbury
805	29 Mar	Jack DAY	31		Bedford
806	25 May	Victor TERRY	20		Wandsworth
807	29 Jun	Zsiga PANKOTIA	31	*Hungarian*	Armley
808	6 Jul	Edwin BUSH	21		Pentonville
809	8 Sep	Henryk NIEMASZ	49	*Polish*	Wandsworth

27 January 1961   Lincoln prison

803

<u>Wasyl GNYPIUK</u>   **34**   *Polish*

Strangled: ***Louise Surgey***, *62, on 17 July 1960, in Worksop, Notts.*
Motive: *Financial; drink related.*

Gnypiuk, *(b.1927),* was married, but was unemployed and flat broke, with numerous debts. He left his lodgings without paying and slept rough on the allotments for three nights, before deciding to call on Louise Surgey, who had been kind to him in the past. He found enough money for some brandy before breaking into Louise's house late at night, and there helped himself to more drink, before falling asleep on the sofa.

When Louise disturbed him, he strangled her to death, and stole several hundred pounds. Gnypiuk claimed that there had been no answer to his knocking, and that all he could remember was a violent nightmare, after which he woke to find the woman dead. In panic, he said, he cut off her head, and buried it in a carrier bag in the woods. Her body was later buried in a shallow grave nearby.

Gnypiuk gave his wife £100, and paid £250 to clear his debts. Louise's body was found on 21 July.

Read: And May The Lord Have Mercy On Your Soul

624

804

George RILEY   21

Bludgeoned:	***Adeline Mary Smith**, 62, on 8 October 1960, in Shrewsbury, Shropshire.*
Motive:	*Financial; drink related.*

George Riley, *(b.1940)*, worked in a butchers. At 14 he had two larceny convictions, and in 1959 had served 9 months for stabbing two youths with a flick-knife in a brawl. So when Adeline Smith, a widow, was found battered to death in her heavily bloodstained bedroom, police crossed the road to interview Riley. Mrs Smith had received six heavy punches to the face. Riley had been out the previous night and had consumed ten beers and eight whiskies, and had been involved in a fight at a dance, to which police were called.
     After being questioned for seven hours, he confessed to the killing, though no trace of blood was found on him or his clothes. He later retracted his statement and claimed his innocence to the end. Mrs Smith had only 3/7 in a purse. He was convicted and executed solely on the strength of an uncorroborated retracted confession.

Read: Master Detective, May,Jun 95.

805

Jack DAY   31

Shot:	***Keith Godfrey Arthur**, 25, on 23 August 1960, in Dunstable, Beds.*
Motive:	*Sexual rivalry.*

Day, *(b.1930),* a married man with two children, was a car salesman who stole a revolver from a prospective customer's car in July 1959. He was convinced his wife was having an affair, and on 23 August returned home to find Keith Arthur at home with Margaret Day. Mr Arthur was shot in the neck with a single bullet and the two men staggered out into the street. By the time Day had got Arthur into his car he was dead. He drove the body to a relative's farm where he dumped it under some sacks in a shed.

A trail of blood led police to the vicinity of Day's house where an 11-year old neighbour of Day's told them she had seen the shooting. The murder weapon was found in the store-room at Jack Day's workplace.

Read: Murder Squad, p220.

25 May 1961   Wandsworth prison, London   *Harry Allen/ Plant*

806

Victor John TERRY   20

Shot: ***John Henry Pull***, *61, on 10 November 1960,*
          in Durrington, Sussex.
Motive: *Financial.*

Terry, *(b.1941)*, had been a violent criminal since the age of ten, and had served a term in borstal at 18 for mugging an old man. A drug addict and schizophrenic, he was obsessed with American gangsters, and claimed to be the reincarnation of Legs Diamond. He was a friend of Flossie Forsyth who had killed a young man the previous June. He heard of Forsyth's execution on his car radio, and just one hour later went into a Lloyds bank near Worthing with a 16-year old accomplice, Philip Tucker. Another friend, Alan Hosier, 20, drove the stolen getaway car.
Terry, 5'8", went straight to the office area and shot the bank guard over the left eye with a sawn-off shotgun. They escaped with £1372. The accomplice was recognised, and he named Terry, who escaped with his girlfriend.
A nationwide manhunt ended in a Glasgow hotel at 1am two days after the murder. Terry claimed unsuccessfully that the gun had gone off accidentally. The jury retired for two and a half hours. Both accomplices were found guilty of non-capital murder, Hosier getting life, Tucker being detained at Her Majesty's pleasure, and the girl receiving probation as an accessory after the fact. Another 16-year old girlfriend of Terry gave birth to his child while he awaited execution.

Read: Master Detective, May 95

807

Zsiga PANKOTIA   31   *Hungarian*

Stabbed: ***Eli Myers**, 50, on 24 February 1961, in Leeds, W.Yorks.*
Motive: *Financial.*

      Pankotia, *(b.1930)*, had come to England in 1949, moving to Leeds in 1952. He learned of Eli Myers' wealth, acquired from a pools win of £1275 in December 1960, from a Hungarian friend who worked for him. Myers was a market trader who owned his own mobile clothes shop, and who made no secret of how well he had done in business.
      Pankotia broke into Myers' house through a french window, and ransacked the place. Myers, who lived alone, arrived home at 10pm and struggled with the Hungarian for thirty minutes. He was beaten with a chair, and stabbed with a breadknife. Pankotia made off in Mr Myers' van with a wallet and some trousers, which he tried to sell the following day. When he was arrested on 26 February, he was wearing Mr Myers' jumper.

      Read: Murderous Leeds

808

Edwin Albert Arthur BUSH   21   *half Indian*

Stabbed: ***Elsie May Batten**, 59, on 3 March 1961, in London WC2.*
Motive: *Financial.*

      Bush, *(b.1940)*, had called into an antique shop off Charing Cross Road on 2 March enquiring about dress swords. He returned the following day and killed Mrs Batten, the shop assistant, with a dagger in the neck and another in the stomach. The weapons were still in her when she was discovered. Bush had stolen a sword and had gone into a nearby antiques shop in an attempt to sell it. He later said he wanted the money to buy an engagement ring for his girlfriend.
      An 'identikit' picture was built up by witnesses and Bush was arrested five days later. He had left behind palm and fingerprints in blood, and was picked out in an identification parade.

He claimed that he murdered on impulse when Mrs Batten had made an offensive racist remark, but the jury went with the prosecution's claim that the crime had obviously been planned.

Read: Murder Squad, p218.

8 September 1961   Wandsworth prison, London   *Harry Allen/ Plant*

809

Henryk NIEMASZ   49   *Polish*

Shot:	***1 Hubert Roderick Twells Buxton**, 35, and*
Bludgeoned:	***2 Alice Buxton**, 37, his wife, on 12 May 1961, in near Ashford, Kent.*
Motive:	*Sexual rivalry.*

Alice Gyesel, a Belgian, had married soldier Richard Bateman in 1944, and had taken in Hubert Buxton as a lodger some time later. Alice and Hubert fell in love and ran away together, finally settling in the village of Aldington, where Hubert got work as a gardener, and Alice as a hotel waitress. Alice was friendly with a Polish woman, Grypa Niemasz, and she and her husband, Henryk Niemasz, *(b.1912),* a labourer, socialised regularly with the Buxtons.

Eventually, Henryk and Alice began an affair, and on the night of 12 May, Niemasz called at the Buxtons' bungalow, only to discover that Buxton had found a love letter and was aware of the relationship. Alice protested that she wanted to end her entanglement.

An hour later, at 10.15pm, Niemasz returned with a shotgun. He shot Buxton through the kitchen window, and battered Alice with the butt as she ran screaming to the door. His weapon broke in two, and police found the second half at the Niemasz house. Grypa lied for her husband, saying he had been in bed with her at the time, but with evidence of fingerprints, and bloody clothing, she admitted the truth.

Read: The Murder Guide to Great Britain, p49

25 July 1961   Crumlin Road Gaol, Belfast   *Harry Allen/ Rickard*

Samuel McLAUGHLIN   **40**

Bludgeoned/ strangled: ***Nellie McLaughlin**, his wife, on 17 October 1960, in Lislabin, Co Antrim*
Motive: *Vengeance; drink related*

Samuel's marriage to Nellie Rogers had been a stormy one. He drank heavily and she nagged incessantly. Her interfering mother Jean did not help matters, but neither did a spell living in Derby. Eventually Nellie left him, and a court ordered him to pay her maintenance. McLaughlin, *(b.1921),* a foundry worker, attempted a recociliation, and the two went out for a drink together, returning to her cottage and going to bed together. Blind drunk, in bed he strangled her with a stocking, and beat her severely about the head with a broom handle. Jean Rogers raised the alarm when she could not gain entry the following morning.

The defence claimed Sam had not known what he was doing, and the jury failed to agree a verdict. At the retrial, the jury took 2 hours and 20 minutes to find him guilty. McLaughlin wet himself on the way to the scaffold.

Read: True Detective, Jan 97.

10 December 1961   Crumlin Road Gaol, Belfast   *Harry Allen*

Robert Andrew McGLADDERY   **26**

Strangled: ***Pearl Gamble**, 19, on 28 January 1961, in Upper Damolly, Co Armagh*
Motive: *Sexual rivalry; drink related*

McGladdery, *(b.1935),* an unemployed labourer, had spent a January evening drinking with a friend, and went on to a dance in Newry where he saw his cousin Pearl with her boyfriend Joe Clydesdale. Pearl worked in a Newry drapers and had gone there with two friends, and got a lift back to her junction at 2am.

McGladdery stole a bike and pursued the car. He grabbed Pearl at the roadside and dragged her into a nearby field. There he stripped her, save for her stockings, and stabbed her in the neck, breasts and heart with a file he had bought the previous week. She suffered a fractured wrist and a broken nose. He finished her off by strangling her with a bootlace. He dragged her further into some gorse bushes and threw her clothes on top of the body. She was found there the following day.

Police were suspicious about scratches on McGladdery's face, and discovered he had lied about the suit he had been wearing. He was followed and clothes and shoelaces were found in a septic tank.

The jury took 40 minutes to decide his fate. McGladdery's execution was the last in Ireland.

Read: True Detective, Jan 97.

1962

total: **3**

810	4 Apr	James HANRATTY	25		Bedford
811	20 Nov	Oswald GREY	20	*Jamaican*	Winson Green
812	28 Nov	James SMITH	26	*Scottish*	Strangeways

4 April 1962   Bedford gaol   *Harry Allen*

810

James HANRATTY   25

Shot:	***Michael John Gregsten,*** *34, on 23 August 1961, near Clophill, Beds.*
Motive:	*To clear impediment.*

Michael Gregsten, a married man with two children, was separated from his wife, and had for some months been having an affair with his research assistant, Valerie Storie, 23. The two were parked in a field near Windsor after an evening out together, when a man approached the car and got in at gunpoint. He eventually forced Gregsten to drive the Morris Minor, by a circuitous route, to the A6.

On Deadman's Hill, on the other side of Clophill, Gregsten was told to pull into a lay-by. There, in the car, the man shot Gregsten twice in the head with a revolver and raped Valerie Storie. Gregsten was dumped in the lay-by and Valerie was shot five times. She survived, though paralysed. The murderer drove off in the car, the victims being found three hours later. The car was found later the same day in Ilford, and the murder weapon the following day on a bus in Peckham. Cartridge cases from the same gun were mysteriously found several weeks later on a chair in a Maida Vale hotel room.

Peter Alphon, 31, had occupied the room the night before the murder, and James Hanratty had booked in the following day. Alphon lied about his whereabouts and was the first suspect, but Miss Storie failed to identify him. He later confessed several times to the murder, and subsequently retracted. He claimed he had been employed to break up the relationship between Gregsten and Storie. Hanratty, however, who had noticeably blue eyes, was identified by Miss Storie and two other witnesses. He was arrested in Blackpool on 11 October and charged with murder.

James Hanratty, *(b.1936),* had spent six of the last ten years in prison for housebreaking and stealing cars. Released in March 1961 he returned to his Irish parents in Kingsbury, London NW9. He soon reverted to stealing and selling jewellery. He told police that he had been in Liverpool on the night of the murder to sell stolen gems. He could not back up his alibi.

During the course of the trial, he changed his story. He now claimed to have been in Rhyl. Witnesses were found who claimed to have seen him there on 22 August.

After England's longest murder trial, 21 days, the jury took nearly ten hours to decide Hanratty's guilt. He maintained his innocence to the last, and his family conducted a long campaign to clear his name. Hanratty's body was exhumed in 2001. The case finally came before the Court of Appeal in May 2002 where it was stated that DNA samples linking him to the crime were conclusive, and the conviction was upheld.

Read: Who Killed Hanratty?

20 November 1962   Winson Green prison, Birmingham
Harry Allen/ Plant

811

Oswald Augustus GREY   **20**   *Jamaican*

Shot: ***Thomas Arthur Bates**, 47, on 2 June
                   1962, in Edgbaston, Warwicks.*
Motive: *Financial.*

Thomas Bates was not married and lived with his 79-year old mother over his newsagent shop. At 6.30pm a short, thin black man entered the store with a handkerchief over his mouth and waited for some school-children to leave. He then shot Mr Bates in the chest and fled empty-handed. Police questioned over 200 local black men before arresting destitute baker Oswald Grey, *(b.1942).* Though he was found with bullets and admitted having a gun, he denied murder. He said he stole the gun from a roommate and sold it to fellow Jamaican Harris Karnfi for £16. Karnfi denied this, and the gun was never found.

Grey continued to protest his innocence and claimed police brutality towards him. Four witnesses stated that Grey was not the man seen, that the suspect was 5'10" and about 40, taller and older than Grey, but the admission of possessing the gun convinced the jury in 50 minutes. Grey spent the hours leading to his execution limbo dancing in his cell.

Read: True Crime Summer Special 97.

James SMITH   **26**   *Scottish*

Bludgeoned: ***Isabella Cross***, *57, on 4 May 1962, in Manchester, Lancs.*
Motive: *Financial.*

James Smith, *(b.1936)*, a rubber moulder from Edinburgh, lived just one mile from where Mr and Mrs Cross had their corner shop. Slim and 6'2" tall, he was married with a baby and two step-children. At 4.20 p.m. Mrs Cross was alone in the shop in Miles Platting, when Smith came in. He battered the shopkeeper to death with five bottles of mineral water from her shelves. He emptied the till and rifled the back rooms before leaving through the rear. Police believed the thief was after Cup Final tickets the Crosses were known to have. Stephanie Howard, 9, discovered her Aunty Bella when she called at 4.30.

Smith, who had a record of crime, was identified by fingerprints which he had left on the kitchen door's wet paint. In his home police found a shard of glass proved to come from the broken bottles. His claim to never have been in the house was proved to be a lie. The jury having taken 20 minutes to decide his fate, Smith's hair turned white in the condemned cell.

Read: Strange Tales from Strangeways.

1963

total: **3**

813	15 Aug	Henry BURNETT	21	*Scottish*	Aberdeen
814	17 Dec	Russell PASCOE	23		Bristol
815	17 Dec	Dennis WHITTY	22		Winchester

15 August 1963   Craiginches prison, Aberdeen   *Harry Allen*

813

Henry John BURNETT   **21**   *Scottish*

Shot: ***Thomas Guyan***, *27, on 31 May 1963, in Aberdeen.*
Motive: Sexual rivalry.

Burnett, *(b.1942),* the fourth of six children, had been in trouble from an early age. He had attended an approved school, and was sent to borstal for threatening to stab his sister. In 1961 he took an overdose when his girlfriend finished with him, and was discharged from the army as unfit after just six months.

Getting a job as a curer in a fish factory, he there met Margaret Guyan, 24, the mother of two children. Her husband was away in the merchant navy, and she and Burnett became lovers, moving in together. She wrote to her husband asking for a divorce, but upon his return told Burnett she would go back to her spouse.

Burnett attacked her, cutting her neck with a knife, and throttling her, though she escaped serious injury. He stole his brother's shotgun and went to Guyan's house, bursting in and blasting his rival in the face, killing him instantly. He dragged Margaret with him and stole a car at gunpoint, later giving himself up when pursued by police.

Though the jury dismissed pleas of insanity in just 25 minutes, even Guyan's family joined the campaign for a reprieve, believing him mad. Burnett's was the first execution in Aberdeen since 1857, and the last in Scotland.

Read: True Crime, Feb 96

17 December 1963	Horfield gaol, Bristol	*Harry Allen*
	Winchester prison	*Stewart/ Robinson*

814, 815

Russell PASCOE   23
Dennis John WHITTY   22

Bludgeoned/ stabbed:	*William Garfield Rowe, 64, on 14 August 1963, near Falmouth, Cornwall.*
Motive:	*Financial.*

Pascoe and Whitty, *(b.1940 & 1941)*, both labourers, lived with three young women in a caravan at Truro, though Pascoe was married with a child. He had worked for recluse Willy Rowe at Nanjarrow Farm, Constantine, near Falmouth, several years previously and suspected him of hoarding money in his house. It was probably he who had robbed Rowe of £200 in 1960.

Willie Rowe had been a deserter in the First World War, and had been presumed dead. His family hid him for nearly forty years, Willy working on the farm at night, until, in an amnesty in 1956, he was at last free. He had lived alone at Nanjarrow since the death of his mother that same year.

Calling at 11pm, the two enticed the old man from his house, Pascoe attacking him with an iron bar, Whitty with a knife, stabbing him eight times in the chest and neck. They netted £4 in cash and two watches, but missed £3000 hidden around the house. Willy was discovered the next morning by a cattle dealer.

Motor cycle tracks led to Pascoe and Whitty being questioned, and the pair were implicated by their girlfriends, Pascoe having been suspected of several previous robberies. Rowe's watches were found in their possession. A plea of diminished responsibility for Whitty, in fear of Pascoe, was turned down.

Read: Settings For Slaughter.

635

| 816 | 13 Aug | Peter ALLEN | 21 | Walton |
| 817 | 13 Aug | Gywnne EVANS | 24 | Strangeways |

13 August 1964

816, 817

Walton gaol, Liverpool
Strangeways prison, Manchester

*Stewart
Harry Allen*

Peter Anthony ALLEN   **21**
Gwynne Owen EVANS   **24**

*(real name: John
Robson Welby)*

Bludgeoned/ stabbed:

Motive:

John Alan West, *53, on 7 April 1964, in
Seaton, Cumberland.*
Financial.

'Ginger' Evans, *(b.1940),* lodged with Peter Allen, *(b.1943),* and his wife in Preston. Both men were of below average intelligence and had been in trouble with the police before. The men stole a car and drove to the home of John West, with whom Evans had previously worked, in Seaton, near Workington. West, a laundry van driver, lived alone.

At about 3 a.m. the two men coshed West and stabbed him in the heart, escaping with a few inconsequential items. West's body was discovered the next day, as was a raincoat left behind by Evans, which contained an inscribed medallion. The two men were arrested two days later, a watch belonging to Mr West being found in Evans' possession. The whole thing seemed to be Evans' idea, though he blamed Allen for the killing.

Allen and Evans were the last men to be hanged in Britain.

Read: Murders of the Black Museum

Analysis

Note: Statistics include only the 817 British hangings this century.

Definition: Sentences of death implemented in Great Britain, by hanging, imposed by British courts or courts-martial.

Not included in statistics:
- The 12 sentences of death in Great Britain carried out by firing squad.
- The 363 sentences of death carried out by British army (1914-20), whether by firing squad (362) or hanging (1 in 1916).
- The 18 sentences of death imposed in Great Britain by US courts-martial (1943-5), whether by firing squad (2) or hanging (16).
- The 2 sentences of death carried out in Jersey by hanging.
- The at least 177 sentences of death carried out in Ireland, whether by firing squad, (at least 27), or hanging.

Crimes of those hanged

Of the 817 hanged:

797 for murder *(98%)*
16 for espionage
4 for treason

Note:

Not included:
- *12 shot for espionage*
- *12 American servicemen executed for murder, 6 for rape*
- *Of 363 executed by the British army 1914-20, 40 for murder, 268 for desertion, 18 for cowardice, 16 for mutiny, 7 for quitting their post, 5 for disobedience, 4 for striking an officer, 2 for casting away arms, 2 for sleeping at their post, and 1 for violence. Note: Executions for desertion etc, were forbidden from 1930.*
- *Excluding army firing squads, the last execution for a crime other than murder, espionage or treason, was for attempted murder in 1861.*

Motives for Murder

		%	% by decade
Vengeance	300	34	47,42,35,28,25,21
Financial	199	22	16,15,20,24,29,31
Sexual rivalry	143	16	18,22,19,15,07,15
To clear impediment	107	12	10,13,13,21,11,08
Sexual	65	7	03,01,05,07,13,14
Sadistic pleasure	55	6	05,06,04,06,09,07
To escape arrest	10		
Political	9		163,333,526,532
Racism	1		222
To escape situation	1		391

Notes:
Numbers refer to those murdered for these reasons, where known.
Key:
- *Vengeance= retaliation for a perceived wrong, revenge*
- *Financial= for monetary gain*
- *Sexual rivalry= jealousy owing to a rival for affection*
- *Clear impediment= to kill those barring the way to betterment*
- *Sexual= for sexual gratification*
- *Sadistic pleasure= only for the sake of causing harm, in anger*
- *Escape arrest= to prevent capture*
- *Political= a strike against the state*
- *Racism= where the victim's race causes offence*
- *Escape situation= the only way out of a dilemma*

Drink related

161, at least, were murdered where alcohol abuse was a contributary factor:
18% of total of 899   % by decade: 23,21,14,07,18,16

Note: Statistics include only the 817 British hangings this century.

Definition: Sentences of death implemented in Great Britain, by hanging, imposed by British courts or courts-martial.

Not included in statistics:
- The 12 sentences of death in Great Britain carried out by firing squad.
- The 363 sentences of death carried out by British army (1914-20), whether by firing squad (362) or hanging (1 in 1916).
- The 18 sentences of death imposed in Great Britain by US courts-martial (1943-5), whether by firing squad (2) or hanging (16).
- The 2 sentences of death carried out in Jersey by hanging.
- The at least 177 sentences of death carried out in Ireland, whether by firing squad, (at least 27), or hanging.

Means to Murder

		%	% by decade
Bludgeoned	202	21	15,19,25,27,22,26
Shot	187	20	19,14,14,12,20,20
Cut throat	152	16	19,35,27,15,03,01
Strangled	146	15	08,08,11,23,25,24
Stabbed	142	15	20,12,12,10,16,20
Drowned	27	3	
Poisoned	25	3	
Suffocated	23	2	
Kicked	12	1	
Punched	10	1	
Blown up	5		
Buried alive	4		327, 435, 483
Dropped	3		154, 355, 771
Traumatised	2		363, 558
Burned	2		125, 448
Gassed	2		477, 584
Run over	1		701
Cut wrists	1		687
Internally	1		116

Note:

Numbers refer to those murdered by these means, out of a known total of 899 victims.

'Means' generally is cause of death, even where other punishment is inflicted.

- *Bludgeoned= death by blow to head with object*
- *Strangled= choking by hand or implement*
- *Suffocated= asphyxiated, blocking of air passages*
- *Dropped= causing to fall and sustain multiple injury*
- *Traumatised= death by secondary effect, eg heart failure or pneumonia brought on by other act.*
- *Internally= death through damage by penetration to internal organs*

Multiple murders

32 did not kill *(16 spies, 4 traitors, 12 accomplices to murder)*
697 killed once *(85%)*
  55 killed twice *(7%)*
  18 killed three times
    4 killed four times   128, 166, 283, 353
    2 killed five times   526, 527
    2 killed six times   563, 677
    2 killed seven times   060, 061
    1 killed eight times   748
    1 killed twelve times   789
    3 killed an unknown number 002, 053, 054

27 paedophiles hanged

031, 049, 130, 148, 215, 259, 264, 302, 326, 353, 359, 363, 369, 456, 463, 468, 543, 583, 663, 674, 718, 754, 759, 763, 769, 784, 789

5 incestuous hanged

405	Knighton
420	Gillon
468	Morse
652	Briggs
673	Cooper

1 transvestite hanged

369	Bressington

4 prostitutes hanged

129	Wiils
396	Calvert
499	Bryant
780	Ellis

6 homosexuals hanged

086	Sullivan
256	Casement
443	Fox
667	Allen *(female)*
719	Bradley
751	Greenway

16 Spies hanged

243, 537, 538, 539, 544, 547, 548, 554, 564, 565, 572, 574, 575, 594, 597, 598
Notes:
~One in 1915, the rest 1940-44
~In addition 12 spies were shot; one in 1941, the rest 1914-16.

4 Traitors hanged

256   Casement
618   Amery
622   Joyce
623   Schurch
Note: One in 1916, the rest 1945-6

12 Accomplices to Murder hanged

025, 053, 280, 316, <u>344</u>, 424, 478, 531, 567, 656, 691, 745

Notes:
~Women underlined
~745 Bentley is the only accomplice to hang alone, without the actual murderer. (Though O'Shea, 1943 in Ireland, suffered the same fate).

4 IRA members hanged

333   Dunn
334   O'Sullivan
526   Barnes
527   Richards

2 hanged for other political murders

163   Dhingra
532   Singh

Note: Many other nationalists, including IRA members, were executed in Ireland, qv.

6 Moslems hanged

103	Benali
298	Caler
352	H. Mohammed
514	J. Mohammed
722	Ali
733	Mattan

9 Jews hanged

155	Reuben
156	Reuben
199	Abromovitch
293	Perdovitch
313	Goodmacher
361	Goldenberg
455	Stein
576	Dobkin
683	Raven

2 Sikhs hanged

532	U. Singh
726	A. Singh

2 Parsees hanged

163	Dhingra
496	Ruxton

1 Gipsy hanged

702	Crosby

12 Blacks hanged

008	Lacey
127	Paterson
250	Hill
298	Caler
459	Michael
590	James
603	Gordon
727	Manneh
733	Mattan
749	Henry
783	Roberts
811	Grey

Note:
~2 Jews, Philips and Beverstein, were shot by the British army 1915/16.
~11 Blacks, Fatoma, Frafra, Mamprusi, Sabongidda, Clarke, Morris, Mitchell, Barama, Denny, Davids, Harris were shot by the British army 1915-19.
~4 US blacks, Davis, Leatherberry, Pearson, Jones, were hanged under US authority 1943-45.

Relations hanged

Brothers
092/093 Potter/Wade
100/101 Stratton
155/156 Reuben
381/382 Fowler

Uncle/Nephew
025/026 Miller

Couples
078/079 Swann/Gallagher
343/344 Bywaters/Thompson

Note: Taylor/Daly, Ireland 1903, were also lovers

28 with disabilities hanged

One eye:	*141, 371, 456, 472*
One arm:	*104*
One leg:	*226, 394*
Legs - malformed, ulcerated, one shorter, crippled:	*139, 262, 324, 392, 440, 550, 570, 577, 717*
Epileptic:	*350, 386, 742, 782*
Hand - paralysed, mutilated:	*237, 570*
Hernia:	*106*
Locomotor ataxy:	*306*
Lupus:	*461*
Albino:	*282*
Dwarfism:	*502*
Stutter:	*618*
Unspecified:	*797*

10 of the cruellest, most callous killers

034, 044, 116, 157, 286, 463, 563, 641, 663, 718

56 who attempted suicide after murdering

by cutting throat: 048, 051, 080, 081, 135, 137, 149, 153, 166, 190, 205, 206, 207, 213, 217, 232, 238, 239, 248, 252, 261, 271, 294, 300, 326, 338, 358, 395, 401, 420, 452, 555

by drowning: 043, 104, 249, 335, 345

by hanging: 467

by stabbing: 391, 760

by gassing: 480

by poison: 214, 644, 665

by shooting: 211, 218, 321 - 240 Quartly, shot and missed!

other/mixture of means:
392, 540, 542, 583, 919

40 hanged for murdering foreigners

019, 023, 060, 061, 084, 103, 110, 152, 179, 222, 250, 273, 274, 275, 276, 291, 342, 383, 400, 433, 469, 514, 576, 591, 600, 610, 611, 612, 613, 614, 616, 617, 621, 630, 631, 704, 727, 748, 773, 809

Notes:
~ 'Foreigners' = non-British or Irish
~underlined = murderers were foreigners themselves
~ also a case in Ireland 1932

30 hanged for murdering prostitutes

011, 072, 074, 075, 083, 149, 154, 221, 237, 254, 287, 350, 352, 377, 408, 455, 497, 507, 518, 563, 636, 648, 653, 697, 698, 709, 748, 758, 779, 785

14 hanged for murdering police officers

006, 064, 065, 210, 219, 423, 424, 530, 531, 715, 720, 745, 795, 798

11 who dismembered their victims

056, 179, 274, 356, 364, 373, 408, 416, 496, 576, 803
Note: Also Ireland 1943

7 who mutilated their victims

098, 148, 286, 291, 563, 641, 658
Note: Also Ireland 1901

10 hanged for murdering Jews

199, 293, 313, 323, 472, 576, 683, 688, 733, 807

Notes:
~underlined=murderers were Jews themselves
~Also a case in Ireland 1929

6 hanged for murdering homosexuals

060, 061, 086, 103, 719, 802

5 hanged for murdering during sex act

167	Murphy
319	Quarmby
376	Winstanley
520	Armstrong
676	Jones
798	Christie

4 hanged for murdering disabled

114	Silk
661	Cross
719	Bradley
799	Constantine

Transport:

11 hanged for murdering on ships
019, 060, 061, 086, 188, 400, 457, 486, 511, 514, 600

4 hanged for murdering on trains
016, 137, 236, 404
Note: The first railway murder was in 1864.

3 hanged for murdering in taxis
347, 606, 734

"Season's Greetings"

6 murders on Christmas Eve: 149, 183, 389, 521, 580, 794

3 murders on Christmas Day: 058, 167, 266

3 murders on Boxing Day: 345, 476, 671

3 murders on New Year's Eve: 031, 459, 488

4 murders on New Year's Day: 265, 346, 394, 789

3 hanged on Christmas Eve: 029, 540, 742

3 hanged on New Year's Eve: 228, 314, 574

4 hanged on New Year's Day: 123, 253, 483, 718

Most prolific murderers

789 **Manuel** killed **12**

748 Christie *probably* killed 8

002 **Chard-Williams,**
053 **Sach** and *054* **Walters** probably exceeded Manuel's total in the number of babies they killed.

Nationality of those hanged

647	English	79%
40	Scottish	5%
28	Welsh	3%
17	Irish	
12	Polish	
7	Canadian	493, 580, 582, 586, 592, 608, 757
7	Chinese	084, 152, 253, 291, 342, 393, 433
5	Belgian	276, 565, 575, 597, 599
5	Dutch	061, 397, 537, 539, 574
5	Indian	163, 400, 496, 532, 726
4	American	179, 243, 250, 606
4	French	001, 023, 274, 362
4	Jamaican	008, 603, 783, 811
4	Russian	095, 199, 293, 576
3	Cypriot	450, 469, 773
3	Greek	266, 566, 591
2	Bengali	514, 722
2	Italian	019, 188
2	South African	317, 697
1	Algerian	103
1	Australian	275
1	Basuto	108
1	Burmese	579
1	Danish	459
1	Gibraltarian	564
1	Hungarian	807
1	Maltese	668
1	Norwegian	162
1	St Vincentian	127
1	Somali	733
1	Spaniard	769
1	West Indian	321
1	Yemeni	352
1	Yugoslav	704
1	Zanzibarian	298

Note: 10 Americans
were executed under
US authority
4 Germans
2 Dutch
1 American
1 Brazilian
1 Latvian
1 Peruvian
1 Swede
1 Uruguayan
were shot as spies

218 English
37 Scottish
25 Irish
19 Canadians
13 Welsh
13 Russians
10 Chinese
6 Cypriots
4 West Indians
3 Americans
3 Australians
3 Gold Coast
3 South Africans
2 New Zealanders
1 Egyptian
1 Nigerian
1 West African,
were shot and
1 South African
hanged by the
British army 1914-20

647

Occupations of those hanged

Most common occupations:

Servicemen	66	*8% of total*
Unemployed	63	
Labourers60		
Miners	35	

Police	*388, 701*
Footballers	*089, 233*
Doctors	*179, 496*
Cricketer	*76*
Teachers	*01, 797*
Boxer	*493*
Solicitor	*331*
Detective	*39*

About 140 different occupations are listed, from advertising agent to yeoman.

Notes:
- *A further 18 US servicemen were hanged under US authority1943-45.*
- *342 servicemen were executed by the British army 1914-20.*

Height and weight of those hanged

Tallest
6'5" *161 Shawcross*
6'4" *554 Richter*

Shortest
4'7"   *502 Haslam*
4'11" *659 Evans*

Heaviest
15 st *419 Power*
15 st *554 Richter*

Lightest
7 st *163 Dhingra*

Note: 16 st Foster was hanged in Ireland 1905.

Ages of those hanged

ave: 34 years   *ave woman: 38*

age 18-19	21	*3%*
age 20-29	360	*45%*
age 30-39	210	*26%*
age 40-49	140	*17%*
age 50-59	59	*7%*
age 60-69	17	*2%*
age >70		1

Oldest

71   *238 Frembd*
67   *025 Miller*
66   *296 Hall*

Oldest woman: 54 - 054 Walters.

Note: Dunphy, Ireland 1900, was 74

Youngest

18 - *332 Jacoby, 379 Bishop, 599 Davidson, 800 Forsyth*

Youngest woman: 28 - 780 Ellis

Earliest and Latest Born
025   Miller, *b.1834*
816   Allen, *b.1943*

Note:
- *3 soldiers aged 17 were shot: Byers 1915, Burden 1915, Morris 1917. A further 3 soldiers aged 18 were also shot 1916 and 1917*
- *In Ireland 1920, Barry, 18, was hanged*
- *Execution of under-16s was outlawed in 1908, though the last case, a 14-year old, had been in 1841. Executions of under-18s was outlawed in 1933, though the last such case had been in 1887.*

Gender of those hanged

Of the 817 hanged: 801 male   *98%*
                          16 female   *2%*

Females hanged:
001 Masset
002 Williams
053 Sach
054 Walters
077 Swann
129 Willis
344 Thompson
354 Newell
396 Calvert
482 Major
495 Waddingham
499 Bryant
667 Allen
750 Merrifield
773 Christophi
780 Ellis

32 hanged though mentally ill

027, 058, 112,198, 230, 238, 286, 297, 302, 335, 367, 374, 393, 405, 412, 413, 420, 426, 439, 445, 471, 541, 658, 672, 684, 718, 746, 754, 796, 797, 806

16 hanged though mentally immature

026, 073, 098, 192, 292, 384, 439, 463, 513, 764, 685, 714, 745, 767, 816, 817

19 hanged though possibly innocent

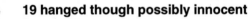

001, 017, 031, 230, 269, 282, 305, 323, 331, 344, 472, 513, 581, 685, 686, 733, 745, 759, 811

Notes:
- *Of these, only 3, 685 Evans, 733 Mattan and 745 Bentley, have had their convictions posthumously quashed.*
- *Gleeson, Ireland 1941, also possibly innocent*
- *Women underlined.*

Hanged despite jury's recommendation to mercy

At least **130** hanged despite such a recommendation. 35 despite a *strong* recommendation to mercy:

003, 007, 027, 037, 040, 042, 096, 097, 111, 149, 182, 192, 206, 231, 255, 290, 348, <u>354</u>, 358, 392, 476, 482, 495, 519, 580, 581, 586, 599, 609, 625, 691, 695, 721, 730, 732

2 hanged despite the *strongest* recommendation:

676	*Jones*
726	*Singh*

- *women underlined*

Shortest trial

4 minutes
385	*Johnson*
752	*Reynolds*

5 minutes
438	*Clark*

Longest trial

21 days
810	*Hanratty*

Shortest jury retirement

The jury did not retire
in 11 cases:
*033, 046, 048, 051,
071, 079, 126, 163,
175, 289, 378*

Longest jury retirement

10 hours – *810, Hanratty*
6h 35m – *777, Robinson*
4h 45m – *788, Teed*

Swiftest justice

Time between murder and execution

27 days
089	*Breeze*

35 days
079	*Starr*

36 days
404	*Stratton*

Slowest justice

9 yrs 11 mths
748	*Christie*

(from 1st murder to execution)
18 yrs
063	*Dougal*

(from his 1st possible murder)

49 Double hangings

006, 048, <u>053</u>, 060, 064, 074, <u>078</u>, 084, 092, 100, 134, 155, 192, 250, 280, 293, 301, 303, 316, 333, 338, 371, 378, 380, 406, 417, 451, 460, 478, 526, 530, 537, 547, 564, 567, 601, 610, 612, 616, 639, 655, 675, 680, 690, 706, 713, 724, 735, 765

Notes:
~The last of these, 765/766 Gilbert and Grant, was on 17 June 1954.
~The last triple hanging took place at Newgate in 1896.
~There were three double hangings of American servicemen in 1944/45.
~The British army carried out 25 double executions by firing squad, also one triple and one quintuple, 1915,17.
~For brevity, only the first of each pair is numbered.
~Women underlined.

Some firsts

First use of fingerprints in securing murder conviction:
1905   Stratton bros   *100, 101*

First women jurors in murder trial:
1921   Bailey   *318*

First appeal against murder conviction:
1908   Dodds   *139*

First full pardon:
1966   Evans   *685*

Incidents before execution

In condemned cell:

Screaming	*026*
Laughing, smiling etc	*115, 372, 390, 414, 465*
Read Koran	*298*
Had to be shaken awake	*330*
Did limbo dancing	*811*
Attacked warders	*567*
Ripped skin from penis	*758*

At scaffold:

Collapsing, carried/supported	*053, 058, 246, 258, 344, 417, 443, 456, 482*
Cried	*246, 258*
Fainted	*114, 250*
'Lost nerve'	*260*
Screamed	*250, 352*
Swearing	*221*
Removed boots or jacket	*055, 176*
Smoked cigar or cigarette	*091, 154, 231*
Bled?	*344*
Knelt to pray	*255*
Dragged	*187, 781*
Fought warders	*187, 554*
Jumped on trap	*364, 554*
Ran to scaffold	*709*
Freed hands, refused hood	*354*
Thanked staff	*742*
Said, 'Don't hurt my neck'	*134*
Soiled themselves	*686, 708*
Rope broke, hanged again	*358*
Assistant hangman fell in trap	*434*
Hangman's genitals remark	*740*
'The bravest'	*778*

Carried to scaffold on board	*Ire 1925*
Caused fight and delay	*Ire 1933*
Prayed	*Ire 1942*
Wet himself	*Ire 1961*

Note: The 'long drop' was introduced in 1888, after hangman Berry had decapitated a prisoner in Norwich in 1885, and almost another in Worcester. However, as late as 1891 a prisoner strangled to death in Liverpool.

1 unidentified victim

448 - murdered by Rouse

Longest survived victims

38 days   *Annie Gillon*   *420*
32 days   *John Duplessis*   *629*

7 months   Frederick Bryant   499
(from first administration of arsenic)

Most remote murder

6500 miles	S Atlantic Ocean	*019*
6000 miles	S Indian Ocean	*086*
4500 miles	Arabian Sea	*188*
4000 miles	off Brazil	*060*

Who Killed Whom?

No. of victims killed by:

A partner	353	*39% of total*
A parent	42	*5%*
A son	11	*1%*
Other relative	40	*5%*
A stranger	171	*19%*

Notes:
- *'Partner' is spouse, lover or those formerly so involved.*
- *Only 4 of the 353 were male victims of female partner, 077, 344, 481, 499*
- *Only 2 were gay partners, 086, 719*

Places for Murder

ENGLAND	**787**	*91% GB total; (cp 83% GB pop 1930)*
Bedfordshire	6	
Berkshire	7	
Buckinghamshire	5	
Cambridgeshire	2	*172, 536*
Cheshire	14	
Cornwall	9	
Cumberland	5	*433, 519, 627, 786, 816*
Derbyshire	14	
Devon	9	
Dorset	3	
Durham	45	
Essex	25	
Gloucestershire	9	
Hampshire	12	
Herefordshire	4	*073,331, 402*
Hertfordshire	3	*197, 242, 584*
Huntingdonshire	2	*224, 491*
Kent	22	
Lancashire	111	*13% of GB total*
Leicestershire	6	
Lincolnshire	10	
London	155	*18% of GB total*
E	26	
EC	6	
N	11	
NW	13	
SE	27	
SW	29	
W	38	
WC	4	
Middlesex	17	
Norfolk	9	
Northamptonshire	5	*028, 087, 110, 239, 448*
Northumberland	18	
Nottinghamshire	18	
Oxfordshire	3	*454, 458, 732*
Shropshire	5	*030, 271, 703, 754, 804*
Somerset	6	
Staffordshire	19	
Suffolk	5	*186, 305, 511, 607, 684*
Surrey	24	
Sussex	27	
Warwicks	36	
Westmorland	2	*467*

Wiltshire	6	
Worcestershire	7	
Yorkshire	102	*12% of GB total*
W Riding	*76*	
N Riding	*18*	
E Riding	*8*	
SCOTLAND	**47**	*5% GB total, (cp. 11% GB pop. 1930)*
Aberdeenshire	1	813
Dumfries	1	715
Fifeshire	2	140, 159
Lanarkshire	33	*70% of Scottish total*
Midlothian	7	
Morayshire	1	133
Perthshire	2	610, 660
WALES	**37**	*4% GB total, (cp. 6% GB pop. 1930)*
Anglesey	1	167
Denbighshire	2	055, 729
Flintshire	1	721
Glamorganshire	27	*73% of Welsh total*
Monmouthshire	4	
Montgomeryshire	1	434
Pembrokeshire	1	689
At sea	10	
Germany	2	*679, 743*
S Africa	1	187

Notes:
- *Murders committed by culprits subsequently hanged only.*
- *Traditional counties, as constituted before reforms of 1960s and 70s.*

Age of those murdered

ave: 35 years

age 0-9	75	*9%*
age 10-19	96	*11%*
age 20-29	218	*26%*
age 30-39	151	*18%*
age 40-49	134	*16%*
age 50-59	75	*9%*
age 60-69	57	*7%*
age 70-79	31	*4%*
age 80-89	14	*2%*
age >90	1	

Oldest

94	Minnie Freeman Lee	*664*
89	Loisa Baguley	*495*
85	Charles Barrett	*796*

Youngest

10 mins	Baby Watkins	*705*
1 day	Baby Treasure	*129*

Gender of those murdered

Of 899 known victims:

264	male	*30%*
630	female	*70%*
5	unknown babies	

Note:
- *A further 7 males & 4 females were victims of those executed under US military authority*
- *A further 18 males and 5 females, (18 unspecified others), were victims of those executed overseas by the British army (1914-20).*

Foreign murder victims

Chinese	5	Canadian	4
American	3	Belgian	3
Cypriot	2	German	2
Indian	2	Armenian	1
Algerian	Australian		
Austrian		Bengali	
Greek		Polish	
Russian		Spanish	
Swedish		Swiss	
Yugoslav			

Dates for Murder

January	54
February	68
March	63
April	68
May	81
June	71
July	84
August	76
September	89
October	73
November	75
December	83
Spring	*205*
Summer	*212*
Autumn	*231*
Winter	*237*

Note: Murders committed by culprits subsequently hanged only.

Longest gap between hangings

1 yr 11 mths	Aug 1955 - Jul 1957

Women:
15 yrs 5 mths	*Aug 1907 - Jan 1923*

Dates for Hanging

By month

January	65
February	47
March	84
April	72
May	52
June	39
July	82
August	101
September	35
October	32
November	64
December	144

Busiest months

January 1928 and December 1903 – 10 hangings

Busiest years

1903 - 27 hangings
1952 - 25

By decade

1870s	*145* hangings
1880s	*155*
1890s	*151*
1900s	166
1910s	125
1920s	151
1930s	83
1940s	157
1950s	116
1960s	19

Places for hanging

ENGLAND	748	First-Last
Armley gaol, Leeds, W.Yorks	68	1900-1961
Bagthorpe prison, Nottingham	8	1905-1928
Bedford gaol	8	1902-1962
Bodmin gaol, Cornwall	2	1901-1909
Cambridge prison	2	1910-1913
Chelmsford gaol, Essex	9	1900-1914
Derby gaol	4	1902-1907
Devizes prison, Wilts	1	1903
Dorchester prison, Dorset	2	1913-1941
Durham gaol	55	1900-1958
Exeter gaol, Devon	10	1914-1943
Gloucester prison	7	1904-1939
Hereford prison	1	1903
Holloway prison, London	5	1903-1955
Horfield gaol, Bristol	13	1925-1963
Hull prison, E.Yorks	10	1903-1934
Ipswich prison, Suffolk	3	1911-1924
Knutsford gaol, Cheshire	4	1905-1911
Lancaster prison	1	1910
Leicester prison	9	1903-1953
Lewes prison, Sussex	4	1913-1914
Lincoln prison	16	1903-1960
Maidstone prison, Kent	11	1901-1930
Newcastle prison, Northumberland	8	1901-1919
Newgate prison, London	9	1900-1902
Northampton prison	3	1901-1914
Norwich gaol, Norfolk	11	1901-1951
Oxford prison	8	1921-1952
Pentonville prison, London	120	1902-1961
Reading gaol, Berks	3	1907-1913
St Albans prison, Herts	2	1911-1914
Shepton Mallet prison, Somerset	4	1914-1926
Shrewsbury prison, Shropshire	8	1902-1961
Stafford gaol	8	1901-1914
Strangeways prison, Manchester	71	1900-1964
Wakefield prison, W.Yorks	10	1906-1915
Walton gaol, Liverpool	54	1900-1964
Wandsworth prison, London	117	1901-1961
Warwick gaol	4	1902-1908
Winchester prison, Wilts	16	1902-1959

Winson Green prison, Birmingham	35	1901-1962
Worcester prison	4	1902-1919

SCOTLAND	**34**	
Barlinnie prison, Glasgow	10	1946-1960
Craiginches prison, Aberdeen	1	1963
Calton gaol, Edinburgh	3	1913-1923
Duke Street prison, Glasgow	12	1902-1928
Perth prison	3	1908-1948
Porterfield prison, Inverness	1	1908
Saughton prison, Edinburgh	4	1928-1954

WALES	**35**	
Cardiff gaol, Glamorgan	20	1900-1952
Carnarvon prison	1	1910
Ruthin prison, Denbighshire	1	1903
Swansea prison, Glamorgan	9	1909-1958
Usk prison, Monmouthshire	4	1902-1910

Notes:
- Since 13 August 1868, all hangings have been carried out in private within prisons. The last public hanging took place at Newgate on 26 May 1868.
- The term 'gaol' in respect of certain prisons is one of style or tradition. All 'gaols' are prisons and could properly be referred to as such.
- Shepton Mallet was also the venue of 18 American military executions 1943-45, 12 by hanging, six by firing squad.
- British Army executions 1914-20 took place as follows:

France	228	Iraq	3	Belgium	96
Egypt	2	Russia	11	Cameroon	1
Greece	9	Italy	1	Turkey	7
Palestine	1	German E Africa	4		

362 by firing squad, 1 hanging in E Africa

- Executions in Irish prisons, where known, was:

Armagh	1	*1904*
Cork	4	*1901-1916, inc 1 by firng squad*
Crumlin Rd	12	*1901-1961*
Galway	1	*1902*
Kilkenny	3	*1903-1904*
Londonderry	3	*1904-1923*
Mountjoy gaol	53	*1901-1954, inc c19 by firing sq.*
Sligo	1	*1902*
Tulamore	1	*1903*
Waterford	1	*1900*

- Hangings in Jersey took place at:

Newgate St. prison, St Helier 2 *1907-1959*

Home Secretaries 1900-1964

	Govt.	Date in office	Hangings/	per mth
Matthew W. Ridley	Con	Jun 1895-Aug 1902	38	1.2
Aretas Akers-Douglas	Con	Aug 1902-Dec 1905	72	1.8
Herbert Gladstone	Lib	Dec 1905-Feb 1910	56	1.1
Winston Churchill	Lib	Feb 1910-Oct 1911	21	1.1
Reginald McKenna	Lib	Oct 1911-May 1915	55	1.3
Sir John Simon	Lib	May 1915-Dec 1916	17	0.9
Sir George Cave	Lib	Dec 1916-Jan 1919	20	0.8
Edward Shortt	Coal	Jan 1919-Oct 1922	59	1.3
William Bridgeman	Con	Oct 1922-Jan 1924	21	1.4
Arthur Henderson	Lab	Jan 1924-Nov 1924	7	0.7
Sir William Joynson-Hicks	Con	Nov 1924-Jun 1929	77	1.4
John Clynes	Lab	Jun 1929-Aug 1931	14	0.5
Herbert Samuel	Nat	Aug 1931-Sep 1932	10	0.8
Sir John Gilmore	Nat	Sep 1932-Jun 1935	26	0.8
Sir John Simon	Nat	Jun 1935-May 1937	14	0.6
Sir Samuel Hoare	Nat	May 1937-Sep 1939	19	0.7
Sir John Anderson	Nat	Sep 1939-Oct 1940	12	0.9
Herbert Morrison	Nat	Oct 1940-May 1945	73	1.3
Sir Donald Somervell	Nat	May 1945-Aug 1945	0	0.0
Chuter Ede	Lab	Aug 1945-Oct 1951	108	1.5
Sir David Maxwell-Fyfe	Con	Oct 1951-Oct 1954	57	1.6
Gwilym LLoyd George	Con	Oct 1954-Jan 1957	13	0.5
Richard A. Butler	Con	Jan 1957-Jul 1962	25	0.4
Henry Brooke	Con	Jul 1962-Oct 1964	7	0.3
Sir Frank Soskice	Lab	Oct 1964-Dec 1965	0	0.0

Note:
- The Home Secretary had the authority to exert his use of the Royal Prerorative of mercy on behalf of the sovereign. We know that in at least 130 cases the above politicians did not follow juries' such recommendations.
- The use of the death penalty in the United Kingdom was limited under the Homicide Act of 1957. Death could be imposed only in cases of murder of a police or prison officer, murder through shooting or explosion, in the furtherance of theft, or in resisting arrest. The death penalty was fully suspended in 1965, and abolished, but for treason, piracy etc, in December 1969.
- At least twenty attempts in Parliament have been made to restore hanging, all were defeated by at least 112 votes.

The Hangmen

	GB	OE	AE	Oth	First-Last	Other Data
Alfred ALLEN	13	3	10		1928-1936	*b.1890*
Brian ALLEN	5	0	5		1961-1963	*son of Harry Allen, career total: 5*
Harry ALLEN	68	24	44	3 *3-0*	1940-1964	*1912-1992, career total: c190*
Herbert ALLEN	2	0	2		1951	
Robert BAXTER	75	37	38	1 *0-1*	1915-1932	
James BILLINGTON	24	24	0	1 *1-0*	1884-1901	*1847-1901, career total: 147*
John BILLINGTON	46	16	30		1900-1905	*1890-1905, son of James*
Thomas BILLINGTON	3	0	3		1901-1902	*1873-1902, son of James*
William BILLINGTON	73	59	14	7 *7-0*	1900-1905	*1874-1934, son of James*
Joseph BROADBENT	2	0	2		1953-1954	
George BROWN	22	0	22		1911-1919	
William CONDUIT	1	0	1		1911	
Henry CRITCHELL	22	0	22		1940-1948	
Stanley CROSS	17	4	13		1933-1941	
Thomas CUNLIFFE	4	0	4		1958-1959	*career total: 4*

Syd DERNLEY	21	0	21		1949-1953	*b.1920*
John EDWARD	1	0	1		1961	
John ELLIS	187	143	44	2 *1-1*		*1874-1992, career total: 203*
William FRY	1	0	1		1905	
J. GRANT	2	0	2		1954	
Herbert HARRIS	2	0	2		1945	
Thomas HYSCOTT	1	0	1		1909	
Harry KIRK	37	1	36		1940-1950	
Albert LUMB	11	0	11		1911-1912	
Lionel MANN	16	0	16		1925-1931	
Seth MILLS	7	0	7		1922-1923	
Herbert MORRIS	18	0	18		1938-1951	
Thomas PHILLIPS	41	2	39		1922-1940	
Albert PIERREPOINT	175	152	23	8 *4-4*	1932-1955	*1905-1992, son of Henry, career total: c490*
Henry PIERREPOINT	99	68	31	3 *3-0*	1901-1913	*1877-1922, career total: 107*
Thomas PIERREPOINT	210	178	32	9 *9-0*	1908-1946	*1868-1954, brother of Henry, career total: c320*
Samuel PLANT	3	0	3		1961-1963	
Henry POLLARD	24	0	24		1925-1937	
Royston RICKARD	11	0	11	1 *0-1*	1953-1961	

Alexander RILEY	9	0	9	1 *0-1*	1940-1946	
Harry ROBINSON	5	0	5		1958-1963	
Thomas Henry SCOTT	1	0	1	3 *3-0*	1900-1902	
Harry SMITH	16	0	16		1952-1959	
Leslie STEWART	23	5	18	1 *0-1*	1951-1964	*d.1988*
Edward TAYLOR	27	0	27		1915-1925	
Steve WADE	55	26	29		1940-1955	
William WARBRICK	3	0	3		1900-1910	
William WILLIS	84	13	71	2 *1-1*	1906-1926	*d.1939, career total: c110*
Robert WILSON	32	0	32	2 *0-2*	1920-1937	
BINNS				1 *0-1*	1901	
JOHNSTONE				1 *1-0*	1947	
ROBINSON				1 *0-1*	1925	

Notes:
- *Figures are incomplete in this section. The hangman at a number of executions remains unknown.*
- *Albert Pierrepoint's career figure also consisted of the hanging overseas of a number of war criminals.*

and finally...

The last hanging on the Isle of Man was..
1 Aug 1872   John Kewish

The last hanging other than for murder was..
4 Jan 1946   Theodore Schurch *(treason)*   *623*

The last execution by firing squad was..
14 Aug 1941   Josef Jakobs *(German)*

The last army execution was..
6 Nov 1920   Richard Flynn *(Irish)*

The last army execution of a UK serviceman was..
11 Aug 1919   Joseph Chandler

The last triple hanging was..
9 Jun 1896   Thomas Fowler, Albert Milsom, William Seaman

The last double hanging was..
17 Jun 1954   Gilbert and Grant   *765/766*

The last hanging on Jersey was..
9 Oct 1959   Francis Huchet

The last woman hanged in Ireland was..
5 Aug 1925   Annie Walsh

The last hanging in Ireland was..
10 Dec 1961   Robert McGladdery

The last hanging in the Irish Republic was..
20 Apr 1954   Michael Manning

The last woman hanged in Wales was..
14 Aug 1907   Rhoda Willis   *129*

The last hanging in Wales was..
5 May 1958   Vivian Teed   *788*

The last woman hanged in Scotland was..
10 Oct 1923   Susan Newll   *354*

The last hanging in Scotland was..
15 Aug 1963   Henry Burnett   *813*

The last woman hanged in Britain was..
13 July 1955   Ruth Ellis   *780*

The last hangings in Britain were..
13 Aug 1964   Allen and Evans   *816/817*

Bibliography

And May The Lord Have Mercy On Your Soul	Eddleston	1997
The Art of Murder	Goodman	1990
The Bedside Book of Murder	Whittington-Egan	1988
The Black Flag	Hepburn	1994
The Book of Executions	Bland	1993
The Cameo Conspiracy	Skelly	1999
The Christmas Murders	Goodman	1986
The Country House Murders	Goodman	1987
Crime Strange But True	Bland	1991
Crimes of the Heart	Marriner	1994
Criminal Justice	Weis	1988,90
The Crippen File	Goodman	1985
The Daily Telegraph Murder File	Goodman	1993
A Date With the Hangman	Leech	1992
Dead Not Buried	Beales	1995
Diary of a Hangman	Ellis	1996
Encyclopedia of Murder	Wilson & Pitman	1961,84
Erskine Childers	Ring	1996
The Essex Triangle	Thurlow	1990
Executioner: Pierrepoint	Pierrepoint	1974,77
Forty Years of Murder	Simpson	1978,80
A Gallery of Poisoners	Vincent	1993
George Joseph Smith	Lyons	1935
Haigh: The MInd of a Murderer	La Bern	1973
Hangman	Bailey	1989,93
The Hangman's Diary	Stockman	1993,94
The Hangman's Tale	Dernley & Newman	1989,90
The Hunting Down of Peter Manuel	Bingham	1973
Ireland Since the Famine	Lyons	1971,85
Landmarks in Twentieth Century Murder	Odell	1995
Let Him Have It, Chris	Trow	1990
Lord Haw-Haw & William Joyce, The Full Story	Cole	1964
Masterpieces of Murder	Goodman	1992
Medical Murders	Goodman	1991
More Murders of the Black Museum	Honeycombe	1993,94
Murder At Marlhill	Bourke	1993
Murder By Gaslight	Piper	1991
The Murder Club Guide to the Eastern and Home Counties	Lane	1989
Murderers' London	Butler	1973

The Murder Guide to Great Britain	Tibballs	1993,94
Murder Guide to London	Fido	1986
Murder in Low Places	Goodman	1988
Murderous Birmingham	Eddleston	1997
Murderous Derbyshire	Eddleston	1997
Murderous Leeds	Eddleston	1997
Murderous Manchester	Eddleston	1997
Murderous Sussex	Eddleston	1997
Murderous Tyneside	Eddleston	1997
The Murders of the Black Museum	Honeycombe	1982,90
Murder Squad	Tullett	1979,81
Murder Under the MIcroscope	Paul	1990
Murder Whatdunit	Gaute & Odell	1982
The Murder Yearbook	Lane	1992
The New Murderers' Who's Who	Gaute & Odell	1989
Notable British Trials #83	Critchley	1959
Nottingham..The Sinister Side	Jones	1996
The Railway Murders	Goodman	1984,89
Roger Casement, The Flawed Hero	Sawyer	
Royal Commission on Capital Punishment Report		1953
Ruth Ellis	Hancock	1963
The Seaside Murders	Goodman	1985
Settings For Slaughter	Wynn	1988,89
Shot at Dawn	Putkowski & Sykes	1989
Shot in the Tower	Sellers	1997
Stinie: Murder on the Common	Rose	1985,89
Strange Tales From Strangeways	Lee	1995
The Supernatural Murders	Goodman	1992
10 Rillington Place	Kennedy	1961,71
They Shot to Slay	Gribble	1986
True Crime	Wilson	1988
True Crime 2	Wilson	1990
True Crime Diary	Bland	1986,88
True Crime Diary, volume 2	Bland	1989,93
The Vintage Car Murders	Goodman	1988
Vintage Murder of the Twenties	Sparrow	1972
Who Killed Hanratty?	Foot	1971
The Wigwam Murder	Trow	1994

Periodicals:

The Daily Mirror
The Guardian
The Mail on Sunday
The Times
Master Detective Magazine
True Crime Magazine
True Detective Magazine

Index of those hanged

Form:
- *Name and case number.*
- *Italics and case number indicate an alias or alternative name.*
- *Italics and year indicate US military, Irish, Jersey or firing squad execution in that year.*

A

B

Charles BACKHOUSE	006
Andrew BAGLEY	503
George BAILEY	318
John BAINBRIDGE	488
Alec BAKERLIS	266
George BALL	229
Fred BALLINGTON	137
Peter BARNES	526
Percy BARRETT	281
Thomas BARROW	046
Kevin BARRY	*1920*
George BARTON	370
William BATTY	624
William BEAL	206
Henry BECKETT	*283*
John BEDFORD	038
Ferat Md BENALI	103
John BENNETT	017
Benjamin BENSON	279
William BENSON	432
James BERGIN	014
Harold BERRY	633
John BERRYMAN	*1908*
Victor BETTS	446
Derek BENTLEY	745
William BIGNELL	368
Edgar BINDON	233
Arthur BIRKETT	202
Arthur BISHOP	379
Edward BLACK	326
Robert BLAINE	621
David BLAKE	484
Charles BLEWITT	009
Herbert BLOYE	*1925*
William BOLTON	051
Francis BOOKER	359
Stanley BOON	524
Alfred BOSTOCK	380
William BOULDRY	144
Herbert BOUNDS	573
Raymond BOUSQUET	493
John BOWES	013
Arthur BOYCE	632
Alfred BRADLEY	719
George BRAIN	518
George BREECKOW	*1915*

George BREEZE	089
William BRESSINGTON	369
John BRIDGE	489
Alfred BRIDGEMAN	099
Eric BRIGGS	652
Leonard BRIGSTOCK	486
Richard BRINKLEY	128
Eliga BRINSON	*1944*
Herbert BROOKER	236
Frederick BROOKS	259
Walter BROOKS	426
William BROOKS	*180*
William BROOME	180
Andrew BROWN	604
Ernest BROWN	475
Ethel BROWN	*482*
George BROWN	692
Joseph BROWN	706
Leo BROWN	*423*
William BROWN	050
William BROWN	074
Frederick BROWNE	423
Heinz BRUELING	613
Horace BRUNT	505
Charlotte BRYANT	499
George BRYANT	498
Richard BUCKHAM	121
Frank BURGESS	731
Frank BURKE	*287*
Henry BURNETT	813
Alfred BURNS	724
William BURRETT	011
Albert BURROWS	353
Herbert BURROWS	388
William BURTOFT	472
William BURTON	216
Fernando BUSCHMAN	*1915*
Edwin BUSH	808
George BUTLER	107
Oliver BUTLER	732
William BUTLER	170
William BUTLER	257
William BUTLER	521
Frederick BYWATERS	343

C

Timothy CADOGAN	*1901*
Charles CALDWELL	512
John CALDWELL	638
Thomas CALER	298
Jeremiah CALLAGHAN	047
Louie CALVERT	396
James CAMPION	*1904*
David CAPLAN	294
George CARDWELL	280
Patrick CARRAHER	632
Horace CARTER	718
George CARTLEDGE	439
Samuel CASE	415
Roger CASEMENT	256
Terence CASEY	587
Daniel CASSIDY	346
William CAVANAGH	270
Eamonn CEANNT	*1916*
Sidney CHAMBERLAIN	674
William CHAMBERS	045
Brian CHANDLER	792
George CHAPMAN	058
Ada CHARD-WILLIAMS	002
Arthur CHARLES	629
Robert E. CHILDERS	*1922*
Joseph CHRIMES	794
John CHRISTIE	748
Stylou CHRISTOPHI	773
William CHURCHER	037
Joseph CLARK	438
Stanley CLARK	662
Sydney CLARK	775
Ernest CLARKE	*1945*
Tom CLARKE	*1916*
James CLARKSON	082
Alick CLAYDON	028
Walter CLAYTON	637
Arthur CLEGG	628
Thomas CLEMENTS	*170*
Percy CLIFFORD	237
Thomas CLINTON	263
David COBB	*1943*
Martin COFFEY	634
Con COLBERT	*1916*
Charles COLCLOUGH	314
Stanley COLE	535

Charles COLEMAN	197
Michael COLLINS	185
Noah COLLINS	*146*
Patrick COLLINS	146
William COLLINS	571
Charles CONLIN	435
Thomas CONNAN	*1907*
James CONNELLY	*334*
James CONNOLLY	*1916*
John CONSTANTINE	799
Bernard COOPER	673
William COOPER	536
William CORBETT	453
James CORBITT	699
John COULSON	175
Harold COURTNEY	*1933*
Ernest COUZINS	682
Thomas COWDREY	075
William COWELL	529
Charles COWLE	463
William COWLE	601
John COX	*1929*
Thomas COX	271
Thomas CRAIG	173
Thomas CRAKE	*173*
Hawley CRIPPEN	179
William CRONIN	378
Nicholas CROSBY	701
Frederick CROSS	781
Walter CROSS	661
John CROSSLAND	284
Raymond CULL	735
Eddie CULLENS	*1932*
Gordon CUMMINS	563
George CUNLIFFE	213
Samuel CURTIS	111
Samuel CUSHNAN	*1930*

D

Hubert DALTON	375
Edward DALY	*1916*
Mary DALY	*1903*
John DAND	711
Sam DASHWOOD	568
John DAVIDSON	599
William DAVIES	678

John DAVIS	123
Joseph DAVIS	230
Lee DAVIS	*1943*
Philip DAVIS	504
Walter DAVIS	158
Jack DAY	805
John DAYMOND	519
Joseph DEANS	261
Francois DE DEEKER	*547*
Sidney DELASALLE	595
Thomas DELANEY	*1923*
John DENNIS	*436*
Arthur DE STAMIR	272
Patrick DEVENEY	728
Eugene DE VERE	394
Arthur DEVEREAUX	105
Edward DEVLIN	725
Madar Lal DHINGRA	163
John DICKMAN	176
Ernest DIGBY	593
Harry DOBKIN	576
Matthew DODDS	139
Daniel DOHERTY	*1941*
James DOHERTY	*1902*
Conrad DONOVAN	*092*
James DOOHAN	761
Lee DOON	342
John DORGAN	589
Thomas DORNAN	*1931*
Samuel DOUGAL	063
Daniel DRISCOLL	418
Johannes DRONKERS	574
Karl DRUCKE	547
Rowland DUCK	350
William DUDDLES	131
James DUFFY	072
John DUNN	414
Reginald DUNN	333
Patrick DUNPHY	*1900*
Charles DYER	083

E

Thomas EAMES	730
Charles EARL	033
John EASTWOOD	357
John EAYRES	239

Frederick EDGE	112
George EDISBURY	341
Douglas EDMONDSON	562
Alexander EDMONSTONE	159
John EDMUNDS	157
Edgar EDWARDS	*056*
Trevor EDWARDS	434
Edmund ELLIOTT	151
Norman ELLIOTT	430
Ruth ELLIS	780
James ELLOR	308
John ELLWOOD	143
Trevor ELVIN	585
Evan EVANS	659
Fred EVANS	*158*
Gwynne EVANS	817
Timothy EVANS	685

F

Michael FAGAN	191
James FARRELL	670
Joseph FEE	*1904*
Frederick FIELD	497
Jack FIELD	316
Frederick FIELDING	411
Charles FINDEN	399
John FISHER	386
John FLEMING	*1933*
Joseph FLETCHER	195
Thomas FLETCHER	218
Frank FLOOD	*1921*
Edmund FOLEY	*1921*
Del FONTAINE	*493*
Frederick FOREMAN	174
Francis FORSYTH	800
John FOSTER	*1905*
Thomas FOSTER	285
Marcel FOUGERON	023
Frank FOWLER	339
Harry FOWLER	770
Lawrence FOWLER	382
Wilfred FOWLER	381
Sidney FOX	443
William FOY	154
Arthur FRANKLIN	490
Albert FRASER	303

John FREEMAN	164
Maurice FREEDMAN	462
Frank FREIYER	643
Charles FREMBD	237
Fredercik FULLER	407

G

Robert GADSBY	267
Jeremiah GAFFNEY	*1924*
James GALBRAITH	600
John GALLAGHER	078
Robert GALLOWAY	204
William GALBRAITH	208
William GAMBON	*1948*
Arthur GARROD	186
John GARTSIDE	654
Henry GASKIN	286
Charles GAUTHIER	586
Christos GEORGHIOU	591
Christopher GERAGHTY	655
Miles GIFFARD	746
Kenneth GILBERT	765
Frederick GILL	447
James GILLON	420
Valeri GIOVANNI	019
Henry GLEESON	*1941*
Edward GLYNN	117
Wasyl GNYPIUK	803
John GODAR	734
William GODDARD	457
Francisco GODHINO	188
Abraham GOLDENBERG	361
Norman GOLDTHORPE	69
Marks GOODMACHER	313
Horace GORDON	603
Arthur GOSLETT	307
Sidney GOULTER	413
Zbigniew GOWER	691
Richard GOWLER	778
Henry GRAHAM	372
Ian GRANT	766
William GRAVES	516
William GRAY	317
Leslie GREEN	741
Norman GREEN	782
Frank GREENING	221

John GREENWAY	751
Roy GREGORY	474
Oswald GREY	811
Alan GRIERSON	494
Frank GRIFFIN	703
John GRIFFITHS	115
Peter GRIFFITHS	663
William GRIFFITHS	351
Marian GRONDKOWSKI	630
Howard GROSSLEY	608
Henry GROVE	003
Augustine GUERRA1945	
Thomas GUNNING	088

H

Harold HAGGER	649
George HAGUE	492
John HAIGH	677
Bikhtyar HAKIM	*496*
Albert HALL	762
Edmund HALL	094
William HALL	296
Lester HAMILTON	321
Louis HAMILTON	476
Ernest HAMMERTON	528
Charlie HAMMOND	*083*
William HAMPTON	160
Jeremiah HANBURY	465
James HANCOCK	172
William HANCOCKS	104
James HANRATTY	810
Ernest HARDING	784
James HARGREAVES	260
William HARKNESS323	
Arthur HARNETT	409
George HARVEY	*485*
Thomas HARRIES	764
Norman HARRIS	801
Paul HARRIS	696
Roy HARRIS	721
Wiley HARRIS	*1944*
Edward HARRISON	097
John HARRISON	029
William HARRISON	*1945*
Edward HARTIGAN	120
Max HASLAM	502

Reginald HASLAM	255
Verney HASSER	275
Lord HAW-HAW	*622*
George HAYWARD	421
William HAYWOOD	073
Alfred HEAL	102
Neville HEATH	641
Joseph HEFFERMAN	*1910*
Thomas HENDREN	636
Philip HENRY	749
William HEPPER	769
Richard HETHERINGTON	467
Sean HEUSTON	*1916*
Arthur HEYS	607
George HIBBS	040
Patrick HIGGINS	223
Alfred HIGHFIELD	004
Edward HILL	189
George HILL	*016*
Harold HILL	561
Young HILL	250
Reginald HINKS	477
Alfred HIRD	*292*
Stanley HOBDAY	473
William HODGSON	269
Joseph HOLDEN	012
Samuel HOLDEN	091
Frank HOLLINGTON	436
Clifford HOLMES	541
Frederick HOLMES	254
Leonard HOLMES	635
William HOLMYARD	437
Frederick HOLT	297
James HONEYLANDS	231
Robert HOOLHOUSE	513
Desmond HOOPER	759
Edward HOPWOOD	211
John HORNER	363
Charles HOUGHTON	402
Dennis HOWARD	787
Charles HOWELL	062
Francis HUCHET	*1959*
Frederick HUDSON	*510*
William HUDSON	059
Leonard HUCKER	523
William HUGHES	055
Karl HULTEN	606
Joseph HUME	133
Edward HUTCHINSON	464

Ernest HUTCHINSON 149
John HUTCHINSON 098
Harry HUXLEY 729

I

James INGLIS . 709
William IRWIN 005
Henry ISON 182

J

Christopher JACKSON 501
Henry JACOBY 332
Josef JAKOBS *1941*
Thomas JAMES 590
Halcke JANSSEN *1915*
Arthur JEFFRIES 096
Wallace JENDEN 500
Albert JENKINS 689
Charles JENKINS 656
David JENNINGS 545
Frederick JESSE 356
Thomas JESSHOPE 171
Oswald JOB 594
Cyril JOHNSON 559
James JOHNSON 440
Reginald JOHNSON *621*
Peter JOHNSON 737
Samuel JOHNSON 385
Edward JOHNSTON 140
Ernest JONES 793
Henry JONES 081
Joseph JONES 124
Joseph JONES 153
Joseph JONES 273
Parson JONES *1945*
Rex JONES 676
William JONES 403
William JONES 679
John JOYCE 022
William JOYCE 622
Stanislaw JURAS 753
Eugeniusz JURKIEWICZ 657
Richard JUSTIN *1909*

K

Matthew KAVANAGH	790
John KAY	090
Thomas KEELEY	*1902*
Frederick KEELING	328
John KEEN	383
Ernest KELLY	227
George KELLY	686
John KELLY	*1904*
Ernest KEMP	596
Reginald KENNEDY	*438*
William KENNEDY	424
Thomas KENT	*1916*
Jose KEY	564
Patrick KINGSTON	570
Bertram KIRBY	412
Robert KIRBY	470
Bernard KIRWAN	*1943*
William KIRWAN	085
Severin KLOSOVSKI	*058*
William KNIGHTON	405
Erich KOENIG	610
Charles KOOPMAN	588
Czeslaw KOWALEWSKI	758
Nenad KOVACEVIK	704
Armin KUEHNE	616
Lee KUN	253

L

William LACEY	008
Francis LAND	449
William LANE	039
Eric LANGE	095
Charles LAKE	485
George LAW	228
Robert LAWMAN	135
Alfred LAWRENCE	207
Lorraine LAX	387
James LEAH	401
John LEATHERBERRY	*1944*
Ronald LEE	*348*
See LEE	152
Patrick LEGGETT	043
James LEHMAN	*1945*
George LEVER	315

Henry LEWIS	671
Pasha LIFFEY	108
John LINCOLN	389
John LIVESEY	740
George LOAKE	198
LOCK Ah Tam	383
Frederick LOCK	422
Carl LODY	*1914*
Harry LONGDEN	217
Eugene LORENZ	*095*
Wilhelm LUBINA	760
Leong LUN	*341*
Ping LUN	084
John LYNCH	763
John LYON	626

M

Sean MacDIARMADA	*1916*
Thomas MacDONAGH	*1916*
Harry MacDONALD	*252*
Harry MACK	044
George MACKAY	*210*
Robert MACKINTOSH	675
John MAGUIRE	442
Patrick MAHER	*1921*
Patrick MAHON	364
Ethel MAJOR	482
James MAKIN	377
Piotr MAKSIMOWSKI	687
Henryk MALINOWSKI	631
Michael MALLIN	*1916*
Antonio MANCINI	551
Backary MANNEH	727
Michael MANNING	*1954*
Peter MANUEL	789
Albert MARJERAM	445
Walter MARRIOTT	244
Walter MARSH	122
George MARSHALL	247
Thomas MARSLAND	035
Aniceto MARTINEZ	*1945*
Walter MARTYN	192
Ronald MARWOOD	795
David MASON	639
Louise MASSET	001
Lewis MASSEY	292

John MATHIESON	645
Mahmood MATTAN	733
Robert MAURI	615
William MAYNARD	428
John McBRIDE	*1916*
Henry McCABE	*1926*
John McCARTNEY	252
Patrick McDERMOTT	*1932*
Thomas McDONAGH	*1923*
James McDONALD	041
John McDONALD	*147*
Mervin McEWAN	592
Simon McGEOWN	*1922*
Robert McGLADDERY	*1961*
Thomas McGUINNESS	268
James McHUGH	*1926*
Miles McHUGH	299
James McKAY	416
Patrick McKENNA	024
Hugh McLAREN	222
Samuel McLAUGHLIN	*1961*
Felix McMULLEN	*1924*
James McNICOL	620
Henry McWIGGINS	*044*
Thomas MEAD	150
William MEFFEN	602
Carl MEIER	537
Ernst MELIN	*1915*
Thomas MELLOR	007
Liam MELLOWS	*1922*
Louisa MERRIFIELD	750
Harold MERRY	569
Josep MERTINS	614
Chung Yi MIAO	433
George MICHAEL	459
Samuel MIDDLETON	036
Anthony MILLER	802
John MILLER	025
John MILLER	026
Herbert MILLS	717
Alex MIRANDA	*1944*
William MITCHELL	*1921*
Jan MOHAMED	514
Hassan MOHAMMED	352
Johannes MOMMERS	397
Alfred MOORE	720
Dennis MOORE	713
Edwin MOORE	125
Robert MOORE	757

Joseph MORAN	*1904*
Patrick MORAN	*1921*
Samuel MORGAN	543
Frederick MORSE	468
Ernest MOSS	509
Thomas MOUNCER	118
Dennis MULDOWNEY	736
Carl MULLER	*1915*
Frederick MURPHY	507
James MURPHY	406
John MURPHY	147
William MURPHY	167
Philip MURRAY	355
James MYLES	*1926*
Stanislaw MYSZKA	660

N

Pierre NEUKERMANS	597
Dennis NEVILLE	672
Susan NEWELL	354
George NEWLAND	756
Oliver NEWMAN	452
George NEWTON	183
James NICHOLLS	142
Thomas NICHOLSON	049
Henryk NIEMASZ	809
Michael NIESCIOR	625
Joseph NOBLE	134
Frederick NODDER	510
Eric NORCLIFFE	739
Matthew NUNN	358

O

John O'BRIEN	*333*
Edward O'CONNOR	322
Jeremiah O'CONNOR	148
John O'CONNOR	716
Rory O'CONNOR	*1922*
Leo O'DONNELL	265
Michael O'HANRAHAN	*1916*
Cornelius O'LEARY	*1925*
William O'NEILL	*1927*
Arthur OSBORNE	666
William O'SHEA	*1943*

Vincent OSTLER	530
Joseph O'SULLIVAN	334
Edgar OWEN	056

P

Joachim PALME-GOLTZ	611
Edward PALMER	069
Edward PALMER	214
William PALMER	187
Zsiga PANKOTIA	807
Ernest PARKER	471
Frederick PARKER	478
George PARKER	016
George PARKER	196
G.T.PARKER	*1915*
Harry PARKER	145
William PARKER	517
John PARR	010
Russell PASCOE	814
Leonard PATCHETT	066
Charles PATERSON	127
Arthur PEACH	556
Patrick PEARsE	*1916*
William PEARSE	*1916*
Robert PEARSON	*1945*
Augustus PENNY	225
Hyman PERDOVITCH	293
Henry PERKINS	110
George PERRY	169
George PERRY	345
Henry PERRY	283
Robert PETTER	548
Henry PHILIPS	194
Sargent PHILIP	203
James PHIPPS	141
George PLACE	052
Joseph PLUNKETT	*1916*
William PODMORE	444
Guenther PODOLA	798
Bernard POMROY	347
George POPLE	458
Thomas PORTER	064
Jospeh POTTER	092
Elijah POUNTNEY	335
James POWER	419
Patrick POWER	374

Michael PRATLEY	*1924*
Charles PRESCOTT	627
Thomas PRESTON	065
Albert PRICE	695
Albert PROBERT	479
Jack PUTTNAM	466
Benjamin PYEGATE	*1944*

Q

Frederick QUARMBY	319
Henry QUARTLY	240
William QUAYLE	583
Ambrose QUINN	290

R

John RAMSBOTTOM	136
Gustav RAU	060
Daniel RAVEN	683
Arthur RAVENY	441
Thomas RAWCLIFFE	177
Charles RAYMOND	582
Dudley RAYNER	579
Roman REDEL	690
William REEVE	248
Edward REID	771
Irving REIS	*1915*
Marks REUBEN	155
Morris REUBEN	156
Alfred REYNOLDS	714
Frederick REYNOLDS	119
Frederick REYNOLDS	650
George REYNOLDS	429
John REYNOLDS	752
George RICE	456
Alfred RICHARDS	515
Eli RICHARDS	550
James RICHARDS	527
Arthur RICHARDSON	032
Thomas RICHARDSON	609
Karel RICHTER	554
William RIDER	340
George RILEY	804
James RILEY	309
Thomas RILEY	461

James RIVETT 684
Benjamin ROBERTS 681
Corbett ROBERTS 783
George ROBERTS 533
John ROBERTS 460
Kenneth ROBERTS 779
Ronald ROBERTS 577
Frederick ROBERTSON 226
George ROBERTSON 768
James ROBERTSON 701
William ROBERTSON 410
George ROBINSON 338
James ROBINSON 777
John ROBINSON 408
William ROBINSON 262
John RODGERS 508
Gerald ROE 584
Augusto ROGGEN *1915*
James ROLLINS 304
William ROONEY 278
William ROONEY *1923*
Johannes ROOS *1915*
Joseph ROSE 282
Robert ROSENTHAL 243
Alfred ROUSE 448
Reginald ROWLAND *1915*
Walter ROWLAND 648
Edward ROWLANDS 417
Samuel ROWLEDGE 087
Albert RUMENS 209
Arthur RUSHTON 644
Frederick RUSHWORTH 483
George RUSSELL 664
Buck RUXTON 496
Bernard RYAN *1921*
James RYDER 220

S

Albert SABIN 647
Amelia SACH 053
Herbert SALISBURY 301
Sampson SALMON 015
William SALT 774
Hashankhan SAMANDER 400
August SANGRET 581
Cyril SAUNDERS 310

William SAUNDERS	*130*
John SAVAGE	349
William SCANLAN	*1911*
Emil SCHMITTENDORF	617
Theodore SCHURCH	623
Edward SCOLLER	540
Ernest SCOTT	289
Ernest SCOTT	*471*
Duncan SCOTT-FORD	572
Frederick SEDDON	201
Eric SEDGEWICK	212
Frederick SEEKINGS	224
George SEMINI	668
Henry SEYMOUR	454
Thomas SEYMOUR	184
George SHARPLES	395
Walter SHARPE	688
William SHAUGHNESSY	710
George SHAW	744
Winston SHAW	776
Mark SHAWCROSS	161
William SHELLEY	451
Thomas SHELTON	371
Stanley SHEMINANT	646
Scottie SHEPHERD	*210*
Joseph SHUTTLEBOTHAM	018
Thomas SIDDLE	138
John SILK	114
George SILVEROSA	567
Arthur SIMMS	367
Donald SIMON	738
Sydney SINCLAIR	*649*
Ajit SINGH	726
Udham SINGH	532
William SLACK	126
Charles SLOWE	068
William SMEDLEY	653
Arthur SMITH	525
Edward SMITH	707
George SMITH	113
George SMITH	246
George SMITH	*1945*
Gilbert SMITH	205
Harold SMITH	*1943*
James SMITH	398
James SMITH	723
James SMITH	812
John SMITH	*503*
John SMITH	549

John SMITH	553
Ralph SMITH	522
Robert SMITH	715
Samuel SMITH	057
Sidney SMITH	080
Sydney SMITH	640
Walter SMITH	511
Willem SMITH	061
William SMITH	366
Willie SMITH	*1944*
William SMYLIE	*1928*
Fred SNYDER	*554*
Frederick SOUTHGATE	365
Edwin SOWERBY	312
Joseph SPOONER	234
Arthur STAMROWSKI	*272*
Henry STARR	079
Frank STEELE	245
Solomon STEIN	455
Frederick STEWART	425
George STILLS	132
Ewen STITCHELL	*394*
Frank STOKES	791
Leslie STONE	506
Frederick STOREY	305
Alfred STRATTON	100
Albert STRATTON	101
James STRATTON	404
Kenneth STRICKSON	669
Daniel SULLIVAN	258
John SULLIVAN	086
William SULLIVAN	325
George SUMNER	*229*
Djang SUNG	291
Emily SWANN	077
Walter SYKES	215

T

Michael TALBOT	*1925*
John TARKENTER	193
Thomas TATTERSHALL	106
Michael TATUM	796
Joseph TAYLOR	*1903*
Milton TAYLOR	767
Vivian TEED	788
Victor TERRY	806

Frederick THOMAS	190
George THOMAS	391
Madison THOMAS	*1944*
Arthur THOMPSON	605
Edith THOMPSON	344
Harry THOMPSON	251
Henry THOMPSON	178
Henry THOMPSON	390
Hiram THOMPSON	330
John THOMPSON	027
John THOMPSON	264
William THOMPSON	*270*
Norman THORNE	373
John THORNLEY	249
Thomas THORPE	555
William THORPE	392
Alphonse TIMMERMAN	565
Gerard TOAL	*1928*
John TODD	747
Edmund TONBRIDGE	329
John TOOLE	*1901*
Thomas TRAYNOR	*1921*
Gordon TRENOWETH	580
Harold TREVOR	557
Chris TRIHAS	*591*
William TUFFEN	067
Henry TUFFNEY	480
Patrick TURNAGE	697
William TURNER	578

U

Robert UPTON	232

V

Louis VAN DE KERKHOVE	276
Charles VAN DEN KIEBOOM	539
Joseph VAN HOVE	598
Jean-Pierre VAQUIER	362
John VICKERS	786
James VIRRELS	708
Louis VOISIN	274